Dimensions of LAW

CANADIAN AND INTERNATIONAL LAW IN THE 21ST CENTURY

GEORGE ALEXANDROWICZ
Queen's University, Faculty of Law

MARION AUSTIN
London Catholic District School Board

ROSEMARY CAIRNS-WAY
University of Ottawa, Faculty of Law

ALLAN HUX
Toronto District School Board

MURRAY LOCKE
Toronto District School Board

GEORGE MAVRAGANIS
Toronto District School Board

AGI METE
Niagara Catholic District School Board

PATRICK MONAHAN
Osgoode Hall Law School, York University

TERRY G. MURPHY
Limestone District School Board (formerly)

LAURENCE OLIVO
School of Legal and Public Administration, Seneca College

LARRY O'MALLEY
Avon Maitland District School Board

NORA ROCK

PHILIP SWORDEN
Humber College Institute of Technology & Advanced Learning

2004
EMOND MONTGOMERY PUBLICATIONS LIMITED
TORONTO, CANADA

Printed in Canada.

We acknowledge the financial support of the Government of Canada through the Book Publishing Industry Development Program (BPIDP) for our publishing activities.

Publisher
Tim Johnston

Coordinating editor
Jenifer A. Ludbrook

Developmental editors
Kate Hawkins
Ed O'Connor
Dayne Ogilvie

Editorial assistant
Joyce Tannassee

Production editor, copy editor, & image researcher
Francine Geraci

Image researcher & permissions editor
Lisa Brant

Interior designer
Jack Steiner Graphic Design

Compositor
Tara Wells, WordsWorth Communications

Proofreader
Cindy Fujimoto, WordsWorth Communications

Indexer
Paula Pike, WordsWorth Communications

Production coordinator
Jim Lyons, WordsWorth Communications

Reviewers
Derek Doolan
Toronto Catholic District School Board

Pat Durst, bias reviewer
York Region School Board (formerly)

Doug Gordon
Thames Valley District School Board (formerly)

Catherine Hough
Peel District School Board

Ian Hundey
University of Toronto/OISE (formerly)

Hazel Keefner
Essex County District School Board

John Myers
University of Toronto/OISE

Ted Shaw
Ontario Human Rights Commission, Policy and Education Branch

Gary Simons
Upper Canada District School Board

About the cover

IUSTICIA

> "Justice, like the bright sun, shall break majestic forth."

An allegorical figure of Justice. She represents the striving of humanity toward higher civilization. Original painting 1995 by Trevor Goring. In the private collection of Powers and Santola, Attorneys at Law, New York. The image is juxtaposed with the contemporary design of Susan Darrach.

National Library of Canada Cataloguing in Publication Data

Dimensions of law : Canadian and international law in the 21st century / George Alexandrowicz ... [et al.].

Includes index.
ISBN 1-55239-087-X

1. Law—Canada. 2. International law.
I. Alexandrowicz, G. W.

KE444.D45 2003 349.71 C2003-904981-7
KF385.ZA2D45 2003

Table of Contents

Unit 2 Rights and Freedoms

CHAPTER 4
Canadian Constitutional Law 102

CHAPTER 5
The Charter and the Courts 128

CHAPTER 6
Human Rights in Canada 158

CHAPTER 7
Majority and Minority Rights 192

Unit 5 International Law

To the Reader

Law is made in the context of a society—of the philosophies and religions that set the standards of behaviour and organization, of its history, and of its ideas of human rights and responsibilities. The first four units of *Dimensions of Law: Canadian and International Law in the 21st Century* explore Canadian law in its social and political contexts, looking first at the roots of our laws, then at the framework Canadians have laid down in the constitution, at criminal law, and at the laws that govern the environment and the workplace. The fifth unit explores how and why international law developed since the mid-20th century, and how it is developing in the 21st century.

These are complex topics, and *Dimensions of Law* has approached the challenge of making this material understandable and interesting to its readers by including features in each chapter that encourage discussion and debate of contemporary issues. These include

- chapter openings that focus attention on the main concepts and issues
- a selection of long and short cases, each supported by questions that guide you through the relevant aspects of the case
- "Turning Points in the Law," which examines key decisions and actions that have led the way to significant change, highlighting the role of individuals and organizations in bringing about such change
- "Personal Viewpoint," which presents the opinions of individuals on issues relevant to each chapter, and opens the door to discussion of contemporary topics of interest
- "Issue," which explores a significant law-related issue through the opinions of supporters and opponents, and requires you to analyze these opinions before coming to your own conclusion
- "Working for Change," which focuses on individuals or groups who promote change to deal with important issues in the law
- Web links, which encourage you to move beyond the text and to interact critically with a wider array of primary and secondary sources
- "Check Your Understanding," which poses questions to assess your understanding at the conclusion of each major section in a chapter
- "Career Profile," which features interviews with individuals associated with implementing the law
- "Methods of Legal Inquiry," which challenges you progressively to organize, summarize, and analyze information
- "Reviewing Main Ideas," which provides assessment tools such as cases to consider and questions that require research, inquiry, and synthesis of information.

We hope that you will be engaged and challenged as you explore the many issues about law in our society that are raised in this book, and that you will gain new insight into the problems that our global society faces in the first years of the 21st century.

Unit 1

Heritage

If you are to take away only one idea from the book you are reading right now, it might be this: that law is not something static and unchangeable, but a dynamic process that renews itself in response to society's evolving needs.

This opening unit in *Dimensions of Law: Canadian and International Law in the 21st Century* focuses on Canada's legal heritage. To emphasize law's dynamic aspect, we open the unit with a chapter on legal change that explores how the law responds to society's needs. You will discover what conditions make legal change possible and necessary. You will also read about different groups and individuals who have fought to reform Canadian law.

Chapter 2 explores the questions: Where does law come from, and how is it organized? You will see that Canada's present legal system has roots not only in the legal systems of other countries and civilizations, but that it can be traced back to religious and moral precepts as well. You will be introduced to the constitution—Canada's main

repository of law—and learn about two other contemporary legal sources: statute law and case law. You will also see it is possible to organize law into various categories that make its purposes easier to understand.

Chapter 3 introduces you to a profound idea: the meaning and purpose of law itself. Do societies create law to make their citizens better people, or to protect them from one another's greed and violence? Great thinkers have meditated on this question; and here, in clear, understandable language, you will discover their conclusions. You will see how the radical ideas of legal philosophers such as John Locke and Karl Marx inspired various revolutions, and you will understand how contemporary law has expanded to incorporate the ideas of feminist thinkers and scholars. Throughout this chapter—and this whole first unit—you will examine the way that ideas and theories about law have been applied to real-life situations in a Canadian context.

Chapter 1 Changes to the Law

CHAPTER Focus

In this chapter, you will

- examine factors that lead to changes in the law
- assess some of the legal and political conditions that make changing the law possible
- evaluate the influence of individual citizens who have fought to change the law
- assess the role of collective action in changing law in democracies
- determine the circumstances under which people have a responsibility to seek legal reform
- examine several court cases involving people seeking to change Canada's laws

Throughout Canadian history, people have sought to change existing laws and to bring new laws into effect. Sometimes these struggles have been violent, as when Louis Riel organized the Red River Resistance and forced the Canadian government to pass the *Manitoba Act*, which established certain legal rights for the Métis. At other times, changes have been made in a gradual fashion, as when women won the right to vote or when penalties were increased for drunk driving. This chapter explores reasons people may have to change the law and examines some of the underlying conditions that make legal change possible. It also considers some specific changes that individuals and groups of people have made to the law in Canada.

The cartoon in Figure 1.1 refers to a controversial change in the law. In 2002, the Supreme Court of Canada handed down a decision that gave prisoners serving lengthy sentences the right to vote in federal elections.

Figure 1.1

At First Glance

1. Who are the characters sitting at the table in this cartoon?
2. Where are these characters speaking, and why are they there?
3. What is the main point the cartoonist is making?
4. One purpose of putting people convicted of serious crimes in prison is to punish them. Do you think that losing the right to vote should be part of this punishment? Explain.
5. Do you think that people who are found guilty of breaking Canada's criminal laws should be able to vote for politicians who make those laws? Why or why not?

Factors Driving Changes in Law

At some point or other, you have probably heard one of your friends say, "There ought to be a law about this!" Some people feel strongly enough that they do more than complain. They use every legal channel open to them to get a law passed that will correct the situation. But most often when laws change, they do so as a response to broad shifts in society that occur over a period of time. These shifts can be the result of *demographic changes, technological changes*, or *changes in values*. There are also times when it is necessary to change the law more quickly, as in response to a *national emergency*.

Demographic Changes

Today, Canada is not the same country it was 100 years ago. Between then and now, there have been several of what social scientists call demographic changes. A demographic change is a change relating to birth and death rates or to trends in immigration, education, and employment.

In Canada in 1900, more people lived in rural areas than in the cities, and few married women were in the paid workforce. Today, Canada is an urban society, and in most households both spouses have to earn salaries to support the family. In the early part of the 20th century, as young men and women left the family farm to take jobs in city factories, laws were passed to respond to this demographic change. For instance, new safety measures were passed to ensure a safer working environment in factories. Over time, laws and regulations were passed to raise standards in sanitation, public health, and housing so that workers could have cleaner and safer places to live.

Another demographic change occurred as more and more women joined the workforce in the 1960s and 1970s. Many of these women objected

Urban Percentages of Population for Regions and Provinces, 1901–1941 (people in cities of 20 000 or more)

	1901	1911	1921	1931	1941
Canada	34.9	41.8	47.4	52.5	55.7
Quebec	36.1	44.5	51.8	59.5	61.2
Ontario	40.3	49.5	58.8	63.1	67.5
Prairies	19.3	27.9	28.7	31.3	32.4
British Columbia	46.4	50.9	50.9	62.3	64.0
Maritimes	24.5	30.9	38.8	39.7	44.1

Source: Wayne W. McVey, Jr. and Warren E. Kalbach, *Canadian Population*. Toronto: Nelson, 1995, p. 149.

Figure 1.2 *This table illustrates a clear demographic trend: over the first half of the 20th century in Canada, the population shifted from being predominantly rural to predominantly urban. Which two areas experienced the most change? How would you explain these shifts?*

to the fact that they earned less on average than men doing similar jobs. Pay equity issues became a matter of public debate, and laws were passed to ensure a woman's right to "equal pay for work of equal value" (see Chapter 13: The Government and the Workplace). As you will learn in Chapter 5: The Charter and the Courts and Chapter 14: Organizing the Workforce, the *Canadian Human Rights Act* now prohibits sexual discrimination in employment, and the *Canada Labour Code* prohibits layoffs or dismissals because of pregnancy.

Technological Changes

In 1867, the British parliament passed the *British North America Act* (now known as the *Constitution Act, 1867*), which made Canada a federal state. This Act gave the federal government in Ottawa jurisdiction over such matters as criminal law, national defence, and trade and commerce. To the provinces, it gave jurisdiction over such areas as hospitals, municipalities, and education. The framers of the Act could not foresee later technological innovations such as the telephone, airplane, radio, television, and the Internet.

New laws have had to be passed over the years to make it clear which level of government—federal or provincial—has jurisdiction over these new inventions. For example, in 1932 the Judicial Committee of the Privy Council in London, England (which until 1949 had to approve amendments to the Canadian constitution), awarded jurisdiction over radio broadcasting to the federal government instead of the provinces. In response, the federal government established the Canadian Radio Broadcasting Commission, which was reorganized as the Canadian Broadcasting Corporation (CBC) in 1936.

Changes in Values

People used to tolerate certain forms of behaviour that would cause outrage today. Often this was because it took time for the public to realize how harmful these behaviours could be. Over time, the terrible toll that drunk drivers were taking in lives and injuries motivated their victims to take action. As these people organized into **lobby groups** and publicized their cases, the Canadian public began to share their outrage. As a result, Parliament made changes to the *Criminal Code* (see Chapter 8: Crime and Criminal Law) that increased the penalties for drunk driving. Similarly, anti-smoking groups worked to publicize the harmful effects of second-hand smoke in restaurants and bars. Cities began to pass bylaws outlawing smoking in these public places. Members of visible minorities who were discriminated against by landlords have been able to effect changes in provincial housing laws. Aboriginal peoples have been able to get laws passed prohibiting construction projects on their ancestral lands and burial grounds. All these legal changes reflect shifts in values held by a broad spectrum of Canadians.

lobby group: a number of people trying to influence legislators on behalf of a particular cause or interest

National Emergencies

Throughout Canada's history, Parliament has passed laws in response to conditions created by national emergencies. Sometimes these laws were meant to be temporary measures but were never repealed when the crisis passed. Two famous examples came into effect after Canada entered World War I: the *War Measures Act* and the *Income Tax Act*. The *War Measures Act*, which gave the federal government the power to restrict the civil liberties of Canadians, was last invoked by Prime Minister Pierre Trudeau during the October Crisis in 1970. Trudeau was responding to a Quebec separatist group's kidnapping of a British diplomat and kidnapping and murder of a Quebec government official. As we all know, the *Income Tax Act* is still a fact of life for every Canadian who earns a paycheque.

Learn more about the October Crisis and the *War Measures Act* at www.emp.ca/dimensionsoflaw

On September 11, 2001, a terrorist attack on the United States demolished the World Trade Center in New York and damaged the Pentagon in Washington, DC. Many Canadians feared their own country was vulnerable to a similar attack. In response, Parliament passed the *Anti-terrorism Act* and has proposed the *Public Safety Act*, which greatly increase the investigative powers of police and security forces. Among other things, these measures

- made terrorism or aiding terrorists a criminal act punishable by up to 10 years in jail
- allowed police to arrest people suspected of terrorist activity without charging them first
- allowed police to force people to testify in secret investigations
- made it easier for police to use wiretaps as an investigative tool
- allowed the Canadian government to freeze and take away the assets of terrorists and their supporters.

For a discussion of Canada's domestic response to terrorism, visit www.emp.ca/dimensionsoflaw

Figure 1.3 *The towers at the World Trade Center in flames on September 11, 2001. Why would an attack on the United States lead to legal changes in Canada?*

issue

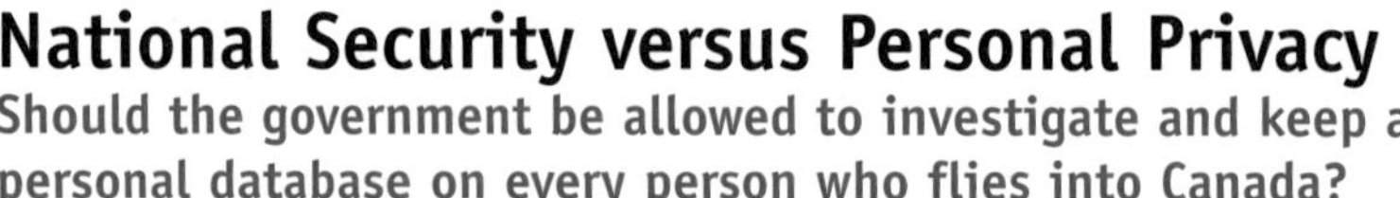

National Security versus Personal Privacy

Should the government be allowed to investigate and keep a personal database on every person who flies into Canada?

One of the Canadian laws that was changed in response to the events of September 11 was s. 107 of the *Customs Act.* The revised law allows customs officers advance access to airline passenger lists. The officers can use these lists to decide who should be closely questioned on arrival in Canada. All the information obtained is placed in a computer database where it will remain for six years. Other government agencies will have access to this database.

Is this change in the law a legitimate response to the threat of terrorism, or is it an unwarranted invasion of privacy on the part of the federal government? The following two excerpts give opposing points of view by government officials.

As a government, we in Ottawa understood the need to search for gaps in our picket fence of protection and intelligence-gathering. At Canada Customs and Revenue we found such a gap: our knowledge of who was flying into Canada by commercial jetliner. With parliamentary approval, we fixed that gap. We now know who is landing at Pearson, Vancouver, Halifax or any other airport receiving international flights. Now we have a legislative mandate that balances the privacy rights of Canadians with everyone's right to security, health and safety. Advance passenger information is just one way that Ottawa is protecting Canadians through the collection and analysis of flight information for all passengers entering the country. ...

Advance passenger information is a major investigative tool. It put investigators hard on the trail of suspected killers and terrorists.

> Similar data collected at our land borders have helped rescue children, and thwarted armed criminals from entering. Advance passenger information significantly increases our ability to track pedophiles, find criminals trying to enter our country, identify potential drug smugglers, and protect the health of Canadians.
>
> —*Elinor Caplan, Minister of National Revenue, December 2002*

> I do not object to customs officers accessing advance passenger information to learn who is flying into Canada and to determine who should be closely inspected upon arrival.
>
> What I do object to ... is allowing [the] Canada Customs and Revenue Agency to retain all this detailed information about the foreign travel activities of every law-abiding Canadian in a massive, six-year "Big Brother" database.
>
> This constitutes the unprecedented creation of government dossiers of personal information about all citizens: Every foreign destination you visit, who you travel with, how long you stay, how you pay for your ticket, what contact numbers you provide—even any dietary preferences or health-related requirements you communicate to the airlines.
>
> All this information will be stored not to provide you with any service, but to have it handy to use against you if it ever becomes expedient to do so. And under the broad information-sharing provisions of section 107 of the *Customs Act*, it will be available for an almost limitless range of governmental purposes that have nothing to do with anti-terrorism.
>
> —*George Radwanski, Privacy Commissioner of Canada, December 2002*

Fyi "Big Brother" is a term used by George Orwell in his novel *1984* to describe an all-powerful government body that keeps the population under surveillance and control.

Questions

1. What are Caplan's arguments in defence of gathering information from passengers arriving in Canada by air? Do you agree with these arguments? Explain your response.
2. In your own words, explain the Privacy Commissioner's main objection to the revised legislation.
3. a) What does Radwanski mean by a "Big Brother" database?
   b) Do you think the reference to "Big Brother" is appropriate here? Explain your view.
4. Could the information gathered be used just for anti-terrorism investigations, or for other purposes as well? If so, what purpose(s)?
5. Should the government be allowed to use this information in situations such as income tax investigations? Why or why not?
6. Do you think the government should be allowed to keep all the information it gathers in this way for six years? If not, then for how long? Explain your position.
7. What is your opinion on this issue? Justify your view in a short written report.

Many people criticized the new anti-terrorism laws on the grounds that they

- gave the government and the police too much power
- violated the civil liberties of Canadian citizens
- would encourage prejudice against Muslim Canadians
- would have a stifling effect on legitimate protests and demonstrations.

After months of criticism, the government withdrew some of the anti-terror legislation, including a law that allowed the minister of defence to declare any place in Canada a military zone and send in the army. Despite these revisions, criticism of the new laws remained widespread.

Check Your Understanding

1. What changes in law might result from the demographic change of an aging population?
2. Use the example of a change from horse-drawn transportation to automobiles to explain how technological change can create a need for new laws.
3. Give two examples, other than those given, of changes in laws that resulted from changing values.
4. Should legal measures passed during national emergencies to protect citizens be of limited duration? Discuss.

Figure 1.4 *The Magna Carta restricted the English monarch's power and safeguarded public rights and privileges.*

The Possibility of Change

For legal change to occur in an orderly fashion, and in a way that reflects the will of a country's people, certain conditions must be in place. In a dictatorship, for example, the people are powerless to change unpopular laws. Instead, any changes that are made come directly from the head of the government and express the will of the dictator, not of the people who are being governed. Fundamental freedoms, such as freedom of speech, of the press, of association, and of assembly, are all prohibited. Protests and demonstrations are violently suppressed, and people have no choice but to obey laws they believe are unjust. To avoid such a situation, three conditions are necessary. The country as a whole must respect what legal experts call the "rule of law," there should be a democratic system of government, and the justice system must be independent of the other branches of government.

rule of law: the fundamental principle that society is governed by laws applying equally to all persons and that neither any person nor the government is above the law

The Rule of Law

The **rule of law** was formulated in the Magna Carta, the list of legal rights that the English barons forced King John to sign in 1215 (see Chapter 2). There are three important parts to the rule of law: first, general recognition that law is necessary in an orderly society; second, that the law applies equally to everyone, including the highest officials in the country; and third, that a person's legal rights will not be taken away except in accordance with the law. Respect for the rule of law is one of the fundamental aspects of our legal system that Canada has inherited from Britain. It means that changes to the law will occur in an orderly fashion and in a way that reflects the decisions of a democratically elected government.

Case MANITOBA LANGUAGE RIGHTS AND THE RULE OF LAW

Re Manitoba Language Rights, [1985] 1 SCR 721

Facts

Provisions in both the *Constitution Act, 1867* and the *Manitoba Act, 1870* stated that it was mandatory for Manitoba to publish its laws in both English and French. This requirement reflected the long struggle of the **Métis** to establish their French language rights and the fact that when Manitoba joined Confederation, its population consisted of anglophones and francophones in roughly equal proportions. By 1890, however, largely because of immigration from Ontario, there were more anglophones than francophones in the province. In that year, the Manitoba legislature passed the *Official Language Act*. This Act made English the only official language of the province and ordered that all provincial laws be printed in English only. On several occasions over the years, this law was challenged in the courts and found to be unconstitutional. Nevertheless, Manitoba continued to print most of its laws in English only. In 1984, the federal government asked the Supreme Court to decide whether the province of Manitoba was obliged to write and publish all its laws in French as well as English.

Métis: French-speaking descendants of fur traders or voyageurs and Aboriginal peoples

Issues

The federal government wanted to know whether (1) the language provisions of the *Constitution Act, 1867* and the *Manitoba Act* were mandatory, and (2) if so, did that mean that all the provincial laws that had not been printed in French as well as English were invalid? If most of the laws of Manitoba that had been published since 1890 were invalid, then how would the province govern itself until it could translate its laws into French and publish them?

Decision

The Supreme Court answered yes to the first two questions. The language provisions of the *Manitoba Act* and the *Constitution Act, 1867* were mandatory. Technically, this did mean that most of Manitoba's laws passed since 1890 were invalid because most of them had been published in English only. To avoid creating a "legal vacuum" in the province and the chaos that would naturally follow, the Court cited the rule of law as a reason for deeming the laws of Manitoba "temporarily valid":

> The principle of rule of law, recognized in the *Constitution Acts* of 1867 and 1982, has always been a fundamental principle of the Canadian constitutional order. The rule of law requires the creation and maintenance of an actual order of positive laws to govern society. Law and order are indispensable elements of civilized life. This Court must recognize both the unconstitutionality of Manitoba's unilingual laws and the Legislature's duty to comply with the supreme law of this country, while avoiding a legal vacuum in Manitoba and ensuring the continuity of the rule of law.
>
> There will be a period of time during which it would not be possible for the Manitoba Legislature to comply with its constitutional duty under s. 23 of the *Manitoba Act, 1870.* It is therefore necessary, in order to preserve the rule of law, to deem temporarily valid and effective the Acts of the Manitoba Legislature, which would be currently in force were it not for their constitutional defect. The period of temporary validity will run from the date of this judgment to the expiry of the minimum period necessary for translation, re-enactment, printing and publishing.

Questions

1. In your own words, state the issues in this case.
2. What reference did the Supreme Court make to the rule of law, and why?
3. What did the Court mean by "legal vacuum"?
4. Do you agree with the Court's decision? Justify your response.

A Democratic Government

It is probably easiest to bring about peaceful and orderly legal change in a country that has a democratic system of government. A democracy gives people the power to change their government by voting in regular and free elections. This means an unpopular government can be voted out of power and replaced by one that has pledged to repeal or reform laws that the voting public considers unjust. If voters feel that the new government fails to live up to its campaign promises, then they can vote it out of power in the next election.

Passage of the goods and services tax (GST) in 1990 by Brian Mulroney's Progressive Conservative government was one of the most unpopular measures in Canadian history. Responding to opinion polls that showed public support for the proposed tax was almost non-existent, the Liberal-dominated Senate delayed approving the bill. Mulroney then appointed eight new Progressive Conservative senators, giving the government the necessary majority to win approval for the bill. In the 1993 federal election, the Liberals campaigned hard on a promise to repeal the GST. The tax's unpopularity was one reason the Liberals beat the Conservatives so convincingly in that election. Once in power, Liberal leader Jean Chrétien refused to honour his campaign promise, and the GST still remains in place.

Some democracies also have the advantage of a constitution and a bill of rights. The constitution can be either written, as in Canada and the United States, or partially unwritten, as in the United Kingdom. With a bill of rights in place, people have a clearer idea of their most fundamental rights and freedoms under the law. They have the right to petition the courts to declare laws that violate these rights and freedoms to be unconstitutional. If the courts do so, then the legislative branch of government must repeal the laws or rewrite them in such a way that they no longer violate the constitution.

A democracy also allows people to advocate for legal change in other ways. They can work for change through lobby groups, and they can make their views heard by signing petitions, by participating in demonstrations, or by voting in a referendum.

An Independent Justice System

If a country's people are to respect the law, the judges in that country must be able to function independently of the other branches of government. Judges cannot be intimidated by the threat of losing their position, or of being jailed. For example, in 1994, the Supreme Court of Canada raised a storm of controversy by ruling, in *R v. Daviault*, that intoxication by drugs or alcohol could be used as a defence in some cases to a charge of sexual assault. The federal government responded to this unpopular decision by enacting a new law, Bill C-72, that denied the defence of intoxication to anyone accused of interfering or threatening to interfere with "the bodily integrity of another person."

Fyi The "R" in a case citation refers to *Rex* (king) or *Regina* (queen) or, generally, the Crown.

It helps the independence of the judiciary for a country's court system to be organized in a hierarchical or pyramidal fashion, with many local courts at the bottom and one highest or supreme court at the top (see Figure 4.5, page 115). This structure allows for a system of appeals. The losing party in a case at a lower level has the right to appeal the court's decision to a higher level. If the higher court accepts the appeal, it will then review the case and deliver its own decision. This decision can also be appealed, and the process can continue right up to the highest court in the land. The appeals process allows for a very thorough review of a case and of the law that applies to it. In theory at least, this means that the most appropriate decision possible will be reached by the end of the process. Sometimes these decisions can bring about changes to **case law** (**common law**) or to the meaning of **statute law**.

case law/common law: a type of law developed in England that is based on following previous judicial decisions and is common to all the people of a country

statute law: laws passed by legislatures

In the case *R v. Ewanchuk*, the defendant was acquitted of sexual assault in an Alberta criminal court, based on a defence of "implied consent." The judge accepted the complainant's testimony that she did not want to be

Crown (attorney): lawyer employed by the state to prosecute a criminal offence

touched, but then found that her conduct gave the accused the impression of "implied consent." The **Crown** appealed the case, and the Alberta Court of Appeal reaffirmed the acquittal. The Crown then appealed to the Supreme Court of Canada, which found there was no basis in Canadian statute law for the defence of "implied consent." The acquittal was overturned and a conviction entered. Without the Supreme Court's decision, "implied consent" would have become a legitimate defence under Canadian case law to a charge of sexual assault.

Just as judges must be able to deliver their judgments free of threats and harassment, lawyers must also have the freedom to defend their clients vigorously, without fear of government reprisals. Defence lawyers must believe that their first obligation is to their clients and not to the government. They can advance arguments or use defences that may require new interpretations of the law.

Check Your Understanding

1. Explain how the principle of the rule of law protects Canadian citizens.
2. What opportunities are there in a democratic state to change unpopular laws? Which of these do you think are most effective?
3. A Cabinet minister phones a judge to discuss a case that is being heard in the judge's courtroom. Explain how this action threatens the justice system and the rule of law.

Change as a Result of Individual Action

Throughout history, there have been examples of individuals who struggled to change unjust laws or to pass new laws they thought necessary in a just society. The best-known example of such a person in recent times is Nelson Mandela. He was born in South Africa in 1918 and grew up under **apartheid**, a government policy of racial discrimination and segregation.

apartheid: a former policy of the South African government that involved discrimination and segregation directed against non-whites

After college, Mandela went to Johannesburg, where he worked as a clerk in a law firm. Every day he saw examples of black people being mistreated and marginalized by the white-dominated society. In 1944, Mandela joined the African National Congress, a group dedicated to overturning the apartheid system. In 1962, he was arrested and sentenced to life in prison, where he spent the next 27 years. While in prison, Mandela organized a system of "self-education" in which the prisoners taught one another a variety of subjects such as politics, economics, and law. He also smuggled messages to the outside world to encourage the black people in South Africa to continue their struggle for justice.

Learn more about Nelson Mandela at www.emp.ca/dimensionsoflaw

Finally in 1990, Mandela was released from prison. With F.W. de Klerk, the president of South Africa, he worked on dismantling the apartheid system. For their efforts, the two men were awarded the 1993 Nobel Peace Prize. In the first multiracial elections in the country's history, Mandela was elected president in 1994. His story has inspired people around the world with the faith that unjust laws, no matter how deeply entrenched, can be overturned and replaced by a system in which all people have equal rights.

In Canadian history, there are many examples of people who have struggled to change laws they considered unjust. Some of them spent time in jail for their beliefs; some even paid with their lives. Perhaps the best-known example in early Canadian history is Louis Riel, who organized the Red River Resistance in 1869 and the Northwest Rebellion in 1885. Riel spent years in exile in the United States, and in 1885 he was hanged for treason in Saskatchewan. Nevertheless, in 1992 Parliament passed a resolution that formally recognized the contributions Louis Riel made to the Canadian nation.

WORKING FOR CHANGE *Louis Riel and the Creation of Manitoba*

The Hudson's Bay Company sold the vast tract of Rupert's Land to the government of Canada in 1869. The deal was signed in London, England, with the approval of the British government, but without consulting the people who lived in Rupert's Land. The Red River settlement, in the area of present-day Winnipeg, was the largest settlement in the territory with about 12 000 people. The largest group in Red River was the Métis. They did not have legal title to the lands they occupied.

Figure 1.5 *Louis Riel, 1875.*

The Hudson's Bay Company withdrew from Rupert's Land in January 1869, but the Canadian government was not authorized to set up its rule until December of that year. For the better part of 12 months, the people at Red River would be without a formal government. In June 1869, before the legal land transfer took place, Ottawa sent surveyors to the area to mark out lands for settlement. The Métis, who had lived on the land for many years as hunters and farmers, feared they were about to have their lands taken over by English-speaking settlers from Ontario. They turned to Louis Riel, a 25-year-old Métis who had been educated in Quebec and was fluent in English and French, to act as their leader.

Riel was a skilled public speaker and a brilliant organizer. He stopped the surveyors and sent them away, then organized the National Committee of the Métis and prevented William McDougal, recently appointed lieutenant governor of the Northwest Territories, from entering the land. While McDougal waited across the border in the United States, Riel took over Fort Garry, the old Hudson's Bay stronghold, which gave the Métis a safe base and plenty of food and ammunition. He then set up a provisional government and announced that only it was authorized to speak for the people of the area and to negotiate on their behalf with the government of Canada.

In Ottawa, Prime Minister John A. Macdonald was perplexed. No one had anticipated such a strong response on the part of the Métis. Macdonald was reluctant to provoke bloodshed. Instead he sent an envoy to Riel, asking what the Métis wanted. In response, Riel drew up a Bill of Rights, demanding, among other things,

- the right to enter Confederation as a province
- the right to send four MPs to Parliament
- the right to use French as well as English in the new province's schools, courts, and legislature.

Before the issue could be settled, Riel approved the execution of a vehemently anti–Roman Catholic, anti-French labourer from Ontario, Thomas Scott, who had been imprisoned in Fort Garry for trying to overthrow the Métis.

Macdonald and Minister of Defence George-Étienne Cartier agreed to meet almost all of Riel's demands. On July 15, 1870, the *Manitoba Act* became law, creating the province of Manitoba and allowing the use of French and English in the schools and government. Riel himself was elected one of the four MPs Manitoba wanted to send to Ottawa. Unfortunately, this man who had struggled so hard for the rights of his people was forced to flee to the United States. In Ontario, the authorities had issued a warrant for Riel's arrest on a charge of murder in retaliation for the execution of Thomas Scott. Riel would eventually settle in Montana and not return to Canada until the 1880s, when the Métis once again sought his help.

Questions

1. In your opinion, did the government of Canada violate the rule of law by sending in surveyors in June 1869?
2. Which of Riel's actions violated the rule of law? Were his actions justifiable? Explain your answer.
3. Riel remained a controversial figure for over 100 years after his death. Investigate the roots of this controversy, and evaluate his role as an individual who changed the law.

Challenging Laws in Court

Many individual Canadians have devoted their lives to pressing for legal reform. Since the passage of the *Constitution Act, 1982*, which included the *Canadian Charter of Rights and Freedoms*, one of the most common ways to do this has been to challenge the constitutionality of a law in the courts. There have been many examples of the courts striking down a law because it was found to violate the rights guaranteed under the Charter. Usually, if the courts declare a law unconstitutional, and this decision is upheld on appeal, the law is no longer valid. Parliament then has the option of writing new legislation that will not conflict with the rights **entrenched in the constitution** and the Charter.

entrenched in the constitution: forming part of the constitution, and amended only through the formal constitutional process

One of the best-known examples of an individual Canadian challenging a law on constitutional grounds is that of Dr. Henry Morgentaler, who spent 10 months in jail for performing illegal abortions in the 1970s. He appealed a later conviction to the Supreme Court of Canada on the grounds that the abortion law in the *Criminal Code* violated a woman's right to security of the person under s. 7 of the Charter. In a landmark 1988 decision, the Court struck down the law. Justice Wilson stated:

> Forcing a woman, by threats of criminal sanction, to carry a foetus to term unless she meets certain criteria unrelated to her own priorities and aspirations, is a profound interference with a woman's body and thus an infringement of security of the person.

Once the Supreme Court declared the abortion law unconstitutional, it was no longer in effect. A new abortion law was introduced into Parliament in 1989. It was approved by the House of Commons but failed to pass the Senate. At this point, the federal government announced it would not pursue any further legislation on abortion.

Other important cases where the courts were asked to rule on the constitutionality of certain laws have involved Sue Rodriguez, who challenged the law on assisted suicide; and the convicted murderer Richard Sauvé, who challenged a law denying the right to vote to prisoners serving lengthy sentences.

Challenging the Law on Assisted Suicide

Not all struggles to change Canadian laws are successful. In 1992, a British Columbian woman, Sue Rodriguez, mounted a court case to establish a person's right to assisted suicide. In Canada, it is a crime, according to s. 241 of the *Criminal Code*, to help another person commit suicide. Rodriguez suffered from a condition called amyotrophic lateral sclerosis (ALS), widely known as Lou Gehrig's disease. A person with ALS experiences a gradual deterioration of the nervous system. Rodriguez knew that at some point she would lose the ability to swallow, speak, walk, or move at all without someone to help her. She would become bedridden, and be unable to eat or breathe without mechanical assistance. She did not want to die as long as she could enjoy life, but she knew that once she was no longer able to enjoy life, she would not have the strength to commit suicide. In 1992, she applied to the British Columbia Supreme Court for an order that would declare s. 241 invalid because it denied her right to security of the person under s. 7 of the Charter (see The Law, page 18).

Fyi Lou Gehrig played first base for the New York Yankees from 1924 to 1939, when ALS forced him to abandon his career. He died in 1941.

To find out more about Sue Rodriguez's case, visit www.emp.ca/dimensionsoflaw

The BC Supreme Court rejected Rodriguez's application, and the following year the BC Court of Appeal dismissed her appeal. She then appealed to the Supreme Court of Canada. By a majority of 5–4, the Supreme Court also decided against Rodriguez.

The Court interpreted the phrase "the principles of fundamental justice" to mean that the government has a fundamental obligation to protect the lives of its citizens. If s. 241 were removed from the *Criminal Code*, then the life of anyone who had been weakened by disease, accident, or age might be threatened by unscrupulous doctors or others.

This split among the judges seemed to reflect a similar division in Canadian society. Many people sympathized with Rodriguez, but many others feared that legalizing physician-assisted suicide would set a dangerous precedent. In its decision, the Court noted that Rodriguez's right to

The Law

From the *Criminal Code*:

241. Every one who
   (a) counsels a person to commit suicide, or
   (b) aids or abets a person to commit suicide, whether suicide ensues or not, is guilty of an indictable offence and liable to imprisonment for a term not exceeding fourteen years.

From the *Canadian Charter of Rights and Freedoms*:

7. Everyone has the right to life, liberty and security of the person and the right not to be deprived thereof except in accordance with the principles of fundamental justice.

Questions

1. What is the restriction on the rights given in s. 7 of the Charter?
2. In your opinion, were Rodriguez's rights under s. 7 violated by s. 241 of the *Criminal Code*? Justify your answer.

security of the person had to be balanced against the sanctity of life, which is another value enshrined in s. 7 of the Charter. The state has an obligation to protect the vulnerable and maintain the sanctity of human life:

> The long-standing blanket prohibition in s. 241(b), which fulfils the government's objective of protecting the vulnerable, is grounded in the state interest in protecting life and reflects the policy of the state that human life should not be depreciated by allowing life to be taken. This state policy is part of our fundamental conception of the sanctity of life.

About four months after the Supreme Court decision, Rodriguez committed suicide with the aid of a doctor whose name is still unknown. A Special Senate Committee in 1995 voted 4–3 against legalizing assisted suicide. The issue remains a controversial one in Canadian society.

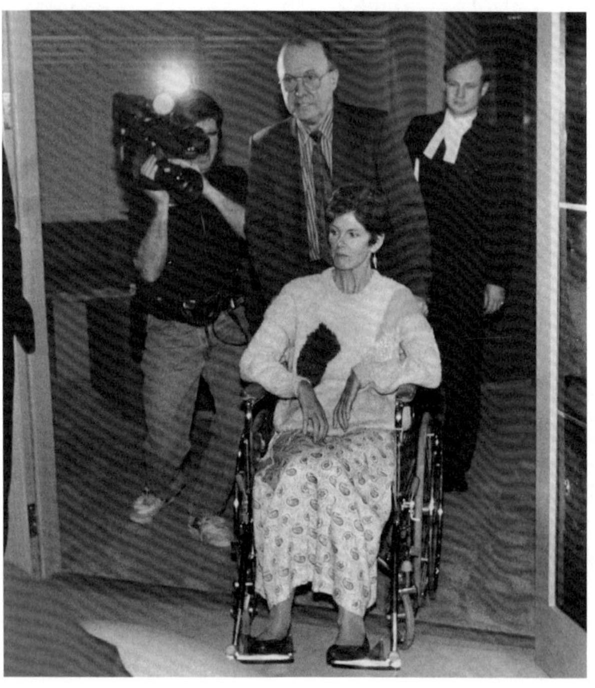

Figure 1.6 *Sue Rodriguez argued that s. 241 of the* Criminal Code *violated her rights under s. 7 of the Charter.*

Turning Points in the Law

The Introduction of Medicare

Polls and surveys show that most Canadians value Canada's universal health insurance scheme—medicare—over any other public policies that have been adopted. Roy Romanow, who was appointed in 2000 to study the system and recommend improvements, found that Canadians consider medicare the "defining aspect of their citizenship."

Under the constitution, hospitals and health care are a provincial responsibility. Pressure on the federal government for universal medical coverage began to build momentum in Canada in the 1950s. British Columbia and Saskatchewan, led by Tommy Douglas, a firm supporter of medicare, already operated public, universal hospital insurance plans. About 50 percent of Canadians in other provinces carried some kind of health insurance to cover ever-growing hospital costs. But there were people who could not afford proper care. Memories of the pre-war Great Depression, when sick people could not afford hospital care or even doctors, were still vivid for some. The general population supported the idea that the federal government should implement a nationwide medical coverage scheme similar to those put in place in Germany, Britain, and other European countries.

A national scheme required the federal government to get the agreement of the provinces. By 1961, in return for the federal government's granting them money, the provinces had all agreed to cover the costs of standard hospital costs and diagnostic services. The next step was to cover the costs of doctors' fees. This was legislated in the *Medical Care Act* of 1966 and was replaced by the *Canada Health Act* in 1984.

The fiscal arrangement between the provinces and the federal government that funded medicare changed in the 1980s. Since then, provinces have more flexibility in how they use federal transfer payments; but even though the costs of medical care have risen, the federal government has cut back on the money it transfers to the provinces.

Figure 1.7 *Tommy Douglas gives a speech, November 1965.*

In 2000, faced with a monetary crisis in medicare, provincial and territorial leaders committed their support for a common vision within the five principles in the *Canada Health Act*. These principles are broadly described as follows.

- *Public administration:* The administration of the health care insurance plan of a province or territory must be carried out on a non-profit basis by a public authority.
- *Comprehensiveness:* All medically necessary services provided by hospitals and doctors must be insured.
- *Universality:* All insured persons must be entitled to public health insurance coverage on uniform terms and conditions.
- *Portability:* Coverage for insured services must be maintained when an insured person moves or travels within Canada or travels outside the country.
- *Accessibility:* Reasonable access by insured persons to medically necessary hospital and physician services must not be impeded by financial or other barriers.

The challenge for governments is to maintain these principles.

Questions

1. How was the *Medical Care Act* a turning point in the law?
2. What factor(s) do you think played a role in promoting change with regard to health insurance?
3. Investigate the role played by Tommy Douglas in promoting medicare. Would you consider him an individual who promoted change? Explain your answer.
4. Do you agree with Romanow's finding about the importance of medicare? Why or why not?

For background on prisoners' right to vote and the Supreme Court decision, visit www.emp.ca/dimensionsoflaw

Restoring to Prisoners Their Right to Vote

Changes in the law are often controversial. This was certainly the case with Richard Sauvé's 10-year struggle to win voting rights for prisoners. A member of the biker gang Satan's Choice, Sauvé was convicted of first-degree murder and received a life sentence. From his cell in a Kingston prison, he decided to challenge s. 51(e) of the *Canada Elections Act*, which denied prisoners the right to vote. Sauvé felt this violated his rights under s. 3 of the Charter, which says that "every Canadian citizen has the right to vote."

Sauvé took his original challenge all the way to the Supreme Court, which in 1993 ruled in his favour and declared s. 51(e) unconstitutional. Parliament then rewrote the law so that it applied only to prisoners in federal penitentiaries. (Usually, people sentenced to less than two years serve their terms in provincial prisons, while those sentenced to more than two years serve their terms in federal penitentiaries.) Sauvé remounted his legal challenge, and in 2002 the Supreme Court, by a margin of 5–4, ruled in his favour once again. In her written decision, Chief Justice Beverley McLachlin used unusually strong language to chastise Parliament for trying to circumvent the Court's earlier decision by rewriting the law: "The healthy and important promotion of a dialogue between the legislature and the courts should not be debased to a rule of 'If at first you don't succeed, try, try again.'"

Some members of Parliament and representatives of victims' rights groups were appalled by the Court's decision. They argued that depriving prisoners of their right to vote was a logical punishment for breaking the law and would encourage greater respect for the law. Chief Justice McLachlin disagreed with this theory, noting that "neither the record nor common sense supports the claim that disenfranchisement [taking away the right to vote] deters crime or rehabilitates criminals."

Return to the cartoon in Figure 1.1, which refers to the Supreme Court's 2002 decision in this case. Now that you know the background, does this knowledge change your answers to any of the questions that follow the cartoon?

CHECK YOUR UNDERSTANDING

1. How were the avenues of change used by Mandela and Riel different from those used by Morgentaler, Rodriguez, and Sauvé?
2. Explain how the Charter can be used to change laws in Canada.
3. Briefly explain why the Supreme Court refused to strike down the law prohibiting assisted suicide. Do you think this law could be repealed in the future? Why or why not?

Change as a Result of Collective Action

You have been looking at cases in which individuals struggled to change laws they considered unjust. It is important to remember that most of these people did not work in complete isolation but relied on the support of other individuals and organizations to help accomplish their goals. Nelson Mandela belonged to the African National Congress, a powerful political party that helped spread his message of equal rights throughout South Africa. Louis Riel used the political and military organization of the Métis buffalo hunt to mobilize the people of the Red River settlement. Henry Morgentaler presented his 1988 case to the Supreme Court of Canada in conjunction with two other doctors who had been charged under the abortion law. He also enjoyed widespread support from feminist groups. Sue Rodriguez won backing from MP Svend Robinson and from groups such as the Right to Die Society of Canada. Richard Sauvé was helped in his long legal battle by prisoners' rights organizations such as the John Howard Society.

To move the government to the point at which it is willing to change one of its own laws, it is necessary to develop a widespread consensus, or broad agreement of opinion, that the law needs to be changed. This is always easier to accomplish when a group of people works together, rather than when one person works alone. In this section, you will look at several of the most effective ways for groups of people working together to change the law. These include the use of lobby groups, Royal Commissions, legal scholarship, and political demonstrations.

Lobby Groups

From the point of view of getting results, lobby groups are the most effective form of collective action for changing the law. There are many different kinds of lobby groups in Canada, but they all share some general characteristics. A lobby group can be defined as a number of people trying to influence legislators on behalf of a particular cause or interest. In Canada, all provincial governments have their own lobby groups in Ottawa. Before the federal government passed legislation ratifying the Kyoto Accord in 2002, for instance, both Alberta and Ontario had very active lobby groups seeking exemptions for the oil and automobile industries, respectively.

In the incident that became known as the Montreal Massacre, a deranged gunman shot and killed 14 women engineering students at Montreal's École Polytechnique in 1989. In the wave of public revulsion that followed, a lobby group called the Coalition for Gun Control was formed and began a campaign to reform Canada's gun laws. As a direct result of this group's efforts, Parliament passed the *Firearms Act* in 1995 (see the Personal Viewpoint in Chapter 3, page 75). Among other requirements, this law made it mandatory for all gun owners in the country to register their weapons. This group was an **ad hoc organization**. Other lobby groups consist of **national organizations** such as the Canadian Association of Chiefs of Police.

ad hoc organization: an organization created for a specific purpose

national organization: an organization that represents a particular group of people on a permanent basis and has more than one purpose or goal

In 1988, 11-year-old Christopher Stephenson was brutally murdered by Joseph Fredericks, a convicted child molester who was on parole from a federal prison. In response, Ontario became the first province in the country to pass a law setting up a sex-offender registry. This legislation made it mandatory for all sex offenders to register with their local police force within 15 days of their release from prison or whenever they changed address. They also had to give the police updated photos and information on the crimes for which they had been convicted. For several years, the Canadian Association of Chiefs of Police lobbied the federal government to set up a national sex-offender registry similar to that in Ontario. In December 2002, the government introduced legislation to implement just such a registration system. The establishment of the registry raises the important question of whether the protection of society should be allowed to overrule the rights of convicted sex offenders.

Much of a lobby group's efforts are directed at legislators in Ottawa. But lobbyists also focus on raising public awareness about their issue of concern. This is part of the consensus-building process that usually takes place before a law is changed. The Canada Council for Tobacco Control (CCTC) is a good example of a lobby group that has excelled in its public awareness campaign.

The CCTC is a coalition of groups that includes the Canadian Cancer Society, the Heart and Stroke Foundation of Canada, and the Canadian Lung Association. Its focus on public education is evident in its mission statement, which says in part that the CCTC's goal is "educating Canadians about the marketing strategies and tactics of the tobacco industry and the adverse effects the industry's products have on the health of Canadians." The CCTC's education efforts have helped make Canadians more open to provincial and municipal laws banning smoking in public places and to the federal law that requires cigarette packages to carry graphic images to deter people from smoking. As a result of these laws, Canada has developed a reputation for being at the forefront of the global campaign to reduce smoking.

Fyi In 2000–2001, 24% of Canadians over 15 were smokers—slightly more than 6 million people. This figure was down from 31% in 1994 and 38% in 1981.

Royal Commissions

Sometimes when a lobby group has succeeded in building public support for its cause, the government will appoint a **Royal Commission** to investigate the issue and publish a report. A Royal Commission usually calls public meetings, gathers testimony from private citizens, calls expert witnesses, and commissions scholarly research. The government does not have to act on the Commission's recommendations, but Parliament will often use them as a basis for passing new legislation or repealing old laws that are perceived to be outdated or unjust.

Royal Commission: a board of inquiry appointed by the government to investigate and report on a particular issue

Feminist activist Laura Sabia played a key role in persuading the government to appoint the Royal Commission on the Status of Women in 1967. The commissioners worked for three years before issuing their report in 1970. Recommendations included establishing certain rights for women that today we take for granted but that at the time seemed revolutionary. Among these were that women should be granted unemployment benefits for maternity leave, that gender and marital status should be prohibited as grounds for discrimination by employers, and that the federal government should appoint more women judges to federal courts. All these and more of the Commission's recommendations have since been implemented.

In 1993, the federal government set up the Commission of Inquiry on the Blood System in Canada, also known as the Krever Commission after its head, Justice Horace Krever. Between 1980 and 1985, about 2000 Canadians were infected with the HIV/AIDS virus after receiving transfusions of blood or blood products. Between 1980 and 1990, more than 60 000 transfusion recipients contracted the hepatitis-C virus. In the report he released in 1997, Judge Krever concluded that a significant number of these infections could have been prevented through proper testing and treatment of blood donations. He noted significant failures on the part of the Canadian Red Cross, officials in the federal government, and some pharmaceutical companies. As a direct result of Krever's recommendations, the government established the Canadian Blood Services to take control of the country's blood supply away from the Red Cross. In 2002, the RCMP laid criminal charges against the Canadian Red Cross, one pharmaceutical company, and four doctors who had previously worked for either the Red Cross or the federal government.

For a timeline on Canada's tainted blood scandal and the final report of the Krever Commission, visit www.emp.ca/dimensionsoflaw

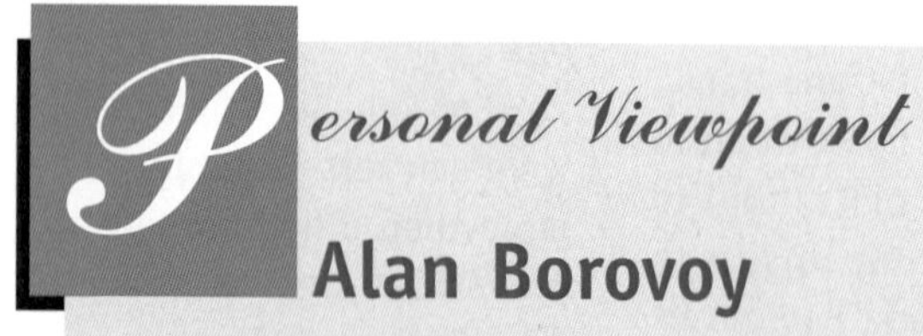

Personal Viewpoint: Alan Borovoy

Alan Borovoy grew up in downtown Toronto in the 1940s, around Grace and Harbord Streets, "a small, upper-working-class island of Jews in a sea of anti-Semitism." One of the most memorable moments of his youth was at his bar mitzvah in 1945, when World War II was almost over and word was filtering out about the horrors of the concentration camps.

"With tears streaming down his face, my grandfather talked about the catastrophe that had befallen European Jewry, and he admonished me never to forget, and always to protect, my people," he recalls. Following that advice, Borovoy became increasingly convinced that "the best way to protect the Jewish people was to promote greater justice for all people."

So the Jewish Labour Committee, where he started working, broadened into combatting discrimination against everyone. That experience led him, in 1968, to the Canadian Civil Liberties Association (CCLA). He has been there ever since, for far less pay than what a legal analyst of his skill and experience would make in private practice, and struggling to run the organization on a shoestring budget.

The CCLA was founded in 1964 by a group of citizens who were alarmed by the growing power of the state and, in particular, by an Ontario bill that would drastically increase the powers of the police. Activists from many walks of life, including universities, journalism, the law, trade unions, and politics, have served on its board.

As general counsel of the CCLA, Borovoy has made presentations to public inquiries and given testimony before parliamentary committees on such issues as mandatory drug testing in the workplace, wiretapping, and race relations between local communities and the police. He has also given lectures and public addresses to students, human rights organizations, and policing agencies. His media work has included a stint as a columnist for the *Toronto Star* and many appearances on public affairs programs and open-line television and radio programs. He is the author of three books.

In addition, Borovoy has played a key role in establishing the right for **intervenors** to participate in cases heard before the Supreme Court of Canada. If granted intervenor status, a group will usually prepare a brief explaining its position on a particular issue. The Court will then review this brief before handing down its decision. Before passage of the *Charter of Rights and Freedoms* in 1982, it was rare for intervenors to participate in court cases, especially at the Supreme Court level. Usually, only provincial governments could gain intervenor status with the Supreme Court.

After the Charter came into effect, many people realized that the Court's Charter decisions had the potential to affect a broad spectrum of Canadians. In 1984, Alan Borovoy wrote to the Supreme Court, asking that it permit more interventions in the Charter cases that came before it. The Court responded in 1987 by changing its rules on interventions to allow more third-party participation in cases involving Charter rights. By 1990, the Supreme Court was allowing intervenors to participate in 58 percent of its Charter cases. This is one example of Borovoy's work as advocate for the CCLA that led to an important change in Canadian legal practice.

In summing up his 35 years of work at the CCLA, Borovoy has said that he tries to focus on what is practical and to resist utopian thinking: "It's a mistake to try and create heaven on earth. We should try instead to reduce the hell on earth. Otherwise you end up being terribly frustrated and give up."

Source: Adapted from Haroon Siddiqui, *The Toronto Star*, June 25 and 29, 2000; and from the CCLA's Web site at http://ccla.org/peop/borovoy.shtml.

Questions

1. Explain why intervenor status in court cases is an important right for parties who want to change the law.
2. What do you understand by the term "civil liberties"?
3. How does an organization like the CCLA protect civil liberties? Do you think an organization like this is needed in Canada? Explain your viewpoint.

Legal Scholarship

Another method of accomplishing law reform is to produce scholarly articles and books on a particular topic or issue. Perhaps no one has used this method more successfully over the past several years than feminist legal scholars. Quarterly publications such as the *Canadian Journal of Women and the Law* contain a variety of articles in every issue that give a feminist perspective on legal matters and events. Feminist research on battered women's syndrome, for example, was key to having this condition accepted as an **exculpating factor** in some murder cases in which a woman was pleading self-defence.

Find out more about the lobbying efforts of the Canadian Civil Liberties Association at www.emp.ca/dimensionsoflaw

intervenor: an individual, agency, or group of people not directly involved in a case but who, as a third party, has a special interest in its outcome; sometimes called "friend of the court"

exculpating factor: a factor that clears a defendant of blame

Case BATTERED WOMEN'S SYNDROME

R v. Lavallee, [1990] 1 SCR 852

Facts

Lavallee was a battered woman in a stormy common-law relationship with Rust. She killed Rust one night by shooting him in the back of the head with a rifle as he left her room. The shooting occurred after a violent argument during which Rust had beaten Lavallee. He also taunted her with the threat that he would kill her if she didn't kill him first. Rust had frequently beaten Lavallee in the past, and she was in the habit of making up excuses for her injuries to medical staff. A psychiatrist with extensive professional experience in the treatment of battered wives prepared an assessment of Lavallee that was used in support of her defence of self-defence. He explained her ongoing terror, her inability to escape the relationship despite the violence, and the escalating pattern of abuse that put her life in danger. He testified that in his opinion, Lavallee's shooting of Rust was the final, desperate act of a woman who believed she would be killed that same night.

At trial, the jury acquitted Lavallee, but the verdict was overturned by the Manitoba Court of Appeal. Lavallee then appealed to the Supreme Court of Canada.

Issue

One of the more important issues in this case was whether expert evidence on Lavallee's condition as a battered woman was relevant to her plea of self-defence.

Decision

The Court's decision was delivered by Justice Bertha Wilson, the first woman appointed to the Supreme Court of Canada. The Court found that expert evidence on the effect of battered woman syndrome was "both relevant and necessary" in Lavallee's case if the members of the jury were to understand her mental state. Otherwise, they might not understand why a battered woman would remain in an abusive relationship, the extent of the violence that she suffered, and her perception that her life was in danger. The Supreme Court overturned the Court of Appeal's ruling and restored Lavallee's acquittal by a decision of 7–0.

In its written decision, the Supreme Court listed several scholarly works it had reviewed before making its ruling. The list included several works by feminist legal scholars, including two books by Lenore E. Walker, *The Battered Woman* and *The Battered Woman Syndrome.* The *Lavallee* case established a **precedent** that recognized battered women's syndrome as a psychiatric condition that a jury should consider in relevant cases.

precedent: a legal decision that is taken as a guide for subsequent cases

Questions

1. Explain what is meant by "self-defence" and "battered women's syndrome."
2. In what sense did feminist legal research have an influence on the Supreme Court's decision in this case?
3. How did the Supreme Court's judgment change the law?

Political Demonstrations

Sometimes people in a democratic society feel that their government has failed to listen to their calls for legal change. When this happens, citizens can exercise the option of participating in political demonstrations, a right guaranteed under s. 2 of the Charter as the "freedom of peaceable assembly." Protest rallies, where large numbers of people gather to march, carry signs, and listen to speeches, are the most common form of political demonstrations. There are two things to note about this form of protest.

First, in regard to having concrete, practical effects on the law, the results of a political demonstration can be mixed. Sometimes the mere threat of a rally will be enough to persuade the government to act. This was the case in 1966 when Laura Sabia threatened to organize a march on Ottawa if the federal government did not authorize a Royal Commission on women. The government acted very quickly to set up the Commission and avoid the spectacle of protesters converging on Ottawa from across the nation. At other times, protest rallies have had little or no effect on government policy. The several marches on Queen's Park organized in the 1990s to protest changes to provincial laws made under the Progressive Conservative party's "Common Sense Revolution" only seemed to strengthen the government's resolve to push through its reforms in the face of public resistance.

Second, protest rallies can often change from "peaceable assemblies" to exercises in **civil disobedience** or even to acts of violence. Mohandas K. (Mahatma) Gandhi used this form of protest to free India of British rule after World War II. In the United States, Martin Luther King, Jr. used lunch-counter sit-ins, bus boycotts, and protest marches to win basic political and legal rights for African-Americans. Boxer Muhammad Ali's refusal to register for the US draft in 1967 is another example of civil disobedience.

civil disobedience: a peaceful form of protest by which a person refuses to obey a particular law as a matter of conscience

Sometimes a few people who believe in using force as a tactic against the government infiltrate a peaceful protest and turn it into a violent one. This was the strategy taken by some of the protesters who participated in the marches and attacks on police barricades at the third Summit of the Americas held in Quebec City in 2001.

The grassroots protest against clear-cut logging on Clayoquot Sound, Vancouver Island, in 1993 is a good example of a political demonstration that involved civil disobedience and had mixed results when it came to changing the law. In 1991, the BC government decided to allow some clear-cutting of old-growth forests on Vancouver Island. Protests began almost immediately, and the lumber company MacMillan Bloedel won a court injunction forbidding protesters to blockade access roads in the Clayoquot Sound area. The protests escalated and the blockades continued until the summer of 1993, when more than 10 000 protesters arrived and 857 of them were arrested for violating the court order.

Figure 1.8 *Protesting fishers and families display signs at a ceremony commemorating the designation of Clayoquot Sound as a UNESCO Biosphere Reserve in May 2000.*

In 1995, the provincial government responded by adopting the recommendations of the Science Panel for Sustainable Forest Practices in Clayoquot Sound. These recommendations included

- ending conventional clear-cutting in the area
- deferring logging in pristine areas until studies and inventories of all species living there had been conducted
- banning logging in areas that had been overcut
- reducing the amount of wood cut each year in Clayoquot Sound.

To learn more about Clayquot Sound, visit www.emp.ca/dimensionsoflaw

At first glance, it seemed as if the protesters had won a decisive victory over the loggers. In 1996, however, the environmental group Greenpeace accused MacMillan Bloedel of resuming logging operations in one of the pristine areas of the Sound, an area that should have been off-limits to logging until impact studies had been completed. The net result of all the protests over the years seems to have been to slow and somewhat restrict the operations of logging companies in Clayoquot Sound, but the drive to stop them completely has failed.

CHECK YOUR UNDERSTANDING

1. Do you agree that lobby groups are the most effective form of collective action for changing the law? Explain your reasoning, giving examples.
2. Give your opinion on the advantages and disadvantages of civil disobedience as a method of trying to effect legal change.
3. What, in your opinion, are the advantages of Royal Commissions in the process of legal change?

METHODS OF *Legal Inquiry*

Using the Internet for Legal Research

By using your home or school computer, you can find legal sites on the Internet that provide cases, legislation, law journals, and government services.

General Principles

When doing research online, it is imperative that you evaluate the Web sites you visit. You must be able to judge the quality and reliability of the legal information you find.

Here are some guidelines on evaluating free Web sites.

- *Authorship:* Be clear on who wrote the material and who owns the Web site. Anyone can publish a Web site. That does not mean that the material provided is accurate and authoritative. Is the site associated with a reliable publisher or organization? Does it provide a mailing address, phone number, and e-mail address?
- *Quality of presentation:* Is the written material free of spelling and grammatical errors? If the site looks as if it were thrown together in an unprofessional manner, then it probably was—and you should beware of using it.
- *Purpose:* Ask yourself why the Web site exists. Is it meant to sell a product? Is the site meant to advocate a particular point of view? If so, then the information it presents will contain an ideological bias. You may use the material to illustrate the point of view the author is advocating, but it would be unwise to accept this information unquestioningly.
- *Currency:* What is the date range of the material on the site? A good Web site is usually updated regularly to keep its information current and accurate. The site will show when a page was last updated, often in a note at the bottom of the page. If the last update was longer than a year ago, try to find another site with more current material.

Source: Adapted from Ted Tjaden, *Legal Research and Writing*. Toronto: Irwin Law, 2001, pp. 94–95.

Applying the Skill

1. Find Web sites for the following organizations. Write up a general evaluation of the legal materials available from each site using the four criteria listed above.
   a) Canadian Civil Liberties Association
   b) Department of Justice of Canada
   c) Greenpeace
   d) Ontario Human Rights Commission
2. Go to the Web site of the Alberta Court of Queen's Bench and locate the case of *Chae v. Min*. Read the case. Discuss what further details you learned about the case, and how these helped you understand the concept of "contributory negligence."

Internet Search Sites

Access to Justice Network
www.acjnet.org/home.cfm
A good source for legal and justice information. The site is supported by governmental, educational, and professional law affiliates.

Alan Gahtan/Canadian Legal Resources
www.gahtan.com/cdnlaw
A comprehensive source for Canadian legal resources. Alan Gahtan is a practising lawyer in the area of information technology and electronic commerce.

Canadian Legal Information Institute (CANLII)
www.canlii.org
A good source for federal and provincial statutes and cases. The site is run by the Federation of Law Societies of Canada, which is the umbrella organization of Canada's 14 law societies.

Duhaime & Company
www.duhaime.org
A comprehensive source for Canadian legal resources, including a legal dictionary. Duhaime & Company is a Vancouver law firm.

Reviewing Main Ideas

You Decide!

BRINGING A KIRPAN TO SCHOOL

Ontario Human Rights Commission and Harbhajan Singh Pandori v. Peel Board of Education (1991), 3 OR (3d) 531 (Div. Ct.)

This case is an appeal by the Peel Board of Education of a ruling by a Board of Inquiry constituted under the Ontario *Human Rights Code*. The Board of Inquiry had ruled that Mr. Pandori, a Sikh teacher, was allowed to wear his kirpan, a ceremonial dagger with a metal blade, to school subject to certain safety restrictions.

Facts

Pandori was a teacher with the Peel Board of Education. As a Khalsa Sikh, he was required to wear a kirpan wherever he went. This created a problem when his employer, the Peel Board of Education, developed a no-weapons policy in response to a number of knife incidents and increasing violence in its schools. The Board stated that this policy also applied to kirpans, and as a result Pandori would not be permitted to wear his on school grounds.

Pandori took his case to the Ontario Human Rights Commission, which set up a Board of Inquiry under the Ontario *Human Rights Code* to investigate the matter. The Board ruled that the school board's policy discriminated against Khalsa Sikhs. It ordered that Pandori be allowed to wear his kirpan to school subject to certain safety restrictions that prevented the kirpan from being easily removed from its sheath. The school board appealed this order.

The Law

The chair of the Board of Inquiry found that the Peel school board's no-weapons policy was contrary to s. 10 of the Ontario *Human Rights Code*, which states:

> 10(1) A right of a person under Part I is infringed where a requirement, qualification or factor exists that is not discrimination on a prohibited ground but that results in the exclusion, restriction or preference of a group of persons who are identified by a prohibited ground of discrimination and of whom the person is a member, except where,
>
> (a) the requirement, qualification or factor is reasonable and *bona fide* [in good faith] in the circumstances... .

Outlawing the carrying of weapons at school is not in itself a prohibited ground of discrimination. However, since the ban has the effect of restricting Khalsa Sikhs in the free expression of their religion, it infringes on one of their human rights. The only question is whether this infringement is reasonable and necessary given the circumstances.

Argument of Pandori and the Ontario Human Rights Commission (Respondents)

Pandori and the Human Rights Commission argued that there had been only three reported incidents of violent kirpan use in the Toronto area, and that none of these happened at a school. They also stated there was no evidence that a kirpan had ever been used as a weapon in any Peel school. In addition, they pointed out that two other Toronto-area school boards allowed students to wear kirpans to school, and that there was no evidence to show that kirpans caused any violence in other schools.

They claimed that the Peel school board's policy was contrary to the Ontario *Human Rights Code* and amounted to religious discrimination.

Argument of the Peel Board of Education (Appellant)

The school board argued that a kirpan, though a religious object, could be perceived by non-Sikhs as a weapon and therefore as something dangerous to bring to school. The board pointed out that kirpans are prohibited on Canadian airplane flights and that judges in Manitoba courts have the power to exclude kirpans from their courtrooms.

The board also contended that its schools were special places, and the Ontario *Human Rights Code* had to be interpreted in light of this fact. It argued that it was reasonable to impose its weapons ban on kirpans to ensure the safety of all students under its jurisdiction, and that it could not accommodate the requirements of Khalsa Sikhs without undue hardship.

Make Your Decision

1. Outline the facts of this case in point form.
2. Re-read the excerpt from s. 10 of the Ontario *Human Rights Code.* Pandori and the Human Rights Commission said that the school board's no-weapons policy clearly contravened this section of the Code. The Peel school board argued that its policy did not contravene the Code. Which part of s. 10 did the school board focus on to justify its policy? Explain why.
3. In your own words, summarize the key points made by both sides in this case.
4. Now make your decision: reject or allow the appeal. Give reasons for your decision.

Key Terms

Review the following terms to show that you understand the meaning of each and how it is applied in a legal context.

ad hoc organization
apartheid
case law/common law
civil disobedience
Crown (attorney)
entrenched in the constitution
exculpating factor
intervenor
lobby group
Métis
national organization
precedent
Royal Commission
rule of law
statute law

Understanding the Law

Review the following legislation mentioned in the text, and be able either to explain why the law was passed or to cite at least one change that has been made to it.

Canada Elections Act
Canada's *Official Languages Act*
Criminal Code, s. 287
Customs Act
Firearms Act
Manitoba Act
Manitoba's *Official Language Act*

Thinking and Inquiry

1. Identify a current demographic trend and explain what effect it may have on the law in Canada.
2. Judging by the material in this chapter, do you think the law on assisted suicide will ever be changed to make this practice legal? Explain why or why not.
3. Research one lobby group that is not mentioned in the text. Use an organizational chart to show
   a) its official name
   b) when it was founded
   c) what issue or issues it is concerned with
   d) how it lobbies public officials
   e) how it increases public awareness
   f) what results it has achieved.
4. Are political demonstrations an effective means for changing the law? Why or why not?
5. Do you think battered women's syndrome should be extended to other people who react violently to long-term physical abuse? Write a one-page brief to argue that either (a) battered child syndrome or (b) battered senior syndrome is a legitimate psychological explanation of an abused person's state of mind that ought to be taken into consideration when that person is pleading self-defence to a murder charge.

Communication

6. Identify a current Canadian law that you think needs to be changed. Draw up an action plan for getting Parliament to make the necessary changes. Remember that your plan should contain strategies for raising public awareness and for direct lobbying of Members of Parliament.
7. Organize into teams to debate the following resolution: "*Louis Riel was justified in using violence to protect the rights of the Métis in the Red River settlement.*" Before the debate begins, make sure that your team has a written list of at least three arguments to support your side of the debate.
8. Find an example of a person (either in Canada or another country) who, like Nelson Mandela, struggled to change unjust laws. Write a brief account of this person's life, making sure to include the following points:
   a) what inspired this person to work for change
   b) what sacrifices this person had to make while working for change
   c) the strategies (violent or non-violent) this person used to achieve change
   d) what results this person achieved

Application

9. Find an editorial cartoon in a newspaper that comments on the need for changing a Canadian law. As a guide, use the questions for Figure 1.1 to explain the cartoon. What is the cartoonist recommending? Do you agree? Explain.
10. Ben Stillmore lives in Belltown, Ontario. Ben owns six cats, which he lets outside every morning for exercise. The city passes a bylaw making it illegal to have more than four cats in a residence. Owners must also register their cats to get special identification collars that cost $50 each. Ben refuses to register his cats, and one morning the city confiscates all six of them. Ben believes the new bylaw is a bad regulation and wants it repealed. Write Ben a letter, advising him of the best way to have this done.

Chapter 2 Sources and Categories of Law

CHAPTER Focus

In this chapter, you will

- trace the development of law from its primary sources in religion, philosophy, and traditional customs
- examine secondary sources of law, such as constitutions, statutes, court decisions, and legal writings
- consider the relationship between law, religion, and morality
- compare historical systems of judgment, such as trial by combat and trial by ordeal
- understand the distinctions among different categories of law, such as common and civil law, substantive and procedural law, domestic and international law, and private and public law
- analyze how society uses law to express its values

In its earliest development, law was closely associated with other aspects of society, including religion and moral values, philosophy, and customs and conventions. Because of these different influences, the law in Canada has developed into a complex system of rules and regulations. In this chapter, you will examine some of the earliest sources of law and the way they came to be codified or written down. You will also consider the organization of law into different categories that can make its purposes easier to understand. Throughout the chapter, you will explore ways in which the law continues to develop in response to contemporary issues, changes in moral values, and concerns.

The cartoon in Figure 2.1 offers a reflection on the way many people feel about their country's written laws.

"As a matter of fact, I have read the Constitution, and, frankly, I don't get it."

Figure 2.1

At First Glance

1. Where is this cartoon set? Identify the roles of the three main figures. Who are the people sitting to the right?
2. Do you think this cartoon indicates a problem that is common in Canada as well as in the United States? Explain.
3. What do you know about Canada's written constitution? Share your knowledge with your group.
4. Do you think it is important for a country's citizens to be familiar with the written laws of the land? Explain.

Primary Sources of Canadian Law

Canada's legal system is the outcome of a historical development that stretches back thousands of years. The system's cumulative values, beliefs, and principles are based on actions and decisions of the past. The parts of the legal system that have the longest historical development are known as **primary sources of law**. For instance, we can see forerunners of some current Canadian laws in religious commandments that were formulated in ancient times in the Middle East.

primary sources of law: those parts of a legal system that have the longest historical development and represent the system's cumulative values, beliefs, and principles

Influence of Religion and Morality

Canada's laws reflect our Judeo-Christian religious heritage. The primary source for this heritage is the Old Testament of the Christian Bible, whose first five books comprise the Jewish Torah. "Torah" means "instruction" in Hebrew. The Torah tells how the Jewish leader Moses went up Mount Sinai. There he had a vision in which God gave him divine laws to guide the Jewish people. The core of these laws, called the Ten Commandments, forbade the people, among other things, to commit murder and theft, "to bear false witness" against their neighbours, and to worship other gods. Much later, the Christian religion, as taught by Jesus and practised by his disciples, included the Ten Commandments and many other aspects of Jewish law.

When Christian missionaries and colonists came to Canada in the 16th and 17th centuries, they brought their religion with them. This religion would have a profound effect on the development of Canadian law. Consider, for example, the *Canadian Charter of Rights and Freedoms*, which was passed into law in 1982. The preamble to the Charter reads: "Whereas Canada is founded upon principles that recognize the supremacy of God and the rule of law." This wording reflects the fact that a majority of Canadians profess a belief system that assumes the existence of God as the supreme being and, as such, the original source of law.

Do you swear (or solemnly affirm) that the evidence to be given by you to the court shall be the truth, the whole truth, and nothing but the truth, so help you God?

Figure 2.2 *Oath administered to witnesses in Ontario criminal courts. Today, witnesses in Canadian courts do not have to swear to tell the truth on the Christian Bible. Muslims, Hindus, Buddhists, and others can swear on their respective sacred texts. Devout Christians who believed that swearing on a holy book was blasphemy were the first to be permitted to make a solemn affirmation to tell the truth. Now, people who do not believe in God are also legally entitled to make a solemn affirmation.*

Canada is not the only country whose laws reflect a religious heritage. Many countries in the Middle East, Africa, and Asia base their laws on the teachings of the Qur'an, the holy book of Islam. Some of the laws of India have been influenced by Hinduism and some of Japan's laws by Shintoism.

In addition to its Judeo-Christian religious heritage, Canada's laws also reflect the influence of moral philosophy or ethics. Moral philosophy deals with the distinction between right and wrong in human behaviour. Although morality is often connected with religion—people speak of "Christian morality" or "Buddhist ethics"—this is not always the case. Atheists, people who do not believe in God, can also have a strong moral sense.

Philosophers such as Aristotle taught that one must use one's reason to understand the difference between acceptable and unacceptable behaviour. Laws are written affirmations of what society as a whole considers good and bad behaviour.

Canada's laws reflect a strong moral sense that there are certain actions, such as taking another person's life, that are wrong by their very

Excerpts from the Ten Commandments	Excerpts from Canada's *Criminal Code*
5. Thou shalt not kill.	s. 235(1) Every one who commits first degree murder or second degree murder is guilty of an indictable offence and shall be sentenced to imprisonment for life.
7. Thou shalt not steal.	s. 344 Every person who commits robbery is guilty of an indictable offence and liable ... to imprisonment for life.
8. Thou shalt not bear false witness against thy neighbour.	s. 132 Every one who commits perjury is guilty of an indictable offence and liable to imprisonment for a term not exceeding fourteen years.

Figure 2.3 *Canada's* Criminal Code *contains laws that reflect some of the restrictions in the Ten Commandments.*

Figure 2.4 *Thanks largely to the* Lord's Day Act, *Sunday streets in Toronto were often deserted in the early 1900s.*

nature. We know murder is wrong not just because religion forbids it, but because human reason tells us so.

Some of our laws, such as laws against public nudity, reflect society's moral values. As moral values change, these laws may be changed. It is hard to imagine now, but Canada's major cities, even through the 1970s, often resembled ghost towns on Sunday afternoons, with their stores locked up and few pedestrians to be seen. This was largely due to a piece of legislation passed at the beginning of the 20th century called the *Lord's Day Act*, which made it illegal to transact business on a Sunday. When the law was passed, many Canadians felt that Sunday, as the Christian sabbath, ought to be a day of worship and rest from work.

The *Lord's Day Act* had its roots in British law, where a similar act had been passed in the 17th century. In Canada, a group of devout Protestants formed the Lord's Day Alliance in 1882 to halt a growing trend to think of Sunday as a workday like any other or as a day for leisure activities, such as going to the theatre or playing games in public places. The Alliance won support from Roman Catholic church officials and from organized labour, which wanted to protect the one rest day its workers still had. In 1906, the Lord's Day Alliance persuaded Wilfrid Laurier's federal government to introduce the *Lord's Day Act.*

Canada's cultural mosaic changed radically over the course of the 20th century, especially after World War II. Immigrants came from Asia and Africa, many of whom were Muslims, Buddhists, or Hindus. As well, more Jewish immigrants arrived, fleeing war-ravaged Europe and the aftermath of the Holocaust. Few of these new Canadians shared the Christian concern with keeping the sabbath on Sunday. (For Jews the sabbath is on Saturday; for Muslims, Friday is the holiest day of the week.)

Section 4 of the *Lord's Day Act* contained a basic prohibition against commercial transactions on Sunday:

4. It is not lawful for any person on the Lord's Day, except as provided herein ... to sell or offer for sale or purchase any goods, chattels, or other personal property, or any real estate, or to carry on or transact any business of his ordinary calling, or in connection with such calling, or for gain to do, or employ any other person to do, on that day, any work, business, or labour.

Section 5 provided that any worker required to work by an employer operating on Sunday in conformity with the Act be given a substitute day of rest. Section 6 prohibited any games or performances for which an admission fee was charged. Section 7 prohibited any transportation operated for pleasure where a fee was charged. Section 8 prohibited advertisement of anything prohibited by the Act. Section 9 prohibited the shooting of firearms. Section 10 prohibited any sale or distribution of a foreign newspaper.

As Canadian society changed, the *Lord's Day Act* became the target of legal challenges. The first significant case was *R v. Robertson and Rosetanni* in 1962. Robertson and Rosetanni owned a bowling alley in Hamilton, Ontario, and when they opened on a Sunday, police charged them with violating the *Lord's Day Act.* In their defence, the two men argued that the Act violated their right to freedom of religion guaranteed by the *Canadian Bill of Rights,* passed in 1960 (see Chapter 5: The Charter and the Courts). The case went to the Supreme Court, which found that the *Bill of Rights* was not concerned with rights and freedoms in a broad sense, but guaranteed only those rights that were already in place when it was passed.

Once the *Canadian Charter of Rights and Freedoms* became law in 1982, it was inevitable that more legal challenges would be mounted. This happened almost immediately, when, on Sunday, May 30, 1982, Big M Drug Mart opened for business in Calgary. After police witnessed several transactions, they charged Big M with violating the *Lord's Day Act.* This case, too, went to the Supreme Court, but this time the result was different. The Court ruled in Big M's favour and struck down the Act as unconstitutional.

Historical Influences

Historical influences have also played a role in the development of Canadian law. Our law reflects British and French laws, both of which were influenced by Greek and Roman laws. These in turn were partly based on such ideas as the concept of private property that came from the ancient kingdoms of Mesopotamia.

Greek Influences

The Greeks were the first European people to practise democratic ideals in their political and legal systems. Today, we would say that they practised a "limited" democracy. In the city-state of Athens, for instance, citizenship was limited to native-born men over the age of 18. Women, foreigners, and slaves were excluded from political life. The Athenians expected citizens to take an active role in politics. Voting was not just a right, but a serious civic responsibility, as was serving in public office and the military.

People accused of crimes were tried by juries of their fellow citizens. To avoid bribery, juries were quite large. In the most famous trial in ancient Athens, a jury of 501 citizens heard the case brought against the philosopher Socrates (see Chapter 3: Theories and Concepts of Law). No judges or lawyers participated in these trials; the defendant acted as his own lawyer, and the jury itself was the judge. Verdicts were decided through a secret ballot. If the defendant was found guilty, his accusers would recommend one penalty and he another. Then the jury would vote again on the sentence.

These two important principles—citizen participation and trial by jury—are entrenched in the *Canadian Charter of Rights and Freedoms.* Section 3 of the Charter guarantees every Canadian citizen the right to vote, and s. 11 guarantees the right to trial by jury.

Roman Influences

The legal system of ancient Rome has also influenced Canadian law. In 449 BCE, a Roman legal commission drew up a **code** of traditional Roman laws. They inscribed this code on 12 tablets that were displayed in the Forum, the largest public square in Rome. The code was called the *Law of the Twelve Tables.* It was organized by topic and covered almost every aspect of Roman life, including marriage, court cases, and property rights. Any Roman who needed to know the law could walk to the Forum and consult this code.

code: a systematic collection of laws, written down and organized into topics

Over time, Roman laws became more numerous, and their interpretation more complex. It was difficult for even the best-informed citizen to know the law thoroughly. At this point, the Romans began to train specialists (what we would now call lawyers) to advise citizens who needed to use the legal system.

By the sixth century CE, there were so many laws and volumes of commentary that even trained lawyers had trouble using them. The Emperor Justinian ordered that all the laws in the Roman empire be collected together and organized into one manageable code. The *Code of Justinian* was published in 529 CE and became the standard body of law throughout the empire.

Canada has adopted these aspects of the Roman legal system: the use of codes and the use of lawyers. For example, most of Canada's criminal laws have been published in the *Criminal Code.* Lawyers are a mainstay of the Canadian legal system, providing assistance to almost everyone who comes in contact with the courts or who needs help with legal matters.

Personal Viewpoint

The Language of Law

The language—sometimes known as "legalese"—used by practitioners of the law is rooted in the past. Words and phrases that are no longer part of everyday language have precise legal meanings. This is the opinion of Sandeep Dave, a lawyer in Mumbai (Bombay), India, on the use of "legalese" in his work.

It is difficult for me to communicate in plain English. Why? Because I am a lawyer!

My everyday correspondence is peppered with *make an application, as you deem fit, in respect of, notwithstanding* and *hereinafter*.

Clients (and good ones at that) come with specific mandates. Give your opinion on this area of law. Draft that document. Summarize this commercial arrangement. Speak to our colleagues on ...

Readers delight in legalese and jargon—and jump with joy facing old French, Latin and Roman words. Their ears ring with history and adventure—and they pay handsomely for that momentary journey to the past.

Am I serious? No, I am not. Clients abhor legalese. They want lawyers to communicate like ordinary mortals—in plain and understandable language. Tongue in cheek, they repeatedly remind us lawyers to shun jargon. But who cares? After all, we are sentries to a thousand year old heritage.

Imagine the plight of thousands of people reading home loan agreements, insurance policies, credit card documents and routine legislation. They cry and plead for some sensibility in legal writing. They revolt. They litigate. BUT NOTHING HAPPENS. On the contrary, some believe that this approach differentiates lawyers—and adds value to their work. What rubbish!

Figure 2.5 *Sandeep Dave specializes in banking, corporate, and commercial law. He maintains the* Global Law Review, *which focuses on India law and international resources.*

I drafted a client-document some years ago. The usual ending (Latin is *testimonium*) was "*In witness whereof the parties have executed these presents the day and year first hereinabove written.*"

The client cancelled this ending, kept some space for signatures and date, and asked me if this change diluted the legal position. There was lesson enough for me. The burden of history and precedent was ruining my thoughts and ability to communicate. While law school taught me law, it apparently forgot the practical aspects of legal life—language, communication, client skills, management, marketing, competition, technology and profits. What should I do?

Now, I am determined to avoid verbal and visual mess. I try to be simple and direct. I focus on the reader and listener. I plan document layout. Most importantly, I think it all through—FIRST.

But all this takes time. It is difficult to unlearn years of legal drilling.

Source: Sandeep Dave, "Plain Language in Law," Law Library Resource XChange, LLC; www.llrx.com/features/plainlanguage.htm.

Questions

1. You will encounter several Latin legal terms in this textbook. Why do you think these terms are still used?
2. Do you agree with Sandeep Dave's opinion? Why or why not?
3. Explore Web sites to find out how successful efforts to introduce "plain language" into legal documents have been, and explain the difficulties in making this change.

Aboriginal Influences

Canada's Aboriginal peoples had their own legal systems before contact with Europeans. The First Nations did not write their laws down like the Romans, but transmitted them orally from generation to generation. This tradition was one of the responsibilities of the elders in each nation's community. Sometimes the tribal laws were transmitted in the form of legends or stories to make them easier to remember and to inspire the listener with respect for the law.

The Iroquois Confederacy, located south of Lake Ontario, was one of the most powerful groups of Aboriginal peoples. Originally it consisted of five nations: the Mohawk, Seneca, Oneida, Onondaga, and Cayuga. The Confederacy was established by two great chiefs, Dekanawida and Hiawatha, around 1142 CE. According to their oral history, it took them 40 years to convince the tribes to form a union bound together by a formal constitution. This constitution was called the *Gayanashagowa*, Iroquois for "great

Figure 2.6 *Interior of a Mohawk longhouse.*

binding law." It provided a system of checks and balances by giving every man and woman in the Confederacy a voice in tribal affairs. The powers of the war chiefs were held in check by those of the peace chiefs. All chiefs were appointed by the clan mothers, who also had the power to remove any chief who did not act in the interests of the people. At some point in the 18th century, the leaders of the Iroquois Confederacy agreed to write down their Great Binding Law. The framers of both the US constitution and the *Charter of the United Nations* referred to the Iroquois Great Binding Law in drawing up their own legal documents.

In Canada today, under the terms of the *Indian Act*, most Aboriginal peoples have the authority to make and enforce the equivalent of municipal

The Law

Excerpt from the Great Binding Law:

68. Should any member of the Five Nations, a family or person belonging to a foreign nation submit a proposal for adoption into a clan of one of the Five Nations, he or they shall furnish a string of shells, a span in length, as a pledge to the clan into which he or they wish to be adopted. The Lords [the chiefs] of the nation shall then consider the proposal and submit a decision.
69. Any member of the Five Nations who through esteem or other feeling wishes to adopt an individual, a family or number of families may offer adoption to him or them and if accepted the matter shall be brought to the attention of the Lords for confirmation and the Lords must confirm adoption.
70. When the adoption of anyone shall have been confirmed by the Lords of the Nation, the Lords shall address the people of their nation and say: "Now you of our nation, be informed that such a person, such a family or such families have ceased forever to bear their birth nation's name and have buried it in the depths of the earth. Henceforth let no one of our nation ever mention the original name or nation of their birth. To do so will be to hasten the end of our peace."

Source: From the Iroquois Constitution, "Laws of Adoption." Available at the University of Oklahoma Law Center, www.law.ou.edu/hist/iroquois.html.

Questions

1. Identify one advantage to having the Great Binding Law in written format.
2. What did the string of shells mentioned in s. 68 signify?
3. Suggest why the Iroquois considered adoption to be a legal matter that had to be approved by the nation's elders.

bylaws on their reserves. Some have negotiated rights of self-government with the federal government in Ottawa. For example, the Nisga'a in British Columbia have the right to make and enforce the equivalent of provincial laws on their own lands, including laws dealing with marriage, education, and health services (see Chapter 7: Majority and Minority Rights). The creation of Nunavut in 1999 granted powers of self-government to the Inuit in this territory of 2.2 million square kilometres. The Nunavut legislature follows the Inuit tradition of making decisions through consensus rather than by a simple majority of votes.

To learn more about the Nunavut government, its people, culture, and land claims, visit www.emp.ca/dimensionsoflaw

Turning Points in the Law

The Creation of Nunavut

Nunavut came into existence on April 1, 1999. It was formed of the eastern two-thirds of the former Northwest Territories and comprises 24 percent of Canada's landmass. The population of Nunavut is distinctive, with a high degree of cultural homogeneity. About 84 percent of the population describe themselves as partially or entirely of Inuit descent. Almost 75 percent of the population claim Inuktitut as their mother tongue.

The creation of Nunavut came about through a long period of negotiation between the government of Canada and the Inuit people. Initially the idea was confined to discussions among Aboriginal groups, both Inuit and other First Nations, and government officials. In 1982, the people of the Northwest Territories were asked if they supported the idea of dividing the territories, and then, in 1992, if they approved the plan developed to achieve such a division. With the support of the population of the Northwest Territories on both of these questions, the Canadian Parliament passed the *Nunavut Act* in 1993.

The language and the culture of the Inuit were central in determining the ways in which the new territory was to be run. Targets were put in place to ensure that Inuit filled positions in government and the civil service. The 19 members of the legislative assembly are not members of political parties, but reach decisions in the traditional manner, by discussing issues until a consensus is reached. The traditional ways of life were recognized in some of the programs that have been established, such as the Nunavut Hunter Support program. This program gives money each year to Inuit families who fish, trap, or hunt for subsistence purposes to help them with expenses such as equipment and fuel related to hunting. As well, the Inuit have powers to control land use in their traditional homeland.

Questions

1. Compare the Aboriginal method of making decisions regarding laws with the decision-making method used in Parliament.
2. What are the advantages of consensus decision making? What are the disadvantages?

Figure 2.7 *Inuit drum dancers perform during the celebration of Nunavut's creation.*

British Influences

Britain has had a greater influence on the government and laws of Canada than any other country. Such fundamental rights as trial by a jury of one's fellow citizens, which Britain adopted from Greek law, presumption of innocence, and the rule of law, adopted from Roman law, were all inherited from Britain. These rights are considered so important that they have all been entrenched in the constitution in the *Canadian Charter of Rights and Freedoms.*

In medieval England there was no standard way of deciding a person's guilt or innocence. Instead, systems of adjudication varied from place to place and were influenced by local custom and superstition. Trial by ordeal involved torturing the accused person to determine guilt or innocence. Sometimes the accused would be forced to hold a hot bar of iron. The burned flesh would then be bound. If the wound was healing when the bandages came off, that meant the person was innocent. If the wound was infected, however, the person was guilty and punishment would follow. In trial by combat, the accused and accuser would fight until one defeated the other. People assumed that God would show favour to the innocent and reveal the guilt of the defeated party.

The faults of these systems are obvious. Usually, the person who was physically stronger would win the fight. In almost all cases when a person's flesh was burned with a hot iron, the wound would not heal because it was not sterilized before the bandages were applied. Many innocent people suffered because of these methods of judgment.

In the 11th century, William the Conqueror gave the authority to judge local disputes to his barons, or landholders. This system did away with some superstitious customs but perpetuated inconsistencies in judgment from place to place. A child who stole a loaf of bread in one place might be fined or beaten, while in another he or she might be hanged for the same crime.

In the 12th century, King Henry II tried to bring greater consistency and fairness to the justice system. He trained a group of circuit judges who went from place to place and held assizes, or travelling courts, to hear local cases. Over time, these judges noted similarities in certain types of cases that allowed for similar judgments to be made and penalties to be assigned. At some point they began to write down their decisions and the reasons for them, so that other judges could consult them. This became what we know today as case law or common law, because it allowed the law to be applied in a common fashion throughout the country.

As part of his legal reforms, Henry also established the jury system. The right to trial by jury was broadened under King John, Henry's son, who was forced to sign the Magna Carta by rebellious barons. As well as recognizing the rule of law, the Magna Carta also guaranteed the right of an accused person to be considered innocent until proven guilty in a court of law.

French Influences

Quebec was settled by people from France, and these settlers brought with them the French civil law. Like other parts of continental Europe that were part of the Roman empire, France's legal system had its roots in Roman law. This meant that its civil laws, or those dealing with personal relationships, were organized into codes arranged by topic. Quebec became part of the British empire in 1763, and in 1774, the *Quebec Act* was passed. This Act established British criminal law and a British colonial government in Quebec, but retained French civil law. In France, Napoleon Bonaparte gathered together all the civil laws into one code, which was called the *Napoleonic Code* or the French *Civil Code*. This Code came into effect in 1804 and forms a foundation of the *Civil Code of Quebec*. Under this Code, precedents are not as important in deciding cases as in a common-law system. Rather, judges must refer to the Code itself, and to scholarly interpretations of the Code, in making their decisions.

Fyi While a common-law system uses juries in certain kinds of cases, a civil-law system does not use juries at all.

Influence of Customs and Conventions

Other primary sources of Canadian law include **customs** and **conventions**. As an example of a custom, for several generations people living in a village close to the ocean may have used a shortcut through someone's ocean-front property to get to the beach. The villagers could cite this customary usage to prevent the owner from suddenly fencing off the property in a way that interfered with their beach access. Not formally a law, this customary right of way could be recognized by a judge as having the force of a law through established usage.

custom: a long-established way of doing something that, over time, has acquired the force of law

convention: a way of doing something that has been accepted for so long that it amounts to an unwritten rule

Conventions are similar to customs but apply mainly to political practices. Since Vincent Massey's tenure as governor general (1952–1959), it has been a convention in Canada for the prime minister to request the monarch to appoint only Canadian citizens to serve as governor general. This practice has not been written down in the constitution or in any collection of Canadian law. Nevertheless, it has become a political convention.

The most significant Canadian case dealing with a political convention involved the constitutional battle between Prime Minister Pierre Trudeau and the provincial premiers in the early 1980s. At that time, Canadian leaders in government had not been able to agree on a procedure for amending the original constitution, so that any changes had to be passed by the British parliament. Trudeau wanted to **patriate** Canada's constitution from Britain—in other words, to place sole authority for amending the constitution in the hands of the federal Parliament and provinces of Canada. Although Trudeau eventually succeeded, he created considerable controversy along the way. Much of it centred around his attempt to pass his constitutional amending formula through Parliament without a majority of the provinces approving the formula beforehand. The provinces argued that this attempt violated a longstanding constitutional convention.

patriate: bring decision-making powers regarding the constitution under Canadian control

Figure 2.8 *Prime Minister Pierre Trudeau in conference with the 10 premiers to work out details of the proposed constitutional package, November 1981.*

Case PATRIATION OF THE CANADIAN CONSTITUTION

Re Resolution to Amend the Constitution of Canada, [1981] 1 SCR 753

Facts

In April 1981, the House of Commons and Senate of Canada passed a joint address to Queen Elizabeth and the British parliament requesting an amendment to the Canadian constitution. This amendment package included the patriation of the constitution to Canada so that all future amendments would be decided within Canada, including the division of powers between the federal and provincial/territorial governments. The package also included an amending formula and the *Canadian Charter of Rights and Freedoms* that eight provinces believed significantly limited their powers. The proposals had been presented to the Canadian Parliament with the consent of only two of the 10 provinces. Three provincial governments mounted court challenges to the actions of the federal government.

Issues

The provinces wanted the Supreme Court to rule on three questions: first, whether the federal government's amending package would have a direct effect on provincial powers; second, whether the package was legal and constitutional, since the federal government had acted unilaterally (by itself) to amend the constitution and without the consent of the provinces; and third, whether a constitutional convention existed that required the federal government to win the agreement of the provinces when it wished to amend the constitution.

Decision

The Supreme Court ruled on these three questions in the following manner.

First, the Court said yes, the amendment package would have an effect on provincial powers and change the relationship between the provinces and the federal government. Second, the Court ruled that the federal government's proposed action to amend the constitution did fall within the bounds of constitutional law and therefore was legal "as a matter of law." Third, the Court ruled that a constitutional convention did exist that required the federal government to seek "a substantial measure of provincial consent" when asking for an amendment to the constitution that affected provincial powers.

Questions

1. In your own words, summarize the issues in this case.
2. What was the convention that Trudeau was challenging?
3. Was the Court's ruling a victory for the provinces or for the prime minister? Explain your answer.
4. Use this case as an example of how the Supreme Court can be used to protect the rights inherited from the Magna Carta.

The effect of the Supreme Court's ruling that a constitutional convention existed was to force Prime Minister Trudeau to negotiate a settlement with the provincial premiers. Over the course of several meetings, nine of the 10 premiers agreed on a package to be submitted to the British parliament as the *Constitution Act, 1982.* Only Quebec refused to approve the new Act. (The political implications of this refusal are explained in Chapter 7: Majority and Minority Rights.) The Supreme Court had not suggested that the constitutional convention had the binding force of a written law, nor that the unanimous agreement of the provinces was required. However, simply acknowledging that a convention existed was enough to bring the parties back to the negotiating table to work out a package acceptable to the majority.

Influence of Social and Political Philosophy

Social movements and political philosophies have also influenced Canada's laws. For example, public reaction to the horrors of the Holocaust during World War II and to the US civil rights movement in the 1950s and 1960s helped create a social movement that eventually ushered in the *Canadian Human Rights Act, 1977.* Similarly, the socialist political philosophy of the Co-operative Commonwealth Federation party (CCF), forged during the

Great Depression in the 1930s, had a direct impact on provincial and federal legislation in such areas as social security, employment insurance, and workers' compensation benefits. More recently, the separatist political philosophy of the Parti Québécois and the Bloc Québécois has sought to bring further changes to Confederation.

Case WHEN ANTI-SEMITISM BECAME INTOLERABLE

Re Drummond Wren, [1945] OR 778 (HC, in Chambers)

Facts

Mr. Drummond Wren bought land in York County, Ontario. The sale agreement contained a "restrictive covenant" or clause that stipulated that if Wren himself sold the property at a later date, the "land [was] not to be sold to Jews or persons of objectionable nationality." Wren applied to a judge for an order declaring this restrictive covenant invalid.

Issue

Wren argued that the restrictive covenant was contrary to public policy because it divided Canadians among religious and ethnic groups and thus violated Ontario's *Racial Discrimination Act, 1944.*

Decision

The judge declared the restrictive covenant void and of no effect. In doing so, he was responding to the ways in which Canadian society had changed since World War II. For example, Canada had recently signed the *Charter of the United Nations*, which pledged to promote "universal respect for, and observance of, human rights and fundamental freedoms for all without distinction of race, sex, language, or religion." The judge also looked at Ontario's *Racial Discrimination Act, 1944*, which prohibited anyone from displaying on their property "any notice, sign, symbol, emblem or other representation indicating discrimination or an intention to discriminate against any person or any class of persons for any purpose because of ... race or creed."

The judge felt he had a "moral duty" to help support national unity:

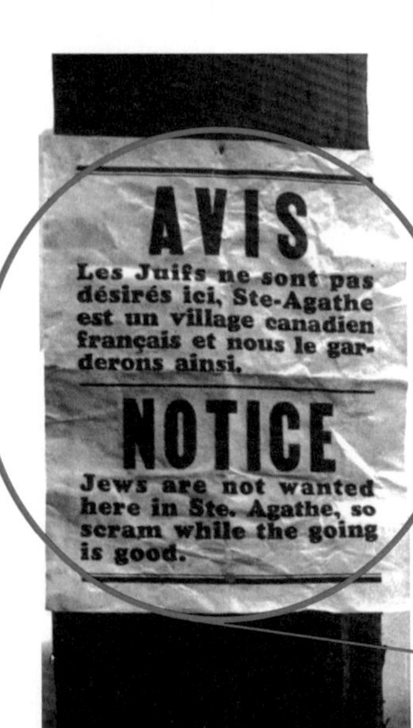

Figure 2.9 *A bilingual anti-Semitic sign in the village of Ste-Agathe, Quebec, in 1939. Such sentiments were not restricted to Quebec, and in parts of Canada they persisted well into the second half of the 20th century. How would a sign like this conflict with Ontario's* Racial Discrimination Act, 1944?

If sale of a piece of land can be prohibited to Jews, it can equally be prohibited to Protestants, Catholics, or other groups or denominations. ... In my opinion, nothing could be more calculated to create or deepen divisions between existing religious and ethnic groups in this province, or in this country, than the sanction of a method of land transfer which would permit the segregation and confinement of particular groups to particular business or residential areas, or, conversely, would exclude particular groups from particular business or residential areas.

Questions

1. a) What was the "restrictive covenant" that Wren was opposing?
   b) Whom do you think might have been considered "persons of objectionable nationality" at that time?
2. What reasons did the judge give for finding the sale agreement discriminatory?
3. What forces do you think were helping to shift attitudes about anti-Semitism at the time of this case?
4. What political philosophy was the judge reflecting in his judgment?

Check Your Understanding

1. Explain the difference between religion and morality. What influences have each of these primary sources had on Canadian law?
2. List the historical influences on contemporary Canadian law. Outline the contributions of each.
3. What evidence is there in the excerpt from the Great Binding Law (see The Law, page 40) of a consensus method of decision making?
4. Based on your understanding, which of the primary sources discussed has had the greatest influence on Canadian law? Justify your view.

Secondary Sources of Canadian Law

Secondary sources of law consist of laws and reported cases that have been written down by various lawmakers. These sources enshrine a society's values, beliefs, and principles in written rules and regulations. In Canada, lawmakers include Members of Parliament and judges who render legal decisions. The constitution, statute law, and case law are the three secondary sources of law in Canada. You can think of these sources as forming a kind of pyramid, with the constitution at the top and case law at the bottom (see Figure 2.10). This hierarchy indicates the level of importance of each source.

secondary sources of law: current laws that enshrine a society's values in written rules and regulations that have been formulated by legislators and judges

The constitution is the most important source of Canadian law. If a statute is found to conflict with it, then that statute must be revised or repealed. Similarly, statute law takes precedence over the judicial decisions that make up case law, except when the courts find that a statute is unconstitutional. You will learn more about constitutional law in Chapters 4 and 5.

Figure 2.10 *Secondary sources of Canadian law.*

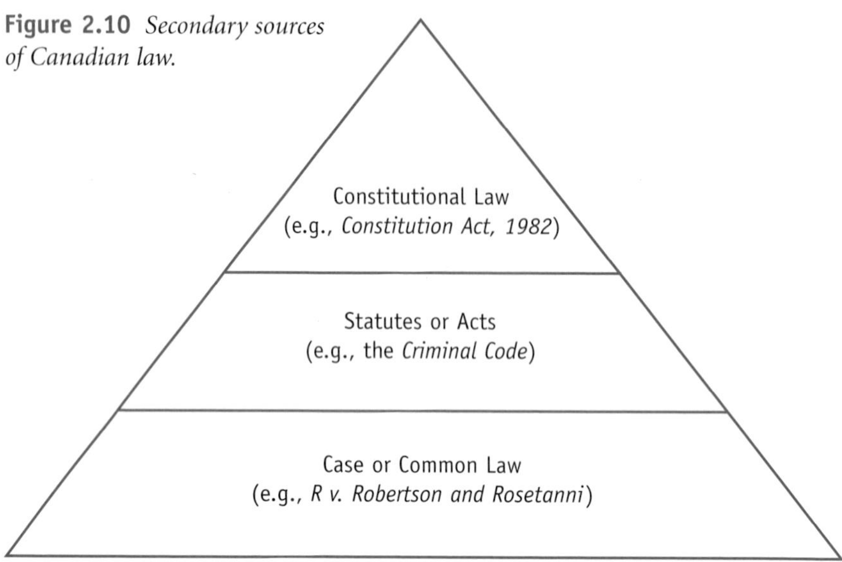

The Constitution

constitutional law: in Canada, the body of written and unwritten laws that set out how the country will be governed. This type of law sets out the distribution of powers between the federal government and the provinces and embodies certain important legal principles

Canada's constitution embodies the values and principles that Canadian law has derived from primary sources such as philosophy, religion, and tradition. In Canada, **constitutional law** may be defined as the body of laws that deals with the distribution of government powers and sets out certain important legal principles. The written part of the Canadian constitution actually consists of several documents, most of which have direct links to the legal traditions of Britain.

The first of these documents is the *British North America Act*, now known as the *Constitution Act, 1867*. Through the passage of this Act, the Dominion of Canada was created in 1867. According to the Act's preamble, Canada was to have "a Constitution similar in Principle to that of the United Kingdom." This meant that Canadians inherited many ideas, customs, conventions, values, and principles of law from Britain that were not always spelled out in written clauses but were understood from centuries of experience and case law.

judicial independence: the principle that judges function independently of the government

parliamentary supremacy: the principle that Parliament has the supreme power of making Canadian laws

Two of the most important principles are judicial independence and parliamentary supremacy. **Judicial independence** means that judges function independently of the government that appointed them. Their decisions reflect their own legal interpretation of the law and not government policy. The principle of **parliamentary supremacy** means that Parliament, as the representative body of the Canadian people, has the supreme power of making Canadian laws.

Over the years, Canada's constitution was amended several times by acts of the British parliament. In 1982, the constitution was patriated, which means that Canada now has the right to amend its own constitution. This right was entrenched in the *Constitution Act, 1982*, one part of which was the *Canadian Charter of Rights and Freedoms*. Besides these documents, the Canadian constitution reflects constitutional law decisions, which are court decisions that have clarified various points of constitutional law (see Chapters 4 and 5).

Note that the *Constitution Act, 1982* has had a direct impact on some of the legal principles embedded in the *Constitution Act, 1867*. If a court finds that any law violates one of the rights listed in the Charter, it has the authority to strike down part or all of the law and direct Parliament either to revise or to repeal it. For this reason, some legal scholars feel that the Supreme Court, not Parliament, now has supremacy in making Canadian law. You will learn more about this issue in Chapter 5.

The Law The *Constitution Act, 1982* contains the following provision:

s. 52(1) The Constitution of Canada is the supreme law of Canada, and any law that is inconsistent with the provisions of the Constitution is, to the extent of the inconsistency, of no force or effect.

Question

How was the constitution of Canada fundamentally changed when the *Canadian Charter of Rights and Freedoms* was entrenched in it?

Statute Law

A statute may be defined as any law passed by the federal or provincial governments. At the federal level, a statute first takes the form of a written bill that has to pass three readings in the House of Commons. Sometimes the bill is revised before its third and final reading to take into account responses from the public or from opposition parties. The bill must then pass three readings in the Senate. If passed, it is then given Royal Assent (signed by the governor general) and proclaimed law. Figure 2.11 illustrates the passage of a bill through Parliament.

Find out more about recently passed Ontario statutes at www.emp.ca/dimensionsoflaw

Provincial legislatures can also enact statutes. Legislative authority in various areas was divided between the federal and provincial parliaments by the *Constitution Act, 1867*. For example, s. 91 of this Act gave the federal government jurisdiction, or law-making authority, in such areas as currency, defence, and criminal law; s. 92 gave the provincial governments jurisdiction over such areas as hospitals, property and civil rights, and municipalities (see Chapter 4). Suppose the government of Alberta passed a new law creating a provincial currency called "Alberta bucks." The federal government would ask the court to strike down this statute on the grounds that Alberta had acted ***ultra vires***, or beyond its power under the constitution, in making a law for which it had no constitutional authority. If a statute is within the power of the province, it is considered ***intra vires***.

***ultra vires*:** (Latin) beyond the power of

***intra vires*:** (Latin) within the power of

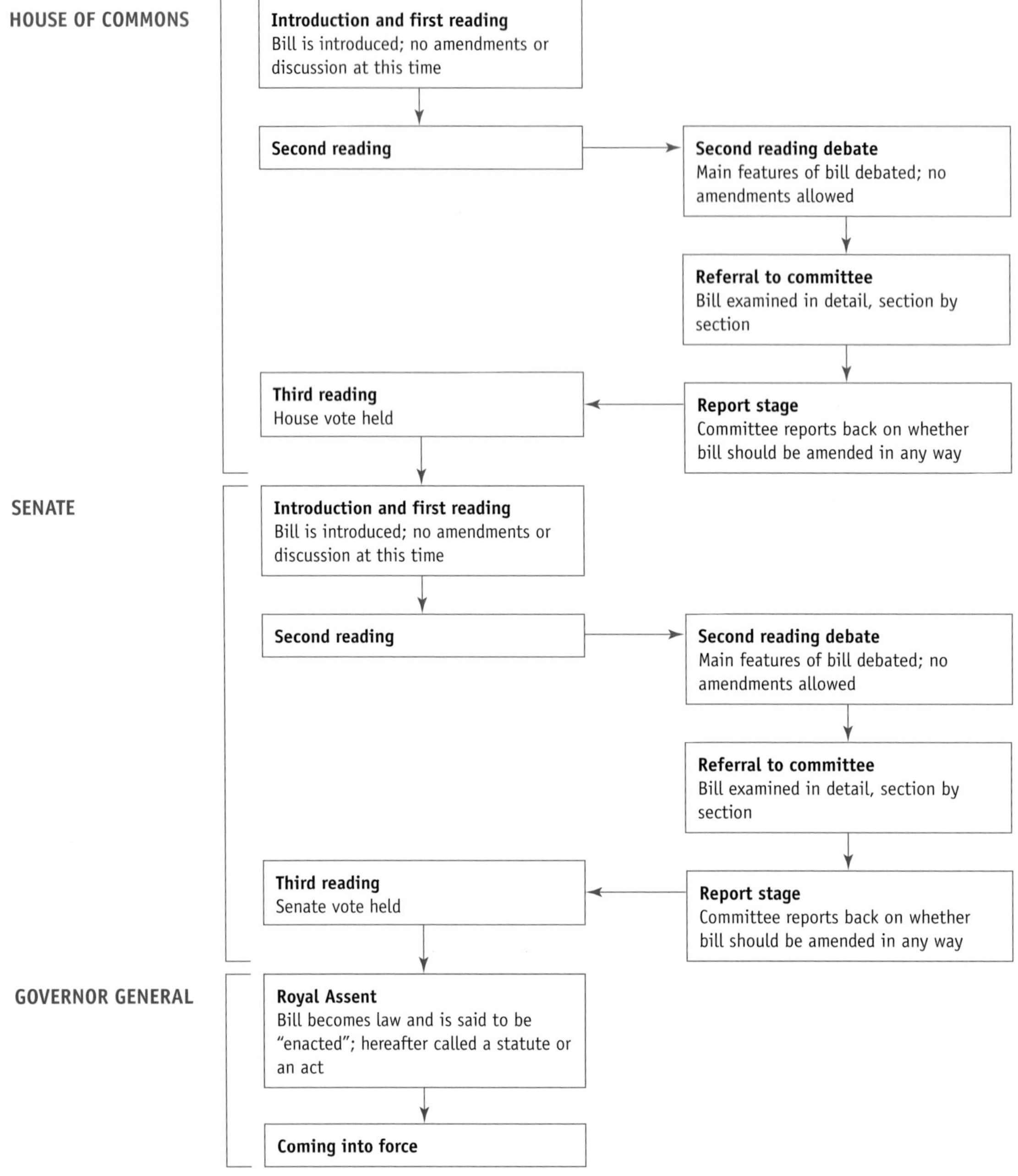

An act or statute may come into force in one of three ways:

1. *Royal Assent* Brings the act into force; no further steps necessary
2. *Particular date* The act comes into force on a date specified expressly within the text of the statute
3. *Proclamation* The act comes into force on a date to be announced later

Note: Different sections of the statute may come into force at different times.

Figure 2.11 *Passage of a bill through Parliament.*

Personal Viewpoint

An Aboriginal View of the Canadian Constitution

Ovide Mercredi was elected National Chief of the Assembly of First Nations in 1991, a position that gave him a high-profile platform from which to promote the rights of First Nations people. Growing up in Grand Rapids, Manitoba, in the 1950s, Mercredi learned at a young age the differences between Aboriginal and "white" Canada. While he spoke Cree at home, he was forced to speak English at school, and he recognized clearly the sharp differences in conditions between reserve schools and local schools. Later, he took advantage of adult learning programs to earn a university degree and then a law degree. For Mercredi, the *Canadian Charter of Rights and Freedoms* does not reflect Aboriginal views of the law.

Figure 2.12 *Among his other roles, Mercredi has served as Commissioner of the Manitoba Human Rights Commission.*

> The traditions of the Ojibwa peoples and the Midewin spirituality don't separate politics and religion. They incorporate both those ideas as part of their way of dealing with the needs of their people and their society ... .
>
> The Charter imposes a particular point of view on how justice should be administered on behalf of Canadians, and it doesn't include our communal vision. It usually involves a Crown attorney, a judge, a defence counsel, recording people, corrections facilities, group homes and, obviously, jails. Our traditional forms of justice do not have to duplicate these practices. We should have the freedom to establish forms of justice that will be acceptable to and workable for our people. We have to tailor them to our social problems, not to the interests of others.
>
> The primary objective of the Charter is to protect individual freedoms, but Aboriginal peoples have individual freedoms through our own forms of government. Who is to say that freedom of conscience and religion, freedom of thought and belief, and freedom of association do not exist in our societies? Of course they exist. We believe in maximizing individual autonomy without sacrificing a sense of community responsibility. Our beliefs and values do not exist because the Canadian Charter says they exist. Our societies and cultures are older than Canada's. Our values are part of who we are. ...
>
> The truth is that our basis for governing our lives has been more consensual than Canada's. It is more directly democratic. Canada's idea of democracy is majority rule. Our idea of running governments is consensus by the people. Who is to say that Canada's principles are better than ours?

Source: Ovide Mercredi and Mary Ellen Turpel, *In the Rapids: Navigating the Future of First Nations*. Toronto: Penguin Books Canada, 1993, pp. 100–102.

Questions

1. Summarize Mercredi's view of the differences between Canadian and Aboriginal views of justice and law.
2. The Canadian justice system is adversarial, which means that there are opposing sides in any case. What is Mercredi's opinion on this form of justice?
3. a) Give examples to explain what Mercredi means by "individual autonomy" and "a sense of community responsibility."
   b) Which principle do you think is reflected more in Canadian law? Explain your answer.

Statutory Interpretation

Judges interpret laws through cases referred to them. They have developed a number of rules to help them with statutory interpretation. For instance, judges sometimes use the "mischief rule" to help them understand a statute better by focusing on the problem or mischief the statute was intended to correct. They also use "internal aids" in the statute itself, such as sections of the statute that define the legal terms used in it, or a preamble that explains the statute's purpose. Judges also use "external aids" such as legal dictionaries and scholarly articles. The following case shows how one judge used the principles of statutory interpretation to broaden the scope of a particular statute, the Ontario *Wages Act.* (For more on statutory interpretation, see Methods of Legal Inquiry, Chapter 12, page 380.)

Case CAN A WAITER'S TIPS BE CONSIDERED WAGES?

Jantunen v. Ross (1991), 85 DLR (4th) 461 (Ont. Div. Ct.)

Facts

The defendant Ross borrowed money from his relatives, the Jantunens, and never paid it back. They sued for repayment and obtained judgment in their favour. Under Ontario's *Wages Act*, the Jantunens had the right to garnishee (seize) 20 percent of Ross's wages. The other 80 percent was exempt under the Act.

Issue

Ross worked as a waiter, a job that paid minimum wage. The Jantunens realized that if they received 20 percent of his salary, it would take a long time to recover their money. They argued that they should also be entitled to garnishee all of Ross's tips. They pointed out that his tips came from customers in the restaurant, not Ross's employer. Therefore, the tips were not protected under the *Wages Act* and the Jantunens, as legitimate creditors, should be entitled to them. Ross claimed he needed his tips to help pay his living expenses. The court had to decide whether tips qualified as wages and therefore came under the protection of the statute.

Decision

Although tips were not mentioned in the *Wages Act*, the court decided that they did qualify as wages and were therefore protected. In reaching its decision, the court felt it had to interpret the term "wages" in accordance with the "underlying intent and spirit" of the *Wages Act.* The intent of the Act was to allow a debtor to pay off creditors while still making enough to maintain a livelihood. Since waiters were paid minimum wage, they had to rely on tips to cover a significant portion of their living expenses. Garnishing a waiter's tips in their entirety would cripple the waiter's ability to make a livelihood and therefore to repay debts.

The court found in favour of Ross and against the Jantunens. Through a process of statutory interpretation, the court extended the reach of the *Wages Act* to include tips.

Questions

1. Summarize the arguments on both sides of this case.
2. If tips were not explicitly mentioned in the *Wages Act*, on what grounds could the judge say they qualified as wages? Explain.
3. This case dealt specifically with waiters who receive tips. Would the decision also apply to, for example, taxi drivers who receive tips? Explain.

Case Law

For most court cases, judges have to render a written decision or explanation of their ruling. These decisions form a substantial body of case law.

Note that case law is distinct from statute law. In Chapter 1 we saw how the Supreme Court of Canada established, in *R v. Lavallee*, that battered women's syndrome is a factor to consider when ruling on a plea of self-defence in certain cases. Even though Parliament has not written this provision into a statute, the need to consider this condition in this type of case has legal force because of the Supreme Court's decision. This is because the Supreme Court set a precedent, a legal decision that must be followed in subsequent similar cases. In law, the concept of ***stare decisis*** means that a precedent must be considered when ruling on a case with similar circumstances. The precedent must be followed if it was set by a court higher than the one in which the case was heard.

***stare decisis*:** (Latin) to stand by the decision

There may be cases in which a precedent does not apply, either because the precedent comes from another province or the circumstances of the case are different, or because times have changed to such an extent that the precedent has become outdated. When this happens, judges have the option of distinguishing the precedent; that is, they decide not to follow the precedent and in their decision they outline the reasons why.

Lawyers and judges prepare for court cases by reading through all the relevant case law, most often found in law reports, which are periodical publications that print judges' written decisions. In Canada, there are national, regional, topical, and provincial law reports. Because of the expense involved in purchasing law reports, the Internet is now used more frequently to conduct legal research. (See the Methods of Legal Inquiry feature later in this chapter and in Chapter 1, page 28.)

You can find the *Supreme Court Reports* at www.emp.ca/dimensionsoflaw

WORKING FOR CHANGE *The National Judicial Institute*

Who educates and trains the judges? How confident are you that a judge will really know the law and the context within which a dispute has arisen?

Judges in Canada are appointed from the practising bar and, from time to time, the academic world. This means that preparation for a career as a judge is the preparation received as a lawyer or as a law professor. Once a person begins judging, he or she is often faced with cases in areas of the law for which they are not particularly well prepared. For example, a person whose pre-judging career was confined exclusively to personal injury disputes may have to deal with family disputes or criminal-law cases. This raises two concerns: the knowledge of a judge in an area of the law in which he or she had no previous experience; and the sensitivity of a judge to the circumstances of one or both of the parties in a case.

This second concern is especially challenging. How does a judge fully understand the social and economic challenges facing a single mother charged with welfare fraud? How does a judge deal with the power imbalance between an abusive husband and a woman who is trying to end the marriage and obtain custody of and financial support for her children? And how does a judge make sense of the cultural aspects of a case involving a First Nations person charged with hunting out of season? Should judges be sensitive to the social, cultural, and power elements of a case? If so, how will they obtain the sensitivity training? And how can society be sure that the training will not bias the judge in favour of or against one of the parties in a case?

In 1988, the National Judicial Institute (NJI) was formed as an independent, non-profit organization that serves the Canadian judiciary by planning, coordinating, and delivering judicial education dealing with the law, the craft of judging, and the social context. The NJI mandate is to "engender a high level of social awareness, ethical sensitivity, and pride of excellence within an independent judiciary." For example, new judges are encouraged to attend a four-and-a-half-day seminar that focuses on the craft of judging and the role of judges in the social context. The program includes such topics as

- judicial independence
- judicial ethics
- equality issues in the courtroom
- Aboriginal law
- persons with disabilities and the judicial system
- introduction to judicial dispute resolution.

The seminars are conducted by experienced judges, legal academics, and experts in the topics addressed at the workshop.

Canada is widely regarded as having one of the finest judiciaries in the world. The NJI's seminars and workshops, together with training and educational programs from other organizations, play a large part in ensuring that Canada's judiciary lives up to its reputation.

Questions

1. What is the role of the National Judicial Institute?
2. In what sense is judging a "craft"?
3. Should judges be sensitive to the social and cultural context within which a legal dispute arises, or should they simply decide the case on the basis of the "facts" and the "law" and attempt to ignore context?
4. What are the advantages and disadvantages of sensitivity training for judges?

Legal Writings

Many law professors, judges, and lawyers write books and articles about Canadian law. These sources are often the best place to look first when researching a topic in Canadian law. The authors generally take care to discuss key examples of statute law and case law pertaining to their subject matter. As you saw in Chapter 1, these books may sometimes be cited by judges in their written decisions and have an impact on these decisions.

Learn more about the National Judicial Institute at www.emp.ca/dimensionsoflaw

CHECK YOUR UNDERSTANDING

1. Distinguish between primary law and secondary law.
2. Why is it important to understand what is meant by (a) judicial independence and (b) parliamentary supremacy?
3. What is the relationship between the *British North America Act* and the *Constitution Act, 1867*?
4. Briefly explain the importance of precedents in case law.
5. What are the rules and aids that judges may use when interpreting a statute?

Categories of Law

Anyone studying Canadian law soon realizes that the subject can be divided into several broad and contrasting categories. Grouping types of laws in this way can help to make their purposes clearer.

Substantive and Procedural Law

Laws may be distinguished by their purpose, or what they are intended to do. In this sense, all laws are either substantive or procedural. For example, much of Canada's *Criminal Code* consists of laws that define the nature or substance of various crimes. The law on first-degree murder indicates that it must be "planned and deliberate" to qualify as this type of crime. This is a **substantive law**.

The *Criminal Code* contains a number of **procedural laws** that explain how arrests, bail hearings, and trials must be conducted. These laws are meant to protect an accused person's legal rights by ensuring that the same procedures are followed in every case.

substantive law: a law that identifies the rights and duties of a person or level of government

procedural law: a law that outlines the methods or procedures that must be followed in enforcing substantive laws

Domestic and International Law

Laws may also be categorized by their territorial jurisdiction or area of influence. In this sense, laws have either a domestic or an international scope. The *Firearms Act*, discussed in Chapter 1, is an example of a Canadian **domestic law** that places certain restrictions on gun owners. It has no application outside Canada. The United States, for instance, has its own laws regarding gun ownership. However, if a US citizen brings an unregistered handgun

domestic law: a law that governs activities within a particular country

Types of Law	
Substantive Law ***(from the* Criminal Code*)***	***Procedural Law*** ***(from the* Criminal Code*)***
s. 231(2) Planned and deliberate murder—Murder is first degree murder when it is planned and deliberate.	s. 515(5) Detention in custody—Where the prosecutor shows cause why the detention of the accused in custody is justified, the justice shall order that the accused be detained in custody until he is dealt with according to law and shall include in the record a statement of his reasons for making the order.

Figure 2.13 *Examples of a substantive law and a procedural law from the* Criminal Code. *What legal procedures must a prosecutor and judge follow in order to detain a suspect in custody?*

into Canada, he or she is no longer under the jurisdiction of American law and may be charged and convicted under Canada's *Firearms Act.*

international law: a law that has jurisdiction in more than one country

International law is usually made when two or more countries sign a treaty in which they agree to enforce the same law in both or all their countries. An extradition treaty is an example of international law. Through such a treaty, each participating country agrees to extradite (send back) someone charged with a designated crime in one of the other countries.

Sometimes international law applies to a geographical area over which no country has exclusive jurisdiction. The *United Nations Convention on the Law of the Sea*, signed in 1982, is an example of this type of law (see Chapter 18: International Law and Common Heritage).

Public and Private Law

public law: the area of law that regulates activities between a state and its citizens

administrative law: the category of public law that governs relations between people on the one hand and government agencies, boards, and departments on the other

criminal law: the category of public law that prohibits and punishes behaviour that injures people, property, and society as a whole

Domestic law can be further divided into the categories of public and private law. The main divisions of **public law** are constitutional law, **administrative law**, and **criminal law**. We looked at constitutional law earlier in this chapter. As an example of administrative law, if you are injured on the job in Ontario, your case will go to the Workplace Safety and Insurance Board (formerly the Workers' Compensation Board), which will decide how much money you may receive as compensation for your injury. Other government agencies can decide whether you are eligible for welfare payments or for certain medical benefits. Administrative rulings by government boards also set precedents that can have wide-ranging impacts on similar cases.

Under s. 91(27) of the *Constitution Act, 1867*, the federal government has the sole authority for passing criminal laws in Canada. The bulk of these can be found in the *Criminal Code* or in related statutes such as the *Controlled Drugs and Substances Act* or the *Youth Criminal Justice Act.* In a criminal case, the state or Crown is represented by the Crown attorney, who prosecutes the defendant, the person accused of a crime. The Crown must prove its case "beyond a reasonable doubt." Criminal law is discussed in detail in Unit 3 of this book.

Decriminalizing Marijuana **Should Canada reduce the penalty for possession of small amounts of marijuana from a prison sentence and criminal record to a fine?**

Learn more about Canada's marijuana law and the debate about decriminalization at www.emp.ca/dimensionsoflaw

First outlawed in Canada under the *Opium and Drug Act* of 1923, marijuana was made illegal under the *Controlled Drugs and Substances Act*. In May 2003, Parliament introduced Bill C-38 to decriminalize the act of possessing small amounts (up to 15 grams) of marijuana. Possession of such an amount would result in a fine if the bill passed.

Those who advocate decriminalizing marijuana include civil libertarians and mental health advocates. They argue that

- penalties for possession are too harsh
- those convicted acquire a criminal record, which creates difficulties when travelling or job hunting
- the money spent on enforcing the law against marijuana use would be better spent on enforcing laws against more serious crimes.

Figure 2.14 *Police with confiscated marijuana. Should someone caught with a small amount of the drug be subject to the same penalty as someone caught with a large amount?*

Opposition to decriminalization remains, especially among law enforcement officers in Canada and officials of the US government, who fear that relaxing Canadian laws could mean more marijuana is smuggled into the United States. Those who oppose decriminalizing marijuana argue that

- marijuana is a "gateway" drug that leads to the use of more harmful drugs, such as cocaine and heroin
- decriminalization will lead to increased drug use and higher addiction rates
- decriminalization will send conflicting messages to young people about the harmful effects of drug use.

Read the two excerpts below that give opposing views on this issue. Then, answer the questions that follow.

> This committee feels this practice [of laying criminal charges for possession of small amounts of marijuana] to be unfair and wasteful of scarce police and judicial resources. ... Moreover, we contend that the penalty of a permanent criminal record represents a case where the punishment exceeds the crime.
>
> *—Paddy Torsney, head of the House of Commons Special Committee on Illegal Drugs, December 2002*

> Marijuana use is associated with poor work and school performance, and [with] learning problems for younger users. Next to alcohol and cigarettes, marijuana is internationally recognized by many competent authorities as the gateway drug for other drug use. To suggest otherwise is to turn a blind eye to the truth.
>
> *—From a brief by the Canadian Police Association to the House of Commons Special Committee on Illegal Drugs, 2002*

Questions

1. Explain the difference between legalizing marijuana and decriminalizing it.
2. Use the Internet to find additional arguments in favour of and opposed to decriminalization of marijuana. Draw up a two-column chart to summarize the arguments. Identify the best argument on each side, and explain your choice.
3. In your opinion, should the use of marijuana be a matter of criminal law, or is it a moral issue? Give reasons for your position.
4. Conduct research to find out whether Bill C-38 became law.

In contrast to public law, **private law** regulates disputes between individuals, businesses, or organizations on one side and other individuals, businesses, or organizations (rather than the government) on the other. Private law is sometimes called civil law, but do not confuse civil law in this sense with the civil codes we considered earlier in this chapter. In a private-law case, the **plaintiff** sues the **defendant**, and each side may be represented by its own lawyer. There is no Crown attorney in civil cases. The plaintiff has only to prove his or her case "on the balance of probabilities," which is a less exacting standard than "beyond a reasonable doubt," the standard used in criminal cases.

Private law is further subdivided into such categories as family law, contract law, tort law, wills and estates, and property law.

private law: the body of law that regulates disputes between individuals, businesses, or organizations; sometimes called civil law

plaintiff: in civil law, the party suing

defendant: in civil law, the party being sued; in criminal law, the person charged with an offence

Family Law

If two people want to get married, the legal procedures they have to follow fall under the heading of **family law**. Family law also sets out the procedures for divorce and its after-effects, such as spousal and child support payments, and visitation rights.

family law: the area of private law that governs relations among members of a family

Contract Law

Under **contract law**, people or companies enter into verbal or written agreements to purchase or provide goods or services. For example, Colleen contracts with the Ready to Ride agency to rent a car for a weekend trip. She is supposed to return the car on Monday, but the transmission breaks down on Sunday, and it takes her two more days to have the repairs done and return to the city. Ready to Ride charges Colleen for the two extra days she had the car. Colleen argues that it is the company's own fault that the transmission broke down and thus she should not have to pay for the extra two days. Under contract law, Colleen may have the right to sue the company to recover her money. A court would, however, look at the terms of the contract in deciding this issue.

contract law: the area of private law that governs agreements between people or companies to purchase or provide goods or services

Tort Law

Some **tort law** cases involve individuals suing companies or corporations for damages, but more often the cases are between one person and another (refer to *Chae v. Min*, on page 60). The damage can be caused either deliberately or through negligence, and the law may allow the plaintiff to sue the defendant for financial compensation.

tort law: the area of private law covering civil wrongs and damages that one person or company causes to another, when the wrongs or damages arise independently of a contractual relationship

Case CONTRIBUTORY NEGLIGENCE

Chae v. Min, 2001 ABQB 1071

Facts

Chae was a front-seat passenger in a car driven by Min. Both men had been drinking at a restaurant and were returning home late at night. Min failed to negotiate a curve, and the car slammed into a ditch. Chae claimed to have suffered catastrophic injuries. These included a brain injury so severe he would never be able to work again. He accused Min of negligence and sued under tort law for damages of more than $2 million. Min was able to prove that Chae was not wearing a seat belt at the time of the accident, and that if he had been he would have suffered only minor injuries.

Issues

To what extent was Chae, through the principle of "contributory negligence," responsible for his own injuries? To what extent should any contributory negligence reduce the amount of damages to which he was entitled?

Decision

The court ruled that Chae was 75 percent responsible for his own injuries. There was an operating seat belt available to him, he knew that the driver of the car had been drinking, and he was aware that the drive home was on a winding, unlit, rural road. If he had been wearing a seat belt, his injuries would probably have been limited to whiplash and abrasions from the seat belt.

The court awarded Chae $345 000, of which he was entitled to only 25 percent because of his contributory negligence.

Questions

1. Identify the plaintiff and the defendant in this case.
2. Explain in your own words the principle of contributory negligence, and how it was relevant to this case.
3. Do you think the court's decision was reasonable? Explain why or why not.

estate law: the area of private law that regulates wills and probates, and determines what happens to a person's property after death

property law: the area of private law that applies primarily to the buying, selling, and renting of land and buildings and the use to which lands may be put

Estate and Property Law

Estate law deals with law governing how a person's property is distributed after death. Estate lawyers assist in drawing up wills that clearly state the individual's wishes. If a person dies without having drawn up a will, that is, intestate, estate law governs how his or her property is distributed. **Property law** applies to many different types of property—intangible property such

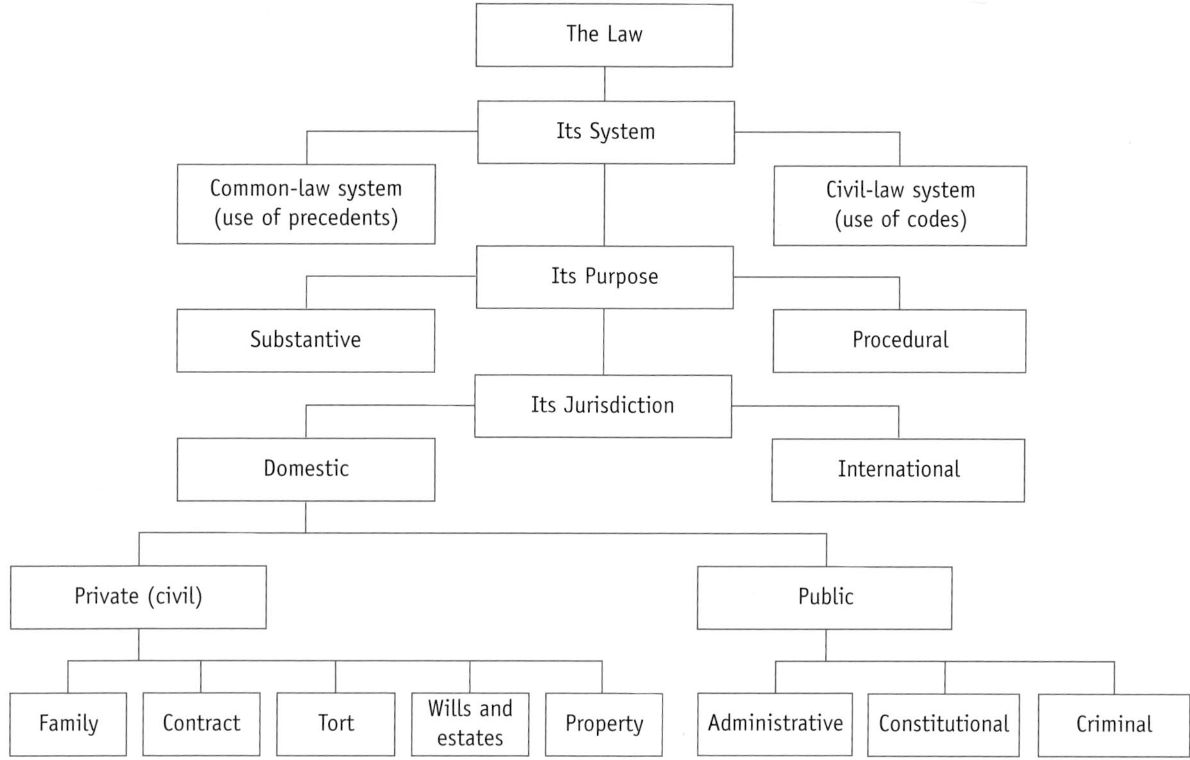

Figure 2.15 *Categories of law. As discussed in Unit 4, labour law and environmental law cross the usual boundaries between domestic and international law and between private and public law.*

as patents and copyright, or stocks and bonds, and tangible property, such as land, buildings, jewellery, and CDs. Tangible property can be divided into real property, such as land and buildings, and personal property, such as jewellery. The most common branch of property law applies to the buying, selling, and renting of land and buildings. Much of this property law is in statute form, such as Ontario's *Conveyancing and Law of Property Act* and *Tenant Protection Act, 1997.*

Check Your Understanding

1. In your own words and giving examples other than those described in the text, distinguish between substantive law and procedural law.
2. Explain how procedural laws protect a person's rights.
3. Identify the three categories of public law, and provide a brief description of each.
4. Why is proof "on the balance of probabilities" a less exacting standard than "beyond a reasonable doubt"?

METHODS OF *Legal Inquiry*

Reading Case Citations

Knowing how to read and interpret case citations is an important skill for law students. A case citation is a reference for locating a specific case, and it allows readers to locate the decision quickly. It also provides useful information about the case, including the style of cause (case title), date, volume number of the case reporter, series number, page number, and court. Each of these components is described below.

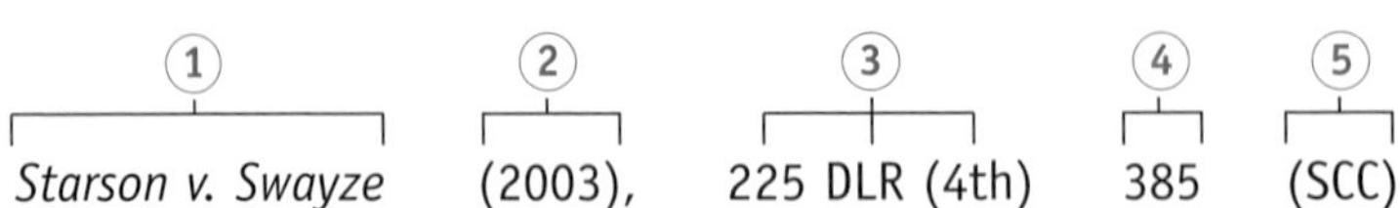

(1) **Style of cause:** The title or name of the case lists the names of the parties involved. Usually, only the last names of the parties involved are listed, and they are italicized and separated by a "*v.*," meaning "versus" in criminal law and "and" in civil law.

Criminal case example: *R v. Tessling*

Civil case example: *Starson* (plaintiff) *v. Swayze* (defendant)

Appeal case example: *Appellant* (person requesting appeal) *v. Respondent* (person opposing appeal)

Other Latin terms you might find in a citation are:

et al. means "and others" and is used when there are multiple parties involved

re means "in the matter of"

(2) **Date:** The year in which the case is decided appears in round brackets ( ). Square brackets [ ] indicate the year of the case reporter volume. Sometimes a case is published in the year after the case is decided.

(3) **Case reporter volume and series number:** Case reporters are referenced by standard abbreviations; for example, DLR refers to *Dominion Law Reports* and SCR refers to *Supreme Court Reports*. Most case reporter series use consecutive volume numbers, beginning at volume one and continuing indefinitely. For example, 225 DLR (4th) indicates volume 225 of the fourth series, or edition, of *Dominion Law Reports*. Many case reporters are in their second, third, or fourth series. A list of other reporters appears in the Appendix.

In some series, the volume is designated first by the year, then by the volume published within the year if there are several new volumes each year. For example, [2003] 2 SCR indicates that this case can be found in volume 2 of the 2003 volumes of the *Supreme Court Reports*.

(4) **Page:** The page number is the first page within the report volume where the case is found.

(5) **Court:** Citations include both the jurisdiction and the court level where the case was decided. These are either obvious in the title of the case reporter (as in SCR) or indicated in round brackets at the end of the citation.

A case may be published in several different reporters, so you may get several different citations. The *McGill Guide*, formerly known as the *Canadian Guide to Uniform Legal Citation*, is the official authority reference for Canadian legal citations.

Internet Case Citations

The Internet has become an invaluable tool in legal research, especially if you do not have access to a law library or case reporters. Many Internet citations, especially for provincial and territorial courts, use the following form or a variation of it:

R v. Tessling (2003-01-27) ONCA C36111

This citation refers to a criminal case heard in the Ontario Court of Appeal with a judgment issued on January 27, 2003. The ending number is the docket reference to a list of cases tried in Ontario courts.

Neutral Citation Standard

Many Canadian courts have adopted a new method of citing judicial decisions. Since 2001, cases are assigned a neutral citation, which gives a unique identifier but does not refer to any case reporter. Use of this standard is increasing, and both traditional and neutral citation standards appear in this textbook.

This "neutral citation standard" has three main elements: the traditional style of cause; the core of the citation, containing the year of the decision, a court or tribunal identifier, and an ordinal number attributed to the decision; and possible optional elements such as paragraph numbers or notes. For example:

Starson v. Swayze, 2003 SCC 32

In this example, *Starson v. Swayze* is the style of cause, 2003 is the year the decision was rendered, SCC is the court identifier (Supreme Court of Canada), and 32 is the ordinal number of the decision. Normally, the numbering sequence restarts each January 1.

Applying the Skill

1. Using *Dimensions of Law* and the Internet as your sources, find examples of the following types of case citations, and explain the meaning of each part:
   a) a civil law case
   b) a criminal law case using a consecutive volume number
   c) a civil case in which the date is the year in which the case was decided
   d) a criminal case in which the date is the year of the case reporter volume
   e) an Internet legal case
   f) a case with a neutral citation standard
2. Using *Dominion Law Reports* or the Supreme Court of Canada Web site, research the *Starson v. Swayze* case. Prepare a short report that contains the following:
   a) the full names of the parties involved
   b) the courts involved in the case
   c) the principal legal issue
   d) the background of the case
   e) the Supreme Court of Canada's decision

Reviewing Main Ideas

You Decide!

WHEN FAITH HEALING RESULTS IN DEATH

R v. Tutton, [1989] 1 SCR 1392

Arthur and Carol Tutton were convicted of manslaughter in the death of their five-year-old son, Christopher, a diabetic. The Tuttons had stopped Christopher's insulin treatments in the belief that he had been miraculously cured of the disease. When they appealed their guilty verdict, the Ontario Court of Appeal overturned the lower court's finding and ordered a new trial. The Crown then appealed to the Supreme Court of Canada.

Facts

The Tuttons had a good reputation in their community for honesty and integrity, and they were known to be loving and responsible parents. They were also deeply religious and belonged to a sect that believed in faith healing. This belief did not prevent them from seeking and acting on medical advice, but they believed that divine intervention could effect cures for illnesses in a way that surpassed the power of medical science.

In 1979, the Tuttons' family doctor diagnosed Christopher as a diabetic and admitted him to hospital, where he remained for several weeks. During this time, Carol Tutton attended classes at a diabetic education centre, where she learned how to give insulin injections and studied the effect of diet and exercise on diabetics.

Both Carol and Arthur believed Christopher would be healed through a spiritual cure. Their doctor told them this was impossible, and a specialist from Toronto's Hospital for Sick Children said that their son would never be able to discontinue his insulin injections. Nevertheless, in October 1980, Carol stopped giving the injections in the belief that her son had been healed by divine intervention. In two days, Christopher became seriously ill and was rushed to hospital. A doctor found the boy suffering from diabetic acidosis, a potentially fatal disorder resulting from the absence of insulin. He admonished the parents, telling them the boy would require regular insulin injections for the rest of his life. Arthur promised that insulin would not be withheld in the future without consulting a doctor.

A year later, Carol stopped the injections again. She believed she had had a vision of God telling her that Christopher was cured, there was no more need for insulin, and God would take care of her son. Christopher sickened quickly and two days later was taken to hospital, where he was pronounced dead on arrival. The autopsy identified the cause of death as diabetic hyperglycemia.

The police charged Arthur and Carol Tutton with manslaughter resulting from a failure to provide Christopher with the necessaries of life and from criminal negligence.

The Law

At the time, the relevant sections of the *Criminal Code* read:

Duties of persons to provide necessaries

197(1) Every one is under a legal duty

(a) as a parent, foster parent, guardian or head of a family, to provide necessaries of life for a child under the age of sixteen years; ...

(2) Every one commits an offence who, being under a legal duty within the meaning of

subsection (1) fails without lawful excuse, the proof of which lies upon him, to perform that duty, if

(a) with respect to a duty imposed by paragraph (1)(a) or (b),

(i) the person to whom the duty is owed is in destitute or necessitous circumstances, or

(ii) the failure to perform the duty endangers the life of the person to whom the duty is owed, or causes or is likely to cause the health of that person to be endangered permanently; ...

Criminal negligence

202(1) Every one is criminally negligent who

(a) in doing anything, or

(b) in omitting to do anything that it is his duty to do, shows wanton or reckless disregard for the lives or safety of other persons.

Argument of the Crown (Appellant)

The Crown argued that, under law, the Tuttons had a duty to provide Christopher with the necessaries of life, namely, his daily injections of insulin and timely medical assistance once he fell ill. They neglected to provide these necessaries without a lawful excuse. (A lawful excuse would be, for example, that they did not have the money to buy the insulin or that they did not know how to administer it.) In neglecting to provide insulin and medical assistance, the Tuttons showed a wanton or reckless disregard for Christopher's life. It was this omission or failure to act that caused his death.

Argument of the Tuttons (Respondent)

At trial, the Tuttons raised the defence of "mistake of fact." In other words, they had an honest though mistaken belief in a circumstance that, if present, would mean that they were not to blame for Christopher's death. As far as the Crown's case rested on their failure to provide Christopher with insulin, they honestly believed that Christopher had been cured by divine intervention and, therefore, that he no longer needed insulin. As far as the Crown's case depended on their failure to provide timely medical assistance for Christopher, the Tuttons argued that they were not aware that he was seriously ill as a result of the withdrawal of the insulin. Consequently, their conduct could not be said to exhibit a wanton or reckless disregard for the life of their son.

On appeal, the defendants' counsel said that the trial judge erred in telling the jury that for any such belief to be effective as a defence, it must have been reasonably held.

Make Your Decision

1. Summarize in point form the facts in this case.
2. Explain in your own words the meaning of the term "criminal negligence."
3. In this particular case, what did the Crown mean by the term "the necessaries of life"?
4. The Tuttons believed they had a lawful excuse for stopping Christopher's insulin injections. What was it?
5. How does this case illustrate possible conflict between religion and law?
6. Dismiss or allow the Crown's appeal, giving reasons for your decision.

Key Terms

Review the following terms to show that you understand the meaning of each and how it is applied in a legal context.

administrative law
code
constitutional law
contract law
convention
criminal law
custom
defendant
domestic law
estate law
family law
international law
intra vires
judicial independence
parliamentary supremacy
patriate
plaintiff
primary sources of law
private law
procedural law
property law
public law
secondary sources of law
stare decisis
substantive law
tort law
ultra vires

Understanding the Law

Review the following pieces of legislation mentioned in the text, and show that you understand the intent of each.

Canadian Charter of Rights and Freedoms
Charter of the United Nations
Civil Code of Quebec
Constitution Act, 1867
Constitution Act, 1982
Criminal Code
Magna Carta
Racial Discrimination Act, 1944

Thinking and Inquiry

1. a) Explain how the need for lawyers developed in ancient Rome.
   b) In what circumstances might you or your family require a lawyer's services?
2. Use your school or local library to find out more about trial by combat in the Middle Ages. Who was usually involved? What weapons did they use? Did they fight on foot or on horseback? In public or in private? Summarize your findings in a visual presentation, either on a poster or in a PowerPoint display. Be able to explain the principle of justice involved in this sort of trial.
3. Identify the category (or categories) of law that would apply in these situations:
   a) You are walking past your neighbours' yard when their pit bull breaks through the unlocked gate and sinks its fangs into your leg. You sue for damages.
   b) You sign up for 10 guitar lessons at your local music store. After four lessons, the teacher moves away and the store does not replace her. When you ask for a refund, the store refuses.
   c) The police suspect you of vandalizing a local business. They arrest you on a charge of public mischief. Before questioning you, they forget to inform you of your right to a lawyer.
4. Select 10 articles dealing with legal issues from newspapers or magazines and classify them into at least five different categories of law. Justify your decision for each article.

Communication

5. On a mind map of your own design, identify and summarize the most important primary sources of Canadian law.
6. Visit the Web site of the Assembly of First Nations (AFN) over a period of at least one month. Prepare a summary report on issues that concern the AFN, and present your findings in a short oral presentation to your group.
7. Working in teams, debate the following proposition. Resolved that: "*Religion is a valid source of legal principles.*"

Application

8. Griffin Grimbly, aged 12, complained to his teacher that his father beat him with a length of nylon clothesline. Police arrested Mr. Grimbly and charged him with assault. At

trial, Mr. Grimbly revealed he was a devout Christian and followed the Biblical injunction on child rearing: "Spare the rod and spoil the child." His lawyer cited s. 43 of the *Criminal Code*, which gives parents the right to use "reasonable force" in disciplining their children. As judge, you must decide whether Mr. Grimbly is guilty or not guilty of assault. In a one-page decision, render your verdict and give reasons to support it.

9. Judaism and Christianity have had a significant influence on the development of legal systems in Europe and North America. Choose one of the following religions: Hinduism, Buddhism, or Islam. In a three-page research report, describe how the religion you have chosen has influenced the legal system of one country in Africa, the Middle East, or Asia.

Chapter 3 Theories and Concepts of Law

CHAPTER Focus

In this chapter, you will

- interpret the concepts of justice, jurisprudence, natural law, and positive law
- explain the views of historical and contemporary philosophers of law
- evaluate the strengths and weaknesses of different theories of law
- analyze contemporary legal situations that illustrate a conflict between what is legally correct but generally viewed as unjust

There is not just one way to define law, but many. As well, there are many philosophical interpretations of law or theories of the way it operates. Reviewing these different definitions and interpretations from the past and present will increase your knowledge of the law and of the important role it plays in bringing order to human society.

The cartoon in Figure 3.1 offers one, somewhat cynical, interpretation of the law: a set of rules formulated by politicians for their own advantage.

THE WIZARD OF ID — Brant parker and Johnny hart

Figure 3.1

At First Glance

1. Who are the two characters in the cartoon? What is their relationship?
2. Does the prisoner in the cartoon have any rights? If so, what are they?
3. Are politicians the only people who make laws? Explain.
4. What role do ordinary citizens have in making the law?
5. Does a citizen have to obey a law that he or she believes to be unfair? Explain.

What Is Law?

If you had to define "law" in your own words, without the aid of a dictionary, what would you say? Do you think your definition would satisfy everyone, or does law mean different things to different people?

Over many centuries, legal scholars and philosophers have formulated various definitions of law. Their writings, theories, and debates are known collectively as jurisprudence. The field of **jurisprudence** covers such topics as definitions of the law, the reasons for making and obeying laws, characteristics of a good law, definition of a crime, and the distinction between law and justice. In this chapter, you will examine several of these philosophical schools of thought, how they developed over time, and the problems they were meant to address.

jurisprudence: philosophical interpretations of the meaning and nature of law

Ancient and Medieval Theories of Law

Until modern times, most theories of law could be grouped under two headings: **natural law** and **positive law**. Parents protecting their offspring is an example of natural law. People become aware of natural laws through their faculty of reason. Human laws that contradict the laws of nature are considered invalid, and people are not morally obliged to obey them. Positive law is illustrated by regulations such as traffic laws.

natural law: the theory that human laws are derived from eternal and unchangeable principles that regulate the natural world, and that people can become aware of these laws through the use of reason

positive law: the theory that law is a body of rules formulated by the state, and that citizens are obliged to obey the law for the good of the state as a whole

Natural Law

Ancient and medieval theories of natural law are based on the notion that a wise and beneficent God created the universe according to eternal and unchangeable laws. Human beings, as part of nature, live according to these laws, both as individuals and as members of society. The closer that human laws mirror the natural law, the better society will function. Although philosophers have generally agreed over the basic features of natural law, each philosopher that we will consider here had his own distinct interpretation of it.

Socrates and Plato

Socrates (470–399 BCE) was a Greek philosopher who lived in Athens during its "golden age," a time when Greek civilization reached its highest development, and the arts of drama, sculpture, and architecture flourished. Socrates never wrote down any of his thoughts, although we know of his teachings from the writings of his pupil, Plato. His philosophic method was to meet people in the streets and marketplaces of Athens and start a discussion about a particular topic, such as justice, knowledge, love, or virtue. Through a process of **dialectic**—questions, answers, and further questions—Socrates would try to arrive at some agreement about the

dialectic: the process of clarifying an idea through discussion

To learn more about Socrates, visit www.emp.ca/dimensionsoflaw

meaning of the term under discussion and an understanding of how the concept functioned in a person's search for the "good life."

In 399 BCE, Socrates was put on trial on a number of charges relating to his teachings. His accusers' speeches have not survived, but Socrates' speech has been reported in the dialogue by Plato called "The Apology." Plato may have been biased in favour of his teacher, but scholars believe "The Apology" gives a reasonably accurate summary of Socrates' defence.

Case THE TRIAL OF SOCRATES

Anytus, Meletus, and Lycos v. Socrates, 399 BCE, Athens

Facts

When he was almost 70 years old, Socrates was brought to court and charged with two crimes that were so serious in the eyes of his accusers that they felt justified in demanding the death penalty. First, they accused Socrates of being a "criminal who corrupts the young." Second, they charged that he "does not believe in the gods whom the state believes in, but other new spiritual things instead."

Socrates' trial was held before a jury of 501 of his fellow citizens. His accusers spoke first, identifying the charges and outlining the evidence against him. Socrates then replied to the charges.

Issues

Did Socrates "corrupt the young" and so break the laws of Athens and thereby earn the death penalty, or were his teachings in agreement with Athenian law and the law of the gods, that is, natural law?

To the first charge, that he had corrupted the youth of Athens, Socrates replied that the accusation had no foundation in truth. It was based on the "envy and malice" of the people whose ignorance he had exposed when questioning them. Young men enjoyed the spectacle of their elders being tripped up by Socrates. These youths imitated his method of cross-examining anyone who had a reputation for wisdom. But why, Socrates asked, would he deliberately harm young men by corrupting them, when he knew that anybody he injured would try to injure him in return?

Socrates said the second charge contradicted itself. His accusers implied that he was an atheist, but at the same time said he believed in "new spiritual things." Since spiritual things include the gods, he could not be an atheist. In truth, said Socrates, everything he did was in obedience to God's command:

> For this is what God commands me, make no mistake, and I think there is no greater good for you in the city in any way than my service to God. All I do is go about and try to persuade you, both young and

Figure 3.2 *Socrates about to drink the hemlock in prison. In "The Apology," Socrates said: "As for death, ... I cared not one jot, but all my anxiety was to do nothing unjust or wrong." In what sense does this statement agree with the theory of natural law?*

> old, not to care for your bodies or your monies first, and to care more exceedingly for the soul, to make it as good as possible; and I tell you that virtue comes not from money, but from virtue comes both money and all other good things for mankind, both in private and in public.

In other words, Socrates felt he was not breaking the law, but fulfilling it by making individual people better. This was the whole point of the law, to encourage people to lead good lives.

Decision

First Decision

After Socrates' defence, the jury held a secret ballot and found him guilty as charged by a vote of 281 to 220. By law, Socrates had to address the jury again and offer an alternative punishment to the death penalty demanded by his accusers. At first, Socrates suggested that he should be rewarded instead of punished, and that he should receive free room and board at the state's expense for the rest of his life. In the end, at the urging of his friends, he said a small fine might be the most appropriate penalty.

Second Decision

The jury voted again and condemned Socrates to death, this time by a margin of 361 to 140. Socrates was made to drink hemlock, a deadly poison.

Questions

1. Explain the process of dialectic that Socrates used as a method of trying to determine truth. How did Athenian society react to this method?
2. How did Socrates' accusers' beliefs place them in opposition to him?
3. What was the chief aim of the law according to Socrates, as recorded by Plato? Do you agree or disagree with this view? Justify your opinion.
4. How does Canadian society in general react to views that challenge our normal way of thinking?

Socrates' defence, as it is portrayed in "The Apology," is a clear and dramatic statement of the theory of natural law: that there is a moral imperative in the law, and it must guide people in right living. Socrates states this most dramatically when he recalls the time he was in charge of a panel of judges who were deciding the trial procedures for 10 generals accused of failing their duties. By law, each general was supposed to be tried separately, but the Athenian government wanted them all tried together. Socrates alone held out against the government:

> Then I alone of the presidents opposed you, and voted against you that nothing should be done contrary to the law; and when the orators were ready to denounce me and arrest me on the spot, and you shouted out telling them to do so, I thought it my duty to risk the danger with law and justice on my side, rather than to be on your side for fear of prison and death.

To learn more about Plato and "The Republic," visit www.emp.ca/dimensionsoflaw

Even in the face of death, says Socrates, the law demands that each person do what is right and avoid what is wrong. This is where true justice lies, in obeying the law that is based on the eternal principles that govern the universe, that is, in natural law.

Plato thought that humans were social by nature and that organized society was a natural institution. Society, or the state, did not exist for economic reasons alone but to help people develop the good life, the life that is led according to principles of justice. But what is justice? Much of Plato's longest dialogue, "The Republic," forms a meditation on this question. Here, Plato writing in the voice of Socrates says that the workings of natural justice (what we would call natural law) should be evident in two places: in the individual and in the state. An individual may be considered "just" when all that person's powers—physical, mental, and spiritual—are working in harmony with one another, with the lower powers subordinated to the higher. A person achieves this state of justice through the use of reason. In the same way, the state is considered just when each class of persons performs its own functions properly and does not interfere with the functions of any other class. As a human being achieves justice through reason, so the state achieves justice through law. For Plato, then, **justice**

justice: in Plato's theory of natural law, the state or condition that exists when all the powers of an individual or society are working together in harmony for the good of the whole exists when all the powers of an individual or society work together for the good of the whole. Human laws must be based on knowledge of the eternal laws that rule the universe.

If we could ask Plato for a particular example of a natural law, what would he say? The first and most basic law is to do good and avoid evil. All the rest of natural law flows from this basic premise. For Plato, law is closely associated with morality.

Aristotle and Rationalism

Just as Plato was a student of Socrates, so Aristotle (384–322 BCE) was a student of Plato. In his philosophy, Aristotle was strongly influenced by Plato, but he disagreed with his teacher in several respects. Aristotle agreed with Plato that humans are political animals. In this sense, they resemble bees, ants, and cranes, all of whom live in colonies with a social organization. What sets humans apart is their reason, which allows them to tell the difference between good and bad, the just and unjust. This process of using reason to analyze the natural world from observation is known as rationalism, and is the root of the modern scientific method.

Fyi Philip of Macedon hired Aristotle for two years to tutor his son, who later became famous for his military conquests and was called Alexander the Great.

Plato thought that education was the answer to making people "good," and that anyone who really knew what good was would do good. Aristotle disagreed. He felt that, morally speaking, people fall into three classes. Some are born good, some can be made good through education; but the majority of people are ruled by their passions, and education alone will not make them good. Only law can do that. It is only through fear of punishment that most people can be persuaded to follow reason and thus do what is right and avoid evil. Since law is so important to the workings of the state, citizens should train as legislators. Only in this way will they learn how to regulate the behaviour of their fellow citizens and ensure the prosperity of the state.

In this sense, Aristotle, like Plato, thought that law had a moral purpose. It forced people to live according to their reason rather than their passions. Reason is a spark of the divine in human beings; by following their reason, people fulfill their greatest potential: "If reason is divine, then, in comparison with man, the life according to it is divine in comparison with human life." Law, which regulates human life in the state, has this as its highest purpose—to help citizens use their faculty of reason to reach their greatest potential, and by doing so to live a good life.

Figure 3.3 *Plato and Aristotle. After studying with Plato for many years at the Academy, Aristotle opened his own school in Athens, called the Lyceum.*

To learn more about St. Thomas Aquinas, visit www.emp.ca/dimensionsoflaw

St. Thomas Aquinas

Aquinas (1224–1274) was a Dominican friar who taught for several years at the University of Paris. He lived at the time in the Middle Ages when Greek philosophy, especially the thought of Aristotle, had just been rediscovered in Europe and was causing a sensation in the universities. Aquinas adapted Aristotle's thought to his own purposes as a Christian philosopher. His teachings on natural law would have a profound influence on the development of legal theory over the following centuries.

Aquinas identified four kinds of law:

- eternal law
- natural law
- divine positive law
- human positive law.

Eternal law is the body of laws by which God created the universe and keeps it in operation. This type of law exists outside time and will never change. It is impossible for humans to have a perfect knowledge of eternal law because it is impossible for them to understand the mind of God. Natural law, on the other hand, is the eternal law as it operates in humans and can be known by them. We know this law through our faculty of reason and can see its workings in the natural world around us. Examples of natural law include the following principles:

- Parents should care for their children.
- Each person should try to preserve his or her own life.
- People should do no harm to others.
- We should all assist the poor, the sick, and the elderly.

The divine positive law is that part of the eternal law that has been revealed in the scriptures. This would include the Ten Commandments in the Old Testament of the Christian Bible and the Sermon on the Mount in the New Testament. Human positive law consists of laws that human beings have made for the proper functioning of society and the state. Though it is evident from natural law that murder is wrong, for the sake of an orderly society there has to be a written law against murder in which the act is defined and penalties are set out.

Figure 3.4 *Aquinas taught that natural law is based on the eternal laws by which God ordered the universe.*

Aquinas agreed with Aristotle that human law has a moral purpose, but he disagreed with the idea that humans can develop their greatest potential within the state. As a Christian philosopher, Aquinas thought that humans were created for a spiritual purpose. People should live in such a way that they will be united with God after death. For this reason, the state or its government is not the ultimate authority on earth; rather, the Roman Catholic Church is, since it has been put in charge of the spiritual needs of the human race. The state, at least in spiritual matters, has to be subordinate to the Church.

Aquinas thought that people are bound by conscience to obey a just law. An unjust law would not have this binding force. People are under no moral obligation to obey any laws that conflict with divine laws. In fact, such laws are not true laws but a perversion of law and an act of violence against the people of a state.

Aquinas defined human law in the following manner: "Law is nothing else than an ordinance of reason for the common good, promulgated by him who has the care of the community." This definition contains the following important aspects:

- The law is a product of human reason (i.e., it is based on natural law).
- It is made for the common good.
- It is made by the ruler, who must have the care of the community at heart.
- It is promulgated, or published, so that everyone knows it.

Laws that fulfill these requirements are just and work for the good of all citizens. As well, they are in harmony with the final end of human life, which is spiritual.

Personal Viewpoint

Should Laws Ever Be Ignored?

In 1995, Parliament enacted the *Firearms Act*, which requires all gun owners in Canada to register their firearms. The legislation has been controversial from the time it was introduced. Here is one opinion on enforcement of the Act.

> Why hasn't Ottawa just killed the joke known as the federal gun registry? It has already cost taxpayers $1 billion, and it's doing little, if anything to enhance public safety.
>
> Is it myopic conviction that Father Knows Best? The empire-building imperative in an ethos where success is measured by money spent? Inability to understand how irredeemably flawed the program is? Or mere inertia?
>
> Whatever the reason, if Ottawa won't officially put this misbegotten monster out of its misery, the provinces should unofficially do so.
>
> Ontario and British Columbia this week joined Nova Scotia, Manitoba, Saskatchewan and Alberta in saying they won't prosecute people who fail to register their rifles and shotguns by the end of the month.
>
> It's the right decision.
>
> We're not in the habit of urging governments not to enforce the law. But respect for this law is ever more difficult to muster.
>
> The feds provided us with yet another reason for disdain and despair on Wednesday. They admitted that a computer crash at the registry last December [2002] may have permanently erased the records of no one knows how many gun owners who thought they were in line for registration certificates.
>
> This is the last of many straws, and it means that prosecuting anyone for failing to register a gun will be difficult, if not impossible.
>
> Yet federal Solicitor-General Wayne Easter still has the temerity to insist Ottawa won't

extend the June 30 [2003] deadline. This is despite the fact that the agency has yet to register half a million licensed gun owners. And that untold thousands more haven't received licenses that may or may not be in the mail.

There are also plenty of old reasons for wishing this boondoggle would end. Originally forecast to cost $2 million, the total is now close to $1 billion and counting. That money could have put hundreds more cops on the beat across the country, a proven way to prevent crimes.

The fact that criminals don't usually register their guns also seems to have escaped the Ottawa braintrust. Or that criminals' usual guns of choice are handguns, which have been registered in Canada for the past 70 years.

Nor should we forget that more than 90 percent of all violent crimes in Canada don't involve firearms. And more than 80 percent of firearm-related deaths are suicides.

So it's a small percentage of deaths—homicides and accidents—where firearms are involved.

It's not surprising, therefore, that a 1994 briefing note from the justice ministry raised serious doubts about the effectiveness of the firearms registry. Specifically, "There are real questions about the extent to which these proposals [gun registry] would improve public safety and whether the high costs could be justified."

It's clear now that the costs aren't justified. This is what led Ontario Attorney-General Norm Sterling to say that Ottawa "should take responsibility for a badly flawed piece of legislation, which really persecutes the wrong people, innocent people, good people, who want to use long firearms for hunting and recreational use."

B.C. Attorney-General Geoff Plant noted that the gun registry is an "unmitigated disaster" and the province won't prosecute those who don't register their guns. Nova Scotia's Justice Minister Jamie Muir said, "It's their law; let them enforce it."

Mr. Easter responds that "Governments have a responsibility to uphold the laws of the land, and it's up to the provinces to prosecute under those laws."

But it's also the responsibility of governments to be cost-effective with their crime control measures. No reasonable person can make the case that this gun registry is a cost-effective crime-busting tool.

And it would be irresponsible to throw good money after bad trying to enforce a badly flawed law when there isn't enough money and manpower to properly enforce so many laws that really matter.

Source: "Federal Gun Registry Doesn't Make Sense, But Ignoring It Does," *The Vancouver Sun*, Saturday, June 7, 2003.

Questions

1. What do you think Aquinas's reaction would have been to this writer's opinion? Explain.
2. List the reasons why the author feels "this boondoggle should end." Which do you think is the strongest argument, and why?
3. The federal Solicitor-General Wayne Easter states that "Governments have a responsibility to uphold the laws of the land, and it's up to the provinces to prosecute under those laws." Given the strong opposition to the gun registry from several provinces, what solution would you propose for this conflict?
4. What is your opinion on the necessity and value of the federal gun registry? Defend your position with a classmate who has an opposing view.
5. Some firearms owners in Canada have stated that they will not obey this law because they do not agree with it. What is your opinion on their stance? Explain.

CHECK YOUR UNDERSTANDING

1. In your own words, differentiate between natural and positive law.
2. According to the philosophers you have studied, do people have the right to oppose what they see as unjust laws? Discuss.
3. Identify one way in which Aristotle's theory of natural law differed from Plato's. Whose view do you favour? Why?
4. What is the difference between divine positive law and human positive law, according to Aquinas?

English Theorists

The Age of Reason was an intellectual movement in 17th-century Europe that emphasized the logical analysis of philosophical problems. Philosophers tried to analyze human nature and society without relying on religious revelation or the teachings of medieval philosophers such as Aquinas. Although the theory of natural law was still an important idea during this time, some thinkers began to challenge it, especially in England. They began to advance a new theory of positive law. This differed radically from natural-law theory in its description of the relationship between citizens and the state and how law worked to regulate this relationship.

Positive Law

The development of positive-law theory in England followed a period of widespread religious, political, and social upheaval in the 16th and 17th centuries that included a civil war and the beheading of the monarch. This period of violence, fear, and confusion affected the way thinkers of the time viewed the origin and purpose of law. The theory of natural law—that law is based on divine revelation and the eternal workings of the universe, and that it was put in place for the moral improvement of human beings—did not seem to accord with contemporary reality. Instead, philosophers put forward the theory of positive law: that law was established by the head of the state and for the good of the state as a whole. It had no moral purpose other than to ensure the survival of the state, and obedience to it was no longer a matter of conscience, as it had been for Aquinas. The law by its nature must be obeyed, and anyone who challenged it was subject to severe penalties.

Thomas Hobbes

Thomas Hobbes (1588–1679) saw some of the violence of the English Civil War at first hand and fled to Paris in 1648. There he wrote his famous book *Leviathan*, which put forward a new purpose for law. The state of nature was nothing more than a state of perpetual war as the strong and

To learn more about Thomas Hobbes, visit www.emp.ca/dimensionsoflaw

Figure 3.5 *Thomas Hobbes believed that law was necessary to curb the greed, fear, and violence that were part of human nature.*

intelligent plundered the weak and the slow, and weak people banded together to attack those they feared. People tried to strengthen their own positions by destroying those around them. "Hereby it is manifest," said Hobbes, "that during the time men live without a common power to keep them all in awe, they are in that condition which is called war; and such a war as is of every man, against every man." The result was that in the state of nature people led lives that were "solitary, poor, nasty, brutish, and short."

In the interests of self-preservation, according to Hobbes, people agreed to surrender their rights to the sovereign or king. The king alone had the power to enforce his will, which was embodied in the law. Refusal to obey the law was an act of folly, since this would only return society to its earlier state of perpetual warfare and anarchy. Hobbes did not think that people formed governments to recognize and defend their natural-law rights. Since all people were prone to violence and disorder, they formed governments to have a strong leader who would rule over them and maintain law and order.

John Locke

The English philosopher and political theorist John Locke (1632–1704) tried to temper the extreme pessimism of Hobbes by incorporating into his own political philosophy some aspects of natural-law theory. In his *Two Treatises of Government* (1690), Locke recommended that if the king violated the natural rights of the people, then the people were justified in rebelling and in replacing the unjust government with one that would respect their rights.

To learn more about John Locke, visit www.emp.ca/dimensionsoflaw

What were these natural rights? The most fundamental were the rights to life, liberty (freedom of thought, speech, and religion), and property. The chief end of the state, and therefore of the state's law, was to preserve these three rights. Even natural law decreed that no person should deny these rights to another. In the state of nature, however, people's passions got the better of their reason, and this led to injustice as the strong took whatever they wanted from the weak. Therefore, it was to a people's advantage to form a civil society in which the majority handed over to the state the authority to preserve their fundamental rights.

Locke's theory that governments were formed through the consent of the people and that the government's laws must not violate the people's natural rights had a strong influence on Thomas Jefferson, the chief author of the *Declaration of Independence* (1776) in the United States. In the preamble to this document, Jefferson echoed the natural-law theory that certain truths are "self-evident," that is, they are universal and can be discerned through reason. These truths included:

> That all men are created equal; that they are endowed by their Creator with certain unalienable [inviolable] rights; that among these are life, liberty,

and the pursuit of happiness; that, to secure these rights, governments are instituted among men, deriving their just powers from the consent of the governed; that whenever any form of government becomes destructive of these ends, it is the right of the people to alter or to abolish it and to institute new government, laying its foundation on such principles, and organizing its powers in such form, as to them shall seem most likely to effect their safety and happiness.

Figure 3.6 *John Locke's legal theories were used to help justify both the American and French revolutions.*

Locke's synthesis of natural- and positive-law theory would influence political and legal philosophers for hundreds of years. It laid the foundation for modern theories on democracy and inspired the leaders of both the American and French revolutions.

Jeremy Bentham and John Austin

Jeremy Bentham's (1748–1832) analysis of human nature led him to believe that people, left to their own devices, tried to achieve the maximum amount of pleasure and happiness in their lives. With this idea in mind, Bentham proposed a novel way to judge whether a law was good or bad: the law should be evaluated by its utility to society as a whole. That is, a truly just law provides "the greatest happiness [for] the greatest number" of people. Bentham's philosophy became known as **utilitarianism**.

utilitarianism: the theory that the law should achieve the greatest good for the greatest number of people

Bentham's ideas had a profound influence on his good friend, the legal philosopher John Austin (1790–1859). While Austin agreed with Bentham that the purpose of the law was to secure the happiness of the majority, he separated law completely from morality. For Austin, it was useless to judge law by a moral or religious code because these were subjective measures. To do so would mean that each person in society had his or her own interpretation of the law and could obey those laws they judged to be good and disobey those they judged to be bad. No society, he said, can function in such a manner. Positive law, on the other hand, provided an objective measure of judgment. Every law that was passed, or "set," had to be obeyed. Individuals had to bend their will to that of the governing body since the purpose of the law, which the governing body set and enforced, was to ensure the happiness of the majority.

To learn more about Jeremy Bentham and John Austin, visit www.emp.ca/dimensionsoflaw

CHECK YOUR UNDERSTANDING

1. What was the natural state of the human race, according to Thomas Hobbes?
2. Identify two ways in which the theory of positive law differs from that of natural law.
3. What was the greatest virtue of positive law, according to John Austin?
4. Review the excerpt from the preamble to the *Declaration of Independence* (pages 78–79). Make a point-form list of the statements in this excerpt that reflect natural-law theory.

Modern and Contemporary Theories of Law

Legal Realism

legal realism: the school of legal philosophy that examines law in a realistic rather than a theoretical fashion; the belief that law is determined by what actually happens in the courts as judges interpret and apply law

At the start of the 19th century, a number of legal scholars and judges in the United States found that they were less interested in legal theory, strictly speaking, than in what actually happened in the justice system. This became known as the school of **legal realism** because it set out to examine the law in a realistic rather than a theoretical fashion. These scholars began to question the assumption that legal cases could best be resolved simply by applying the procedural rules found in statute law. Why, they asked, do people go to court at all if they need only apply the relevant rules to their cases to resolve them? If the answer to this question is that only a judge—someone trained in the law—knows how to apply those rules, then why do some judges decide cases differently from others?

To answer this question, the legal realists decided they had to look more closely at the discretionary power and creativity of judges and at the way individual judges applied the law once a case was in court. The American Supreme Court justice, Oliver Wendell Holmes, summarized this new position by observing that "law is a prediction of what courts will decide."

This view of law encourages a keener focus on the temperament of individual judges and how their backgrounds might influence their judgments. This focus could involve, for instance, the type of law the judge practised before coming to the bench and where he or she practised it. Legal realists believe that these factors and others can have an impact on the decisions that judges make in court, and thus in the way the law is applied in individual cases. The United States has developed a system of confirmation hearings in the selection of judges, taking the principle of legal realism into account.

Figure 3.7 *Karl Marx developed a radical theory of law that was based on his economic analysis of English society during the Industrial Revolution. Why would Marx's legal theory have a strong appeal for people living in impoverished countries?*

Marxism: An Economic Analysis of Law

Karl Marx (1818–1883) was born in Germany and attended the University of Bonn. There he studied law, history, and philosophy. In 1841 he completed a doctoral degree at the University of Jena. For a while he edited a newspaper in Germany and then went to France, where he immersed himself in the working-class movement and became involved with various radicals and revolutionaries. In 1848 he collaborated with Frederick Engels on the *Communist Manifesto*. In the same year he was arrested for sedition (inciting rebellion) and expelled from France. Marx settled for the rest of his life in England, where he spent his time studying the capitalist economy, advocating for workers' rights, and writing his major work, *Das Kapital*.

At that time, England was still experiencing the dramatic effects of the Industrial Revolution, a great technological and demographic shift that

Turning Points in the Law

The Brandeis Brief: Using "Non-Legal" Evidence in Court

Legal realists say that the law can best be understood by examining the temperament of judges and the creative ways in which they apply legal rules to the cases before them. This understanding is even more important in cases where no rules apply or where the rules are vague or in conflict with one another. How will the judge decide which rules to apply?

The point is illustrated by the career of Louis Brandeis, a famous American lawyer and later justice of the US Supreme Court. Brandeis believed that judges had to be made aware of the social consequences of their decisions. Such consequences would help them to make wise decisions on behalf of the public good. As a lawyer, Brandeis developed a novel way to help judges decide cases—by examining non-legal social and economic evidence. He began including this sort of information in his brief (written argument) for various cases.

Brandeis first presented such a brief in the 1908 Supreme Court case of *Muller v. Oregon.* Acting to defend an Oregon statute that limited working hours for women, he presented a brief that contained extracts from more than 90 committee reports and a great deal of testimony from expert witnesses about the dangerous effects that working long hours had on female employees. The judges were so impressed by this "Brandeis brief" that they upheld the Oregon law, even though they had struck down a similar statute previously.

In the United States, this landmark decision led to the widespread use of "Brandeis briefs" as a means of persuading judges to consider the social consequences of various laws and their own decisions. For example, in *Brown v. Board of Education* in 1954, it was a Brandeis-style brief that helped convince the US Supreme Court to rule against school segregation. The brief showed in some detail the psychological harm suffered by black children when they were forced to attend segregated schools.

Questions

1. Explain what sort of material a typical "Brandeis brief" contains.
2. Do you think a judge should be influenced by socio-economic rather than strictly legal materials?
3. In what sense can the Brandeis brief in *Muller v. Oregon* be considered a turning point in the law?

saw the bulk of the working population turn from farming to industry and from rural to urban living. Marx became fascinated by the class struggle he observed taking shape between the unprecedented number of workers employed in factories, mills, and mines and the relatively small numbers of the capitalist class who controlled these "means of production." He concluded that British law favoured the capitalist class by strengthening its power over the working class. He noted, for instance, that there were laws that made the act of forming a labour union a criminal offence.

Marxism: an economic and political theory that states that law is an instrument of oppression and control that the ruling classes use against the working classes

Based on his observations, Marx developed a new theory of law, one that was rooted in the inequalities he detected in the new economic system. According to **Marxism,** "Law is simply class rule. The 'ruling class' controls

To learn more about Karl Marx, visit www.emp.ca/dimensionsoflaw

the formation of law. Law is an instrument used for maximizing ruling class interests in society and controlling the working classes."

Ever since Marx made this famous observation, it has come under intense criticism. Political scientists, historians, economists, and others have all debated its validity as an explanation. Because of its unique perspective, however, this definition of law still has historical importance. Marxism continues to appeal to many people.

Feminist Jurisprudence

feminist jurisprudence: the theory that law is an instrument of oppression by men against women

The development of **feminist jurisprudence** is a product of the women's liberation movement of the 1960s. As with Marxism, feminist theory argues that the law has been used as an instrument of oppression. Where Marx said that the law oppresses workers on behalf of the capitalist ruling class, feminist theorists argue that it oppresses women on behalf of men. Feminist scholars thus directly challenge the idea that the law is objective and neutral in its application and that everyone is treated equally under it. They argue that this is not the case for women, who have traditionally been treated differently from men under the law.

This treatment takes at least three forms, according to some feminist legal scholars. First, they cite historical examples of explicitly discriminatory laws. In Canada, for instance:

- women were not considered "persons" under the law until 1929 (see Chapter 4: Canadian Constitutional Law)
- the *Women's Franchise Act*, giving women over 21 the right to vote in federal elections, was not passed until 1918
- women could not vote in Quebec provincial elections until 1940
- until 1925, a man could file for divorce on grounds of adultery but a woman could not; she had to be able to prove desertion as well as adultery.

The second form of unequal representation is the law's historical failure to respond to women's needs as distinct from those of men. For example, only in 1989, in *Brooks v. Canada Safeway Ltd.*, did the Supreme Court of Canada rule that provisions in group insurance plans denying benefits to pregnant women were illegal. Third, feminist theorists say legal institutions are systemically biased against allowing women to attain positions of power and prestige.

Issue

Is the Law Gender Neutral? Do judges view the law differently depending on their gender?

In 1982, Justice Bertha Wilson became the first woman ever appointed to the Supreme Court of Canada. Justice Wilson presented a paper in 1990 at the Osgoode Hall Law School entitled "Will Women Judges Really Make a Difference?" In this famous speech, Justice Wilson reflected on the lack of gender equality in the legal system that she had noticed during her long career on the bench.

> Taking from my own experience as a judge of 14 years' standing, working closely with my male colleagues on the bench, there are probably whole areas of the law on which there is no uniquely feminine perspective. ... In some other areas of the law, however, a distinctly male perspective is clearly discernible. It has resulted in legal principles that are not fundamentally sound and that should be revisited when the opportunity presents itself. Canadian feminist scholarship has done an excellent job of identifying those areas and making suggestions for reform. Some aspects of the criminal law in particular cry out for change; they are based on presuppositions about the nature of women and women's sexuality that, in this day and age, are little short of ludicrous.
>
> *—Bertha Wilson, "Will Women Judges Really Make a Difference?"* Osgoode Hall Law Journal *(1990), vol. 28, p. 515*

Ten years after Justice Wilson delivered her paper, the *National Post* published an editorial that argued against any sort of "gendered perspective" in the courts, be it male or female.

> A "gendered perspective" is necessarily a biased one and, by its very nature, antithetical to judging. As Lord MacMillan, eminent jurist of Great Britain, once wrote, judges must approach their job with detachment; they must purge their minds "not only of partiality to persons, but of partiality to arguments." If it is true, as some feminists maintain, therefore, that the law is "systemically sexist," offsetting male bias with female bias would only compound injustice. The sensible response would be to correct the existing bias, not supplement it.
>
> *—"Gender Bending,"* The National Post, *Wednesday, January 12, 2000*

Questions

1. If you agree with Justice Wilson's views, what aspects of criminal law do you think "cry out for change"?
2. In your opinion, is it possible for judges to "purge their minds" and be completely impartial? Defend your argument.
3. Identify the best argument used by each side in this issue, and explain your choices.
4. How should Canada deal with this issue in law? Explain the reasons for your position.

Personal Viewpoint

Beverley McLachlin

Chief Justice of the Supreme Court of Canada

Beverley McLachlin was sworn in as chief justice of the Supreme Court of Canada in January 2000, the first woman to hold that position. McLachlin had already served on the Supreme Court for 10 years before being named chief justice, and had been a judge since 1981. As a result of some of the decisions she wrote, she was no stranger to controversy. On the one hand, the Canada Family Action Coalition branded her a "radical feminist" for writing the decision that barred a boy from suing his mother for prenatal injuries. On the other, feminist groups assailed her decision striking down the so-called "rape shield" law that kept rape victims from being asked about their sexual history. McLachlin felt the law made it difficult for men charged with rape to defend themselves in court.

At her swearing-in ceremony as chief justice, McLachlin identified a new openness in Canadian society as one of the factors that allowed her to rise to such a prestigious position.

"The fact that I am in this seat today is more than anything else a testament to the justice of Canadian society—a society where people without money or connections or the usual gender for a certain job will be allowed to do it, and having done it, will be allowed to succeed.

"When I grew up, there were few women lawyers and no women judges. But there was an increasing awareness that fairness required equal opportunities for women and that the law must work to ensure this. I am the beneficiary of that sense of fairness and of the laws and practices that cast it in concrete form. Today's youth will benefit from these [even more]."

McLachlin has a special interest in seeing that the law remains responsive to social changes in Canada. One example is the way in which family law responds to new norms of parenting and to custody questions in cases of divorce.

Figure 3.8 *Beverley McLachlin, the first woman to serve as chief justice of the Supreme Court of Canada.*

"In the old days, things were simple. Mother got custody, period," she said in a 2002 speech to Ontario lawyers. "But that approach does not always square with new norms of equality and parenting and the realities of our multicultural society. Issues like culture, race, mobility, and new family structures will become the flashpoints for family law during the next decade. Ready or not, we will have to deal with them."

Does she think the Supreme Court has been too "activist" in using the Charter to strike down laws that conflict with the rights of individuals?

"Judges have always made law and I suppose been 'activist' in the common law tradition," she said in an interview with the *Toronto Star*. She cited the law of negligence as a good example. In 1932, after a woman found a snail in a bottle of ginger beer she was drinking, a British court ruled that manufacturers had a "duty of care," that is, they had to take reasonable measures to avoid harming consumers with their products.

"That was judge-made law and it was very activist. It's been accepted in the British model, which we inherited, that courts can and do and must make law in the sense that they're applying older precedents to new situations. And they have to keep up with the realities of society when they are applying them.

"Judges have always been doing this, point number one. Now, when you do have constitutional issues of rights and collective interests, and you have this balancing, certainly there's a dimension of judicial activity that was not there before."

Source: Adapted from Tonda MacCharles, *The Toronto Star*, Tuesday, April 16, 2002, p. A18, and Wednesday, April 17, 2002, p. A7; and Juliet O'Neill, *The National Post*, Tuesday, January 18, 2000.

Questions

1. How many years did McLachlin serve as a judge before being appointed to the Supreme Court of Canada? What inference can you draw from this?
2. What does McLachlin mean by her statement, "Judges have always made law"? Give an example other than the one she cites.
3. Explain how "judge-made" law differs from statute law.
4. How might "legal realists" view Chief Justice McLachlin?

Concept of Procedural Justice

Harvard law professor Lon Fuller (1902–1978) taught that law is a special body of procedures that must be carefully analyzed to ensure that the citizens of a country are provided with the best legal system possible. Fuller's standard in judging the quality of a law was whether the procedures used to administer it actually worked. To illustrate this idea, he wrote a parable about a young king called Rex who noticed that his subjects were having problems with the kingdom's legal system. To solve these problems, Rex abolished the current system completely and started over from scratch.

First, Rex decided he would hear all the cases himself and draw up a system of legal principles as he went along. He soon noticed, however, that there was no consistency in the decisions he made, and therefore it was impossible to draw any principles from them. Next, he drew up a code of laws to guide himself in his decisions, but he kept the code secret from everybody else. When this system failed, he published a code of laws, but then repealed many of them at later dates. This system failed, too. Altogether, Rex failed in eight different ways to formulate a workable legal system:

1. He failed to create rules at all and made all his decisions to suit the particular case in his judgment.
2. He failed to promulgate (publicize) the rules his subjects were expected to obey.
3. He passed retroactive rules that applied to the past as well as to the future, threatening to invalidate his existing rules.
4. He failed to express the rules in understandable terms.
5. His rules contradicted one another.
6. He made rules that were beyond the ability of his subjects to obey.
7. He changed the rules so often that his subjects could not rely on them.
8. He failed to administer the rules in a way that was consistent with their wording.

The point of Fuller's parable is that a country's laws must have a procedural fairness that makes them workable. The law is meant to guide human behaviour in such a way as to create and maintain social order. This order is impossible to accomplish if the rules by which the laws are administered are not fair.

For Fuller, the question that sets the standard by which we can judge the validity of law is: are its procedures fair and workable?

Concept of Restraint of Power

Philip Selznick taught for many years at Stanford University's faculty of law. He developed a standard to assess the quality of a country's laws that was very different from Fuller's. Selznick argued that the law's essence does not lie in "the exercise of power and control, but in the predictable restraint on those using that power." In other words, a country will have the best laws, and justice will be achieved, only when there is an independent body or branch of government that can challenge, review, and limit the laws made by the ruling power.

Selznick would argue that one reason a dictator is so powerful is that there is no one else in the country to challenge his or her authority. The law represents the will of the dictator, who controls the armed forces to ensure there is no opposition to the law no matter how unjust it may be. Selznick would say that by his standard of judgment, the quality of law must be very poor in a dictatorship precisely because there is no independent body to review and restrain the dictator's laws.

WORKING FOR CHANGE *Association in Defence of the Wrongly Convicted (AIDWYC)*

One of the great challenges facing any criminal justice system is to ensure that the courts convict only the guilty and protect the innocent. People must have confidence that their courts function properly in this respect; otherwise the system will lose its validity.

In England, legal experts recognized very early the problems that citizens face when the power of the state is organized against one person. Over time, English jurists put in place a number of safeguards to protect the rights of people accused of crimes. Among other things, in British (and Canadian) law, an accused now has the right

- to be presumed innocent until proven guilty
- to retain and instruct counsel
- to have a fair and public hearing
- to be assessed reasonable bail
- to be tried by an impartial tribunal, including a right to trial by jury for serious offences.

These are all examples of ways in which the law itself restrains the power of the courts.

Unfortunately, legal systems are administered by human beings who are far from perfect. Some guilty people go free, and some innocent people go to jail. Well-known Canadian examples of people who were wrongfully convicted include:

- David Milgaard, sentenced to life in prison in 1970 for murder. Milgaard served 23 years before the Supreme Court of Canada set aside his conviction.
- Donald Marshall, sentenced to life in prison in 1971 for murder. Marshall served 11 years before being acquitted by the Nova Scotia Court of Appeal.

Figure 3.9 *Boxer Rubin "Hurricane" Carter served as the first executive director of the Association in Defence of the Wrongfully Convicted.*

- Thomas Sophonow, convicted of murder in 1981. Sophonow served almost four years before Winnipeg police announced he had been cleared by DNA evidence.

In 1984, police arrested Guy Paul Morin for the murder of his next-door neighbour Christine Jessop. A jury acquitted Morin at his first trial, but the Crown appealed. When the jury at his second trial convicted Morin, a group of concerned citizens raised money to continue investigating the case and to pay for DNA tests. In 1995, these more advanced tests proved Morin was innocent, and his conviction was overturned.

The informal committee of volunteers that had worked to free Morin afterward created a non-profit organization to lobby on behalf of other people the group felt had been wrongfully convicted. The new organization was known as the Association in Defence of the Wrongfully Convicted (AIDWYC). The American prizefighter Rubin "Hurricane" Carter was named executive director of AIDWYC. Carter had himself been wrongfully convicted for a triple murder in Paterson, New Jersey, in 1966. He moved to Toronto after his release from prison in 1985.

AIDWYC is committed to two goals:

- to reduce the likelihood of future miscarriages of justice
- to review and, where warranted, attempt to overturn wrongful convictions.

The organization receives support from lawyers and other volunteers who help research cases and raise money for scientific tests. AIDWYC's campaigns on behalf of the wrongfully convicted, in addition to freeing the innocent, have also revealed the dangers of relying on "jail-house informants," the limitations of eyewitness evidence, and the importance of scientific tests—especially DNA tests—in establishing an accused person's guilt or innocence. AIDWYC is a good example of a non-governmental organization that acts as a restraint on the power of the state in its criminal justice system.

Questions

1. Identify three provisions of Canadian law that exercise a restraint on the power of the government in the criminal justice system.
2. Why is it necessary to have such restraints as part of the law?
3. If the law itself already acts as a restraint on the power of the courts, why is it advantageous to have further restraints, such as AIDWYC?

Check Your Understanding

1. Judge A came from a wealthy background, attended a prestigious law school, and practised corporate law before he was called to the bench. Judge B had to work her way through law school and practised criminal law before being called to the bench. According to the theory of legal realism, will these two judges deliver similar judgments in similar cases? Why or why not?
2. What led Karl Marx to conclude that "law is simply class rule"?
3. Identify three ways in which the law, according to feminist theory, is biased against women.
4. Explain in your own words the standard that Lon Fuller developed to judge the validity of a law.

James Lockyer, a Toronto lawyer, writes columns on new cases that are available at the AIDWYC Web site, which you can access at www.emp.ca/dimensionsoflaw

Application of Legal Theory to Canadian Law

Rule of Law and Restraint of Government Power

Suppose for a moment that we applied Philip Selznick's legal standard to Canada instead of to a dictatorship. What would we learn about the Canadian legal system? As already noted, Selznick argued that the quality of a body of laws was not to be judged by the lawmakers' ability to exercise power and control. Rather, the quality of law hinged on the existence of an independent body to review and (if necessary) recommend changes to the government's laws. In Canada, which body performs this vital function?

Traditionally, most challenges to Canadian law or government actions have been mounted in the court system. It is tempting to think that the *Canadian Charter of Rights and Freedoms*, with its stated purpose of protecting individual rights from unjust laws, created this situation. But even well before the passage of the Charter in 1982, Canadian citizens mounted court challenges when they felt the government (whether federal, provincial, or municipal) had violated their legal rights. The case *Roncarelli v. Duplessis* provides a famous example of a private citizen using the courts to obtain redress when he felt the premier of Quebec had violated his rights in an arbitrary fashion.

Case A GROSS ABUSE OF LEGAL POWER

Roncarelli v. Duplessis, [1959] SCR 121

Facts

Roncarelli owned a Montreal restaurant and belonged to the Jehovah's Witnesses. In 1946, other members of this religious group began distributing two of their periodical publications, *The Watchtower* and *Awake!*, on the streets of Montreal. This action disturbed the authorities in this predominantly Roman Catholic city and province. The provincial police arrested about 1000 Jehovah's Witnesses and charged them with distributing printed matter without a licence.

After Roncarelli posted bail for 400 Jehovah's Witnesses, provincial Premier Maurice Duplessis ordered the Quebec liquor commission to cancel the liquor licence for Roncarelli's restaurant. Roncarelli sued Duplessis for damages arising from a subsequent loss of business and was awarded $25 000 by the Superior Court of Quebec. The Quebec Court of Appeal overturned the judgment and ruled in favour of Duplessis. Roncarelli then appealed to the Supreme Court of Canada.

Issue

Was the premier's action against Roncarelli legal, or was it an abuse of the power granted to the premier under law?

Decision

The Supreme Court overturned the Court of Appeal's judgment in favour of Duplessis. The court found the premier's action to be a "gross abuse of legal power" because it was "dictated by ... the arbitrary [random] likes, dislikes, and irrelevant purposes of public officers acting beyond their duty." To let the premier's action stand would be to "signal the beginning of disintegration of the rule of law as a fundamental postulate [principle] of our constitutional structure."

Questions

1. Explain how this case illustrates Philip Selznick's theory of the need for restraint of power in a legal system.
2. What powers did Premier Duplessis have that Roncarelli did not have?
3. In what sense was Duplessis's action against Roncarelli "arbitrary"?
4. Review the definition for rule of law in Chapter 1. Explain how Duplessis's action violated this fundamental principle of Canadian law.
5. How long did it take to resolve this case? Do you agree with the saying, "Justice delayed is justice denied"? Explain your answer.

In *Roncarelli v. Duplessis*, the Supreme Court acted as a restraining influence on the sovereign power of the premier of Quebec. The case illustrates the idea that in Canada, public officials hold conditional power. If they exceed the power granted them under the law, then citizens have the right to challenge their actions in court. In noting that the rule of law is a fundamental principle of the Canadian justice system, the Supreme Court made it clear that even the highest government officials were not above the law and had to obey it.

Positive Law in the Canadian Constitution

Generally, Canadians have been more sympathetic than Americans to the idea of direct state intervention in their lives. This difference is evident from the earliest days of European settlement, when the government in the royal colony of New France assumed an active and paternalistic role over citizens in the colony. As well, the United Empire Loyalists who left the rebellious American colonies held to the positive-law theory that the authority of the king was absolute and that rebellion was not to be tolerated.

The Fathers of Confederation also took a positive-law stance in their insistence on a strong central government at the expense of provincial powers. Canada's first prime minister, John A. Macdonald, wanted a strong central government, but other political leaders insisted that a provincial level of government also be established in 1867. At the same time, they agreed to strengthen the new federal government by giving it jurisdiction over trade, taxation, defence, transportation, criminal law, and the appointment of higher-level judges. In s. 91 of the *Constitution Act, 1867*, the founders also gave the federal Parliament the general power "to make laws for the peace, order, and good government of Canada."

The federal government has exercised this power during times of war and insurrection, as when it invoked the *War Measures Act* during World War I and World War II and during the October Crisis in 1970 (see Chapter 1, page 7). Although the government has taken a less interventionist stance during peacetime, there have been occasions when it asserted its general power in response to a perceived crisis. In 1975, the Canadian economy was being battered on two fronts: by rapidly rising inflation rates and by high levels of unemployment. In response, the government under Prime Minister Pierre Trudeau passed the *Anti-Inflation Act*, granting it the right to set wage and price controls. The provinces agreed with the program and entered into agreements with the federal government. At this point, however, several public service unions in Ontario mounted a legal challenge to the federal legislation.

Case CHALLENGING WAGE AND PRICE CONTROLS

Reference re Anti-Inflation Act, [1976] 2 SCR 373

Facts

The *Anti-Inflation Act* in 1975 gave the federal government the authority to regulate the economy for three years by setting limits on incomes, prices, and profits. The provinces agreed to support this restraint program. When several Ontario public service unions challenged the law in court, the federal government referred the *Anti-Inflation Act* to the Supreme Court of Canada.

Issues

Was inflation a problem of such national dimensions at the time that it was necessary for the federal government to control wages and prices? Was the federal government's intervention justifiable under s. 91 of the *Constitution Act, 1867*, which granted it the authority to "make laws for the peace, order, and good government of Canada"?

Decision

The Supreme Court found that the *Anti-Inflation Act* was valid as emergency legislation, since the federal government had the power to pass such legislation under s. 91. However, the Court ruled that the Ontario government's agreement to place its employees under the Act was illegal. The agreement between the two levels of government effectively amended provincial labour legislation, and this required the provincial legislature to pass an amending act. The government of Ontario subsequently passed the required legislation.

Fyi Since 1892, there have been 76 federal references to the Supreme Court of Canada. The most recent in 2003 was a draft bill concerning same-sex marriages.

Questions

1. Why did the federal government secure the agreement of the provinces before passing the *Anti-Inflation Act*?
2. Explain why some unions opposed this Act.
3. How does this case illustrate the theory of positive law?

In this case, the Supreme Court confirmed that the federal government had the power to pass emergency legislation on economic issues in peacetime. Under the *War Measures Act*, the government also had the power to pass emergency legislation on security issues in peacetime. These two pieces of legislation meant that the government had the power to override the rights of individuals and companies in both the private and the public sectors during designated national emergencies. In other words, under Canadian law, individual rights could be set aside in the interests of society as a whole under certain defined circumstances.

Canadian Charter of Rights and Freedoms

When Canadian politicians set out, in the early 1980s, to amend the constitution and provide increased protection for the rights of individuals and minorities, they made sure to preserve the power of the federal and provincial governments. The *Canadian Charter of Rights and Freedoms* lists many fundamental freedoms that reflect a natural-law perspective. These include the right to "freedom of conscience and religion" and the "right to life, liberty and security of the person."

The Charter also reflects a positive-law perspective, however, in its insistence on the legislatures' right to limit those individual rights and freedoms. Section 1, for instance, states that any rights guaranteed by the Charter may be limited by "reasonable limits prescribed by law." Section 33, known as the "notwithstanding clause," also permits Parliament or one of the provincial legislatures to declare a law to be operational even when it violates a right guaranteed by the Charter. Sections 1 and 33 are discussed in Chapter 5: The Charter and the Courts.

CHECK YOUR UNDERSTANDING

1. Does the concept of restraint of government power operate in the Canadian legal system? Explain.
2. How is the theory of positive law represented in the Canadian constitution?
3. Is the theory of natural law represented in the *Canadian Charter of Rights and Freedoms*? If so, in what way?

CAREER PROFILE

The Honourable R. Roy McMurtry

In the course of his legal career, R. Roy McMurtry, now Chief Justice of Ontario, has had the opportunity to work with the law in three very different ways: as a trial lawyer, as a legislator, and as a judge.

Q. Can you comment on how changing social values influence the law?

A. I was fortunate to have been appointed Attorney General in 1975, when many serious issues of law reform were being considered.

For example, in 1975, the traditional family generally involved an income-earning husband and a wife who maintained the household and provided primary care for the children. The home was usually purchased by the husband and registered in his name. The husband was therefore generally the only legal owner of the only significant family asset. Furthermore, a wife in an abusive relationship often felt constrained to remain in the home as she might lose any right to support if she left.

My *Family Law Reform Act* created a legal presumption of equal ownership of the home between husband and wife. Support obligations were created on the basis of need, and the often futile process of fault finding was eliminated. [These] reforms reflected ... values ... related to equality and fairness, although I was widely criticized for disturbing traditional property ownership rights and support obligations.

Q. Does a lawyer's work on behalf of an individual client serve the broader community?

A. The right to legal representation is intimately connected with the most important principle of our criminal law, the presumption of innocence. However, this is often a difficult principle for many people to support, let alone embrace, when the public has made up its mind, for example, as to the guilt of someone in a particularly brutal crime.

However, the requirement that the prosecution establish the guilt of an accused beyond a reasonable doubt does serve the broader community. As a society we decided a long time ago that it is preferable to risk the acquittal of perhaps morally guilty persons than to risk the conviction of innocent people. ... The power and resources of the state generally far outweigh the resources available to an individual faced with a criminal prosecution. The law seeks to provide a level playing field and, notwithstanding this fundamental objective, innocent persons are still sometimes convicted.

Q. What is the most important thing high school students should know about the functions of law in society?

A. The law provides the absolutely essential underpinning of any civilized society. It is the legal infrastructure that is particularly essential to a democracy. There are horrendous examples of brutal dictatorships where there is no independent judiciary and legal profession.

It matters not what code of law may exist if its application is not subject to review by a neutral and impartial judiciary aided by independent lawyers. For example, the *Bill of Rights* in the formerly totalitarian Soviet Union contained impressive-sounding guarantees of human rights, but was quite meaningless in the absence of a bar and a judiciary that was independent of government.

Q. Why is legal education important for people who do not work directly with the law?

A. A well-informed public is vital for an effectively functioning democracy. The parliaments and legislatures of Canada are essentially law-making bodies, and it is important that individual citizens are able to understand and participate in the public debates that often revolve around legislation.

Equally important is creating a level of respect for the rule of law. While the term "rule of law" may have oppressive overtones for some people, the expression is intended to convey the fact that the rule of law is to prevail over the "rule of" a government or powerful corporation when the government or corporation is not acting according to law created by a democratic process and an independent and neutral judiciary.

We live in an increasingly impersonal society where selfishness, arrogance, and even rage can overtake respect and civility. A broader understanding of the law is an essential foundation for a civil society where respect for the individual rights of others is strongly supported.

METHODS OF *Legal Inquiry*

Identifying Point of View

It is very important to be able to identify and classify an author's point of view. This ability will be of great help in writing research papers on legal topics. It will aid your understanding of unfamiliar writers and help you develop and test your own hypotheses on what a writer is saying. You have read about the views of several different philosophers, each belonging to one or another of the schools of jurisprudence you have examined.

You know that Aristotle was in the natural-law tradition because he thought the main purpose of law was to help citizens lead good lives. Thomas Hobbes was in the positive-law tradition because he thought the chief purpose of law was to maintain order in society. The definitions of the various legal theories that you can find in the marginal notes for this chapter outline very briefly the main points of each theory. They can help you identify an author's point of view.

Read selections from the works of other writers on the law and identify their points of view.

Applying the Skill

Read the following brief excerpts from various legal writers. In an organizational chart similar to the one in Figure 3.10, identify the school of jurisprudence to which each belongs and give reasons for your identification.

1. True law is right reason in agreement with nature; it is of universal application, unchanging and everlasting.—Cicero
2. An unjust law is no law at all.—St. Augustine
3. We aim to replace the present capitalist system, with its inherent injustice and inhumanity, by a social order from which the domination and exploitation of one class by another will be eliminated.—*The Regina Manifesto*, Co-operative Commonwealth Federation

4. A just law is a manmade code that squares with the moral law or the law of God. An unjust law is a code that is out of harmony with the moral law.—Martin Luther King, Jr.
5. It is not so much that laws must be changed; it is patriarchy [a society of male dominance] that must be changed. Actions taken within the legal system cannot by themselves eliminate patriarchy, which is a pervasive social phenomenon.—Diane Polan
6. Law is governmental social control.—Donald Black
7. No free man shall be taken or imprisoned or disseised [be dispossessed of his property] or outlawed or exiled or in any way ruined, nor will we go or send against him, except by the lawful judgement of his peers or by the law of the land.—Clause 39, Magna Carta
8. Scarcely any political question arises in the United States that is not resolved, sooner or later, into a judicial question.—Alexis de Tocqueville
9. All human beings are born free and equal in dignity and rights.—*Universal Declaration of Human Rights*
10. Law is a union of primary and secondary rules.—H.L.A. Hart
11. Law is not some "thing," an entity unto itself to be studied in isolation. ... Law is best understood as a human activity, a set of relationships between humans and between humans and their world.—Linda Medcalf
12. The challenge that the Charter presents lies in securing for people the rights embodied in the Charter. Courts, practising lawyers, and legal academics together, face the necessity of shaping laws, which give order, form and reality to social relationships within the new constitutional and political infrastructure and in guarding the supremacy of law and the rights and freedoms assured by law.—Brian Dickson
13. An order shall be called law where it is guaranteed by the likelihood that (physical or psychological) coercion aimed at bringing about conformity with the order, or at avenging its violation, will be exercised by a staff of people especially holding themselves ready for this purpose.—Max Weber

Schools of Jurisprudence

Author	*School of Jurisprudence*	*Justifications*
1. Cicero	Natural law	• He says that law agrees with nature.
2. St. Augustine		

Figure 3.10

Reviewing Main Ideas

You Decide!

TRYING TO CATCH THE "BALCONY RAPIST"

Jane Doe v. Metropolitan Toronto (Municipality) Commissioners of Police (1998), 160 DLR (4th) 697 (Ont. Ct. (Gen. Div.))

This case was an action for damages for negligence and for violation of the plaintiff's rights under the *Canadian Charter of Rights and Freedoms* and relates to feminist jurisprudence.

Facts

"Jane Doe" is a pseudonym assigned by the court to protect the identity of the rape victim in this case. In 1986, Jane Doe was living in a second-floor apartment in a downtown area of Toronto when an intruder broke into her apartment from the balcony and raped her. Prior to attacking Jane Doe, the "balcony rapist," as he became known, had raped four other women who lived in the same downtown area. In each case, the rapist broke into the woman's apartment through the balcony.

Before Jane Doe was attacked, officers of the Metropolitan Toronto Police Force (MTPF) had deduced that the four other rapes were linked. They concluded that these attacks were the work of a serial rapist who was preying on the women in this particular neighbourhood and always using the same *modus operandi*: climbing onto the balcony and from there gaining access to the apartment.

Officers did not, however, issue any warnings to women living in this area to safeguard themselves against this serial rapist. When MTPF officers interviewed Jane Doe after she was raped, she learned of the four previous attacks against women in her neighbourhood. She then sued the MTPF for damages for negligence and for violating her Charter rights.

The Law

The trial judge noted that the police are legally obligated to prevent crime under s. 57 of the Ontario *Police Act*, which stated: "members of police forces ... are charged with the duty of preserving the peace, preventing robberies and other crimes... ."

The judge also held that ss. 7 and 15 of the Charter applied to this case:

7. Everyone has the right to life, liberty, and security of the person and the right not to be deprived thereof except in accordance with the principles of fundamental justice.

15(1) Every individual is equal before and under the law and has the right to the equal protection and equal benefit of the law without discrimination and, in particular, without discrimination based on race, national or ethnic origin, colour, religion, sex, age or mental or physical disability.

Argument of Jane Doe (Plaintiff)

Jane Doe argued that the MTPF failed to protect her from a serial rapist (a) when they already knew his prior pattern of behaviour, and (b) when she lived under similar conditions to his four previous victims and was, therefore, a prime target for his next attack.

She claimed that the MTPF had a duty to warn women in her neighbourhood about the rapist and that, had she been warned, she would have taken steps to protect herself.

She also claimed that the MTPF had stereotypical views about rape, about women in general, and about women who had been raped in particular. She charged that these views had an adverse impact on the police investigation and caused it to be done incompetently. As a result, the police discriminated against her because of her gender.

Argument of the MTPF (Defendant)

Although MTPF officers suspected there was a serial rapist at work in this case, they decided not to warn women living in the neighbourhood of the attacks for fear of alerting the rapist and causing him to flee. They also decided against increasing the police presence in the area except covertly. In making these decisions, officers were influenced by a previous police investigation of the "Annex Rapist." In that case, a large police presence coupled with a media alert had caused the suspect to flee to Vancouver. Police did not want something similar to happen in this case.

Make Your Decision

1. Outline the facts of the case in point form.
2. In your own words, summarize the arguments made by both sides in this case.
3. In what sense does Jane Doe's argument agree with principles of feminist jurisprudence?
4. Now make your decision: allow or dismiss the action by Jane Doe. Give reasons for your decision.

Key Terms

Review the following terms to show that you understand the meaning of each and how it is applied in a legal context.

dialectic
feminist jurisprudence
jurisprudence
justice
legal realism
Marxism
natural law
positive law
utilitarianism

Understanding the Law

Review the following pieces of legislation mentioned in the text, and show that you understand the intent of each.

Anti-Inflation Act
Canadian Charter of Rights and Freedoms
Constitution Act, 1867
Preamble to the US *Declaration of Independence*

Thinking and Inquiry

1. Based on the discussion of legal realism in this chapter, do you think that the perspectives and judgments of the Supreme Court of Canada would be affected by the appointment of one or more justices
   a) from a visible minority group?
   b) from one of the Aboriginal communities?
   c) who were confined to a wheelchair?
   Explain your answer.
2. Create an organizer to compare the following schools of jurisprudence or theories of law: natural law, positive law, utilitarianism, legal realism, Marxism, and feminism. Describe the following aspects of each theory of law: the source of law, the purpose of law, the role assigned to the state, and the role assigned to private citizens.
3. Which of the philosophers you have studied would support the concept of civil disobedience? What arguments do they give to support this concept?
4. How could John Locke's theories be used to justify the overthrow of government?

Communication

5. In small groups, investigate the impact of feminist jurisprudence on the following areas of law in Canada:
   a) property rights
   b) spousal support
   c) sexual assault (formerly, rape law)
   Present a short oral report on your findings, citing legal decisions where appropriate.
6. Aquinas believed that law should be for the "common good" (see page 75). How would you define the "common good"? Discuss this concept as a group, and then prepare a list of rules or laws that you think should govern the education system for it to operate for the "common good."
7. Scientific developments in recent years have made cloning of human cells possible. In the United Kingdom, under an amendment to the *Human Fertilisation and Embryology Act, 1990*, human cells can be cloned for therapeutic measures to help replace diseased human cells with healthy ones. Canada at present has no such law.
   a) For each of the philosophers you have studied, give what you think his opinion would be, stating your reasons, on whether this law is acceptable according to his views.
   b) As a group, research the topic of human and animal cloning, and form an opinion on whether (i) Canada needs a law to govern these scientific developments, and (ii) if it does, what the aims of the law should be.
8. Select one philosopher mentioned in this chapter and conduct a search of Internet and library sources to compile a point-form summary of his views on law. Summarize this philosopher's main arguments about the

source and purpose of law, and present these arguments in a brief oral presentation to the class.

Application

9. Re-read Lon Fuller's list of eight ways to fail when formulating laws (page 86). Then convert the list to eight positive statements that would increase the ruler's chances of success in creating a workable legal system. Add any ideas you might have yourself.
10. Use media sources and the Internet to research conditions of law and government in a country where civil war is raging. Consider:
    a) Who is making law or rules for governance?
    b) Who is enforcing law or these rules?
    c) What methods of enforcement are being used?
    d) Which of the philosophers you have studied would say that the conditions resulting from the war validate his theories of law and governance? Explain your answer.
11. Write a short report to explain what Chief Justice Roy McMurtry means by his statement, "It matters not what code of law may exist if its application is not subject to review by a neutral and impartial judiciary aided by independent lawyers."
12. Selznick recommends an independent body to review and recommend changes to government's laws. Assume that such a body (apart from the courts) was set up to fulfill this function in Canada.
    a) What kind of background should the participants have?
    b) Should the general public have input into such a body?
    c) What kinds of controls would be needed to limit the influence of powerful lobby groups?
    d) In your opinion, would such an independent body be useful in Canada?

Unit 2

Rights and Freedoms

This second unit of *Dimensions of Law: Canadian and International Law in the 21st Century* focuses on Canadians' rights and freedoms and the significant change that has occurred in Canadian law since Canada's constitution was patriated from Britain in 1982 with a "revolutionary" *Canadian Charter of Rights and Freedoms* entrenched within it.

Chapter 4 examines the role of the constitution in Canada's legal system and how our constitutional law developed. Why is a constitution necessary, and why was it so important to patriate the constitution? You will also be introduced to key events in Canadian constitutional history, including attempts to bring Quebec back into the constitutional fold.

Chapter 5 traces the evolution of civil rights legislation from English common law to the *Canadian Charter of Rights and Freedoms*, one of the most significant pieces of legislation passed by Parliament in the last 50 years. Your basic rights under the Charter are examined, but you will learn that these rights are not absolute; they may be legally limited in certain circumstances. Are judges "making" law, or is that Parliament's role? You will examine the courts' role in interpreting and enforcing the Charter and the ever-

increasing debate about current procedures for the appointment of superior court judges and the pleas for change. Should something different be done?

Chapter 6 focuses on the historical development of human rights in Canada and highlights some embarrassing examples of human rights discrimination in Canada within the last century. Being aware of these incidents, among others, you will understand the need for protection provided by the *Canadian Human Rights Act* and provincial legislation like the Ontario *Human Rights Code*. The Charter's impact on human rights is also examined. Finally, what does "equality" mean? The concept and meaning of equality rights are explored, recognizing that no one definition of "equality" is acceptable to everyone. Some landmark cases are provided to illustrate how courts are interpreting this basic right.

Chapter 7 narrows the focus on three key areas of majority and minority rights: the Quebec sovereignty and language debate, Canada's treatment of our Aboriginal peoples and their respective land claims, and the need for affirmative action programs to overcome aspects of discrimination for disabled and challenged persons. How are rights balanced in a democracy, and what must governments do to protect minority rights? The role of referenda, courts, and tribunals is also examined as a means of resolving these conflicts.

Chapter 4 Canadian Constitutional Law

CHAPTER Focus

In this chapter, you will

- explain the role of a nation's constitution and the reasons it is necessary
- explain how constitutional law developed in Canada
- distinguish among the law-making powers of the federal, provincial, and municipal governments
- explain the role of the courts in determining law-making jurisdiction
- demonstrate an understanding of key events in Canadian constitutional history

The constitution is often said to be the most important law of any country because it provides the fundamental framework on which all other laws are based. This chapter examines the role of the constitution in Canada's legal system. It looks at the law-making powers of the federal, provincial, and municipal governments, as well as the role of the courts. Canada has had a long history of constitutional struggles, which continue to this day. In order to understand these struggles, you will look at several important cases that have helped to shape our constitution, and consider some individuals who have influenced the development of Canada's constitutional law.

The cartoon in Figure 4.1 reflects the strains that have always existed between Canada's levels of government.

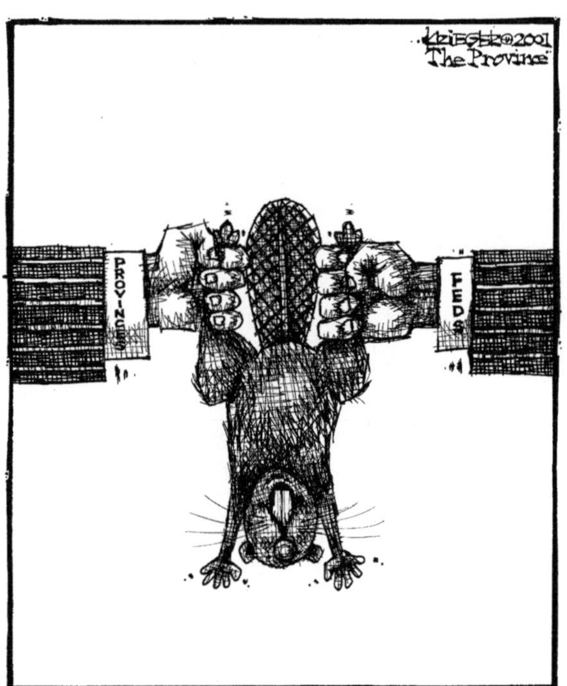

Figure 4.1

At First Glance

1. What kind of relationship between the federal and provincial levels of government does this cartoon depict? What might be the consequences of this relationship, according to the cartoon?
2. What are some current sources of strain between the two levels of government?
3. Which level of government, federal or provincial, do you think is more powerful in Canada today? Explain.
4. The third level of government, municipal government, is not even shown in this cartoon. What is its relationship to the other two? If it were added to the cartoon, how might it be shown?

The Importance of a Constitution

A constitution provides the basic framework for a nation's form of government and its legal system. In Canada, for example, our constitution describes the structure of the federal and provincial governments and allocates powers to each level of government. A constitution also sets out the procedures for making laws and defines who will be involved in making them.

A constitution can be thought of as a nation's rulebook, containing the rules that the political players must observe in order to adopt, amend, or revoke a law. These rules reflect the values and beliefs of a people. For example, Canada's constitution is founded upon ideas of freedom, equality, and democracy. However, the mere fact that a nation has a constitution proclaiming these ideas does not guarantee that it will abide by them. The citizens and government of a nation must have a continuing commitment to the values laid out in their constitution and actively demonstrate a respect for the rule of law.

Constitutions may be written or unwritten. The United States, for instance, has a written constitution that explicitly sets out the various branches of government and the powers of each. Britain has a largely unwritten constitution; its government principles are laid out in a series of customs and conventions, court decisions, and statutes. Canada has both a written and an unwritten constitution.

Sources of Canada's Constitution

There are three main sources of Canada's constitution. The first is the written constitution: the *Constitution Act, 1867* (originally called the *British North America Act*) and the *Constitution Act, 1982*. Our written constitution sets out the basic structure for Canada's system of government, which divides power between the federal and provincial governments. The second source of our constitution is the unwritten set of rules or conventions by which our system of government operates. The third source of constitutional law comes from court rulings that interpret the written constitution. These rulings become precedents, guides to be used in settling subsequent constitutional cases.

The *British North America Act*

Canada became a country in 1867, when the provinces of Canada (now Ontario and Quebec), New Brunswick, and Nova Scotia were united under the terms of the *British North America* (BNA) *Act*. The BNA Act was passed by the British parliament in March 1867. The Act was a piece of British legislation, since it concerned British colonies. It had, however, been drawn up by the Canadian Fathers of Confederation to serve as the written constitution for the new dominion that the Act created. Changes to the BNA Act had to be passed by the British parliament until the Act was patriated (brought home to Canada) in 1982 and renamed the *Constitution Act, 1867*. The 1982 amendments and additions to the constitution, which included the *Canadian Charter of Rights and Freedoms* and an amending formula, are known as the *Constitution Act, 1982*.

Although Canada was much smaller geographically in 1867, it was still a diverse country. In particular, it had large populations with French and British origins. In order to meet the requirements of its varied peoples and regions, the Fathers of Confederation adopted a federal structure of government for the new nation, in which power would be divided between a central (federal) government and regional (provincial) governments. George Brown, representing the Province of Canada, stated in the **Confederation debates** that a federal system was the only possible form of union that would be acceptable for the new country:

Confederation debates: debates held in the legislative assembly of the Province of Canada to discuss the terms of Confederation drafted at conferences held by the Fathers of Confederation in Charlottetown and Quebec

> We had either to take a Federal union or drop the negotiation. ... There was but one choice open to us—Federal union or nothing. ... We have thrown over on the localities all the questions which experience has shown lead directly to local jealousy and discord, and we have retained in the hands of the General Government all the powers necessary to secure a strong and efficient administration of public affairs.

The federal system would allow the central government to look after issues of national concern, such as defence and economic development. Issues that might cause conflict between competing interests would be handled by the provinces. It was clear, for example, that Quebec, which was largely French speaking, would want French-language schools, while Ontario would want English schools. The Fathers of Confederation hoped to avoid disruption by assigning power over education to the provinces. The federal system, however, was not able to remove all conflict between the various levels of government. As you will see, the courts would need to become involved in settling constitutional disputes.

Canada's Unwritten Constitution

The unwritten portion of the constitution also plays a vital role in Canadian law. For instance, the *Constitution Act, 1867* made no mention of a prime minister, even though Canada has had a prime minister since Confederation. However, the Act did contain the phrase that Canada would be federally united with "a constitution similar in principle to that of the United Kingdom." It is from this phrase that we get many of the ways in which our government functions, including the Cabinet system, the party system, and our parliamentary democracy. Since our constitution is similar in principle to that of the United Kingdom, many of the conventions built up in the UK were adopted here. The British parliamentary system included a prime minister and Cabinet and a party system, and these became part of Canada's system of government as well.

Conventions are unwritten rules of political conduct. Over time, such conventions generally become binding (that is, obligatory, not optional) on political representatives, and develop into important principles by which the government operates. An example of such a convention, again inherited from the British parliamentary system, is the idea that a Cabinet minister must resign if she or he does not agree with a decision reached by the Cabinet. This convention is often referred to as Cabinet solidarity, and Canadian governments follow it even though it is not formally entrenched in law. In 1990, for example, Lucien Bouchard left Brian Mulroney's Cabinet after the collapse of the Meech Lake Accord and the failure to recognize Quebec in the constitution as a distinct society.

Court Decisions

Court decisions are the third source of Canadian constitutional law. When there is a dispute over the meaning or intent of certain sections, phrases, and even individual words in the constitution, the courts are called upon to resolve it. Governments must comply with these judgments, which create precedents that become part of our legal system. The role of the courts in shaping our constitution is discussed in detail in Chapter 5: The Charter and the Courts.

Check Your Understanding

1. From what you have learned in Unit 1, what characteristics do you think need to exist in society to ensure that the rights and values expressed in the constitution are safeguarded?
2. What are the three main sources of Canada's constitution?
3. What led the Fathers of Confederation to choose a federal system of government?

The Division of Powers

As we have seen, the *Constitution Act, 1867* divided powers between the two levels of government in Canada. The most sweeping powers were given to the federal government, since the Fathers of Confederation wanted this to be the more important level of government in the new country. The federal government, for example, was given unlimited powers of taxation. By contrast, the provinces were assigned only the power of direct taxation, which left them largely dependent on the federal government for money. The federal government would also regulate the country's economy, based on the first four powers assigned to them under s. 91 of the Act. The provinces, on the other hand, were given control over matters that were merely of local interest.

The Law From the *Constitution Act, 1867*, s. 91; selected powers of the federal government:

It shall be lawful for the Queen, by and with the Advice and Consent of the Senate and House of Commons, to make Laws for the Peace, Order, and good Government of Canada, [and] ... it is hereby declared that (notwithstanding anything in this Act) the exclusive Legislative Authority of the Parliament of Canada extends to all Matters coming within the Classes of Subjects next hereinafter enumerated; that is to say,

1. The Public Debt and Property.
2. The Regulation of Trade and Commerce.
3. The raising of Money by any Mode or System of Taxation.
4. The borrowing of Money on the Public Credit.
5. Postal Service. ...
7. Militia, Military and Naval Service, and Defence. ...
12. Sea Coast and Inland Fisheries. ...
14. Currency and Coinage.
15. Banking, Incorporation of Banks, and the Issue of Paper Money. ...
20. Legal Tender. ...
24. Indians, and Lands reserved for the Indians. ...
26. Marriage and Divorce.
27. The Criminal Law, except the Constitution of Courts of Criminal Jurisdiction, but including the Procedure in Criminal Matters.

From the *Constitution Act, 1867*, s. 92; selected powers of provincial governments:

In each Province the Legislature may exclusively make Laws in relation to Matters coming within the Classes of Subject next hereinafter enumerated; that is to say,

5. The Management and Sale of the Public Lands belonging to the Province and of the Timber and Wood thereon. ...
7. The Establishment, Maintenance, and Management of Hospitals, Asylums, Charities, and Eleemosynary [charitable] Institutions in and for the Province, other than Marine Hospitals.
8. Municipal Institutions in the Province. ...
10. Local Works and Undertakings other than such as are of the following Classes:
    (a) Lines of Steam or other Ships, Railways, Canals, Telegraphs, and other Works and Undertakings connecting the Province with any other or others of the Provinces, or extending beyond the Limits of the Province:
    (b) Lines of Steam Ships between the Province and any British or Foreign Country:
    (c) Such Works as, although wholly situate within the Province, are before or after their Execution declared by the Parliament of Canada to be for the general Advantage of Canada or for the Advantage of Two or more of the Provinces. ...
12. The Solemnization of Marriage in the Province.
13. Property and Civil Rights in the Province. ...

Questions

1. In general terms, state the powers of the federal and provincial governments.
2. Examine the powers listed. Is there evidence of overlapping powers, or any contradiction in the division of powers that you feel would have led to disagreement between the two levels of government? Explain your response, using specific examples.

Figure 4.2 *According to the* Constitution Act, 1867, *postal services (left) fell under the jurisdiction of the federal government, while education (right) would be administered by the individual provinces.*

Case LIMITS ON SEAL HUNTING

Ward v. Canada (Attorney General), 2002 SCC 17

Facts

Ford Ward, a licensed fisherman and sealer, lived in the town of La Scie on the north coast of Newfoundland. Ward held a commercial sealing licence issued under the authority of the federal *Fisheries Act* that permitted him to harvest hooded and harp seals. In March and April 1996, Ford participated in the seal hunt and took approximately 50 seals, including some "blueback" seals. In November 1996 he was charged with selling blueback seal pelts, contrary to s. 27 of the *Marine Mammal Regulations.* These regulations prohibit the sale, trade, or barter of both whitecoat (immature harp seal) and blueback (immature hooded seal) pelts. Ward applied to the Supreme Court of Newfoundland to have s. 27 of the *Marine Mammal Regulations* declared *ultra vires* the Parliament of Canada (outside the federal government's powers).

Issue

The issue in this case became whether or not the *Marine Mammal Regulations* were a valid exercise of federal authority. These regulations had been introduced in 1993 in response to the public outcry over the killing of baby seals. The European Community's ban on the import of the seal skins in 1983 and a public boycott against Canadian fish were having an economic impact on Canada. In response to this pressure, the government of Canada passed the regulations prohibiting the sale, trade, or barter of whitecoat and blueback pelts.

Decision

The original decision in the Supreme Court of Newfoundland found that s. 27 was a valid exercise of the federal government's power. The trial judge found that the federal jurisdiction over fisheries could be used not only for conservation measures but also for more general socio-economic goals.

On appeal, however, the Newfoundland Court of Appeal, in a 2–1 ruling, overturned the trial judge's decision. The Court of Appeal decided that the federal power over fisheries was limited to issues of conservation, while the *Marine Mammal Regulations* were drafted in such broad terms that their purpose was left unclear, and thus they were unenforceable.

The Court of Appeal's decision was then appealed to the Supreme Court of Canada. The Court allowed the appeal and restored the original decision of the Supreme Court of Newfoundland. The federal Supreme Court found that the purpose of the regulations was to stop the commercial hunting of whitecoats and bluebacks. It recognized that the legislation did not ban the killing of these seals, since it was almost impossible to distinguish a blueback from another seal in the water. However, once a seal hunter realized he had killed a blueback, it would be reasonable for him to stop harvesting other seals in the area, knowing that the pelts could not be sold. The regulations, therefore, have the practical effect of stopping the commercial hunting of these seals, and this legislation was passed to protect the Canadian fishing industry in general. This purpose, the Court ruled, fell within the jurisdiction of the federal government.

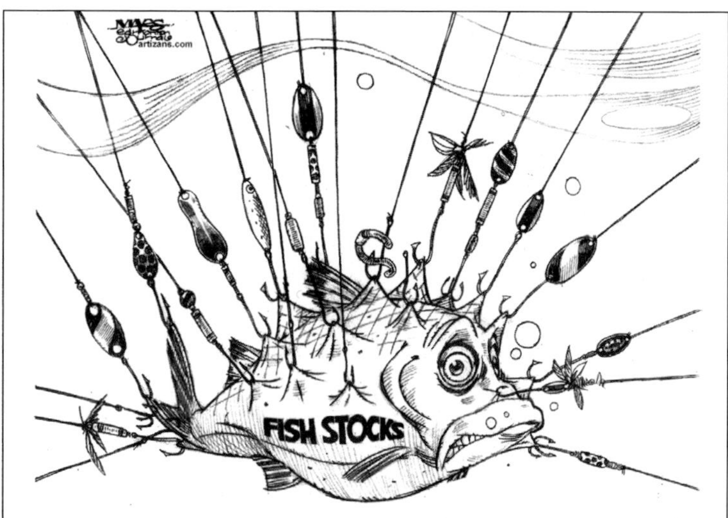

Figure 4.3 *The collapse of the Atlantic fisheries in the 1990s resulted in accusations that the federal government mismanaged them, and that they should be jointly managed with the provinces.*

Questions

1. According to the constitution, which level of government controls the fisheries?
2. The defence (Ward) argued that the federal law was *ultra vires* Parliament because it fell under provincial jurisdiction over "property and civil rights." Explain how control of the sale, trade, or barter of seal pelts could fall within the area of "property and civil rights."
3. The Court ruled that the purpose of the regulations could not be separated from their effect. What does this ruling mean?
4. Do you agree with the decision in this case? Why or why not?

To learn more about the joint management of fisheries, visit www.emp.ca/dimensionsoflaw

The Importance of Education

The importance of education in the Canadian constitution can be seen in the fact that it received a separate section (s. 93) of the *Constitution Act, 1867*. Education was important to the Fathers of Confederation because control of the school system meant control of the socialization of future generations. In Quebec, for example, provincial control of education meant that the French language would be used as the language of instruction and the schools would continue to be run by the Roman Catholic Church. In addition, the educational rights of Roman Catholics and Protestants, as they existed at the time of Confederation, were guaranteed under the constitution.

issue

Funding of Religious Schools Should all religious schools receive government funding?

The public funding of Roman Catholic schools in Canada came about through special circumstances in Canada's history. In recent years, other religious groups in Canada's multicultural society have argued that their schools should also be publicly funded. Some provinces have provided such funding. However, in Ontario at the end of the 20th century, only Roman Catholic separate schools were funded. Arieh Waldman of Toronto believed it was unfair that his children could receive a Jewish religious education only in private schools, even though he paid taxes that supported the public school system. After the Supreme Court of Canada ruled that public funding of Ontario's Roman Catholic schools, to the exclusion of other religions, was legal, Waldman took his case to the United Nations' Human Rights Committee. On November 3, 1999, the Committee found his situation to be in violation of the *International Covenant on Civil and Political Rights*, stating that

For the full text of the United Nations decision, visit www.emp.ca/dimensionsoflaw

[i]n the [Waldman] case, the author has sent his children to a private religious school, not because he wishes a private non-government–dependent education for his children, but because the publicly funded school system makes no provision for his religious denomination. ... On the basis of the facts before it, the Committee considers that the differences in treatment between Roman Catholic religious schools, which are publicly funded as a distinct part of the public education system, and schools of the author's religion, which are private by necessity, cannot be considered reasonable and objective.

> —*Section 10.5, views of the UN Human Rights Committee under article 5, paragraph 4, of the optional protocol to the* International Covenant on Civil and Political Rights, *67th session, concerning communication no. 694/1996 on behalf of Arieh Hollis Waldman*

One fully funded public education system is the answer to the United Nations finding today that Ontario is in violation of the International Covenant on Civil and Political Rights. ... In our multicultural society, the best way to protect the rights of all citizens is for the Ontario government to fund one public system that provides for heritage religion courses for all religious groups in the same manner that it now provides heritage language instruction.

The public system provides equal access and opportunity for all students in Ontario. Any other solution would further dismantle the public system and would not serve the needs of multicultural Ontario. It would simply foster a greater segregation of Ontario's society.

> —*Earl Manners, President, Ontario Secondary School Teachers' Federation, statement in response to the UN ruling in* Waldman v. Canada

> The Charter cannot provide for the automatic repeal of any provisions of the Constitution of Canada. Although the Charter is intended to constrain the exercise of legislative power conferred under the *Constitution Act, 1867* where the delineated rights of individual members of the community are adversely affected, it cannot be interpreted as rendering unconstitutional distinctions that are expressly permitted by the *Constitution Act, 1867*. The Charter, therefore, is not available to disallow the implementation of s. 93(1), or legislation for the protection of the rights embedded by s. 93(1), or legislation contemplated in s. 93(3).
>
> —*Supreme Court of Canada, 1987* Reference Re Bill 30 *(which extended full funding to Roman Catholic separate schools)*

In 2001, the Ontario government announced that it would grant tax credits to parents who sent their children to private schools, including privately funded religious schools. The *Catholic World News* on May 28, 2001 reported on a press conference by a coalition of groups fighting the tax credit:

> The group was furious that Ontario was even considering a partial tax credit for parents who send their children to private, religiously based schools. However, according to a report by the Canadian Press, Ontario is the only Canadian province not funding private religious schools, at least partially.
>
> [Alan] Borovoy [of the Canadian Civil Liberties Association] said that "the situation is a bad one when you have only one religious group funded publicly for its schools," but publicly funding all religious schools would make the situation even worse, because it further "undermines the ability of public schools to do the all-important job of integration." [Lawyer Clayton] Ruby said, "One wonders why the Constitution, which at the moment requires funding for Catholic schools, has to remain that way."

Questions

1. What is the constitutional basis for funding separate schools in Ontario?
2. What are the main arguments against funding religious schools?
3. What are the main arguments in favour of funding religious schools?
4. Working in small groups, list two or three different solutions that the government could use to deal with the United Nations ruling. Which solution would your group recommend? Why?

ersonal Viewpoint

The Challenge for Toronto

In 2001, the chief administrative officer and the chief financial officer for the city of Toronto prepared a report calling for a new relationship between Toronto and the provincial and federal governments.

> The global economy is composed more and more of competing city regions. Toronto is in competition with other city regions in North America and around the world. The City is in a financial squeeze that threatens its international position. It is caught between limited growth in its revenue base and high demands for unique services that are a consequence of its position as Canada's largest metropolis. This squeeze is worsened by the impact of ongoing transfer of responsibilities from the province.
>
> The City's ability to gain access to alternative sources of revenue is curtailed by provincial legislation. Provincial legislation also does not permit City Council to develop policy responses to critical problems within the City's boundaries.
>
> For the past few decades, the senior levels of government have been steadily withdrawing from or reducing their commitment to a number of policy fields that have a profound impact on Toronto. For example:
>
> - The federal government's changes to the Employment Insurance program had an impact on applications for welfare, which in Ontario is cost-shared with the municipal government. A cutback to a federal program can increase the cost to the municipality.
> - The City's 2000 Report Card on Homelessness showed that the combination of lack of investment in social housing by the provincial and federal governments and cuts in welfare rates correlate statistically with observable increases in homelessness. There is a direct impact on the demand for municipal services from hostels and public health to policing.
>
> The importance of sustainable cities has been recognized internationally. Increasingly, city government is recognized as an order of government with entrenched rights. In some cases, for example, in Brazil and many European countries, municipalities are formally recognized constitutionally. Several US states provide municipalities with the option to adopt Home Rule status, which allows them to draft, adopt and amend constitutional charters and govern their own affairs independent of the state government.
>
> In Europe, the United States and some parts of Canada, a fixed share of senior government revenues is earmarked for municipalities. In Germany, local governments receive fifteen percent of national income and wage tax revenues. Manitoba allocates revenues from two percentage points of the personal income tax and one percentage point of the corporate income tax to municipalities in the form of a per capita grant.

Figure 4.4 *Three people live in this parking booth-turned-shelter near Toronto's lakeshore.*

How Does Toronto Compare?

- Toronto has limited legislative powers. Toronto has twice the population of Manitoba. It has more people than all the Atlantic provinces combined. Yet, unlike Montreal, its Council does not even have the power to raise money by mortgaging an asset.
- Toronto has fewer revenue options.
- Toronto experiences little federal government involvement, primarily because of the inability to work through the federal–provincial relationship.
- Toronto lacks a formal voice on critical issues. The City government is often not consulted on the development of federal and provincial policies and actions that have a profound impact on the City.

Source: Adapted from "Canada's Cities: Unleash Our Potential," June 2000; www.canadascities.ca/caoreport_062000_2.htm.

Questions

1. Under the *Constitution Act, 1867*, what level of government controls municipal institutions?
2. Why would cities not have been considered a third level of government that needed its own powers under the *Constitution Act, 1867*?
3. Should we amend the constitution to give large urban centres such as Toronto more power? Explain your reasoning.

The Municipal Level of Government

When the Fathers of Confederation drafted the *British North America Act*, three out of four Canadians lived in rural areas. Today, over three-quarters of Canadians live in cities and towns, and the three largest cities—Toronto, Montreal, and Vancouver—account for a third of Canada's population. Yet, Canadian cities have no constitutional rights of their own. The *Constitution Act, 1867* made cities the responsibility of provincial governments. The provinces then enacted municipal acts, which gave cities the authority to provide basic services and to pay for them by levying property taxes and imposing service charges. The ability of a city or town to pass local laws, known as bylaws, was strictly limited by the provincial legislation that created the municipality. In recent years, leaders of Canada's cities have pushed for a new relationship between cities and the other levels of government.

Learn more about Toronto's tent city at www.emp.ca/dimensionsoflaw

CHECK YOUR UNDERSTANDING

1. Refer to Figure 4.1 again. Have your answers to questions 3 and 4 changed as a result of learning more about the division of powers in the Canadian constitution? Explain.
2. a) Why was education given a separate section in the BNA Act?
   b) How does the constitution make it difficult for Canada to adopt a national education policy?
   c) Do you think such a policy would be desirable? Why or why not?

The Role of the Courts

As we have seen, the role of the courts is to interpret the constitution and to solve disputes between the levels of government. If the provinces and the federal government are unable to reach agreement, then the courts will determine which level of government has jurisdiction over a particular subject matter. When the *British North America Act* was written in 1867, the Fathers of Confederation could not foresee the social changes and scientific advances that would transform the world. Telephone, radio, television, airplanes, and the Internet were not even in the realm of possibility when Canada became a nation, and so they were not covered in the division of powers under the BNA Act.

Furthermore, in 1867 government played a much more limited role in the lives of Canadians than citizens expect today. Health care, employment insurance, and other matters that we now put into the category of the "social safety net" were not thought to be government responsibilities until the Great Depression of the 1930s, and other historical events, changed our views about the role of government. Again, when constitutional disputes arose in these areas, it often fell to the courts to rule on which level of government had the power to deal with the issue.

The Structure of the Courts

The Canadian judicial system is based on the British model. The court structure follows a hierarchical pattern starting from the lowest courts—the provincial courts—to the highest, the Supreme Court of Canada.

In each province, the highest level of court is the provincial Court of Appeal, which hears appeals from lower provincial courts. The name of the next highest provincial court varies by province—the Supreme Court, the Superior Court, or the Court of Queen's Bench. A case appealed from the highest court in a given province might be heard by the Supreme Court of Canada. The federal and Ontario court systems are illustrated in Figure 4.5.

The Historic Role of the JCPC

Today, our highest court of appeal is the Supreme Court of Canada, but until 1949, Canada's final court of appeal for constitutional matters was the Judicial Committee of the Privy Council (JCPC) in Britain. The Privy Council is one of the oldest parts of the British government. Its judicial committee was, among other things, the final court of appeal for Britain's overseas possessions and dominions, a role it still plays for some Commonwealth nations to this day. In the years following Confederation, the JCPC made over 100 judgments relating to the distribution of legislative power alone, and its decisions had a dramatic impact on the relationship between Canada's federal and provincial governments. Sir John A. Macdonald and

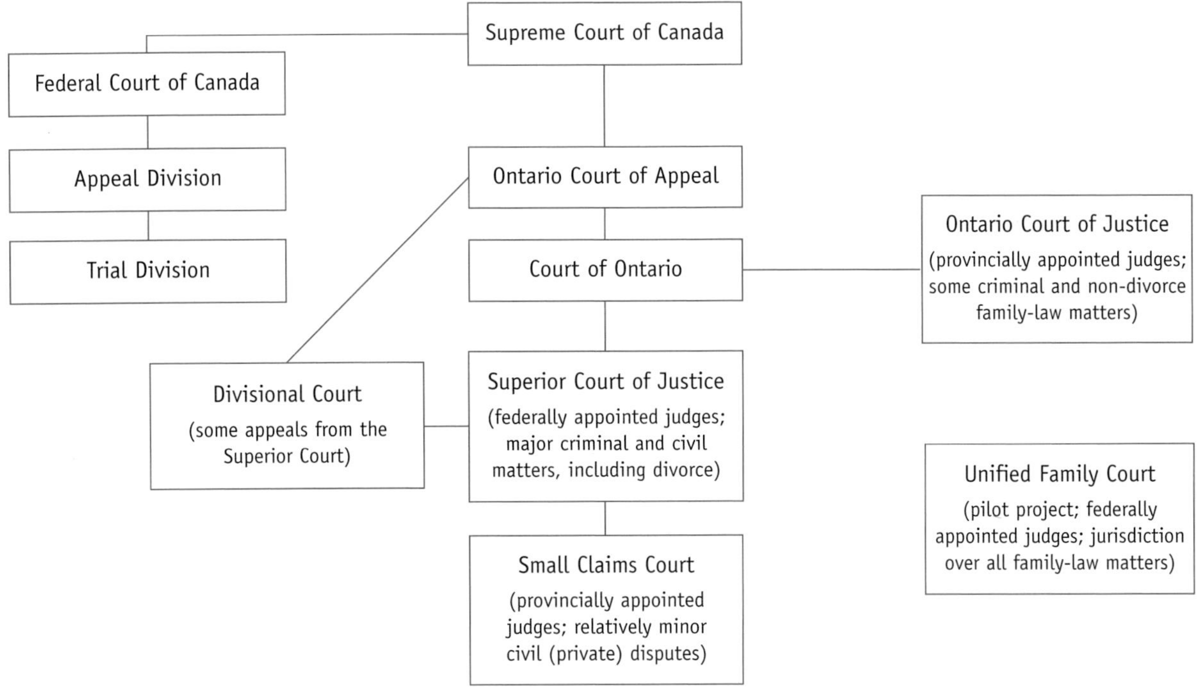

Figure 4.5 *Structure of the federal courts and those of Ontario.*

many of his colleagues believed that they had created a federal union in which the central government was the most important and powerful level of government. The JCPC, however, limited the powers of the federal government and expanded the role of the provincial governments by more narrowly defining the federal powers outlined in the BNA Act.

The JCPC changed the course of Canadian history with its decision in the "persons" case in 1929, overturning a ruling by the Supreme Court of Canada. The JCPC based its decision on the "living tree" approach to judicial review. As Lord Sankey of the JCPC put it, "the *British North America Act* planted in Canada a living tree capable of growth and expansion within its natural limits." In other words, judicial interpretation of the Act had to reflect the great changes, unforeseen by the Fathers of Confederation, that had occurred in Canada since Confederation.

Find out more about the "persons" case at www.emp.ca/dimensionsoflaw

The Supreme Court of Canada

The Supreme Court is the highest level of court in Canada. It is an appeal court that hears cases from the provincial court system and from the Federal Court of Canada. Section 101 of the BNA Act authorized the Parliament of Canada to create "a general court of appeal for Canada," but it wasn't until 1875 that Parliament used this provision to create the Supreme Court. (Before that, appeals from provincial courts went directly to the

For background information on the Supreme Court of Canada, visit www.emp.ca/dimensionsoflaw

Turning Points in the Law

The Persons Case: *Edwards v. A.G. of Canada*, [1930] AC 124 (JCPC)

Under British common law, women were considered to be "persons only in terms of pains and penalties, and not rights and privileges." Thus, for decades after Confederation, Canadian women could be sent to jail for committing a crime ("pains and penalties") but were cut off from such "rights and privileges" as voting and holding public office. It was an important breakthrough for Canadian women when Emily Murphy was appointed a judge in the city of Edmonton in 1916. She was the first female judge in the entire British empire. Murphy, with support from many women, then began a drive to become the first female senator in Canada. Unfortunately, the response from successive federal governments remained the same: they were unable to appoint Murphy because, as stated in the BNA Act, only "qualified persons" could be appointed to the Senate.

From s. 24 of the BNA Act:

> The Governor General shall from Time to Time, in the Queen's Name, by Instrument under the Great Seal of Canada, summon qualified Persons to the Senate; and, subject to the Provisions of this Act, every Person so summoned shall become and be a Member of the Senate and a Senator.

In 1927, Murphy employed a new strategy in her quest to become a senator. She used s. 60 of the *Supreme Court of Canada Act*, which stated that any five citizens acting as a unit could make an appeal through the federal Cabinet to the Supreme Court for a ruling on a constitutional issue. Murphy—along with Henrietta Muir Edwards, Louise McKinney, Irene Parlby, and Nellie McClung—forced Prime Minister Mackenzie King's Cabinet to submit a question to the Supreme Court. The question referred to the Court was, "Does the word 'persons' in s. 24 of the *British North America Act* include female persons?" On April 24, 1928, the Supreme Court ruled against the five women, who had become known as the "Famous Five" or the "Alberta Five."

Figure 4.6 *This larger-than-life bronze sculpture by Barbara Paterson stands on Parliament Hill in Ottawa. It depicts an imaginary moment when the "Famous Five" received word that women were indeed "persons" under s. 24 of the BNA Act.*

The women then appealed to the Judicial Committee of the Privy Council in Britain. On October 18, 1929, the JCPC ruled that women were persons and that they were eligible to be appointed to the Canadian Senate.

Murphy was finally triumphant. However, political circumstances kept her from becoming the first female senator in Canada. She was a supporter of the Conservative Party, and when the first Senate vacancy opened in Ontario, Liberal Prime Minister Mackenzie King appointed Liberal Cairine Wilson to the post. Murphy, who had fought so hard for this right, was never appointed to the Senate herself.

Questions

1. Record your initial reaction to the idea that women were not considered "persons" in Canada until 1929. Share your reaction with a partner.
2. Why was it important for women to be recognized as "persons" under Canadian law?
3. What equality issues are Canadian women dealing with today?

Judicial Committee of the Privy Council.) The Court consists of nine justices appointed by the federal Cabinet. Three of the judges must come from the province of Quebec, to ensure that the Court has a solid understanding of the *Civil Code*, derived from the *Civil Law Code* of France, that governs Quebec civil law. Once appointed, the judges may serve to age 75.

The Supreme Court must grant leave to appeal, which means that the Court agrees to hear a case. The Court hears important cases that deal with civil, criminal, and constitutional law. Once the Supreme Court of Canada makes a decision, it becomes binding on all lower courts across Canada. Decisions of the Supreme Court are "final," and there is no way for the case to be further appealed.

Fyi By tradition, three of the Supreme Court judges come from Ontario, three from Quebec, two from Western Canada, and one from the Atlantic provinces.

Case WHO CONTROLS TOBACCO ADVERTISING?

RJR–MacDonald Inc. v. Canada (Attorney General), [1995] 3 SCR 199

Facts

The *Tobacco Products Control Act* came into effect on January 1, 1989. This Act regulated the advertisement of tobacco products and the health warnings that had to be placed upon tobacco products. The first part of the Act (ss. 4–8) prohibited the advertising of tobacco products and any form of activity designed to encourage their sale. Section 9 of the Act regulated the labelling of tobacco products and stated that all tobacco packages had to carry health warnings. Prior to this Act, the public health warnings on tobacco packages had been attributed to "Health and Welfare Canada," but the new regulations required the warnings to be carried without any reference to their source. The purpose of the Act was set out in s. 3, which stated:

> 3. The purpose of this Act is to provide a legislative response to a national public health problem of substantial and pressing concern and, in particular,
>   (a) to protect the health of Canadians in the light of conclusive evidence implicating tobacco use in the incidence of numerous debilitating and fatal diseases;
>   (b) to protect young persons and others, to the extent that is reasonable in a free and democratic society, from inducements to use tobacco products and consequent dependence on them; and
>   (c) to enhance public awareness of the hazards of tobacco use by ensuring the effective communication of pertinent information to consumers of tobacco products.

RJR–MacDonald Inc., a tobacco company, challenged the constitutional validity of the *Tobacco Products Control Act* on the grounds that it was *ultra vires* the Parliament of Canada and invalid because it violated s. 2(b) (freedom of expression) of the *Canadian Charter of Rights and Freedoms*.

RJR–MacDonald was successful at trial in the Quebec Superior Court. Justice Chabot ruled that the dominant characteristic of the *Tobacco Products Control Act* was the control of tobacco advertising, and that the protection of public health was only an incidental objective of the Act. Since the Act regulated the advertising of a particular product, a responsibility of the provincial government, the law was *ultra vires.* Justice Chabot also ruled that the Act violated s. 2(b) of the Charter because it limited freedom of expression.

The federal government appealed this ruling to the Quebec Court of Appeal. The Court of Appeal ruled that the main characteristic of the Act related to public health, and therefore the Act was *intra vires* (within the jurisdiction of) Parliament because it had been enacted for the "peace, order, and good government" of Canada. Further, the Court of Appeal ruled that although the Act infringed on s. 2(b) of the Charter, it was justified under s. 1 of the Charter, which states that the Charter guarantees rights and freedoms "subject only to such reasonable limits prescribed by law as can be demonstrably justified in a free and democratic society." RJR–MacDonald then appealed to the Supreme Court of Canada.

Decision

The Supreme Court was split in its decision in this case. RJR–MacDonald was unsuccessful in one part of the appeal, since the Court ruled that the Act was *intra vires* Parliament. In a 7–2 ruling on the question of the division of powers, the Court found that "[t]he *Tobacco Products Control Act* is, in **pith and substance**, criminal law." This ruling was based, in part, on the Court's finding that

pith and substance: the main purpose of a law, as opposed to its incidental effects

> [t]he legislation, while not serving a "public purpose commonly recognized as being criminal in nature," is nevertheless a valid exercise of the criminal law power. The definition of the criminal law is not "frozen as of some particular time" and the criminal law power includes the power to create new crimes.

RJR–MacDonald was successful in winning the Charter argument that the Act violated freedom of expression. Again, the Court was split, but in a 5–4 decision it ruled that forcing the tobacco companies to place unattributed warnings on packages infringed on freedom of expression, and that this infringement could not be justified under s. 1 of the Charter.

Fyi In 1999, Parliament passed the *Tobacco Act,* which prohibits most tobacco advertising and requires health warnings on the packages of tobacco products.

Questions

1. Summarize the main arguments used by RJR–MacDonald in this case.
2. Explain why this case involved both the *Canadian Charter of Rights and Freedoms* and the division of powers in the *Constitution Act, 1867.*
3. Explain the Supreme Court's decision in this case.
4. Do you agree with this decision? Why or why not?

CHECK YOUR UNDERSTANDING

1. How did decisions by the JCPC change the division of powers that the Fathers of Confederation believed they had established between the federal and provincial governments?
2. When was the Supreme Court of Canada established, and what is its current role in the Canadian judicial system?
3. What role does the Supreme Court of Canada play in shaping the Canadian constitution?

The Evolution of Canada's *Constitution Act*

The constitution of Canada, like those of other members of the British empire, including Australia and New Zealand, was enacted by the British parliament rather than passed under Canadian legislative authority. Any amendments made to the *British North America Act* had to be passed through the British parliament. This requirement had two important consequences. First, Canada remained subject to British law and bound by the foreign policy of Britain. It was for this reason that Canada was automatically at war with Germany when Britain declared war on August 4, 1914. Second, our final court of appeal was not the Supreme Court of Canada, but the Judicial Committee of the Privy Council in Britain. In these ways, Canada was not yet an independent nation prior to World War I.

The war, which lasted from 1914 to 1918, had a tremendous impact on the nations of the world, Canada included. By the time the armistice took effect on November 11, 1918 (Remembrance Day), about 600 000 had served in the military and, of these, over 60 000 had died. The war brought about a turning point in Canada's relations with Britain. Canada's wartime prime minister, Sir Robert Borden, forcefully argued that Canada's tremendous contributions to the war effort and our sacrifices on the battlefield should earn the nation an independent seat at the negotiating table where the peace treaty to end the war was hammered out. Canada had been automatically involved in the war in 1914, but when the *Treaty of Versailles* was signed in June 1919, Canada signed the treaty on its own. A first full step toward nationhood had been taken.

Statute of Westminster, 1931

In the decades after World War I, Imperial Conferences were held every four years. The leaders of the member countries of the British empire met at these conferences to discuss issues of common concern. In 1926, a report by a committee at the Imperial Conference declared that Canada and the other dominions, including Australia, New Zealand, and the Union of South Africa, would no longer be subservient to Britain. The *Statute of Westminster*, passed in 1931, was the logical extension of that 1926 report (known as the Balfour Report). Under the provisions of this statute, Britain could no longer legislate for a dominion unless it was specifically asked to do so by that dominion. Canada was no longer subject to British laws and could pass laws that contradicted those of Britain. Furthermore, Canada was now independent of Britain in terms of foreign policy. The most dramatic sign of the new independence came in 1939, when Canada's Parliament declared war on September 10, a full week after Britain had declared war on Germany.

Patriation of the Constitution

Although Canada had become independent in foreign policy, our constitution remained a British statute. An important reason for this impasse was that no agreement could be made on patriating the constitution with a Canadian amending formula. An **amending formula** is a way to change parts of a constitution when its member constituencies—in this case, the Canadian provinces—agree to do so. Constitutional amending formulas commonly have a minimum proportion of members—such as two-thirds or three-quarters—who must agree before a change can be made. An amending formula must also take care to protect minority constituencies. For example, in Canada, the province of Quebec would want a guarantee that French language rights could not be taken away by the nation's English-speaking majority.

amending formula: a method for making changes to a constitution; in Canada's case, a method that would no longer involve the British parliament

Liberal Prime Minister Pierre Trudeau, first elected in 1968, was determined to reform the Canadian constitution. In 1971, a meeting of first ministers produced a draft called the Victoria Charter, a written guarantee of rights that was initially accepted by the provinces and the federal government. However, the Quebec government of Robert Bourassa withdrew its agreement after it faced harsh criticism within the province of Quebec.

In 1976 the Parti Québécois, whose goal was the independence of Quebec, became the governing party in that province. Trudeau, a long-time foe of the independence movement, was defeated in the 1979 federal election, but was returned to power with a majority government in February 1980. Trudeau led the fight against the PQ referendum on **sovereignty-association** in May 1980. Under Trudeau's leadership, the "no" side scored an impressive victory over the sovereigntists by a margin of almost two to one. See Chapter 5 for more detail.

sovereignty-association: the concept put forth by the Parti Québécois government of René Lévesque, whereby Quebec would become a sovereign jurisdiction in all areas of law making, but would maintain economic association with the rest of Canada

In his speeches leading up to the referendum, Trudeau had promised a renewed federalism. The federal government was committed to constitutional renewal and patriating the constitution from Britain. The next 18 months brought a great deal of intense debate about the constitution to Canadian public life. In addition to the amending formula, one of the most controversial issues became the **entrenchment** of a bill of rights in the constitution. Finally, in November 1981, the federal government and nine of the 10 provinces agreed to the patriation of the constitution with an entrenched charter of rights and freedoms. The province of Quebec, however, which had felt excluded from key discussions and ignored in some of its concerns, refused to sign the agreement.

entrenchment: protecting a portion of a constitution by ensuring that it can be changed only through constitutional amendment

On April 17, 1982, over 115 years after it had been originally passed, the *British North America Act*, renamed the *Constitution Act, 1867*, was brought home to Canada. Canada's written constitution now also included the *Constitution Act, 1982*, containing an amending formula that would allow all future constitutional amendments to be made within this country, as well as the *Canadian Charter of Rights and Freedoms*. The nation was now fully independent in all areas of the law.

Figure 4.7 *The* Canada Act, 1982 *was passed by the parliament of the United Kingdom and brought into effect as the* Constitution Act, 1982, *which included the* Canadian Charter of Rights and Freedoms.

The Meech Lake Accord

The failure to persuade the province of Quebec to agree to the patriation of the constitution in 1981 left many critics arguing that the constitutional deal was flawed. In 1984, Progressive Conservative leader Brian Mulroney became the new prime minister of Canada, and one of his objectives was to return the province of Quebec to the constitutional fold. The government of Quebec, under the leadership of Robert Bourassa, put forth a series of proposals that would have led to Quebec's signing of the constitution. In 1987, at Meech Lake near Ottawa, Prime Minister Mulroney managed to get all 10 provincial premiers to agree to a constitutional package based on these proposals. The new deal, the Meech Lake Accord, would recognize Quebec as a "distinct society" and would give the provinces more power relative to the federal government. Some of the changes included giving the provinces the right to supply nominees for the Senate and the Supreme Court. It is not surprising that all provinces agreed with enhancing their constitutional power.

The Meech Lake Accord, although hailed as a major breakthrough by many, faced harsh criticism as well. Critics of the accord included former Prime Minister Pierre Trudeau, who saw any type of special recognition of Quebec as a "distinct society" as being unnecessary and dangerous. Aboriginal leaders were also upset at the lack of consultation with them over the proposed changes, and the fact that the accord did not address Aboriginal concerns. Dissatisfaction with the terms of the accord mounted after its passage. By early June 1990, Prime Minister Mulroney called a special meeting of the premiers to ensure that the Meech Lake Accord would receive the consent necessary from each of the provincial legislatures. All the premiers agreed to ratify the accord based on the guarantees that some outstanding matters, such as an elected Senate and Aboriginal issues, would be dealt with at future constitutional conferences. However, despite the agreement of all premiers to pass the accord, it was not ratified within the necessary time frame.

Figure 4.8 *Elijah Harper sits in the Manitoba legislature holding an eagle feather for spiritual strength as he opposes the Meech Lake Accord. Harper served in the Manitoba legislature from 1981 to 1992, and was later elected to the House of Commons in Ottawa. In recent years, he has taken the lead in promoting greater understanding between Aboriginal and non-Aboriginal Canadians.*

Under the constitutional amending formula in the accord, it would have to be ratified by all the provinces plus the federal government within three years. (The final deadline was June 23, 1990.) Under the laws of Manitoba, public hearings would be necessary before holding a ratification vote. The necessity of public hearings could be waived with the unanimous consent of the province's Legislative Assembly. That unanimous consent could not be achieved because Elijah Harper, an Aboriginal member of the Manitoba legislature, refused his consent to waive the public hearings. Therefore, the Meech Lake Accord could not be brought to a ratification vote before the June 23 deadline. Also, Premier Clyde Wells of Newfoundland did not bring the accord to a vote in his province's Legislative Assembly. The Meech Lake Accord would not be passed.

Aboriginal peoples had not been given a chance for input into the Meech Lake Accord, despite the fact that their concerns needed to be addressed. Some would say that it was fitting that an Aboriginal legislator ensured that the accord would not pass.

The Charlottetown Accord

The Mulroney government did not give up on constitutional renewal, despite the failure of the Meech Lake Accord. In 1992 a new proposal, called the Charlottetown Accord, was put before the people of Canada in a national referendum. The Charlottetown Accord, like the Meech Lake Accord, dealt with a number of constitutional issues including the division of powers in such areas as forestry, mining, and cultural affairs. In general, the Charlottetown Accord enhanced provincial power so that, for example, the federal **power of disallowance** was abolished. This time, Aboriginal concerns were addressed, including the issue of Aboriginal self-government. The new accord would also make changes to the Supreme Court by formally entrenching the composition and appointment process. The Senate would be changed from an appointed body to an elected body having equal representation from each of the provinces. The Charlottetown Accord, like its predecessor, was doomed: it was defeated in six provinces and one territory.

power of disallowance: a power granted to the federal government by s. 90 of the *Constitution Act, 1867* that gave it the right to disallow provincial legislation (declare it void) within one year of its passage; a type of veto power that has not been used since World War II and that is generally considered to be no longer valid

The 1995 Quebec Referendum

The failure to reach a deal that would have allowed Quebec to sign the constitution led to another referendum in Quebec. As with the earlier referendum, Quebeckers would decide on whether or not they wished to remain a part of Canada. Unlike the referendum of 1980, however, the 1995 vote would have resulted in an immediate declaration of sovereignty. The outcome of the 1995 referendum was also dramatically different from the results in 1980. This time, the "no" forces won by a razor-thin majority—50.56 percent of the popular vote. (For more detail, see Chapter 7, pages 200–201.)

At the beginning of the 21st century, Canada remained intact, but Quebec still had not signed the constitution.

CHECK YOUR UNDERSTANDING

1. Explain the significance of the *Statute of Westminster*.
2. Why did it take so long for Canada's constitution to be patriated?
3. What was the Meech Lake Accord, and why did it fail?
4. Outline the major difference in the results of Quebec's 1980 and 1995 referenda.

METHODS OF *Legal Inquiry*

Developing a Thesis and Outline

In July 2003, provincial premiers met for their annual meeting in Charlottetown. The newly elected premier of Quebec, Jean Charest, proposed that premiers form a Council of the Federation. The Council would focus on common provincial concerns regarding their relationship with the federal government. The premiers planned to meet in Quebec City in October 2003 to agree on the Council's mandate. Here is one commentator's opinion on Charest's proposal.

Council of the Federation May Be Effective

by Larry Cornies

I think creation of the council [of the federation] is a positive development. ...

On Thursday, we saw representatives of Canada's provinces forge a mechanism they hope will strengthen the federation. The council would provide a strong voice for the provinces—the entities whose antecedents founded the country in the first place. Born in Charlottetown, largely of Quebec Premier Jean Charest's persuasion, the body would be located in Quebec City. ...

[The Council's] importance ... could come in two areas: first, as a check and balance against the federal government, which derives its authority from the House of Commons, and second, as a means of distilling pan-provincial concerns, giving them focus, impetus and direction.

The entrenchment of the Liberal party as the federal government of the foreseeable future, the lack of a truly effective opposition and the ineffectual nature of Canada's Senate could make an institution such as the Council of the Federation a useful counterweight to Ottawa's power.

It's only a council, not an elected body, but at least it's one more forum in which the provinces, which carry the lion's share of responsibility for ministries such as health care, social assistance and education, can voice legitimate concerns. Together, the provinces and territories are Canada, expressed through a different political prism. ...

The point is that the provinces deserve a strong voice in how their constitutional responsibilities are discharged. Canadians, meanwhile, want their politicians at both senior levels to act constructively in the interests of the country. We're all tired of seeing arrogance, one-upmanship, sullenness and posturing on display.

> The fact this week's agreement was the pet project of Charest, who promised Quebec a new kind of dialogue with Canada short of reopening the painful debate over the Constitution, is an added bonus and mutually beneficial for him and his fellow premiers.
>
> So give the council a chance. We'll learn very quickly if it will work.

Source: *The London Free Press*, July 12, 2003.

Suppose you were asked to evaluate this writer's opinion in an oral presentation or an essay. Do you agree with Cornies that "the provinces deserve a strong voice in how their constitutional responsibilities are discharged"? Does the power of the federal government need to be checked?

Applying the Skill

What steps do you need to take to organize information for a speech or essay?

The Research Stage

The first step is to find out as much as you can about the proposal for the Council. Make a list of the questions you would want answered, such as: What were the details of the proposal? Why did the premiers support the idea? Were any political commentators opposed to the proposal? What were their arguments?

The Thesis

On the basis of your research, you will soon have a clear idea of the main points to consider in preparing your thesis. A thesis is a statement of your point of view. For example, your thesis could be *"The proposed Council of the Federation could result in a 'renewed federalism' that will address the concerns of the provinces"*; or *"The proposed Council of the Federation will be a tool that the provincial premiers can use to take even more powers from the federal government."*

The Outline

The next stage is to organize the information you have gathered into as detailed an outline as possible. In any argument, you will need to include a defence of your opinions to answer those who disagree with your thesis. At this stage, you will probably find that there are some gaps in the information you have gathered, and that you will need to do further research.

Here is an example of an outline.

[Main heading] **The Proposal:** Describe what the Council of the Federation is, and what its role is to be.

[Sub-heading] **Background of the Proposal:** Explain the role of previous annual meetings of first ministers, and why a proposal for the Council was made.

[Sub-heading] **The Role of Quebec:** Describe the significance of participation by Quebec.

[Main heading] **Evaluation of the Proposal:** Describe your opinion of the proposal, using a separate paragraph and sub-heading for each reason for your support or opposition. Deal with opponents' arguments, using a sub-heading for each argument, if necessary.

[Main heading] **Assessment:** Give a final summary of your opinion on the proposal.

*R*eviewing *M*ain *I*deas

You Decide!

WHO CAN MAKE LAWS ABOUT GUNS?

Reference re Firearms Act (Can.), 2000 SCC 31

Facts

The controversial issue of "gun control"—that is, the registration and control of distribution of firearms—has been in the public spotlight for many decades. Supporters of gun control argue that registering guns reduces the number of weapons used in crimes and keeps Canadians safe. They use Canada's low homicide rate as evidence of the success of gun control, especially in comparison to the United States, where firearms are much more readily available. Critics of gun control, however, see such legislation as an infringement on their fundamental right to possess weapons. In particular, hunters and those who use guns for target shooting argue that criminals will not obey gun control legislation and, therefore, any attempts to restrict guns only harm legitimate owners.

In 1995, the federal government passed an amendment to the *Criminal Code* known as the *Firearms Act*. This Act was commonly referred to as the "gun control law" because it required gun owners to obtain licences and register their guns. In 1996, the province of Alberta challenged Parliament's power to pass the gun control law. However, the Alberta Court of Appeal, in a 3–2 decision, upheld Parliament's power to enact this law. The government of Alberta then appealed this decision to the Supreme Court of Canada.

The Law

The issue before the Supreme Court was whether Parliament had the constitutional authority to pass the *Firearms Act*. The Court was not determining whether gun control legislation is good or bad, whether it is effective in reducing gun violence, or even whether it is unfair to gun owners. The only basis for making the decision in this case was the division of powers as set out in the *Constitution Act, 1867*.

The Court had to examine three important areas of constitutional law. The first two are from s. 91, which assigns powers to the federal government:

> 91 ...to make Laws for the Peace, Order, and good Government of Canada. ...
>
> 91(27) The Criminal Law, except the Constitution of Courts of Criminal Jurisdiction, but including the Procedure in Criminal Matters.

The third is from s. 92, which assigns powers to the provincial government:

> 92(13) Property and Civil Rights in the Province.

In order to resolve the dispute, the Supreme Court would have to determine what the *Firearms Act* was really about (its "pith and substance"). Once this was established, the Court could determine under which head or heads of power (in the constitution) the law would fall.

Arguments of the Government of Alberta

The basic argument of the government of Alberta was that the legislation impinged on the province's power over property and civil rights. Although the federal law claimed to fall under criminal law (protection of the public, for example), the attorney general of Alberta noted that the law could not achieve this purpose for a number of reasons. These included the fact that criminals would not register their guns and thus would not advance the fight against crime. Instead, the *Firearms Act* would simply create more bureaucratic red tape for legitimate owners. Although the Act may claim to protect the public (through criminal law), it may not actually accomplish this goal.

The Federal Government's Arguments

The Court considered both the wording of the legislation and the statements made by government members when examining the law. The *Firearms Act* states that its purpose is "to provide ... for the issuance of licences, registration certificates and authorizations under which persons may possess firearms" and "to authorize ... the manufacture of" and "transfer of" ordinary firearms. The federal minister of justice had stated that "[t]he government suggests that the object of the regulation of firearms should be the preservation of the safe, civilized and peaceful nature of Canada." In addition, the minister explained the purpose of the legislation during debate in the House of Commons as follows: "First, tough measures to deal with the criminal misuse of firearms; second, specific penalties to punish those who would smuggle illegal firearms; and third, measures overall to provide a context in which the legitimate use of firearms can be carried on in a manner consistent with public safety."

Make Your Decision

1. Outline the basic facts of this case.
2. What is the central issue on which this case would be decided?
3. Summarize the arguments presented by the government of Alberta.
4. Summarize the purpose of the legislation as outlined by the federal government.
5. Decide whether the appeal should be allowed or dismissed. Explain the legal reasoning behind your decision.

Key Terms

Review the following terms to show that you understand the meaning of each and how it is applied in a legal context.

amending formula
Confederation debates
entrenchment
pith and substance
power of disallowance
sovereignty-association
"persons" case
Statute of Westminster
Supreme Court of Canada

Understanding the Law

Review the following terms related to Canada's constitution, and show that you understand the significance of each:

British North America Act
Judicial Committee of the Privy Council
patriation of the constitution

Thinking and Inquiry

1. Sir John A. Macdonald and many of the Fathers of Confederation believed that the provincial governments would be relatively unimportant and that the federal government would be the paramount government. Through the years, the provinces have assumed more and more responsibility for the well-being of Canadians. Working in groups of four, develop a mind map to come up with suggestions and ideas as to why the provinces have become more powerful.

2. You and a partner are given the task of designing a constitutional proposal that would meet the aspirations of Quebeckers and have them agree to sign the constitution. Outline the main points that you would include to satisfy Quebec's wishes.
3. New technologies are constantly developing and evolving. In today's high-tech world, all countries are forging closer ties and becoming less isolated. With a partner, consider the following statement, and then write down your thoughts: *The 20th century saw the power of the provinces increase as they expanded their impact on Canadian society under the "property and civil rights" section of the BNA Act. In the 21st century, the federal government's control over international treaties will result in these treaties' becoming the most important force in the lives of Canadians as we move closer to what Marshall McLuhan called the "global village."* You may agree or disagree with this proposition. Use chart paper and markers to record your ideas, and then share your thinking with the rest of the class.

Communication

4. Locate a recent case involving the interpretation of the powers of the provincial or federal government. You can use newspaper or magazine articles, or find case summaries on court Web sites (such as the Web site of the Supreme Court of Canada). Use the format followed in the text to write a case summary. Make an oral presentation of the case to the class. Include visual aids to enhance your presentation.
5. Some people have argued that the Judicial Committee of the Privy Council wrongly interpreted the BNA Act. Use your library resource centre to research commentary on this issue. You can use magazines, journals, books, and Internet sources to find your information. Decide whether you agree or disagree with this critique. Write a three-page essay to present your position. Include specific examples and evidence to support your analysis.
6. Work with a partner to research the final results of the 1980 and 1995 referenda held in Quebec. For each, identify the question asked, the main participants, and the outcome. Explain what influenced the final vote in each case.

Application

7. Locate a political cartoon that deals with federal–provincial conflict. Identify the symbols used in the cartoon and the main issue involved, and explain the cartoonist's perspective. If possible, find a second cartoon on the same issue that illustrates a different perspective. Identify possible reasons for the differences in perspectives. Present your findings to the class.
8. Research one constitutional change that occurred to the BNA Act between 1867 and 1945. Identify the change, explain the reason for it (including the groups that supported and opposed it), and describe the impact that this constitutional change had on Canada.
9. Use resources such as the Internet, newspapers, magazines, and books to find information on constitutional change that is currently occurring in another country. Outline the key features of the country's constitution and explain the philosophy behind it.

Chapter 5 The Charter and the Courts

CHAPTER *Focus*

In this chapter, you will

- trace the evolution of civil rights legislation from English common law to the *Canadian Charter of Rights and Freedoms*
- outline the main categories of rights under the Charter
- explain the significance of the entrenchment of rights in Canada's constitution
- explain how rights may be limited or overruled by the Charter
- explain how citizens exercise their rights under the Charter
- analyze the role of the courts in defining, interpreting, and enforcing Charter rights

This chapter traces the evolution of civil rights legislation in Canada from English common law to the *Canadian Charter of Rights and Freedoms*, one of the most significant pieces of legislation passed by Parliament in the last half of the 20th century. The Charter is organized around the protection of fundamental freedoms and other categories of rights and is an essential part of our constitution. You will also examine two key sections of the Charter that may limit or overrule our rights and freedoms in certain circumstances. Finally, you will consider the role of the legislature in making law and that of the courts in interpreting that law. A potential for conflict exists between these bodies.

Figure 5.1 gives one view of the Alberta government's position on same-sex marriages after the Ontario Court of Appeal's 2003 judgment recognizing the legality of these unions.

Figure 5.1

At First Glance

1. What is the cartoonist saying about same-sex marriages in Alberta?
2. What symbols are used in the cartoon? What is their significance to the issue?
3. Does this cartoon deliver an effective message? Explain.
4. Is preventing same-sex partners from marrying discriminatory? Why or why not?
5. Do you think that same-sex partners should legally be able to marry? Why or why not?

The Charter's Evolution

The evolution of the *Canadian Charter of Rights and Freedoms* falls into four periods:

- English common law and customs
- the *Canadian Bill of Rights*
- the Victoria Charter
- the *Canadian Charter of Rights and Freedoms.*

Each is discussed in the following pages.

English Common Law and Customs

As you learned in Chapter 2: Sources and Categories of Law, much of Canadian law is based on English common law, customs, and traditions inherited from the United Kingdom. That chapter introduced the principle of parliamentary (or legislative) supremacy. This principle states that the parliamentary branch of government—the Cabinet, House of Commons and Senate, and the provincial and territorial legislatures—is the highest political and law-making body in the country. In fact, this principle forms much of the basis of responsible government in Canada even today. Also, until patriation in 1982, our constitution was under the control of the British parliament and could be amended only by that legislative body.

The *Canadian Bill of Rights*

The atrocities committed during World War II focused attention not only on the worth of humanity as a whole but also on the worth of the individual as a human being. Individual rights were withdrawn during the war, and the subsequent publicity surrounding the withdrawal of individual rights angered people around the world.

Figure 5.2 *As the first Canadian prime minister who was not of either British or French descent, Diefenbaker had experienced discrimination because of his "foreign" name.*

In Canada, there was a growing recognition that Canadians needed formal protection against unfair treatment by governments. The debate as to whether Canadians needed a bill of rights began in 1945 when John Diefenbaker, Member of Parliament, first raised the issue in the House of Commons. During the next decade, a controversy arose between those people who favoured the traditional English common law to protect citizens and those who believed that formal written legislation would be more effective. During the general election campaigns of 1957 and 1958, Diefenbaker, by then leader of the Progressive Conservative party, promised Canadians a federal bill of rights as his highest priority if his party formed the next government.

In 1960, Prime Minister Diefenbaker introduced the legislation, and the *Canadian Bill of Rights* became law on August 10, 1960. It was an important achievement in Canadian law and a precursor to the *Canadian Charter of Rights and Freedoms*. It was not, however, a revolutionary piece of legislation because it only put into writing basic rights that were already recognized. The main significance of the Bill was the codification of these rights, in that it reminded Canadians of the rights they had and still have.

Limitations of the Canadian Bill of Rights

The impact of the Bill was limited for several reasons.

- The *Canadian Bill of Rights* was an ordinary statute like any other act of Parliament, and so could easily be changed by Parliament.
- It was not entrenched (included) in the constitution (unlike the US *Bill of Rights*), so it did not take precedence over any other federal statute.
- It applied only to areas of federal jurisdiction and did not offer protection against unfair treatment in areas of provincial jurisdiction. For example, if you worked at a bank, you were covered by the Bill because banking fell under federal jurisdiction. If, however, you worked at the local supermarket, you were not covered by the Bill because retail business fell under provincial labour law.
- Finally, judges were reluctant to use the Bill to strike down existing laws or to expand rights, again because it was not part of the constitution.

The Law The *Canadian Bill of Rights*, s. 1:

1. It is hereby recognized and declared that in Canada there have existed and shall continue to exist without discrimination by reason of race, national origin, colour, religion or sex, the following human rights and fundamental freedoms, namely,
   (a) the right of the individual to life, liberty, security of the person and enjoyment of property, and the right not to be deprived thereof except by due process of law;
   (b) the right of the individual to equality before the law and the protection of the law;
   (c) freedom of religion;
   (d) freedom of speech;
   (e) freedom of assembly and association; and
   (f) freedom of the press.

Questions

1. What is the meaning and significance of the phrase "have existed and shall continue to exist without discrimination"?
2. Compare the freedoms listed above with the Charter's fundamental freedoms (see the Appendix). What are the similarities and the differences?

Read the *Canadian Bill of Rights* at www.emp.ca/dimensionsoflaw

Only one federal statute, the *Indian Act*, was rendered partially inoperative by the *Canadian Bill of Rights*. The case of *R v. Drybones* involved the defendant's challenge to s. 94(b) of the *Indian Act*, which specified harsher penalties for Aboriginal persons intoxicated off a reserve, compared to non-Aboriginal persons intoxicated in a public place. Drybones claimed this provision denied him "equality before the law" under s. 1(b) of the *Canadian Bill of Rights*. The Supreme Court of Canada found this provision discriminatory and rendered it inoperative. (This case is discussed in greater detail in Chapter 7: Majority and Minority Rights.)

The *Canadian Bill of Rights* remains in force today and still has application to federal statutes, but it is never argued in court because of the Charter.

The Victoria Charter

In 1968, Pierre Trudeau became Canada's prime minister, and he believed that Canada's constitution needed to be modernized and reformed. In June 1971, he and the provincial premiers debated a package of changes to the constitution in Victoria, British Columbia. The anglophone provinces sought such changes as an entrenched charter of rights, the patriation of the constitution from the United Kingdom to Canada, and an amending

Figure 5.3 *Quebec Premier René Lévesque (right) shrugs and walks away from Prime Minister Pierre Trudeau (left) during the Constitutional Conference of 1980.*

formula for future changes. Quebec was more interested in substantive changes, clarifying and enlarging that province's legislative and fiscal autonomy. After considerable debate, no agreement was reached, as Quebec could not accept the terms of the Victoria Charter.

In 1980, the federal and provincial governments resumed discussion and negotiations. In late 1981, they reached a compromise on patriation and the entrenchment of a charter of rights. All provincial premiers accepted the compromise except for Quebec Premier René Lévesque, who demanded stronger French-language rights.

The Charter as Law

For a guide to the 20th anniversary edition of the Charter, check www.emp.ca/dimensionsoflaw

On April 17, 1982 on Parliament Hill, Queen Elizabeth II signed legislation changing the name of the *British North America Act* to the *Constitution Act, 1867* and adding the *Constitution Act, 1982* to it. Included was an amending formula and an entrenched *Canadian Charter of Rights and Freedoms* setting out those rights and freedoms that Canadians believe are essential in a free and democratic society. As part of the constitution, the Charter protects Canadians at all levels of government—federal, provincial, and territorial. This means that Canadians can seek redress in court if they are treated unfairly by the actions of any government. This is an expensive and seldom-used form of redress. Because of the expense, it is usually pursued only by groups or on behalf of groups; for example, gays and lesbians or persons with disabilities.

The Charter celebrated its 20th anniversary in 2002. Because of its impact on Canadian law at that time and its continuing significance in the future, you will examine key sections of the Charter and some landmark cases in greater detail in the next section.

CHECK YOUR UNDERSTANDING

1. What is the principle of parliamentary supremacy?
2. Why was the *Canadian Bill of Rights* an important step in protecting Canadians' rights?
3. Outline three criticisms of the *Canadian Bill of Rights*.
4. What are the two key components of the *Constitution Act, 1982*?

The *Canadian Charter of Rights and Freedoms*

Section 52 of the *Constitution Act, 1982* states that "the Constitution of Canada is the supreme law of Canada, and any law that is inconsistent with the provisions of the Constitution is ... of no force or effect." Many Canadians believe that the Charter is the most important part of our constitution, and for this reason, the entire text of the Charter is included in the Appendix.

The Section 1 Guarantee

Although Charter rights and freedoms are fundamental, they are not absolute or unlimited. Section 1 "guarantees the rights and freedoms set out in it subject only to such **reasonable limits** prescribed by law as can be demonstrably justified in a free and democratic society." This means that any limits imposed on rights and freedoms by s. 1 must meet two basic tests: (1) the limit must be important, and (2) the limit must be reasonable and justified for the benefit of society as a whole.

reasonable limits: restrictions on rights and freedoms that are imposed if the merits of the limits are determined to advance society's interests

Courts must determine whether any limit meets these requirements; judges must balance the benefits of the limitation against the well-being of society in general. The benefits must be greater than the harm resulting from the violation of the right, and the law must interfere as little as possible with the right or freedom in question. For example, freedom of expression may be limited by laws against hate or against pornography, if what is expressed incites hatred against an identifiable group of people (that is, distinguished by colour, race, religion, or ethnic origin) or constitutes obscenity under the *Criminal Code* of Canada.

In 1986, in *R v. Oakes*, the Supreme Court of Canada set out a general framework that could be used to decide whether a law found to violate a Charter right can be justified under s. 1. This case was to yield an important decision regarding the application and interpretation of the Charter and the "reasonable limits" that may be placed on Charter rights.

Case BALANCING RIGHTS

Learn more about the Charter and landmark cases at www.emp.ca/dimensionsoflaw

R v. Oakes, [1986] 1 SCR 103

Facts

David Oakes was charged with possession of a narcotic for the purpose of trafficking, contrary to s. 8 of the *Narcotic Control Act* (now the *Controlled Drugs and Substances Act*). Oakes had been found in possession of eight one-gram vials of hashish oil and $619.45 in cash. He claimed that he had purchased 10 vials of hashish oil for $150 for his own use and that the money came from a Workers' Compensation cheque. In the first part of the trial, the Crown easily proved that Oakes was in possession of the narcotic. Section 8 of the *Narcotic Control Act* stated: "[I]f the court finds that the accused was in possession of the narcotic he shall be given an opportunity of establishing that he was not in possession for the purpose of trafficking." So, in the second part of the trial, Oakes would have to prove that he was not in possession of the hashish oil for the purpose of trafficking. He argued that this "reverse onus" principle violated his presumption of innocence under s. 11(d) of the Charter, which states that any person charged with an offence has the right "to be presumed innocent until proven guilty according to law in a fair and public hearing... ."

Issue

If there seems to be a conflict between a Charter right (the presumption of innocence) and existing criminal law (s. 8 of the *Narcotic Control Act*), how does s. 1 of the Charter apply to this conflict? Will the Charter right prevail over the criminal law?

Decision

Oakes's argument was accepted by the trial judge and upheld by the Ontario Court of Appeal. The Ontario Court of Appeal agreed with Oakes, but the judgment noted that rights may sometimes be overridden if they are subject to "reasonable limits" as can be "demonstrably justified in a free and democratic society." This provision meant that the limitation of rights had to meet the criteria set out in s. 1 of the Charter.

The Crown appealed this decision to the Supreme Court of Canada. In a 7–0 decision, then Chief Justice Dickson wrote:

> To establish that a limit is reasonable and demonstrably justified in a free and democratic society, two central criteria must be satisfied. First, the objective, which the measures responsible for a limit on a Charter right or freedom are designed to serve, must be of sufficient importance to warrant overriding a constitutionally protected right or freedom. Second, once a sufficiently significant objective is recognized, then the

party invoking section 1 must show that the means chosen are reasonable and demonstrably justified.

The Court decided that a law limiting a Charter right is "reasonable" if

- it enforces an important government objective
- the limitation of individual rights or freedoms is minimal
- the law is clear and sets precise standards (for example, specific laws on materials that are obscene).

The Court found that although the first criterion existed, the second did not. Section 8 was too sweeping in scope to be considered a reasonable connection between its objective (stopping trafficking) and its effect (forcing people with even a small amount of narcotics to prove themselves innocent). The earlier court rulings were upheld, the Crown's appeal was dismissed, and s. 8 of the *Narcotic Control Act* was found to be unconstitutional.

Questions

1. Why did all three courts that heard the *Oakes* case rule that s. 8 of the *Narcotic Control Act* was unconstitutional?
2. How did the *Oakes* decision change the trial process for accused persons charged with trafficking?
3. In the Court's decision, Chief Justice Dickson stated: "The presumption of innocence confirms our faith in mankind; it reflects our belief that individuals are decent and law-abiding members of the community until proven otherwise." Explain the meaning of this statement.
4. a) Outline the criteria established in *R v. Oakes* to determine whether a law limiting a Charter right is "reasonable."
   b) What is the significance of the *Oakes* case?

Charter rights will not always prevail over criminal law. Section 1 of the Charter provides the basis for governments to limit Charter rights as long as those limits are acceptable in a free and democratic society.

Rights and Freedoms

The main rights and freedoms that form the nucleus of the Charter fall into the following seven categories:

1. fundamental freedoms (s. 2)
2. democratic rights (ss. 3–5)
3. mobility rights (s. 6)
4. legal rights (ss. 7–14)

5. equality rights (s. 15)
6. official language rights (ss. 16–22)
7. minority language rights (s. 23).

Each is discussed in the following pages. To see how these rights and freedoms work in real-life situations, you must examine how courts have interpreted and applied these sections of the Charter.

Fundamental Freedoms

Section 2 of the Charter provides the framework of what is commonly referred to as our "free society." It outlines the four fundamental freedoms of all Canadians:

- freedom of conscience and religion
- freedom of thought, belief, opinion, and expression, including freedom of the press and other media of communication
- freedom of peaceful assembly
- freedom of association.

Fundamental freedoms are sometimes referred to as "civil liberties"; they allow us to function as citizens of a parliamentary democracy. For example, freedom of expression is one of the most important rights that we have in a democratic society. Our ability to express our ideas, without fear of reprisal, allows us to criticize government actions, voice our opinions, and influence the choice of who will run our governments.

The rights outlined in s. 2 allow Canadians to enjoy a free life. However, these rights are accompanied by corresponding responsibilities. For example, we have the right to freedom of opinion and expression, but this does not give us the right to say whatever we want, whenever we want. Defamation laws prevent us from damaging another person's reputation with lies. We are free to express our opinions openly on any topic and to believe whatever we wish, but criminal law establishes censorship of obscene materials and of communications that willfully promote hatred against identifiable groups. We have freedom of the press, but courts have upheld most *Criminal Code* provisions that allow judges to restrict access to courts and the publication of names or descriptive events that might affect an accused's right to a fair trial. We are free to gather together and to associate with whomever we wish, but such assembly must be done peacefully and lawfully.

While these freedoms are considered fundamental, they are not absolute. Rather, they are subject to "reasonable limits" that are "justifiable in a free and democratic society," as s. 1 of the Charter states. For example, in Chapter 2, you read about a Charter challenge to the *Lord's Day Act*, prohibiting the Sunday sale of goods (see pages 35–36). The Act was struck down, as it was contrary to freedom of conscience and religion because it required a Sunday observance as a day of rest. It could not be saved by s. 1 of the Charter.

Figure 5.4 *Thousands of people protesting the US invasion of Iraq participate in a peaceful demonstration through the streets of Toronto in March 2003.*

Over the years, fundamental freedoms have led to many legal disputes and Charter challenges. In a high-profile case in 1990, *R v. Keegstra*, the Supreme Court of Canada weighed a high school teacher's right to freedom of expression against the *Criminal Code* offence of willfully promoting hatred against an identifiable group.

Case FREE SPEECH VERSUS HATE PROPAGANDA

R v. Keegstra, [1990] 3 SCR 697

Facts

Jim Keegstra was a high school teacher in Eckville, Alberta, from the early 1970s until his dismissal from teaching in 1982. As a history teacher, he taught that the Holocaust had never happened and that it was a fabrication, part of a Jewish conspiracy to rule the world. In repeated anti-Semitic remarks, he told his students that Jews were "power hungry," "subversive," and "money loving." He expected students to repeat his beliefs in class and on exams. In 1984, Keegstra was charged under s. 319(2)—then s. 281.2(2)—of the *Criminal Code*, which prohibits willfully promoting hatred against an identifiable group. He argued that this law violated his right to freedom of expression guaranteed in s. 2(b) of the Charter.

The accused was tried and convicted in the Alberta Court of Queen's Bench. Keegstra appealed his conviction to the Alberta Court of Appeal, where his Charter arguments were unanimously accepted. The Court held that s. 319(2) infringed Keegstra's Charter right to freedom of expression, that the *Criminal Code* section was too broad, and that it was not a reasonable limit under s. 1 of the Charter. The Crown appealed this decision to the Supreme Court of Canada, where the appeal was heard in December 1989.

Issues

Are we free to state absolutely anything we wish, regardless of whom we offend? If there is a limit to freedom of expression, what is that limit?

Decision

In a 4–3 decision released in December 1990, the Court upheld the Crown's appeal. All seven judges agreed that the hate law violated s. 2(b) of the Charter, but the majority of the Court believed this violation of Charter rights could be justified under s. 1. Recognizing Canada's multicultural society, the majority of the Court stated that we are not free to say absolutely anything that we wish. We are free to think whatever we want, but once we begin to express our opinion—and if that opinion has an impact on others—then the law may prevent us from publicly proclaiming those views. In this case, the greater good of the majority of society overrode Keegstra's basic right to free expression.

Questions

1. Outline the basic conflict in this case.
2. Why was the *Keegstra* case a landmark decision?
3. Does a teacher have the right to free expression of his or her opinion of historical events, even if that opinion contradicts the accepted viewpoint? Explain.
4. Why do you think it took the Supreme Court one year to release its judgment in this case?
5. Ultimately (in 1996), Keegstra's sentence was a $3000 fine, a one-year suspended sentence, and 200 hours of community service. Do you feel that this sentence was fair and reasonable? Why or why not?
6. David Matas, Honorary Senior Legal Counsel for B'nai Brith Canada, the Jewish service and cultural organization, issued the following statement in response to Keegstra's sentence: "The Supreme Court's ... findings ... for the constitutionality of the provisions against hate propaganda should have sent a clear message ... of the severity of Keegstra's actions. Today's decision reveals the extent to which the Alberta Court of Appeal is oblivious to the dangers of hate speech. Hate speech was among the root forces driving the greatest crimes of the 20th century, a fact which seems to have been lost on the court." Write a paragraph that defends or refutes this statement.

Democratic Rights

Canada is a democracy; we choose our government. The democratic rights part of the Charter regulates the functions of our democratic system. Sections 3 to 5 of the Charter set down the basic rights of being eligible to vote and to run for election. At the beginning of Chapter 1 (page 4), you saw a cartoon related to the Supreme Court of Canada's 2002 decision giving inmates in federal institutions (serving two years or more) the right to vote in federal elections. Sections 3 to 5 also limit the duration of legislative bodies and ensure that legislative assemblies sit at least once every 12 months.

Fyi In 1918, women (excluding Asian, Inuit, and Aboriginal women) were given the right to vote in federal elections.

Mobility Rights

Section 6 of the Charter guarantees our mobility rights, making it easier for Canadians to move from one province to another. Canadian citizens have the right to enter, remain in, and leave Canada. Thus, all Canadians who have permanent residence in the country have the right to move and pursue a livelihood in any other province or territory.

Legal Rights

The Charter plays a critical role in the criminal justice system. As you saw in *R v. Oakes*, it was a criminal-law case in which the meaning of s. 1 of the Charter was first determined. Sections 7 to 14 of the Charter set out the rights that protect us in our dealings with the justice system, especially if we are charged with a criminal offence. These rights, guaranteed under the Charter, help protect individuals from any arbitrary measures by the state; this provision, in turn, helps ensure that justice prevails.

Section 7 guarantees everyone "the right to life, liberty and security of the person" that will not be taken away except in accordance with "the principles of fundamental justice." Section 8 protects citizens from unreasonable search and seizure; that is, the police cannot enter people's homes without a valid reason. Sections 9 to 11 include the right not to be arbitrarily detained or imprisoned, the right to a lawyer on arrest or detention, the right to be tried within a reasonable time, and the right to be presumed innocent until proven guilty.

Section 12 guarantees our right "not to be subjected to any cruel and unusual treatment or punishment." Section 13 gives us the right against self-incrimination (a section that Canadians often confuse with the expression "pleading the fifth," which refers to the Fifth Amendment to the US Constitution, a guarantee against self-incrimination). Section 14 ensures that everyone who is a "party or witness" in legal proceedings can have an interpreter so that he or she can understand what is going on at the trial.

The Charter's legal rights and case law applications will be discussed in greater detail in Unit 3: Criminal Law.

Equality Rights

Section 15 of the Charter provides the right to equality, that is, freedom from discrimination. It states that everyone has the right to equal protection and equal benefit of the law without discrimination on the basis of race, national or ethnic origin, colour, religion, sex, mental or physical disability, or age. During Charter negotiations, governments, lawyers, and special-interest groups debated what "equality" meant. Although the Charter became law on April 17, 1982, s. 15 did not come into effect until three years later. The delay was intended to allow governments time to revise any laws that did not conform to these equality rights.

Equality rights can be restricted if it is believed that the restrictions are reasonable in a free and democratic society. For example, you must be a certain age to drive a car, to vote, and to sign a contract.

Equality rights are examined in greater detail in Chapter 6: Human Rights in Canada and Chapter 7: Majority and Minority Rights.

Fyi New Brunswick is designated a bilingual district for federal services, making it the only bilingual province in Canada.

Official Languages Rights

Sections 16 to 22 of the Charter guarantee both French and English as the two official languages of Canada. For example, s. 17(1) states, "Everyone has the right to use English or French in any debates and other proceedings of Parliament." Canadians also have the right to use either language when dealing with federal government offices. Both languages have equal status and equal rights pertaining to their use.

Minority Language Rights

Section 23 outlines minority language rights that apply only to French and English. Although French is the official language in Quebec, parents may have their children educated in English—the minority language—if the parents' own primary education was in English.

Because our constitution gives jurisdiction for education to the provinces, provincial governments may make decisions about providing education in minority languages other than French or English—Japanese, Mandarin, Ukrainian, and so on.

Check Your Understanding

1. What effect can s. 1 of the Charter have on our rights and freedoms?
2. Explain, with examples, the meaning of this statement: "Charter rights are accompanied by corresponding responsibilities."
3. How have the Charter's legal rights sections played a critical role in our criminal justice system?
4. Why did the equality rights section of the Charter not come into effect until three years after the rest of the Charter?
5. List three examples of reasonable restrictions on equality rights.
6. How does the Charter deal with Canada's two official languages?

Turning Points in the Law

Entrenching the Charter in the Constitution

Shortly after passage of the *Canadian Bill of Rights*, many politicians, lawyers, and concerned citizens advocated that Canada should adopt an entrenched charter of rights, similar to the *Bill of Rights* incorporated as part of the US constitution. This movement continued through 1970 and the Victoria Charter; it took until 1982 before Canada finally had an entrenched constitution.

Why was this a turning point in the law? Once the Charter was entrenched, it was part of the constitution, Canada's supreme law, and could be changed only by a formal constitutional amendment. Changes would not be easy to make: amendments require the consent of the federal Parliament and two-thirds of the provinces, with 50 percent of the population approving any change. Thus, all levels of government must ensure that any legislation they pass is consistent with the Charter. A law that limits Charter rights may be challenged in court and ruled invalid. However, earlier in this chapter you saw that s. 1 of the Charter allows governments to pass a law limiting Charter rights, as long as those limits are acceptable in a free and democratic society. Canadian courts may thus interpret Charter rights and freedoms broadly. For example, courts have ruled that some laws violate a person's freedom of expression, but they also have upheld many of these laws under s. 1.

An important provision of the Charter is s. 32, which states that the Charter applies to acts of Parliament, the federal government, and provincial and territorial governments and their legislatures. In other words, the Charter applies only to relations between governments and citizens. It does not apply to actions between private persons such as neighbours, landlords and tenants, employers and employees, and so on. (Such actions between private parties are protected by human rights legislation—the focus of Chapters 6 and 7—or common-law traditions.)

Questions

1. What is the key distinction between the *Canadian Bill of Rights* and the *Canadian Charter of Rights and Freedoms*?
2. Outline Canada's amending formula.
3. Why is s. 1 of the Charter referred to as a "reasonable limits" provision?
4. What is the significance of s. 32 of the Charter?

Limits on Charter Application

Although the Charter is part of Canada's supreme law, it contains three major limitations on the protection that it offers. First, as you have seen, under s. 32 the Charter applies only to the public sector, namely, all levels of government, and not to relationships between private citizens. Next, any violation of a Charter right may be justified under s. 1. Finally, there is the Charter's s. 33—the "notwithstanding" clause.

The Notwithstanding Clause

In 1980 and 1981, there was a lack of agreement between supporters and opponents of entrenching the Charter in a patriated constitution. Thus, in

The Law The *Canadian Charter of Rights and Freedoms* contains the following provision:

33(1) Parliament or the legislature of a province may expressly declare in an Act of Parliament or of the legislature, as the case may be, that the Act or a provision thereof shall operate notwithstanding a provision included in section 2 or sections 7 to 15 of this Charter. ...

(3) A declaration made under subsection (1) shall cease to have effect five years after it comes into force or on such earlier date as may be specified in the declaration.

Questions

1. What does "notwithstanding" mean?
2. Name the three subheadings of Charter rights to which s. 33 applies.
3. To which groups of rights does s. 33 not apply?

notwithstanding clause: a clause in the Charter that may be invoked by Parliament or provincial legislatures to override basic Charter provisions

the final stages of negotiations surrounding patriation, Prime Minister Pierre Trudeau introduced, in s. 33, the **notwithstanding clause**, which allows governments to pass legislation notwithstanding (in spite of the fact) that it might violate one of a certain group of rights.

Use of the Notwithstanding Clause

If there is an important issue that the federal or a provincial government believes needs to be dealt with in a manner that infringes on Canadians' rights, then it may be passed using s. 33. The government passing the legislation must specifically indicate which rights are being ignored or infringed in spite of the Charter protections. There are, however, Charter rights (for example, ss. 3 to 6 and ss. 16 to 23) that cannot be avoided through the use of s. 33.

Governments are reluctant to invoke s. 33, because it is difficult to justify overriding Charter rights to voters who have elected you to protect their interests. Also, use of the notwithstanding clause has a time limit of five years. If the legislature wants a piece of rights-offending legislation to continue, it must re-enact the measure. The five-year limit requires the government to review and restate its rights-offending legislation at least once in an election period, possibly risking loss of the election if that measure does not receive the support of the electorate.

To date, s. 33 has had very limited use. In the first 16 years of the Charter, the notwithstanding clause was used only three times. Its first use occurred in Quebec when the government passed *An Act Respecting the Constitution Act,*

1982, which declared that all Quebec statutes would operate notwithstanding ss. 2 and 7 to 15 of the Charter. This use of s. 33 was a form of political protest against the fact that the Charter was entrenched in the constitution without Quebec's consent. (This Act lapsed a few years later following the election of a new provincial government.) The second use of s. 33 occurred in Saskatchewan in 1986 to protect back-to-work legislation.

The third and most controversial use again occurred in Quebec. In the late 1980s, the Supreme Court struck down five statutes prohibiting the use of English on outdoor signs. However, Quebec Premier Robert Bourassa's government believed that protecting Quebec's linguistic and cultural concerns was very important, and so in 1988 it brought in new legislation requiring signs to be in French only, this time invoking s. 33 of the Charter. This measure meant that the legislation could not be struck down by the courts even though it was clearly in violation of the Charter. (This case, *Ford v. Quebec*, is discussed in Chapter 7: Majority and Minority Rights.)

The federal government has never invoked the notwithstanding clause to uphold any federal legislation that has been struck down by the courts. In a highly controversial decision in 2001, the Supreme Court allowed the appeal of John Sharpe, who lived in British Columbia. Sharpe had been charged with two counts of possession of child pornography under s. 163.1(4) of the *Criminal Code* and two counts of possession of child pornography for the purposes of distribution or sale under s. 161.1(3). The decision of the trial judge and the majority of the British Columbia Court of Appeal, which ruled that the prohibition of the simple possession of child pornography as defined under s. 163.1 of the *Criminal Code* was not justifiable in a free and democratic society, was upheld. Sharpe's own writings were deemed to be of artistic merit and could therefore not be prohibited; and the Court upheld the sections of the *Criminal Code* that dealt with child pornography in other forms, such as pictures.

To learn more about John Sharpe and Canada's pornography law, visit www.emp.ca/dimensionsoflaw

Victims' groups and child advocacy groups from across the country were outraged by this decision. Many Canadians called on the federal government to invoke, for the first time, the notwithstanding clause so that the entire ban on child pornography could be upheld. The federal government did not use the notwithstanding clause to reintroduce this section of the *Criminal Code*, but new legislation was introduced that restricted the use of the artistic-merit exception on which the *Sharpe* case had depended.

CHECK YOUR UNDERSTANDING

1. Outline the three ways in which Charter rights may be limited or overruled.
2. Why are governments reluctant to invoke s. 33 of the Charter?
3. Why does use of the notwithstanding clause have a five-year time limit? Do you agree with this limitation? Explain.
4. Why was Quebec's application of s. 33 in 1988 a controversial action?

ersonal Viewpoint

The Wrong Use of Section 33

Patrick Nugent, an Edmonton lawyer and a former project director of the Centre for Constitutional Studies, says that "the notwithstanding clause is a powerful tool and should not be invoked lightly." Nugent expressed this strong opinion on March 31, 2000, after the Alberta government passed the *Marriage Amendment Act*, which defines marriage as a union between a man and a woman, and invoked s. 33. As Nugent stated, "How many Albertans know a law was passed on March 15 that represented Alberta's use of the notwithstanding clause? I would guess not too many."

To support his position, Nugent noted that Bill 202 (the proposed *Marriage Amendment Act*) was a private member's bill. Such a bill is introduced by a private member in the legislature rather than by a Cabinet minister. Strict time limits are imposed on debate, and most such bills die long before being passed. Nugent went on to say that "it is never appropriate for the notwithstanding clause to be invoked in a situation where debate is so seriously limited. ... This serious legislative tool by definition overrides the rights of individuals and should only be used after a full and open public debate and an equivalent debate in the legislature."

Newspaper reports indicated that use of the notwithstanding clause received little public notice before or after the bill was passed. When the bill came forward at its third reading, neither Premier Ralph Klein nor the leader of the official opposition was present. Of the 83 members in the Alberta legislative assembly, only 47 participants voted on the third reading: 32 for, 15 against.

Patrick Nugent questions whether the Alberta legislature had the authority to pass such a bill in the first place. The *Constitution Act, 1867* divides the jurisdiction for marriage between the federal and provincial governments. The provincial governments have the authority to legislate the solemnization of or procedures for marriage, while the federal government has the authority to determine the capacity to marry or who may marry whom. Nugent contends that Bill 202 concerned itself with the capacity to marry, and therefore was possibly unconstitutional. In fact, Alberta's minister of justice, who voted against the bill, acknowledged this possibility during debate and in his comments to the media after the bill's passage.

Red Deer South MLA Victor Doerkson introduced the bill, stating: "I've presented a positive statement about the value of marriage, reflective of our legal history, also a reflection of religious history. ... That history is that marriage is between a man and a woman, and I've restated that in the preamble." Doerkson further stated: "Section 33 is the only mechanism that legislatures have to assert themselves in this area. I think that in some matters, legislatures do have the responsibility to make the decisions. Ultimately, if people don't like the decisions that we've made, they have the opportunity to unelect us, which you can't do with the courts."

Source: Patrick Nugent, "Wrong Use of the Notwithstanding Clause," Opinion Guest Column, *University of Alberta Folio* (Vol. 37, No. 15), March 31, 2000; www.ualberta.ca/~publicas/folio/37/15/opinion.html.

Questions

1. What Charter rights might be infringed by Alberta's *Marriage Amendment Act*?
2. List three reasons why Patrick Nugent feels that passage of the *Marriage Amendment Act* was the wrong use of s. 33.
3. How is the responsibility for marriage divided between levels of government in the *Constitution Act, 1867*? (See Chapter 4: Canadian Constitutional Law.)
4. Formulate a personal opinion of MLA Doerkson's quotation above, and be prepared to defend it.

The Role of the Courts

In 1982, no one knew what effect the Charter would have on Canadian law. Prior to 1982, the *British North America Act* outlined the division of powers between Parliament and the provincial legislatures in ss. 91 and 92, respectively (see Chapter 4, pages 106–107). The majority of constitutional cases considered by the courts concerned these two sections of the constitution and which government had jurisdiction over what. A court could find that a provincial law was invalid only if the court found that the subject matter of the law fell within the s. 91 jurisdiction of the federal government. The Supreme Court of Canada was often called upon to resolve any disputes over jurisdiction.

Since 1982, the Charter has expanded the scope of judicial review significantly. Because the Charter is entrenched in the constitution, any Canadian law can now be challenged in court, not only on the grounds that the law was enacted by the wrong level of government, but also on the grounds that the law violates Charter rights. All laws, regulations, and programs established by governments must, therefore, adhere to the Charter's principles.

Fyi Canada's Supreme Court is unanimous in about three-quarters of its decisions, compared to 45% for the US Supreme Court.

Governments and their lawyers had to start building legislation that complied with the Charter, and they needed to review existing legislation to remove any clauses that infringed on Charter rights. The Charter has thus expanded the courts' role in protecting the basic human rights and civil liberties of Canadians. Because of the increased role played by the courts in the judicial interpretation and application of law, it is important to be aware of how our judges, especially those at the level of the Supreme Court of Canada, are appointed.

The Appointment of Canadian Judges

There are about 750 courts across Canada. Section 92(14) of the *Constitution Act, 1867* gives the provinces jurisdiction over the administration of justice, including the constitution, organization, and maintenance of provincial courts, both criminal and civil. This provision does not extend to the appointment of judges to all provincial courts. Although provincial and small claims court judges are appointed by provincial governments, all provincial and territorial superior court judges are appointed by the federal government.

For more information on judicial appointments, visit www.emp.ca/dimensionsoflaw

The highest court in the land is the Supreme Court of Canada, sitting only in Ottawa, with a chief justice and eight other justices. This court has final authority over all municipal, provincial, and federal laws, all common law, and constitutional interpretations. Its decisions are binding on all lower courts in Canada. The Supreme Court tries to reach unanimous decisions, but if this does not happen, then both majority and minority judgments are released. These judgments are often examined closely by lawyers and legislators to see the direction in which the Court might be moving.

All judges in Canada come from the legal profession; judges appointed by the federal government must have practised law for at least 10 years. Lawyers must apply to become judges, and their applications are reviewed by independent committees established for that purpose. However, after consultation with provincial law societies and judicial councils, professional colleagues, and members of the public, the federal minister of justice and the prime minister have the final say. All Supreme Court of Canada appointments are major news events announced by the prime minister. Judges serve until they resign or reach mandatory retirement (at age 70 or 75, depending on the court), or are removed "for cause" (which seldom happens).

In contrast to the Canadian system, although US Supreme Court justices are appointed by the president after scrutiny by elected politicians in public confirmation hearings, most other judges are elected. Do we, as Canadians, want to elect our judges as our American neighbours do? One high-profile critic of the US system is (Canadian) Chief Justice Beverley McLachlin, who made the following comment in a speech to the Canadian Club at Toronto's Royal York Hotel in 2003:

> Images of judges running campaigns in which they hand out doughnuts and gasoline coupons, buy drinks for voters or speak at political rallies may seem far-fetched, yet they occur south of the border. ... Elected officials owe, or at least can be seen to owe, their position to particular segments of the community. ... How can a judge function impartially and ... be seen to function impartially, when her very job is at stake? ... One may gain accountability, but one loses judicial impartiality.

Fyi On July 31, 2003, Prime Minister Jean Chrétien appointed Morris Fish, a Jewish anglophone from the Quebec Court of Appeal, to the Supreme Court of Canada. Fish is the first Quebec anglophone since the 1950s and the first Jewish member of the court since the late Chief Justice Bora Laskin.

strike down: to rule that a piece of legislation is inconsistent with the Charter and is no longer valid

issue

Appointing Our Judges **Should our Supreme Court justices be appointed, or elected, or chosen by some other means?**

Since the entrenchment of the Charter in the constitution, judges have had a stronger role to play in the Canadian justice system, especially since they can **strike down** a law or declare that a law is of no force or effect if it conflicts with Charter rights. Parliament, or provincial legislatures, must then decide how to redraft the law so that the Charter is not breached. The Supreme Court has become especially powerful because it is now the guardian of constitutionally guaranteed rights of Canadians. Our superior courts, and especially the Supreme Court of Canada, help to protect Canadians' rights, including those of small or unpopular minorities whose viewpoints and voices might otherwise be ignored or trampled by political majorities.

Many Canadians strongly believe that the appointment process for Supreme Court justices should be changed because courts are becoming too powerful; citizens oppose the idea that nine appointed judges can strike down or overrule laws passed by elected representatives. They want to see a major change in the way in which our superior court judges are appointed, as they believe that judges are becoming unelected legislators and are "making law" these days. An Environics poll released in early 2002 found that two out of three Canadians surveyed favoured the election of Supreme Court judges. The poll, which surveyed 2000 Canadians, found support for election of justices to be lowest in Ontario, with 65 percent in favour, and highest in the West and Atlantic Canada at 71 percent.

Figure 5.5 *Supreme Court justices look on as Justice Marie Deschamps is sworn in on September 30, 2002.*

A possible compromise between the current appointment system and the US election system is the continuance of the appointment system, but with the modification that the prime minister's nominee to the Supreme Court be required to answer questions before a standing committee of the House of Commons. It would not be a US-style confirmation because the prime minister would still retain the authority to appoint the nominee, regardless of the committee's recommendations.

The following excerpts express the opinions of Canadians on this issue.

> Unlike politicians, judges do not have agendas. They take the laws and the cases as they find them, and apply their interpretative skills to them as the constitution requires. ... Contrary to popular myth, ... judges do not pluck meanings from the air according to their political stripe. ... The image of the judicial cowboy riding amok among the carefully planted legislative garden is just that, an image—and a distorted one at that. The judge is more like a gardener, shaping and nurturing plants so that they grow as intended, occasionally pulling out a weed that offends the plan on which the garden is based.
>
> —*Chief Justice Beverley McLachlin, in a speech to the Canadian Club at Toronto's Royal York Hotel, June 17, 2003*

> **Judicial activism** is alive and well. This latest intrusion by the courts into social policy making [a reference to the Ontario Court of Appeal's decision regarding same-sex marriages on July 10, 2003] ... only affirms that courts are usurping Parliament's responsibility to legislate.
>
> —*Vic Toews, Canadian Alliance justice critic, quoted in Dimitry Anastakis, "Alliance Hypocritical on Judiciary,"* The Toronto Star, *July 22, 2003*

judicial activism: the perception that judges, rather than Parliament, are making laws and imposing their personal values in their judgments

> We support the concept of having a say in federal court appointments, because the court rulings can have such an impact on provincial legislation.
>
> —*Fay Orr, spokesperson for Alberta Premier Ralph Klein, quoted in John Ibbotson and Steven Chase,* The Globe and Mail, *October 25, 1999*

Fyi As of August 1, 2003, Prime Minister Jean Chrétien had appointed six of the nine Supreme Court justices. This number is unprecedented in the Court's history.

How does informal, unaccountable consultation cure the obvious democratic deficit and the fact that a limited-term politician can determine the composition of the Supreme Court and the future course of judicial adjudication without even a modicum of public scrutiny of a candidate before an appointment is announced? How can we justify vesting such extraordinary power in the head of an executive that is itself the most frequent litigator before the Supreme Court?

> —*Jacob Ziegel, professor of law emeritus at the Faculty of Law, University of Toronto, quoted in "The Rule of Law and Appointments to the Supreme Court,"* Law Times, *July 21, 2003, p. 7*

At the very least, there needs to be some review of these appointments by elected officials. ... These justices are straying further and further away from legal doctrine and implementing policy by legal fiat. And are in the job until age 75. Given all that, it would be useful to know what their inclinations are before we appoint them to the court.

> —*Vic Toews, Canadian Alliance justice critic, quoted in Chris Cobb, "Canadians Want to Elect Court,"* The National Post, *February 4, 2002*

I can understand the attraction [for a different selection process] because it appears more democratic. But it would severely undermine the Supreme Court's independence. Think of it. If a judge runs for election, he or she needs a platform and then has to go out campaigning. The winner would go into the court with a preconceived agenda and severely tarnish the independence of the judiciary. ... Canadian governments have a long record of appointing effective, independent Supreme Court appointees.

> —*Edward Ratushny, University of Ottawa law professor, quoted in Chris Cobb, "Canadians Want to Elect Court,"* The National Post, *February 4, 2002*

Questions

1. In your own words, explain the meaning of "judicial activism."
2. Create a table in your notebook to compare arguments used in favour of the status quo in judicial appointments with arguments used to oppose the status quo. Use the material presented in this chapter and your own viewpoint to complete your table.
3. What do you think of the compromise solution, and why?
4. In a paragraph, summarize your position on the appointment of justices to the Supreme Court of Canada. Explain the reasons for your position.

Resolving Charter Disputes

If Canadians feel that their rights have been infringed, they can seek redress through the courts. When a court finds that a law violates a Charter right and cannot be saved by s. 1, there are remedies available. It is possible to strike down a law (in part or in total), making the offending legislation no longer in effect, as happened in *RJR–MacDonald* (see Chapter 4, pages 117–118).

It is also possible to **read down** a law, forcing it to comply with the Charter. That is, a court may find that the piece of legislation is generally acceptable, but not acceptable in the particular case before the court.

A further option, ruling on the admissibility of the evidence under s. 24 of the Charter, will be discussed later in this chapter.

read down: to rule that, while a piece of legislation may generally be consistent with the Charter, it is inconsistent in the particular case at hand

The Increasing Role of the Supreme Court

Courts have been willing to define Canadian values and to change parts, or all, of some Canadian laws when required to make them comply with the Charter. The Supreme Court of Canada has played an ever-increasing role in the interpretation of Canadians' rights and freedoms. It has moved front and centre in Canada's political system by attempting to balance the goals of legislators and lawmakers with the Charter's rights and freedoms. Since 1982, the Charter has been the focus of many difficult court decisions involving considerations of social values and, to some extent, Canadians have come to expect the courts to protect their Charter rights and freedoms. One of the best examples of this is the case of *M. v. H.*

Fyi Between 1982 and 1998, 58 statutes (31 federal, 27 provincial) were struck down by the courts, and 125 out of 373 claimants won their cases before the Supreme Court. This compares to only one section of one federal statute being struck down by the *Canadian Bill of Rights*.

Case CHANGING THE LAW(S)

M. v. H., [1999] 2 SCR 3

Facts

Two Toronto women, M. and H., began living together in a spousal relationship in 1982. Over the course of that relationship, they shared a home that H. had owned since 1974, started their own business, and bought business and vacation property. Although H.'s direct contribution to the business was greater than that of M., they continued to be equal partners. M. assumed more of a role in managing the home and assisting H. by doing considerable business entertaining. Because of the economic decline in the late 1980s, the couple ran into financial difficulty. The relationship began to deteriorate and, in 1992, M. left the home she had shared with H. The breakup left M. financially disadvantaged, and she filed for support payments under Ontario's *Family Law Act.*

Under s. 19 of this Act, a spouse is entitled to support payments when a relationship ends. The definition of spouse, however, was limited to those who were married, namely, a man and a woman, or "either of a man and woman who are not married to each other and have cohabited ... continuously for a period of not less than three years." M. made the support claim knowing that same-sex couples were not included in the definition of "spouse," but she intended to launch a Charter challenge based on s. 15, arguing that her equality rights were infringed by this definition of "spouse" and could not be saved by s. 1 of the Charter.

Issues

Did the denial of support to M., because she and H. were not a man and a woman, infringe her equality rights guaranteed in s. 15 of the Charter? Was Ontario's *Family Law Act* discriminatory in its definition of spouse as "a man and a woman"?

Decision

M. won her case before the Ontario Superior Court in early 1996. Madam Justice Gloria Epstein ruled that the definition of spouse discriminated against same-sex couples and their equality rights, and could not be saved by s. 1. The remedy ordered by the court was to have the words "a man and a woman" replaced with "two persons" so that same-sex couples would be included in the definition. H. appealed, and the Ontario Court of Appeal upheld the trial judgment in a 2–1 decision in December 1996. Soon afterward, M. and H. reached a private settlement of their financial concerns.

In March 1998, the Supreme Court of Canada heard the appeal of this decision because the Ontario government wanted to resolve the constitutional issue of equality versus same-sex couples' rights to seek spousal support. In May 1999, in an 8–1 judgment, the Court affirmed (agreed with) both lower court decisions. The Ontario government was given six months to rewrite provincial laws to ensure equal treatment of same-sex partners.

Questions

1. The Supreme Court stated in its ruling that the purpose of the *Family Law Act* was to provide financial support for spouses when a relationship broke down, and that excluding same-sex couples was contrary to the purpose of the law. Explain what the Court meant by this statement.
2. Why was *M. v. H.* a landmark judgment?
3. Review the case of *R v. Oakes* (page 134). It could be said that the *Oakes* case is significant from a legal perspective and that *M. v. H.* is important from a social perspective. Explain.
4. Do you agree with the Supreme Court's ruling in this case? Why or why not?

In its ruling in the case of *M. v. H.*, the Supreme Court sent a very clear message to all Canadian governments that laws excluding same-sex partners would likely infringe s. 15 of the Charter (equality rights). *M. v. H.* is significant for two reasons. First, the case created an important precedent in changing the definition of spouse in Ontario to include same-sex partners, thus requiring the Ontario and federal governments to change their definition of spouse in many pieces of legislation. Second, the fact that governments were forced to change their laws, based on the Supreme Court ruling, shows how substantial the Charter's impact is on the legal system.

The Ontario government reluctantly responded to this decision by promptly proclaiming the *Amendments Because of the Supreme Court of Canada Decision in M. v. H. Act, 1999.* (The name of the legislation certainly suggests the government's reluctance to make these changes.) This legislation forced the government to amend 67 Ontario statutes. In July 2000, the federal government passed the *Modernization of Benefits and Obligations Act*, which ensures that same-sex and opposite-sex relationships are treated equally under federal law. This Act necessitated changing nearly 60 federal statutes.

Fyi A June 2003 survey, done for the *Globe and Mail* and CTV by Ipsos-Reid, found that 54% supported same-sex marriages, 44% were opposed, and 2% were undecided. Seventy-one percent of surveyed Canadians aged 18 to 34 supported the concept, compared to 36% of those over 55.

The Admissibility of Evidence

Besides considering s. 1 of the Charter and striking down or reading down laws, courts have another option in enforcing Charter rights: consideration of s. 24 of the Charter.

Section 24(2) of the Charter plays a key role, especially in criminal cases. When a Charter challenge arises, the court must first determine whether the police have violated an accused's rights at some point in the investigation. For example, if the police did not obtain a proper search warrant before conducting an extensive search of a suspect's residence, the suspect might argue that a s. 8 Charter violation had occurred, namely, an unreasonable search and seizure, and that the results of that search should not be admitted as evidence at a later trial.

The Law Section 24(2) of the Charter states:

(2) Where, in proceedings under subsection (1), a court concludes that evidence was obtained in a manner that infringed or denied any rights or freedoms guaranteed by this Charter, the evidence shall be excluded if it is established that, having regard to all the circumstances, the admission of it in the proceedings would bring the administration of justice into disrepute.

(For s. 24(1), see the Appendix.)

Questions

1. To whom and when does s. 24 of the Charter apply?
2. In your own words, explain the meaning of the phrase "would bring the administration of justice into disrepute."

WORKING FOR CHANGE *The Two Michaels*

On Tuesday, June 10, 2003, the Ontario Court of Appeal released a unanimous landmark decision stating that the exclusion of same-sex partners from marriage is illogical, offensive, unjustifiable, and a definite denial of a couple's equality rights under the *Canadian Charter of Rights and Freedoms.* A few hours later, two Ontario men who had been partners for 22 years became Canada's first same-sex couple to wed legally. For a major constitutional issue, the Ontario Court of Appeal's decision was released quickly, just six weeks after a complex four-day hearing. The ruling was a personal victory for seven same-sex couples defending a lower court decision that said Canadian law violated their Charter rights by denying them the right to marry.

Earlier in 2003, the BC Court of Appeal and a Quebec Superior Court judge had issued similar rulings, but those decisions gave Parliament until July 2004 and September 2004, respectively, to change the law and the definition of marriage. The Ontario ruling legalized gay and lesbian marriages immediately, because the court felt that changing the definition of marriage from "one man and one woman" to "two persons" would not create any public harm.

Toronto Crown attorney Michael Leshner and Michael Stark, manager of a graphics design firm, were married in a civil ceremony. The couple paid $110 for their marriage licence at city hall, crossing out part of the form that read Bride/Groom, replacing it with Spouse/Person. Afterward, celebrating with a champagne toast, Leshner told reporters, "This is the culmination of a personal 20-year battle to end legally sanctioned homophobia. ... Now, nobody else will have to go through the nonsense of fighting a court battle to marry!"

As well, the appeal court ordered the province to register marriage certificates to Kevin Bourassa and Joe Varnell, and to Elaine and Anne Vautour, who were married by Reverend Brent Hawkes in a double ceremony at Toronto's Metropolitan Community Church in January 2001, under the Christian tradition of the publication of banns. Their marriages had not been legally recognized.

Figure 5.6 *Michael Leshner (left) and Michael Stark (centre) hold their marriage licence after being married by Superior Court Justice John Hamilton (right) in Toronto on June 10, 2003.*

Within days, Prime Minister Jean Chrétien announced that the federal Cabinet did not intend to appeal the BC and Ontario appellate court rulings. Instead, the government planned to draft a bill changing the legal definition of marriage to recognize the union of same-sex couples and their equality rights, while protecting religious freedom and "the right of churches and religious organizations to sanctify marriage as they define it." This draft legislation would then be referred to the Supreme Court of Canada for an opinion on its constitutionality, after which the bill would be put to a free vote in the House of Commons. If passed, this bill would make Canada only the third country in the world to recognize same-sex marriages. The Netherlands was the first country to legalize same-sex marriages, on April 1, 2001; Belgium became the second in early 2003.

Not all Canadians accepted the government's position. After the prime minister's announcement, Alberta Premier Ralph Klein stated: "Alberta law is very clear. If there's any move to sanctify and legalize same-sex marriages, we will use the notwithstanding clause. Period. End of story."

And the two Michaels? After asking the men to place rings on each other's fingers, Mr. Justice Hamilton stated: "By the power vested in me by Ontario's *Marriage Act*, I pronounce you, Michael, and you, Michael—affectionately known as 'the Michaels'—to be lawfully wedded spouses."

Questions

1. Why was the Ontario Court of Appeal's decision a landmark judgment?
2. Explain the meaning of Leshner's statement: "This is the culmination of a personal 20-year battle to end legally sanctioned homophobia."
3. Why do you think the federal government decided not to appeal the court's decision to the Supreme Court of Canada? Do you agree? Defend your position.
4. Prepare an argument to defend or refute Premier Klein's position.

It is important to note that the exclusion of evidence is not automatic under s. 24(2). Just because the police might have violated that right during their search does not mean that the evidence will not be used in court. The test for exclusion involves consideration of the fairness of the trial, the seriousness of the violation of Charter rights, and the effect that the exclusion of evidence will have on the administration of justice. A judge must make a subjective determination, weighing Charter rights against police actions. If the evidence were to be admitted at trial, how would this look? Would the public feel that the police had abused their powers and lose faith in the justice system, or would it feel that the police actions were warranted? Would "the administration of justice be brought into disrepute," as s. 24 states, if the judge allowed the admission of the evidence? This subjective decision, considering existing case law as precedent, is a key factor in resolving Charter disputes and is examined more in Chapter 9: Rules of Criminal Procedure. An application of s. 24 in an actual trial, *R v. Tessling*, is presented at the end of this chapter.

For more on the "two Michaels" and the fight for gay rights in Canada, visit www.emp.ca/dimensionsoflaw

Check Your Understanding

1. How has the Charter expanded the role of judicial review? In your answer, contrast the courts' role before and after 1982.
2. Briefly describe the current procedure for the appointment of Supreme Court of Canada judges. Should this prodecure be changed? Why or why not?
3. What is the difference between "striking down" and "reading down" a law?
4. What impact did the case of *M. v. H.* have on federal and provincial legislation?
5. List three options that courts have in enforcing Charter rights.
6. Why is s. 24(2) of the Charter a significant factor in Canadian law?

METHODS OF *Legal Inquiry*

Analyzing and Interpreting Data

Statistical data are useful "raw materials" for identifying trends and reinforcing arguments. What patterns do you need to identify in order to interpret statistics, and what questions should you ask to explain the patterns?

Figure 5.7

Success Rate of Charter Claimants, 1991–2001*

Year	Charter Challenges	Claimant Successes	Success Rate
1991	35	15	43%
1992	38	12	32%
1993	42	9	21%
1994	26	11	42%
1995	33	8	24%
1996	35	8	23%
1997	20	10	50%
1998	21	8	38%
1999	14	5	36%
2000	11	3	27%
2001	16	8	50%
Total	**291**	**97**	**33%**

* A successful case is defined by reference to its outcome, where the claimant either obtains a declaration that a law or regulation is inconsistent with a provision in the Charter and cannot be justified under s. 1, or obtains some other relief under s. 24 of the Charter.

Source: Patrick J. Monahan, *Constitutional Law*, 2nd ed. Toronto: Irwin Law, 2002, p. 393.

Applying the Skill

1. Plot the statistics from the first two columns of Figure 5.7 in a bar graph. What trends do you notice in the data? Write short statements summarizing these trends.
2. Make a list of questions that you would need to answer to explain these trends.
3. Over 75 percent of the cases involved claims based on ss. 7 to 14, involving legal rights in the criminal process. Working in small groups, discuss why the majority of Charter cases in these years involved rights related to criminal law.
4. From what you have learned in this chapter, what differences might there be in the statistics for the period 1982–1990? Explain your answer.

Reviewing Main Ideas

You Decide!

COURT EXAMINES USE OF HEAT-SEEKING CAMERAS

R v. Tessling (2003-01-27) ONCA C36111

This case involves an appeal by the accused, Walter Tessling, to the Ontario Court of Appeal. At trial, Tessling was convicted and sentenced to six months' imprisonment for possession of marijuana for the purpose of trafficking, six months concurrent for related drug offences, and a total of 12 months for weapons offences. Tessling appealed, primarily arguing that the use of heat-seeking cameras was an unreasonable search and seizure and a violation of s. 8 of the *Canadian Charter of Rights and Freedoms.*

Facts

The RCMP began investigating Tessling in February 1999, based on information from two confidential informants, A. and B. A. was an "unproven source," meaning that A. had not previously provided information leading to a criminal charge. A. told police that Tessling and a partner, Ken Illingworth, were producing and trafficking in marijuana. B., a proven informant, told the police that a known drug dealer was buying large quantities of drugs from a man named Ken in the area in which Illingworth had a farm. B. did not give the police any information about Tessling. Visual surveillance of Tessling's and Illingworth's residences revealed nothing that indicated that a marijuana-growing operation was being run at either location.

On April 29, 1999, police used an RCMP airplane equipped with a forward-looking infra-red (FLIR) camera to conduct a "structure profile" of the two residences. The FLIR camera is used to detect heat emanating from buildings. It takes an image of the heat radiating from the exterior of a building and can detect heat sources within a home, although it cannot identify the exact nature of the heat source, nor see inside the building. The FLIR camera indicated that Tessling's property, and one of Illingworth's properties, had heat emanations that might indicate a marijuana-growing operation. Based on this information, the RCMP applied for a warrant on May 5, 1999; the application was denied.

Later that day, the RCMP applied for a warrant before a different judge. The second warrant application differed from the first in that the information provided to the judge included the testimony of the two confidential informants as well as the FLIR readings. The second application was successful, and police executed the search warrant at Tessling's home. During the search police found a large quantity of marijuana, two sets of scales, freezer bags, and some weapons. Tessling was charged.

The Law

Section 8 of the Charter states: "Everyone has the right to be secure against unreasonable search or seizure." But s. 24(2) permits a person who feels that rights or freedoms have been "infringed or denied" the opportunity to a trial where "the evidence shall be excluded if ... the admission of it ... would bring the administration of justice into disrepute."

Arguments of the Defence (Appellant)

At trial, the defence brought an application under s. 24(2) of the Charter to exclude the evidence. Their argument was based on the contention that the warrant could not be based only on the information supplied by A., and that the use of the FLIR technology was an unlawful search (an invasion of privacy). According to the defence, this meant that the warrant was not valid and thus the search was unreasonable. Evidence obtained in such a manner would bring the administration of justice into disrepute and must therefore be excluded under s. 24 of the Charter.

Arguments of the Crown (Respondent)

The Crown argued that, based on the circumstances, A.'s information was reliable and, when combined with the FLIR evidence, was reason enough for the warrant to be issued. Furthermore, the Crown argued that the FLIR technology was a recognized and accepted surveillance tool, not a search, and thus did not violate s. 8 of the Charter.

Make Your Decision

1. Outline the basic facts in this case.
2. Summarize the defence arguments, carefully explaining how s. 24 of the Charter is applied in the case.
3. Summarize the Crown's arguments in the case.
4. Dismiss or allow the appeal, and provide reasons for your decision.

Key Terms

Review the following terms to show that you understand the meaning of each and how it is applied in a legal context.

judicial activism
notwithstanding clause
read down
reasonable limits
strike down

Understanding the Law

Review the following pieces of legislation mentioned in the text, and show that you understand the intent of each.

Canadian Bill of Rights
Canadian Charter of Rights and Freedoms, ss. 1, 2, 24, and 33

Thinking and Inquiry

1. Working with a partner or in a small group, interview at least two persons who were born before 1960, the year the *Canadian Bill of Rights* was passed. Ask them how they feel Canadian society has changed in the decades since then. Summarize your interviews in posterboard format. Set up displays in the classroom. Visit each display to find out about the various perspectives given. Share your impressions with the class.
2. There is still debate about whether the *Canadian Charter of Rights and Freedoms* has had a favourable or an unfavourable impact on Canada. Use your library research centre to locate a newspaper or magazine article that examines the impact of the Charter. Write a one-page summary of the article. In class, divide into groups (maximum of five people each) based on whether the article assessed the Charter's impact favourably or unfavourably. Each group is to summarize the main arguments presented in its articles. Record these arguments on chart paper. Share your group's findings with the class.
3. Use your library research centre to conduct research dealing with the Charter's impact in a specific area (for example, expanding same-sex rights). Based on your research, outline whether you feel that this impact has had a favourable

or an unfavourable effect on Canadian society. Present your ideas in a formal essay of about 1000 words. Include specific examples and supporting evidence to justify your position.

Communication

4. Visit the Web site of the Supreme Court of Canada to research a recent case involving the *Canadian Charter of Rights and Freedoms* in one of the following areas: freedom of religion, freedom of speech, freedom of assembly, mobility rights, or equality rights. Summarize the case using the format presented in this textbook. Present your case to the class. Conclude with a discussion of the case.
5. On the 10th anniversary of the Charter in April 1992, former Chief Justice Antonio Lamer stated: "The Charter represents a revolution on the scale of the introduction of the metric system, the great medical discoveries of Louis Pasteur, and the invention of penicillin and the laser." With a partner, prepare oral arguments that support or refute Lamer's statement, and present your opposing viewpoints to the class.
6. On the 20th anniversary of the Charter in April 2002, Justice Rosalie Silberman of the Ontario Court of Appeal delivered a speech entitled "Canadian Rights and Freedoms Under the Charter" at the closing session of the Association for Canadian Studies in Ottawa. In it she stated: "Twenty years from now a new generation of children will have grown up with the values of the Charter as moral tutors and the pre-eminence of rights as the core of their civic curriculum. That makes me feel very positive about the future and, at the same time, very lucky." Decide whether you agree or disagree with Justice Silberman. Write a minimum of 500 words to support your position. Present your viewpoint to the class.

Application

7. Working in groups of four, design a survey for students within your school to see how much they know about their rights, freedoms, and responsibilities. Present your findings in an oral presentation to the class. Include graphics illustrating the information gathered.
8. The editorial page of a newspaper gives that newspaper's point of view on a current public issue. Read the editorials in a newspaper to get an impression of how the editors present their ideas and the approximate length of a typical editorial. As a class, brainstorm the criteria for an editorial. After determining the requirements, each student is to prepare an editorial on a current, controversial aspect of the Charter. (This topic can be determined by the class.) Submit the best editorials to a local newspaper.
9. As a class, select a recent case from the Supreme Court of Canada, or provincial court of appeal, that deals with the *Canadian Charter of Rights and Freedoms.* Conduct an analysis of the case selected. The class is to be divided in two, and each group is to prepare arguments for both sides of the case.

Chapter 6 Human Rights in Canada

CHAPTER Focus

In this chapter, you will

- outline the historical development of human rights legislation in Canada
- evaluate the protections provided by federal and provincial human rights legislation
- demonstrate an understanding of equality rights under the Charter and in human rights legislation
- outline the historical and contemporary barriers to the equal enjoyment of human rights faced by individuals and groups in Canada
- explain how citizens can exercise their rights under the Charter
- assess the role of the courts and tribunals in protecting human rights

In 1993, Barbara Turnbull went to a cinema in downtown Toronto with some friends. After she had purchased her ticket, a theatre employee asked her if she "could get out of that thing"—her wheelchair. Turnbull could not because she is paralyzed from the shoulders down, the result of having been shot in 1983 during a robbery at the store where she worked. Because she could not climb the long flight of stairs inside the theatre, she did not get to see the movie. Turnbull, along with several other people who use wheelchairs, lodged a complaint with the Ontario Human Rights Commission, seeking full access for the disabled at Famous Players Cinemas. In September 2001, an Ontario Human Rights Board of Inquiry (now called the Human Rights Tribunal of Ontario) ruled that Famous Players had discriminated against the complainants by not providing wheelchair-accessible services.

Turnbull took action because she felt her human rights had been violated. She was able to do so because Ontario, like every other Canadian province and territory, has legislation designed to protect those rights. However, as you will see in this chapter, the human rights that Canadians enjoy did not come easily or automatically.

The cartoon in Figure 6.1 makes a statement about the rights of the disabled.

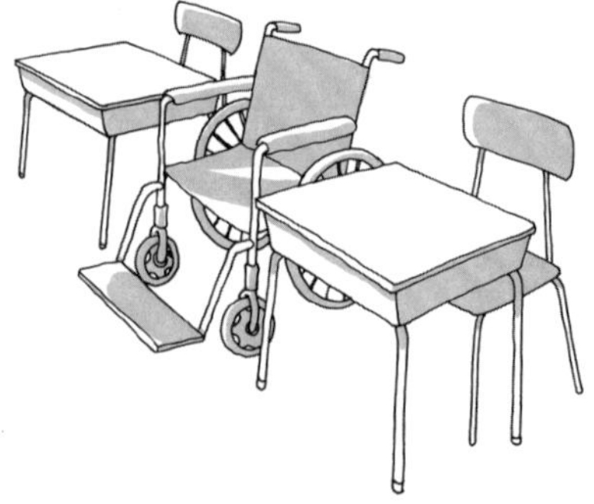

Figure 6.1

At First Glance

1. In one sentence, summarize the cartoonist's message. How has he chosen to convey this message?
2. How are the rights of the disabled part of the broader issue of human rights?
3. In what ways might using cartoons be an effective medium to communicate ideas about human rights?
4. How important is the protection of human rights for you, personally?
5. In your opinion, are human rights adequately protected in Canada? Explain your point of view.

The Historical Development of Human Rights

Barbara Turnbull won her case against Famous Players Cinemas because she was a victim of discrimination. **Discrimination** results when people base their actions on stereotyping and prejudice and treat others unfairly. **Stereotyping** occurs when the characteristics of one member of a group are applied to all members of a group. If, for example, you saw your next-door neighbour back her car into the utility pole at the end of the driveway and, from that observation, concluded that all women are bad drivers, then you would be stereotyping. Many stereotypes are based on oversimplifications along racial or gender lines.

Prejudice occurs when individuals or groups are pre-judged based on a stereotype of the group. Continuing the example from the previous paragraph, if a stereotype is that women are bad drivers and you assume that a person is a bad driver because she is a woman, then your attitude toward that woman would be prejudiced. Usually, prejudiced opinions are based on ignorance and are often negative and cruel.

In a free society such as Canada, we are all entitled to hold our own beliefs and opinions. However, if you act on a prejudicial belief and treat someone in a discriminatory manner, then you are not treating that person fairly. For example, if a taxi company owner believes that all women are bad drivers (a stereotype) and when a woman applies for a job the owner assumes that she must be a bad driver (a prejudice) and refuses to give her one, then discrimination has occurred. Although stereotyping and prejudice are not illegal, discrimination is. Human rights legislation prohibits discrimination and helps protect society against it.

The right to fair and equitable treatment is referred to as **human rights**. In one sense, the definition of human rights is simple: they are the benefits and freedoms to which all people are entitled, not because they are citizens of a particular country, but because they are human beings. Human rights ensure that everyone has adequate access to such basic needs as food

discrimination: treating a person differently or adversely for no valid reason

stereotyping: judging one person of a group and applying that judgment to all group members

prejudice: an opinion or judgment, especially an unfavourable one, based on irrelevant considerations or inadequate knowledge

human rights: the rights of an individual that are considered basic to life in any human society, including the right to religious freedom and equality of opportunity; when such rights require protection, intervention by the state is necessary and shelter. But, most importantly, human rights involve respecting one another and not discriminating against others. Beyond this broad definition, however, detailing the nature of human rights and how they should be protected is problematic and has generated much discussion.

WORKING FOR CHANGE *Canadian Coalition for the Rights of Children*

In November 1989, the United Nations General Assembly ratified the *Convention on the Rights of the Child*, an agreement described as the most comprehensive human rights document in history. This agreement set out the fundamental freedoms and rights to which all children are entitled from birth. It was then up to the government of each member country to accept this Convention and commit to implementing its principles. All countries except Somalia and the United States have ratified the Convention in their own legislatures.

In Canada, organizations that were committed to the well-being of children came together to promote the ratification of the Convention. The mandate of the Canadian Coalition for the Rights of Children was to ensure that the vision set out in the UN agreement was implemented here in Canada. Once the Convention was ratified by Parliament in December 1991, the member groups of the Coalition set about to

- monitor Canadian domestic and international policies to ensure that they respect the directions of the Convention
- establish local, provincial, national, and international networks with organizations concerned about the well-being of children
- promote awareness of the rights of children among Canadians
- encourage the federal government to support leadership roles for Canadians on the UN Committee on the Rights of the Child.

Within a short period of time, over 50 groups became members of the Coalition.

The Canadian Coalition for the Rights of Children has criticized the federal government for its treatment of children. In a stinging report issued in 1999, the Coalition argued that Canada had failed to live up to the UN Convention. The report concluded that Canadian legislation rarely recognizes children and allows adults to place arbitrary limits on children's fundamental freedoms. Specific complaints included the facts that children with disabilities are not guaranteed basic educational and social services, that the *Criminal Code* allows corporal punishment for children, and that Canada was not meeting its foreign aid obligations.

Questions

1. Why was the Canadian Coalition on the Rights of Children founded?
2. Identify three strategies that the Coalition might use to promote greater public awareness about children's rights. Explain your ideas.
3. Visit the Coalition's Web site through the link at www.emp.ca/dimensionsoflaw and determine the three current and top priorities of this group. Do you agree with their choices? Why or why not?
4. The Coalition would like to see an end to the legal use of corporal punishment of children. Spanking is a form of corporal punishment. Would you support making the spanking of children an illegal act? Explain. (See also You Decide! "Correcting Children by Force," Chapter 8, page 256.)

History of Human Rights

Our concept of human rights has a long history. The idea that human beings have inherent dignity and worth dates back to the ancient world. Over the centuries, ideas about human rights began to be incorporated into law.

- In 1215, the Magna Carta (discussed in Unit 1: Heritage) contained references to what we now think of as human rights, such as equal treatment before the law.
- In 1689, the *Bill of Rights* required that all future monarchs had to obey parliament and its laws, and reaffirmed the rights that had been won since the Magna Carta, such as freedom from cruel and illegal punishments.
- In 1776, when Britain's colonies in America sought political independence, their *Declaration of Independence* contained a ringing statement of human rights: "We hold these truths to be self-evident, that all men are created equal, that they are endowed by their Creator with certain unalienable Rights, that among these are Life, Liberty and the pursuit of Happiness." These, and other rights, became part of the American *Bill of Rights* entrenched in the US constitution and are still very much the basis of American civil rights and freedoms.
- In 1789, France's *Declaration of the Rights of Man* stated that the "natural rights of man" included "liberty, property, security, and resistance to oppression," and went on to cover other human rights such as freedom of religion and freedom of speech.
- In 1833, Britain's *Emancipation Act* abolished slavery throughout its empire.

In Britain, the step-by-step accumulation of human rights was protected and enforced under the common-law system, which eventually was inherited by Canada. Thus, the rights won by British subjects also applied to Canadians.

The Impact of World War II on Human Rights

During World War II (1939–1945), some 60 million people, more than half of them civilians, were killed. Millions of Europeans were forced to work in labour camps by the Nazi German state. Jews in particular were targeted, first deprived of their properties and legal rights, and then sent to camps where millions died.

The terrible crimes against humanity committed during this war caused the nations of the world to reflect on how they could prevent such atrocities from happening again. As one of its important early steps, in 1948, the United Nations General Assembly proclaimed the *Universal Declaration of Human Rights* (UDHR). This was the first international agreement intended

The Law From the *Universal Declaration of Human Rights*:

Article 2
Everyone is entitled to all the rights and freedoms set forth in this Declaration, without distinction of any kind, such as race, colour, sex, language, religion, political or other opinion, national or social origin, property, birth or other status. ...

Article 24
Everyone has the right to rest and leisure. ...

Article 25
Everyone has the right to a standard of living adequate for the health and well-being of himself and of his family, including food, clothing, housing and medical care and necessary social services, and the right to security in the event of unemployment, sickness, disability, widowhood, old age or other lack of livelihood in circumstances beyond his control.

Questions

1. In your opinion, which of the articles listed here is the most important? Explain your point of view.
2. Some people argue that there are aspects of human rights that should have been included in the UDHR, but are not there, such as equal treatment based on sexual orientation and freedom from poverty. In your opinion, are these "rights"? Explain your answer.

solely for the promotion and protection of human rights. The UDHR included fundamental freedoms and legal rights, equality rights, and economic, social, and cultural rights. Member states were obligated to meet "the common standard of all achievements and all nations" on the topic of human rights. Most nations took up the challenge and incorporated some or all of the UDHR's principles into their own constitutions. By signing this Declaration, a country commits itself to protecting the rights of its citizens and to respecting the rights of all human beings. (The UDHR and the role of the United Nations in international law are examined in Chapter 17: International Organizations.)

Human Rights Discrimination in Canada

As Canadians, we often take for granted the rights and freedoms that are afforded us. We often assume that everyone in Canada is, and has always been, treated equally, but there have been times in our history when rights were, and still are, denied to certain groups living in Canada.

Shortly after the outbreak of World War I in 1914, Parliament passed the *War Measures Act* granting extraordinary powers to the government during war or invasion; for example, the power to pass legislation without debate, to arrest without laying charges, to detain indefinitely, and to seize and sell private property. The Act also defined immigrants from Austria–Hungary (Britain's enemy during the war) as "enemy aliens." This designation resulted in the **internment** of about 8600 people in camps in Canada, including about 5000 Ukrainians. Another 80 000 had to carry identification cards and report regularly to the police. Those interned were forced to help develop provincial parks, build roads, clear land and cut wood, and work in mines in British Columbia, Ontario, and Nova Scotia. (This program worked so well for the government that it continued until 1920, two years after the end of World War I.) These internments exposed some of the anti-immigrant feeling that existed among the general Canadian population.

internment: confinement, such as in wartime, when a country forces people considered enemies to live in a special area or camp

A similar form of racial discrimination occurred during World War II, when Canada was at war with Japan. After the Japanese attack on US warships in Pearl Harbor in 1941, the federal government—under pressure from the British Columbia provincial government—used provisions of the *War Measures Act* to intern about 22 000 Canadians of Japanese descent, citing security risks. Within weeks of the Pearl Harbor attack, the Canadian government seized all Japanese-Canadian fishing boats and began to round up these citizens, placing them in internment camps in the BC interior.

Fyi In 1988, the *War Measures Act* was replaced by the *Emergencies Act*. Laws made under the new legislation are subject to the *Canadian Charter of Rights and Freedoms*, and Parliament has to approve the declaration of an emergency.

Because most of these citizens worked in the fishing industry, they automatically lost their means of livelihood. Their property, homes, and belongings were confiscated and sold at a fraction of their value. The men were forced to work building roads in the interior or on farms, while women, children, and the elderly were confined to camps until the end of

Figure 6.2 *Internment camp for Japanese-Canadians, 1942. Human rights were not well protected during World War II, as the internment of people of Japanese origin indicates. Much later, in 1988, the government of Canada officially apologized for this action and gave survivors money to help compensate them for their losses.*

For more on factors regarding the internment of Japanese-Canadians and Ukrainian-Canadians, visit www.emp.ca/dimensionsoflaw

the war in 1945. At that time, there was no human rights legislation to protect Japanese-Canadians from the actions of the Canadian and British Columbia governments, which barred them from voting, working in professions, and participating fully in Canadian society.

Racial discrimination of a different kind is the subject of the following case.

Case JUST FOLLOWING "HOUSE RULES"

Christie v. York Corp., [1940] SCR 139

Facts

Fred Christie was a Montreal Canadiens fan. On the night of July 11, 1936, he had gone with some friends to the Montreal Forum to see a hockey game. After the game, they entered the Forum's tavern. However, when Christie ordered a beer, the barman refused to serve him. Fred Christie was black, and the barman explained that "house rules" of the tavern prohibited serving "coloured persons." Christie brought an action against York Corporation, the owners of the tavern, for damages for the humiliation he suffered. His suit was for $200. York Corporation argued that, in giving instructions not to serve black persons, it was merely protecting its business interests. The company maintained that, as a private enterprise, it was free to deal with anyone it chose.

At the trial, Christie won his case and was awarded $25. The judge based his decision on ss. 19 and 33 of the *Quebec Licence Act*, which made refusing service illegal. However, the Court of King's Bench (as the Quebec Court of Appeal was then called) overturned this decision. The appeal court ruled that the sections of the *Quebec Licence Act* did not apply, and that in the absence of any specific law, merchants were free to carry on business in the manner that they believed to be best. Fred Christie then took his appeal to the Supreme Court of Canada.

Decision

The Supreme Court ruled against Christie. The judgment stated:

> The general principle of the law of Quebec is that of complete freedom of commerce. Any merchant is free to deal as he may choose with any individual member of the public. It is not a question of motive or reasons for deciding to deal or not to deal: he is free to do either. The only restriction to this general principle would be the existence of a specific law, or, in the carrying out of the principle, the adoption of a rule contrary to good morals or public order; and the rule adopted by the respondent in the conduct of its establishment was not within that class. Also, as the law stands in Quebec, the sale of beer in that province was not either a monopoly or a privileged enterprise. Moreover, the appellant

cannot be brought within the terms of section 33 of the *Quebec Licence Act*, as he was not a traveller asking for a meal in a restaurant, but only a person asking for a glass of beer in a tavern. As the case is not governed by any specific law or more particularly by section 33 of the *Quebec Licence Act*, it falls under the general principle of the freedom of commerce; and, therefore, the respondent, when refusing to serve the appellant, was strictly within its rights.

Questions

1. Summarize the facts in this case.
2. Why did Christie lose the case?
3. Do you agree with the Supreme Court's decision? Why or why not?
4. Would this case have the same outcome today? Explain.

Until well into the 20th century, Canada's history was marred by instances of discrimination against women, persons of colour, persons of Asian and Jewish descent, and many other minorities. In Chapter 3, you saw an example of religious discrimination in the lengthy battle between members of the Jehovah's Witnesses faith and the Quebec government in *Roncarelli v. Duplessis* (page 89). An example of gender discrimination occurred when women were not considered to be "persons," as you saw in the "persons case" in Chapter 4 (page 116).

The protection of human rights in Canada also has a long history (see Figure 6.3). Since the *Canadian Charter of Rights and Freedoms* came into effect, there has been a great deal of activity geared toward making laws consistent with its requirements.

Fyi The BC legislature took the right to vote away from Chinese men in 1872, from Japanese men in 1895, and from East Asian men in 1907. This meant they could not vote in federal elections either. These groups were not given the right to vote until 1947.

Important Events in the History of Human Rights in Canada

1944 • Ontario passes the *Racial Discrimination Act*.
1947 • *Saskatchewan Bill of Rights* becomes the first human rights statute in Canada.
1948 • *Universal Declaration of Human Rights* is adopted and proclaimed by the United Nations.
1951 • Canadian government enacts fair accommodation and fair employment practices acts.
1960 • *Canadian Bill of Rights* is passed.
1961 • Ontario Human Rights Commission is established.
1975 • All provinces have enacted human rights legislation by this date.
1976 • Canada ratifies the *International Bill of Rights*, making it binding upon Canada in international law.
1977 • Canadian Parliament passes the *Canadian Human Rights Act*.
1978 • Canadian Human Rights Commission is set up to administer this Act.
1982 • *Canadian Charter of Rights and Freedoms* comes into effect.

Figure 6.3

ersonal Viewpoint

Not on the "Hebrew List"

Barnet Berris graduated from the University of Toronto Faculty of Medicine in 1944. In 1951, he became the first Jewish doctor appointed as a teacher in the Clinical Department of Medicine at the University of Toronto; he was Chief of Medicine at Toronto's Mount Sinai Hospital from 1964–1977. Dr. Berris retired in 1987 after 50 years in medicine and, in 1999, published a memoir called *Medicine, My Story*. In it, he recalled the anti-Semitism that hampered his progress early in his career.

> In 1944, my final year of medical school, I was looking forward to interning. Since most of my student hospital experience had been at the Toronto General and Toronto Western Hospitals, these were the only hospitals to which I applied. I felt quite certain that I would be accepted by one of them, because in a class of 126, my standing ranged between four and ten. However, when the appointments were announced, I discovered to my dismay that I was the only person in my class who had not been accepted for internship by a hospital. I couldn't understand how this could have happened and was certain it was a mistake. I went to both hospitals to which I had applied and asked to see the list of students they were prepared to accept. At first there was some resistance to my request, but when I persisted, I was allowed to see them. I was stunned by what I saw. The Toronto General Hospital had two lists on one page. On the left was a long list of students they were prepared to accept, and this included a number of students who were near the bottom of the class. On the right was another, very short list. It was titled "Hebrew list" and on it were three names. The first was the name of the gold medallist in our class, and the second was another Jewish student who also had a very good record. Below the two names was the heading "Alternate Hebrew" with my name. The Toronto Western list had the name of only one Jewish student, the gold medallist in our class, but he had chosen to go to the Toronto General. As a consequence, the Toronto Western Hospital took no Jewish intern that year. It was the first time I recognized anti-Semitism in the medical hierarchy.

A few years later, having found a small hospital in which to serve his internship, Dr. Berris sought a residency to train as a specialist in internal medicine:

> I was surprised and pleased when I received a letter of acceptance from McGill University. In this letter I was told that it was necessary for me to come to Montreal to formalize the appointment. When I arrived in Montreal, I went to the department chair's office and, as was very common those days, one of the questions asked was religious affiliation. I filled in this line with the word "Jewish." The secretary took my completed application form into the department chair's office, and a few minutes later she came out and said that she had been instructed to tell me that all the positions were filled. I was taken aback and I asked her to show the letter to the department chair and to ask if I might see him. She entered his office again and came out soon after. She said, "The department chairman told me to tell you again that the positions are all filled."
>
> I knew there was nothing more that I could do; I left the office and went back to Toronto. You might ask why I accepted overt anti-Semitism from a medical school without taking any action. The reason was that in the 1940s there was no

mechanism available to bring about any change in this area. There were no laws prohibiting such activities, and minority groups at that time had very little influence, political or otherwise.

Source: Barnet Berris, *Medicine, My Story*. Toronto: University of Toronto Press, 1999.

Questions

1. What is anti-Semitism?
2. What was your personal reaction when you first read Dr. Berris's account? Explain.
3. Why didn't Dr. Berris do something about the racial discrimination he faced?
4. Is such discrimination likely to occur today? Explain your views.

CHECK YOUR UNDERSTANDING

1. Of stereotyping, prejudice, and discrimination, which is prohibited by law, and why?
2. Why are human rights important?
3. What is the significance of the *Universal Declaration of Human Rights*?
4. List three examples of the denial of human rights in Canada.
5. List two reasons why the *Emergencies Act* is a significant improvement over the *War Measures Act*.

Canada and Human Rights

Much of the material in this textbook involves the *Canadian Charter of Rights and Freedoms* and its significant impact on many areas of the law, but it is important to understand that rights didn't just suddenly appear in our constitution on April 17, 1982. Since signing the *Universal Declaration of Human Rights* in 1948, the Canadian government has succeeded in making universal human rights an essential part of Canadian law. In Chapter 5, you learned about the *Canadian Bill of Rights*, the freedoms that it recognized, and its role as a precursor to the *Canadian Charter of Rights and Freedoms.* But the Bill was limited in its application and did not offer protection against unfair treatment in areas of *provincial* jurisdiction. To provide Canadians with comprehensive protection of their rights, something more was needed.

Currently, there are four important mechanisms in Canada to protect human rights: the Charter, the *Canadian Human Rights Act*, provincial human rights legislation, and human rights commissions. The Charter provides a list of rights to which Canadians are entitled and outlines the government's responsibility in upholding those rights (see Chapter 5). An important difference between the Charter and human rights legislation is that the Charter applies to the actions of "public" laws and bodies, including acts of the federal Parliament and provincial legislatures. In contrast, human rights legislation applies to "private" laws and parties. The application and administration of human rights legislation is discussed in the following pages.

For more on a variety of Canadian human rights Web sites, visit www.emp.ca/dimensionsoflaw

Federal and Provincial Human Rights Legislation

The *Canadian Human Rights Act* (CHRA) came into force in 1978, and applies to federal government departments and businesses that fall under federal jurisdiction. For example, Canada's armed forces and Crown corporations, such as Canada Post and the CBC, must follow the CHRA. Some private companies—such as chartered banks, telecommunications companies, radio and television stations, railroads, and airlines—must also adhere to the CHRA. The Act states that all Canadians have the right to equality, fair treatment, and a life free of discrimination. The CHRA prohibits discrimination on 11 grounds (see Figure 6.4).

Each province and territory has its own human rights law, usually called a code. Each provincial and territorial code is slightly different, and prohibited grounds of discrimination vary. Restaurants, retail stores, schools, hospitals, unions, and governments themselves are among the institutions covered by provincial human rights legislation. For example, the Ontario *Human Rights Code* (OHRC), proclaimed in 1962, prohibits discrimination on 16 grounds (see Figure 6.4).

Fyi In 1997, the Ontario Human Rights Commission introduced mediation. All individuals filing complaints are first offered mediation, a voluntary process in which a neutral third party works with parties to resolve their issues at the outset. Between 65 and 70% of complaints in which mediation has been attempted have been successfully settled.

Human Rights Commissions and Tribunals

To implement and administer human rights legislation, the federal, provincial, and territorial governments have established human rights commissions. Their function is to investigate complaints concerning possible human rights violations, to provide legal procedures to hear the complaints, and to try to find solutions. For example, if you use a wheelchair and your local Canada Post outlet or your neighbourhood bank is not wheelchair-accessible, you can file a complaint with the Canadian Human Rights Commission. If you have experienced any kind of discrimination or sexual or racial harassment in your community, you can file a complaint with your provincial human rights commission (as did Barbara Turnbull to the Ontario Human Rights Commission against the movie theatre that did not provide wheelchair accessibility). Most complaints filed with provincial commissions are resolved at that level.

Sometimes a human rights complaint requires further investigation, and the parties cannot resolve their differences and reach an agreement. Then, the commission will send the case to the Ontario Human Rights Tribunal for a formal hearing, where the principles of human rights legislation are applied. Cases are referred by various human rights commissions. To give an analogy, the commission's role is similar to that of police, who receive and investigate complaints; the tribunal's role is similar to that of a court, although it is less formal and hears cases related to discrimination only. A human rights tribunal has more flexibility than a court of law because it allows the parties and witnesses to plead their cases without having to follow strict rules of evidence. All parties are given an opportunity to make submissions and to present evidence.

Fyi After the shooting, Barbara Turnbull earned an honours degree in journalism and has been a reporter at the *Toronto Star* since 1991. Since 2001, the Barbara Turnbull Award has been presented annually to recognize outstanding research in the field of spinal cord injuries.

Comparison of Grounds for Discrimination

Canadian Human Rights Act	Ontario *Human Rights Code*
Race	Race
National or ethnic origin	Place of origin (country or region)
	Ethnic origin
	Ancestry (family descent)
	Citizenship
Colour	Colour (associated with race)
Religion	Creed (religion or faith)
Age	Age
Sex (including pregnancy, childbearing)	Sex (includes pregnancy, breastfeeding, gender identity)
Sexual orientation	Sexual orientation
Marital status	Marital status (cohabitation, separation)
Family status	Family status (parent–child relationship)
	Same-sex partnership status
Physical or mental disability	Disability (physical, learning, developmental, psychiatric)
Pardoned criminal conviction	Record of offences (employment only)
	Receipt of public assistance (accommodation only)

Figure 6.4

Turning Points in the Law

The Founding of the Ontario Human Rights Commission

The Ontario Human Rights Commission was established in 1961 and was the first human rights commission in Canada with a mandate to administer and enforce a human rights code protecting the rights of individuals, namely the Ontario *Human Rights Code*. The Code, one of the first in Canada, was used as the model for many of the human rights codes developed by other provinces and territories and, to some extent, the federal CHRA.

The Commission's first director was Dan Hill (1923–2003), a black civil rights activist; he held this position through the 1960s. From 1971–1973, Hill served as the Commission's first full-time chairman. When he moved to Toronto in 1953, he had faced racial discrimination. As one of his sons said: "As an interracial couple, my parents could not find an apartment to rent in Toronto. Dad was obliged to step aside while his wife hunted for an apartment with a white friend who pretended to be her husband." Instead of

Figure 6.5 *Daniel Grafton Hill (left) talks with Ian Wilson of the Ontario Archives.*

becoming embittered by such an experience, Dan Hill resolved to change things and became known as the founding father of human rights in Ontario.

Years later, Hill stated:

Those who have settled in Ontario comprise every nationality, race, creed, and colour, drawn by the promise of a fuller and freer life. Some have escaped religious persecution, some racial discrimination and others poverty—but all have cherished the dream of a land where equality and opportunity are prized. Yet, human rights issues from the past are still with us—native rights, women's rights, the treatment of

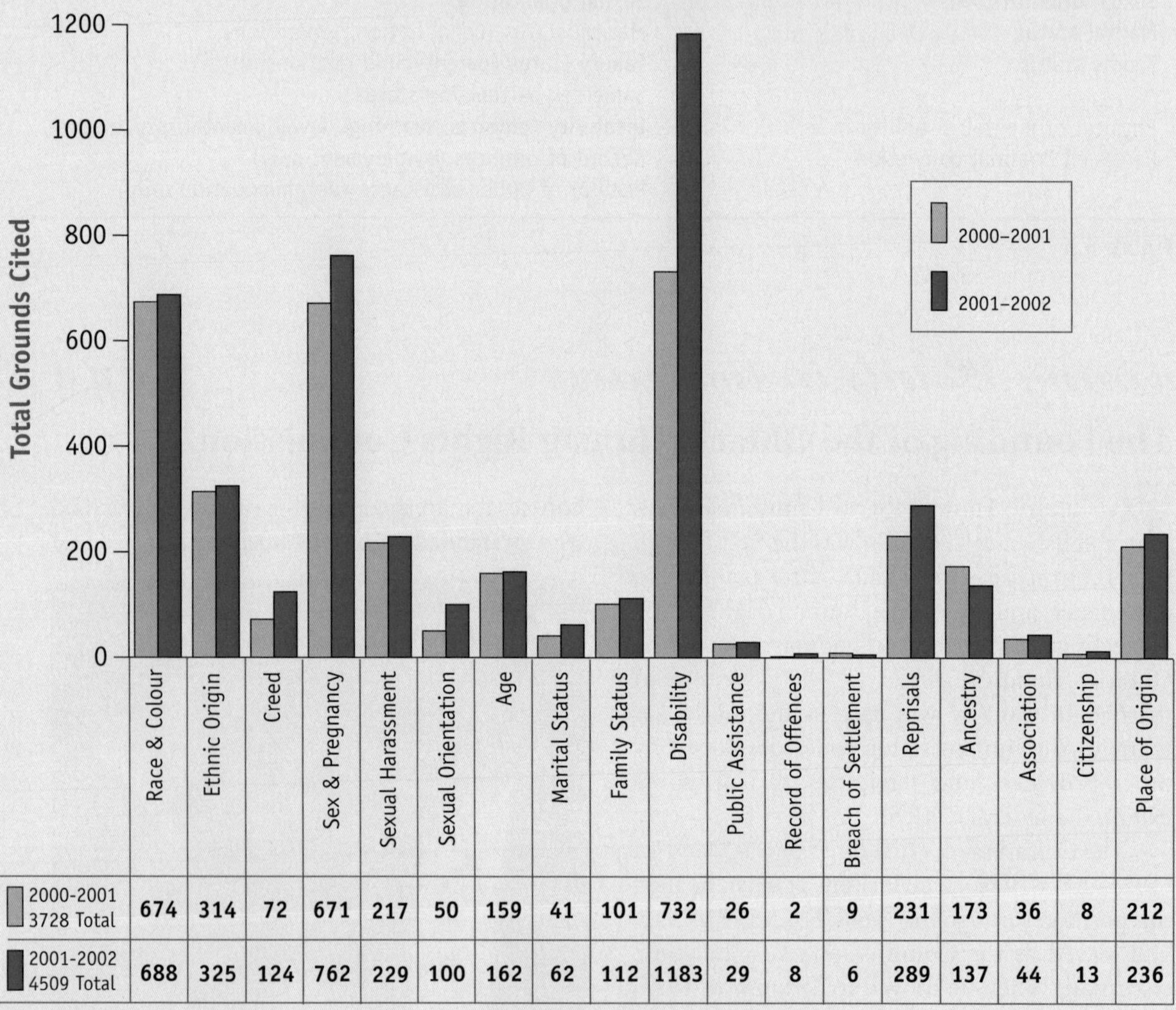

Figure 6.6 *Grounds of discrimination cited in human rights claims filed in Ontario in 2000–2001 and 2001–2002.*

	Race & Colour	Ethnic Origin	Creed	Sex & Pregnancy	Sexual Harassment	Sexual Orientation	Age	Marital Status	Family Status	Disability	Public Assistance	Record of Offences	Breach of Settlement	Reprisals	Ancestry	Association	Citizenship	Place of Origin
2000-2001 3728 Total	674	314	72	671	217	50	159	41	101	732	26	2	9	231	173	36	8	212
2001-2002 4509 Total	688	325	124	762	229	100	162	62	112	1183	29	8	6	289	137	44	13	236

Note: Some human rights claims were filed citing more than one ground of discrimination.

Source: Adapted from Ontario Human Rights Commission; www.ohrc.on.ca/english/publications/2001-2002-annual-report_4.shtml.

visible minorities, Francophone rights, and the rights of the handicapped—to mention just a few, a very few. That we have not reached the promised land of the just society is known to every person who has toiled for security and social justice. But that is no reason to abate [put an end to] our efforts. There is simply too much at stake. From the hindsight of history, one lesson is very clear—so long as the rights of even one are abused, abridged [shortened] or abrogated [abolished]—then the freedom of all is in peril.

Prior to 1962, Ontario's efforts to protect human rights had been piecemeal. Ontario's first effort at protecting human rights was the *Racial Discrimination Act, 1944*, the first Canadian legislation to provide protection against racial and religious discrimination. This legislation was specifically passed to prevent discriminatory practices such as the "No Jews or Dogs Allowed" signs that were sometimes posted in stores, on beaches, and in other public places. (Review the *Re Drummond Wren* case in Chapter 2, page 46.) In 1950, the provincial government amended the Ontario *Labour Relations Act* so that racial discrimination in collective agreements was outlawed. In 1951, the province passed the *Fair Employment Practices Act*, prohibiting discrimination based on race and religion in employment. In 1954, the *Fair Accommodation Practices Act* prohibited discrimination in public places on ethnic, racial, or religious grounds. With the passage of the OHRC in 1962, these and other acts that the province had put in place over the previous two decades to combat discrimination were consolidated into one comprehensive and inclusive law.

The Commission's mandate under the OHRC includes

- investigating complaints of discrimination and harassment
- making efforts to settle complaints between parties
- looking into situations where discriminatory behaviour exists
- preventing discrimination through public education and public policy.

The Commission presently has an annual budget of about $12 million and is the largest human rights agency in Canada, handling the greatest number of complaints. In 2001–2002, the Commission opened 2438 cases, representing a general rise in complaints across most grounds of discrimination, and closed 1932 cases.

Questions

1. Why was the creation of the Ontario Human Rights Commission a turning point in the law?
2. Why is it important to have human rights commissions?
3. Why was Dan Hill an important person in Ontario's human rights history?
4. Identify two general trends that you notice in the graph in Figure 6.6.
5. What issues is the Ontario Human Rights Commission currently trying to resolve? Visit its Web site through the link at www.emp.ca/dimensionsoflaw and examine the most recent data on complaints filed. Summarize the highlights.

■ ■ ■ ■

The major distinction between criminal law, civil law, and human rights legislation is the different standards of proof. In criminal law, the Crown must prove the charges beyond a reasonable doubt; this is a very high and demanding standard. Under the Ontario *Human Rights Code*, as in civil

balance of probabilities: the basis of greater likelihood; the degree of proof in civil law, in comparison with proof beyond a reasonable doubt in criminal law

bona fide: (Latin) "in good faith"; legitimate, genuine

undue hardship: the result of a change that would affect the economic viability of an employer or produce a substantial health or safety risk that outweighs the benefit of accommodating someone

law, the complainant's standard of proof is the **balance of probabilities**. Of the parties involved, who is more believable, and did the alleged discrimination more likely occur or not? If the tribunal believes that discrimination has occurred, then the respondent must prove that there was a **bona fide** reason for the discrimination and that to act otherwise would bring **undue hardship**.

Following a tribunal's judgment, any of the parties involved may appeal the decision, and an appeal sometimes may go all the way to the Supreme Court of Canada. For example, in the case *Ontario Human Rights Commission and O'Malley v. Simpsons-Sears Ltd.*, the Supreme Court of Canada recognized for the first time in 1985 the concept that the workplace would remain closed to minorities if steps were not taken to accommodate different needs. In this case, O'Malley was a member of the Seventh Day Adventist faith, which requires strict observance of the sabbath from sundown Friday to sundown Saturday. Her employer, Simpsons-Sears Ltd., argued that it was not intentionally discriminating by requiring her to work Friday evenings and Saturdays, because this was a term of full-time employment. However, the Supreme Court, in a unanimous judgment, found that O'Malley was discriminated against because of her creed, as her employer had not made reasonable adjustments to normal work schedules in order to accommodate her special needs. Even though the discrimination was unintentional, Simpsons-Sears Ltd. did not show that accommodating O'Malley would have created undue hardship.

However, all human rights codes or acts provide only civil remedies, not criminal penalties such as imprisonment. Companies or individuals found to have discriminated against others may be required to compensate persons filing human rights complaints or to make major changes in the way they operate. In Chapter 1, You Decide! "Bringing a Kirpan to School" (page 29) provides a good example of a successful complaint. Another example is seen in the following case.

Case JOB DISCRIMINATION

Kearsley v. City of St. Catharines, Ontario Human Rights Commission, April 2002

Facts

Tony Kearsley applied for a position as a firefighter with the City of St. Catharines. He was accepted on condition that he pass a medical examination by a doctor specified by the city. During the medical exam, the doctor discovered that Kearsley had an atrial fibrillation (an irregular heartbeat) and refused to pass him. However, Kearsley consulted medical specialists who advised him that his condition would not affect his ability to perform his job as a firefighter. Kearsley then filed a complaint against the city with the Ontario Human Rights Commission.

At the Commission's Board of Inquiry hearing, the doctor who had originally examined Kearsley testified that atrial fibrillation led to increased risk for stroke. He further testified that Kearsley's heart could fail to pump sufficient blood to his organs during the extreme rigours of firefighting.

The Board of Inquiry called a medical expert in atrial fibrillation. The expert testified that the increased risk for stroke in someone of Kearsley's age was inconsequential. The expert further testified that there was no increased risk for heart failure in someone like Kearsley, who was otherwise in good general health. Meanwhile, after being turned down by the St. Catharines fire department, Kearsley had become a firefighter in the City of Hamilton, achieving the rank of first-class firefighter in October 2001.

Issue

Did Kearsley suffer job discrimination, or were the requirements for firefighters in St. Catharines such that he did not meet a bona fide job requirement?

Decision

The Board of Inquiry accepted the evidence of the expert in atrial fibrillation over that of the medical doctor who had originally conducted Kearsley's physical, since the latter was a general practitioner with no particular expertise in this area. The Board of Inquiry further noted that it would have been appropriate for the City of St. Catharines to seek an expert opinion when confronted with a medical condition such as that found in Kearsley. The Board indicated that this was the procedure used in other municipalities. Since the Board found the risk of impairment to be "minuscule" and "insignificant," it ruled that Kearsley had suffered discrimination. The Board of Inquiry ordered the following remedies:

- The city was to hire Kearsley as a first-class firefighter (with his work to commence within 75 days of the decision).
- The city was to pay the difference between what Kearsley earned and what he would have earned had he been hired originally.
- The city was to reimburse Kearsley for his travel expenses to Hamilton from his home in St. Catharines (during the time that he was employed by the City of Hamilton).
- The city was to pay general damages of $4000.

Questions

1. Summarize the facts of this case.
2. Why did the Board of Inquiry rule in Kearsley's favour?
3. Do you agree with the decision in this case? Why or why not?
4. In what ways is this case a question of human rights?

ombudsman: an official appointed to receive and investigate citizens' grievances against the government

The provinces also put in place measures to protect citizens from governmental actions. The position of provincial **ombudsman** was established to investigate complaints about provincial governmental organizations. Where an ombudsman finds wrongdoing, he or she can make recommendations to resolve the problem and, if necessary, report on the issues to the legislature. The ombudsman is independent of both the government and of political parties. The position of Ontario's ombudsman was established in 1975. In 1984, Dan Hill was appointed Ontario ombudsman, a position he held until his retirement in 1989.

Human rights codes, like all legislation, are now subject to the provisions set out in the *Canadian Charter of Rights and Freedoms.* If a section of a human rights code is found to contravene the Charter, then the provision can be struck down by the courts. One famous case involving the striking down of a section of a human rights code took place in Ontario. Twelve-year-old Justine Blainey wanted to play boys' hockey, as she was very skilled in the game, but she was not allowed to do so. She addressed a discrimination complaint to the Ontario Human Rights Commission, but it failed because, at that time, the Ontario *Human Rights Code* allowed sexual discrimination in sports. This forced Blainey to work her way through the Ontario court system, and finally, in 1986, the Ontario Court of Appeal struck down a section of the Ontario *Human Rights Code* that allowed athletic organizations to restrict membership based on gender. In this particular case, the court ruled that this restriction violated her equality rights guaranteed under s. 15 of the Charter. As a result, the province of Ontario had to amend its human rights code to comply with the court's ruling.

Justine Blainey-Broker is now a doctor of chiropracty at the Justine Blainey Wellness Centre in Brampton. She manages the clinic with her husband Blake and brother David, and she is the mother of two.

Personal Viewpoint

Justine Blainey: "She Shoots! She Scores!"

Justine Blainey went all the way to the Supreme Court of Canada to win the right to play on a boys' hockey team.

> I was a traditional little girl when it came to sports and hobbies—figure skating, ballet, tennis, arts and crafts—until the roaring cheers at my brother David's hockey games led me to discover my first enduring passion, hockey. I fell in love with the swish of the ice, the bumps, and being able to say, "This puck is mine," and then using my mental and physical power to make it so.
>
> Hockey school and practising with my brother's teams came next. Soon his coaches asked me to cut my hair and call myself Justin so that I could play for them. I declined, saying, "Take me as I am." David stood by me, left defence to my right, reminding me that there is no reason a girl should have to fight to do whatever a boy can do. As more hockey organizations refused to let their coaches sign me because I was a girl, controversy swirled—everyone had an opinion, mostly negative.

Figure 6.7 *Justine Blainey raises her hockey skates in victory after the Supreme Court of Canada rejected an Ontario Hockey Association bid to keep her from playing on a boys' team.*

People spat on me, harassed me, grabbed at me, and insulted me. "She must be sleeping with all those boys," they said in arenas. Coaches threw my bags out of dressing rooms—"No girls on my ice!" Even some of my friends turned against me: my girlfriends told me that they would no longer play or talk with me because their parents said that I was a troublemaker.

I quickly learned how much better men's teams were with respect to the availability and level of play, length of season, range of age categories, ice time, sponsorships, and scholarships. I originally wanted to play hockey for the fun of it, but a sense of fairness and a desire for equality for women soon became an important part in my fight. Lawyer J. Anna Fraser volunteered her services to help me win the right to play with male teams, and a series of five court cases began. The cases seemed interminable, so to pass the time I joined a girl's hockey league. To improve my skills I practised with boys' teams, played exhibition games incognito, and went to hockey schools.

The battle wasn't easy, but it was important. With every physical attack I experienced or threat I received, I realized that females need to be mentally and physically tough in order to stand up to any threats. Hockey taught me to get up when I was knocked down. I realized that equality of access and opportunity should be a fundamental right for every person, not just in sport, but in all aspects of life. The court battles fostered my determination to fight for a society where we can all work and play as equals.

The law may uphold equality but sometimes the rest of the world is slow to change. I continue the battle for equality through public speaking and private encouragement. And when I play hockey with my young daughter, practising shooting, bodychecks, falling down, and jumping up to try again, we can always hear that triumphant cry, "She shoots, she scores!"

Questions

1. Although Blainey could have played on girls' teams, why do you think she wanted to play on a boys' team?
2. Why was Blainey's case an example of an issue concerning "equal protection and benefit of the law"?
3. "The law may uphold equality, but sometimes the rest of the world is slow to change." Defend or refute this statement.
4. Should there be integrated sports events in which men and women compete with, and against, each other? Why or why not?

CHECK YOUR UNDERSTANDING

1. What is the major difference between the *Canadian Human Rights Act* and the Ontario *Human Rights Code*?
2. List the three main functions of a human rights commission.
3. What is the relationship between a human rights commission and a human rights tribunal?
4. What is the main distinction between criminal law and civil law in terms of the standard of proof required?
5. What is the function of an ombudsman?
6. Why was Justine Blainey's case significant?

To find out more about important rulings in the development of human rights in Canada, visit www.emp.ca/dimensionsoflaw

issue

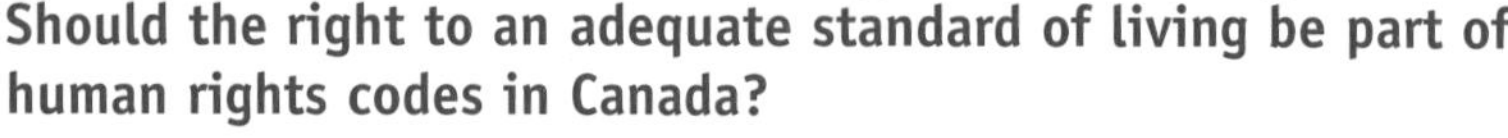

The Extent of Human Rights Coverage

Should the right to an adequate standard of living be part of human rights codes in Canada?

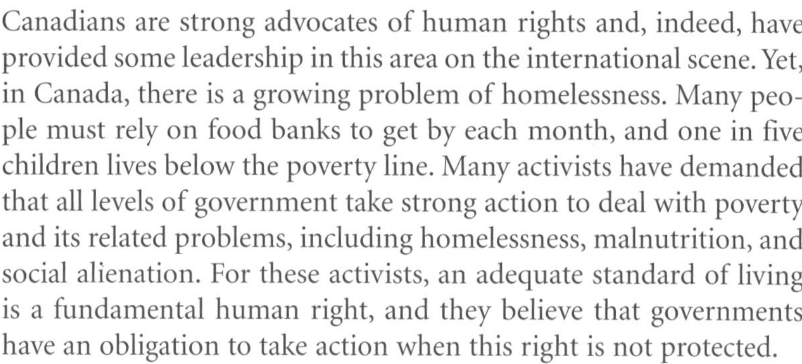

Canadians are strong advocates of human rights and, indeed, have provided some leadership in this area on the international scene. Yet, in Canada, there is a growing problem of homelessness. Many people must rely on food banks to get by each month, and one in five children lives below the poverty line. Many activists have demanded that all levels of government take strong action to deal with poverty and its related problems, including homelessness, malnutrition, and social alienation. For these activists, an adequate standard of living is a fundamental human right, and they believe that governments have an obligation to take action when this right is not protected.

The following excerpts outline the positions of some individuals and groups on this issue.

> Twenty-five years ago [1976] Canada ratified the *International Covenant on Economic, Social and Cultural Rights*, recognizing that all levels of government in Canada have an obligation to ensure that everyone enjoys the rights to an adequate standard of living. ... Since 1976, we have experienced unprecedented economic growth, ... yet at the same time we have witnessed the emergence of an unprecedented crisis of homelessness and poverty. ...
>
> This "epidemic" of homelessness is the direct and predictable result of changes in government programs and legislation. ... At CERA we believe that it is important to apply a human rights framework to these violations of fundamental human rights by governments. ... The *Canadian Charter of Rights and Freedoms* guarantees the right to "security of the person" and protection from discriminatory policies that fail to address the needs of disadvantaged groups. Ontario's *Human Rights Code* guarantees equality to groups such as single mothers, social assistance recipients and youth, who are increasingly denied access

to housing. CERA believes it is time for those who are denied adequate housing in Ontario and across Canada to claim these fundamental rights.

> *—Centre for Equality Rights in Accommodation, "Challenging Homelessness and Poverty as Human Rights Violations: An Update on CERA's Test Case Litigation," Winter 2002; www.equalityrights.org/cera/docs/tcupdate.rtf*

I believe that Canadians have serious doubts about claims of widespread poverty in this country. Skepticism is wholly justified. These estimates of the extent of poverty in Canada are grossly exaggerated. The fact is that poverty, as it has been traditionally understood, has been virtually eliminated. It is simply not a major problem in Canada.

> *—Christopher A. Sarlo,* Poverty in Canada *(2nd ed.), Chapter 1: Introduction. Vancouver: The Fraser Institute, 1992, 1996; http://oldfraser.lexi.net/publications/books/poverty/chapter_1.html*

The challenge of finding ways to raise the minimum wage here in Ontario and across the country to a wage above the poverty line is an important part ... [of] lessening poverty and inequality. A society that cannot pay people who work full time all year a wage above the poverty line—i.e. a living wage—cannot make any claims to being either just or fair.

> *Christopher Schenk,* From Poverty Wages to a Living Wage. *Toronto: The CSJ Foundation for Research and Education/Ontario Federation of Labour, November 2001, pp. 11–12*

Being homeless in Canada doesn't mean just being denied the right to an adequate standard of living, it also means being denied the right to life. ...

The roots of the current housing and homelessness crisis in Ontario can be traced to a distinct shift in policy by the federal and provincial governments... . "Since 1984, the national and provincial governments have cut funding, programs, and legislative protections at the lowest-income households," said the Toronto Disaster Relief Committee report. "In addition, these governments have deliberately and consistently refused to take action when presented with evidence of the lethal impact of their policies on the maintenance of life itself."...

Meanwhile, activists and observers warn that without a substantial shift in public policy, Canada will continue to be a human rights offender.

> *—Mira Oberman, "Human Rights Hypocrites?"* The Varsity *(University of Toronto), September 27, 1999*

In *Gosselin v. Quebec (Attorney General)*, the first case to consider whether governments have positive obligations under Canada's Charter to ensure adequate financial assistance for food, clothing, housing, and other necessities, the majority of the Supreme Court left the critical question formally undecided.

> The Court was deeply divided on the evidence in the case, with four of nine judges finding that a dramatically lower rate of assistance available prior to 1989 for employable singles not enrolled in workfare or training programs had profound effects on the dignity of recipients such as Louise Gosselin. Justice Louise Arbour, supported by retiring Justice L'Heureux-Dubé, wrote a strong dissent [disagreement], finding that the right to adequate food, clothing, housing, and other necessities recognized as central to international human rights is a component of the right to "life, liberty and security of the person" in section 7 of the Charter.
>
> Justice Arbour finds positive obligations to address poverty and homelessness clear from both the architecture and the wording of the Charter.
>
> —*Charter Committee on Poverty Issues, "Press Release:* Gosselin *Decision from Supreme Court," December 19, 2002; www.povnet.org/press_releases/ccpi_gosselin.htm*

Questions

1. Summarize the grounds offered for claiming that freedom from hunger and homelessness is a human right.
2. Given the direction provided in the *Universal Declaration of Human Rights* and the *Canadian Charter of Rights and Freedoms*, for what reasons might the Supreme Court of Canada not have been able to make a clear ruling on Canadians' right to freedom from hunger and homelessness?
3. Should governments be obligated to protect citizens from hunger and homelessness? Prepare a one-page argument to answer this question.
4. Research the case of Louise Gosselin, referred to above. Summarize her argument to the Supreme Court and the Court's decision.

Human Rights and the *Canadian Charter of Rights and Freedoms*

Many human rights complaints involve equality rights, and that is the focus of this section of the chapter. Although the *Canadian Charter of Rights and Freedoms* was discussed in Chapter 5, equality rights are highlighted here, since many human rights issues deal with various forms of discrimination and with equality rights.

Since s. 15 of the Charter came into effect on April 17, 1985, the right to equality has become a fundamental principle of Canadian law. Groups and individuals use equality rights in order to guarantee that their diverse needs are accommodated before and under the law. It should be noted that the guarantee of equality rights is a human right extended to "individuals"; compare this with the legal rights sections of the Charter (ss. 7–14; see the Appendix), where the term "everyone" is often used. Clearly, s. 15 does not apply to corporations.

The Law *Canadian Charter of Rights and Freedoms*, s. 15:

(1) Every individual is equal before and under the law and has the right to the equal protection and equal benefit of the law without discrimination and, in particular, without discrimination based on race, national or ethnic origin, colour, religion, sex, age or mental or physical disability.
(2) Subsection (1) does not preclude any law, program or activity that has as its object the amelioration [improvement] of conditions of disadvantaged individuals or groups including those that are disadvantaged because of race, national or ethnic origin, colour, religion, sex, age or mental or physical disability.

Questions

1. In your own words, what does s. 15 of the Charter guarantee?
2. Why have these particular groups been singled out for protection?
3. What is the significance of the words "in particular"?
4. What is guaranteed or recognized under s. 15(2)?

What Is Equality?

For an equality rights glossary, visit www.emp.ca/dimensionsoflaw

There is no definition of "equality" acceptable to everyone; it lacks precision more than any of the Charter's other rights and freedoms. Equality is an evolving concept that our courts continue to define and reinterpret. Traditionally and historically in Western societies, it was believed that only certain people had equality rights—landowners and adult males. Over time, this changed to a belief that equality meant treating all individuals similarly or equally, regardless of circumstances. That is, if you treat similar people in a similar manner ("treating likes alike"), then you cannot be accused of discrimination. This is "equality before the law." ("Equality under the law" refers to the substance of the law itself.)

However, equality may not mean identical treatment. Treating all persons equally without recognizing their different needs may lead to discrimination. Laws that seem fair may violate equality principles if they have a negative impact on individuals on the basis of the grounds listed in s. 15(1) of the Charter. Indeed, the principles of equality may require that individuals receive distinctive treatment, in order to provide "equal protection and benefit of the law." A publication of the Ontario Human Rights Commission states that "in some cases, *same treatment* will lead to *unequal results* while *different treatment* will sometimes be required to accomplish an *equality of results*."

Enumerated and Analogous Grounds of Discrimination

Section 15 enumerates (lists) grounds of discrimination that, according to a decision from the Supreme Court of Canada, "reflect the most common and probably the most socially destructive and historically practised bases of discrimination and must, in the words of section 15(1), receive special treatment." These enumerated grounds have been linked to disadvantage or oppression in Canadian society and around the world. But these grounds are not exclusive—that is, there are other grounds of discrimination.

Our courts have determined that the basic goal of s. 15 is to protect human dignity by ensuring that lawmakers view all people, right from the beginning, as being of equal value and worth and as full and equal participants in Canadian society. Thus, since 1985, the Supreme Court of Canada has identified analogous (similar) grounds to those formally enumerated in s. 15(1). These analogous grounds that warrant protection include marital status, off-reserve Aboriginal band member status, and sexual orientation. According to Canada's Court Challenges Program (a national non-profit organization set up in 1994 to provide financial assistance for important court cases that advance language and equality rights under Canada's constitution), to decide whether a personal characteristic is an enumerated or analogous ground of discrimination, the court will ask some of the following questions:

- Does the ground of discrimination describe a group that has experienced and/or is now experiencing social, legal, or economic disadvantage?
- Does it describe a group that is vulnerable to prejudice or stereotyping?
- Is this group vulnerable to being mistreated or having its needs/conditions overlooked?
- Is this group being prevented from participating fully in society?
- Is this group a minority community within the broader society?

For details on the Court Challenges Program, visit www.emp.ca/dimensionsoflaw

A "yes" answer is not required to all these questions to determine that discrimination exists.

Deciding an Equality Case

It is impossible to prove an infringement of s. 15(1) of the Charter without first proving discrimination. The Supreme Court of Canada has developed guidelines for determining whether an action offends s. 15. These guidelines involve asking the following questions:

1. Does the action deny an equal benefit or impose an unequal burden on an individual or group?
2. Is the action discriminatory? An action will be discriminatory only if it is made on the basis of an enumerated or analogous ground.
3. Is the action discriminatory on the facts of the case?

For example, does the decision of a provincial medical services commission not to provide sign language interpretation for deaf patients in hospitals and medical clinics unjustifiably infringe the equality rights of deaf persons? The "equality before the law" theorists would say "no," because all persons receive the same treatment with the same care and the same doctors. But the "equal protection and benefit of the law" theorists would disagree. If deaf patients cannot understand or communicate properly with their doctors, then those patients are not receiving the full protection and equal benefit of the law. Thus, to ensure full equality, such patients must have the services of a sign language interpreter to improve their health care conditions.

After answering the questions that determine whether an equality claim exists, the government is given a chance to defend its policy or law, based on s. 1 of the Charter, as being "reasonable in a free and democratic society." The following landmark judgment from the Supreme Court of Canada is an excellent example of this process.

Case EQUALITY RIGHTS AND SEXUAL ORIENTATION

Vriend v. Alberta, [1998] 1 SCR 493

Facts

Delwin Vriend worked as a lab co-coordinator at King's College, a private Christian college, in Edmonton and was given permanent, full-time employment in 1988. During his time at the college, he was given positive evaluations, salary increases, and promotions based on his work performance. In 1990, the college found out that Vriend was homosexual; shortly afterwards, he was asked to resign. He refused, and his employment was terminated. The reason given for this termination was his non-compliance with the college's policy on homosexual practices. Vriend tried to be reinstated but was refused.

He attempted to file a complaint with the Alberta Human Rights Commission, but was told that he could not because Alberta's *Individual's Rights Protection Act* (IRPA) did not include sexual orientation as a protected ground. Vriend, along with other appellants, filed a motion in the Alberta Court of Queen's Bench; the trial judge found that the omission of sexual orientation as a protected ground against discrimination violated s. 15(1) of the Charter. The trial judge ordered that the words "sexual orientation" be read into the IRPA as a prohibited ground of discrimination.

To learn more about the *Vriend* case and gay rights, visit www.emp.ca/dimensionsoflaw

The government of Alberta appealed this decision. The majority of the Court of Appeal sided with the Alberta government that the omission of sexual orientation in the IRPA was not a s. 15(1) violation, and the lower court ruling was overturned. Vriend's appeal of this decision to the Supreme Court of Canada was heard in November 1997, and the judgment was released in April 1998.

Issue

Was the omission of sexual orientation from Alberta's IRPA an infringement of equality rights under s. 15 of the Charter?

Decision

The Supreme Court ruled that the Charter did apply to the IRPA and concluded that the omission of sexual orientation as a protected ground violated s. 15(1) because it created a distinction between heterosexuals and homosexuals:

> The deliberate exclusion of sexual orientation, considered in the context of social reality to discriminate against gays and lesbians, clearly has a disproportionate impact on them as opposed to heterosexuals. This, in turn, denies significant equality to the former group. ... The Alberta provincial human rights legislation creates a distinction which results in the denial of the equal benefit and protection of the law on the basis of sexual orientation, a personal characteristic which is analogous to those enumerated in section 15(1). This, in itself, is sufficient to conclude that discrimination is present, and that there is a violation of section 15.

Once the Court determined that there had been a violation of s. 15, the justices had to determine whether or not the infringement could be justified under s. 1. They found that the omission of sexual orientation "constitutes total, not minimal, impairment." As a result, the Court found that the government of Alberta failed to demonstrate that there was a reasonable basis for excluding sexual orientation from the IRPA. Since the infringement could not be upheld under s. 1, the Court then had to consider an appropriate remedy.

Figure 6.8 *Delwin Vriend (right) and his partner Andrew Gagnon leave the Supreme Court during a break in Vriend's case.*

The written decision of the Court noted that the infringement in this case arose from an omission in the legislation, and thus to "read down" or "strike down" the legislation would not be a suitable remedy. Instead, the Court concluded that "reading sexual orientation into the impugned [challenged] provision of the IRPA is the most appropriate way of remedying this underinclusive legislation."

Questions

1. Summarize the facts in this case.
2. Do you agree that the omission of sexual orientation violated s. 15 of the Charter? Why or why not?
3. Do you agree with the Court's remedy of "reading in" sexual orientation to the IRPA? Why or why not?
4. Do you feel that the courts should take an active role in changing legislation, or should this be left up to our elected representatives? Defend your position.

Thus, the Supreme Court ruled that the deliberate exclusion of sexual orientation resulted in serious discriminatory effects, including denial of access to remedial procedures and psychological harm from the implicit message that gays and lesbians were not worthy of protection under Alberta's IRPA. Such legislation most definitely infringed equality rights under the Charter and could not be saved under s. 1.

Fyi Nearly all provincial and territorial governments have legislated "sexual orientation" into their respective human rights codes. Quebec has done so since 1977, Ontario since 1986.

An example of a different infringement of equality rights occurred in British Columbia. In June 2003, in *Trociuk v. BC (Attorney General)*, a father secured a victory for paternity rights from the Supreme Court of Canada when the Court ruled unanimously that BC's *Vital Statistics Act*, which allows single mothers the right to decide on their children's surname, was discriminatory and violated his Charter equality rights. When the children's mother registered their births, she marked the father as "unacknowledged by the mother." Darrell Trociuk had visitation rights and paid monthly support for his children, and he wanted them to have hyphenated surnames. The BC Director of Vital Statistics refused him, and the BC Supreme Court and the Court of Appeal, in a majority judgment, dismissed his claim. However, the Supreme Court of Canada ruled in Trociuk's favour, agreeing that this was discrimination based on sex and could not be saved by s. 1 of the Charter. The Court gave the BC government 12 months to change the law and bring it into line with the constitution.

In order to achieve equality, legislators have recognized that, to assist disadvantaged groups to overcome discriminatory practices, it may sometimes be necessary to devise special programs—for example, s. 15(2) of the Charter and s. 14 of the OHRC. Without these sections, affirmative action programs (discussed in greater detail in Chapter 7: Majority and Minority Rights) would constantly be challenged in courts as examples of discrimination.

CAREER PROFILE

The Honourable Madam Justice Maryka Omatsu
Ontario Court of Justice

Maryka Omatsu became a lawyer in the 1970s when very few Canadian women—let alone women of Asian descent—were practising criminal law. But her efforts soon earned the trust of clients in several high-profile cases. Her best-known victory led to government compensation for Japanese-Canadians who were held in detention camps, stripped of their possessions, and forced to relocate or even emigrate during and after World War II. In 1993, Ms. Omatsu became the first Asian Canadian woman appointed to the bench (sworn as a judge).

Q. Why do you have to be a lawyer before becoming a judge?

A. Actually, it is not that way everywhere. In Europe and in Japan, you can actually start out as a judge, by studying, being accepted, and serving an apprenticeship period. Here, you have to be a lawyer for 10 years first. Canadian law incorporates so much information. Our law is huge and growing, and increasingly specialized. You almost have to practise law to absorb and be able to apply it.

Q. What aspect of your work is the most challenging?

A. Being even-handed and fair to all of the parties—victim, accused, the lawyers—within the context of the large volume of cases we handle, and within the "box" of the law. Sentencing is very challenging, also.

Q. What do you mean by the "box"?

A. The scope of a judge's decision is confined not only by the law, but also by factors like the rules of evidence. In a criminal case, the amount of evidence you get to hear is closely restricted to protect the rights of the accused.

Q. Which personal qualities are key to being a good judge?

A. I mentioned even-handedness before, but another important one is the ability to listen. A friend of mine once said that while lawyers make a career out of talking, becoming a judge means learning to keep your mouth shut. I can even see it in my personal life—I listen more now, and speak less.

Q. As a lawyer, you used law for social justice, and to enforce individual rights. Now that you are a judge, are there similar opportunities to work for change?

A. Yes. About five years ago, I established a "mediation court." It is a separate process that is appropriate for less serious cases, especially involving parties such as neighbours who have an ongoing relationship. The victim actually speaks about how the crime has affected him or her, and the accused (who must admit fault to participate) tells his or her side, apologizes, and makes reparations (for example, by paying for property damage). Cases handled in this way are often healing for everyone—the accused learns about the impact of the crime on the victim, and the victim gets to articulate his or her feelings. The degree of victim satisfaction in these cases is much higher than in a traditional trial.

Check Your Understanding

1. To whom does s. 15 of the Charter apply? To whom does it not apply?
2. Why is there no definition of "equality" that is acceptable to everyone?
3. Explain the meaning of this statement in the OHRC: "In some cases, same treatment will lead to unequal results while different treatment will sometimes be required to accomplish an equality of results." Do you agree? Explain.
4. With examples, distinguish between enumerated and analogous grounds of discrimination.
5. What guidelines did the Supreme Court of Canada develop to prove that an infringement of s. 15(1) might exist?
6. Why was *Vriend v. Alberta* a landmark judgment?
7. What was the significance of *Trociuk v. BC (Attorney General)*?

Methods of *Legal Inquiry*

Determining Factual Relevance

A case is a kind of story about past events in which the judge who conducts the trial writes a decision that summarizes the facts, notes "the law," and then comes to a conclusion about who is right and wrong, or whether a person is guilty or not guilty by applying the law to the facts. Which facts are relevant—that is, essential to the judge's decision—and which are not? This question is best answered by examining an actual case. Here is a brief summary of the *Eaton* case.

Eaton v. Brant County Board of Education, [1997] 1 SCR 241

Facts

Emily Eaton, a 12-year-old girl with cerebral palsy, was unable to communicate through speech, sign language, or otherwise. Emily had some visual impairment, and her mobility was also impaired; she had to use a wheelchair, but could use a walker for short distances. Before starting kindergarten, Emily was recognized by the Identification, Placement and Review Committee (IPRC) of the Brant County Board of Education as an "exceptional pupil" under Ontario's *Education Act*. However, at her parents' request, Emily was placed in her local public school in a regular classroom with a full-time educational assistant. Three years later, Emily's teachers and assistants concluded that this arrangement was not in Emily's best interests and might cause her harm. They recommended that Emily be placed in a special education class.

Emily's parents unsuccessfully appealed the IPRC's decision through a local tribunal, a provincial Special Education Tribunal, and a provincial court. However, on a further appeal in 1995, the Ontario Court of Appeal allowed the appeal and set aside the tribunal's order. The court held that s. 8(3) of the *Education Act*, which deals with identification programs and special education programs and services, infringed Emily's equality rights under s. 15 of the Charter. The court concluded that the

Charter implied a presumption in favour of integration and that s. 8(3) should be read to include a direction that, unless the parents of a disabled child consent to the placement of that child in a segregated environment, the school board must provide a placement that is the least exclusionary from the mainstream and is still reasonably capable of meeting the child's special needs. The school board appealed this decision to the Supreme Court of Canada. The Court released its decision in February 1997.

Figure 6.9 *Carol and Clayton Eaton look over some school work with daughter, Emily.*

Issue

Did the school board's decision to place Emily in a special education class violate her equality rights under s. 15 of the Charter?

Which facts in this story are relevant or essential to the case? One way to summarize the relevant facts is to answer the "how, when, where, and why" questions as if you were writing the synopsis of a television program for a TV guide. If you have a doubt whether any particular fact is relevant, ask yourself whether the absence or presence of that fact (an event, a person, or an action) would have changed the Court's decision. If the answer is no, then the fact is not relevant.

Decision

In the *Eaton* case, the Supreme Court of Canada reversed the Court of Appeal's decision. The Court observed that disability, as a prohibited ground of discrimination, differs from other grounds such as race, because of the vastly different circumstances of each individual:

> Avoidance of discrimination on the ground of physical and mental disability will frequently require distinctions to be made taking into account the actual personal characteristics of disabled persons. ... While integration should be recognized as the norm ... because of the benefits it generally provides, a presumption in favour of integrated schooling would work to the disadvantage of pupils who require special education in order to achieve equality. Integration can be either a benefit or a burden depending on whether the individual can profit from the advantages that integration provides.

The Court concluded that Emily's special needs had been carefully and thoroughly considered by the special education tribunals and that their actions had not violated her equality rights:

> To reach the conclusion that Emily's best possible placement was in the special class, they had balanced her various educational interests appropriately, taking into account her special needs. ... The integration of Emily had produced the counterproductive effect of isolating her, of segregating her in the theoretically integrated setting. ... It

seems incongruous that a decision reached after such an approach could be considered a burden or a disadvantage imposed on a child.

Finally, the Court held that decisions involving the welfare of disabled children ought to be made on a case-by-case basis and should consider the best interests of the individual child. The appropriate accommodations for an exceptional child are determined from a child-centred approach and not from the perspective of the adults in her life.

Once you know the Court's reasoning, you have a very good idea as to what is and is not relevant. Based on the Court's decision, the following facts were not relevant:

- Emily's age and gender.
- When the IPRC review was conducted.
- The length of time between the original placement and the conclusion by Emily's teachers and assistants that the placement was not in her best interests.

These facts are interesting and paint a fuller picture of the case, but they are not relevant to the Court's reasoning or decision. As a result, they can be ignored in the same way that you can ignore facts about Emily's parents, such as where they work or how long they have been employed.

Applying the Skill

1. What is the test for determining whether a fact is relevant?
2. Using the technique of writing a synopsis of a television program, list the facts from a recent event reported in the newspaper. Prioritize the facts into the categories of "very relevant" and "less relevant."
3. The concept of relevance requires judges to ignore many factors in a case, such as the financial position of the parties or their past behaviour. What are the advantages and disadvantages to ignoring these facts about the parties to a lawsuit?

Reviewing Main Ideas

You Decide!

EQUALITY RIGHTS AND SIGN LANGUAGE INTERPRETATION

Eldridge v. British Columbia (Attorney General), [1997] 3 SCR 624

This case involved an appeal to the Supreme Court of Canada concerning three deaf appellants and their claim that the BC public health system failed to provide sign language interpretation in their dealings with hospitals, medical appointments, and doctors. The appellants had been unsuccessful in the BC Supreme Court, and a majority of the BC Court of Appeal dismissed an appeal of the trial judgment.

Facts

Each of the appellants, Robin Eldridge and Linda and John Warren, was born deaf; their preferred means of communication was sign language. Robin Eldridge suffers from several medical conditions, including diabetes. The medical personnel whom she sees don't know sign language. When she had surgery in hospital, she hired an interpreter. She would continue to do this for important medical appointments, but she could not afford an interpreter for every visit.

Although Linda and John Warren planned to hire an interpreter for the birth of their twin daughters, they were unable to do so owing to lack of time due to the girls' premature birth. During the birth, the nurse communicated to Linda through gestures that the heartbeat of one of the babies had slowed. After the babies were born, they were immediately taken from Linda, and other than writing a note that they were "fine," no one explained their condition to her.

At trial in the BC Supreme Court, Eldridge and the Warrens argued that the absence of sign language interpreters compromised the accuracy of the information they received, that this was very frustrating, and that their equality rights were infringed. The trial judge dismissed their application, stating that the Charter does not require governments to implement programs to assist disabled persons. In a majority decision, the BC Court of Appeal held that the lack of interpreting services in hospitals is not discriminatory because the *Hospital Insurance Act* does not provide "any benefit of the law" within the meaning of s. 15(1) of the Charter, and the absence of interpreters results not from the legislation but rather from each hospital's budgetary discretion.

The appellants then took their case to the Supreme Court of Canada.

The Law

The BC *Hospital Insurance Act* funds hospitals for the medically required services that they provide to the public. Funding for medically required services delivered by doctors and other health practitioners is provided by the province's Medical Services Plan, established by the *Medical and Health Care Services Act* (now the *Medicare Protection Act*). Neither program pays for sign language interpretation for the deaf.

However, s. 15 of the Charter guarantees equality rights and the equal protection and equal benefit of the law without discrimination.

Arguments of Eldridge and the Warrens (Appellants)

The appellants argued that the provincial health insurance plan did not cover sign language interpretation for the deaf. Because of this, they were unable to communicate effectively with their doctors and other health care providers, and this increased the risk of misdiagnosis and ineffective treatment. In Linda Warren's case, difficulties in communication occurred during the premature birth of twin daughters and, without an interpreter, she found the birth process difficult to understand and frightening.

The appellants contended that the failure to provide sign language interpreters as an insured benefit under the Medical Services Plan violated their s. 15 Charter rights "to equal benefit of the law without discrimination." They argued that if deaf patients cannot understand or communicate effectively with their doctors, they are not receiving the full and equal benefit of medical care.

Arguments of the BC Government (Respondent)

Government lawyers argued that the government does not provide any services directly. It pays for medical services provided by medical practitioners on a fee-for-service basis. Although the BC Medical Service Plan covers most health services, some services are not included, or are only partly funded. These include such services as occupational and speech therapists, clinical psychologists, and nutritional counsellors. As well, the Ministry of Health allots lump-sum payments to hospitals that they are, for the most part, free to allocate as they see fit; hospitals are seldom ordered to provide specific services. Furthermore, it would be too difficult to bring in interpreters on short notice, and it was far too expensive to have sign interpreters available 24 hours a day. Finally, the government argued that discrimination did not, in fact, exist—all patients received the same care by the same doctors.

Make Your Decision

1. What were the key facts in this case?
2. With which argument do you agree, and why?
3. Does the Charter apply to a non-governmental institution, such as a hospital, performing a "governmental action"? Why or why not?
4. Dismiss or grant the appeal, and provide reasons for your decision.

Key Terms

Review the following terms to show that you understand the meaning of each and how it is applied in a legal context.

balance of probabilities
bona fide
discrimination
human rights
internment
ombudsman
prejudice
stereotyping
undue hardship

Understanding the Law

Review the following pieces of legislation mentioned in the chapter, and show that you understand the intent of each.

Canadian Charter of Rights and Freedoms, s. 15
Canadian Human Rights Act
Emergencies Act
Ontario *Human Rights Code*
War Measures Act

Thinking and Inquiry

1. Give one example each of *stereotype, prejudice,* and *discrimination.* Explain how these three terms are connected. How does human rights legislation relate to these terms?
2. In a small group, examine each of the following scenarios and explain how you would respond. Take into account the appropriate laws.
   a) The vice-principal and another staff member search your locker.
   b) You work at a local fast-food restaurant and the other employees are constantly telling racist jokes and making sexually explicit comments.
   c) You see the family from the apartment next to yours parking their car in a "wheelchair users only" spot.
   d) Your friend's mother is not given a job because the manager of the company claims that "this is a man's job."
   e) You overhear a group of tow-truck drivers laughing about how "the Chinese" are their best customers.
3. Use your library resource centre and the Internet to obtain more information about human rights legislation in another country. Find out how human rights are protected and enforced; include the types of prohibited grounds of discrimination. Conclude with a discussion on how Canada's human rights legislation compares with that of the country you selected. What factors might account for the differences in the methods for protecting human rights?
4. Research a group that has organized to lobby for changes in Canadians' human rights protection. Produce a short report in which you identify the group's
   a) origin and purpose
   b) focus on human rights
   c) actions that have been taken to protect human rights.

Communication

5. Working with a partner or in a small group, interview a person who was born before 1978 (the year the *Canadian Human Rights Act* came into force). Ask him or her how Canadian society has changed in the decades since the Act was passed. Summarize your interview in a posterboard format. Set up the classroom with the displays, and visit each display to find out about the various perspectives given. Share your impressions with the class.
6. Interview someone in your school who is familiar with IPRC procedures. Determine the Ministry of Education's requirements and your school board's implementation of those policies. Before conducting your interview, in small groups, formulate questions to ask. Discuss the *Eaton v. Brant County Board* case with the person you interview and ask his or her opinion of the Supreme Court's decision. After your interview, prepare a report for the class on equality rights in your school board.
7. Survey your school's neighbourhood to note possible human rights violations in your area. (Are major retail areas and your school accessible to wheelchair users? Is there parking for handicapped drivers? Are elevator buttons in Braille for blind persons? Are visible minorities represented throughout the workforce? etc.) Prepare a report to share with the class.
8. Your school is holding a Human Rights Day, and your class has been asked to develop and present an assembly and related displays highlighting significant events in the area of human rights in Canada over the past 50 to 100 years. Choose a group (for example, women, same-sex partners, disabled persons, immigrants) and prepare a presentation using PowerPoint if available, posterboard displays, and other vehicles to illustrate the information you have obtained concerning the protection of human rights as it relates to the group you researched.

Application

9. Use the Internet or news reports to locate a recent human rights case. Find the full case report, if possible, by visiting the Web site of the appropriate court or human rights commission. Present the case to the class using the format followed in this textbook ("Facts," "Issues," "Decision," and "Questions"). You are responsible for leading the class in a discussion of the case you researched.
10. Visit the Web site of the Ontario Human Rights Commission and research the procedures for making a complaint about possible discrimination, or locate an actual human rights case. Then, in small groups, role-play and present this information to the class.
11. Over five million Canadians live in poverty. What are the federal and provincial or territorial governments doing to combat this problem? What can you and your classmates do? Use the Internet to research government action, and brainstorm to determine what actions you and your peers can take.

Chapter 7 Majority and Minority Rights

CHAPTER *Focus*

In this chapter, you will

- understand the conflicts between rights and freedoms and between minority and majority rights in a democratic society
- assess historical and contemporary examples of conflicts between minority and majority rights, such as the Quebec sovereignty debate, Aboriginal land claims, and affirmative action programs
- demonstrate an understanding of the difficulty of balancing rights in a democracy
- evaluate the available political and legal avenues, such as courts, tribunals, and referenda, for resolving these conflicts

As a society, we constantly seek to protect the interests of those in minority positions in our country. This is a difficult task. For example, Canada is largely a nation of immigrants, and our indigenous peoples represent only a small percentage of our overall population; also, many Quebeckers feel that their French language, culture, and heritage are threatened in a sea of English-speaking people. Although all Canadians are entitled to equal treatment, winning equality for some groups has been a battle. This chapter examines three important areas in which the balance between majority and minority rights warrants special attention: the French–English conflict, Aboriginal land claims, and the rights of disabled and challenged persons.

Figure 7.1 offers a commentary on the first of these issues.

Figure 7.1

At First Glance

1. What symbols are represented in this cartoon?
2. What message is the cartoonist conveying?
3. How reflective is this cartoon of Quebec's current relationship with Canada? Explain your answer.
4. Does this cartoon deliver an effective message? Why or why not?

The French–English Conflict

Canada has had a long history of trying to balance the rights of its English-speaking and French-speaking populations. With the fall of New France in 1759, the British chose to accommodate the needs and rights of the French-speaking Roman Catholic majority. As the British proportion of the population grew in the years after the American Revolution, **francophones** became a smaller percentage of the population. By Confederation in 1867, the French were a minority in Canada, but their language was protected under the terms of Confederation in s. 93 of the constitution.

francophone: in a bilingual country, a person whose principal language is French

anglophone: in a bilingual country, a person whose principal language is English

The relationship between the francophones in Quebec and **anglophone** Canadians has not always been harmonious. Conflicts have arisen throughout our history over the protection of the French language and culture, and over differing visions of the country's future. In Ontario in 1911, for example, the government prohibited French-language schools; this assault on the French language created controversy. Similarly, the imposition of conscription (the compulsory enlistment of people in the armed forces) during World War I led to riots in Quebec. During World War II, the country experienced another conscription crisis that split the nation's English- and French-speaking populations. The most serious challenges, however, came after 1960.

Fyi The French *Civil Code* (as opposed to English common law) was and is still used in the province of Quebec.

Quebec's Quiet Revolution, 1960–1966

The Quiet Revolution refers to the period of social, cultural, and political upheaval that occurred in Quebec between 1960 and 1966, when the province moved from being isolationist, politically influenced by the Roman Catholic clergy, and rural-focused, into an open and industrialized society under the leadership of Liberal Premier Jean Lesage. Prior to the Quiet Revolution, an anglophone minority controlled the major leadership positions in Quebec's business and industry. Although about 80 percent of Quebeckers listed French as their first language, English was still the main language of business. To be successful, French-speaking Quebeckers had to be fluently bilingual.

The francophone population quietly began to resist the prevailing English economic and social dominance. They wanted equal partnership with English Canada, but a partnership in which Quebec would determine its own role and fate, ensuring the survival of the French language and culture.

During this period, the provincial Liberals enacted several policies to help French-speaking Quebeckers become "maîtres chez nous," that is, "masters in our own house." Many new government departments, including the first provincial Department of Cultural Affairs, were created. As well, the political and social influence of the Roman Catholic church began to decline. Federal efforts to make Quebec an integrated part of Canada continued with the election of Pierre Trudeau as prime minister in 1968. His vision of a bilingual Canada in which French and English would hold equal stature was reflected in Parliament's passage of the *Official Languages Act* in 1969, which required all federal government services to be delivered in both languages.

Separatism

separatism: the desire to establish a politically independent Quebec and to withdraw from Confederation

sovereignty-association: the concept put forth by the Parti Québécois government of René Lévesque, whereby Quebec would become a sovereign jurisdiction in all areas of law making, but would maintain economic association with the rest of Canada

federalism: Canada's form of political organization in which the federal government governs the country as a whole, while the provinces and territories have specific, limited powers

During the 1960s, many Quebeckers increasingly questioned their province's role within Confederation. **Separatism**, however, meant different things to different groups of Quebeckers. For some, it meant total independence as a political state and the severing of all ties with the federal government and the rest of Canada. For others, it meant **sovereignty-association** in a limited partnership with Canada. Yet others believed, as Trudeau did, that **federalism**—a strong federal government with supporting provincial governments—was the best system for Canada; each level of government would provide a check on the use and misuse of power by the other.

In the 1966 Quebec provincial election, the Liberal government was defeated by a revitalized Union Nationale party. However, the separatist movement gained strength and importance in Canadian politics with the formation in 1968 of the Parti Québécois (PQ) under the leadership of René Lévesque. By 1973, the PQ was the official opposition in Quebec. Pressure increased for legislation to preserve the French character of Quebec, and in 1974, Liberal Premier Robert Bourassa introduced the *Quebec Official Languages Act* (Bill 22). It proclaimed French as the only official language in Quebec and promoted the teaching of French in English schools. The bill also restricted the admission of immigrant children into English schools unless they could pass an English language test. Yet, for many Quebeckers, Bill 22 fell short of requiring French to be the language of instruction and everyday use for all Quebec citizens.

Bill 101

After the 1976 provincial election, the victorious Parti Québécois government led by René Lévesque passed Bill 101, the *Charter of the French*

Figure 7.2 *A Quebec war veteran demonstrates against the passage of Bill 101, January 1982.*

Learn one historian's view of the development of language laws to protect the French language in Quebec at www.emp.ca/dimensionsoflaw

Language, one of the most radical pieces of language legislation ever seen in Canada. From the perspective of the PQ, this legislation was necessary to address longstanding inequities between francophones and anglophones in Quebec. Because Quebec is the only predominantly French-speaking society in North America, the PQ believed it had to impose these language restraints by law to ensure the survival of the French language and French culture. French became the official language not just for government, but for most facets of public life. For example, under Bill 101, all companies in Quebec with 50 or more employees had to conduct business mainly in French, and employees in all industries were to be addressed in French by their employers. Companies were given four years to comply, and required a "Francization" certificate to prove that they were working toward these goals.

The Sign Law

One of the most controversial sections of Bill 101 prohibited the use of English on commercial and road signs. Government arguments in defence of this provision held that

- the use of other languages on signs would marginalize the French language in Quebec
- immigrants to Quebec would recognize the predominantly French character of the province
- French would be preserved as Quebec's official language.

Fyi About one million people in Quebec identify themselves as part of the English-speaking community.

Critics of Bill 101 suggested a lack of solid evidence for the first argument, and a slight to the intelligence of immigrants in the second. As to the third argument, critics felt that the bill ignored the gains that the French language had already made in Quebec (and in Canada as a whole) from the federal government's recognition of two official languages in Canada.

Court challenges to Bill 101 have occurred since the passage of the *Canadian Charter of Rights and Freedoms* in 1982. One of the most significant cases was *Ford v. Quebec* (see below). In response to the Supreme Court's landmark judgment, Quebec Premier Robert Bourassa invoked the Charter's notwithstanding clause. As you saw in Chapter 5, by making use of s. 33 of the Charter, the original law concerning the use of French only on signs could not be struck down.

For background on language rights in Quebec, visit www.emp.ca/dimensionsoflaw

Bill 101 has been amended several times since its passage. In the early 1990s, amendments to the sections relating to signage permitted the limited use of languages other than French on commercial signs. A further modification in 1993 allowed English to appear on outdoor signs as long as French was predominant.

Case THE SIGN LAW CONTROVERSY

Ford v. Quebec (Attorney General), [1988] 2 SCR 712

Facts

Valerie Ford was one of five retailers who, in 1984, challenged the validity of two sections of Bill 101 (the *Charter of the French Language*). Ford carried on business under the company name of Les Lainages du Petit Mouton Enr. Since 1981, she had displayed an exterior sign that said LAINEWOOL (*laine* is French for wool). Under Bill 101, public signs, posters, and commercial advertising were required to be in French only. Moreover, only the French version of a company's name could be used. Bill 101, however, did permit bilingual signs where health and safety were concerned. Ford had been informed by the Language Commission that her sign did not conform to the provisions and that she was to change it. She challenged the validity of the law on the basis that it infringed on her freedom of expression, guaranteed by s. 2(b) of the *Canadian Charter of Rights and Freedoms* and by s. 3 of the *Quebec Charter of Human Rights and Freedoms.*

Ford and the other retailers were successful at trial. The Quebec Attorney General appealed this decision to the Quebec Court of Appeal, where the trial judgment was unanimously affirmed, and sections of Bill 101 were declared of no force or effect. The Quebec Attorney General appealed this decision to the Supreme Court of Canada.

Issues

Did Bill 101's sign law violate Ford's freedom of expression? Does freedom of expression include the freedom to express oneself in the language of one's choice?

Decision

In a unanimous decision, the Supreme Court of Canada ruled that two sections of Bill 101 were invalid. The Court found that, while the province was justified in requiring the use of French, it was not justified in prohibiting the use of other languages. Both sections challenged were found to infringe on s. 3 of the *Quebec Charter of Human Rights and Freedoms*, and the provision concerning the use of the French language in signs and commercial advertising was found to infringe on the right to freedom of expression guaranteed by the *Canadian Charter of Rights and Freedoms*. In its ruling, the Supreme Court of Canada stated that "freedom of expression" includes the freedom to express oneself in the language of one's choice. The evidence presented by the Attorney General of Quebec did not demonstrate that the requirement of the exclusive use of French was either necessary for the achievement of the legislative purpose or proportionate to it. Hence, the two sections of Bill 101 could not be saved by s. 1 of the Charter. Although Bill 101 had a very significant objective, it was unnecessary to ban all languages other than French from signs.

Questions

1. Outline the basic conflict in this case.
2. Why was this case a landmark judgment?
3. Do commercial speech and expression deserve legal protection? Why or why not?
4. Do you think there still is a need for Bill 101 in the 21st century? Why or why not?

Access to Schools

Although Bill 101 had enormous implications for all of Quebec, allophones (people whose principal language is neither English nor French) were most affected by it. Under Bill 101, their children could no longer attend English schools. The Bill reversed the longstanding tradition of children of anglophone and allophone immigrants being able to attend English schools. Only children who were born in Quebec and used English as their first language could attend English schools. This limiting of access to English schools resulted in an enrolment drop of nearly 50 percent between 1976 and 1990 and the closing of several hundred English schools.

Turning Points in the Law

Bill 101 and the Protection of the French Language in Quebec

Quebec nationalists were thrilled and proud of their government's strong action to protect the French language. On the other hand, an immediate result was the withdrawal of numerous anglophone and American-based head offices from Montreal to Toronto; their working language, English, conflicted with the requirements of Bill 101. In addition, it was necessary for everyone in the Quebec workforce to be able to speak and write French, or risk losing their jobs. An estimated 100 000 Quebec anglophones and immigrants left to settle elsewhere in Canada. The language legislation, so important to the PQ government, had a major negative impact on the provincial economy. Because Canadian and multinational corporations were reluctant to invest in the province, Quebec's unemployment rate increased substantially.

Bill 101 was regarded as a major and significant victory by Quebec nationalists because it had a wide-ranging impact on Quebec society. However, anglophone Quebeckers condemned the legislation, and it aroused anger and hostility in much of English-speaking Canada. The aspects of Bill 101 that so offended English Canada and new immigrants to Quebec included

- making French the official language ("Francization")
- requiring the exclusive use of French on signs
- requiring new immigrants to send their children to French-language schools
- requiring all children to attend French-language schools unless their families were born in Quebec and spoke English as their first language.

But from the perspective of the province's struggle to protect French language rights, Bill 101 remained an important symbol of Quebec's resolve to maintain French as a strong, viable language on a North American continent that is predominantly English-speaking.

Questions

1. Why was Bill 101 a turning point in the law?
2. What were the most controversial elements of Bill 101?
3. What were the immediate results of the passage of Bill 101?

Check Your Understanding

1. How was the French language protected in Confederation and in the Canadian constitution?
2. What was the significance of the federal *Official Languages Act*, 1969?
3. What was the significance of the *Quebec Official Languages Act*?
4. Why were many Quebeckers disappointed with the *Quebec Official Languages Act*?
5. Why did the Parti Québécois government feel that Bill 101 was necessary?
6. Some commentators think Bill 101 may, in the long run, undermine the aims of the separatists. Do you agree? Why or why not?

The Sovereignty Issue

Between 1980 and 2003, the controversy over Quebec's role in Canada did not abate. There are four critical and significant events in these years that must be highlighted: the sovereignty referenda of 1980 and 1995; the *Clarity Act*, in which the federal government set forth terms for any future referenda on provincial sovereignty; and the subsequent shift toward "cooperative federalism."

The Quebec Referendum: Round One

The Quebec government set May 20, 1980, as the date for a promised referendum on Quebec's future within Canada. The Lévesque government campaigned for sovereignty-association; that is, Quebec would acquire the exclusive power to make laws, levy taxes, and establish relations abroad—all powers of a sovereign state—while maintaining an economic association with Canada (including a common currency). Prime Minister Pierre Trudeau appointed his Minister of Justice, Jean Chrétien, to coordinate the federalist position, emphasizing the economic costs of separation to Quebeckers. Emotions in this debate ran high. Not only in Quebec but all across Canada, hundreds of thousands of Canadians signed petitions proclaiming, "We Love You, Quebec."

The question asked of Quebeckers in the referendum was:

> The Government of Quebec has made public its proposal to negotiate a new agreement with the rest of Canada, based on the equality of nations; this agreement would enable Quebec to acquire the exclusive power to make its laws, levy its taxes and establish relations abroad—in other words, sovereignty—and at the same time to maintain with Canada an economic association including a common currency; no change in political status

Figure 7.3 *René Lévesque reacts to news of defeat in the 1980 Quebec referendum.*

> resulting from these negotiations will be effected without approval by the people through another referendum; on these terms, do you give the Government of Quebec the mandate to negotiate the proposed agreement between Quebec and Canada?

Voter turnout on May 20 slightly exceeded 80 percent. When the ballots were all counted, nearly 60 percent had voted "non" to separation. This was a stunning defeat for René Lévesque and his PQ government.

Patriation and Beyond

Backed by the referendum result, Prime Minister Trudeau now turned his passion and energy to his long-time goal, patriation of the Canadian constitution. As you read in Chapter 2, the provinces could not come to an agreement. In late 1981, Trudeau and the provincial premiers met in Ottawa for one last attempt at reaching consensus. After four days of heated debate and ultimate compromise, an agreement was reached among nine provinces, excluding Quebec. On April 17, 1982, the constitution was patriated despite Lévesque's strong objections. He and many Quebeckers saw this action as one more betrayal of Quebec by the rest of Canada.

Chapter 4 outlined two further attempts to end Quebec's isolation and to recognize the province as a distinct society because of its language and culture. But, as you learned, both attempts—the Meech Lake Accord and the Charlottetown Accord—failed.

To learn more about the second Quebec referendum, visit www.emp.ca/dimensionsoflaw

The Quebec Referendum: Round Two

The 1994 Quebec election brought Jacques Parizeau, a long-time nationalist and new leader of the PQ, to power. He took this electoral victory as a mandate for a second referendum. Federalists again argued the economic costs of separation, and the Aboriginal peoples in Quebec, especially the Cree,

Figure 7.4 *"Yes" supporters cheer during a speech by Bloc Québécois leader Lucien Bouchard a few days before the referendum vote on October 30, 1995.*

opposed separation because they were not certain that they could remain part of Canada if Quebec seceded. The question asked in this referendum was:

> Do you agree that Quebec should become sovereign after having made a formal offer to Canada for a new economic and political partnership within the scope of the bill respecting the future of Quebec and of the agreement signed on June 12, 1995?

On October 30, 1995, over 90 percent of eligible voters in Quebec turned out. This vote was much closer than in 1980: 50.6 percent voted "non"; 49.4 percent voted "oui." Sovereignty had been rejected once again, but by an extremely narrow margin. Part of the federal government's response to this slim majority included efforts to convince Quebeckers that life in a separate Quebec would be difficult and costly—Quebeckers would not have, among other benefits, a common currency with the rest of Canada, or the use of Canadian passports. The federal Parliament then passed a resolution recognizing Quebec as a distinct society in Canada.

Figure 7.5 *Jean Charest, at the time the leader of the federal Progressive Conservative Party, flashes his Canadian passport at a pre-referendum rally, asking Quebeckers if they want to lose the benefits of Canadian citizenship.*

The *Clarity Act*, 2000

In 1996, the federal government referred a series of questions to the Supreme Court of Canada asking the Court's advice on whether Quebec had the legal authority to secede from Canada unilaterally. On August 20, 1998, the Supreme Court ruled that Quebec could not secede without consulting the rest of Canada. This ruling seemed a victory for the federal government. However, the Court also stated that Ottawa would have to negotiate with Quebec in good faith if a "clear majority" voted in favour of secession in response to a "clear question." This qualification pleased the separatists. (The reference to "clear question" should be seen in the light of evidence that some Quebeckers had not understood the implications of the questions asked in the previous referenda.) But the Court did not define what a "clear majority" was. It merely stated: "It is for the political actors to determine what would constitute a clear majority on a clear question in the circumstances under which a future referendum vote may be taken."

For more information on the *Clarity Act*, go to www.emp.ca/dimensionsoflaw

Wanting to have a framework and process in place if Quebec (or any other province) sought to secede from Canada, Jean Chrétien's Liberal government tabled Bill C-20 (the *Clarity Act*) on December 13, 1999. This Act outlined the rules and conditions to be met should the Canadian government enter into negotiations following a referendum that could lead to the break-up of Canada. It set out the principles and procedures that would guide Parliament in determining what would constitute a sufficiently clear question and a clear majority.

The Law Selected sections of the *Clarity Act*:

NOW, THEREFORE, Her Majesty, by and with the advice and consent of the Senate and House of Commons of Canada, enacts as follows:

1(1) The House of Commons shall, within thirty days after the government of a province tables in its legislative assembly or otherwise officially releases the question that it intends to submit to its voters in a referendum relating to the proposed secession of the province from Canada, consider the question and, by resolution, set out its determination on whether the question is clear. ...

(3) In considering the clarity of a referendum question, the House of Commons shall consider whether the question would result in a clear expression of the will of the population of a province on whether the province should cease to be part of Canada and become an independent state.

(4) For the purpose of subsection (3), a clear expression of the will of the population of a province that the province cease to be part of Canada could not result from

(a) a referendum question that merely focuses on a mandate to negotiate without soliciting a direct expression of the will of the population of that province on whether the province should cease to be part of Canada; or

(b) a referendum question that envisages other possibilities in addition to the secession of the province from Canada, such as economic or political arrangements with Canada, that obscure a direct expression of the will of the population of that province on whether the province should cease to be part of Canada. ...

2(2) In considering whether there has been a clear expression of a will by a clear majority of the population of a province that the province cease to be part of Canada, the House of Commons shall take into account

(a) the size of the majority of valid votes cast in favour of the secessionist option;

(b) the percentage of eligible voters voting in the referendum; and

(c) any other matters or circumstances it considers to be relevant.

Fyi Section 2(2)(a) of the *Clarity Act* refers to "valid votes" because some of the 86 000 votes rejected in the 1995 referendum may in fact have been valid but not counted by overly zealous scrutineers.

Questions

1. Why does the *Clarity Act* emphasize a "clear question"? What do you think a clearly worded question would be?
2. Why did the federal government think this Act was needed?
3. Within what period of time must Parliament decide whether a province's referendum question is clear?
4. What factors must the House of Commons consider about referendum results before entering negotiations?
5. Should 51 percent be considered a sufficient majority for Ottawa to begin secession negotiations with a province? Why or why not? If not, what percentage would you recommend, and why?

Cooperative Federalism

With the election of Jean Charest and his Liberal Party in Quebec in 2003, the thinking on Quebec's role in Canada and sovereignty versus federalism changed and entered a much less combative stage. For the first time in many years, Quebec had a federalist-leaning premier. In 2002, a committee of Quebec's Liberal Party issued a report, "Quebec: Affirmation, Autonomy and Leadership," which called for a revived spirit of cooperative federalism. Ideas in this report have been advanced as a basis for reopening the constitutional debate. The report recognized that a federal Canada is the necessary key constitutional component. But it also stated that Quebec, and other provinces, must be able to make cross-border or cross-global dealings as part of a North American and global economy.

At a First Ministers' conference held in Charlottetown in July 2003, Premier Charest proposed a Council of the Federation. This permanent committee of the federal and provincial governments would coordinate major policies affecting Canada, the provinces, and the territories. This proposal was unanimously endorsed by all in attendance and will be implemented over the next several years. (For more information on the Council of the Federation, see Methods of Legal Inquiry in Chapter 4, pages 123–124.)

Fyi Jean Charest resigned as leader of the federal Progressive Conservative Party in 1998 to become leader of the Quebec Liberal Party. He gained a high profile as an anti-separatist during the 1995 referendum campaign.

CHECK YOUR UNDERSTANDING

1. What was the major difference between the 1980 and the 1995 Quebec referenda?
2. In its 1988 decision in *Ford v. Quebec*, how did the decision of the Supreme Court of Canada help both sides of the sovereignty debate?
3. Who joined the 1995 sovereignty debate, and what were their positions?
4. Why do you think more Quebeckers voted "oui" in the 1995 referendum than in the 1980 referendum?
5. What was the purpose of the *Clarity Act*? In your opinion, was this Act necessary? Explain your answer.
6. What is the purpose of the Council of the Federation?
7. Why might the post-2003 period be a positive and calming time in Quebec–Ottawa relations?

Aboriginal Rights

When questions of **Aboriginal rights** are addressed, discussions generally focus on the **collective rights** of the people, rather than on individual rights and freedoms. Aboriginal peoples argue that their collective rights come from having occupied the land that is now Canada for thousands of years as distinct nations. These collective rights concern the right to self-government and control and use of land. Over one million people of Aboriginal ancestry live in Canada today. They are divided into 12 distinct language families and are further separated into 50 different linguistic groupings.

Aboriginal rights: rights that some Aboriginal peoples of Canada hold as a result of their ancestors' longstanding use of the land. Aboriginal rights vary from group to group depending on the customs, practices, and traditions that have formed part of these distinct cultures

collective rights: rights acquired as a result of membership in a group; all members of the group share the same rights

Aboriginal–European Relations

As you saw in Chapter 2, Canada's Aboriginal peoples had well-established communities with traditions and social structures when European settlers came to Canada. Although a detailed history of Aboriginal–European relations is beyond the scope of this text, a brief background is necessary in order to understand many of today's Aboriginal concerns and claims.

The French and British were eager to gain the cooperation of the Aboriginal peoples in the pursuit of economic ventures and their support as military allies. Historically, the Mi'kmaq had allied themselves with the French, but formed a new alliance with the British and signed the *Peace and Friendship Treaty* on March 10, 1760. This **treaty** was not a land treaty but rather one of mutual protection and support. In exchange for agreeing to keep the peace and to respect British law, the Mi'kmaq were promised that they could fish and hunt, and continue their customs and religious practices. They could also trade with the British for food, clothing, blankets, and gunpowder and shot in "truckhouses" (approved trading posts). In 1762, the British replaced the expensive truckhouses with licensed traders, and then discontinued the system of licensed traders in the 1780s. Together, the 1760 treaty and trading procedures played a key role in a controversial landmark Supreme Court of Canada judgment, *R v. Marshall*, discussed later in this chapter.

treaty: a formal agreement between two autonomous entities to conduct themselves in certain ways or to do certain things

Then, in 1763, at the end of the Seven Years' War between France and Britain, the *Treaty of Paris* was signed. The days of New France were over, and the French were required to relinquish their claims to all land in North America. A few months later, King George III issued the *Royal Proclamation of 1763*.

Aboriginal Treaties

To learn more about Aboriginal treaties, law, and land claims, visit www.emp.ca/dimensionsoflaw

The *Royal Proclamation of 1763* recognized Aboriginal peoples as autonomous political units or nations and established the framework for future treaties. It declared that

- Aboriginal peoples were entitled to lands in their possession until or unless they gave or traded them away
- no one could purchase or settle on land recognized as Aboriginal territory with the exception of the British Crown, which served as the only agent for transferring land between Aboriginal peoples and settlers.

The belief was that Aboriginal lands would, therefore, be safe from any efforts to cheat indigenous peoples out of their land. This proclamation has been called the "Magna Carta of Aboriginal rights" and has been held by the courts to have the force of a statute that has never been repealed. It remains fundamental even today to any discussion of Aboriginal rights, land claims, and Aboriginal law in Canada as it is referenced in s. 25 of the *Canadian Charter of Rights and Freedoms.*

In 1867, after Confederation and the *British North America Act*, which gave the federal government authority over "Indians and lands reserved for Indians" in s. 91(24), this federal authority was codified in 1876 with the passage of the *Indian Act*. But Aboriginal peoples were not included in the formulation of the Act, a statute that did not recognize Aboriginal self-government. Subsequent treaties had the effect of peacefully removing Aboriginal peoples from their lands in order to provide settlement areas for a flood of European immigrants. In exchange for giving up their lands, Aboriginal peoples were to have exclusive use of some land, set aside as reserves, and other benefits. However, it is likely that the Aboriginal peoples did not fully comprehend the implications of these land treaties.

The official government policy that began in 1830 and continued during this post-Confederation period was assimilation (absorption) of Aboriginal peoples into the broader Canadian society. The government believed

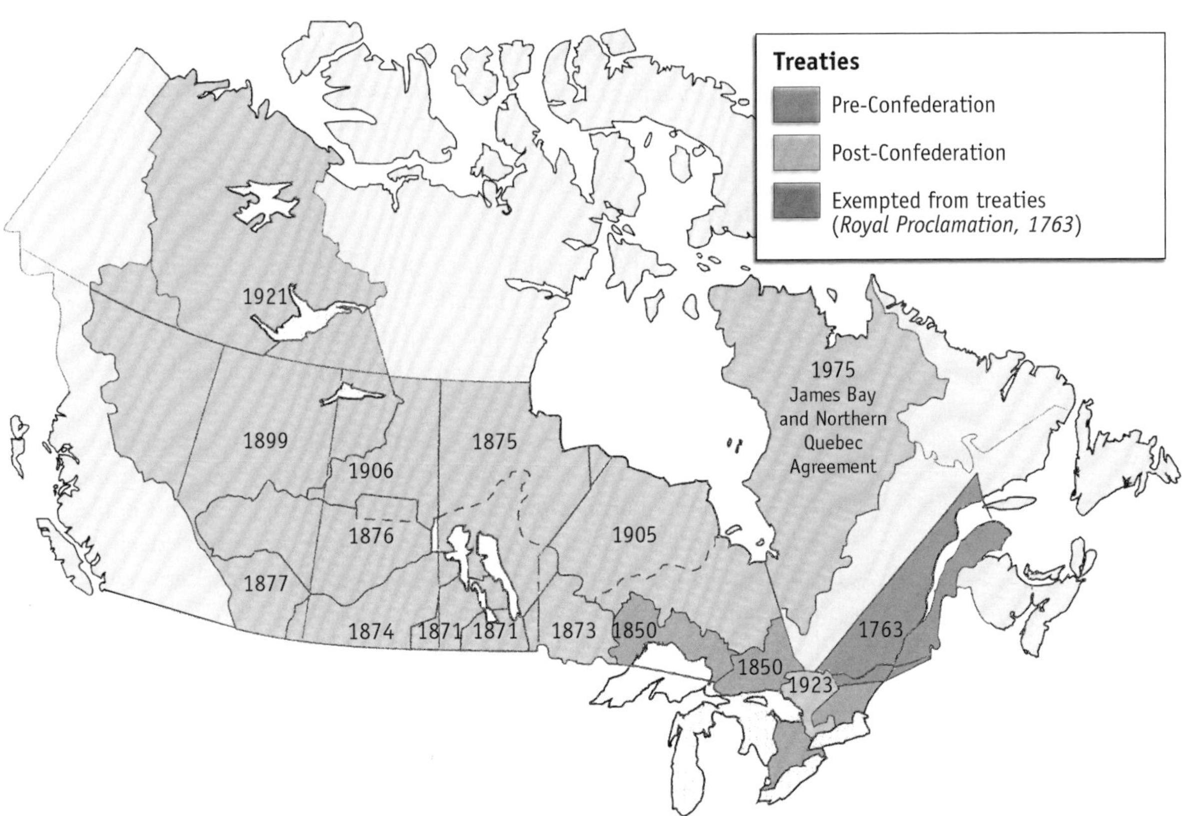

Figure 7.6 *Treaties signed with Aboriginal peoples, pre-Confederation to 1975. Which major areas were not covered by treaty arrangements?*

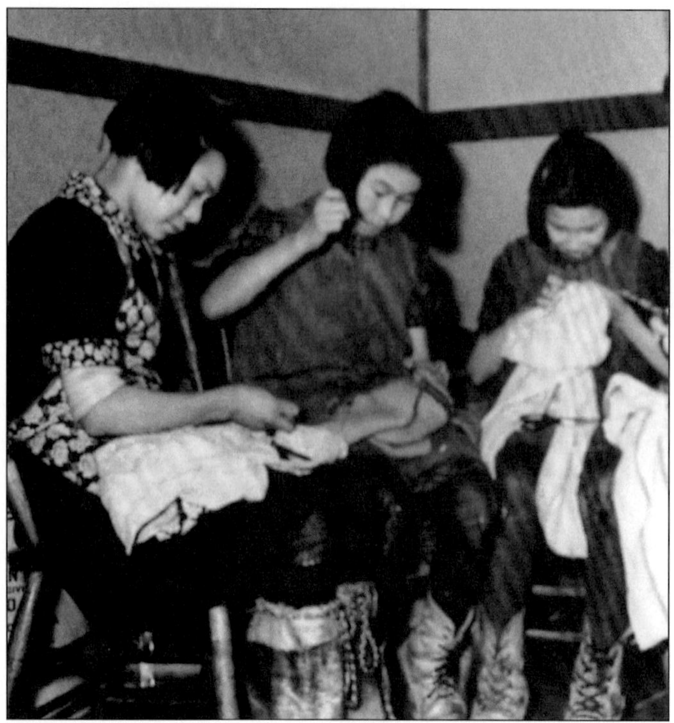

Figure 7.7 *Aboriginal girls learn sewing at St. Phillip's School, Fort George, Quebec, in the 1930s.*

that the Aboriginal peoples were dying out from diseases introduced by the new settlers and that their future lay in assimilation. The theory was to provide Aboriginals with Euro-Canadian cultural and social ways so that they could successfully adapt to the changing times. For example, children were removed from their villages and housed in church-run residential schools, where they were forced to speak English and behave in "European" ways. Among the negative effects of this policy were a staggering number of incidents of physical and sexual abuse of Aboriginal children in these schools. Currently, these abuses are the basis of numerous legal actions and private compensation packages between former abused residents and church hierarchies. Aboriginal people have described the life experienced by their children in these schools, and the negative effects on the children and Aboriginal communities, as **cultural genocide**.

cultural genocide: deliberate and systematic destruction of the culture, traditions, language, and customs of a specific cultural group

The *Indian Act*

Prior to passage of the *Indian Act* in 1876, tribal bands followed their own forms of self-government and made decisions for their people. All of this changed with the advent of the Act. It defined who was "Indian," and imposed major changes in the way Aboriginal chiefs and their councils could be elected and could operate.

The Act also "protected" Aboriginal lands by appointing non-Aboriginal agents to be responsible for executing the Act's conditions; these agents were authority figures, financial managers, and enforcers of the law. Thirdly, the Act gave the authority to make final decisions over health care, social services, and education to the federal government. All other Canadians have these services provided by provincial governments.

Another section of the *Indian Act* dictated that it was illegal for Aboriginals to manufacture, possess, or sell liquor, and that they could be arrested if found in an intoxicated state. Other Canadians had no such restrictions. As you saw in Chapter 5 (page 131), a challenge to this section of the *Indian Act* provided the first test of the strength of the 1960 *Bill of Rights*: the landmark *Drybones* case questioned the meaning of "equality before the law."

Case ABORIGINAL RIGHTS VERSUS THE *BILL OF RIGHTS*

R v. Drybones, [1970] SCR 282

Facts

Joseph Drybones, an Aboriginal, was found intoxicated on the premises of the Old Stope Hotel in Yellowknife, Northwest Territories (NWT). The charge against him read: "On or about the eighth day of April, 1967, at Yellowknife, [he] being an Aboriginal, was unlawfully intoxicated off a reserve, contrary to section 94(b) of the *Indian Act*, a federal statute."

Section 94 of the *Indian Act* stated:

> 94. An Indian who
> (a) has intoxicants in his possession,
> (b) is intoxicated, or
> (c) makes or manufactures intoxicants off a reserve,
> is guilty of an offence and is liable on summary conviction to a fine of not less than ten dollars, and not more than fifty dollars or to imprisonment for a term not exceeding three months or to both fine and imprisonment.

The important issue raised in this case was that in the NWT it was not an offence for anyone except an Aboriginal to be intoxicated in a non-public place. Because there were no reserves in the territories within the meaning of the *Indian Act*, an Aboriginal could be found to be intoxicated anywhere, even in his own home. A non-Aboriginal, however, could be convicted only under the *Liquor Ordinance Act* for being intoxicated in a "public place." Also, unlike s. 94 of the *Indian Act*, the *Liquor Ordinance Act* made no provision for a minimum fine; the maximum term of imprisonment was only 30 days.

Decision

Drybones, who spoke no English, pleaded guilty and was sentenced to the minimum fine of $10 plus costs or, in default of payment, three days in jail. Drybones appealed his conviction to the Territorial Court of the NWT on the ground that it violated his right to equality under the law in s. 1(b) of the *Bill of Rights*, and was acquitted. The Crown then appealed the acquittal to the NWT Court of Appeal, where it was dismissed. The Crown then further appealed this decision to the Supreme Court of Canada. In a 6–3 judgment, the Court declared s. 94(b) of the *Indian Act* invalid and acquitted Drybones. In this case, the *Bill of Rights* was given its first formal recognition by the courts.

Fyi Under the *Indian Act,* Aboriginal women who married non-Aboriginal men lost their Indian status. Aboriginal men who married non-Aboriginal women kept their status and passed Indian status along to their children. A non-Aboriginal woman who married a status Indian automatically gained her husband's status.

To find out more about the Assembly of First Nations, go to www.emp.ca/dimensionsoflaw

Fyi On July 16, 2003, Phil Fontaine was elected National Grand Chief of the AFN. Second-place runner-up was Roberta Jamieson. Jamieson was Canada's first female Aboriginal lawyer and was Ontario ombudsman for 10 years.

Questions

1. Why was this a landmark judgment?
2. Outline the reasons that this case concerned questions of Aboriginal rights rather than unlawful behaviour by an individual.
3. Review the section on the *Bill of Rights* in Chapter 5, pages 129–131, and explain how it relates to this case.

The *Drybones* case was the first legal test of the *Bill of Rights,* and courts gave the Bill its first formal recognition. With this case, only one portion of a federal statute, s. 94 of the *Indian Act,* was rendered inoperative by the *Bill of Rights.* Two years later, another section of the *Indian Act* that covered the status of Aboriginal women who married non-Aboriginal men was challenged in *Canada v. Lavell,* but in a 5–4 decision, the Supreme Court of Canada rejected the challenge.

Aboriginal leaders were resentful of the government's administration of the *Indian Act.* For example, there were instances where reserve land was sold or leased by Indian Affairs agents without the approval of local bands. Aboriginal peoples struggled for involvement in constitutional discussions and for input to the *Indian Act,* which controlled much of their lives. Leaders began to press governments on Aboriginal rights. A lobby group, the National Indian Brotherhood (NIB), was formed in the 1960s to give voice to their concerns. This group's name was changed in 1982 to the Assembly of First Nations (AFN). It has become a very visible and vocal organization on such concerns as treaty rights, social development, and housing, justice, and health issues for the over 600 First Nations across Canada.

The 1969 White Paper

In the late 1960s, the federal government still expected the Aboriginal peoples to assimilate fully into Canadian life. Meanwhile, Aboriginal communities were concerned about their unique status as peoples and with securing rights to the land that once belonged to them.

In 1969, the government released a White Paper for discussion on the importance of individual human rights over collective rights. The government proposed to repeal the *Indian Act* and amend the *British North America Act* to end the distinction between Aboriginal peoples and other Canadians. This move would bring Aboriginal peoples into mainstream Canada and would treat them as individuals, not communities. But they would also lose compensation for the surrender of their ancestral lands. And they would be subject to provincial laws and no longer be a federal responsibility.

Aboriginal leaders vigorously opposed the White Paper and the government's continuing attempt at their assimilation. A high-profile leader at that time, Harold Cardinal, argued that in spite of its flaws, the *Indian*

Act still gave Aboriginal peoples a strong sense of community. Opposition to the White Paper was so intense and hostile that the government withdrew the proposal in 1971.

CHECK YOUR UNDERSTANDING

1. How diversified is Canada's Aboriginal population? Give examples.
2. What was the significance of the 1760 *Peace and Friendship Treaty*?
3. Why was the *Royal Proclamation of 1763* called the "Magna Carta of Aboriginal rights"? List its major features.
4. Outline the major highlights of the *Indian Act*.
5. What is the Assembly of First Nations?
6. Why did the federal government withdraw its White Paper in 1971?

To learn more about the Nisga'a Agreement, visit www.emp.ca/dimensionsoflaw

Aboriginal Land Claims

In recent decades, various Aboriginal groups have attempted to establish control over their traditional lands based on the argument that the land still belongs to them because title to it was never extinguished. This reasoning held especially true in British Columbia, where treaties had not been negotiated. Non-treaty Aboriginal peoples believe that they have a legal right to the land because past governments never enacted specific legislation to eliminate Aboriginal title to it. The settlement of **land claims** has become an ongoing major cause of dispute between Aboriginal peoples and both levels of government. An evolving understanding of human rights and pressure from lobby groups combined to produce a crucial turning point for Aboriginal rights in 1973.

land claims: formal demands made by Aboriginal peoples for ownership and control of lands on which they live or have traditionally lived

Turning Points in the Law

Aboriginal Title to the Land: The Nisga'a Claim

The Nisga'a people of British Columbia have always felt strongly about their ties to the land. As far back as 1887 they protested the loss of their ancestral lands to outsiders, and in 1913 they sent a petition to the Privy Council of Great Britain seeking to resolve the land question. Over the years, the Nisga'a kept raising the question of "Indian title" in spite of formidable odds, including a law that prevented them from raising money in support of land claims. By the middle of the 20th century, opinions in society had become more tolerant, and the Nisga'a were able to launch a lawsuit that transformed Indian land policy in this country. In 1968, the Nisga'a Tribal Council began litigation in the BC Supreme Court; this case was known as the *Calder* case, named after Frank Calder, Nisga'a chief at the time.

In 1973, in its decision in *Calder v. Attorney General of British Columbia*, six out of seven Supreme Court justices supported the view that English law—in force in British Columbia when colonization began—had recognized Aboriginal title to the land. In support of the Nisga'a,

Mr. Justice Hall wrote: "What emerged from the ... evidence is that the Nishgas [common spelling of name at the time] in fact are and were from time immemorial a distinctive cultural entity with concepts of ownership indigenous to their culture and capable of articulation under the common law." This case affirmed that Aboriginal title, as a legal concept, exists in Canada.

The minority Liberal federal government was in a difficult position: opposition parties were pressing it to settle Aboriginal claims. In 1973, the government announced a land claims policy that established a process for negotiating Aboriginal land claims. The Nisga'a entered into negotiations with the federal government. The government's goal was to replace undefined Aboriginal rights with a clearly defined package of rights and benefits that were set out in settlement agreements. The BC provincial government, however, was less willing to recognize the Nisga'a claim, and it was not until 1991 that it created the BC Treaty Commission. In August 1998, the Nisga'a, the provincial government, and the federal government reached a final agreement.

Questions

1. Why was the 1973 *Calder* case significant in spite of the fact that it did not resolve the Nisga'a claim?
2. In what ways did the federal political situation affect Aboriginal land claims in Canada in 1973?
3. In 2001, a newly elected BC Liberal government promised to hold a provincial referendum on the issue of treaty negotiations. Research the outcome of this promise.

Figure 7.8 *Nisga'a Tribal Chief Dr. Joseph Gosnell addresses a crowd after the historic signing of the Nisga'a Agreement in New Aiyansh, BC. The signing culminated more than 100 years of negotiations.*

specific land claims: claims that deal with specific grievances that Aboriginal peoples may have regarding the fulfillment of treaties and administration of lands and assets under the *Indian Act*

Two types of land claims can be brought before Canadian courts. **Specific land claims** apply to Aboriginal groups that have signed treaties but feel that the government has failed to fulfill its obligations under the *Indian Act*. These claims may include such concerns as mineral and timber rights that were improperly or poorly administered by the government, or land that was sold without a band's consent. Specific land claims seek redress for particular problems covered by signed treaties. **Comprehensive land claims** apply when Aboriginal groups have never signed treaties but have lost access to ancestral land and resources. Ownership and use of these lands were assumed without legal justification by the federal or provincial governments, or some other party. These claims invoke negotiation of treaties long overdue.

Land claims usually include demands for full ownership of some lands, rights to harvest natural resources, full participation in resource management efforts, and financial compensation for lost resources. Comprehensive land claims are aimed at ensuring that Aboriginal groups will become economically self-sufficient. Treaties were not signed by Aboriginal groups in a large part of British Columbia, the Atlantic provinces, and much of northern Canada (see Figure 7.6, page 205).

While the process to resolve Aboriginal land claims seems straightforward, land claims have, in fact, proven difficult to settle. Boundaries are often difficult to establish and are frequently subject to disagreement. Also, until 1986, settlement of land claims required the Aboriginal group to agree to the loss of their rights and titles, something they were unwilling to do. In addition, non-Aboriginal Canadians own property in the land-claim areas and have legal title to the land. They resist Aboriginal land settlements that may affect their use of their property. Between 1973 and 2003, only 15 claims had been finalized, while about 70 remained in negotiation.

Criticism has also been levelled at the bureaucracy that exists to deal with comprehensive land uses, to the extent that Canada's Auditor General reported "fundamental issues" with the negotiation process in her 2001 report.

comprehensive land claims: claims based on the recognition that there are continuing Aboriginal rights to lands and natural resources; these claims occur where Aboriginal title has not been previously dealt with by treaty or other means

Fyi In August 2003, the Inuit of Labrador signed an agreement with the federal and provincial governments, creating a 73 000 km^2 area to be governed by the Inuit. The agreement, 25 years in the making, included a one-time payment of $140 million to the Inuit.

Comprehensive Land Claims Agreements as of 2003

Name of Agreement	Area Covered	Year
James Bay and Northern Quebec Agreement	From the shores of James Bay and Hudson Bay to Labrador	1975
Northeastern Quebec Agreement	A large part of northeastern Quebec	1978
Inuvialuit Final Agreement	The islands and part of the mainland along the Beaufort Sea	1984
Gwich'in Agreement	Parts of northern Yukon and northwestern portion of the NWT	1992
Nunavut Land Claims Agreement	Eastern part of NWT, including Baffin Island	1993
Sahtu Dene and Métis Agreement	Northwestern part of the District of Mackenzie	1994
Vuntut Gwich'in First Nation Agreement	Part of Yukon Territory	1995
Teslin Tlingit Council Agreement	Part of Yukon Territory	1995
Champagne and Aishihik First Nation Agreement	Part of Yukon Territory	1995
Na-cho Ny'ak Dun Agreement	Part of Yukon Territory	1995
Little Salmon/Carmacks First Nation Agreement	Part of Yukon Territory	1997
Selkirk First Nation Agreement	Part of Yukon Territory	1997
Tr'ondek Hwech'in First Nation Agreement	Part of Yukon Territory	1998
Nisga'a Agreement	Lower Nass River valley of northwestern British Columbia	2000
Ta'an Kwach'an Council Agreement	Part of Yukon Territory	2002

Figure 7.9 *The comprehensive land claims settled by 2002 have focused on Canada's North.*

Aboriginal Rights and the Charter

Before 1982, Canada's Aboriginal peoples continually lobbied the federal government for involvement in the process of patriation. Inclusion in the constitution would give them recognition as Canada's first citizens and protection for their treaty rights that were being eroded by the federal government. Thus, Aboriginal rights and freedoms were included in s. 25 of the *Canadian Charter of Rights and Freedoms* and in s. 35 of the *Constitution Act, 1982* as a means of resolving some of the problems that had hindered Aboriginal–Crown relationships over the decades.

The Law

From the *Constitution Act, 1982*:

Part I. *Canadian Charter of Rights and Freedoms*

25. The guarantee in this Charter of certain rights and freedoms shall not be construed so as to abrogate or derogate from any aboriginal, treaty or other rights or freedoms that pertain to the aboriginal peoples of Canada including
    (a) any rights or freedoms that have been recognized by the Royal Proclamation of October 7, 1763; and
    (b) any rights or freedoms that now exist by way of land claims agreements or may be so acquired.

Part II. Rights of the Aboriginal Peoples of Canada

35(1) The existing aboriginal and treaty rights of the aboriginal peoples of Canada are hereby recognized and affirmed.

(2) In this Act, "aboriginal peoples of Canada" includes the Indian, Inuit and Métis peoples of Canada.

(3) For greater certainty, in subsection (1) "treaty rights" includes rights that now exist by way of land claims agreements or may be so acquired.

(4) Notwithstanding any other provision of this Act, the aboriginal and treaty rights referred to in subsection (1) are guaranteed equally to male and female persons.

Questions

1. Distinguish between the terms "abrogate" and "derogate."
2. What three groups does s. 35 identify as the "aboriginal peoples of Canada"?
3. To whom are these rights guaranteed?
4. Under what circumstances might the phrase "notwithstanding any other provision of this Act" come into play in dealing with rights?

Section 25 of the Charter makes it clear that other rights in the Charter must not interfere with the rights of Aboriginal peoples. For instance, where Aboriginal peoples are entitled to particular benefits negotiated in their treaties, others who do not have these benefits cannot argue that they have been denied the right to be treated equally. As well, s. 35 recognizes that Aboriginal people were Canada's first citizens and that this early occupation gives them certain rights.

The Charter protects "existing Aboriginal and treaty rights," but these rights are poorly defined and understood. The task of defining Aboriginal rights has passed to Canada's Supreme Court, which has tried to balance those rights with those of the Crown. Through several decisions, the Court has established guidelines that can be used to determine whether an Aboriginal right exists in a particular case and whether the government can restrict that right under any circumstances.

The issue of which rights were "existing" as set out in s. 35 of the *Constitution Act, 1982* was first answered by the Supreme Court of Canada in 1990 in *R v. Sparrow.* At issue was an Aboriginal right to fish salmon with a net for food and for social and ceremonial purposes. Ronald Sparrow was a member of the Musqueam Band. He was charged with exceeding the net length restriction imposed on the band's food fishing licence under British Columbia legislation based on the federal *Fisheries Act.* Sparrow argued that, according to Aboriginal rights, the net length restriction was invalid. In its unanimous decision, the Supreme Court ruled that any person or group claiming an Aboriginal right must prove that a treaty right existed, that he or she was following that right, and that the right had been affected or frustrated by government regulations. If all these conditions could be proven, and if the government still wanted to pursue a legal action, then the government would have to justify the infringement. The Court overturned Sparrow's conviction and ordered a new trial. After this decision, the Crown withdrew charges against Sparrow; thus, there was no retrial.

In 1999, a major decision was reached in *R v. Marshall.* In a 5–2 judgment, the Supreme Court of Canada recognized the constitutionally protected treaty rights of the Mi'kmaq to catch and sell fish. The judgment affirmed the treaty right to earn a "moderate livelihood" from fishing and hunting. However, the Court's minority position felt that once the Mi'kmaq lost the benefit of the truckhouses (see page 204) and gained the right to fish and trade freely like any other inhabitants of the colonies, they also lost the benefit of the treaty-protected right to fish and trade.

To find out more about the fishing dispute at Burnt Church, go to www.emp.ca/dimensionsoflaw

Ongoing disputes between Aboriginal fishers and the federal Department of Fisheries and Oceans (DFO) have developed since the *Marshall* decision. Although the decision involved the catching and selling of eels, the Mi'kmaq have used it as justification for increased activity in the more lucrative lobster fishery. Several Aboriginal groups in the Maritimes and Eastern Quebec immediately began fishing lobster out of season, saying the ruling gave them complete, unregulated fishing rights (this activity led

WORKING FOR CHANGE *Donald Marshall, Jr.*

In 1993, Donald Marshall, Jr. went fishing for eels in Pomquet Harbour, Nova Scotia. The problem was that he did not have a fishing licence and it was not eel season. The Department of Fisheries and Oceans charged him with fishing out of season, fishing without a licence, and selling fish without a licence. Marshall admitted that he had done all these things. But he did not simply accept the results of what appeared to be an open-and-shut case. Instead, he fought the charges all the way to the Supreme Court of Canada.

Marshall is a member of the Mi'kmaq people. He argued that he had the right to fish because of a 1760 treaty giving the Mi'kmaq the right to earn a "moderate living" by fishing and hunting year round without a licence. In 1999, Marshall was acquitted by the Supreme Court, and the 1760 treaty was upheld.

The controversy surrounding the case was enormous. The decision unleashed pent-up tensions among First Nations people, non-Aboriginal people, and the federal and provincial governments. It led to confrontations about who ultimately would control the fishing industry. Tensions were so high that, in a rare move, the Supreme Court issued a follow-up clarification to *R v. Marshall*, known as "Marshall 2." This ruling said that the federal government had the right to regulate Aboriginal fishing for such purposes as conservation, and that the Supreme Court's decision was not to mean that Aboriginal peoples could regulate their own industry, fishing wherever and whenever they wanted.

Bernd Christmas, a Mi'kmaq lawyer, explained the key role that Marshall had played when he stated that "[Donald Marshall] ... has been the catalyst for getting Ottawa to the table to talk about Aboriginal rights in Atlantic Canada."

Figure 7.10 *Donald Marshall's name first came to the attention of Canadians in the early 1980s when it was revealed that, in 1971, he had been wrongfully accused and convicted of murder. He spent 11 years in prison before being exonerated of the crime in 1983. In 1987, a Royal Commission indicated that the criminal justice system had committed serious errors in the case: the police and the justice system had acted in a manner that was unprofessional and incompetent, and racism had played a role in Marshall's conviction.*

Questions

1. What legal precedent was set by the decision of the Supreme Court?
2. Explain why non-Aboriginal fishers and government agencies were disturbed by the Supreme Court's ruling in the *Marshall* case.
3. Did the Court's majority judgment give the Mi'kmaq unlimited opportunities to fish, trade, and accumulate wealth from fishing? Explain.
4. Should a 1760 treaty still be considered valid and binding in the 21st century? Why or why not?
5. In what ways might Marshall's wrongful conviction for murder have been a significant element in the struggle for Aboriginal fishing rights?

to the "Marshall 2" clarification). Non-Aboriginal workers in the fishing industry demanded that the federal government impose limitations and a ban on the catch so that lobster stocks would not be depleted.

By the end of 2002, 30 of the 34 First Nations affected by the *Marshall* decision had reached agreements with the federal government concerning their fishing practices, and the government provided $160 million to help them establish a commercial fishing industry. But in Burnt Church, New Brunswick, an agreement was not reached. Hundreds of Aboriginal lobster traps were destroyed by angry non-Aboriginal fishers, and three fish processing plants were vandalized. The issue was not resolved by federal intervention.

Learn more about the *Marshall* decision and the Maritime Canadian fishery at www.emp.ca/dimensionsoflaw

Control of the Fishing Industry **Do Aboriginal rights mean that non-Aboriginals have limited access to fishing areas?**

The Supreme Court decision in the *Marshall* case resulted in tension and conflict in fishing areas where the Mi'kmaq had a traditional claim. The ruling affirmed the right of Aboriginal peoples to fish when they wanted without a licence. The non-Aboriginal fishing industry cried foul, claiming that it would effectively be shut out of a livelihood and way of life that it had known for hundreds of years. Federal conservation officials worried that their ability to protect fish stock was seriously limited by the decision. Angry voices were heard on all sides, as the following excerpts illustrate.

Aboriginal and non-Aboriginal peoples in the Maritimes feel that the federal government, the RCMP, and the media have let them down. The peaceful co-existence and reconciliation they seek can be achieved only through constructive dialogue and education and only if the federal government is willing to honour and uphold Aboriginal rights. ...

The problem is not that the federal government was unprepared for the *Marshall* decision, but that the federal government is unprepared to recognize Aboriginal rights. Clearly, the government's strategy of stalling to wear down Aboriginal peoples ... is frustrating for Aboriginal peoples who are harvesting natural resources and for [non-Aboriginals] who feel threatened by what appears to be a situation of anarchy. This divisive strategy creates a lack of confidence in Canadian institutions and breeds contempt for the law.

—*Summary of the* Marshall *case, Aboriginal Rights Coalition of British Columbia, 2000; http://members.tripod.com/arcbc/marshall_summary.htm*

[T]his gets into some very complicated stuff but we shouldn't get too abstract in our debate. ... I've just come from the Miramichi, it's a very, very serious business what's going on down there. It's far beyond a local lobster dispute. The communities are upset on both sides. National organizations like the Assembly of First Nations, in a sense, [are] asking the Burnt Church people to carry a struggle that's really a national struggle which is based on ... years and years of national ineptitude with respect to our founding people, and a tiny little Burnt Church community of 1100 people are being asked to carry this on. Relationships between the [inaudible] people and the Burnt Church people in that whole area are breaking down. If you ... were down there for a minute, I'm not sure that you would get into the kind of abstract conversations you want to get into.

> *—Mike Belliveau, Maritime Fishermen's Union, speaking on CBC's* Counterspin, *September 12, 2000; www.afn.ca/Burnt%20Church/cbc_counterspin_burnt_church_dic.htm*

The federal and provincial governments have the authority within their respective legislative fields to regulate the exercise of a treaty right where justified on conservation or other grounds. The *Marshall* judgment referred to the Court's principal pronouncements on the various grounds on which the exercise of treaty rights may be regulated. The paramount regulatory objective is conservation and responsibility for it is placed squarely on the minister responsible and not on the Aboriginal or non-Aboriginal users of the resource. The regulatory authority extends to other compelling and substantial public objectives which may include economic and regional fairness, and recognition of the historical reliance upon, and participation in, the fishery by non-Aboriginal groups.

> *—From the statement of clarification produced by the Supreme Court (also known as "Marshall 2") following the turmoil generated by the* Marshall *decision; cited by Disparities in Law and Power at www.rism.org/isg/dlp/bc/introduction*

Questions

1. From the information presented here, state the positions of the Aboriginal peoples, the non-Aboriginal fishing industry, and government officials.
2. People on both sides of the issue were critical of the federal government's handling of the situation. From your perspective, what should the federal government have done to deal more effectively with the *Marshall* decision? Explain your answer.

On July 28, 2003, a BC judge handed down a landmark decision that is likely to have far-reaching implications for the West Coast's fishing industry. Mr. Justice Kitchen dismissed charges against a group of non-Aboriginal fishers who had challenged Ottawa's Aboriginal Fisheries Strategy (which followed the decision in *R v. Sparrow*) by fishing on a day designated for Aboriginals only. He ruled that Aboriginal-only commercial salmon fisheries are a form of racial discrimination and therefore a violation of the *Canadian Charter of Rights and Freedoms.* In this ruling he cast doubt on the fishing provisions of the Nisga'a Treaty, other proposed West Coast treaties, and Aboriginal fishing provisions for the East Coast.

Fyi In August 2003, the federal government announced that it planned to appeal Justice Kitchen's judgment.

CHECK YOUR UNDERSTANDING

1. Identify some ways in which historical circumstances shaped conditions for Aboriginal peoples in Canada.
2. Distinguish between specific land claims and comprehensive land claims.
3. In what ways are Aboriginal rights the same as those of all Canadians? In what ways are Aboriginal rights different from those of other Canadians?
4. Explain how land claims agreements help to establish Aboriginal rights for the peoples involved.

Affirmative Action

Throughout Canada's history, many groups have been the subject of racial discrimination, either through official, government-supported means, or in a more informal manner through social conditions and traditions. Discrimination against Aboriginal peoples has existed since European contact; slavery was legal in Canada until it was abolished by Britain in 1833; racial groups such as blacks, Japanese, and Chinese have been systematically repressed; and cultural groups such as the Irish have been declared unwanted. In addition, discrimination has occurred because of gender, religion, age, sexual orientation, and physical abilities. The *Canadian Charter of Rights and Freedoms* seeks to guarantee that all people will be treated equally. It also recognizes that discrimination did occur in the past, and that corrective measures are now necessary to ensure equality of opportunity. Such corrective measures are referred to as **affirmative action**, which is another way of dealing with people who have been treated unequally.

affirmative action: a policy designed to increase the representation of groups that have suffered discrimination

Affirmative action programs cannot violate the equality provisions of s. 15(1) of the Charter. Generally, this means that an affirmative action program cannot discriminate on the basis of a prohibited ground. Discrimination is permitted, however, if the program benefits a group that was previously discriminated against. How should governments achieve the equality goals of the Charter? Some suggest that governments should set policies or create laws that treat some individuals and groups more favourably than others. For example, building codes could require facilities such as access ramps and washrooms for wheelchair users, or hiring quotas based on race or gender could be required for public sector agencies.

The Law

From the *Canadian Charter of Rights and Freedoms*:

Equality Rights

15(1) Every individual is equal before and under the law and has the right to the equal protection and equal benefit of the law without discrimination and, in particular, without discrimination based on race, national or ethnic origin, colour, religion, sex, age or mental or physical disability.

(2) Subsection (1) does not preclude any law, program or activity that has as its object the amelioration of conditions of disadvantaged individuals or groups including those that are disadvantaged because of race, national or ethnic origin, colour, religion, sex, age or mental or physical disability.

Questions

1. Specific types of discrimination are listed in s. 15(1). Are there other types of discrimination that you would like to see included in the list? Are there types of discrimination that you think should be deleted from the list? Explain your point of view.
2. What wording in s. 15(2) might lead to problems in interpretation and application? Explain your answer.

Section 15(2) has generated some questions of interpretation. What does equality mean? To some, equality implies a numerical sameness. That is, if a particular group represents 50 percent of the population, then it should represent 50 percent of any particular sector of the government, economy, and so on. Others have rejected this formal equality and have argued that s. 15(2) implies the equality of opportunity: people should have equal access. However, many variables may affect the representation of a particular group in any sector.

Another question raised under s. 15(2) is the meaning of the term "disadvantaged." Most would agree that groups who have been historically under-represented in positions of power and prestige in society have been disadvantaged. The courts have to use historical and sociological studies of Canadian society to determine the degree to which groups have been disadvantaged, and the impact of this discrimination. In many situations the studies are incomplete or inconclusive, or there are significant differences in the interpretation of findings.

Learn more about the ODA Committee at www.emp.ca/dimensionsoflaw

ersonal Viewpoint

David Lepofsky: Fighting for Rights of Ontarians with Disabilities

David Lepofsky is a blind lawyer and Chair of the Ontarians with Disabilities Act Committee, Toronto.

When I studied law in high school, I knew I wanted to be a lawyer and that I had poor vision. I didn't know I'd become totally blind, and that I'd volunteer much of the time outside my day job fighting for the rights of people with disabilities.

As my eyesight worsened, I discovered many unfair barriers that block people with disabilities from fully participating in life. New buses are too often made with steps, creating physical barriers, when accessible buses can be bought. Most Web sites lack simple features that would make them accessible to special computers for blind or dyslexic people. Different kinds of barriers impede people with other physical or mental disabilities.

Removing these barriers would help everyone. Ontario has 1.9 million people with disabilities. Everyone has a disability or gets one later in life. We all should be able to ride public transit, shop in stores, get an education, use our health-care system, and get a job based on [our] abilities, without facing barriers.

In 1980, while finishing lawyer training, I volunteered with disability groups fighting to amend the *Canadian Charter of Rights and Freedoms* and the Ontario *Human Rights Code* to make it illegal to discriminate against people with disabilities. We were excited when grassroots teamwork won us those new legal rights.

Yet by the 1990s, we realized that those important new rights were not enough to achieve a barrier-free society where all people with disabilities can fully participate. A person in a wheelchair who is prevented from entering a store to shop, due to a single step at the doorway, must file a lawsuit, perhaps hire a lawyer, and fight for years. People with disabilities have to fight such barriers one at a time.

I and others decided we needed a new law to achieve a barrier-free society. We named it the *Ontarians with Disabilities Act* (ODA). We launched a grassroots coalition, the ODA Committee, to fight for it. Our Web site shows what we want and how to get involved. We knew that all barriers can't be removed overnight. We wanted the ODA to let everyone know what they must do to become barrier-free and to give organizations reasonable time to act.

In 2001 the Ontario government passed an ODA. It was a first step, but it didn't go far enough. The government left out most ingredients we needed. It lets government organizations like city hall and schools decide what barriers to remove and when, if ever, to remove them. It doesn't make the private sector (stores, restaurants, and other companies) do anything.

Our effort continues. We want the government to fully implement its ODA, and we want the ODA strengthened.

I learned important lessons from this rewarding activity. Everyone can have a huge impact, by volunteering for a cause to improve society.

Questions

1. Using the Internet, locate information on the *Ontarians with Disabilities Act, 2001*. What is its purpose, and to whom does it apply?
2. Why was the ODA Committee disappointed with the Ontario government's legislation passed in 2001?
3. What barriers impede persons with disabilities in your school and community?
4. How would society benefit from removing and preventing these barriers?
5. How could the *Ontarians with Disabilities Act, 2001* be rewritten to be strong and effective?

The Charge of Reverse Discrimination

Affirmative action programs have been controversial. For many people, the treating of some groups more favourably than others in order to rectify historical inequities runs contrary to the principles of free enterprise and democracy. They believe that ability and hard work should be the relevant criteria for determining social and economic rewards in Canadian society. Affirmative action programs and laws are seen as reverse discrimination—the practice of advancing one group's interests by treating everyone else "unfairly."

Another concern about affirmative action programs is that those who receive preferential treatment are not usually those who were originally discriminated against, and those who are at a disadvantage because of affirmative action are not generally those who were responsible for past discrimination. Critics argue that today's middle-class, heterosexual, white males are paying the price in the workforce for attitudes and behaviours of their ancestors toward the poor, homosexuals, non-white races, and women.

Case PRISONERS' RIGHTS

Conway v. The Queen, [1993] 2 SCR 872

Facts

Phillip Conway was an inmate at Collins Bay Penitentiary in Kingston, Ontario, in 1986. He objected to frisk searches (the hand search of a clothed inmate from head to foot) and cell patrols that were conducted by women guards. Conway argued that the cross-gender touching during searches "feels wrong" and that there was opportunity for women guards to see him undressed. He began a court action alleging that the performance of these duties by women violated his rights to security of the person, privacy, and equality. The Federal Court Trial Division held that the frisk searches did not violate the Charter, but that cell patrols were an invasion of male inmates' privacy and therefore violated s. 8 of the Charter. The Federal Court of Appeal ruled that neither practice was unconstitutional. Conway appealed to the Supreme Court.

The case had implications for women because affirmative action programs were in place to increase the number of women working as correctional officers. Simply removing women from male prisons and reassigning them would discriminate against them. The outcome of the case could have had repercussions for other affirmative action programs based on s. 15(2) of the Charter.

Decision

The Supreme Court dismissed Conway's appeal, ruling that frisk searches and cell patrols are practices necessary in a prison for the security of the institution and the safety of inmates. Training of correctional officers ensures that these duties are carried out in a professional manner with regard for the dignity of the inmate. In addition, prisoners should expect a substantially reduced level of privacy while incarcerated.

The Supreme Court went on to comment that its decision in this case did not mean that female prisoners should also be subject to cross-gender searches and surveillance. They argued that the requirement for equality in s. 15(1) of the Charter does not mean identical treatment. Historical, sociological, and biological differences between men and women mean that cross-gender touching is different and more threatening for women than men. The decision states:

> Biologically, a frisk search or surveillance of a man's chest area conducted by a female guard does not implicate the same concerns as the same practice by a male guard in relation to a female inmate. Moreover, women generally occupy a disadvantaged position in society in relation to men.

Questions

1. Summarize the issues and arguments in this case.
2. Why did the Supreme Court dismiss Conway's appeal of earlier decisions?
3. This case is also known as *Weatherall v. The Queen.* The Women's Legal Education and Action Fund (LEAF) intervened in this case because of the implicit equality issues for women. Conduct research to find out the arguments presented by LEAF in this case.

Learn about LEAF at www.emp.ca/ dimensionsoflaw

Check Your Understanding

1. In your own words, explain the rationale for affirmative action programs.
2. What are some of the concerns or criticisms of affirmative action programs?
3. In your view, are affirmative action programs justifiable? Explain your point of view.
4. Suppose you reject the view that affirmative action is justifiable. What are some other strategies or approaches that could be used to rectify the problems of historic discrimination against some groups in society?

METHODS OF *Legal Inquiry*

Dissecting a Statute: The *Ontarians with Disabilities Act, 2001*

Read the *Ontarians with Disabilities Act* at www.emp.ca/dimensionsoflaw

Once a bill is given Royal Assent by the governor general (for federal bills) or the lieutenant governor (for provincial bills), it becomes enacted and is referred to as a statute or act. A statute such as the *Ontarians with Disabilities Act, 2001* ("the Act") is made up of a number of parts, some of which are official and a part of all statutes, and some of which are unofficial. Each part is described briefly below.

Chapter Number

A statute is commonly identified and located by its chapter number. Federal and provincial statutes are given consecutive chapter numbers in the year in which they are enacted. Every 10 to 20 years in most jurisdictions, statutes are consolidated into one publication (called the Revised or Consolidated Statutes), organized alphabetically, and assigned a new chapter number. The Act was passed in 2001 and assigned chapter number 32. Statutes are described as chapters because, historically, all acts of a session of Parliament were considered to be one statute, and chapters were used to distinguish one particular act from another. Today, not only is an act a separate chapter, it is also a separate statute.

Long Title

The long title of a statute usually appears after the chapter number. Because these titles were often too long for purposes of citation, a shorter form was introduced in the 19th century. The long title may be used as an aid to understanding or interpreting a statute where a provision is ambiguous. The long title of the Act is: *An Act to improve the identification, removal and prevention of barriers faced by persons with disabilities and to make related amendments to other Acts.*

Date of Royal Assent

The date of Royal Assent is usually stated after the long title of the statute. The date is important because, unless the statute states otherwise, this is the date on which the statute "comes into force" or becomes effective as a statute. A statute may also come into force on a particular date or on a date to be named by proclamation. Section 33(1) of the Act provides that the Act "comes into force on a day to be named by proclamation of the Lieutenant Governor." The Act received Royal Assent on December 14, 2001, but the government has still not proclaimed into force all of the Act.

Words of Enactment

Words of enactment usually appear after the date of Royal Assent and serve to indicate that Parliament is exercising its royal authority.

Short Title

Both federal and provincial statutes have sections that confer a short title on the statute. Section 34 enacts the short title of the Act as the *Ontarians with Disabilities Act, 2001*.

Definitions

Most statutes contain a definition section at the beginning of the act. Definitions are important, especially where "everyday" words have a different or specific legal meaning in a statute. Section 2(1) of the Act defines such key words as "barrier" and "disability." "Barrier," for example, is defined to include physical and architectural barriers as well as attitudinal and policy barriers.

Parts, Sections, Subsections, and Paragraphs

Every statute is divided into principal units called sections, which are numbered consecutively. Sections may be further divided into subsections, paragraphs, and subparagraphs. (The federal *Income Tax Act* goes beyond subparagraphs to clauses, subclauses, and even sub-subclauses.) Canadian statutes usually indicate subsections by numbers in parentheses, paragraphs by lowercase letters in parentheses, and subparagraphs by roman numerals in parentheses. For example, the requirement of the Act that municipalities consult with persons with disabilities in preparing an accessibility plan as found in s. 11, subsection (1), paragraph (6), subparagraph (ii). A statute may also have larger divisions than sections, called parts. The Act is divided into five parts: three parts deal with the duties of the government of Ontario, municipalities, and "other organizations, agencies and persons," and the other two parts deal with interpretation and general matters.

Marginal Notes

Marginal notes appear alongside the sections of a statute and are designed to provide a summary of each section. Marginal notes are not formal parts of an act and, therefore, may not be used to assist in interpreting it. While these notes are meant to be useful, they can also be misleading. For example, the summary may be inaccurate, or it may summarize only a part of the section, or it may fail to reflect the fact that the section has been changed.

Amendments

Statutes may be amended by subsequent statutes, which follow the same pattern as the main statute. The Act was amended in 2002 by the *Municipal Statute Law Amendment Act, 2002*, c. 17, Schedule c, s. 18. The amended provisions of the principal statute are noted at the end of the section or subsection that has been amended.

Applying the Skill

Dissect a statute from this chapter. Go to www.emp.ca/dimensionsoflaw to locate the respective sites for searching federal and Ontario statutes.

Reviewing Main Ideas

You Decide!

EVIDENCE IN SEXUAL ASSAULT CASES

R v. O'Connor, [1995] 4 SCR 411

This case raises issues related to the fairness of trials when a criminal trial gains notoriety because of the nature of the charges, the parties charged, or any other reason. The accused's constitutional rights to a fair trial must be balanced with the complainants' constitutional rights to privacy and gender equality.

Facts

In February 1991, the accused, Hubert Patrick O'Connor, a Roman Catholic bishop, was charged with rape (now sexual assault) and indecent assault alleged to have occurred between 1964 and 1967. The complainants, four Aboriginal women, had attended Williams Lake, a residential school in British Columbia where O'Connor was the principal and priest. The women had been students and, later, employees at the school. O'Connor did not deny sexual relationships with two of the women, but he claimed the relationships were consensual.

In preparing to defend O'Connor, the defence counsel requested the complainants' entire medical, therapeutic counselling, and school records from the Crown and third parties. By November 1992, the Crown still had not complied with the order to provide these records to the defence. The trial judge stayed the proceedings (ordered the trial to stop until certain conditions were met) because he found that the delay in providing the records had irreparably damaged the integrity of the defence case. The Crown appealed to the British Columbia Court of Appeal and, on March 30, 1994, the Court overturned the stay and ordered a new trial on the basis that a stay was an improper remedy in such a case. O'Connor appealed this decision to the Supreme Court, where the appeal was heard in February 1995. A decision was rendered in December 1995.

The Law

Part of the Crown's case focused on the equality rights stipulated in s. 15 of the Charter. An argument was presented that suggested that legal practices around sexual assault cases have discriminated against females, especially Aboriginal females, and denied them equality rights guaranteed by s. 15 of the Charter.

Arguments by the Crown and Intervenors (Appellants)

The Crown was reluctant to disclose the therapeutic records, motivated by a desire to protect the complainants' privacy, and argued that the defence's demand to examine the extensive records on the complainants' backgrounds reinforced discriminatory stereotypes about the sexuality of women and Aboriginal peoples, and perpetuated myths about rape. It was argued that the defence was employing a line of reasoning that presumes that the evidence provided by individual members of disadvantaged groups may not be as worthy as evidence provided by others. This presumption undermined the complainants' right to equality guaranteed in the Charter. The use of this line of reasoning in the past was a form of systemic inequality in the law.

Intervenors in the case also focused on the relationship between O'Connor and the complainants. Studies presented indicated that the two most important characteristics of sexual assault victims are vulnerability and availability. People who are dependent, relatively powerless, or disadvantaged are vulnerable to sexual exploitation, especially by someone who knows them. O'Connor was in a position of power in that he had been priest, principal, and, later, employer of the four Aboriginal women since they were eight years old.

Arguments for the Defence (Respondents)

There is an implicit need to protect the rights of the accused. In cases of sexual assault that are brought to the courts long after the alleged offences have occurred, there is no physical evidence to establish guilt or innocence. Cases must be decided on the credibility of the complainants and accused—in other words, which stories are more likely to be accurate or closer to the truth. A fair defence can be presented only if counsel has an understanding of the motivations and behavioural patterns of the accusers. For this reason, the defence needs as much information as possible about the backgrounds of the complainants, including details about education, medical histories, therapeutic treatments, and employment. Much of this information may be irrelevant to the defence of the accused for sexual assault; however, it is difficult to determine what is relevant or irrelevant until the records have been examined. In the past, disclosure practices in sexual assault cases have made mental health and medical records accessible to the defence. In this case, the need for the records was recognized by the 1991 court order to make the information available to the defence counsel.

Make Your Decision

1. Outline the basic facts in this case.
2. Explain the meaning of the term "systemic inequality." Do you agree with the argument that women have been systemically discriminated against by the justice system on sexual assault cases? Explain your viewpoint.
3. Dismiss or allow the appeal, and provide reasons for your decision.
4. Write a one-page opinion in response to the following statement: "Female victims of sexual assault are victims twice over, first at the hands of their rapist, and then in the legal system."

Key Terms

Review the following terms to show that you understand the meaning of each and how it is applied in a legal context.

Aboriginal rights	federalism
affirmative action	francophone
anglophone	land claims
collective rights	separatism
comprehensive land claims	sovereignty-association
cultural genocide	specific land claims
	treaty

Understanding the Law

Review the following pieces of legislation mentioned in the text, and show that you understand the intent of each.

Canadian Charter of Rights and Freedoms, ss. 15 and 25
Charter of the French Language (Bill 101)
Clarity Act, 2000
Official Languages Act, 1969
Part II of the *Constitution Act, 1982*, s. 35
Quebec Official Languages Act (Bill 22)

Thinking and Inquiry

1. Should Prime Minister Trudeau and the nine provincial premiers have patriated the constitution without Quebec's approval? Was this action really beneficial to Canada? Write an essay with a minimum of 1000 words expressing your reasoned opinion, or debate the issue in class.
2. Using the Internet, research the status of the Council of the Federation, proposed by Quebec Premier Jean Charest at the 2003 First Ministers' conference. Prepare a critical report on its organization and purpose, its mandate, and its operational procedures, and evaluate its overall effectiveness. (See Methods of Legal Inquiry, Chapter 4, pages 123–124, for further information.)
3. What forces in society seem to operate to discourage the resolution of Aboriginal land claims in a timely fashion? What are some strategies that could be used to speed up the process?
4. Research to find an example of an affirmative action program. Determine its effectiveness in rectifying past discrimination of the target group of people.
5. Investigate how minority groups such as First Nations view the idea of Quebec separatism.
6. Are there Aboriginal land claims in your area? Conduct research to determine if Aboriginal groups near where you live have initiated the land claims process. If so, outline the grievances and claims by the group.

Communication

7. Organize a round-table discussion for a local television station on the following topic: "Parents in Quebec should be able to educate their children in the language of parental choice, be it English or French." Form groups of four, with each person assuming one of the following roles:
   a) a separatist member of the provincial legislature
   b) an anglophone Quebecker
   c) an immigrant parent of non-French background
   d) the panel discussion moderator

   Organize your panel discussion and present it to the class.
8. Conduct a survey of people in your community about their attitudes toward Aboriginal self-government. Summarize your findings in a written report.
9. Prepare arguments to debate the following proposition: *"Resolved that: Affirmative action programs are necessary in order to create a just society."*

Application

10. Choose a partner. One of you is the prime minister, the other is the separatist premier of Quebec. Prepare arguments for your government's position, and present your debate to

the class. (As background information, you might look at speeches by Pierre Trudeau and René Lévesque, and note their arguments for and against separation.)

11. In 2003, the federal government introduced the *First Nations Governance Act* (Bill C-7) in another effort to overhaul the 127-year-old *Indian Act.* Analysts find some very good aspects in this bill, while many critics condemn the entire package of changes. Working with a partner, prepare a list of the key changes being proposed and the strengths and weaknesses of the proposed legislation. If you were a Member of Parliament, would you give approval to this legislation? Why or why not?
12. Working in small groups, decide on three to five criteria for judging the effectiveness of organizations' Web sites. (See Methods of Legal Inquiry, Chapter 1, page 28, for further information.) Use your criteria to evaluate the Web site of the Assembly of First Nations, another Aboriginal organization, or an organization supporting affirmative action. Select the best evaluation from each group, and send it and your comments to the organization. Also, place a copy of your suggestions in your notebook.
13. Within your school, determine a situation in which an affirmative action program might be helpful in creating greater equality. Write a plan for putting such a program in place, including justifying its implementation to the broader school community.

Unit 3

Criminal Law

This third unit in *Dimensions of Law: Canadian and International Law in the 21st Century* focuses on the Canadian criminal justice system. Most of you probably believe that this is one area of law you are fairly familiar with. You probably recognize the players in the human drama that is criminal law—the police, the prosecutor, the defence lawyer, and the judge—and, further, have an idea of what a criminal trial looks like. Unfortunately, much of our public knowledge is both superficial and misinformed, based more on television drama than real life. The reality of the criminal justice system is far more complex than the world portrayed by crime novels, police shows, law-firm soap operas, and sensationalized journalism. Your study of the following chapters will help you clear away any misconceptions you may have and deepen your understanding of the Canadian criminal justice system.

Your introduction to the criminal justice system in Chapter 8 begins with an examination of what crime is and how society's views of crime have evolved. You will also consider who commits crimes and against whom crime is committed.

Chapter 9 explores what takes place before a trial occurs. You will learn about crime scene investigation and the use of forensics to gather evidence. This chapter will also examine arrest and search powers. You will become familiar with how we ensure an accused's appearance in court and what methods of trial are available.

In Chapter 10, you will look at the trial process itself. Your study will include an examination of the role of juries, the use of evidence, and several defences an accused may introduce.

In Chapter 11, you will first examine the area of plea bargaining. Your study of sentencing will include a look at the principles judges consider when imposing a sentence and the variety of sentences available for imposition. The chapter concludes with an examination of wrongful convictions in Canada.

Chapter 8 Crime and Criminal Law

CHAPTER *Focus*

In this chapter, you will

- explain the legal definition of crime
- outline the relationship between criminal law and morality
- explain the purpose of criminal law
- demonstrate an understanding of some theories that psychologists, sociologists, and criminologists use to explain deviant behaviour
- explain the concepts of *mens rea, actus reus,* absolute liability, and strict liability

The criminal justice system is perhaps the most familiar part of our legal system. Most people could, if asked, give examples of criminal behaviour. Theft, assault, and murder, for instance, are acts that Canadian citizens generally believe to be wrong and deserving of punishment. But what about other acts, such as possessing an unregistered firearm or correcting a child by force? In this chapter, you will examine what crime is and how our society's notions of crime have changed over time. You will consider who commits crime and against whom crime is committed. And you will ponder the relationship between crime and morality.

The cartoon in Figure 8.1 asks you to consider who is a criminal and who is a victim of crime.

Figure 8.1

At First Glance

1. What point is the cartoonist making?
2. The law concerning "theft" of music from the Internet is currently unclear. Do you think that lawmakers should be concerned about this?
3. Who suffers when music is enjoyed without payment?
4. If you were unable to afford food or medicine, would you be justified in stealing it? Why or why not?

What Is Crime?

The simplest legal definition of "crime" is "whatever Parliament defines as crime." Under s. 91(27) of the *Constitution Act, 1982*, federal lawmakers have the sole authority to legislate in relation to criminal law. Criminal offences differ from regulatory offences, such as traffic and pollution offences, which may be created by both provincial and federal lawmakers. The minimal legal definition provided above can usefully be expanded into a socio-legal definition. Consider the words of Justice McDermid in the 1993 case of *R v. Ssenyonga*:

> Crimes are wrongful acts that the State recognizes as deserving of control and punishment in the interests of society as a whole. When such wrongs are detected, the State prosecutes the alleged perpetrators to ensure the safety of the public and to preserve the rule of law, which is the foundation of our democratic society.

In other words, there is a public dimension to the criminal law. Alleged criminals are prosecuted by the state on behalf of us all. The prosecution of a criminal offence is not the responsibility of the victim, who often remains uninvolved or minimally involved.

The *Criminal Code*

The *Criminal Code* is a statute, passed and amended by the federal Parliament, that outlines which actions are considered crimes, how offences are prosecuted, and what penalties are imposed. The Code is not the only federal statute to deal with crime. Consider, for example, the *Controlled Drugs and Substances Act*, which deals specifically with drug offences. However, the *Criminal Code* is the most comprehensive statement of the law of crime and punishment in Canada. It applies in every Canadian province and territory.

Fyi The following is taken from Canada's first *Criminal Code*: "Whenever whipping may be awarded for any offence ... the number of strokes shall be specified in the sentence and the instrument to be used for the whipping shall be a cat-o'-nine-tails unless some instrument is specified in the sentence. Whipping shall not be inflicted on any female."

Regular amendments to the Code reflect societal concerns, emerging issues, and the preoccupations of the federal government. The first Canadian *Criminal Code*, which was enacted in 1892, was based on the English common law of crimes. Patchwork changes to the Code have been made almost annually, but the statute itself has never undergone a fundamental overhaul. As a result, some of the offences that remain in our present-day Code seem irrelevant to modern society. Section 71, for example, prohibits duelling, and s. 365 prohibits the fraudulent practice of witchcraft, sorcery, enchantment, or conjuration (casting spells).

Judge-Made Criminal Law

While the Code sets out offences, judges interpret them. In doing so, judges rely on legal precedents to assist in the interpretation of provisions that are often ambiguous. We saw, in Chapter 1 (*R v. Lavallee*, page 25), how judges expanded the concept of self-defence to include the experiences of women who have been battered. In Chapter 2, we examined the process of statutory interpretation in the non-criminal context of Ontario's *Wages Act* (page 52). In this section, we will explore how judges expand definitions of crime to cover behaviour not specifically addressed by the drafters of the *Criminal Code.*

Knowingly transmitting HIV during an otherwise consensual sexual contact is an example of harm-causing activity that is not clearly covered by the Code. Various courts have struggled with the question of whether the transmission of AIDS by a person who knows that he or she is infected should be criminalized and, if so, which provision of the Code should apply.

ambit of the offence: scope of a legal prohibition

One of the first cases to grapple with these questions was *R v. Ssenyonga.* Charles Ssenyonga knew that he had AIDS. Despite being advised by doctors and public health officials to refrain from unprotected sexual contact, he had unprotected sexual intercourse with at least three women without telling them that he was infected. Tragically, all three women subsequently contracted the virus. Uncertain as to what offence to charge Ssenyonga with, the Crown proceeded on several different charges, one of them being aggravated sexual assault. Justice McDermid was reluctant to extend the **ambit of the offence**. He observed: "The purpose of the assault provision is to control the non-consensual application of force by one person to another. What the Crown is asking this court to control is the transmission of HIV and the spread of AIDS rather than the application of force." He concluded that "the law of assault is too blunt an instrument to be used to excise AIDS from the body politic. If no other section of the *Criminal Code* catches the conduct complained of, which remains to be seen, then it is a matter for Parliament to address through legislation."

Ssenyonga died before the case was completed. In the end, it took a decision of the Supreme Court of Canada, *R v. Cuerrier*, to resolve the question.

Turning Points in the Law

Crime or Private Morality?

In October 2002, after police raids on two Montreal "swingers' clubs," 70 Montrealers were charged with being found in a bawdy house (brothel). Almost immediately, the press reported the group's defence: "The state has no place in the bedrooms of the nation." This memorable remark was first made by Prime Minister Pierre Elliott Trudeau when he was justice minister. Trudeau was responding to press questions after he introduced a bill proposing a wide range of amendments to the *Criminal Code*, including the decriminalization of homosexuality.

The movement to liberalize criminal laws related to sexuality began in 1957 in Britain with the publication of the Wolfenden report on homosexuality and prostitution. The report expressed the view that both homosexuality and prostitution should be decriminalized. It stated that "there must remain a realm of private morality which is not the law's business." Trudeau believed that Canada's *Criminal Code* needed to be amended because "there is a difference between sin and crime, and it is not the business of the lawmaker or of the police to check sin. This is a problem for each person's conscience, or his priest, or his God, but not for the police."

On December 21, 1967, Trudeau tabled the 72-page, 104-clause omnibus *Criminal Code* reform bill that proposed, among other amendments, the decriminalization of homosexuality between consenting adults. Trudeau gained a tactical advantage by placing the more controversial changes regarding homosexuality in a bill dealing with a variety of unrelated matters. The timing of the introduction of the bill was also well calculated. It was tabled days before the Christmas holidays. Because the opposition was caught off guard, Trudeau was able to expedite the legislation through its first reading on the same day.

Even more skillful was Trudeau's handling of the bill in the media through his famous remark banishing government from the nation's bedrooms. Political scientist F.L. Morton has commented in his book *Morgentaler v. Borowski* that this "offhand, almost flippant remark would subsequently permeate the consciousness and political vocabulary of the entire society. It seemed to justify in a single sentence the new sexual freedom of the sixties, the ultimate rejoinder to an attempt by society to control the sexual behaviour of its citizens." The reverberations of Trudeau's comment are still felt today.

Questions

1. What did Trudeau mean when he drew a distinction between crime and sin? What other words might he have used to describe "sin"?
2. Are there areas of morality that you believe the state should control through its criminal laws? If your answer is yes, name one and argue a justification for state control. If your answer is no, argue against state control, using examples.

Figure 8.2 *Pierre Trudeau, John Turner, Prime Minister Lester B. Pearson, and Jean Chrétien are photographed together upon joining Pearson's Cabinet in 1967. All three ministers went on to become prime ministers of Canada.*

The Law

In the case of *R v. Cuerrier*, the Supreme Court of Canada was required to consider the following sections of the *Criminal Code*:

265(1) A person commits an assault when
  (a) without the consent of another person, he applies force intentionally to that other person, directly or indirectly; ...
(2) This section applies to all forms of assault, including ... aggravated sexual assault.
(3) For the purposes of this section, no consent is obtained where the complainant submits or does not resist by reason of ...
  (c) fraud; ...

268(1) Every one commits an aggravated assault who wounds, maims, disfigures or endangers the life of the complainant.

Questions

1. How does a victim's consent or lack of consent affect the possibility of an accused's conviction under s. 265(1)? Explain your answer.
2. Why would the Crown choose to prosecute an HIV-positive person who has unprotected sex with another person under s. 268(1) instead of s. 265(1)?

Case HIV, SILENCE, AND SEX

R v. Cuerrier, [1998] 2 SCR 371

Facts

When Henry Cuerrier tested positive for HIV in August 1992, a public health nurse told him to use condoms every time he had sexual intercourse and to tell all prospective sexual partners that he was HIV-positive. Cuerrier rejected this advice, complaining that he would never be able to have a sex life under these circumstances.

Three weeks later, Cuerrier met KM and began a sexual relationship with her. He assured KM that he had tested negative for HIV eight or nine months earlier. The couple had unprotected sexual intercourse on a regular basis. When KM contracted hepatitis, both she and Cuerrier were tested for HIV. KM tested negative, but she was advised that Cuerrier had tested positive. For several months, KM continued to have unprotected sex with Cuerrier. She explained that she loved him and that she did not want another woman put at risk. The couple's relationship ended 18 months after it began.

Shortly after the end of his relationship with KM, Cuerrier began another sexual relationship. He did not tell his new partner, BH, that he had HIV, nor did he regularly use condoms. When BH discovered Cuerrier's HIV-positive status, she ended the relationship. Both KM and BH testified at trial that they would never have had unprotected sex with Cuerrier if they had known that he was HIV-positive.

Cuerrier was charged with two counts of aggravated assault. At the time of trial, neither complainant had tested positive for the virus. The trial judge acquitted Cuerrier, and the British Columbia Court of Appeal refused to set aside the acquittals. The Crown's appeal from Cuerrier's acquittal was allowed by the Supreme Court of Canada, and a new trial was ordered.

Issues

Should Cuerrier be convicted of aggravated assault? Was the women's consent to engage in unprotected sex with Cuerrier true consent, or was it **vitiated by fraud**? Is consent to sexual contact fraudulently obtained when one partner fails to disclose or deliberately deceives the other about his or her HIV-positive status?

vitiated by fraud: made invalid as a result of fraud on the part of the accused

Decision

Three different Supreme Court judges wrote reasons in this case. All judges agreed that Cuerrier should be convicted of aggravated assault, even though this judgment required a reinterpretation of the law. All agreed that Cuerrier failed to obtain the true consent of his partners to unprotected sexual intercourse. All agreed that failure by one partner to disclose HIV-positive status vitiated the consent of the other partner.

Questions

1. What facts support a finding of guilt in Cuerrier's case? Are there any facts to support a finding of not guilty?
2. What is the difference between the approach taken by the Supreme Court in *Cuerrier* and the approach taken by Justice McDermid in *Ssenyonga*?

Check Your Understanding

1. Give two definitions of crime.
2. Name and describe two sources of criminal law.
3. What did Justice McDermid mean when he said the law of assault is "too blunt an instrument"? Do you agree with his assessment?
4. Should judges extend the criminal law to respond to new social problems, or should they wait for a parliamentary response? Give reasons for your answer.

Purpose of the Criminal Law

Why do we have criminal law? The question is deceptively simple. The answers are complex and immensely controversial. At the end of a successful criminal prosecution, the state inflicts punishment in the name of us all. As a society, we need strong justification for such a profound intervention in our lives. At its most basic, the criminal law exists to label wrongful behaviour, to identify violations, and to impose **sanctions**. Labelling, identifying, and sanctioning wrongful behaviour achieves two purposes: retribution and the protection of society.

sanctions: penalties

Retribution

Retribution involves the public denouncing and punishing of wrongful behaviour. It is meant to reaffirm social values and deliver "justice." The retributive purpose of criminal law focuses on providing a fitting response by society to wrongdoing. This means that the criminal law should punish and denounce in a way that respects the rights and liberties of an accused person. Retribution should be fair.

Protection of Society

The protective purpose of the criminal law is more forward looking. The concern is to make society safer by deterring future wrongdoing and by rehabilitating wrongdoers (see Chapter 11: Delivering Criminal Justice). The focus is on public security and the prevention of crime. The question is how far the protective principle extends in justifying a state's use of the criminal-law power. Philosophers, politicians, and criminal theorists have struggled with this question for centuries and have offered the following principles of justification:

- *private harm principle:* the prevention of harm to individuals
- *public harm principle:* the prevention of harm to public institutions and practices
- *offence principle:* the prevention of offence to others
- *legal paternalism:* the prevention of harm to the self
- *legal moralism:* the prevention of immorality.

Some of these principles may provide more obvious justification for a state's exercise of the criminal-law power than others. It is apparent to most citizens that the criminal law should prevent and punish the infliction of physical harm. But what do we mean when we talk about harm, either private or public? Are there different perspectives on the harmfulness of certain behaviours? Should the criminal law prevent people from harming themselves? Should it be used to enforce morality? If so, whose morality should it enforce?

WORKING FOR CHANGE Canadian Association of Elizabeth Fry Societies

Elizabeth Fry, born into a family of Quakers in 1780 in England, played an important role in prison reform. Throughout her life, Fry advocated the humane treatment of prisoners and was viewed by many as a leading expert in the field. As a result of her efforts, the treatment of women and children in London's Newgate Prison was significantly improved. To honour her memory, Elizabeth Fry societies were established. The first Canadian society was founded in 1939 in Vancouver. Eventually, in 1969, the Canadian Association of Elizabeth Fry Societies (CAEFS) appeared. Today there are 23 member societies across Canada.

Figure 8.3 *Elizabeth Fry reading to inmates of Newgate Prison.*

CAEFS works with and for women involved with the justice system. Its key principles stress the Charter right of equality before the law and the right to equal benefit of the law without discrimination. It operates on the principles that women have the right to obtain justice without fear of prejudice or gender discrimination, and that they have the right of access to all opportunities and programs in the justice system.

CAEFS also lobbies different levels of government and their agencies to institute reforms in the prison system. It advocates that offenders should be corrected within their communities unless there are compelling reasons for doing otherwise, and that offenders should retain all the rights and privileges enjoyed by ordinary citizens, except those expressly removed by law.

One of CAEFS's key goals is to ensure quality programs, services, and facilities for marginalized women in conflict with the law. These are based on individual needs, including programs directed toward the improvement of conditions for disadvantaged people and groups. The programs exist "in courts, institutions, or in the community," and are provided by paid workers or volunteers.

CAEFS advocates for legislative and administrative reform and provides avenues to inform the public about areas of the justice system that affect women. In furtherance of this goal, the association hosts National Elizabeth Fry Week, which is always held the week before Mother's Day. The association deliberately chose this week to draw attention to the fact that the majority of women who come into conflict with the law are mothers who are the sole supporters of their families. For many of these women, CAEFS is the only place they can turn to for help and for hope.

Questions

1. Suggest reasons why the majority of women in conflict with the law are mothers who are solely responsible for their family's support.

2. Why do you think that CAEFS supports the principle that the correction of offenders should take place within the community, unless there are compelling reasons to the contrary? Do you agree with this principle? Why or why not?

3. Locate and visit CAEFS's Web site. Read some of the briefs that the society has presented to the federal government in an effort to improve conditions for women incarcerated in Canadian prisons. Discuss your findings in small groups.

Personal Viewpoint

Velma Demerson: An Incorrigible Law

In 2003, Velma Demerson was in her 80s. When she was 18, she suffered an injustice so huge that it took her 60 years to speak of it in public.

When Demerson was 17, she fell in love with Harry Yip, a young Chinese-Canadian. She moved in with him, and the couple made plans to marry.

One morning, while the lovers were in their pyjamas, Demerson's long ordeal began. In her own words, "two policemen came in, followed by my father. I was ordered to get dressed and [was] taken to a place where I was put in a barred cage.

"Shortly, I was taken into a room and interviewed by a woman. She asked me if I had ever slept with anyone else. I felt I would have to damage my character to save my boyfriend from any blame. I said, 'Yes.' She asked, 'How many?' I said, 'Two.' ... Although I wasn't sure, I told her I was pregnant, hoping that would help. I had never told anyone I was pregnant before.

"Almost immediately, I was taken to a courtroom. I stood with my back toward the judge who sat about 10 feet away. ... The judge asked me, 'Are you pregnant?' I said, 'Yes.' He asked, 'How far along?' I said, 'Three months—I'll get married if you'll just let me out of here long enough.' The judge said, 'Remanded one week for sentence.' ... When I returned to court, the judge said, 'You are charged with being incorrigible and I sentence you to one year in the Belmont Home.'"

Figure 8.4 *Velma Demerson giving a news conference in 2002.*

Demerson learned later that "I had been sentenced under the *Female Refuges Act*. Section 15 states: 'Any person may bring before a judge any female under the age of 35 years who ... is leading an idle and dissolute life.' It further states that: 'Any parent or guardian may bring before a judge any female under the age of 21 years who proves unmanageable or incorrigible, and the judge may proceed as provided in s. 15.'" Other offences under this Act included promiscuity, being illegitimately pregnant, and consorting willingly with a Chinese man.

Belmont Home was an industrial refuge run as a commercial laundry by the Protestant church. All such refuges operated some type of industry in which women laboured long hours without pay. Six weeks after Demerson arrived, the laundry was shut down for failing to make a profit, and its 47 inmates were transferred to Mercer Reformatory.

Demerson and the other Mercer inmates were housed in windowless cells equipped with enamel buckets for toilets. She recalls, "There were no clocks, so we never knew the time, and no newspapers. We were forbidden to talk. We had to walk in strict lines to the sewing machines, and to the dining room. They purposely broke up any friendships."

While in Mercer, Demerson gave birth to a boy. She attempted to escape from the maternity ward but failed. She was sent back to prison to labour in the sewing factory while her baby spent his days on a "sleeping porch." One day, Demerson was told that her baby had been "removed to hospital." She did not hear of him again until she retrieved him after her release.

Demerson was freed after nine months of imprisonment and reunited with Yip and her baby. The baby, Harry Jr., suffered from severe eczema and asthma, and the couple was unable to afford medicine. The marriage disintegrated several years later. Harry Jr. drowned at age 26. As Demerson later observed, "The ... stigma, and family turmoil that ensues from confining a woman in prison, passes down through the generations."

"I want justice," says Velma Demerson. "I was estranged from my family to this day. I'm on the books as guilty, and so are the other girls. Some of them lost their babies."

In December 2002, Demerson received an apology from the Ontario government. She has not received any compensation because an Ontario Superior Court judge ruled that the provincial government was immune from lawsuits based on events that happened before 1963. The offence provisions of the *Female Refuges Act* were repealed in 1958, largely as a result of the work of the Toronto Elizabeth Fry Society.

Source: Adapted from "The Female Refuges Act," *Opening the Doors: The Newsletter of the Council of Elizabeth Fry Societies of Ontario*, Spring 2001, www.web.net/~efryont/SPRING%202001.pdf; and Michelle Landsberg, "Plight of 'Incorrigible' Women Demands Justice," *The Toronto Star*, Sunday, May 6, 2001.

Questions

1. Consider the words "incorrigible," "unmanageable," "idle," "dissolute," and "refuge." Discuss the potential for injustice in enforcing laws based on terms such as these.
2. Columnist Michele Landsberg concluded an article on Demerson with these words: "[W]e should remain alert to the potential for terrible harm and abuse when men in power pass laws to 'protect' girls and women." Consider this comment in relation to the principles of legal paternalism and legal moralism discussed on page 236.
3. Do you believe that the 2002 apology of the Ontario government adequately compensated Velma Demerson for her ordeal? Why or why not?

CHECK YOUR UNDERSTANDING

1. Name and describe two purposes of the criminal law.
2. Can you think of any situations where these purposes might be in conflict? In the event of a conflict, which purpose should be given priority? Why?
3. Explain the "offence principle." How far might the term "offence" extend? Do you think the offence principle is a good justification for the imposition of criminal sanctions? Why or why not?

Find out more about theories of criminology at www.emp.ca/ dimensionsoflaw

Who Commits Crimes?

Theories about the causes of crime are as plentiful as criminal behaviour itself. Different explanations have focused on different aspects of human existence: physiology, biology, psychology, sociology, politics, economics. Both the perspective of individual theorists and the intellectual fashions of the era are reflected in different explanations. Some theories now seem silly. For example, in the late 19th century, Cesare Lombroso tried to relate certain physical characteristics, such as jaw size, to criminal behaviour. Other theories now seem better founded, although no single approach has proven universally valid.

During the late 19th and early 20th centuries, two streams of theory emerged. One linked criminality to underlying social and economic factors, while the other linked it to individual psychology. The first was typified by a group of theorists known as the Chicago School, which argued that social and environmental factors were important in examining deviant behaviour. The other was best expressed by Sigmund Freud, who believed that all humans have criminal tendencies, but that these are modified through inner controls learned during childhood. Freud believed that faulty identification by the child with the parent was the most common factor contributing to criminal behaviour.

As the 20th century progressed, criminologists looked for more complex explanations, particularly given the fact that crime continued to grow even though individuals were generally better off and protected by a more elaborate social safety net. The following excerpt discussing the causes of crime is taken from a report published by the National Council of Welfare in 2000 entitled *Justice and the Poor.*

You can read the complete report *Justice and the Poor* at www.emp.ca/ dimensionsoflaw

> Until the 1960s, it was widely assumed that poverty bred crime and that most crimes were committed by young men with lower-class backgrounds. This assumption was based on statistics showing that the majority of those arrested, convicted, and imprisoned were then, as they are now, males under the age of 25 from families in which the parents had little education and low incomes and held inferior jobs or no jobs at all. To account for this, criminologists developed many explanations. One was the social disorganization theory, which said that specific neighbourhood conditions, such as poverty, high mobility, and multi-ethnicity, caused a breakdown of traditional values which led to crime. Another was the opportunity theory, according to which lower-class people were more likely to engage in crime because they were blocked from achieving financial success by legal means.
>
> Everyone was therefore surprised in the 1960s when US researchers discovered that criminal behaviour was not linked exclusively to lower-status people and poor neighbourhoods. Using self-report studies, which asked (mostly young) participants to reveal, in total confidence and without

fear of punishment, what illegal actions they had committed, researchers made two shocking discoveries.

First of all, the vast majority of all male participants reported having committed illegal acts that could have landed them before youth courts. Girls were much less likely to engage in illegal behaviour. When Canadian criminologist Marc LeBlanc questioned 3000 young Montrealers, he found that more than 90 percent had committed delinquent acts in the previous year and that more than 80 percent had contravened the *Criminal Code.* The most common offences were shoplifting, vandalism, driving a car under the influence of alcohol, or taking mild drugs, especially marijuana. Nine percent had committed more serious crimes such as robbery.

The second surprise was that the children of parents with professional jobs were as likely to report having committed illegal acts as the children of poorer parents with low-status jobs. Contrary to the strong link between crime and social class of origin that had been taken for granted until then, it seemed that they were not related at all. This finding caused huge controversies in criminology circles that continue to this day. It also inspired dozens of other self-report studies, which produced contradictory and inconsistent results and therefore failed to establish that young people from low-status or poverty backgrounds were more likely to get involved in crime or to commit more serious crimes. ...

Most experts now agree that the social status and income of the parents have little or no *direct* effect on the likelihood that children will turn to delinquency, although they may in some cases have *indirect* effects by amplifying life problems that can lead to crime. ...

Research has found that children most at risk of becoming delinquents and criminals face the following circumstances:

> (1) they receive little love, affection, or warmth, and are physically or emotionally rejected and/or abandoned by their parents;
>
> (2) they are inadequately supervised by parents who fail to teach them right from wrong, and who do not monitor their whereabouts, friends, or activities, and who discipline them erratically and harshly; and
>
> (3) they grow up in homes with considerable conflict, marital discord, and perhaps even violence. Families at greatest risk of delinquency are those suffering from limited coping resources, social isolation, and (among parents) poor parenting skills.

Given the lack of resources and greater vulnerability of young people from disadvantaged backgrounds, it is a tribute to their parents that the differences in criminal behaviour between youths from low-income and more affluent families are not evident. ...

[T]here has been an increasing awareness in the last few decades that official crime statistics immensely underestimate white-collar and corporate crimes. These include a huge range of offences, including tax fraud and bank embezzlement at the simpler end, and enormously complex corporate stock and securities fraud and antitrust violations at the other end, as well as numerous types of criminal negligence causing occupational injury or death. In her book about corporate crime in Canada, Laureen Snider writes that:

> Although corporate crime receives much less publicity than the assaults, thefts and rapes most people think of when they hear the word "crime," it actually does more harm, costs more money, and ruins more lives than any of these. Corporate crime is a major killer, causing more deaths in a month than all the mass murderers combined do in a decade. Canadians are killed on the job by unsafe (and illegal) working conditions; injured by dangerous products offered for sale before their safety is demonstrated; incapacitated by industrial wastes released into the air or dumped into lakes and rivers; and robbed by illegal conspiracies that raise prices and eliminate consumer choice. ... Canadians are 28 times more likely to be injured at work than by assault. ... People are 10 times more likely to be killed by conditions at their workplace than to be victims of homicide ... .

What are we to conclude from all this about the people who commit crimes in Canada? The answer appears to be that almost all Canadians break the law at some point in their lives, but that most of these illegal acts are not serious and are usually committed in adolescence. Among older youths and adults, those who commit most criminal offences are men who are at the extremes of the social spectrum. At one end are criminals who were not necessarily from poor families, but who are now without legitimate employment and sometimes destitute. They are most feared by the public and are responsible for a large share of common or street crimes. At the other end are higher-class, white-collar criminals, who are responsible for more deaths and steal much more money than the poor, but are seldom called criminals and are seldom condemned by a society in which many people believe that "greed is good."

CHECK YOUR UNDERSTANDING

1. Briefly describe a biological, a sociological, and a psychological theory used to explain criminal behaviour.
2. Choose at least one finding in the National Council of Welfare's report *Justice and the Poor* that surprised you. Explain your choice.
3. What characteristics are shared by children who are most at risk of becoming delinquents? What could society do to alter these circumstances?
4. Suggest reasons why official statistics have immensely underestimated white-collar and corporate crimes.

Issue

Life on City Streets **Should the government legislate against squeegee kids and aggressive panhandlers?**

In 2000, the Ontario government responded to squeegee kids and panhandlers by enacting the *Safe Streets Act*. The Act makes it illegal to solicit in an "aggressive manner," which is defined as "a manner that is likely to cause a reasonable person to be concerned for his or her safety or security."

Section 2(3) of the Act cites the following examples of aggressive solicitation:

1. Threatening the person solicited with physical harm, by word, gesture or other means, during the solicitation or after the person solicited responds or fails to respond to the solicitation.
2. Obstructing the path of the person solicited during the solicitation or after the person solicited responds or fails to respond to the solicitation.
3. Using abusive language during the solicitation or after the person solicited responds or fails to respond to the solicitation.
4. Proceeding behind, alongside, or ahead of the person solicited during the solicitation or after the person solicited responds or fails to respond to the solicitation.
5. Soliciting while intoxicated by alcohol or drugs.
6. Continuing to solicit a person in a persistent manner after the person has responded negatively to the solicitation.

Section 3(2) outlines places where solicitation is no longer allowed to take place:

3(2) No person shall,
- (a) solicit a person who is using, waiting to use, or departing from an automated teller machine;
- (b) solicit a person who is using or waiting to use a pay telephone or a public toilet facility;
- (c) solicit a person who is waiting at a taxi stand or a public transit stop;
- (d) solicit a person who is in or on a public transit vehicle;
- (e) solicit a person who is in the process of getting in, out of, on or off a vehicle or who is in a parking lot; or
- (f) while on a roadway, solicit a person who is in or on a stopped, standing or parked vehicle.

Figure 8.5 *Police officers on bike patrol talk to a squeegee kid at a Toronto intersection.*

Some of the arguments raised in the Ontario Legislature to oppose or support the *Safe Streets Act* are set out below.

> When a person, young or elderly, can enter a store without being blocked by someone aggressively soliciting, we have quality of life in Ontario. When parents can pull up in the car at an intersection with the children in the back seat and not feel worried about being approached by someone selling a service with a squeegee, to perform unwanted services, we have quality of life in Ontario.
>
> *—Jim Flaherty (Whitby–Ajax), attorney general and minister responsible for Native affairs, November 18, 1999*

> [I]t's this government's priority that ... police officers ... are going to spend their time chasing after squeegee kids. No effort for wife assault, no effort for hate crime, no effort to deal with home invasion. ... It is an insult. It is an embarrassment. But even worse, what we see is a government that wants to use the criminal law to go after a social problem. We see young people who want a real job ... trying to make do with squeegeeing to make a few bucks.
>
> *—Howard Hampton (Kenora–Rainy River), leader of the New Democratic Party, November 2, 1999*

> How does bringing this law into place now that will force you to jail squeegee kids or homeless people if they persist in being squeegee kids or persist in being homeless ... deal with the underlying problems that are there? How does this deal with the potential mental health problems many of our homeless face? ... How does it help the young person who's on the street, has no home and this is their only means of survival?
>
> *—Dominic Agostino (Hamilton East), November 15, 1999*

> Many of my constituents do not feel safe walking down their own streets because of fear of harassment. ... Mothers with children and seniors are particularly vulnerable to harassment from aggressive panhandlers. Certainly we owe it to them to protect them from this sort of unnecessary harassment.
>
> *—Julia Munro (York North), November 16, 1999*

Questions

1. Which parts of the new law specifically target squeegee kids? Which parts target aggressive panhandlers?
2. List the arguments used by people on each side in the issue. Choose the best argument, and explain your choice.
3. In a paragraph, summarize your own position on the need for the *Safe Streets Act*. Give at least two reasons for your position.

Who Are the Victims of Crime?

Most people live with some fear that they will be the victim of a criminal offence. We all make adjustments in our daily routines that are designed to avoid or prevent victimization. Fear of being victimized makes some people choose to stay inside their homes at night. It makes others purchase expensive alarm systems or take classes in self-defence. In other words, fear of victimization sometimes limits our choices. In Chapter 11: Delivering Criminal Justice, you will consider victims' rights and the role of victims in the criminal process. Here, you will examine the kinds of precautions you and your family may take to avoid being victims of a criminal offence.

What criminal offences do you protect yourself against? Do you fear an assault by a stranger, or loss of personal property? Now, consider the following information about the risks of victimization compiled by statisticians Sandra Besserer and Catherine Trainor. It is based on figures compiled by Statistics Canada in 1999. Do the strategies you use to avoid victimization make sense?

- Twenty-five percent of Canadians aged 15 or older reported that they were victimized during 1999; 23 percent reported victimization in 1993.
- Fifty percent of the incidents involved personal crimes (theft of personal property, assault, sexual assault, and robbery). About 35 percent of the incidents involved household crime (breaking and entering, vandalism, theft of household property). The remaining 15 percent fell outside these categories.
- Women and men had similar overall risks of personal victimization (189 per 1000 women and 183 per 1000 men). However, women were four times more likely to be the victims of sexual assault, and men were more likely to be the victims of assault and robbery.
- Young persons aged 15 to 24 reported the highest rate of personal victimization. Senior citizens reported the lowest rate of personal victimization. Young persons were 21 times more likely to be the victims of violent crime and nine times more likely to be the victims of personal property theft than seniors.
- People who frequently engaged in evening activities outside the home were at the greatest risk of personal victimization.
- Low household income was associated with a greater risk of violent victimization and a smaller risk of personal theft.
- Urban dwellers reported higher rates of personal victimization than residents of rural areas.
- Suspects in most violent crimes were male and acted alone. For example, 92 percent of sexual assaults and 60 percent of assaults were committed by a lone male. Most violent crimes were committed by someone known to the victim.

- Approximately 60 percent of offences were not reported to the police. Reasons given for not reporting included the insignificance of the incident, the impotence of the police, and the decision to deal with the incident in another way. Victims who reported crimes to police commonly did so because they believed it was their duty.
- Women reported the fear of crime more often than men. Twice as many women as men reported feeling worried while waiting for or using public transportation alone after dark. Three times as many women as men felt unsafe while walking alone in their neighbourhood after dark.

Check Your Understanding

1. Describe the differing rates of victimization for young people and for seniors. Can you suggest reasons for the difference, using facts derived from the Statistics Canada survey?
2. Did reading the statistics change your ideas about your personal safety strategies? Explain your answer.
3. Examine the reasons given for not reporting offences. Which do you believe is the most valid? Why? What other reasons might people have?

Elements of an Offence

To obtain a conviction, the Crown must prove beyond a reasonable doubt that each and every element of the offence with which the accused is charged was in fact committed by the accused. Criminal offences are made up of two basic elements: a prohibited act, known as the *actus reus*, and a criminal intent, known as the *mens rea.*

Actus Reus

actus reus: the wrongful act or omission in a criminal offence

The ***actus reus*** of a *Criminal Code* offence is the act or omission (failure to act) that has been identified by Parliament as sufficiently harmful to warrant state intervention. It is usually simple to identify the *actus reus* of a crime by reading the definition of the offence set out in the Code. Consider, for example, s. 222(1), which provides that "a person commits homicide when, directly or indirectly, by any means, he causes the death of a human being." The *actus reus* of homicide is causing the death of a human being.

Now consider s. 90(1), a more complicated prohibition. Section 90(1) provides that "[e]very person commits an offence who carries a weapon ... concealed, unless the person is authorized under the *Firearms Act* to carry it concealed." The *actus reus* for s. 90(1) has several components: *carrying* a *weapon* that is *concealed* without *authorization.* Each of these four elements of the *actus reus* may raise questions of interpretation. Is an accused "carrying" a weapon when the weapon is in the trunk of a car being driven by the accused? Is an ice pick a weapon? What about a nail file or a tire iron? What constitutes concealment? What counts as an authorization under the *Firearms Act*? Must the accused have physical possession of the authorization? The answers to these interpretive questions are found in the decisions of judges who have applied s. 90(1).

Generally speaking, most criminal offences require that the accused take some action, such as possessing, applying force, causing death, taking, stealing, shouting, or harassing. Some provisions, however, make it a criminal offence to fail to act in circumstances where a duty to act exists. Parents, for example, have a duty to provide the "necessaries of life" for their dependent children. Failure to provide such necessaries may lead to criminal liability.

It is understood, but not explicitly written into the *Criminal Code*, that the *actus reus* must be committed voluntarily—that is, it must be the conscious choice of an operating mind. Our criminal law does not hold people criminally responsible for actions that they cannot control. Take, for example, the driver of a motor vehicle who is stung by a bee, has an allergic reaction, and as a result drives into another vehicle. While the manner of driving may be dangerous, the accused has not committed that *actus reus* voluntarily. The Crown, in these circumstances, cannot prove the *actus reus* of the offence of dangerous driving. More complex questions arise when one considers the impact of mental illness or the consumption of alcohol or drugs on a person's ability to act voluntarily. You will examine these questions in Chapter 10: The Criminal Trial.

Mens Rea

The ***mens rea*** of a criminal offence is the mental element that accompanies the commission of the *actus reus*. A famous Latin maxim, "*actus non facit reum nisi mens sit rea*" (an act does not become guilty unless the mind is guilty), summarizes the fundamental idea that mere commission of the prohibited act is insufficient for criminal liability. The act must be done with a "guilty mind." *Mens rea* is the technical term for the blameworthy state of mind that must be proven, beyond a reasonable doubt, by the Crown.

***mens rea*:** the blameworthy mental element in a criminal offence

Sometimes the offence-creating provisions in the *Criminal Code* state the specific *mens rea* that must be established in order to convict an accused. For example, s. 319(2) makes it an offence to "wilfully" promote hatred "by communicating statements, other than in private conversation." The word establishing the *mens rea* in s. 319 is "wilfully." The accused will be convicted only if the Crown can prove that the accused promoted hatred "wilfully." It is not enough for the Crown to prove that the accused behaved "carelessly" or "knowingly" or "recklessly."

Clues to the technical meaning of the word "wilfully" are found in cases interpreting s. 319(2). Other provisions use words such as "intentionally," "negligently," or "fraudulently." Some provisions use no *mens rea* words at all. As a result, much of the law on *mens rea* is found in the decisions of judges interpreting the language of the *Criminal Code*. The best place to start any *mens rea* analysis is in the case law interpreting a particular offence.

Analyzing a Criminal Offence

You have already encountered the offence of assault in discussing the case of *R v. Cuerrier*. Here, you will analyze the *actus reus* and *mens rea* of that offence. Section 265(1)(a) of the *Criminal Code* states, "A person commits an assault when ... without the consent of another person, he applies force intentionally to that other person, directly or indirectly."

There are two aspects to the *actus reus* of assault: the direct or indirect application of force to a person and the lack of that person's consent. If either of these elements is absent, a conviction is impossible because the *actus reus* cannot be established. Therefore, if force is directly applied to a person who has consented to the application of force, as in a hockey game, the *actus reus* is missing. If force is applied directly to an animal, the *actus reus* is missing as well. In neither case can the person who directly applied the force be convicted of assault.

Assuming that the *actus reus* can be proven, what *mens rea* is required in order to convict for assault? Section 265(1)(a) tells you that the application of force must be intentional; however, it says nothing about the lack of consent. There are a number of conclusions that can be drawn from the ambiguity of the provision. You could interpret the failure to specify a *mens rea* with respect to non-consent as an indication that no *mens rea* is required. In this case, the Crown would not have to establish anything about the accused's knowledge of the victim's lack of consent. However, general principles of criminal liability developed at common law suggest that such an approach is wrong. There is an **interpretive presumption** when dealing with *Criminal Code* offences that *mens rea* is required with respect to each and every element of the *actus reus*.

interpretive presumption: inference that must accompany the interpretation of a law

Assuming that some *mens rea* with respect to consent is required, there are still a number of options. You could insist that the prosecution prove that the accused actually knew that there was no consent at the time that force was applied. This is a subjective assessment of **culpability** because it focuses on the actual knowledge of the individual accused. Alternatively, you could interpret the provision as requiring the Crown to establish that a reasonable person would have realized that there was no consent at the time that force was applied. This standard of culpability is objective because it is less concerned with the actual knowledge of the accused. The objective standard reflects the belief that those who apply force should act reasonably.

culpability: guilt

Subjective or Objective?

At various times in the history of criminal law, courts have preferred one approach over the other. In the late 19th century, questions about *mens rea* were straightforwardly objective. People were presumed to intend the natural consequences of their acts. A natural consequence was defined as a consequence that a reasonable person would foresee. Therefore, if a reasonable person would foresee an *actus reus*, that *actus reus* was intended. If a reasonable person would foresee the *actus reus* that the accused committed, the accused was guilty as charged. No one worried about what was in the mind of the accused person at the time of the offence. Blame was based on the accused's failure to live up to the standard of the reasonable person, an "objective" standard that was external to the accused.

More recently, courts in Canada have developed a preference for the subjective standard. Subjective theory requires the Crown to prove that the accused himself or herself had the **requisite intention** at the time the offence was committed. Many judges and criminal theorists believe that subjective theory is the fairest way to allocate blame since it links fault to the accused's own choices. These advocates of the subjective approach believe that criminal liability should be reserved for those who consciously choose to behave criminally.

requisite intention: the *mens rea* that the Crown is required to establish in order to convict an accused of an offence

Whether culpability is based on objective or subjective *mens rea* is a question of law that must be addressed with respect to each criminal offence. Once it has been authoritatively decided that the *mens rea* for a certain offence is objective or subjective, that decision governs all trials of that offence. In other words, it cannot be argued that *mens rea* should be subjectively (or objectively) measured for a particular accused. Any argument must be directed toward whether *mens rea* should be subjectively (or objectively) measured for the particular offence with which the accused is charged.

The following facts, based on the English case of *R v. Lamb*, demonstrate why the choice between subjective and objective standards is important. Larry Lamb was a young man who owned a revolver that had a five-chambered cylinder that rotated clockwise each time the trigger was pulled. As a joke and with no intention of doing harm, Lamb pointed the revolver at his best friend. There were two bullets in the chambers, but neither bullet was in the chamber opposite the barrel. Lamb did not intend to fire the gun, but when he pulled the trigger, the cylinder rotated and placed a bullet opposite the barrel so that it was struck by the striking pin. Lamb killed his best friend.

Assume that Lamb is charged with a homicide offence, the *actus reus* of which is causing death. Clearly Lamb has committed the *actus reus*. His culpability depends on an assessment of *mens rea*.

Did Lamb subjectively intend to cause death? If your answer is no, does that mean that Lamb is blameless with respect to his friend's death?

Was Lamb's behaviour reasonable—that is, would a reasonable person have pointed a loaded gun at the head of his best friend? If you conclude that Lamb behaved unreasonably, do you believe that his unreasonableness is sufficiently culpable to find him criminally responsible for the death?

Would it matter if Lamb were to convince you (perhaps by calling expert evidence) that the mistake he made was a reasonable mistake for anyone unacquainted with guns? If your answer is yes, why is the reasonableness of Lamb's mistake significant? If your answer is no, what is it about Lamb's behaviour that you believe is blameworthy?

For the outcome of *R v. Lamb*, see www.emp.ca/dimensionsoflaw

CHECK YOUR UNDERSTANDING

1. Name two components of a criminal offence and describe them.
2. Distinguish between subjective and objective *mens rea*.
3. Determine what the *actus reus* and *mens rea* are for each of the following *Criminal Code* offences:

242. A female person who, being pregnant and about to be delivered, with intent that the child shall not live or with intent to conceal the birth of the child, fails to make provision for reasonable assistance in respect of her delivery is, if the child is permanently injured as a result thereof or dies immediately before, during or in a short time after birth, as a result thereof, guilty of an indictable offence and is liable to imprisonment for a term not exceeding five years.

346(1) Every one commits extortion who, without reasonable justification or excuse and with intent to obtain anything, by threats, accusations, menaces or violence induces or attempts to induce any person, whether or not he is the person threatened, accused or menaced or to whom violence is shown, to do anything or cause anything to be done.

Absolute and Strict Liability

Traffic offences, pollution offences, and offences relating to unfair or dangerous commercial practices are all examples of regulatory offences. These offences regulate otherwise desirable behaviour (such as driving, manufacturing, or selling goods and services) where such behaviour could cause harm to individuals or the public if carried out improperly. Both the provinces and the federal government have the constitutional authority to create regulatory offences.

The distinction between regulatory offences and crimes is reflected in the way in which the Crown is required to prove its case. Until the mid-1970s, regulatory offences were treated as **absolute liability** offences. All that the prosecution had to establish was that the accused committed the *actus reus* of the offence. Questions about *mens rea* were, by definition, irrelevant.

absolute liability: culpability based on the commission of an *actus reus* without regard to the *mens rea*

However, in 1978, the Supreme Court of Canada decided that absolute liability was unfair. In *R v. Sault Ste. Marie*, the Court set out a new approach to regulatory offences. Henceforth, these offences were to be treated as strict liability offences. When prosecuting a **strict liability** offence, the Crown must establish that the accused person or corporation committed the *actus reus* of the offence. It is then open to the accused person or corporation to avoid liability by proving that it took all reasonable care to avoid committing the *actus reus*. If the accused cannot prove that it was "duly diligent" (took all reasonable care), it will be convicted. The Court saw strict liability as a compromise between absolute liability and full-blown criminal liability based on *mens rea*.

strict liability: culpability based on the commission of an *actus reus* and inability to prove the defence of due diligence

The difference between the three approaches can be illustrated by the example that follows. Assume that it is an offence under environmental protection legislation to discharge pollutants into a waterway. Assume also that the Crown can prove that Company X discharged pollutants into a river.

- If the offence is an absolute liability offence, Company X will be found guilty (and probably fined) once the Crown establishes that it committed the *actus reus* of discharging pollutants.
- If the offence is a full *mens rea* offence, the Crown will have to prove not only that Company X committed the *actus reus* of discharging pollutants but also that Company X did so with the requisite *mens rea*—that is, that Company X discharged pollutants intentionally or recklessly.
- If the offence is a strict liability offence, the Crown will have to prove that Company X committed the *actus reus* of discharging pollutants. Company X then has the option of avoiding liability by demonstrating that it was duly diligent because it made all reasonable efforts to avoid discharging the pollutants. It is the court's duty to determine what amounts to "reasonable efforts" in the circumstances.

Case DUE DILIGENCE AND ENVIRONMENTAL CONTAMINATION

R v. MacMillan Bloedel, 2002 BCCA 510

Facts

The possibility of a leakage from the accused company's underground pipes at its Skidegate operation in the Queen Charlotte Islands came to its attention in 1993, when it received a complaint from the Ministry of the Environment. At that time, the pipes, which had been installed in the 1960s, were dug up and tested. No leakage was discovered. The accused's equipment supervisor and its manager were of the opinion that the pipes were sound.

In September 1995, an environmental inspector with the accused's environmental services department prepared a comprehensive report. The report identified the use of underground fuel lines by the accused as a significant environmental problem. The inspector recommended that the pipes either be installed above ground or be contained in a secondary sleeve to allow early detection of leaks. The accused's personnel reviewed the report. As a result, underground lines were replaced at some locations.

The accused had replaced underground lines at some of its operations before receiving the report. There was some evidence that replaced pipes were found to be in good condition. The Skidegate pipes were regarded as low on the accused's list of environmental concerns, and there was no evidence as to when it intended to take any action with respect to them.

In May 1997, when a fisheries officer observed diesel fuel, the accused was charged with the offence of permitting a deleterious (harmful) substance to be deposited in water frequented by fish. The accused was convicted at trial, but an appeal was allowed, and the conviction was set aside. The Crown then appealed to the British Columbia Court of Appeal.

Issue

Did the accused exercise due diligence?

Decision

The Crown's appeal was dismissed. The majority of judges held that the conditions that produced the leak were not carelessly created by the accused. The accused honestly believed that the pipes were sound. The leak was caused by microbiological corrosion, which was not reasonably foreseeable. The accused did not foresee, and could not reasonably have foreseen, the particular event.

The minority held that the fact that the spill was not foreseeable was not a sufficient defence. There was no evidence that the accused had in place any specific plan to protect against the environmental risk of leaks from the pipes. The absence of a plan was not justified by the fact that the risk that materialized was not the precise risk contemplated by the accused.

Questions

1. Was the accused charged with an absolute liability offence, a strict liability offence, or a full *mens rea* offence? Explain your answer.
2. Over what issue did the court split? Do you prefer the majority or the minority opinion? Why?
3. Who should pay for the cost of cleanup? Does your answer depend on whether the accused company was found to have violated the regulations? Why or why not?

Check Your Understanding

1. Explain the difference between absolute and strict liability offences.
2. Explain the difference between regulatory offences and offences found in the *Criminal Code*. Give two examples of each type of offence.
3. What does it mean to be "duly diligent"?

Mens Rea and Fundamental Justice

When the *Canadian Charter of Rights and Freedoms* was entrenched in 1982, most commentators predicted that it would have an immense effect on criminal law. Many of the Charter's guarantees deal specifically with the administration of criminal justice. Sections 7 to 14, the legal rights provisions, are primarily concerned with the rights of individuals being investigated, charged, arrested, detained, or tried by the state. The unifying thread in these guarantees is the recognition that citizens caught up in the criminal process are entitled to fair treatment from the state. Fair treatment requires rules that redress the power imbalance between the accused and the state. These Charter guarantees reflect the reality of the risk of human rights violations in criminal-law enforcement. Section 7 contains the broadest of the legal rights guarantees. The scope of the s. 7 guarantee was one of the most important issues in *Re British Columbia Motor Vehicle Act* (see the case that follows).

Case ABSOLUTE LIABILITY VERSUS RIGHT TO PERSONAL LIBERTY

Re British Columbia Motor Vehicle Act, [1985] 2 SCR 486

Facts

On August 16, 1982, the lieutenant governor in council of British Columbia referred the following question to the British Columbia Court of Appeal: "Is s. 94(2) of the *Motor Vehicle Act* consistent with the *Canadian Charter of Rights and Freedoms*?" The British Columbia Court of Appeal found that s. 94(2) of the Act was inconsistent with s. 7 of the Charter. The Crown appealed to the Supreme Court of Canada.

Issue

Is the following legislation consistent with s. 7 of the Charter?

> 94(1) A person who drives a motor vehicle on a highway or industrial road while
>
> (a) he is prohibited from driving a motor vehicle under section 90, 91, 92 or 92.1 ...
>
> commits an offence and is liable ...
>
> (c) on a first conviction, to a fine of not less than \$300 and not more than \$2000 and to imprisonment for not less than 7 days and not more than 6 months. ...
>
> (2) Subsection (1) creates an absolute liability offence in which guilt is established by proof of driving, whether or not the defendant knew of the prohibition or suspension.

Decision

A law that has the potential to convict a person who has done nothing wrong offends the principles of fundamental justice. If imprisonment ensues, such a law violates a person's right to liberty under s. 7 of the Charter. Absolute liability and imprisonment cannot be combined. Justice

Lamer, writing for the majority of the Supreme Court, commented, "It has from time immemorial been part of our system of laws that the innocent not be punished. This principle has long been recognized as an essential element of a system for the administration of justice which is founded upon a belief in the dignity and worth of the human person and on the rule of law."

Questions

1. Explain the significance of this decision.
2. In his judgment, Justice Lamer quotes former Chief Justice Dickson when he writes, "there is a generally held revulsion against punishment of the morally innocent." What does Justice Lamer mean by moral innocence? Do you agree with this statement? Explain.

CHECK YOUR UNDERSTANDING

Review the wording of ss. 7 to 14 of the *Canadian Charter of Rights and Freedoms* (see the Appendix). What makes s. 7 a broader provision than ss. 8 to 14?

METHODS OF *Legal Inquiry*

Reading Statistics Critically

British Prime Minister Benjamin Disraeli once said, "There are lies, damned lies, and statistics." What did he mean?

Figure 8.6 was published on the Statistics Canada Web site. Statistics Canada is respected worldwide for the quality of its statistics. You would think that you could use these figures as printed if you had to write a report on the types of crimes committed in Canada in 2001. But can you?

You need to know how data are gathered to understand the figures. The Web site gives some of this information: "As of December 2001, 154 police forces/detachments were providing incident-based crime data, representing approximately 59% of the national volume of crime." The figures, for example, do not include the numbers of offences charged by the RCMP. The Web site also states, "Some urban municipalities are excluded because community size was less than 100 000, although they had a police force."

There are other questions you need to ask as you read this table. For instance, what is the definition of a youth? (Under the *Youth Criminal Justice Act*, a youth is a male or female between the ages of 12 and 17. At 18 years of age, people are considered adults.) You also need to read the explanatory notes beneath the table to understand the different definitions of crimes. Even then, you may have to research how the statistics have been categorized. What is the difference between "attempted murder," for example, and the third level of assault that endangers the life of a complainant?

These questions do not mean that you cannot use these statistics. They do indicate that you have to understand just how the figures were gathered and what they show.

Applying the Skill

1. Why is it important always to include the source for statistics that you use in a report?
2. Read Figure 8.6 carefully and draw up a list of questions to answer before you can be sure you understand what the figures represent.
3. Note that the table shows *charges laid*. What limitations does this table have for use in a report on crimes committed in Canada?
4. Write a letter to a newspaper, using parts of this table to argue that crime rates in Canada rose between 2000 and 2001.

Figure 8.6

Youths and Adults Charged by Type of Offence, Canada, 2001

	Youths Charged		Adults Charged	
	Rate per 100 000 population	% change from 2000 to 2001	Rate per 100 000 population	% change from 2000 to 2001
All incidents	**4656.9**	**0.5**	**2240.6**	**2.8**
Criminal Code offences (excluding traffic offences)	4140.6	0.7	1661.8	3.2
Crimes of violence	940.4	1.8	510.9	3.4
Homicide	1.2	-30.9	1.7	2.4
Attempted murder	2.9	30.5	2.4	-3.3
Assaults (level 1 to 3[1])	673.9	0.7	406.1	3.2
Sexual assault	64.9	-6.0	33.0	-0.4
Other sexual offences	6.5	3.2	2.7	-17.2
Robbery	145.8	9.5	28.9	6.8
Other crimes of violence[2]	45.2	6.8	39.3	9.7
Property crimes	1824.0	-3.3	518.7	-1.4
Breaking and entering	479.2	-6.2	85.6	-5.1
Motor vehicle theft	249.4	7.2	35.6	1.9
Theft over $5000	11.8	-2.1	8.6	4.7
Theft $5000 and under	780.8	-4.7	228.8	-0.2
Possession of stolen goods	224.3	-1.4	67.7	0.2
Frauds	78.5	-6.0	92.5	-3.5
Other *Criminal Code* offences	1376.2	5.6	632.2	7.1
Criminal Code offences (traffic offences)	0.0	**	357.4	3.2
Impaired driving	0.0	**	296.3	1.4
Other C.C. traffic offences[3]	0.0	**	61.1	12.9
Federal statutes	516.3	-0.6	221.4	-1.1
Drugs	338.5	5.9	196.7	-0.5
Other federal statutes	177.8	-11.0	24.8	-6.1

1. "Assault level 1" is the first level of assault. It constitutes the intentional application of force without consent, attempt or threat to apply force to another person, and openly wearing a weapon (or an imitation) and accosting or impeding another person. "Assault with weapon or causing bodily harm" is the second level of assault. It constitutes assault with a weapon, threats to use a weapon (or an imitation), or assault causing bodily harm. "Aggravated assault level 3" is the third level of assault. It applies to anyone who wounds, maims, disfigures, or endangers the life of complainant.
2. Includes unlawfully causing bodily harm, discharging firearms with intent, abductions, assaults against police officers, assaults against other peace or public officers, and other assaults.
3. Includes dangerous operation of motor vehicle, boat, vessel, or aircraft; dangerous operation of motor vehicle, boat, vessel, or aircraft causing bodily harm or death; driving motor vehicle while prohibited; and failure to stop or remain.

Source: Statistics Canada, CANSIM II, table 252-0014. Last modified: 2003-02-28. Available at www.statcan.ca/english/Pgdb/legal17a.htm.

Reviewing Main Ideas

You Decide!

CORRECTING CHILDREN BY FORCE

Canadian Foundation for Children, Youth and the Law v. Canada (Attorney General) (2002), 161 CCC (3d) 178 (Ont. CA)

This case is an appeal by the Canadian Foundation for Children, Youth and the Law from a decision of the Ontario Superior Court of Justice. The Ontario Superior Court ruled that s. 43 of the *Criminal Code*, which authorizes the correction of children by force in certain circumstances, does not violate s. 7 or s. 15(1) of the *Canadian Charter of Rights and Freedoms.*

Facts

The Canadian Foundation for Children, Youth and the Law is a not-for-profit organization that advocates on behalf of children. The foundation applied to the court for a declaration that s. 43 of the *Criminal Code* is unconstitutional and of no force and effect. The foundation was supported by the Ontario Association of Children's Aid Societies.

The Attorney General of Canada, arguing that s. 43 was constitutional, was supported by the Canadian Teachers' Federation and the Coalition for Family Autonomy.

The application did not arise from specific facts. The parties presented a significant volume of affidavit evidence from experts in child protection, children's rights, and social science research.

At trial, the judge made the following findings:

1. Hitting a child under two is wrong and harmful.
2. Corporal punishment of teenagers is not helpful and is potentially harmful.
3. Corporal punishment using objects such as belts and rulers is potentially harmful, both physically and emotionally, and should not be tolerated.
4. Corporal punishment that causes injury is child abuse.
5. Experts do not recommend spanking or other forms of corporal punishment as a form of child discipline.
6. The consensus among the experts is that not every instance of physical discipline by a parent should be criminalized.
7. There is no empirical evidence establishing a definitive long-term causal link between corporal punishment and negative outcomes for children.

The Law

Section 43 of the *Criminal Code* provides as follows:

> Every schoolteacher, parent or person standing in the place of a parent is justified in using force by way of correction toward a pupil or child ... who is under his care, if the force does not exceed what is reasonable under the circumstances.

Sections 7 and 15(1) of the Charter, the fundamental justice and equality provisions respectively, are set out in the Appendix of this text.

Arguments Supporting Section 43

Section 43 puts a limited aspect of family life beyond the reach of the criminal law. It provides a defence for what would otherwise be criminal assault to a small group—parents, surrogate parents, and teachers—who interact with children on a daily basis. The section is strictly limited in its application. It exempts the use of force only when it is reasonable in the circumstances and when it is applied by way of correction. The section is reasonably tailored to permit parents and teachers to carry out their responsibilities without the harm that criminal sanctions would bring to them and their families.

The section strikes a fair balance between the interests of children and the state. The issue is not whether the correction of children is good or bad, but whether the state is entitled to create a limited defence for a small group. The state has many mechanisms in place to protect children from abuse and is vigorously pursuing educational programs to discourage all physical punishment of children.

Section 43 can be justified under s. 1 of the Charter. It recognizes that parents and teachers have important responsibilities with respect to children and that they should be allowed to exercise those responsibilities without undue state interference. The area of conduct decriminalized by the section is so strictly limited that it could not be narrowed further without eliminating the defence entirely.

Arguments Against Section 43

The purpose of the criminal law is to protect members of society from harm. Section 43 violates that principle of protection by explicitly legitimating the use of force against children. Children have the right to security of the person under s. 7 of the Charter. Section 43 is vague and ambiguous. It legitimates the "reasonable" use of force for "correction." Both of these concepts defy definition. The provision has been used in the past to justify the criminal assault of children. There is no reason to believe that it will not be used in this way in the future.

Section 43 violates equality rights under s. 15(1) of the Charter. It specifically decriminalizes assaults against only one group in society: children. The section differentiates on the basis of age and subjects children to differential, demeaning, and potentially dangerous treatment.

The differential treatment of children is not justifiable under s. 1 of the Charter. There is no evidence that the physical correction of children serves any useful purpose. The legislation draws an unjustifiable line around the family and the classroom, insulating potentially abusive parents and teachers. It puts children at risk and sends the message that corporal punishment is acceptable and appropriate.

Make Your Decision

1. Who are the parties and their supporters in this case?
2. What are the issues that the court was required to decide?
3. Summarize the arguments in support of and against the constitutionality of s. 43.
4. Decide whether the appeal should be allowed or dismissed. Explain your legal reasoning.
5. The Supreme Court of Canada granted leave to appeal this decision on October 17, 2002, and the appeal was heard on June 6, 2003. Judgment was reserved. Using the case number 29113, follow the progress of the appeal at the Supreme Court of Canada's Web site.

Key Terms

Review the following terms to show that you understand the meaning of each and how it is applied in a legal context.

absolute liability	*mens rea*
actus reus	requisite intention
ambit of the offence	sanctions
culpability	strict liability
interpretive presumption	vitiated by fraud

Understanding the Law

Review the following pieces of legislation mentioned in the text, and show that you understand the intent of each.

British Columbia *Motor Vehicle Act*
Canadian Charter of Rights and Freedoms, ss. 1 and 7–14
Constitution Act, 1982, s. 91(27)
Controlled Drugs and Substances Act
Criminal Code, ss. 43, 71, 90, 163.1, 175, 222, 242, 265, 268, 319, 346, 365, and 446
Female Refuges Act
Firearms Act
Safe Streets Act

Thinking and Inquiry

1. What purpose do the following offences serve? What principles justify the state in sanctioning the prohibited behaviour?
   - Possession of child pornography under s. 163.1(4) of the *Criminal Code*, where "child pornography" is defined as "a photographic, film, video or other visual representation, whether or not it was made by electronic or mechanical means ... that shows a person who is or is depicted as being under the age of eighteen years and is engaged in or is depicted as engaged in explicit sexual activity."
   - Cruelty to animals under s. 446(1)(a) of the *Criminal Code*: "Every one commits an offence who … wilfully causes or, being the owner, wilfully permits to be caused unnecessary pain, suffering or injury to an animal or a bird."
   - Disorderly conduct under s. 175(1)(a) of the *Criminal Code*: "Every one who ... not being in a dwelling-house, causes a disturbance in or near a public place ... by fighting, screaming, shouting, swearing, singing or using insulting or obscene language ... is guilty of an offence."
   - Possession of cannabis, under s. 4 of the *Controlled Drugs and Substances Act*, except as authorized by the regulations.
2. Research the current status of the law relating to homosexuality. How have the laws changed since 1968? Explain your findings in a short report.
3. Elizabeth Fry wrote: "When thee builds a prison, thee had better build with the thought ever in thy mind that thee and thy children may occupy the cells." Using the story of Velma Demerson or information of your own, respond to Fry's words.
4. Design two profiles comparing and contrasting criminals responsible for street crime with white-collar criminals. What conclusions can you draw?

Communication

5. With a partner or in a small group, interview a person who has been a victim of crime to gain an understanding of the impact of crime on people's lives. Alternatively, find an article in the newspaper that describes a crime, imagine the feelings of the victim, and interpret them. In either case, present your findings in an oral report or a video.
6. Prepare arguments supporting either the retributive or the protective purpose of criminal law. Participate in a classroom debate on which of these two purposes is more important.
7. Use the Statistics Canada Web site or other source to locate criminal statistics relating to the types of offences committed by females.

Convert this information into a graph to display in the classroom. Comment on the graph and any trends that it shows.

8. Select an offence from the *Criminal Code*. In a small group, create a dramatic scene to illustrate the *actus reus* and *mens rea* of this offence. Present this scene to the class, who will deduce the *actus reus* and *mens rea* from your performance.

Application

9. Use resources such as the Internet, newspapers, and news magazines to find information on several criminal cases currently before the courts. For each case, determine the offence, the *actus reus*, the *mens rea*, and the facts of the case. Present arguments that you believe the Crown and the defence will raise. Speculate on the outcome of each case.
10. Review the research from *Justice and the Poor* on pages 240–242 that addresses the conditions faced by children most at risk of becoming delinquents and criminals. What types of intervention programs could be put in place to help these children? Focus on one program and prepare a brief on why your program should receive government funding.
11. Refer to the case *Re British Columbia Motor Vehicle Act* on page 253. Suppose the government wanted to enact new legislation that would survive a Charter challenge. What would the drafters have to change? Redraft the provision to make it "Charter-proof." Does your redrafted provision achieve the same objectives as the original legislation?

Chapter 9 Rules of Criminal Procedure

CHAPTER *Focus*

In this chapter, you will

- explain the processes of police investigation, including collection of evidence and forensic testing
- compare the rules of arrest for both police and private citizens
- explain the procedure for obtaining a search warrant
- analyze the procedures for ensuring an accused person's attendance in court
- demonstrate an understanding of the methods of trial
- assess the role of Crown disclosure in the trial process

Each moment in the chain of events from crime to trial is subject to the laws of criminal procedure. These laws balance two sometimes conflicting objectives: to discover the truth about a criminal event and to protect civil liberties. The rules of criminal procedure mark the boundary between legitimate police investigative practices and every person's right to liberty, privacy, and personal security. They reflect the beliefs that state power should be limited, that the rule of law applies as much to police as to people accused of crimes, and that the ends do not always justify the means. The entrenchment of the *Canadian Charter of Rights and Freedoms* has confirmed our commitment to fair process by making Canadian criminal procedure a matter of constitutional law.

The cartoon in Figure 9.1 asks you to consider the question of rights.

"I can read you your rights, or you can listen to your rights on tape."

Figure 9.1

At First Glance

1. Why do police officers "read" people "their rights"?
2. Why has the cartoonist referred to listening to rights on tape?
3. What rights do you think the young person in the cartoon has?
4. What rights do you think the police officer has?
5. Should young people have more rights than adults on arrest? Why or why not?

Crime Scene Investigation

Police play a crucial role in the initial phase of criminal investigations as a result of their responsibility to investigate crime scenes and to collect and secure evidence. The strength and integrity of ensuing criminal procedures depend to a large extent on the competence of police officers during the investigative stage. Lapses can contaminate the proceedings that follow and result in miscarriages of justice.

The Crime Scene

A crime scene, which may be the residence of a suspect or a location in which a crime occurred, is often a rich source of physical evidence. It is crucial that the scene be secured so that evidence is not lost or tampered with. This requirement places a heavy responsibility on the officers who arrive first at the scene. After attending to the most pressing duties (arresting suspects, assisting the injured, and eliminating potential risks), the first officers at the scene of a crime must determine the boundaries of the crime scene. They must take steps to protect the area from accidental or intentional contamination by anyone, including police officers and other official personnel.

Police officers have the authority to cordon off and refuse entry to a crime scene under s. 129 of the *Criminal Code*, which provides for the arrest and punishment of any person obstructing a police officer in the lawful execution of his or her duties. The 1973 case *R v. Knowlton* has established that police officers are lawfully executing their duties when they refuse admittance to anyone attempting to enter an area cordoned off by police.

Determination of the point at which a crime scene may safely be removed from police control is made by the officer in charge of the investigation, unless the incident involves a death. In this case, the security of the scene falls under the coroner's authority. In Ontario, cases falling under the jurisdiction of the coroner include

- sudden or unexpected deaths
- deaths of persons in custody

To find out more about the Ontario *Coroners Act*, visit www.emp.ca/dimensionsoflaw

- deaths occurring in institutions, including homes for the aged
- deaths from violence
- suicides
- deaths occurring in a suspicious, unusual, or unnatural manner.

The *Coroners Act* allows police officers and others acting under their control to seize anything relevant to the investigation at the crime scene and to maintain the security of the scene until it is ordered released by the coroner following the post mortem examination.

To find out more about the collection of evidence at crime scenes, visit www.emp.ca/dimensionsoflaw

Processing the Crime Scene

Once the crime scene has been secured, the focus of a police investigation moves to the collection of physical evidence. Some physical evidence, such as a knife left at the scene of a homicide, is readily identifiable. Other evidence—fingerprints, for example—requires detection, collection, and interpretation by experts. Crime scene investigation is carried out by members of a mobile crime lab or identification officers who are trained in the analysis of physical evidence. These officers are responsible for preparing a description of what they find, photographing the scene, preparing diagrams or sketches, and collecting evidence. Because the field of forensic evidence is so broad, police departments often hire specialists, such as anthropologists or blood pattern analysts.

continuity of evidence: continuous chain of possession designed to ensure the safekeeping of evidence

Police departments have also established procedures for the seizure, handling, and storage of evidence. Procedures may vary slightly from department to department, but all are designed to safeguard the **continuity of evidence**. Figure 9.3 distills some of the procedures followed by most police departments.

Figure 9.2 *A police detective dusts for fingerprints at a crime scene.*

Crime Scene Procedures

- No exhibit is left unattended from the time of its seizure until it is deposited in the police property-storage facility.
- The officer who seized the item, or the **case officer**, must secure the evidence in the police property locker, which is under the control of the property clerk.
- The transfer of any evidence to the forensic laboratory is the responsibility of the case officer and/or his or her designate.
- The transfer of evidence to and from court is the responsibility of the case officer.
- No exhibit can be removed from the control of the property clerk without appropriate authority and signatures.

Figure 9.3

case officer: officer in charge of an investigation

Processing Physical Evidence

Physical evidence collected at a crime scene is like the pieces of a puzzle. It is the job of forensic scientists to put the pieces together correctly. In their laboratories, forensic scientists examine, test, and analyze the physical evidence. Analysis may involve biology, chemistry, physics, anthropology, geology, and computer science. Forensic scientists are often called on to give expert testimony in court.

Fyi Forensic science has a long history. In 1248, a Chinese book entitled *His Duan Yu (The Washing Away of Wrongs)* described how to distinguish between drowning and strangulation. The first documented use of physical matching occurred in 1784 in Lancaster, England, where John Toms was convicted of murder on the basis of a torn piece of newspaper in a pistol that matched a second piece found in Toms's pocket.

Fingerprints

Along with DNA, fingerprints are considered by many to be the best way to identify a suspect and place him or her at a crime scene. Fingerprints never change and are unique to each person. All fingerprint patterns can be identified as one of three types (see Figure 9.4 on page 264):

1. *arches*, forming ridges that run from one side of the print to the other and curve up the middle
2. *loops*, showing stronger curves than arches with ends that start on one side of the finger, loop around, and end up in the same place
3. *whorls*, forming complete ovals, often in a spiral pattern around a central point.

Some fingerprints are created when a person's fingers come into contact with an object such as a piece of glass or a plastic bag. A residue of oil and perspiration from the fingertip is deposited on the object's surface. This type of print, called a *latent fingerprint*, is usually invisible and requires the application of chemicals or laser light. Fingerprints known as *visible impressions* are the result of a finger's contact with a surface where blood, dust, or grease has been previously deposited. Another type of print, called a *moulded fingerprint*, leaves a visible impression in a soft substance such as clay, wax, or putty.

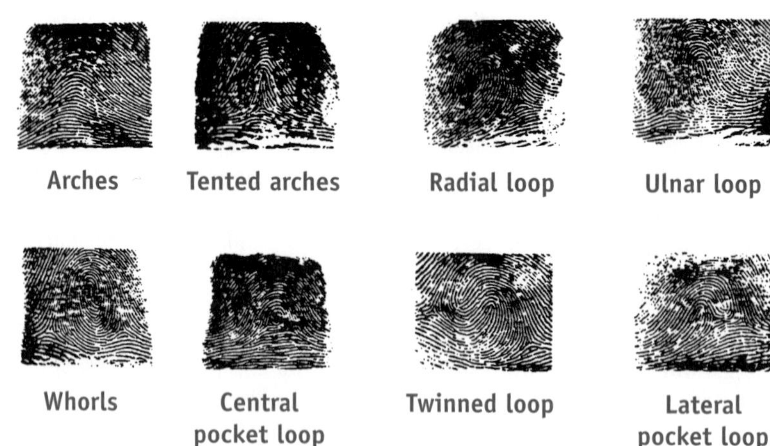

Figure 9.4 *Different patterns found on fingerprints.*

Fingerprints taken from a crime scene are sent to a central repository administered by the RCMP in Ottawa. If an individual has prints on file as a result of a previous arrest or conviction, and if the quality of the fingerprint is adequate, the individual's identity can be determined through comparison with the prints submitted by the police. The characteristics of each print are examined by experts. When a sufficient number of characteristics are thought to be identical (usually 10 to 12 points of comparison), an expert may form the opinion that the print submitted is that of the individual whose prints are on file.

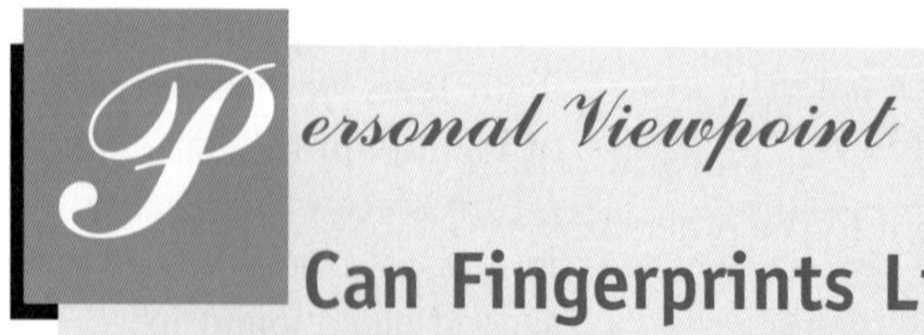

Can Fingerprints Lie?

In 1998, at a murder scene in a small Scottish town, forensic experts made an unexpected discovery: a fingerprint found in the victim's house matched that of Shirley McKie, a young police officer assigned to the case. The problem was that McKie had never been in the victim's house. McKie testified to that effect at the subsequent trial of the victim's handyman, whose conviction depended on fingerprint evidence. Prosecutors, enraged that McKie had cast doubt on the validity of their fingerprint evidence, charged her with perjury.

At McKie's request, Allan Bayle, arguably the foremost fingerprint expert in the United Kingdom, examined the print. Bayle asserted that it was not McKie's. How could such an error have been made? In the words of journalist Michael Specter, who investigated the case, "When fingerprints are properly recorded (inked, then rolled, finger by finger, onto a flat surface, or scanned into a machine that captures and stores each finger as a digital image), identification works almost flawlessly. The trouble is that investigators in the field rarely see the pristine prints that can be quickly analyzed by a computer ... . Crime scenes are messy, and the average fingerprint taken from them represents only a fraction of a full fingertip—about 20 per cent. They are frequently distorted and hard to read, having been lifted from a grainy table or a blood-stained floor."

McKie was eventually acquitted of perjury, but she was unable to return to work on the police force. Later, she told the Fingerprint Society that the system it represents is "incestuous, secretive, and arrogant. ... You are indicted on the basis of a fingerprint. You are not innocent till proven guilty; if the police have a print, you are assumed to be guilty. We need to start a new culture. The view that the police and fingerprint evidence are always right, the rest of the world be damned, has to end."

Bayle's involvement in McKie's case caused a furor and forced him from his job with the Metropolitan Police after 25 years' service. He commented, "When you know something is wrong, how can you stay silent? It's a valuable craft, but is it a science like physics or biology? Well, of course not. ... It is such a subjective job."

Source: Adapted from Michael Specter, "Annals of Crime: Do Fingerprints Lie?," http://www.michaelspecter.com/ny/2002/2002_05_27_fingerprint.html.

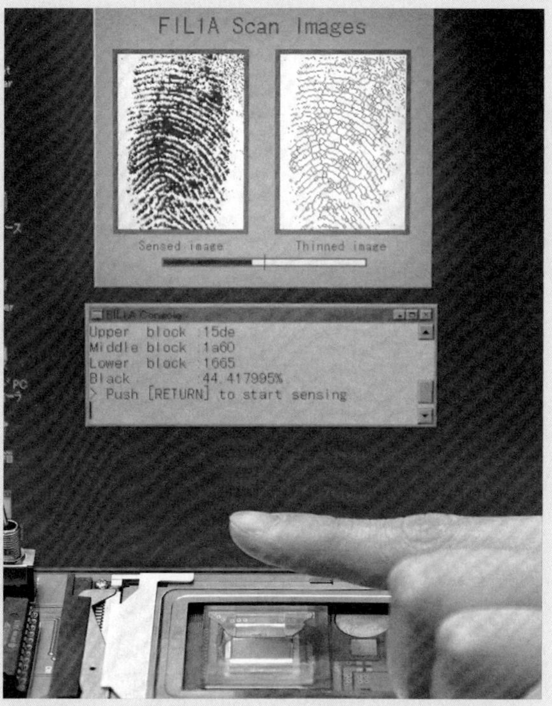

Figure 9.5 *An image sensed by a microchip capable of identifying fingerprints. The image shown at right is the computerized thinned image of the left image, for ease of identification.*

Questions

1. Suggest reasons why fingerprint analysis is not an exact science.
2. Examine your fingerprints. What type of fingerprint patterns do you have? Check a classmate's. Are the patterns different?
3. Are there dangers in presenting the evidence of fingerprint experts in court? Give reasons for your answer. Suggest ways in which any dangers might be overcome.

Trace Elements

Dirt, dust, and residue, even in the minutest quantities, are known as *trace elements.* The origin of these elements may provide a link between a suspect and a crime. For example, wood or other materials at an arson scene may produce trace elements of the accelerant used to start or maintain a fire. Further examination by experts may uncover the specific chemical composition of the fluid, thus linking it to a suspect who possesses the same material. During an investigation into a series of fires in Hamilton, experts linked the fluid used to start fires to fluid found in the garage of one of the suspects. Both samples were mixed in exactly the same proportions and were not sold by any manufacturer.

The transfer of trace elements such as hair and fibres between perpetrator and victim is common in crimes such as homicide, aggravated assault, and kidnapping. Finding hair as a trace element on either the accused or the victim may link the two individuals. Although hair alone cannot positively identify someone, expert analysis may reveal a person's racial background if the sample contains the root, shaft, and tip. Experts can also determine the area of the body from which the hair originated and, if the root is present, the person's blood type.

Expert examination of fibres may determine their point of origin or manufacturer. During the Atlanta child murder investigation of the 1970s, experts were able to determine that fibres found on the soles of the shoes of one of the victims were left behind after contact between the victim and a rug in the accused's residence. In contrast, however, fibre evidence led by the Crown was no doubt partially responsible for the wrongful conviction of accused child murderer Guy Paul Morin in Ontario in 1992.

Blood

The evidentiary value of blood is paramount in impaired-driving cases, since the offence of impaired driving is based on the percentage of alcohol in the suspect's blood. Blood is also relevant in cases where a suspect's *mens rea* is in issue as a result of the ingestion of intoxicating substances.

Because it is a fluid, blood conforms to the laws that govern the motion and properties of other fluids. A study of the size and shape of blood drops on a floor can indicate the height from which they fell and thus the location of the wound that produced the drops. The shape of the drop may indicate movement. A person who is in motion while bleeding produces a tear-shaped drop, with the narrow end indicating the direction of travel and the rounded end pointing toward the bleeder. An examination of blood spatters on a wall may indicate the force and direction of a blow. It may also indicate how far the victim was from the wall when the wound was inflicted.

Gunshot Residue

gunshot residue (GSR): trace substances left on surfaces, including the hand of the shooter, after the discharge of a firearm

When a firearm is discharged, many materials other than the bullet are expelled from the muzzle. These materials, known as **gunshot residue (GSR)**, include gases, unburned or partially burned powder grains, carbon particles, traces of the bullet lubricant, traces of primer components (lead, barium, nitrates), fragments of soft bullets (lead, antimony), fragments of the bullet jacket, and metal traces from the cartridge case or gun barrel. These trace elements are deposited on the hands of the person discharging the gun and are, under certain circumstances, detectable and identifiable.

At one time, a procedure known as a paraffin test was used to detect GSR; however, because of its lack of specificity, this test has been replaced by a *handwash test.* It requires the suspect to wash his or her hands in a chemical solution that is then sent to the laboratory for analysis. This test is able to detect elevated levels of lead, barium, and antimony, which may indicate that the suspect has fired a gun recently. However, handling a weapon after it has been fired may contaminate the hands, thus leading to an incorrect conclusion. The GSR test cannot determine the time at which the suspect may have fired the gun. It is also less effective when the time between firing the gun and taking the handwash sample exceeds four hours.

A newer test for GSR shows promise. The *scanning electron microscopy (SEM) test* provides results that appear to be more accurate and consistent than those of the handwash test. Acquiring a sample is also less cumbersome. A special utensil containing a gummed substance is held against the skin and then removed. The GSR adheres to the gummed substance, which is then prepared for examination by the scanning electron miscroscope.

DNA

All human beings have a distinctive genetic code within their 46 chromosomes, which are composed of **deoxyribonucleic acid (DNA)**. Laboratory analysis of blood stains, semen, saliva, vaginal secretions, skin, and hair follicles can lead to the identification of an individual through his or her distinctive genetic code. When DNA is properly analyzed, it can identify an individual with a certainty exceeding one in several billion. Minute samples of human material are sufficient to produce reliable results even when a sample combines two or more substances. For example, blood taken from a homocide victim may have several of a suspect's skin cells mixed with it. This apparent contamination does not affect the reliability of the test. DNA testing has also been used to rule out suspects.

deoxyribonucleic acid (DNA): biological compound that forms cell chromosomes, from which genetic information can be obtained

Turning Points in the Law

The Discovery of DNA

DNA testing has been available since the early 1980s. Despite its relative newness, it has had a dramatic impact on the collection of evidence at crime scenes. In Canada, it has been used to prove the innocence of accused murderers Guy Paul Morin and David Milgaard.

DNA testing was invented by Alec Jeffreys, a geneticist at Leicester University in England. In the early 1980s, as Jeffreys experimented with removing DNA from human muscle tissue, he discovered that certain segments of human DNA were genetic markers, each as unique to an individual as his or her fingerprints. Realizing that his discovery could benefit law enforcement, Jeffreys found a way to process these genetic markers by using electricity and radioactive labelling to form a distinctive bar code pattern on x-ray film.

Since the 1980s, the process of extracting DNA has become much easier. Today testing takes hours to complete. Laboratory technicians can now use minute amounts of DNA to create a genetic marker. Crime scene technicians can retrieve DNA from a small drop of blood or the slightest residue of a suspect's sneeze.

In Canada, DNA was first used in 1989 by the RCMP while investigating a sexual assault. The victim had identified her attacker, but the suspect denied involvement. Halfway through the trial, after the DNA evidence was presented, the suspect changed his plea to guilty.

The forensic use of DNA is a powerful tool, but caution is called for. Consider the case of Josiah Sutton, a man wrongfully convicted of rape in 1999 on the basis of DNA evidence. An audit of the Texas laboratory responsible for the DNA testing found that "technicians had misinterpreted data, were poorly trained and kept shoddy records. In most cases, they used up all available evidence, preventing defense experts from refuting or verifying their results. Even the laboratory building was a mess, with a leaky roof having contaminated evidence." The files of 25 convicted people, seven of whom were on death row, were reopened as a result of the revelations of faulty DNA testing. William Thompson, a criminology professor who studied the laboratory's work, stated: "The likelihood that there are more innocent people convicted because of bad lab work is almost certain."

In 1995, the government of Canada added s. 487.05 to the *Criminal Code* to allow a judge to issue a warrant authorizing police to obtain DNA evidence from suspects. Five years later, the government established the National DNA Data Bank and enacted the *DNA Identification Act*, which allows judges to authorize the collection of DNA samples from offenders. As of January 27, 2003, the National Data Bank has entered 34 103 DNA profiles into the convicted offender index (CODIS) and 7782 into the crime scene index (CSI).

Questions

1. Should police be empowered to obtain DNA evidence from persons suspected of committing crimes or from other citizens? Why or why not?
2. Suggest procedures for quality control that might eliminate DNA testing errors.

Figure 9.6 *British Prime Minister Tony Blair has a DNA swab taken for Britain's national DNA database in 1999.*

CHECK YOUR UNDERSTANDING

1. Why is it essential that police be well trained in the investigation of crime scenes? Give an example of how lack of attention to detail may lead to a miscarriage of justice.
2. How do police safeguard the continuity of evidence? Why are these safeguards necessary?
3. Name five different types of physical evidence that experts might be required to examine. Describe how each type might be relevant in a criminal proceeding. Describe how this evidence could prove deceptive.

Impact of the Charter on Police Powers

The primary challenge for the rules of criminal procedure is balancing the efficient enforcement of the law with the protection of individual rights. Some commentators contend that the entrenchment of the *Canadian Charter of Rights and Freedoms* in 1982 shifted the balance in favour of individual rights. However, constitutional rights, such as the right to be secure from unreasonable search or seizure and from arbitrary detention or imprisonment, are not new.

In common law, police powers are limited, and the right to privacy in the home has been recognized since Magna Carta. Similarly, the **writ of *habeas corpus*** is an ancient common-law remedy whose purpose is to test the legality of a detention or imprisonment. In interpreting the Charter, courts have had the benefit of centuries-old common-law precedents.

writ of *habeas corpus*: common-law remedy to test the legality of detention or imprisonment

What is different now is that, under the Charter, courts have the power to enforce compliance with constitutionally guaranteed rights and freedoms. The Charter not only proclaims and guarantees rights; it also provides a remedy when these rights are violated. Section 24(2) provides courts with a new power: the **discretion** to exclude evidence from the trial of an accused person. Illegally or unconstitutionally obtained evidence is not excluded automatically. Rather, a court must determine if the administration of justice would be brought "into disrepute" by its admission.

discretion: freedom to decide a matter in accordance with the principles of fairness

When the Charter was enacted, many commentators were concerned that courts might exclude evidence even when rights violations were "mere technicalities" and that guilty people might be acquitted. Most analysts now agree that the Charter has not had this effect. However, the Charter has changed the debate about the nature and limits of police powers. It has forced courts to grapple with difficult questions about what brings the administration of justice into disrepute, and whose perspective governs this issue.

Consider the case of *R v. Stillman.* A 17-year-old accused was arrested for a brutal murder. His lawyers informed the police that he refused to consent to providing any bodily samples or statements. Once the lawyer left the station, the police took hair samples and plasticine teeth impressions from the accused under threat of force. He was subsequently released but arrested several months later. New teeth impressions were taken by a dentist without the accused's consent. Samples of bodily substances were also taken.

The Supreme Court of Canada found that the police had shown a blatant disregard for the accused's fundamental rights. The accused had been compelled to incriminate himself by providing evidence of his bodily substances. Such evidence was tantamount to a forced confession. The evidence, obtained in violation of s. 8, was excluded under s. 24(2) of the Charter.

The following factors were considered relevant in applying s. 24(2).

- Will admission of the evidence render the trial unfair?
- Was the breach of the Charter committed in good faith? Was it inadvertent or trivial, or was it deliberate and flagrant?
- Was the Charter breach motivated by urgency or the need to prevent the loss or destruction of the evidence?
- Will the administration of justice be brought into disrepute as a result of the exclusion of the evidence?
- How serious is the offence?
- How important is the evidence?

Check Your Understanding

1. What is the origin of the right to be free from unreasonable search of one's home? How has the Charter affected this right?
2. Explain how s. 24(2) of the Charter can be used to control police misconduct in gathering evidence.
3. Can the administration of justice be brought into disrepute when persons who commit violent crimes are found not guilty because of insufficient evidence? Can the administration of justice be brought into disrepute when persons who commit violent crimes are convicted because of illegally obtained evidence? Explain your answers.
4. Using the factors enumerated by the court in *R v. Stillman,* discuss how a society's commitment to the rule of law is tested when brutal measures are applied by the police to obtain evidence from a person who committed a brutal offence.

Working for Change *When Emotionally Disturbed Persons Break the Law*

On February 20, 1997, Edmond Yu, a 35-year-old former medical student suffering from paranoid schizophrenia, was shot and killed by a police officer in Toronto. Shortly before, he had assaulted a woman at a bus stop, and police were called to intervene. The officers found him sitting at the back of a bus, and after talking with him for some minutes learned he was schizophrenic. Yu became agitated, stood up, pulled a hammer from his coat, and brandished it. The officers drew their guns and told Yu to drop the hammer. When he did not respond, one fired his gun, killing Yu instantly.

The coroner's inquest that followed this tragedy recommended steps that should be taken to try to avert such incidents. Of the 24 recommendations, 12 concerned the police. One of the most important recommendations was that the Ontario solicitor general amend the *Police Services Act* to require annual crisis-resolution training for police officers. Although this recommendation was not implemented, the Toronto Police Service nevertheless set up special training for its officers. New recruits receive a five-day course in crisis resolution automatically, and gradually all other officers have been required to take this instruction.

Mental health professionals and others were consulted to put the course together. Officers are trained especially in de-escalation techniques that can be used to defuse a crisis. "Active listening skills" are part of this technique. Evidence at the Yu inquest showed that a crisis team of professionals would have helped handle the situation if they had been called. Another recommendation, therefore, was that a list of crisis teams with telephone numbers should be available to all dispatchers and at all police divisions. A pamphlet has been put together to address this concern.

Another recommendation concerned the use of force. Since the time of the inquest, the Taser—a "stun gun" that can restrain persons who become aggressive, threatening violence to themselves and others—has been introduced. It temporarily incapacitates people by electromuscular disruption, but without side effects, and can be used with emotionally disturbed people like Yu.

Emotionally disturbed people cannot be made to undergo treatment, including taking drugs, for their condition. Since the mid-1990s in Ontario, government policy has recommended that these people be treated within the community rather than in hospitals, and treatment too is voluntary under the *Mental Health Act*. Yu had stopped taking medications because of their side effects.

Nine mental health implementation task forces have been set up across Ontario to make recommendations to the Ontario minister of health on how to restructure the mental health system to improve delivery of services. One goal is to develop a service continuum that will lessen the likelihood that people like Yu will come into contact with police.

Questions

1. Do you think it is appropriate that police should be called to intervene in situations such as the one that involved Yu? Why or why not?
2. Make suggestions as to how a situation such as that involving Yu could be handled without police involvement.

The Arrest Power

Common sense suggests that an "arrest" involves the physical taking of a suspect into custody. The legal definition of arrest is more expansive: it includes touching with a view to detention and/or using words of arrest to which a suspect submits. Arrests may take place either with or without the authority of a judicial **warrant**. They may be made by police officers or, in limited circumstances, by private citizens. The primary purpose of an arrest is to compel an accused person's appearance at trial. Sections 494 and 495 of the *Criminal Code* establish the rules for effecting a warrantless

warrant: grant of judicial authority to arrest or search arrest. These sections are best understood by examining the way in which *Criminal Code* offences are classified.

indictable: term used to describe a serious offence under the *Criminal Code*, prosecuted in a manner more complex and carrying penalties more severe than a summary conviction offence

summary conviction: term used to describe an offence under the *Criminal Code*, prosecuted in a manner less complex and carrying penalties less severe than an indictable offence

hybrid offence: term used to describe an offence under the *Criminal Code*, prosecuted as either an indictable or a summary conviction offence at the discretion of the Crown

information: sworn statement setting out reasonable and probable grounds to believe that an offence has been committed; used as a basis for obtaining a warrant

In Canada, we use the terms **indictable** and **summary conviction** to distinguish between serious and less serious offences. Offences are classified in offence-creating or penalty sections of the Code. For example, s. 235(1) states that murder is an indictable offence, while s. 175(1) states that causing a disturbance is "punishable on summary conviction." Procedures for the prosecution of indictable offences are more complex, and the penalties are more severe than for summary conviction offences. Some offences give the Crown a choice of proceeding "by indictment" or "by summary conviction." These offences, called **hybrid offences** or "dual procedure" offences, cover a range of activities from relatively trivial to extremely serious. Assault is an example of a hybrid offence.

The *Criminal Code* also contains provisions for the arrest of suspects under judicial warrants. These warrants are usually issued after a police officer lays an **information** before a justice of the peace that sets out reasonable and probable grounds to believe that an offence has been committed.

The Law Some arrest provisions of the *Criminal Code* are set out below.

494(1) Any one may arrest without warrant
- (a) a person whom he finds committing an indictable offence; or
- (b) a person who, on reasonable grounds, he believes
  - (i) has committed a criminal offence, and
  - (ii) is escaping from and freshly pursued by persons who have lawful authority to arrest that person.

(2) Any one who is
- (a) the owner or a person in lawful possession of property, or
- (b) a person authorized by the owner or by a person in lawful possession of property,

may arrest without warrant a person whom he finds committing a criminal offence on or in relation to that property.

(3) Any one other than a peace officer who arrests a person without warrant shall forthwith deliver the person to a peace officer.

495(1) A peace officer may arrest without warrant
- (a) a person who has committed an indictable offence or who, on reasonable grounds, he believes has committed or is about to commit an indictable offence;
- (b) a person whom he finds committing a criminal offence; or
- (c) a person in respect of whom he has reasonable grounds to believe that a warrant of arrest or committal ... is in force within the territorial jurisdiction in which the person is found.

(2) A peace officer shall not arrest a person without warrant for
  (a) an indictable offence mentioned in section 553,
  (b) an offence for which the person may be prosecuted by indictment or for which he is punishable on summary conviction, or
  (c) an offence punishable on summary conviction,

in any case where
  (d) he believes on reasonable grounds that the public interest, having regard to all the circumstances including the need to
    (i) establish the identity of the person,
    (ii) secure or preserve evidence of or relating to the offence, or
    (iii) prevent the continuation or repetition of the offence or the commission of another offence,

may be satisfied without so arresting the person, and
  (e) he has no reasonable grounds to believe that, if he does not so arrest the person, the person will fail to attend court in order to be dealt with according to law.

Questions

1. Create a chart that illustrates the circumstances under which: a peace officer may arrest without a warrant; a peace officer may not arrest without a warrant; and a private citizen may make an arrest.
2. Why do you think these distinctions exist?

Arrest and the Charter

Sections 9 and 10 of the *Canadian Charter of Rights and Freedoms* have added a constitutional dimension to the arrest process. Both provisions apply not only to individuals who have been arrested—a formal legal process—but also to individuals who have been detained.

In *R v. Therens*, a police officer demanded that the accused driver provide samples of his breath for analysis. The driver accompanied the officer to the police station and there complied with the breathalyzer demand without being advised of his right to counsel under s. 10(b) of the Charter. The Supreme Court of Canada dismissed the Crown's appeal from a decision upholding the trial judge's exclusion of evidence of the accused's blood-alcohol level. The Supreme Court held that the accused had been detained. The Court examined the meaning of detention from the perspective of the detained individual: would that person reasonably have believed that he or she was not free to leave? The Court's broad approach to the concept of detention means that the rights guaranteed by ss. 9 and 10 are triggered in a wide range of investigative circumstances—for example, roadside screening, border searches, and customs interviews.

Fyi The Charter applies to all arrests, whether undertaken by the police, private security officers, or private citizens. The Charter does not apply when a private citizen merely detains another private citizen.

Arrest and detention are infringements of individual liberties. Both the Charter and the *Criminal Code* recognize that any infringement of liberty by the police must be justified. The Code uses "reasonable grounds" as the litmus test for a legitimate infringement of liberty, and the Charter guarantees the right to be free from arrests or detentions that are "arbitrary." Of course, what constitutes "reasonable grounds" depends on the perspective of the observer, and one person's "arbitrary detention" is another's "legitimate investigative tool."

racial profiling: a practice relying on racial stereotypes rather than reasonable suspicion to single out persons for greater scrutiny in law enforcement

One of the most challenging investigative issues currently facing Canadian law enforcement is racial profiling. The Ontario Human Rights Commission, which launched an inquiry into this practice in February 2003, defines **racial profiling** as "any action undertaken for reasons of safety, security or public protection, that relies on stereotypes about race, colour, ethnicity, ancestry, religion, or place of origin, or a combination of these, rather than on reasonable suspicion, to single out an individual for greater scrutiny or different treatment." Was Decovan Brown a victim of this practice?

Case YOUNG, BLACK, MALE ... AND AFFLUENT?

R v. Brown, 2003 ONCA C37818

Facts

On November 1, 1999, Decovan Brown, a young black man wearing a baseball cap and jogging suit, was driving an expensive new car on an urban highway. Brown was driving at a speed slightly in excess of the posted limit in an area where speeding was a common practice. He was stopped by a police officer, given a roadside screening test, and subsequently arrested under s. 253 of the *Criminal Code* for driving with an excessive blood-alcohol level.

At trial, Brown's lawyer applied for an order excluding Brown's breathalyzer results on the basis that the defendant's right to freedom from arbitrary detention under s. 9 of the Charter had been violated. Brown alleged that he had been stopped by the arresting officer not because of his driving, but because of racial profiling. Brown maintained that his arrest was based on the stereotypical assumption that young black men driving expensive cars must have obtained these cars by crime or must be implicated in recent criminal activity.

The defence presented a significant amount of evidence to support its application. This evidence included an attack on the credibility of the arresting officer, which was arguably substantiated by reliable independent evidence and by the testimony of Brown himself. Brown was presented to the court as a respectable man who played professional basketball for the Toronto Raptors and had no prior criminal record.

Throughout Brown's trial, the judge frequently intervened. During cross-examination of the arresting officer, the judge showed, in the words of the Ontario Superior Court of Justice, "a tendency to prejudge the merit of the application" and "an inclination to assist the officer at critical stages of the cross-examination." After Brown's lawyer made his final submissions, the trial judge offered these remarks: "You have made such serious allegations, really quite nasty, malicious ... accusations based on, it seems to me, nothing and you are going to have to persuade me that there is some appropriate basis on which to make this kind of accusation about an alleged racist motivation on the part of the officer." During sentencing, the trial judge made the extraordinary suggestion that Brown apologize to the arresting officer. The trial judge convicted Brown.

Issues

Was Brown a victim of racial profiling? Was there a reasonable apprehension of bias on the part of the trial judge?

Decision

Brown's appeal of his conviction to the Ontario Superior Court of Justice was allowed by Justice Trafford on the basis that the trial judge's comments gave rise to a reasonable apprehension of bias. Brown's application for the exclusion of evidence based on his arbitrary detention as a result of racial profiling was "clearly one of arguable merit." Justice Trafford commented:

> It is helpful to emphasize that racism, whether it be conscious or subconscious, will rarely, if ever, be proven directly. If it is to be proven in court, it will be proven most often through circumstantial evidence.
>
> In my opinion, judges must be particularly vigilant in their efforts to impartially determine applications like this one. Ample scope must be given to counsel attempting to prove such an allegation. Interjections by trial judges ... must be undertaken with a keen sensitivity for the requirements of impartiality, the appearances of justice and the undeniable value of imposing just and appropriate sanctions against racism in the administration of justice where it is proven.

The Crown's appeal from the judgment of Justice Trafford was dismissed by the Ontario Court of Appeal. The court determined that "there was evidence before the trial judge which was capable of supporting a finding of racial profiling" and affirmed the decision of Justice Trafford respecting the existence of a reasonable apprehension of bias.

Questions

1. What is racial profiling?
2. Do you believe that Decovan Brown was stopped because of racial profiling? Why or why not?

3. Justice Trafford commented: "No defendant need apologize to anyone for an application brought at trial by a competent defence counsel where the application is of arguable merit, even if it does not succeed." Why do you think the trial judge suggested that an apology was appropriate?
4. The judgment of the Ontario Court of Appeal quotes the trial judge's interventions at length. Read these remarks at www.emp.ca/dimensionsoflaw and comment on their appropriateness.

issue

Racial Profiling **Should arrest statistics concerning race be monitored regularly to ascertain whether racial profiling exists in Ontario?**

It is a scene that, according to *The Toronto Star*, is repeated with great regularity in the city of Toronto. A young black man driving a late-model car is pulled over by the police. Has this young man been stopped because of racial profiling? *The Toronto Star*, in its examination of police arrest statistics, says yes. The Toronto Police Force, on the other hand, vehemently denies the allegations.

Consider the comments that follow.

We do not do racial profiling. We do not deal with people on the basis of their ethnicity, their race, or any other factor. We deal with people in situations for that is what we're mandated to do. We're not perfect people but you're barking up the wrong tree. There's no racism.

—Julian Fantino, Toronto chief of police in an interview with The Toronto Star, *October 18, 2002*

I'm not disputing that the phenomenon does exist. The reason I'm not disputing that is because there is significant social science research done at the behest of the Commission on Systemic Racism in the Ontario criminal justice system that it does occur.

—James Stewart, senior Crown prosecutor, addressing the Ontario Court of Appeal in R v. Brown

My conclusion is that [*Star* journalists] did not clear up the data adequately, that there's a lack of transparency and there are inconsistencies in their methodology which lead me to have serious reservations about the conclusions that it derived on the basis of research that is conducted in this way.

—Professor Edward Harvey, sociologist, University of Toronto, hired by the Toronto police to review the analysis of The Toronto Star

I looked at the data in many different ways and the effect of race never went away. … The claims that the *Star* made were supported by the data.

> —*Professor Michael Friendly, statistician, York University, at a meeting held between* The Toronto Star*'s publisher and the Toronto Police Services Board*

I don't believe that the Toronto police engage in racial profiling in any way, shape or form. Quite the opposite, they're very sensitive to our different communities.

> —*Mel Lastman, mayor of Toronto, quoted in "Analysis Raises Board Hackles,"* The Toronto Star, *October 20, 2002*

In the long run you have to look at the facts, and the facts are, there is racial profiling.

> —*Lincoln Alexander, former Ontario lieutenant governor and honorary chief of the Toronto Police Services Board, quoted in Catherine Porter, "Action Urged on Race Profiling,"* The Toronto Star, *January 19, 2003*

Questions

1. Which speakers invoke statistics to justify their position? How do the others justify theirs?
2. Whose argument do you find most compelling? Why?
3. In a paragraph, present your own position on the need for public monitoring of arrest statistics based on race.

Check Your Understanding

1. What is the primary purpose for arresting people? Can you think of any other purposes?
2. What is a hybrid offence? How is it different from an indictable or summary conviction offence?
3. What constitutes a legal arrest? Distinguish between arrest and detention.
4. How have ss. 9 and 10 of the Charter affected the arrest process? Refer in your answer to the cartoon in Figure 9.1 (page 260).

The Search Power

Like the power to arrest, police powers of search and seizure are exceptional in that they authorize the police to do what individuals in ordinary circumstances are forbidden from doing. Twenty years ago, the Law Reform Commission of Canada commented: "[T]he interests with which these powers conflict are among the most critical accorded to individuals in a liberal democracy: interests involving the inviolability and dignity of the person, the concept of privacy, the security of possessions and self-expression." Nevertheless, the power to search is an essential tool in the investigative armoury of the police. Successful prosecutions require evidence, and evidence is often obtained as a result of a search.

Searches must be explicitly authorized, either by statute or at common law. The police have no general right to search an individual or a place because they hope to discover evidence. The most important source of the statutory power to search is s. 487 of the *Criminal Code*. This provision authorizes a justice of the peace to issue a search warrant in specified circumstances. The warrant is the grant of authority to conduct the search.

Section 487 of the *Criminal Code* provides prior authorization for specified searches where reasonable grounds exist. The requirements of just cause for the search, judicial authorization of the search, and specificity of objects to be searched for are the key elements of s. 487. These requirements have also been the focus of the courts' interpretation of s. 8 of the Charter, which guarantees the right to be free from "unreasonable search or seizure."

In the landmark case of *Hunter v. Southam*, the Supreme Court of Canada was required to consider the reasonableness of a warrantless

The Law Read the following warrant-issuing provision of the *Criminal Code*, and answer the questions below.

487(1) A justice who is satisfied by information on oath ... that there are reasonable grounds to believe that there is in a building, receptacle or place

(a) anything on or in respect of which any offence against this Act or any other Act of Parliament has been or is suspected to have been committed,

(b) anything that there are reasonable grounds to believe will afford evidence with respect to the commission of an offence, or will reveal the whereabouts of a person who is believed to have committed an offence, against this Act or any other Act of Parliament,

(c) anything that there are reasonable grounds to believe is intended to be used for the purpose of committing any offence against the person for which a person may be arrested without warrant ...

may ... issue a warrant authorizing a peace officer ... who is named in the warrant

(d) to search the building, receptacle or place for any such thing and to seize it.

Questions

1. Before issuing a warrant, of what must a justice of the peace be satisfied?
2. What items can a justice of the peace authorize police to search for?

search authorized under the *Combines Investigation Act*. The Court determined that prior authorization of a search is a precondition to the search's reasonableness. Prior authorization provides an opportunity for an assessment, before a search, of the conflicting interests at stake in the search. Should the citizen's reasonable expectations of privacy give way to the government's interest in law enforcement? The Court held that the general standard to determine a search's legitimacy should be the establishment, on oath, of reasonable and probable grounds that an offence has been committed and that there is evidence to be found at the place of the search.

One major exception to the requirement of prior judicial authorization is the power of **search incidental to arrest**. At common law, a police officer has the power to search an accused as part of the process of arrest. This is not an unlimited power. For the search to be lawful, the police must be attempting to achieve a valid purpose connected to the arrest. The three main purposes of search incident to arrest are (1) to ensure the safety of the police and the public, (2) to protect evidence from destruction at the hands of the arrested individual or others, and (3) to discover evidence. Consider the case of *R v. Caslake* in this regard.

search incidental to arrest: search following an arrest that must be conducted to achieve a valid purpose connected to the arrest

Case WHAT IS THE PURPOSE OF A SEARCH?

R v. Caslake, [1998] 1 SCR 51

Facts

Natural Resources Officer Kamann observed Terence Caslake's car parked by the side of a highway. On investigating, Kamann saw Caslake in high grasses 10 to 12 metres from the road. Suspecting that he might be hunting, Kamann asked Caslake what he was doing. Caslake replied that he was relieving himself in the bushes. After a short conversation, they returned to their respective vehicles, and Caslake drove away. Kamann then went to the area where he first observed Caslake and found a yellow garbage bag containing approximately four kilograms of marijuana. He returned to his vehicle and contacted the RCMP to request backup. He then pursued and arrested Caslake for possession of narcotics.

A few minutes later, RCMP Constable Thomas Boyle arrived on the scene, took Caslake to the RCMP detachment, and had his car towed to a garage. Approximately six hours after the arrest, Boyle unlocked and searched Caslake's car. Caslake had not given permission for the search, and Boyle had no warrant. Boyle found $1400 in cash and two packages of cocaine. Boyle testified that he conducted his search for the sole reason that an RCMP policy requires an inventory to be taken of the condition and contents of an impounded vehicle. The purpose of the policy, according to Boyle, was to safeguard the valuables belonging to the owner and to note the general condition of the vehicle.

Issue

Was Boyle's search reasonable, or did it contravene s. 8 of the *Canadian Charter of Rights and Freedoms*?

Decision

Caslake was convicted at trial, and his appeal to the Manitoba Court of Appeal was dismissed. The Supreme Court of Canada also dismissed his appeal. A majority of the Supreme Court held that the search was unreasonable. To justify a search incidental to arrest, there must be an objectively reasonable purpose for the search. Here, there was such a purpose: obtaining evidence to use against Caslake on the marijuana charge. However, since Boyle did not have this purpose in mind at the time he undertook the search, the Crown could not rely on it to justify the search. Nevertheless, the Court held that the admission of the evidence would not bring the administration of justice into disrepute, and Caslake's conviction was upheld.

Questions

1. Why was the search of Caslake's car unreasonable?
2. Why must s. 8 of the Charter be considered?

Check Your Understanding

1. Give examples of how police arrest powers interfere with the interests identified by the Law Reform Commission of Canada: "the inviolability and dignity of the person, the concept of privacy, the security of possessions and self-expression."
2. Explain how just cause, judicial authorization, and specificity of objects of a search are the basis of s. 487 of the *Criminal Code*.
3. What are the main purposes of a search incidental to arrest? Why are these purposes important?
4. When, if ever, should police be authorized to search without a warrant? Why?

Ensuring the Accused's Appearance in Court

Despite the impression created by most television dramas—that accused persons enter courtrooms in shackles and under guard—the *least* common method of ensuring an accused's attendance at trial is incarceration. Our reluctance to incarcerate individuals before trial reflects the system's fundamental commitment to the presumption of innocence. Simply being charged with a criminal offence is not a sufficient reason to take away a person's liberty.

An individual accused of a criminal offence is likely to attend court on the day of his or her trial as a result of a legally enforceable promise to do so. The process employed to ensure the accused's attendance at court varies with the nature of the offence charged (whether it is indictable, summary conviction, or hybrid), whether a warrant for arrest exists, whether an arrest without warrant has been made, and whether there are reasons to detain the accused in custody. The general presumption underlying the entire procedural structure is that accused persons should be released as soon as possible, unless there are reasonable grounds to believe that they should be detained in custody in order to establish their identity, to secure or preserve evidence, to prevent the continuation or repetition of the offence or the commission of another offence, or to ensure the accused's attendance in court. The procedural options are set out below.

1. **Appearance notice**. This document, which is issued by a police officer when no arrest is made, informs accused persons of the offence with which they have been charged, the date to appear for fingerprinting (if required), and the date to attend court. It is issued under s. 496 of the *Criminal Code.*
2. **Summons**. This document, which is issued by a justice or judge after an arrest has been made, serves the same function as an appearance notice. It is issued under s. 493 of the *Criminal Code.*
3. **Promise to appear** or **recognizance**. These documents are issued by the officer in charge of a police station after an accused has been arrested and taken to the station. A promise to appear is an agreement by the accused to appear in court at a stated time and place. A recognizance is a promise that the accused will pay a certain amount of money if he or she fails to appear. These documents are issued under s. 493 of the *Criminal Code.*

These three procedural options apply to those charged with summary conviction offences, hybrid offences, and indictable offences of a less serious nature (those listed in s. 553 of the Code). People charged with more serious indictable offences are detained in custody to await a judicial interim release or bail hearing. This hearing must be held within 24 hours of an accused's detention or as soon as possible. Usually, with the exception of a small group of extremely serious offences, it is up to the Crown to prove that detention in custody is necessary. Section 515 of the Code deals with **judicial interim release**.

appearance notice: a document designed to ensure an accused's attendance in court; issued by a police officer where no arrest is made

summons: a document designed to ensure an accused's attendance in court; issued by a justice or judge after an arrest is made

promise to appear: a document designed to ensure an accused's attendance in court; issued by the officer in charge of a police station after an arrest

recognizance: a document designed to ensure an accused's attendance in court; issued by the officer in charge of a police station after an arrest in which the accused promises to pay a sum of money if he or she fails to appear

judicial interim release: release of an accused pending trial or appeal

The Law Read the following judicial interim release provisions of the *Criminal Code*, and answer the questions that follow.

515(1) [W]here an accused who is charged with an offence ... is taken before a justice, the justice shall, unless a plea of guilty by the accused is accepted, order, in respect of that offence, that the accused be released on his giving an undertaking without conditions, unless the prosecutor, having been given reasonable opportunity to do so, shows cause, in respect of that offence, why the detention of the accused in custody is justified. ...

(10) For the purposes of this section, the detention of an accused in custody is justified only on one or more of the following grounds:

(a) where the detention is necessary to ensure his or her attendance in court in order to be dealt with according to law;

(b) where the detention is necessary for the protection or safety of the public, including any victim of or witness to the offence, having regard to all the circumstances including any substantial likelihood that the accused will, if released from custody, commit a criminal offence or interfere with the administration of justice; and

(c) on any other just cause being shown and, without limiting the generality of the foregoing, where the detention is necessary in order to maintain confidence in the administration of justice, having regard to all the circumstances, including the apparent strength of the prosecution's case, the gravity of the nature of the offence, the circumstances surrounding its commission and the potential for a lengthy term of imprisonment.

Questions

1. What happens to accused people if the Crown fails to convince a justice that they should be detained under s. 515 of the *Criminal Code*?
2. Give three reasons that justify the detention of accused people under s. 515. For each of these reasons, give an example of a situation that would convince you to detain an accused person if you were the presiding justice.
3. What does s. 515(10)(c) mean? List circumstances in which confidence in the administration of justice would be diminished as a result of granting bail.

Case PUBLIC CONFIDENCE OR PUBLIC FEAR?

R v. Hall, 2002 SCC 64

Facts

Compelling forensic evidence linked David Hall to a brutal murder in Sault Ste. Marie. At his bail hearing, Hall was required to show just cause why bail should be granted. The judge was satisfied that Hall's community and family ties, plus the ample security proposed, would ensure that he would appear for his trial if he were released on bail. The judge was also satisfied that Hall would not commit an offence while on bail. The judge noted, however, that there was a great deal of fear in the community and that the community looked to the courts for protection. He concluded that Hall's detention was necessary to maintain confidence in the administration of justice in view of the highly charged aftermath of the murder, the strong evidence implicating Hall, and the other factors referred to in s. 515(10)(c) of the *Criminal Code.*

Issues

Did the bail judge err in denying bail on the basis that this was necessary "to maintain confidence in the administration of justice"? Is s. 515(10)(c) of the *Criminal Code* constitutionally valid?

Decision

A majority of the Supreme Court of Canada held that there was no error in the reasoning of the bail judge. It also held that the portion of s. 515(10)(c) permitting detention "on any other just cause being shown" is unconstitutional because it confers an open-ended judicial discretion to refuse bail; is inconsistent with s. 11(e) of the Charter, which guarantees a right "not to be denied reasonable bail without just cause"; and is inconsistent with the presumption of innocence. The balance of s. 515(10)(c), which authorizes the denial of bail in order "to maintain confidence in the administration of justice," is valid "because public confidence is essential to the proper functioning of the bail system and the justice system as a whole."

The minority held that the bail judge erred in considering the subjective fears of the public after determining there was no risk of flight or any threat to the public. It also held that s. 515(10)(c) is constitutionally invalid in its entirety. The minority reasoned that at the heart of a free and democratic society is the liberty of its subjects, which is embodied generally in the right to be presumed innocent until proven guilty and specifically in the right to bail. The reference to "just cause" in s. 11(e) of the Charter requires that bail be denied only in a narrow set of circumstances and where necessary to promote the proper functioning of the bail system. The phrase "any other just cause" in s. 515(10)(c) allows for open-ended judicial discretion to deny bail that does not promote the proper functioning of the bail system. The phrase "confidence in the administration of justice" in s. 515(10)(c) of the Code is impermissibly vague. It is ripe for misuse and allows irrational public fears to be elevated above an accused's Charter rights.

Questions

1. In what respect does the majority judgment differ from the minority judgment?
2. Which approach do you prefer? Why?

Check Your Understanding

1. What general presumption underlies the procedural structure for ensuring an accused person's attendance in court?
2. Name and define four factors that affect the process employed to ensure the accused's attendance in court.
3. Name and describe four legal documents that are used to ensure the accused's attendance in court.
4. When must a bail hearing be held?

Method of Trial

There are two courts that hear criminal trials in Ontario. The first is the Ontario Court of Justice (formerly known as Provincial Court); this is a court of **inferior jurisdiction** whose judges are appointed by the provincial government. The second is the Ontario Superior Court of Justice; this is a court of **superior jurisdiction** whose judges are appointed by the federal government. The terms "inferior" and "superior" reflect the nature of the jurisdiction exercised by the courts—that is, the types of offences they have jurisdiction to try and the nature of the trial process they have jurisdiction to supervise.

inferior jurisdiction: jurisdiction exercised by court with provincially appointed judges

superior jurisdiction: jurisdiction exercised by court with federally appointed judges

The method of trial in criminal cases depends on the type of offence. All summary conviction offences (and hybrid offences in which the Crown elects to proceed summarily) are tried by a judge of the Ontario Court of Justice. In most cases, an accused charged with an indictable offence has the choice to be tried in this court or in the Ontario Superior Court of Justice. At either end of the spectrum of seriousness for indictable offences, the accused does not have a choice. The least serious indictable offences (such as theft, fraud, and possession of stolen property) are within the exclusive jurisdiction of the Ontario Court of Justice. The most serious indictable offences (such as murder and sedition) are within the exclusive jurisdiction of the Ontario Superior Court of Justice.

Only a Superior Court judge can preside over a jury trial. All trials in the Ontario Court of Justice are conducted before a judge alone.

Accused persons charged with indictable offences (other than those within the exclusive jurisdiction of the Ontario Court of Justice) are entitled to a preliminary inquiry held before a judge of the Ontario Court of Justice. A **preliminary inquiry** is a hearing held for the purpose of ensuring that sufficient evidence exists to commit the accused for trial before the Ontario Superior Court of Justice.

preliminary inquiry: a hearing held to determine whether sufficient evidence exists to commit an accused for trial in a court of superior jurisdiction

pre-trial conference: conference attended by judge, Crown, and the accused or accused's lawyer to promote a fair and expeditious trial

Section 625.1 of the *Criminal Code* provides for a **pre-trial conference** attended by a judge, a Crown attorney, and the accused or the accused's lawyer. The purpose of the conference is to "consider the matters that, to promote a fair and expeditious hearing, would be better decided before the start of the proceedings." Pre-trial conferences are mandatory in all jury trials and may be used in non-jury trials at the request of the judge, the Crown, or the accused.

Crown Disclosure

The objective of the pre-trial phase is to ensure both fairness and efficiency. Crown prosecutors, acting as officers of the court, have an obligation to promote fairness in all their dealings with accused people. In most cases, the resources available to the Crown far exceed those available to accused people, particularly those who rely on Legal Aid, as many do.

In 1991, the Supreme Court of Canada decided in *R v. Stinchcombe* that fairness requires that the Crown disclose all relevant information to the accused before trial. In this case, the RCMP took statements from Patricia Lineham, the former secretary of lawyer William Stinchcombe. Lineham had testified favourably for Stinchcombe at the preliminary inquiry. The Crown informed Stinchcombe of the existence, but not the contents, of the statements. The Court held that the Crown has a duty to disclose all relevant information, including all incriminating and exonerating evidence. The Court reasoned as follows: "The fruits of the investigation are not the property of the Crown for use in securing a conviction, but the property of the public to be used to ensure that justice is done." Full disclosure by the Crown protects the accused's constitutional right to make full answer and defence in a "fair and public hearing" under s. 11(d) of the Charter.

Check Your Understanding

1. What are the differences between the Ontario Court of Justice and the Ontario Superior Court of Justice?
2. Explain how the method of trial in a criminal case depends on the type of offence with which the accused is charged.
3. Suggest reasons why offences that are considered by Parliament to be the most serious are tried by a judge and a jury.
4. Explain the role of the pre-trial conference.
5. Why must the Crown disclose all relevant information to the accused before the trial?

METHODS OF *Legal Inquiry*

Detecting Bias in the Media

When we read or watch the news, we often assume that we are getting an objective report of events, but this is not always true. Just as we all have certain biases, so too do the media. You can become a more critical reader or viewer by reflecting on certain journalistic techniques that are used to promote a point of view.

1. *Bias in selection and omission.* An editor can express a bias by choosing whether or not to use a particular story. Within that story, some details can be ignored and others included to prompt a desired response in readers.
2. *Bias in placement.* Where a story is placed influences what a reader or viewer thinks about its importance. For example, page 1 stories are often presumed to be more significant than stories on page 16.
3. *Bias in headlines.* As the most-read part of a newspaper, headlines can convey excitement where little exists. They can express approval or condemnation, and they can present carefully hidden bias.
4. *Bias in choice of words.* The use of words that have either positive or negative connotations can subtly influence a reader or viewer. Does the writer want the reader to think "terrorist" or "freedom fighter"?

The following excerpts are from three different newspapers, all reporting on the Supreme Court's judgment in *R v. Hall*. Examine each carefully.

Excerpt 1

Public fear overrides right to bail: court

Judges split 5–4: McLachlin says citizens' confidence in judicial system must be preserved

Public fear is a good enough reason to refuse bail to accused criminals, even if they are not considered a flight risk or safety threat, the Supreme Court of Canada declared yesterday in a sharply divided ruling.

In a 5–4 decision, the court upheld federal legislation that had dramatically limited the application of bail. The change was part of a sweeping law-and-order package ushered in just before the 1997 general election.

The judgment underscored a deep philosophical divide in the court regarding the rights of the accused, with Chief Justice Beverley McLachlin carrying the majority with her contention that judges can take public sentiment into account when considering bail.

"Where justice is not seen to be done by the public, confidence in the bail system and, more generally, the entire justice system may falter," Chief Justice McLachlin warned. "When the public's confidence has reasonably been called into question, dangers such as public unrest and vigilantism may emerge."

Excerpt 2

Public concern sufficient to deny bail, court rules

Accused people can be denied bail solely for the purpose of quelling public fears, the Supreme Court of Canada said yesterday in a ruling that reveals a bitter clash between ideological factions on the court.

Over objections from the dissenting members, a five-judge majority said that, even in cases where an accused person is unlikely to flee or commit another offence, public concern is reason enough to keep that person behind bars.

"Where justice is not seen to be done by the public, confidence in the bail system and, more generally, the entire justice system may falter," wrote Chief Justice Beverley McLachlin. "When the public's confidence has reasonably been called into question, dangers such as public unrest and vigilantism may emerge."

Excerpt 3

Public fear can now deny bail to accused

Should public sentiment alone be a valid enough reason to deny bail to accused criminals? The Supreme Court of Canada thinks so—by a whisker.

People accused of crimes are usually kept in custody because they are considered flight risks, they are believed to be a threat to public safety or it is thought they will tamper with witnesses.

But the law also permits judges to deny bail based on "any other just cause" or to "maintain confidence in the administration of justice."

It is that clause that split the Supreme Court justices into two camps last week. The winning side in the 5–4 decision ruled that public fear is enough to keep an accused behind bars.

The dissenting side argued emotional public views have no place in a courtroom when there is no risk of flight or threat to community safety.

Applying the Skill

1. Using the four guidelines given above for detecting bias, analyze the three headlines and articles. What evidence of bias did you find?
2. In your opinion, which newspaper excerpt presents the most neutral report? Why?
3. Using the skills you have developed, choose any section of this book and analyze it for bias. Write a short report outlining your findings.

Reviewing Main Ideas

You Decide!

SEARCHING STUDENTS AT SCHOOL

R v. M.R.M., [1998] 3 SCR 393

This case is an appeal by the accused student from a judgment of the Court of Appeal for Nova Scotia. The appellate court had allowed a Crown appeal from a finding by a trial judge that a vice-principal's search of a student violated the student's rights under the *Canadian Charter of Rights and Freedoms.*

Facts

A vice-principal of a junior high school received reasonably reliable information that the accused, a 13-year-old student, was intending to sell drugs on school property. The student and his companion accompanied the vice-principal to his office, where the vice-principal asked them if they were in possession of drugs and searched them. A plain-clothed RCMP constable, called by the vice-principal pursuant to school policy, was present but said nothing. The vice-principal seized a hidden bag of marijuana and gave it to the constable, who advised the accused that he was under arrest for possession of a narcotic. The constable read the accused the police caution and his right to counsel, and advised him that he had the right to contact a parent or adult. The accused tried but failed to contact his mother by telephone. He stated that he did not wish to contact anyone else. The constable and the accused then went to the accused's locker and searched it, but found nothing.

The Law

Section 8 of the *Canadian Charter of Rights and Freedoms*, the search or seizure provision, is set out in the Appendix.

Arguments Supporting the Search

It is the job of teachers and others in charge of schools to provide an orderly and safe environment that encourages learning and protects all students. School authorities must be able to react swiftly and effectively when faced with a situation that could unreasonably disrupt the school environment or jeopardize the safety of students. Although students have a reasonable expectation of privacy while in school, this expectation may be diminished in some circumstances. Students know that the responsibility of school authorities to provide a safe environment and to maintain order and discipline sometimes requires searches of students and their personal effects and the seizure of prohibited items.

Evidence found by a teacher or principal should not be excluded because the search would have been unreasonable if conducted by the police. It is not in the best interests of teachers and students to require that a warrant or prior authorization be obtained before a school official is entitled to search a student. If school officials have reasonable grounds to believe that a school rule has been violated, if they reasonably believe that evidence will be found on the student's person, and if the search itself is conducted reasonably having regard to the seriousness of the alleged infraction and the age and sex of the student, then the search does not violate the student's Charter rights.

Arguments Against the Search

Section 8 of the Charter guarantees all Canadians the right to be free from unreasonable search. The Supreme Court of Canada has held that a search conducted without a warrant or prior authorization is *prima facie* unreasonable. The Court has also held that a reasonable search requires reasonable and probable grounds. The pre-authorization requirement ensures an objective assessment of the grounds that purport to justify a search before individual rights are seriously violated by a personal search. The rights of students should be protected in the same way as the rights of all other Canadians. There is no compelling evidence to suggest that schools require a lower standard of search.

Schools have a duty to foster the respect of their students for the constitutional rights of all members of society. These values are best taught by example and may be undermined if the students' rights are ignored by those in authority. In this case, the lack of urgency surrounding the search was demonstrated by the fact that the vice-principal was able to contact the police, who then observed the search and relied on the evidence obtained to arrest the accused. The police relied on the principal's in-school authority to avoid the warrant requirement. The creation of a modified search standard for students diminishes students' Charter rights while encouraging the abuse of power by school authorities.

Make Your Decision

1. Summarize the arguments in support of and against the right of school authorities to search students.
2. Decide whether the appeal should be allowed or dismissed. Explain your legal reasoning.
3. The Supreme Court held that there is no specific authorization to search provided in the Nova Scotia *Education Act*. Research the Ontario *Education Act* to determine the powers of teachers and principals with respect to searches.

Key Terms

Review the following terms to show that you understand the meaning of each and how it is applied in a legal context.

appearance notice
case officer
continuity of evidence
deoxyribonucleic acid (DNA)
discretion
gunshot residue (GSR)
hybrid offence
indictable
inferior jurisdiction
information
judicial interim release
preliminary inquiry
pre-trial conference
promise to appear
racial profiling
recognizance
search incidental to arrest
summary conviction
summons
superior jurisdiction
warrant
writ of *habeas corpus*

Understanding the Law

Review the following pieces of legislation mentioned in the text, and show that you understand the intent of each.

Canadian Charter of Rights and Freedoms, ss. 8, 9, 10, 11, and 24(2)
Criminal Code, ss. 129, 175, 235, 253, 487, 487.05, 493, 494, 495, 496, 515, 553, and 625.1
DNA Identification Act
Nova Scotia's *Education Act*
Ontario's *Coroners Act*

Thinking and Inquiry

1. Select an area in the forensic testing field that interests you, and research its strengths and weaknesses. Present your findings in a short written report.
2. On the subject of racial profiling, law professor Sujit Choudry has written: "For the people who are profiled, the indignity is real. In essence, profiling requires them to establish their legitimacy to the satisfaction of state officials. The cumulative effect on individuals of bearing this burden ... [undermines] fundamental principles of equal dignity and worth and respect for the presumption of innocence." Write a paragraph giving your opinion on this statement.
3. As a citizen of Canada, you have certain rights on arrest. Research the rights of citizens in two other countries. Create a chart comparing these rights with those in Canada.
4. Re-read the facts of the car search in the *Caslake* case (page 279).
   a) Make an argument that the search was justified as incidental to a lawful arrest.
   b) Assume the search was illegal. Should the evidence be excluded? Use the principles in the *Stillman* case (pages 269–270) to support your opinion.

Communication

5. Imagine that an individual who committed a violent offence has been released on bail in your neighbourhood. How do you feel about it? Write a letter to the editor of your local newspaper outlining your views.
6. With a partner, assume the roles of a police officer who is seeking an arrest warrant and a justice of the peace who must decide whether to issue this warrant. Find and complete forms 1 and 5, which are issued pursuant to s. 487 of the *Criminal Code.*
7. In small groups, create a short drama to illustrate when a private citizen may make an arrest. Present your drama to the class.
8. In small groups, debate the following statement: "The *Canadian Charter of Rights and Freedoms* has given too much protection to individual rights and as a result has made effective law enforcement more difficult."

Application

9. You have been asked by the teacher of an adult ESL class to prepare a pamphlet outlining how an individual may be compelled to appear in court by means of an appearance notice, a summons, a promise to appear, and a recognizance. Use clear and simple terms in your description.
10. Movies and television present us with dramatized versions of criminal procedure that are often inaccurate. Select a television show or movie that deals with police arrests and searches. Make notes about the procedures used. Create a chart comparing the media portrayal with reality.

Chapter 10 The Criminal Trial

CHAPTER *Focus*

In this chapter, you will

- explain evolving principles of the criminal justice system
- explain the criminal trial process, including jury selection, roles in the courtroom, and steps in a trial
- demonstrate an understanding of the rules and use of evidence
- outline legally acceptable defences to criminal conduct
- explain defence disclosure

The criminal trial is at the heart of society's perception of the administration of justice. It is seen to be essential because the criminal justice system is based on the presumption of innocence—that is, an accused person is "innocent until proven guilty according to law before an impartial and independent tribunal" (s. 11(d) of the *Canadian Charter of Rights and Freedoms*). A full trial, complete with accused, victim, opposing lawyers, jury, and judge, is the system's most complex and costly method of trying to guarantee that only the guilty are convicted and punished. It is also the exception. More than 80 percent of all criminal charges are dealt with by way of guilty pleas before cases ever go to trial. Despite this reality, an understanding of the principles and processes of the criminal trial is vital for a full appreciation of the law.

The cartoon in Figure 10.1 asks you to consider the complex relationship between society and those it criminalizes.

"We find that all of us, as a society, are to blame, but only the defendant is guilty."

Figure 10.1

At First Glance

1. The person making the statement is speaking for what group in the courtroom? What is her statement called?
2. What role does the courtroom group portrayed play in a criminal trial? How do you think its members are selected, and what criteria might be used?
3. What is the difference between being "to blame" and being "guilty"?
4. For what aspects of a criminal offence might society be responsible? Should society be found "guilty"? Why or why not?

Criminal Trial Principles and Processes

The way in which a society tries an individual accused of a crime is a measure of its core values and its criminal justice system. The criminal trial reflects societal notions of fairness and due process. It puts a public face to the legal system and identifies the circumstances under which it is acceptable to take away perhaps the most important civil right of all—the right to liberty.

Criminal Trial Principles

Certain principles underlie all criminal trials in Canada. These principles are intended to guarantee fairness and, in particular, to strike a balance between the power of the state and the civil liberties of the accused. A brief overview of these trial principles follows.

Rule of Law

In the criminal context, the rule of law means that individuals can be punished only for breaches of the law. It requires that the law be easily discoverable by citizens, who can then choose to act—or not to act—according to its dictates. The rule of law provides that all citizens are equal before the law, which is the only legitimate authority for the exercise of power.

Specific Allegation

People accused of a criminal offence are entitled to know exactly which *Criminal Code* offence they are charged with, and what specific circumstances are alleged to make up the offence. This information allows them to prepare for trial. Imagine trying to prepare a defence without knowing the nature of the charge against you.

Case to Meet

case to meet: a case for the Crown that is sufficiently strong to support a conviction

Accused people need not respond to a mere allegation of wrongdoing. They cannot be made to answer for their conduct until the state presents a plausible case against them. The requirement for presenting a **case to meet** has procedural implications:

- The state (the Crown) always presents its evidence first in any criminal trial.
- The state bears the burden of proof; that is, the Crown must convince the court that the accused should be convicted. The accused does *not* have to convince the court that he or she should be **acquitted**.
- The state cannot compel the accused to testify as a witness against him- or herself. The accused has the absolute right to remain silent. Therefore, the Crown must prove its case without relying on the accused to testify. Accused people, however, may choose to testify in their own defence.

acquitted: found not guilty of offence

Presumption of Innocence

The state must establish the guilt of the accused to a moral certainty before it is appropriate to punish. This means that the Crown must prove its case beyond a reasonable doubt. If there is a reasonable doubt as to whether the accused committed the offence, the accused is entitled to an acquittal.

Open and Public Trial

Justice must not only be done; it must also be seen to be done. As a rule, criminal trials must be open to the public and to the media. A reasonable person, observing a trial, should perceive it as fair and unbiased.

Independent and Impartial Adjudication

Judges must be impartial and must have no personal interest in the outcome of a trial. If a jury is present, each juror must also be impartial. The jury selection process, described below, is designed to ensure that this is so.

Criminal Trial Process

directed verdict: a verdict acquitting the accused after the Crown closes its case where there is insufficient evidence to support a conviction

Most criminal trials are held before a judge, without a jury. When this is the case, the judge decides on both the facts and the law. The judge makes findings of fact and then applies existing law to those findings. Most criminal trials hinge on facts. Only when the law is unsettled or unclear will the judge make legal findings.

The presumption of innocence requires the Crown to present its evidence first. Once the Crown does so, the defence can ask for a **directed verdict**

Figure 10.2 *A CBC camerawoman shoots video in the BC Supreme Court during the trial of nine people accused of smuggling Chinese migrants into Canada. Members of the media made legal history when they used cameras and recording devices at this July 2000 trial. Proponents of televised courtroom proceedings say cameras will democratize the justice system by making trials more public. Critics say the practice could turn the courts into a public spectacle.*

of acquittal. Such a request is based on whether the Crown's evidence is sufficient. The trial judge must determine whether a reasonable person, properly instructed in the law, could find the accused guilty. If the trial judge concludes that no reasonable person could do so, the case is immediately dismissed.

Successful motions for a directed verdict are infrequent. Because Crown attorneys are both officers of the court and public servants, they are responsible for ensuring that cases proceed only when the evidence is sufficient.

If the Crown presents a case to meet, the defence may then produce evidence that raises a reasonable doubt about whether the accused committed the offence. The judge listens to both the Crown's and the defence's evidence and decides which facts have been proven. Again, because the burden of proof rests with the Crown, the judge's primary task is to assess the sufficiency of the Crown's case: Are the witnesses credible? Is the forensic evidence convincing? In short, does the evidence establish beyond a reasonable doubt that the accused committed each and every element of the offence charged? If at the end of the trial a reasonable doubt exists as to any of the elements of the crime, the accused is entitled to an acquittal.

Fyi Canada's criminal justice system follows the *adversarial* system. For a person charged with a criminal offence the sequence of events that applies is (1) suspicion, (2) investigation, (3) arrest, and (4) charge. In Europe, the *inquisitorial* system is used: the process is (1) suspicion, (2) arrest, (3) investigation, and (4) charge. In other words, a citizen can be arrested and imprisoned without the state's having to produce any evidence.

CHECK YOUR UNDERSTANDING

1. How does the rule of law operate in a criminal context?
2. Explain the meaning of a "case to meet" and why this principle is important in a criminal trial.
3. Describe the role of the judge in a criminal trial without a jury.
4. What is the burden of proof, and why does it rest with the Crown?
5. Explain the term "directed verdict."

The Jury

People who are charged with certain serious indictable offences have the option of trial before a judge and a jury. In a jury trial, findings of fact are made by the jury. At the end of the case, the judge instructs the jury about the law, and the jury retires to apply the law to the facts as it finds them.

Trial by jury is seen as an essential part of the criminal justice system and as a constitutional guarantee protecting individual rights. In *R v. Sherratt*, Justice L'Heureux-Dubé made these remarks about juries:

> The jury, through its collective decision making, is an excellent fact finder; due to its representative character, it acts as the conscience of the community; the jury can act as the final bulwark [barricade] against oppressive laws or their enforcement; it provides a means whereby the public increases its knowledge of the criminal justice system and it increases, through the involvement of the public, societal trust in the system as a whole.

In Canada, the jury in a criminal trial comprises 12 members. Because the jury must be an impartial finder of fact and must also represent a cross-section of society, it is chosen by both the Crown and the defence. The early part of the jury selection process, called the generation of the **jury array**, is governed by provincial legislation.

jury array: pool of potential jurors assembled under provincial legislation; also called jury panel or jury roll

Under Ontario's *Juries Act*, Canadian citizens resident in Ontario who are 18 years of age or over are generally eligible to serve as jurors. However, people in certain occupations are ineligible, for example, lawyers, law students, doctors, veterinary surgeons, and people engaged in law enforcement.

Once the array has been assembled by the sheriff, groups of potential jurors are convened for selection. This process is called **empanelling a jury** and is governed by ss. 631 to 642 of the *Criminal Code*. The jury array may be challenged by the Crown or the defence, but only on the grounds of partiality, fraud, or willful misconduct by the sheriff.

empanelling a jury: process of jury selection for individual trials, governed by the *Criminal Code*

Jury Challenges

Both the defence and the Crown have a statutory right to challenge potential jurors. The purpose of challenges is to create an impartial jury and to give the Crown and the defence equal opportunity to participate in its selection.

Potential jurors can be challenged in two ways. The first, the **peremptory challenge**, allows the Crown or the defence to reject a juror without giving a reason. The Crown and the defence have an equal number of peremptory challenges. The number itself varies, depending on the seriousness of the offence. Lawyers make peremptory challenges on the basis of minimal information: the potential juror's name, occupation, address, physical appearance, and demeanour.

peremptory challenge: the procedure by which the defence or Crown can reject a potential juror without giving reasons, as authorized by the *Criminal Code*

Challenge for cause is the second type of challenge. Here, potential jurors are challenged if either the Crown or the defence believes they will not fulfill the responsibilities of jury duty. The grounds justifying a challenge for cause are set out in s. 638 of the Code. The most frequently used ground is that "the juror is not indifferent between the Queen and the accused." In other words, the challenge claims that the juror is not impartial. If the other party disputes the challenge, the judge will appoint two jurors to hear arguments from both parties and determine whether the challenge for cause should succeed.

challenge for cause: procedure for challenging a potential juror for a reason listed in s. 638 of the *Criminal Code*

What factors might justify a challenge on the basis that a potential juror is not "indifferent between the Queen and the accused"? In Canada, courts have long accepted that a prior knowledge of, or association with, one of the parties involved in the trial might prejudice a potential juror. Exposure to media coverage of the case could also be cited. But what about jurors' personal characteristics, such as their gender or race?

R v. Parks, a second-degree murder case, is perhaps the most influential recent court decision on jury selection. In this case, defence counsel applied to challenge prospective jurors for cause with the following question: "Would your ability to judge the evidence in the case without bias, prejudice, or partiality be affected by the fact that the person charged is black and the deceased is white?" The trial judge refused to allow the question, and the accused was convicted of manslaughter.

The Ontario Court of Appeal concluded that the question was relevant, and that there was a realistic potential that "one or more jurors drawn from the Metropolitan Toronto community would consciously or unconsciously come to court possessed of negative stereotypical attitudes towards black persons." It ordered a new trial on the basis that the accused had been wrongly denied an opportunity to challenge for cause. *R v. Parks* triggered a host of jury selection cases. In 1998, the issue reached the Supreme Court of Canada in *R v. Williams*.

Case JURY SELECTION: CHALLENGING RACIAL BIAS

R v. Williams, [1998] 1 SCR 1128

Facts

Victor Daniel Williams, an Aboriginal, pleaded not guilty to robbing a Victoria pizza parlour, and elected trial by judge and jury. His defence was that someone else had committed the robbery. Williams applied to challenge potential jurors for racial bias under s. 638 of the *Criminal Code*.

The trial judge found that the evidence tended to support the view "that natives historically have been and continue to be the object of bias and prejudice" and that this situation "has become more overt and widespread in recent years as the result of tensions created by developments in ... land claims and fishing rights." He acknowledged that there was a reasonable possibility that a potential juror would be biased against an Aboriginal person charged with robbing a white person.

The trial judge rejected the argument that such bias was sufficient to support a challenge for cause because there was no reasonable possibility that it would translate into partiality at the trial. Jurors, he reasoned, can be expected to put aside their biases, and the jury system has effective safeguards against bias. The judge also buttressed his conclusions with a cost–benefit analysis. He held that the cost and disruption caused by allowing challenges for cause on the basis of racial bias would far outweigh the benefit of potentially fairer trials. Williams was convicted of robbery and was unsuccessful in his appeal to the British Columbia Court of Appeal.

Issue

Did Williams have the right to challenge potential jurors for cause to determine whether prejudice against Aboriginals might impair their impartiality?

Decision

Williams's appeal was allowed, and a new trial was ordered. The Supreme Court held that the trial judge should have allowed the challenge for cause. The aim of s. 638 of the Code is to ensure a fair trial. Instructions from a judge, or other safeguards of the jury system, will not eliminate biases that are deeply ingrained in the minds of jurors. Where doubts about biases are raised, it is better to permit prejudices to be examined. The challenge for cause is an essential safeguard of the accused's s. 11(d) Charter right to a fair trial and an impartial jury. It may also be an anti-discrimination right under s. 15 of the Charter.

Questions

1. Describe the trial judge's reasons for rejecting the defence's application to challenge potential jurors for racial bias.
2. What was the decision of the Supreme Court? Do you agree or disagree with it? Explain your answer.
3. a) Define "impartial."
   b) What is the most effective way of ensuring that members of a jury are impartial?
   c) Is it possible to find a truly impartial juror? Explain your answer.
4. With a partner, develop a list of characteristics that are relevant to a juror's impartiality.

Check Your Understanding

1. Explain the purpose of a jury and its role during a trial.
2. On what grounds can a jury array be challenged?

3. Differentiate between a peremptory challenge and a challenge for cause.
4. If you were a Crown attorney at a murder trial, how would you use your peremptory challenges? Would it depend on the nature of the offence, on the characteristics of the accused, or on the kind of evidence you intend to present? Would your strategy differ if you were defence counsel? Explain your answers.
5. Do you believe that the Ontario Court of Appeal made the correct decision in *R v. Parks*? Why or why not?

Evidence

Evidence provides a way for the Crown and the defence to reconstruct the legally relevant aspects of a criminal act. This reconstruction is intended to tell the court a story so that the facts of the case can be determined by the **trier of fact** and a judgment can be rendered. The rules of evidence ensure that the fact-finding process is fair and reliable.

trier of fact: the determiner, whether judge or jury, of the facts on the basis of admissible evidence

Generally, only relevant evidence is admissible. This requirement is intended to eliminate extraneous evidence and to contribute to the efficiency and rationality of the fact-finding process. At first glance, the relevance requirement hardly seems controversial. In reality, however, relevance is a complex concept. It depends on assumptions about what particular pieces of information tend to prove or disprove. For example, let us say that a person was convicted of theft when she was 18. Is this fact relevant to the Crown's case against her on a theft charge when she is 40? Is the fact that a victim of sexual assault told nobody about the assault for three weeks relevant to the defence claim that the sexual assault did not occur?

Evidence given by a witness is usually a verbal description of what the witness knows about an event. A lawyer, however, elicits that description, thus shaping the story being told. The way in which witnesses describe situations or interpret what they saw, heard, smelled, or felt about an event depends on how each individual assimilates information. Each witness uses different mental filters to sort information; these in turn influence perception, memory, and ability to recount.

examination in chief: oral examination of a witness by the lawyer who summonsed the witness to testify

Once a witness has told his or her story to the court in **examination in chief**, the witness is subjected to **cross-examination** by the opposing lawyer. The purpose of the cross-examination is usually to challenge a witness's credibility and the reliability of the evidence. Eventually, the trier of fact determines which facts are "true."

cross-examination: oral examination of a witness by a lawyer who did not summons the witness to testify, designed to challenge the witness's evidence

Rules of Evidence

Many of the rules of evidence are designed to prevent the trier of fact from being misled. For example, the rule against **hearsay** means that a witness cannot testify about indirect knowledge. Imagine a trial in which Malcolm

hearsay: evidence consisting of matters that a witness was told is charged with assaulting Anatoli. Alejandra, testifying for the Crown, says that she saw Malcolm and Anatoli arguing on the night the alleged offence occurred. Her evidence is admissible. Its relevance and significance depend on inferences drawn by the trier of fact. However, if Alejandra testifies that her friend Zhou told her that he saw Malcolm assault Anatoli, this evidence is clearly inadmissible. It is second-hand, or hearsay, and tends to prove only that Zhou told Alejandra of an assault, not that an assault actually occurred. If the Crown wants to introduce evidence about what Zhou saw, Zhou himself will have to testify.

Much of the law of evidence is concerned with the exclusion of evidence. Generally speaking, there are two kinds of exclusionary rules. The first rule is designed to ensure that only reliable evidence is admitted. Hearsay falls under this rule. The second rule is designed to promote fair trials and the proper administration of justice. One example of this rule is described in Chapter 9. Any evidence obtained in violation of Charter rights is inadmissible if its admission would bring the administration of justice into disrepute.

Voir Dire

voir dire: trial within a trial to determine whether evidence is admissible

When a question about admissibility of evidence arises in court, a hearing called a ***voir dire*** is held. If the main proceedings include a jury, the jury is removed for the duration of the *voir dire.* If the evidence is deemed admissible, the jury is given the opportunity to consider it. If deemed inadmissible, the jury will not be told of the evidence. In trials conducted before a judge alone, the judge remains in the courtroom during the *voir dire.* If the evidence is ruled inadmissible, the judge "instructs" him- or herself to disregard evidence heard during the *voir dire.*

Check Your Understanding

1. Explain the purpose of an examination in chief and a cross-examination.
2. What are the two kinds of exclusionary rules, and how do they differ?
3. What is the purpose of a *voir dire*? Briefly describe how a *voir dire* is conducted in a jury trial and a non-jury trial.

Defences

After the Crown presents its case, the accused is entitled to raise a defence. Two types of defences are available: a negativing defence and an affirmative defence.

negativing defence: a defence that raises a reasonable doubt about whether the accused committed the offence charged

A **negativing defence** raises a reasonable doubt about whether an accused committed the *actus reus* of an offence or had the necessary *mens rea* to support a conviction. In effect, this is a defence that negates an essential element in the Crown's case. Four negativing defences will be examined next: (1) mistake of fact, (2) mental disorder, (3) automatism, and (4) intoxication.

An **affirmative defence** admits that the Crown has established the elements of the offence but claims that the accused's criminal act was justified in the circumstances, or that the accused should be excused from punishment because criminal conduct was the only reasonable option. Two affirmative defences—self-defence and compulsion (or duress, in common law) will be covered later in this chapter.

affirmative defence: a defence that justifies an accused's criminal conduct

Mistake of Fact

An accused person who is mistaken about the factual context in which an alleged offence was committed may not possess the *mens rea* (guilty mind) required for a conviction. For example, the *mens rea* for the offence of possession of property obtained by crime requires that the accused knew the property was obtained by crime. Any individual accused of this offence who mistakenly believed that the property was lawfully obtained has a mistake-of-fact defence: the Crown will not be able to prove one of the required elements of the crime if the defence is successful.

Although the mistake-of-fact defence applies in many circumstances, it appears most often in cases of sexual assault. Section 265 of the *Criminal Code* defines the offence of assault (see Chapter 8, page 234). A sexual assault is an assault committed in circumstances of a sexual nature and in which the sexual integrity of the victim is violated. The *actus reus* of sexual assault has two parts: the application of force of a sexual nature, and lack of consent. Accused people who claim they believed the sexual contact to be consensual have a potential mistake-of-fact defence.

Canadian courts have ruled that a mistaken belief must be honestly held to negate *mens rea*. However, whether the mistake needs also to be reasonable has been far more controversial. Some argue that the relevant issue is what the accused thought or knew at the time of the offence, not what a reasonable person would have thought or known. Of course, the more unreasonable the mistake, the less likely it is that the trier of fact will believe that the accused actually made a mistake.

Suppose an individual is charged with trafficking in cocaine. The evidence: the accused was seen on a street corner selling a white, powdery substance to another individual. The substance was tested and found to be cocaine. The accused claims he believed he was selling a herbal supplement meant to increase energy. The willingness of the trier of fact to accept this story will depend on how credible the accused sounds as a witness and on the inherent believability, or reasonableness, of the story.

In the 1980 case *R v. Pappajohn*, which involved the offence of rape (now called sexual assault), the Supreme Court ruled that a mistaken belief did not have to be reasonable, only honestly held. Mistake of fact was a defence that negatived *mens rea. Mens rea* was subjectively measured—the question therefore was what was in the mind of this particular accused, not what should have been in the mind of a reasonable person in the same circumstances.

The case became a lightning rod. For some, it brought welcome clarity to the law by establishing the general rule that mistake of fact is a defence that negates *mens rea.* For others, it confirmed that the Court had no understanding of the reality of rape and was offering accused men legal licence to make unreasonable mistakes about the existence of consent.

The Law

Women's groups across Canada had been working for years to identify and combat sexist stereotypes in the law of sexual assault when the decision in *R v. Pappajohn* was released. The case shocked them into greater action. As a result of their work, the laws on sexual assault changed significantly. In 1992, the *Criminal Code* was amended to clarify the law of consent and to limit the availability of the mistaken-belief defence.

273.1(1) "[C]onsent" means ... the voluntary agreement of the complainant to engage in the sexual activity in question.

(2) No consent is obtained ... where

(a) the agreement is expressed by the words or conduct of a person other than the complainant;

(b) the complainant is incapable of consenting to the activity;

(c) the accused induces the complainant to engage in the activity by abusing a position of trust, power or authority;

(d) the complainant expresses, by words or conduct, a lack of agreement to engage in the activity; or

(e) the complainant, having consented to engage in sexual activity, expresses, by words or conduct, a lack of agreement to continue to engage in the activity.

273.2 It is not a defence ... that the accused believed that the complainant consented to the activity that forms the subject-matter of the charge, where ...

(b) the accused did not take reasonable steps, in the circumstances known to the accused at the time, to ascertain that the complainant was consenting.

Questions

1. What specific problem was each subsection designed to overcome?
2. What reasonable steps could a person take to ascertain whether consent exists?

WORKING FOR CHANGE *LEAF: The Women's Legal Education and Action Fund*

As the *Canadian Charter of Rights and Freedoms* was being drafted, it became abundantly clear that women had no real influence over the process. In early 1981, a national women's group known as the Ad Hoc Committee on the Constitution was formed to do something about that exclusion. It succeeded in having s. 28 included when the Charter became law in 1982: "Notwithstanding anything in this Charter, the rights and freedoms referred to in it are guaranteed equally to male and female persons."

In the three years it took for the Charter to be fully implemented, studies indicated that a fund must be established to (1) support educational programs to increase public awareness of gender inequality and (2) ensure that the legislation was not discriminatory. Women from across Canada responded, and in 1985, the Women's Legal Education and Action Fund (LEAF) was created as a non-profit organization.

LEAF's mandate is (1) to ensure that the Charter rights of girls and women are upheld in courts, human rights commissions, and government agencies and (2) to provide public education on issues of gender equality.

Since being formed, LEAF has intervened in more than 140 cases in appeal courts and at the Supreme Court of Canada to establish important equality principles. LEAF has helped win landmark victories in such areas as:

- violence against women
- bias in employment
- pension reform
- sexual harassment
- pregnancy discrimination
- parental leave
- reproductive choice
- social assistance.

LEAF also takes seriously its mandate to educate on gender equality rights. One project, No Means No for Teens, raises awareness among students in grades 7 to 9 about Charter equality rights, gender power dynamics, and consent with respect to sexual assault. The legal foundation for the project is the Supreme Court decision in *R v. Ewanchuk*, which focused on equality rights under sexual assault law. The No Means No project

- promotes awareness of rights and responsibilities with respect to sexual assault and consent
- encourages students to critically examine social conventions, myths, and stereotypes around what constitutes consent and sexual assault
- familiarizes students with the Charter's equality provisions
- asks students to examine responsibilities under the Charter and the school's code of conduct.

More than 50 volunteers from the University of Ottawa's law faculty have been working on the No Means No program since October 2002. In the first six months, they presented the project to more than 1000 local students in 33 classrooms. Chris Collmorgen, a volunteer law student with the project, says this about the experience:

> LEAF's No Means No program introduces kids to a real case, with myth-busting ramifications. It encourages them to draw parallels with their own experiences with friends, authority figures, and popular culture and to identify and challenge stereotypes.
>
> Kids know all about stereotypes, fairness, respect, equality, and injustice. ... The issues we cover are serious, and I am impressed with how the program allows students to grasp the

implications of the *Ewanchuk* decision. In a sad sort of way, I was very aware of how [my] being a male presenter validated the message for the boys in the classroom. But in a world of conflicting messages, it feels good to be part of an education program that helps kids understand that when sexuality is involved, there is no such thing as implied consent. It explains that it is their responsibility to ask first and to respect the answer.

Questions

1. What led to the formation of LEAF?
2. Describe the content and nature of LEAF's mandate. What might you add to it?
3. Outline the goals of the No Means No for Teens project.

Find out more about LEAF and its work at www.emp.ca/dimensionsoflaw

Mental Disorder

Criminal law works on the assumption that society should punish people who choose to do wrong. Yet individuals living with certain mental disorders that affect their ability to understand either the nature or consequences of their criminal behaviour may not be able to exercise that choice. At the same time, society needs to protect itself. The defence of mental disorder attempts to identify individuals whose disorder renders them blameless and to identify individuals who might pose a continuing danger to society.

An accused person who is found to be not criminally responsible (NCR) is not simply acquitted; rather, a verdict of "NCR on account of mental disorder" is imposed. Once the NCR verdict is imposed, the court, or a special review board, turns its attention to how it can best deal with the **NCR acquittee**. The focus is on whether treatment is needed and whether the acquittee's freedom must be restricted for public safety.

NCR acquittee: a person found not criminally responsible at trial

Mentally ill people have long been stereotyped as inherently dangerous. For many years, Canada's criminal law perpetuated this prejudice by subjecting mentally ill offenders to indefinite detention based on perceived risks. In 1991, the *Criminal Code* provisions dealing with mental disorder were completely overhauled. The new provisions were intended to ensure that NCR acquittees are treated fairly and are not incarcerated unless there is reason to suspect they present an ongoing risk to the community.

Section 672.54 sets out the factors that the court or review board must consider when dealing with an NCR acquittee. These include "the need to protect the public from dangerous persons, the mental condition of the accused, the reintegration of the accused into society and the other needs of the accused." The court or review board must choose the disposition that is least restrictive and least onerous for the accused.

To be tried, an accused person must be able to instruct counsel, understand the proceedings and their consequences, and communicate with counsel and the court. An accused who cannot do this because of mental disorder is placed within the jurisdiction of the review board, and the board decides how best to enable the accused eventually to stand trial.

Turning Points in the Law

From Juvenile Delinquents to Young Offenders

In Canada's early history, anyone 14 or older charged with a criminal offence was tried and sentenced as an adult. Late in the 19th century, reform movements pressured governments to treat youths differently and to try them separately from adults. When the *Criminal Code* was enacted in 1892, it created courts for youths (generally defined as between the ages of seven and 13, inclusive).

In 1908 the *Juvenile Delinquents Act* became law. The age range of "delinquents" varied across the country, but was generally between seven and 15. The Act gave police, judges, and probation officers enormous powers. As you saw in the case of Velma Demerson in Chapter 8 (page 238), youths had no rights to due process, legal representation, appeal, or cross-examination of witnesses. Youths had no right to be informed about charges against them, or to participate in legal proceedings. The judge assumed the role of parent. Options for disposition (sentence) included probation, fines up to $25, placement in foster care, and committal to a training school. The court based its decision on what was "best for the child," not on law. This practice meant that an impoverished child could spend years in custody for stealing a candy bar. The people who ran the training schools decided on the length of time children spent in facilities.

In 1984, after the *Canadian Charter of Rights and Freedoms* had become law, the *Young Offenders Act* replaced the old Act. It gave special rights and protections to youths under arrest. Under s. 26, during police interrogations youths

Figure 10.3 *A group of youths lead a parade in downtown Calgary during a 1998 rally calling for changes to the* Young Offenders Act.

Fyi A child as young as seven could be charged under the *Juvenile Delinquents Act*. Under the *Young Offenders Act*, the minimum age was raised to 12.

Find out more about youth justice in Canada today at www.emp.ca/dimensionsoflaw

(1) must be told of their rights in understandable language, (2) do not have to make a statement, and (3) have the right to have a parent or other adult present. Youths who decided to make a statement had to sign a written form saying that they knew of their rights but did not wish to take advantage of them.

The Act established the basics of how young people are still treated under criminal law in Canada. It set a national age of criminal responsibility (12 to 17, inclusive) and limited the jurisdiction of youth courts to federal criminal laws, such as the *Criminal Code*. The judge must make impartial decisions based on law. The range of dispositions increased to include absolute discharges; community service; probation; open custody in a community residential centre, group home, or childcare institution; and secure custody. It also required that young offenders be sentenced to definite terms. The Act emphasized rehabilitation and was considered progressive. It was a major turning point in the law.

In 1998, the federal government established the Youth Justice Renewal Initiative to consider changes to the *Young Offenders Act*. On April 1, 2003, the *Youth Criminal Justice Act* replaced the *Young Offenders Act*. By then, Canada had one of the highest youth incarceration rates among Western nations. The new Act maintained the 12-to-17 age range of criminal responsibility. It stressed community-based sentences for less serious crimes, but introduced adult sentences for serious crimes. Most observers have said it represents a much less dramatic legal change than either the *Juvenile Delinquents Act* or the *Young Offenders Act*.

Questions

1. Explain why the *Juvenile Delinquents Act* had to be replaced when the *Canadian Charter of Rights and Freedoms* became law.
2. a) The *Youth Criminal Justice Act* applies to youths between 12 and 17. Some argue that the age should be lowered. What is your opinion? Explain your answer.
   b) If you think the age should be changed, describe what age is appropriate and why.
3. What is your opinion on community-based service as a form of rehabilitation for young offenders? Draw up a chart to summarize the pros and cons of this measure.

Automatism

Fyi Under *Criminal Code* provisions for mental disorder, a person can serve more time in custody than the maximum prison sentence for the offence committed. Recent amendments (ss. 672.64–672.66) include a system of capping to limit the time a mentally disabled person can be detained. The amendments have yet to be proclaimed in force.

One fundamental principle of criminal liability is voluntariness. For the accused to be found guilty, the *actus reus* of an offence must be committed voluntarily—that is, it must be the conscious choice of an operating mind. The criminal law does not hold people responsible for actions they cannot control. The defence of mental disorder discussed earlier in this chapter is one example of the voluntariness principle. Another example is the defence of automatism.

The Supreme Court of Canada has defined automatism as "a state of impaired consciousness, rather than unconsciousness, in which an individual, though capable of action, has no voluntary control over that action." A successful defence of automatism leads to a finding of not guilty.

Much of the case law in this area focuses on whether the automatism was caused by a mental disease or was of the "non-insane" variety. The distinction is critical because it determines how the accused is treated by the system.

If the automatism is deemed to be caused by mental disease, the defence of mental disorder applies, and the accused may be subjected to custodial treatment. If the automatism is deemed to be "non-insane," the acquittal leads to freedom. Automatism has been recognized in cases involving stroke, psychological trauma, hypoglycemia, and a severe blow to the head. One of the most famous Canadian cases, *R v. Parks*, involved sleepwalking.

Case SLEEPWALKING OR MURDER?

R v. Parks, [1992] 2 SCR 871

Facts

Kenneth Parks drove approximately 23 kilometres in the middle of the night, entered his in-laws' home, and attacked them both with a knife, killing his mother-in-law and seriously injuring his father-in-law. Immediately after the attacks, Parks drove to the nearest police station and made the following statement: "I just killed someone with my bare hands; oh my God, I just killed someone; I've just killed two people; my God, I've just killed two people... ."

At trial on charges of first-degree murder and attempted murder, Parks claimed that he was sleepwalking and offered evidence about his sleep patterns: he always slept heavily, had trouble waking up, and other family members suffered from sleep disorders, including sleepwalking. Other evidence suggested that his relationship with his in-laws had been good and that they had been particularly supportive of him during the previous year, when he had experienced many difficulties, both at work and because of a gambling habit.

The jury accepted the automatism defence, and Parks was acquitted. After Parks's acquittal was upheld by the Ontario Court of Appeal, the Crown appealed the case to the Supreme Court of Canada.

Issue

Was the defence of non-insane automatism available to Parks?

Decision

The Supreme Court upheld Parks's acquittal because the defence of non-insane automatism was available. It focused on whether Parks's sleepwalking was likely to recur and, if it did, whether he presented a danger to society. The Court also considered whether allowing the defence would diminish respect for the justice system. Would courts be filled with alleged sleepwalkers trying to get away with murder?

The Court concluded:

> Sleepwalking has been recognized as a possible defence for at least a century, and there is no apparent problem with baseless claims of auto-

matism due to sleepwalking. ... Some people think that freeing the accused because of sleepwalking or automatism impairs the credibility of the justice system. A fundamental rule of criminal law, however, is that only those who act voluntarily, intending to commit an offence, should be punished.

Questions

1. a) What facts support a defence of automatism?
   b) What facts, if any, detract from this defence?
2. Why did the Supreme Court uphold Parks's acquittal?
3. Do you support the Supreme Court's decision? Why or why not?

Intoxication

In dealing with criminal offences, society seems to have less sympathy for intoxicated people than it does for people living with mental disorders or suffering from automatism. The public accepts that alcohol or drugs may adversely affect an individual's behaviour, but it is not entirely prepared to excuse individuals for committing offences while intoxicated. Most often, intoxication results from choices the accused has made. But personal choice is not involved in the conditions of mental disorder or automatism.

Courts have fashioned a complicated and controversial rule to deal with intoxication. Offences are divided into two categories: general intent and specific intent. For **general intent offences**, intoxication is not a defence. Intoxication may, however, be used as a defence for **specific intent offences**. Such a defence would use evidence of intoxication to establish that the accused did not possess the specific intent to commit the offence.

general intent offence: an offence in which the accused's intent is limited to the prohibited act itself, with no other criminal purpose

specific intent offence: an offence in which the accused's intent goes beyond the prohibited act itself to include another, criminal purpose

In general intent offences, the intent involves only the prohibited act itself. Assault, for example, is a crime of general intent. The Crown need only prove that the accused intended to apply force. Intent can be inferred from the fact that the accused actually did apply force. With specific intent, the offender's intent goes beyond committing the act in question. For example, "break and enter with intent to commit an indictable offence" is a specific intent offence. It includes a general intent offence (break and enter) plus the hidden, or ulterior, specific intent to commit an indictable offence (perhaps robbery). The defence could present evidence that the accused was too intoxicated to be able to form the specific intent. If this evidence raises a reasonable doubt about the required *mens rea*, the accused is acquitted of the specific intent offence. For example, the person charged with "break and enter with intent to commit an indictable offence" would be acquitted of "intent to commit an indictable offence," but would still be convicted of simple break and enter.

The legal distinction between specific and general intent was created by judges, and many commentators have found it confusing. They argue that if evidence of intoxication is admissible for some mental states, it should be admissible for all mental states. If criminal law is concerned with the dangerous behaviour of drunken offenders, why not create an offence of being drunk and dangerous? Others argue that the distinction makes sense: an individual can be too intoxicated to anticipate cause and effect and the future, but still be able to understand what he or she is doing and perceiving in the moment. The distinction has served the law well, this argument continues, and it reflects a societal sense that drunken offenders are blameworthy.

In 1994, the Supreme Court of Canada introduced a gloss on the distinction between specific and general intent in *R v. Daviault.* Henri Daviault, a chronic alcoholic, was charged with the general intent offence of sexual assault after having consumed a bottle of brandy and several beers. The trial judge had reasonable doubt whether Daviault's conduct was voluntary, owing to extreme intoxication, and acquitted him. The Court of Appeal for Quebec convicted Daviault. The Supreme Court restored Daviault's acquittal, fashioning an exception to the rule regarding intoxication and specific and general intent.

In essence, the Supreme Court decided that evidence of extreme intoxication equivalent to automatism is admissible in general intent offences. The public was outraged. The minister of justice reacted quickly, and the *Criminal Code* was amended. Section 33.1, proclaimed in force in 1995, overruled the judgment in *R v. Daviault* for all offences that involve assault or interference with the bodily integrity of the victim.

issue

Defence Disclosure **Should the defence be obligated to disclose physical evidence in its possession when to do so might unnecessarily damage the case for the accused?**

In Chapter 9, you learned that the Crown must disclose all relevant evidence before trial to respect the Charter rights of the accused. Obviously, defence lawyers respect the rights of the accused, their clients; but what about the needs of the justice system? Should the defence disclose vital evidence in its possession to the Crown, even if this disclosure will incriminate the accused? The answers—there is no single answer—depend on circumstances and provincial rules of professional conduct. During the first-degree murder trial of Paul Bernardo in 1995, this issue triggered an explosive debate.

Bernardo was being tried for the slayings of two schoolgirls. Almost two years earlier, he had given written instructions to his second lawyer, Ken Murray, about where to locate incriminating videotapes that police had failed to find. Murray retrieved the tapes and believed he had no obligation to disclose them to the Crown or to enforcement authorities. He planned to introduce them in his cross-examination of Karla Homolka, Bernardo's former wife, who faced related murder charges. Murray intended to portray her as the mastermind behind the killings. Before that could happen, Murray resigned from the case and sought guidance from the Law Society of Upper Canada. On their advice, he handed the tapes over to John Rosen, Bernardo's new lawyer, in August 1994. Rosen gave the tapes to the Crown a month later.

In 1995, Bernardo was found guilty of first-degree murder. Earlier, before the tapes were available to the Crown, Homolka was convicted of manslaughter. In February 1997, Murray was charged under s. 139(2) of the *Criminal Code* for willfully attempting to obstruct the course of justice by failing to disclose the videotapes. The central issue revolved around the responsibility of the defence lawyer to disclose information.

Consider the following viewpoints on this issue.

> The rule provides no guidance as to the nature of evidence that "ought to be disclosed." It is of small help either to counsel or to clients who may believe that both their secrets and their evidence are safe with lawyers. ... If I make the assumption that Murray intended to use the tapes in the defence, I have no difficulty with the proposition that he may well have believed under the circumstances that he had no legal duty to disclose the tapes until resolution discussion or trial.
>
> —*Ontario Superior Court Justice Patrick Gravely, from the 52-page decision acquitting Ken Murray*

Figure 10.4 *Ken Murray (left) and his lawyer, Austin Cooper, are surrounded by media outside Ontario Provincial Court in St. Catharines, Ontario, following Murray's acquittal.*

> I am very proud of what I did and I would not do a thing differently now than I did three years ago, or seven years ago.
>
> —*Ken Murray, quoted in the Canadian Press, July 22, 2003*

> ...There comes a time when you have to draw the line. I would have never done what [Murray] did.
>
> —*Barry Fox, Bernardo's first lawyer, in an interview with the Canadian Press, July 22, 2003*

> [T]he defence in Canada is under no legal obligation to cooperate with or assist the Crown by announcing any special defence, such as an alibi, or by providing documentary or physical evidence.
>
> —*Supreme Court Justice Antonio Lamer, in the 1984 Supreme Court case* R v. P.

> Hopefully the Law Society, or the legislature or Parliament will do something about the rules because the rules up until now haven't been very clear.
>
> —*Austin Cooper, Ken Murray's lawyer, quoted in the Canadian Press, July 22, 2003*

Questions

1. List the arguments on each side of the issue. Choose the best argument and explain your choice.
2. What do you believe defence lawyers should do with evidence? Write your view in a short paragraph.
3. How did the fact that Karla Homolka was dealt with by the justice system before it had access to the tapes complicate the situation for (a) the defence and (b) the Crown?
4. Conduct research to find out more about how the Law Society of Upper Canada deals with the issue of defence disclosure of physical evidence in its rules of professional conduct.

Find out more about the Law Society of Upper Canada's evolving rule on defence disclosure of physical evidence at www.emp.ca/dimensionsoflaw

Self-defence

As an affirmative defence, self-defence provides a justification for the reasonable use of force in certain situations. These include defending oneself against an assault and defending one's property against trespass. An accused who claims self-defence is asking to be completely excused for otherwise criminal activity. Society is prepared to excuse self-defenders, but only if their behaviour is objectively reasonable. Section 34 of the *Criminal Code* establishes the framework for the defence.

Find cases involving each defence covered in this chapter from ss. 34(1) and (2) at www.emp.ca/dimensionsoflaw

The Law Read the self-defence section of the *Criminal Code* below and answer the questions that follow.

34(1) Every one who is unlawfully assaulted without having provoked the assault is justified in repelling force by force if the force he uses is not intended to cause death or grievous bodily harm and is no more than is necessary to enable him to defend himself.

(2) Every one who is unlawfully assaulted and who causes death or grievous bodily harm in repelling the assault is justified if

(a) he causes it under reasonable apprehension of death or grievous bodily harm from the violence with which the assault was originally made or with which the assailant pursues his purposes; and

(b) he believes, on reasonable grounds, that he cannot otherwise preserve himself from death or grievous bodily harm.

Questions

1. What are the requirements for successfully raising the defence of self-defence?
2. How does the requirement of reasonableness influence both ss. 34(1) and (2)?
3. How does the requirement of reasonableness differ in ss. 34(1) and (2)? Suggest reasons why the difference exists.

The traditional model of self-defence is a single, violent quarrel between two men of similar size and strength who are strangers to each other. In this context, the two requirements in s. 34(2) of the *Criminal Code*—that the threat is imminent and that no alternative to the defensive action is possible—make sense. However, in the context of abusive relationships, these requirements must be reconsidered. In *R v. Lavallee*, the Supreme Court of Canada accepted expert testimony on battered women's syndrome (see Chapter 1, page 25) and made headlines. Although the legal issue in *Lavallee* was evidentiary, the legacy of the case is in the way the Court reconceptualized self-defence.

While hearing the case, the Supreme Court examined *R v. Whynot*, in which the accused shot her abusive husband while he was asleep. Evidence in *Whynot* established that the husband had repeatedly abused his wife and children and had threatened to kill every family member if his wife left him. On the night of the shooting, he had threatened to kill his wife's son. Whynot was convicted because, in the trial judge's opinion, she had acted in anticipation of an assault, not in response to an assault that was imminent.

The Supreme Court rejected this approach in *Lavallee*, concluding that it would condemn battered women to "murder by instalment." In the

Court's view, society gains nothing by insisting that the battered woman wait until the gun is pointed or the knife uplifted. The issue is whether the fear that motivated the defensive action is reasonable. In some situations, the immediacy of the threat provides a way of answering that question. In other situations, the reasonableness of the fear must be assessed using different criteria, ones that take into account the dynamics of the abusive relationship.

The Court in *Lavallee* also re-examined the no-alternative requirement—that is, that the self-defender must reasonably believe that there is no alternative but to defend. In *Lavallee*, the Court pointed out that the relevant question is, "Did the accused reasonably believe that she had no alternative?" In answering this question, the Court acknowledged that the nature of the relationship between the accused and the abuser is relevant.

R v. Lavallee is a landmark case because it recognized that assessing reasonableness and relevance requires attention to context. The Court accepted evidence on battered women's syndrome, but the case is about much more than this aspect alone. As Justice L'Heureux-Dubé explained recently in *R v. Malott*:

> The legal inquiry into the moral **culpability** of a woman who is, for instance, claiming self-defence must focus on the reasonableness of her actions in the context of her personal experiences, and her experiences as a woman, not on her status as a battered woman and her entitlement to claim that she is suffering from "battered woman syndrome." ... By emphasizing a woman's "learned helplessness," her dependence, her victimization, and her low self-esteem, in order to establish that she suffers from "battered woman's syndrome," the legal debate shifts from the objective rationality of her actions to preserve her own life to those personal inadequacies which apparently explain her failure to flee from her abuser. Such an emphasis comports too well with society's stereotypes about women. Therefore, it should be scrupulously avoided because it only serves to undermine the important advancements achieved by the decision in *Lavallee*.

culpability: blameworthiness

Compulsion

The defence of compulsion excuses individuals whose criminal conduct is compelled by threats and who have no realistic choice but to commit a criminal offence. As with self-defence, compulsion is an affirmative defence that, if successful, leads to an acquittal. The defence is codified in s. 17 of the *Criminal Code*, and its use is restricted. The accused person must be subjected to serious threats by a person who has the present capacity to act on the threats. These are known as the requirements of immediacy and presence. In addition, s. 17 contains a list of offences for which the defence of compulsion is unavailable.

The Law From s. 17 of the *Criminal Code*:

A person who commits an offence under compulsion by threats of immediate death or bodily harm from a person who is present when the offence is committed is excused for committing the offence if the person believes that the threats will be carried out and if the person is not a party to a conspiracy or association whereby the person is subject to compulsion, but this section does not apply where the offence that is committed is high treason or treason, murder, piracy, attempted murder, sexual assault, sexual assault with a weapon, threats to a third party or causing bodily harm, aggravated sexual assault, forcible abduction, hostage taking, robbery, assault with a weapon or causing bodily harm, aggravated assault, unlawfully causing bodily harm, arson or an offence under sections 280 to 283 (abduction and detention of young persons).

Questions

1. What are the essential elements of the defence of compulsion?
2. What purposes do the requirements of immediacy and presence serve?
3. Can a person who commits a serious assault because there is a gun pointed at his or her head raise a compulsion defence?

Personal Viewpoint

Clayton Ruby: Advocate at Large

Since being called to the bar in 1969, Clayton Ruby has served as counsel in countless human rights, Aboriginal rights, environmental, and criminal cases. He has mentored scores of young lawyers and is widely admired as a tireless advocate for social justice. As a defence lawyer, Ruby has also caught the attention of various security agencies.

One of his longest battles has been to gain access to files that federal police and security agencies have kept on him since the early 1970s. Ruby asked the RCMP to hand the files over in 1988 and was given documents heavily edited by the Canadian Security Intelligence Service (CSIS). He was flatly refused access to other files. Under the *Privacy Act*, material deemed too sensitive to be made public must be viewed in secret hearings. This meant that only judges could see many of the files. Ruby launched a challenge. In 2002, the

Figure 10.5 *Representing an environmental group, Clayton Ruby announced at a 1997 news conference that he would launch a complaint with the federal government for its failure to protect endangered species.*

Supreme Court ruled that portions of judicial hearings in national security cases should be held in public. Ruby called it a minor victory. He planned on returning to federal court to ask for another look at documents that had been withheld.

Perhaps the best way to appreciate Ruby's principles is to examine some of the cases and issues he has taken on.

> *Laws passed in haste are too often bad laws. Our fundamental freedoms cannot be permitted such cavalier treatment and require this bill be subjected to critical and thorough analysis. ... The value a democracy places upon the right of its citizens to say it is wrong is the hallmark of freedom. ... Freedom need not be undermined in the name of protecting it.*

—Clayton Ruby and Peter Tabuns, on the proposed federal anti-terrorism bill, in an open letter published in *The Globe and Mail*, October 17, 2001, p. 6.

> *Had we been told that a year ago we were going to cage an entire city, no one would have believed it for a minute. ... The Canadian government cannot tell the difference between democratic protest and criminality, but clearly Canadian citizens can.*

—Ruby responding to the decision to place a security barrier in Quebec City during the 2001 Summit of the Americas.

> *...there is an increasing trend by large corporations to file complex cases with large damage claims where they couldn't hope to recover damages. Their objective is to silence. The court struck an important blow today for free speech in Canada. ... If it had gone the other way, it would mean free speech for corporations and a muzzle for everyone else. You have to allow ordinary citizens who have no power, who haven't got the money of corporations and their power, some way of talking to other citizens... . If you can't do that, this isn't much of democracy.*

—Clayton Ruby, on the initial decision in the landmark case *Daishowa v. Friends of the Lubicon*. (The Lubicon First Nation had organized a boycott of the multinational forestry corporation's logging of land they claimed, and Daishowa launched a lawsuit to stop them.)

Questions

1. What do you believe would happen if society did not have people like Clayton Ruby challenging issues?
2. Take one of the issues mentioned in this feature and do some in-depth research to find out what the final outcome was.
3. What issues in the areas of human rights and environmental protection do you believe require action? What actions would you undertake if you felt strongly about an issue?

Recently, the statutory requirements of immediacy and presence have been subjected to analysis. Many commentators have suggested that the requirements are unfairly restrictive and breach s. 7 of the Charter—"the right to life, liberty and security of the person." And the Supreme Court of Canada has ruled that a serious threat made before the commission of an offence by a person who is not present at the time of the offence can reasonably be considered a dangerous threat.

duress: illegal threats; coercion through threats

The common-law defence of **duress** is also available to excuse criminal acts that are compelled by threats. The common law, however, excludes no offences. In theory, even a party to murder could successfully rely on the common-law defence of duress.

Check Your Understanding

1. Differentiate between a negativing defence and an affirmative defence, and give two examples of each.
2. Explain, using an example, the defence of mistake of fact. Why is this defence used most often in the context of sexual assault?
3. What is the rationale behind the defence of mental disorder?
4. a) What happens to an accused person who is found to be not criminally responsible (NCR)?
   b) What factors need to be considered by the court or review board in deciding what should be done with an NCR acquittee?
5. Explain what automatism is and why it constitutes a defence to a criminal charge.
6. Name two kinds of automatism.
7. Differentiate between general intent and specific intent offences, and give an example of each.
8. What impact does the defence of intoxication have on general intent and specific intent offences?
9. What exception to the rule concerning general intent and specific intent offences resulted from *R v. Daviault*? How did the government respond to this exception? Which approach do you prefer—the government's, or the Supreme Court's? Why?
10. Explain the immediacy requirement in the case of self-defence. How did the Supreme Court approach this requirement in *R v. Lavallee*?

METHODS OF *Legal Inquiry*

Writing a Legal Case Brief

It is often helpful to summarize a case once you have read it. A legal case brief is a summary of the essential points of a court decision. A case brief gives readers a good understanding of the case without having to read the case themselves.

A case brief begins with a case citation (review "Reading Case Citations" in Chapter 2, pages 62–63, for the components of a case citation). This is followed by the brief itself, which is organized into five parts under the headings Facts, Issue, Arguments, Decision, and Rationale.

Facts

In this part of the case brief, you state the circumstances involved in the case as simply as possible. In briefing a criminal case, for example, you summarize the incidents leading up to the crime, the crime itself (including when and where it happened), and what the defendant was alleged to have done or not done. You must read the court's opinion very carefully to determine which facts were crucial to its decision. You will often find these facts described at the beginning of the opinion, but they may also be scattered throughout the opinion.

Two important things to keep in mind when you summarize the relevant facts are neutrality and evidence. Each party (in a criminal case, the defendant and the Crown) will have a different perspective on what happened. These perspectives, or *arguments*, will mix facts and interpretations of facts (see below). However, the court's decision will be based only on facts that are agreed on by both parties (these may be listed near the beginning) or that are described as being proven by the evidence. In your case brief, you should list only agreed or proven facts.

Issue

The issue is the legal question that the court must determine in the case. You phrase the issue as a question in a single sentence. The issue may be one of fact ("Did the defendant meet the legal conditions for commission of the crime?") or of law ("Can the defendant use a legal or common-law defence to excuse his actions?") or of both fact and law ("Did the police conduct a valid search of the defendant's premises?").

Arguments

Once you have identified the issue, it can be useful to summarize the argument(s) made by each party's lawyer with respect to how it should be answered, because these arguments often reflect the legal precedents on which the decision will be based. You can often express each side's argument in a single sentence. For example, "Counsel for the defendant argued that *mens rea* was not proven because the defendant did not know he was buying a stolen stereo," or "The prosecution argued that the defendant was wilfully blind to the fact that the stereo was stolen."

Decision

The decision of the court is usually expressed in one sentence. In a civil case, the court finds in favour of one of the parties; in a criminal case, the defendant is convicted or acquitted.

Rationale

In this part of the case brief, you summarize the court's *rationale*, or the reason(s) why the court decided the case in the way that it did. The rationale is usually the lengthiest part of the court's opinion. There are numerous grounds on which a court can base its ruling. An important consideration for common law courts is *stare decisis* (Latin for precedent). According to this principle, if one court has already decided an issue in a particular way, other courts of the same level or a lower level must decide the issue in a similar way.

Applying the Skill

1. Using these guidelines for writing a legal case brief, complete a one-page analysis of *R v. Cox*, 2003 ONSC 10351. (An abbreviated version of the case is available at www.emp.ca/dimensionsoflaw.)
2. Research a case that interests you and write a legal case brief on it. Present your brief to the class.

Reviewing Main Ideas

You Decide!

THREATS AND FUNDAMENTAL JUSTICE

R v. Ruzic, [2001] 1 SCR 687

Facts

In 1994, Marijana Ruzic, a Yugoslavian citizen, landed at a Canadian airport with a false Austrian passport and two kilograms of heroin strapped to her body. She was arrested, charged, and tried for possessing and using a false passport and importing narcotics. Ruzic admitted having committed the offences but claimed she had acted under duress.

Ruzic testified that two months before her arrest, she had been approached by Mirko Mirkovic in Belgrade, where she lived with her mother. She believed Mirkovic to be a "warrior," someone who had been paid to kill people in the war. An expert witness testified that in 1994, paramilitary groups had roamed Belgrade engaged in organized criminal activities, and that people in Belgrade felt unsafe and did not trust the police.

During a series of encounters, Ruzic alleged that Mirkovic's behaviour became more intimidating, escalating to threats, physical violence, sexual harassment, and threats against her mother. He eventually told Ruzic to pack a bag, strapped packages of heroin to her body, gave her the false passport, and instructed her to take the packages to a Toronto restaurant.

Ruzic told no one of Mirkovic, fearing that he would harm whomever she told. She did not seek protection from Belgrade police because she believed they were corrupt and would do nothing. Ruzic maintained that she followed Mirkovic's instructions out of fear for her mother's safety. She made no attempt to seek help from police or other authorities. Ruzic asserted that she believed the only way she could protect her mother was to obey Mirkovic's orders.

At trial, Ruzic's lawyers argued that s. 17 of the *Criminal Code* was too narrow and that the immediacy and presence requirements violated s. 7 of the Charter.

The Law

Section 7 of the *Canadian Charter of Rights and Freedoms* states:

> Everyone has the right to life, liberty and security of the person and the right not to be deprived thereof except in accordance with the principles of fundamental justice.

(Refer also to s. 17 of the *Criminal Code*, which can be found in the Law feature on page 312 of this chapter.)

Arguments Supporting Section 17 of the Criminal Code *(Crown)*

The accused's claim of duress did not meet the immediacy and presence requirements of s. 17 of the Code. A successful argument of compulsion leads to a complete acquittal for someone who has in fact committed a criminal offence. Section 17 is carefully drafted in order to ensure that only those individuals who truly had no choice are acquitted. Therefore, its provisions do not violate fundamental justice. There were realistic alternatives available to Marijana Ruzic.

Arguments Supporting Section 7 of the Charter (Defence)

Ruzic's conduct was "morally involuntary" in that she had no realistic choice but to commit the offence. Section 17 narrows the defence of compulsion in a way that violates the principle of fundamental justice that involuntary behaviour should not be punished. Ruzic should be entitled to rely on the less restrictive common-law version of the defence, which requires an assessment of whether any realistic choice existed at the time she committed the offence.

Make Your Decision

1. What are the issues that the Court was required to decide?
2. Summarize the arguments in support of and against the constitutionality of s. 17 of the *Criminal Code.*
3. Decide whether the defence of compulsion should be allowed. Explain your legal reasoning.
4. To find out what happened in this case, visit www.emp.ca/dimensionsoflaw.

Key Terms

Review the following terms to show that you understand the meaning of each and how it is applied in a legal context.

acquitted
affirmative defence
case to meet
challenge for cause
cross-examination
culpability
directed verdict
duress
empanelling a jury
examination in chief
general intent offences
hearsay
jury array
NCR acquittee
negativing defence
peremptory challenge
specific intent offences
trier of fact
voir dire

Understanding the Law

Review the following pieces of legislation mentioned in the text, and show that you understand the intent of each.

Canadian Charter of Rights and Freedoms, ss. 7 and 11
Criminal Code, ss. 17, 33.1, 34, 265, 273.1, 273.2, and 672.54
Ontario *Juries Act*

Thinking and Inquiry

1. Do you believe that all citizens are equal before the law? Explain your views.
2. After re-examining criminal trial principles, rank them in order of importance. Explain the reasons for your ranking.
3. Examine s. 11 of the *Canadian Charter of Rights and Freedoms* (see the Appendix). If you could add or delete one right, which would it be? Explain your decision.
4. Some critics of the decision in *R v. Williams* have expressed concern that if challenges for cause are permitted on grounds of widespread prejudice in the community, the Canadian approach to jury selection will quickly mirror that in the United States, with routine and sometimes lengthy challenges for cause of every juror in every case, attendant increased costs and delays, and invasion of jurors' privacy. Do you share this concern? Develop an argument supporting one view or the other.
5. Re-examine Justice L'Heureux-Dubé's statement in *R v. Malott* (page 311). What does she say must be scrupulously avoided in the future? Do you agree with her? Why or why not?

Communication

6. In the jury selection process, lawyers make their peremptory challenges based on minimal information (potential juror's name, occupation, address, appearance, and demeanour). As the Crown attorney for a sexual assault case, construct a list of the types of jurors you would like empanelled. Then do the same as the defence lawyer. Present your lists to the class, and be prepared to defend them.
7. Visit a courtroom and prepare a visual of what you see. Explain the responsibilities of the people involved in the trial process. Be sure to include the following people: judge, Crown attorney, defence lawyer, and, if possible, jury.
8. Working in small groups, re-examine the various defences that have been discussed in this chapter. Create a dramatic scenario in which one of the defences is raised. Present your scenario to the class.

Application

9. Conduct research into how a country of your choice deals with courtroom procedures. Create a chart outlining how these courtroom procedures differ from those in Canada. In point form, describe which system you believe best protects the rights of the accused.
10. Conduct research and prepare a report on defences (other than those covered in this chapter) that may be raised in a Canadian court. Your report should describe what the defence is and how it may be raised in court. You should also find a case in which the defence was used successfully, and describe how it was used. Some possible defences include: artistic merit, colour of right, double jeopardy, officially induced error, and provocation.

Chapter 11 Delivering Criminal Justice

CHAPTER *Focus*

In this chapter, you will

- explain the process of plea bargaining and why it remains controversial
- describe and evaluate the types and purposes of sentences imposed in criminal law
- explain the concepts and principles of criminal justice
- analyze situations in Canadian law in which principles of justice conflict
- demonstrate an understanding of competing concepts of justice, such as Aboriginal concerns and principles, as they apply to the criminal justice system
- analyze cases in which there has been a miscarriage of justice

The Supreme Court of Canada has said that, for most offenders, sentencing is "the only significant decision the criminal justice system is called on to make." Sentencing is also significant in the public's perception of justice: it not only reflects social values, but exposes conflicts within the purposes and principles of the criminal justice system and within communities. This chapter considers questions at the heart of these conflicts. How can the justice system both punish and rehabilitate offenders? Do concerns for such principles as fairness, accountability, due process, and restraint truly shape the criminal justice system? Or are costs, efficiency, and public protection more important? What about accessibility? Who participates in the delivery of criminal justice and why? Is the system sensitive to diversity? To victims of crime? And what redress is there for victims of the justice system itself, those who have been wrongfully convicted?

The cartoon in Figure 11.1 reflects a fundamental requirement that must be met for justice to be done.

"I don't know about you, but my confidence in the judge as an impartial guardian of the rule of law wasn't that high even before the Supreme Court ruling."

Figure 11.1

At First Glance

1. What point is the cartoonist making?
2. What is meant by the phrase "the judge as an impartial guardian of the rule of law"?
3. Why might the character speaking in the cartoon lack confidence in the criminal justice system?
4. What cases do you know of that would support the criticism found in this cartoon?

Plea Bargaining

The criminal justice system is far more complex than the world portrayed in crime novels, television shows, and sensationalized journalism. As you learned in Chapter 10, the full criminal trial, complete with reluctant witnesses, dramatic cross-examinations, and mind-bending legal arguments, is the exception. The system disposes of more than 80 percent of all criminal charges through **plea bargaining**, in which the accused pleads guilty in return for some promise from the Crown. Once the accused pleads guilty, a formal sentencing hearing will normally be held almost immediately. For accused people, this hearing could be their only in-court experience or contact with a judge.

plea bargaining: a process in which the accused (defence) negotiates with the Crown, usually agreeing to plead guilty in exchange for a lesser charge and a recommendation for a lighter sentence

To understand why an accused person would bargain away the right to a trial, one should understand what concessions a Crown prosecutor can offer. Accused people are often charged with multiple offences: a Crown prosecutor might offer to drop one or more charges in return for a guilty plea on another. An accused may be facing the most serious potential charge, for example, a charge of aggravated assault as opposed to "simple" assault. A Crown prosecutor might offer to reduce the charge in exchange for a guilty plea. Crown prosecutors might also use the potential sentence as a bargaining tool. For example, the Crown might offer to recommend leniency in sentencing in exchange for a guilty plea.

In plea bargaining, the accused exchanges the presumption of innocence for some certainty over conviction and sentencing. A plea bargain may also mean avoiding public exposure, delays, stress, and the high legal costs of a trial. On the other hand, the state no longer has to prove its case beyond a reasonable doubt, and so plea bargaining clearly benefits the Crown. It saves time and money and frees up courts, presumably for the most serious offences.

Fyi Many people believe that most offences heard by Canada's adult criminal courts involve violence. In reality, the figure is about 20%, and almost 60% of these cases are minor assaults. Homicide and attempted murder account for less than 1%.

Plea bargaining is certainly efficient, but a 1975 study by the Law Reform Commission of Canada declared that it had "no place in a decent criminal justice system." Two decades later, attitudes had changed. The Commission then described plea bargaining as necessary and routine. The Canadian

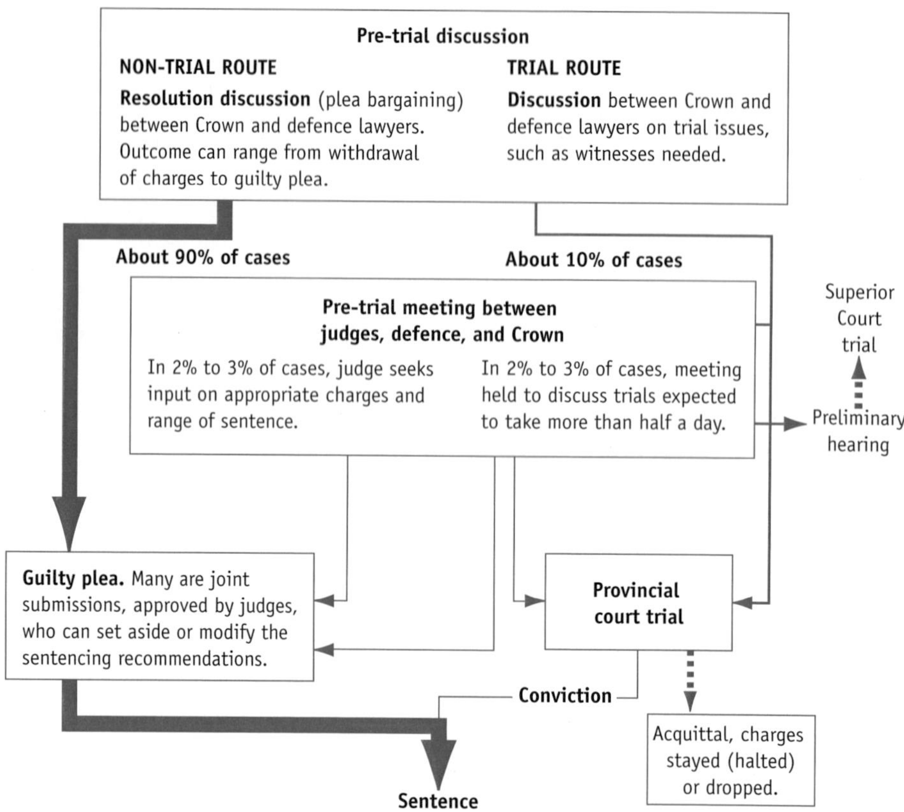

Figure 11.2 *Routes to sentencing. How does this diagram support the view that the criminal justice system is an "assembly line"?*

Bar Association also approves of the practice. Its *Rules of Professional Conduct* suggest that defence lawyers should ensure that clients are advised of the strength of the Crown's case and of the implications of a guilty plea. If a client voluntarily admits the necessary elements of the offence, and voluntarily instructs the lawyers to enter into an agreement, the lawyer is allowed to bargain. A commentary in the rules raises a caution: "the public interest in the proper administration of justice should not be sacrificed in the interest of expediency."

Plea bargaining can stir public outrage when acts of violence and murder are involved. In 1993, for example, Karla Homolka's defence counsel plea bargained with the Crown. Homolka received a sentence of manslaughter rather than face first-degree murder charges in connection with the slayings of two schoolgirls (see the Issue in Chapter 10, pages 307–309).

For an article that appeared in the *Toronto Star* on March 10, 2001, reporters Nick Phon and Donovan Vincent spent four months following 107 cases through Ontario's provincial trial courts. Almost 80 percent of the cases were plea bargained:

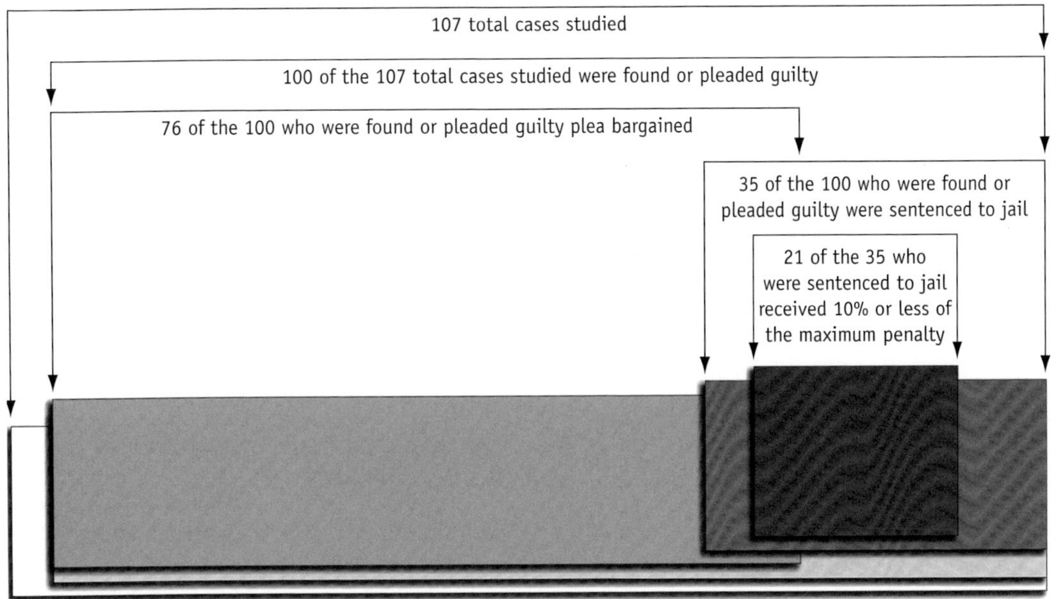

Figure 11.3 *This diagram summarizes facts from Phon and Vincent's survey of a total of 107 cases. What impact might these findings have on public perceptions of the criminal justice system?*

> Prosecutors have become ***de facto*** judges. Defence lawyers ... know the pressure is on prosecutors to resolve cases quickly and keep the justice assembly line moving. ... Forget the thrust and parry of competing lawyers, sobbing witnesses and silent juries. Prosecutors are encouraged to avoid clogging the courts with the less serious cases, even if it means, as Chief Crown Attorney Paul Culver says, "occasionally holding your nose and accepting a sentence you feel is too light."

***de facto*:** (Latin) exists in actuality, whether legally accepted or not

Phon and Vincent concluded that justice was "up for negotiation." They suggested the government's overriding goal was to prevent backlogs, and cited the fact that prosecutors were aiming to resolve 90 percent of charges without going to trial. Ontario's policy manual for Crown attorneys explicitly instructs prosecutors to request a sentence at the bottom end of the normal range when there is an early guilty plea.

Check Your Understanding

1. Explain what a plea bargain is.
2. What are some of the concessions a Crown attorney may make?
3. Why is a plea bargain worth the cost to an accused?
4. Summarize Phon and Vincent's findings on plea bargaining.
5. Is plea bargaining a "necessary evil"? Support your point of view with a chart that lists its advantages and disadvantages.
6. Do you think plea bargaining sacrifices justice for expediency? Explain your view.

Sentencing

The Canadian Sentencing Commission has defined sentencing as "the judicial determination of a legal sanction to be imposed on a person found guilty of an offence." In all cases, whether plea bargained or heard at trial, a sentencing hearing is held to help the judge determine a just sentence for the particular offender and the particular offence.

Traditionally, sentencing in Canada has focused on achieving four aims:

- denunciation (unacceptable behaviour is labelled and condemned)
- deterrence, specific and general (offenders are prevented from committing other offences, deterring others from engaging in criminal activities)
- separation (offenders are separated from society to protect the public)
- **rehabilitation** (offenders are trained and treated).

rehabilitation: a sentencing goal that seeks to restore a person to moral, physical, social, and mental health through training and treatment

Like the criminal trial itself, sentencing involves a conflict between the interests of the state and those of the individual being judged. Separation, deterrence, and denunciation serve state interests by protecting society from dangerous offenders. Rehabilitation is more attuned to the needs of the offender.

judicial discretion: freedom of judges to determine a sentence

Historically, sentencing in Canada has been primarily an exercise of **judicial discretion**. The *Criminal Code* provides minimal guidance by setting a maximum term of imprisonment for each offence. However, the type of sentence (custodial or in the community) and its quantum (the length of the prison term and probation order; the amount of the fine) are at the judge's discretion.

statutorily prescribed minimum: the minimum penalty set by a statute

incarceration: imprisonment

The only exception to the principle of judicial discretion is for offences that carry a **statutorily prescribed minimum** penalty (usually a period of **incarceration** or a fine). For these offences, the judge must impose at least the minimum. The mandatory minimum penalty for first-degree murder is life imprisonment without eligibility for parole for 25 years; for second-degree murder, the penalty is life imprisonment without eligibility for parole for 10 to 25 years, depending on a number of factors. Some offences carry a four-year minimum if a firearm is involved, for example, manslaughter, robbery, and aggravated sexual assault. Other well-known mandatory minimum sentences apply to impaired driving. Section 255 of the *Criminal Code* sets a minimum $600 fine for individuals convicted of a first impaired driving offence. A second conviction carries a mandatory 14-day sentence, and third and subsequent offences have a mandatory minimum sentence of 90 days.

Fyi There is a popular misconception that a life sentence does not mean life. But in Canada, anyone sentenced to life will be subject to conditions and supervision for the rest of his or her life, whether in prison or not.

Offences that carry a mandatory minimum penalty are the exception in Canada. Since the early 1990s, however, the number of offences with mandatory minimums has increased dramatically. There is no clear logic that determines which offences carry such penalties. Often, legislators use the mandatory minimum to send a message to the public that they are taking a strong position on a serious issue.

Case ARE MANDATORY MINIMUM SENTENCES CRUEL AND UNUSUAL PUNISHMENT?

R v. Latimer, [2001] 1 SCR 3

Facts

Robert Latimer was charged with first-degree murder following the death of Tracey, his 12-year-old daughter. Tracey suffered from a severe form of cerebral palsy, was completely immobile, and was said to have the mental capacity of a four-month-old baby. She communicated only through facial expression, laughter, and crying, and was completely dependent on others. She suffered five to six seizures daily, and it was thought that she suffered great pain. Tracey was spoon-fed, but a lack of nutrients caused weight loss. Medical evidence suggested that a feeding tube into Tracey's stomach could improve her nutrition and health and allow for more effective pain management. However, the accused and his wife rejected this option. After learning that doctors wished to perform additional surgery, which he perceived as mutilation, Mr. Latimer carried Tracey to his pickup truck. He placed her on a seat and then inserted a hose from the exhaust pipe into the cab. Tracey died of carbon monoxide poisoning. At first, the accused maintained Tracey had died in her sleep. Later, he confessed to police investigators that he had ended her life. Latimer was found guilty of second-degree murder and sentenced to life imprisonment without parole eligibility for 10 years. He appealed this decision to the Saskatchewan Court of Appeal and, finally, to the Supreme Court of Canada.

Figure 11.4 *The family of Matthew Dolmage (in wheelchair) have followed the* Latimer *case and are opposed to any kind of mercy killing.*

Figure 11.5 *Sheila Noyes says she is willing to help serve the life sentence of Robert Latimer.*

Issues

Does imposing the mandatory minimum punishment upon Robert Latimer violate the Charter guarantee against "cruel and unusual" punishment (s. 12)? Should he be granted a constitutional exemption from the mandatory minimum sentence?

Decision

To learn more about the *Latimer* case, visit www.emp.ca/dimensionsoflaw

The Supreme Court upheld Latimer's conviction and sentence. In its unanimous ruling, the Court stated:

> The law has a long history of difficult cases. We recognize the questions that arise in Mr. Latimer's case are the sort that have divided Canadians and sparked a national discourse. This judgment will not end that discourse.
>
> Mr. Latimer perceived his daughter and family to be in a difficult and trying situation. ... [H]e faced challenges of the sort most Canadians can only imagine. His care of his daughter for many years was admirable. His decision to end his daughter's life was an error in judgment. The taking of another life represents the most serious crime in our criminal law. ...
>
> The mandatory minimum sentence for second-degree murder in this case does not amount to cruel and unusual punishment within the meaning of s. 12 of the *Canadian Charter of Rights and Freedoms*. ... In applying s. 12, the gravity of the offence, as well as the particular circumstances of the offender and the offence, must be considered. Here, the minimum mandatory sentence is not grossly disproportionate. Murder is the most serious crime known to law. ... On the one hand, due consideration must be given to the accused's initial attempts to conceal his actions, his lack of remorse, his position of trust, the significant degree of planning and premeditation, and Tracey's extreme vulnerability. On the other hand, the accused's good character and standing in the community, his tortured anxiety about Tracey's well-being, and his laudable perseverance as a caring and involved parent must be taken into account. ... [But these] do not displace the serious gravity of this offence. Although in this case the sentencing principles of rehabilitation, specific deterrence and protection are not triggered for consideration, the mandatory minimum sentence plays an important role in denouncing murder. Since there is no violation of the accused's s. 12 right, there is no basis for granting a constitutional exemption. ...
>
> Furthermore, denunciation becomes much more important in the consideration of sentencing in cases where there is a "high degree of planning and premeditation, and where the offence and its consequences are highly publicized, [so that] like-minded individuals may well be deterred by severe sentences."

Questions

1. Do you think judges' discretion should be limited in sentencing for certain offences? Why or why not?
2. What factors complicated the *Latimer* case for the Supreme Court?
3. What two sentencing objectives did the Supreme Court reinforce?
4. In light of the Supreme Court's decision in this case, describe some arguments that would support a constitutional exemption for Robert Latimer.

The Sentencing Hearing

Once an individual is found guilty of committing an offence, the court's focus shifts to determining a fit sentence. In some cases, sentencing happens immediately after a finding of guilt. In others, the case will be adjourned for a period of time so that the lawyers can gather evidence and develop arguments about an appropriate sentence. The judge can also adjourn the hearing and ask for more information about the offender.

Sentencing hearings are much less formal than trials, and the rules of evidence are relaxed. The judge can participate actively by asking for information or by questioning the lawyers. Such interaction supports the purpose of the sentencing hearing: to craft a sentence appropriate for the particular offender and offence. The more information the judge has, the more likely it is that the sentence will accomplish the aims as set out in the *Criminal Code.*

One main source of information is the **pre-sentence report**, most often prepared by a probation officer at the request of the sentencing court. It will contain observations on the offender's background, family situation, employment, education, and attitude, as well as information about the offence. A pre-sentence report may also contain a recommendation or assessment of the kind of sentence appropriate for the offender. In addition to the pre-sentence report and the submissions of the Crown and the defence, a **victim impact statement** may be filed with the court. This statement gives victims, or families of victims, the opportunity to describe the emotional and physical impact of the crime for the court's consideration in sentencing. (See the Turning Points in the Law feature later in this chapter.)

pre-sentence report: a report that describes the offender and the offence and that may also recommend a sentence; usually prepared by a probation officer

victim impact statement: verbal or written statement given by a victim or victim's family to describe the personal consequences of the crime

CHECK YOUR UNDERSTANDING

1. What have been the traditional aims of sentencing in Canada?
2. Why has sentencing for the most part been an exercise of judicial discretion?
3. What is the only exception to the principle of judicial discretion?
4. Reconsider both the principle of judicial discretion and the use of mandatory sentencing. After carefully examining the positive and negative aspects of both, develop an argument that supports one or the other.
5. Why is the judge an active participant in a sentencing hearing?

6. Explain what a pre-sentence report is and who prepares it.
7. a) What is a victim impact statement?
   b) Why is a victim impact statement important in a sentencing hearing?
   c) Do you agree with the practice of allowing victim impact statements in sentencing hearings? Explain your answer.

Sentencing Reform

Fyi Many Canadians believe that parole means a sentence has been reduced. In fact, parole only affects how the sentence is served. Inmates released on parole serve the remainder of their sentence under supervision in the community.

As Canadian society became more complex and diverse, dissatisfaction over sentencing grew. In 1987, the Canadian Sentencing Commission issued a report urging reform. It was concerned that too many people were being jailed and that wide disparities existed in sentences across the country. It also found that the traditional aims of sentencing—denunciation, deterrence, separation, and rehabilitation—were too limited.

In 1996, the federal government enacted Bill C-41. This was a comprehensive reform package that provided a consistent national framework for sentencing policy and process. Perhaps most importantly, the new provisions included a legislative statement of the purposes and principles of sentencing in ss. 718, 718.1, and 718.2. Before this amendment, the *Criminal Code* contained no codified statements of sentencing principles.

Section 718 of the *Criminal Code* lists six sentencing objectives:

> The fundamental purpose of sentencing is to contribute, along with crime prevention initiatives, to respect for the law and the maintenance of a just, peaceful and safe society by imposing just sanctions that have one or more of the following objectives:
> (a) to denounce unlawful conduct;
> (b) to deter the offender and other persons from committing offences;
> (c) to separate offenders from society, where necessary;
> (d) to assist in rehabilitating offenders;
> (e) to provide reparations for harm done to victims or to the community; and
> (f) to promote a sense of responsibility in offenders, and acknowledgment of the harm done to victims and to the community.

The United Nations' *Declaration of Basic Principles of Justice for Victims of Crime and Abuse of Power* was adopted by the General Assembly in 1985 and can be found at www.emp.ca/dimensionsoflaw

The first four objectives in s. 718 had guided judges for decades, even though they were not codified within the Code. The last two objectives were new concepts. Paragraph (e) concerns the victim and the community and suggests that offenders should compensate the people they have victimized. Paragraph (f) states that sentencing should encourage offenders to take personal responsibility for the harm their wrongdoings cause. These new concepts marked a dramatic change in sentencing philosophy. For one thing, they acknowledged victims.

Paragraphs (e) and (f) of s. 718 also moved Canadian sentencing policy away from a system based primarily on blame and retribution toward a system that is more "restorative."

Turning Points in the Law

The Rights of Victims of Crime

The rights of crime victims have only recently been recognized in Canada's criminal justice system. In the past, victims often had little input into the system. That situation started to change in 1981 with the appointment of the Canadian Federal–Provincial Task Force on Justice for Victims of Crime. Two years later, the Task Force reported that often "the victim is twice victimized: once by the offence and once more by the process." It recommended compensation for victims, development of victim services, and the use of victim impact statements in court.

At the same time, groups for victims were forming in Canada. For example, Victims of Violence—Canadian Centre for Missing Children was established in March 1984 by the families of abducted and murdered children. The son of two founding members, Gary and Sharon Rosenfeldt, had been murdered by serial killer Clifford Olson in April 1981. This group and others gave victims a voice and a means to lobby (pressure) governments for change.

In 1988, justice ministers across Canada adopted the Canadian Statement of Basic Principles of Justice for Victims of Crime. Today, Canada's criminal justice system is guided by its principles, which state that victims should

1. be treated with courtesy and compassion by the criminal justice system
2. receive prompt and fair redress for harms suffered
3. have access to information about remedies and the mechanisms to obtain them
4. have access to information about participating in proceedings, and their scheduling, progress, and disposition
5. be assisted throughout the criminal process and, when appropriate, consulted about their views and concerns
6. have their concerns brought to the attention of the court, where appropriate and consistent with criminal law and procedure
7. be protected from intimidation and retaliation, along with their families, when necessary
8. have their needs and concerns understood by criminal justice personnel through sensitivity training and guidelines, where appropriate
9. be informed of available health and social services and assisted in receiving medical, psychological, and social assistance through existing programs and services
10. report the crime and cooperate with law enforcement authorities.

The *Criminal Code* now also recognizes the rights and needs of victims of crime (see Figure 11.6).

Criminal Code Provisions for Victims of Crime

Victim's Right	*Criminal Code* Section and Provision
Safety	s. 486(1.4): court may prohibit accused from communicating with victim
	s. 515(10)(b): court must consider victim's safety when granting bail
Privacy	s. 278: judge may order publication ban on information about victim
	s. 486(1): judge may exclude public from trial
A Voice	s. 722(1): victim can submit victim impact statement to court and read it at sentencing hearing
	s. 722(3): court must consider victim impact statement in sentencing
Reparations	ss. 718(e) and (f): sentence must acknowledge harm to victim and provide reparations
	s. 738: victim may receive restitution from offender

Figure 11.6

Questions

1. Re-examine the extract from the Canadian Statement of Basic Principles of Justice for Victims of Crime. Which principle do you believe is the most important? Why?
2. Why do you think it has taken so long for the rights of victims to be recognized?
3. Examine Figure 11.6. Under what circumstances do you believe a judge should be able to (a) issue a publication ban and (b) exclude the public from court?

restorative justice: a philosophy of criminal law that views offences as conflicts among offenders, victims, and their communities that should be resolved through the broad and active participation of all involved

What exactly is **restorative justice**? The Law Reform Commission of Canada has described its central characteristics. Perhaps the chief idea is that crimes should be viewed as conflicts between two or more people, not simply as transgressions against the state. Thus, the justice system should deal with the harms inflicted by wrongful acts. Restorative justice asks victims, offenders, and the community to take part in resolving conflict and in dealing with any harm done by the offence. The restorative approach to justice fosters respectful relationships among wrongdoers, victims, the community, and the state. It has its roots in Aboriginal cultures.

The Law The new sentencing provisions of the *Criminal Code* set out principles to guide judges in balancing the needs of the offender, the victim, and society:

718.1 A sentence must be proportionate to the gravity of the offence and the degree of responsibility of the offender.

718.2 A court that imposes a sentence shall also take into consideration the following principles:

(a) a sentence should be increased or reduced to account for any relevant **aggravating** or **mitigating circumstances** relating to the offence or the offender, and, without limiting the generality of the foregoing,

(i) evidence that the offence was motivated by bias, prejudice or hate based on race, national or ethnic origin, language, colour, religion, sex, age, mental or physical disability, sexual orientation or any other similar factor,

(ii) evidence that the offender, in committing the offence, abused the offender's spouse or common-law partner or child,

(iii) evidence that the offender, in committing the offence, abused a position of trust or authority in relation to the victim,

(iv) evidence that the offence was committed for the benefit of, at the direction of or in association with a criminal organization, or

aggravating circumstances: factors that increase criminal responsibility, for example, the use of violence

mitigating circumstances: factors that reduce criminal responsibility, for example, a first offence

(v) evidence that the offence was a terrorism offence shall be deemed to be aggravating circumstances;

(b) a sentence should be similar to sentences imposed on similar offenders for similar offences committed in similar circumstances;

(c) where consecutive sentences are imposed, the combined sentence should not be unduly long or harsh;

(d) an offender should not be deprived of liberty, if less restrictive sanctions may be appropriate in the circumstances; and

(e) all available sanctions other than imprisonment that are reasonable in the circumstances should be considered for all offenders, with particular attention to the circumstances of aboriginal offenders.

Questions

1. Describe some of the implications of s. 718.1.
2. According to s. 718.2(a), what would be an aggravating factor? a mitigating factor?
3. How does s. 718.2 address the question of uneven sentencing across Canada?
4. In your opinion, why would the new provisions explicitly recommend that "sanctions other than imprisonment" be considered when dealing with Aboriginal offenders?
5. If you could add one principle to the philosophy of restorative justice, what would it be? Why would you want it included?

Restorative Justice Programs

Today, Canada has a variety of restorative justice programs. The specific roles of the police, Crown attorneys, and the judiciary vary from program to program, but the key idea is that they help to settle the conflict to the satisfaction of the parties involved. Victim–offender mediation is one such program. It brings together victims, wrongdoers, and trained facilitators. Conflicts are discussed, strategies and schedules for reparations are devised, and follow-ups and monitoring are arranged. In the controlled environment of these programs, victims can express their anger and question their wrongdoers. This process helps offenders learn to accept full responsibility for their actions.

Fyi Many people believe that severe sentences deter criminals from reoffending. Yet, studies conducted in Canada, the United States, and Europe over the past 30 years indicate just the opposite: longer sentences may be related to a small increase in offenders returning to crime.

Restorative justice is based on establishing a respectful relationship among all parties. This relationship, in turn, will help offenders to be reintegrated, or restored, into their communities. All restorative justice initiatives share three core principles:

Learn more about restorative justice programs across Canada and the world at www.emp.ca/dimensionsoflaw

1. Crime violates a relationship among victims, offenders, and the community.
2. Responses to crime should encourage the active participation of victim, offender, and community.
3. A consensus approach to justice is the most effective response to crime.

In *R v. Gladue*, decided in 1999, the Supreme Court of Canada confirmed that restorative ideals were included in s. 718 of the *Criminal Code*. It also noted that the new legislation directed judges first to consider sanctions other than imprisonment that are appropriate in the circumstances. This movement away from incarceration and toward community-based sanctions reflects a restorative approach to justice.

Check Your Understanding

1. How do paragraphs (e) and (f) of s. 718 of the *Criminal Code* represent a change in sentencing philosophy in Canada?
2. Under restorative justice, how should crimes be viewed? Where should the focus of the criminal justice system be?
3. Describe how victim–offender mediation works. Why are programs such as this important to victims?
4. Upon what three principles are restorative justice initiatives based?

Changing the Process: Circle Sentencing

Historically, Canada's criminal justice system imposed Western legal values on Aboriginal individuals and communities, often with devastating results. The case of Donald Marshall, for example, shocked Canadians in 1983 when he was acquitted after serving 11 years in prison for a murder he had not committed. His case exposed widespread racism and mistreatment of Aboriginals within the criminal justice system.

Report after report has documented how Canada's criminal justice system has failed Aboriginal peoples. Aboriginals are disproportionately arrested, denied bail, and unrepresented in court. If convicted, an Aboriginal person is much more likely to be imprisoned. In Saskatchewan, for example, one study found that a 16-year-old Aboriginal male was nine times more likely to spend time in prison than a non-Aboriginal 16-year-old male. The study concluded that prison, for young Aboriginal men, is the equivalent of what their parents experienced in residential schools.

To find out more about sentencing circles, visit www.emp.ca/dimensionsoflaw

Judge Barry Stuart, who sits on the Yukon Territorial Court, is one of the most innovative and outspoken voices for change within Canada's justice system. He has worked extensively with Aboriginal communities and has found within them traditional models of justice that he has recognized and respected. In his decision in *R v. Moses*, Stuart spoke out powerfully for sentencing reform based on these models and for changes to the criminal justice system. That decision has had an enormous impact in Canada, the United States, and other nations.

Figure 11.7 *Clare McNab, Kikawinaw (Cree for "mother") of the Okimaw Ohci Healing Lodge in Saskatchewan, talks about the spiritual healing aspects of restorative justice. The minimum-security facility, which opened in 1995, was built to recognize the cultural values and special needs of Aboriginal women offenders.*

Case CRIME AND COMMUNITY RELATIONSHIPS

R v. Moses (1992), 71 CCC (3d) 347 (Yuk. Terr. Ct.)

Facts

The offender, Philip Moses, was found guilty of theft and of carrying a weapon (a baseball bat). At the time of the offence, he was a 26-year-old member of Na-cho Ny'ak Dun First Nation. Moses's life had been one of poverty, abuse, neglect, addiction, and criminality. Most of it had been spent in jails, juvenile detention centres, and foster and group homes. For his last offence, Moses had received a 15-month jail sentence.

Issue

What would be an appropriate sentence for Moses's most recent offence?

Decision

The following is an extract from Judge Stuart's ruling.

> The reasons for this sentence will take us on an unusual journey. Unusual, because the process was as influential in moulding the final decision as any substantive factors. ... In sentencing, ... the process influences not just what and how matters are addressed, but who participates and what impact each person has in shaping the final decision.

In this case, by changing the process, the primary issues changed, and consequently, the decision was substantially different from what might have been decided had the usual process been followed.

The justice system['s] rules and procedures provide a comfortable barrier for justice professionals from fully confronting the futility, destruction, and injustice left behind in the wake of circuit courts [courts that travel to communities]. For those who dared in this case to step outside this comfortable barrier, I hope these reasons capture their input and courage. ...

It was late in the evening, everyone was tired. The police plane waited to return Mr. Moses to jail. The charter plane waited to return the court circuit to Whitehorse. Everyone—including myself—expected the sentencing hearing would be short... . Numerous factors which never appear in sentencing decisions but often affect sentencing, pressed the court to "get on with it." We didn't. Somehow, the pernicious cycle plaguing the life of Mr. Moses had to be broken before he tragically destroy[ed] himself or someone else. ...

Mr. Moses had for 10 years travelled from alcohol abuse, to crime, and then to jail. Each time emerging from jail angrier, more dysfunctional. ... His long history with the criminal justice system had proven two unmistakable conclusions.

First, the criminal justice system had miserably failed the community of Mayo. Born and raised in Mayo, his family in Mayo, Philip instinctively returned to Mayo after each of the previous seven jail sentences ... less capable of controlling either his anger or alcohol abuse; more dangerous to the community and to himself. The criminal justice system had not protected, but had endangered the community.

Secondly, the criminal justice system had failed Mr. Moses. After 10 years, after expending in excess of a quarter of a million dollars on Mr. Moses, the justice system continues to spew back into the community a person whose prospects, hopes and abilities were dramatically worse than when the system first encountered Philip... .

If the criminal justice system had failed, what could the community do? It was hardly the model case to experiment with community alternatives. What could be lost in trying! Court was adjourned for three weeks. ... Another special circuit to Mayo was set for January 9 to sentence Philip and to thereafter hold an open community meeting to discuss how the community, especially the First Nation, might constructively participate in the justice system. ...

For centuries, the basic organization of the court has not changed. Nothing has been done to encourage meaningful participation by the accused, the victim, or by the community... . If the objective of the sentencing process is now to enhance sentencing options, to afford greater concern to the impact on victims, to shift focus from punishment to rehabilitation, and to meaningfully engage communities in sharing responsibility for sentencing decisions, it may be advantageous for the justice system to examine how court procedures and the physical arrangements within courtrooms militate [work] against these new objectives. It was, in this case. ...

For court, a circle to seat 30 people was arranged as tightly as numbers allowed. When all seats were occupied, additional seating was provided in an outer circle for persons arriving after the "hearing" had commenced.

Defence sat beside the accused and his family. The Crown sat immediately across the circle from defence counsel to the right of the judge. Officials and members from the First Nation, the RCMP officers, the probation officer and others were left to find their own "comfortable" place within the circle.

By arranging the court in a circle without desks or tables, with all participants facing each other, with equal access and equal exposure to each other, the dynamics of the decision-making process were profoundly changed.

Everyone ... around the circle introduced themselves. Everyone remained seated when speaking. After opening remarks from the judge and counsel, the formal process dissolved into an informal but intense discussion of what might best protect the community and extract Philip from the grip of alcohol and crime. ...

The circle significantly breaks down the dominance that traditional courtrooms accord lawyers and judges. ... All persons within the circle must be addressed. Equally, anyone in the circle may ask a direct question to anyone. ... The circle denies the comfort of evading difficult issues through the use of obtuse, complex technical language. ...

In this case the circle promoted among all participants a desire to find ... something unlike the sentences imposed in the past 10 years, something everyone could support, something they believed would work. ...

A struggle for a safe community must be led by the community. They, not the justice system, must be in the front line of defence against crime. All members of the community must appreciate and accept responsibility to carry their share of the burden in establishing and maintaining a safe community. ... Conflict will always be a part of community life. Creating constructive processes for dealing with conflict is the primary challenge facing society and the criminal justice system.

The current justice system is a very expensive failure... . There is an increasing recognition ... that something more than mere tinkering must be done to create a criminal justice system that is just and offers genuine protection to the community. The existing system notoriously does neither. ...

> In the justice system, too much is made of "professional objectivity." We are not processing agents solely worried about backlogs and budgets. Crimes expose conflicts that cut to the heart of families and communities. If we insulate ourselves with procedures and rules ... from the pain, tragedy and desperateness inherent in all of these conflicts, we will forever fail. We cannot succumb to simply doing "our jobs," passing criminals, victims, and communities from one part of our truncated system to another. ...
>
> Philip's road to recovery will be tougher than most people appreciate... . It is a miracle that despite so much destruction, so much pain, with so little to work with, Philip still clings to the hope he can survive, that he can prevail. Courage and the ability to persevere must be measured in the context of each person's overall life circumstance. ... [Philip's] very survival manifests a formidable will and prodigious courage to prevail. ...
>
> Tragically, Philip's is not a unique story. There are many other victims of the current justice system and [there] will be many more if we irresponsibly believe simply keeping the current machinery of justice in gear defines ... our "professional" responsibility. Unless the system is changed, the community will be victimized by the very system charged with the responsibility of protecting it. We must find a way to change. We must find communities, First Nations, professionals and lay people willing to work together to explore "truly new ways." We will; we have no choice. In making the circle work, the Na-cho Ny'ak Dun First Nation took an important first step. Can we follow?

Moses's sentence was two years' probation, to be served in the community under the following conditions: time spent on the trap line with his family; attendance at a residential treatment centre for Aboriginal alcoholics; return to the community under the supervision of family, probation officer, and Aboriginal elders. The sentence was to be continually monitored by the probation officer and, if necessary, the circle would be recalled to review Moses's progress and restructure the plan.

Questions

1. In sentencing, how does the process influence the result?
2. According to Judge Stuart, how had the criminal justice system failed both the community of Mayo and Philip Moses?
3. Why was it important to place all participants in a circle?
4. Why does Judge Stuart believe too much is made of "professional objectivity"?
5. What was Moses's sentence? Do you agree or disagree with the decision? Why or why not?
6. Create a table listing the differences between circle sentencing and typical courtroom sentencing.

CHECK YOUR UNDERSTANDING

1. How did Canada's justice system deal with Aboriginal peoples historically?
2. What evidence is there that Aboriginal people have been mistreated by the criminal justice system?
3. What have judges such as Judge Barry Stuart discovered in their work within Aboriginal communities? How has this experience shaped sentencing reform in Canada?

Sentencing Options

Once all relevant evidence and information have been presented by lawyers, witnesses, and victims, including any pre-sentence reports, the judge must decide on a sentence for those found guilty. Again, as s. 718.1 of the *Criminal Code* stipulates, the sentence must be "proportionate to the gravity of the offence and the degree of responsibility of the offender." With the exception of offences with mandatory minimum penalties, sentencing is entirely within the judge's discretion. The judge will choose from the following alternatives: absolute and conditional discharges, probation, fines, intermittent sentences, conditional sentences, and imprisonment.

Absolute and Conditional Discharges

Judges can reduce the stigma of a criminal record by granting absolute and conditional discharges. An **absolute discharge** is granted with no qualifications. A **conditional discharge** carries conditions, such as reporting to a probation officer, attending a program, abstaining from alcohol, and so on. An offender can request a discharge as long as the offence does not carry a mandatory minimum or a maximum penalty of 14 years or life. The discharge must not, however, go against the public interest.

absolute discharge: a sentence that frees the offender with no conditions and no criminal record

conditional discharge: a sentence that frees the offender with no criminal record but with court-ordered conditions that must be followed

Discharges are often requested for immigration or employment reasons. For example, an individual with a criminal conviction may be denied professional certification. An offender who receives a discharge is "deemed not to have been convicted." A person granted a discharge can answer "no" if asked whether he or she has a criminal record or a previous conviction. However, if asked whether he or she has ever been found guilty, the person granted a discharge should answer "yes."

Probation

Probation orders allow correctional services to maintain jurisdiction over offenders who are at liberty in the community. They can also be combined with fines and imprisonment and be part of suspended sentences. They often carry conditions that are intended to help reintegrate and rehabilitate offenders, and can be in effect for up to three years. All probation orders have mandatory conditions that require the offender to

- keep the peace and be of good behaviour
- appear before the court when required to do so
- notify the court or the probation officer in advance of any change of name, address, or employment or occupation.

The sentencing judge may also impose optional conditions. For example, the offender may be required to

- report to a probation officer
- abstain from alcohol or drugs
- provide for the support and care of dependants
- perform community service
- make restitution
- participate in a treatment program, if agreeable
- comply with other reasonable conditions as the court considers desirable for securing the offender's good conduct and preventing the commission of another offence.

Fines

Fines are monetary penalties that judges impose for less serious offences. For example, offenders found guilty of summary conviction offences are subject to fines of not more than $2000. There is no upper limit on fines for indictable offences. The 1996 *Criminal Code* amendments made major changes to fine provisions. Perhaps the most significant was that judges must consider whether an offender can actually pay any fine imposed. Previously, the offender's financial situation was often ignored. Prisons filled up with people who were poor rather than dangerous. Financial status, not blameworthiness, determined the impact of a fine.

garnisheeing wages: taking money directly from a defendant's wages under court order

The 1996 amendments also created more payment options, including extended schedules, **garnisheeing wages**, and fine option programs that allow offenders to work off a fine at a statutorily prescribed rate, rather than pay cash.

Parliament also created a victim fine surcharge to fund services for victims. Section 737 of the *Criminal Code* states that whenever a court convicts or discharges an offender after a finding of guilt, it must impose a victim fine surcharge equivalent to up to an additional 15 percent of a fine, or a maximum of $10 000 where no fine is imposed. The only reason for not imposing the surcharge is "undue hardship to the offender." Moneys collected are directed toward provincial victims' services.

Intermittent Sentences

The *Criminal Code* allows sentences of imprisonment of 90 days or less to be served intermittently. This provision gives judges some flexibility. Offenders can be ordered to serve custodial sentences in segments, which means they can continue with work or school. For example, an offender might be ordered to serve a 60-day sentence for two days a week over 30 weeks (i.e., on weekends).

Judges often impose intermittent sentences for offences with short mandatory minimum sentences. For example, a second impaired driving conviction carries a minimum 14-day sentence. By imposing an intermittent sentence, the judge can help ensure that the offender keeps a job, continues with education or training, or is available to support dependants. When not in custody, offenders are subject to probation orders.

Conditional Sentences

The conditional sentence was introduced as part of the 1996 reform package. As a sentencing option, it allows judges to order that a prison term of less than two years be served in the community. Clearly, this provision supports the objective of reducing the use of incarceration. Now incarceration is to be used as a last resort for the worst crimes and most dangerous offenders, when no other reasonable alternatives exist. Section 742.1 provides:

> Where a person is convicted of an offence, except an offence that is punishable by a minimum term of imprisonment, and the court
>
> (a) imposes a sentence of imprisonment of less than two years, and
>
> (b) is satisfied that serving the sentence in the community would not endanger the safety of the community and would be consistent with the fundamental purpose and principles of sentencing set out in sections 718 to 718.2,
>
> the court may, for the purpose of supervising the offender's behaviour in the community, order that the offender serve the sentence in the community... .

An offender serving a sentence in the community is subject to the conditional sentence order, which is similar to probation. Commonly, he or she will also be under some form of house arrest, which may or may not include **electronic monitoring**. The conditional sentence allows judges to denounce criminal conduct by imposing a prison sentence and also to recognize that incarceration is unnecessary with non-dangerous offenders.

electronic monitoring: a device or system that ensures an offender follows a court order; usually used to regulate home confinement (also known as house arrest)

Figure 11.8 *Vancouver inventor Eric Caton holds a model of his electronic monitoring device.*

Fyi Electronic monitoring was first used in British Columbia as part of a 1987 pilot program in Vancouver to create a less costly alternative to incarceration for selected offenders. Early studies indicated that it did save money. Soon, other provinces were also using it.

Imprisonment

To learn more about the protection of human rights in Canadian prisons and about Correctional Service Canada, visit www.emp.ca/dimensionsoflaw

Although imprisonment is the harshest punishment under criminal law, Canada has not used it sparingly. Canada's incarceration rate is very high, usually ranking second or third in the Western world (see Figure 11.9). Since the early 1990s, as a result of reforms, demographic changes, and other factors, that rate has fallen to some degree.

Both the federal and provincial levels of government run correctional institutions. Offenders sentenced to less than two years of imprisonment serve their time in provincial institutions. Longer sentences are served in federal penitentiaries. Although many people view imprisonment as the appropriate response to criminal behaviour, some people who study imprisonment or who work within the system are not convinced it is an effective response. They observe that prison makes people more dangerous, not less, and that prison cannot rehabilitate or promote moral reform.

Consider these 1999–2000 incarceration facts and figures from a recent report of the Canadian Centre for Justice Statistics:

- Canada imprisons approximately 123 adult individuals per 100 000, a decrease of 3.5 percent from 1998–1999.
- Most inmates are incarcerated for non-violent offences.
- On any given day, on average, 152 800 adults are incarcerated, on parole, on probation, or serving a conditional sentence.
- Approximately one in five adult offenders under supervision is in custody.

Figure 11.9 *International incarceration rates, 1999–2000.*

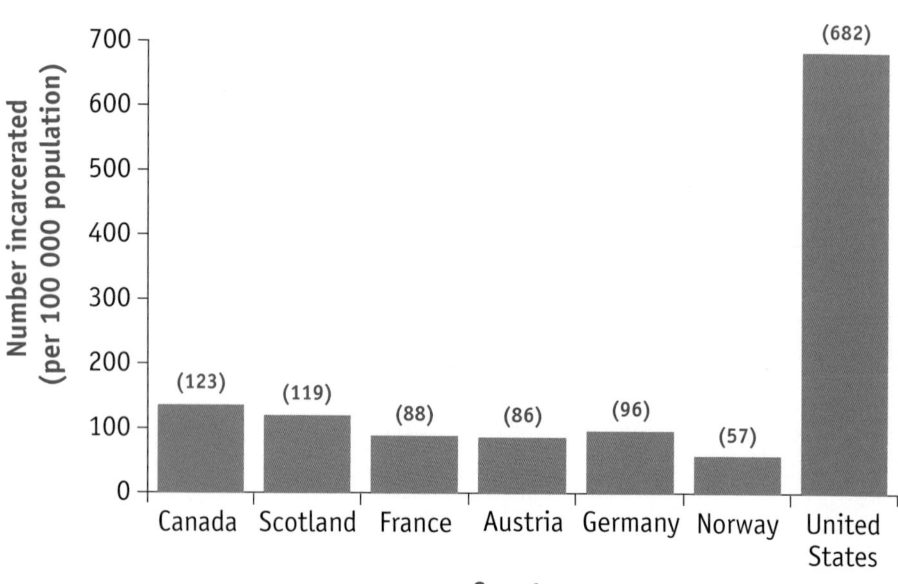

- The number of adults admitted into custody decreased for the seventh year in a row.
- Spending on correctional services totalled $2.4 billion in 1999–2000, a 5 percent increase over 1998–1999.
- An adult offender entering a custodial facility is most likely to be a male, aged 18 to 34. Women constitute about 7 percent of all admissions.
- It costs approximately $67 700 a year to keep an offender in a federal penitentiary, compared to $14 500 to supervise an inmate on parole.

Learn more about Canada's prisons at www.emp.ca/dimensionsoflaw

issue

Strict-Discipline Facilities **Do boot camps have a place in the youth criminal justice system?**

When Project Turnaround was launched as a pilot project in 1997, it sailed straight into public controversy. It was Ontario's first strict-discipline facility. According to the Ministry of Public Safety and Security, it would "provide young offenders with an intensive, regimented program to instill self-discipline, personal responsibility, and accountability for their actions and to reduce the rate of **recidivism** for male, high-risk, repeat young offenders ages 16 to 17 years." Project Turnaround was also privately run. Studies suggested it could cost taxpayers 20 percent less to run than a regular custodial facility for youths.

recidivism: returning to crime

Similar facilities in the United States were being criticized as ineffective and too harsh. In 1999, a 14-year-old female inmate died of exposure in a US facility when she collapsed and was left unconscious in the sun during exercises. Controversy struck Project Turnaround in February 2003, after mould was found in several buildings. Facilities had to be temporarily closed because of health concerns.

Project Turnaround is based on a military model, evidenced by the uniforms and the titles given to staff and youth (sergeants and cadets). The day begins with reveille at 06:00, followed by inspections. Youths are also involved in academic, vocational, and recreational programs. When the lights go out at 21:45, inmates have had very little free time.

Figure 11.10 *A resident of Camp Turnaround, in Barrie, Ontario, scales a wall during obstacle course training under guidance from an instructor. Following orders is part of daily life in strict-discipline facilities. In your opinion, does this approach support rehabilitation? Why or why not?*

Consider the following comments expressing opinions on this issue.

[Project Turnaround] applies, within the environment of a strict-discipline context, the appropriate rehabilitation programs for young offenders so they can learn to have some respect for themselves, respect for society, respect for the people who live in society and carry the responsibility for their actions.

—Hon. Rob Sampson, Ontario Minister of Correctional Services, December 16, 1999

What ... can you expect when you shave young offenders' heads, make them wear paramilitary uniforms and do military-style exercises? It's certainly not about rehabilitation. It's more about turning them into more dangerous criminals with the public paying the price.

—Leah Casselman, President, Ontario Public Service Employees Union, August 1997

We've always maintained that [Project Turnaround] consisted of more than just a place where kids paraded around and were made to wear uniforms. The camp offers a blend of military discipline and education and treatment.

—Ross Virgo, spokesperson for the Ontario Ministry of Correctional Services, to Eye Weekly, *January 20, 2000*

Ontario should not be using resources—both in terms of energy and money—to pursue these models of correctional intervention, such as boot camps, that current research evidence and experience [tell us are] ineffective.

—John Howard Society Fact Sheet #14; www.johnhoward.on.ca/Library/library.htm

Almost 65% of the individuals in the youth justice system are repeat offenders, so clearly we have to look at new initiatives. ... Project Turnaround will have ... programs such as substance abuse, anger management and a variety of courses which will be available to repeat young offenders. ... [T]he outline ... was made public some time ago, [and was] endorsed by the London Family Court Clinic, the Clarke Institute, a number of very well respected organizations and institutions.

—Hon. Robert W. Runciman, Ontario Solicitor General and Minister of Correctional Services, June 18, 1997

Our grave concern about strict discipline programs is that when administered by strangers out of context from the young person's real life, it increases the sense of rage, injustice and lack of control over one's own life. No self-esteem or desire to change for the better is likely to make inroads on the offender in such a case. Discipline that is administered in a non-violent manner by those who genuinely care for the young person is more effective.

—*Church Council on Justice and Corrections, from "Getting Tough or Getting Serious: A Restorative Perspective on Youth Justice"*

Questions

1. List the arguments used by people on each side of this issue.
2. In a paragraph, summarize your own position on the need for correctional facilities such as Project Turnaround. Give at least two reasons for your position.
3. Using the Internet or library resources, conduct research on the effectiveness of "boot camps" in reducing costs and the rate of recidivism in Ontario and other jurisdictions. Compare your findings, using tables and graphs, to the claims quoted above.

CHECK YOUR UNDERSTANDING

1. a) When can absolute and conditional discharges be given?
   b) What kind of criminal record and conditions are attached to each?
2. Describe probation and the optional conditions that may be imposed.
3. What is the maximum fine for (a) a summary offence? (b) an indictable offence?
4. What is the victim fine surcharge, and how is the money it raises used?
5. What does it mean to serve a sentence intermittently?
6. What happens to a prisoner when a conditional sentence is imposed?
7. Examine the facts and figures on incarceration. Choose one or two pieces of information that surprised you. Explain why.

Wrongful Convictions

Find out more about wrongful convictions at www.emp.ca/dimensionsoflaw

One of the most important characteristics of Canada's criminal justice system is its concern with procedural fairness. Obtaining a conviction is important for the Crown, but only if it results from procedures that respect the rights of the accused. In other words, the ends do not justify the means. This principle is captured in a proverb familiar to lawyers and judges: "It is better to let nine guilty persons go free, than to convict one innocent person."

When an innocent person is wrongfully convicted, it is a double failure: the innocent individual is wronged, and a guilty person goes free. As you learned in Chapter 3, Donald Marshall, Guy Paul Morin, and David Milgaard were convicted of murders they had not committed. All spent years in prison and were eventually exonerated. All three cases were examined by the justice system so that wrongful convictions might be avoided in the future. Commissioner Fred Kaufman, who headed an investigation into Guy Paul Morin's wrongful conviction, concluded his report as follows:

> The case of Guy Paul Morin is not an aberration [abnormal or atypical]. ... [T]he causes of Mr. Morin's conviction are rooted in systemic problems, as well as the failings of individuals. It is no coincidence that the same systemic problems are those identified in wrongful convictions in other jurisdictions worldwide.

Wrongful convictions are rarely the result of deliberate misbehaviour. Rather, they are the product of problems within the system. In all three cases cited above, once the suspects were identified, police investigations were characterized by a kind of tunnel vision that focused on obtaining and manipulating evidence to prove guilt that was assumed. According to law professor Dianne Martin, there is a classic pattern to wrongful convictions. They begin "with a heinous, unsolved crime [that] pits an unpopular or minority accused, assisted by an inadequate defence, against a determined prosecution zealously seeking a conviction to resolve community concern."

Personal Viewpoint

Rubin Carter: Standing Up to Injustice

Rubin "Hurricane" Carter's road to justice was long, brutal, and twisted, and it crossed the Canada–US border. Carter was famous in the United States, his homeland, as a "contender," a top-ranked boxer. Then, in 1966, he was arrested, tried, and found guilty by an all-white jury of murdering three white patrons in a New Jersey bar. He was sentenced to life in prison. End of story? Not quite.

In 1974, Carter published *The Sixteenth Round*, an account of his wrongful conviction. He had some support for his claim, but not enough to get the case reopened. In 1980, Lesra Martin, a young black American living in Toronto, found a copy of the book. It convinced him, and the Canadians he was living with, of Carter's innocence. Working with the help of Carter and his lawyers, they took on the US justice system—and won. On November 7, 1985, Federal District Judge H. Lee Sarokin ordered Carter released.

As you learned in Chapter 3, Carter moved to Toronto and helped found the Association in Defence of the Wrongfully Convicted (AIDWYC). He is also on the boards of the Southern Center for Human Rights in Atlanta, Georgia, and the Alliance for Prison Justice in Boston, Massachusetts. Carter has become a voice for the wrongfully convicted. His talks have moved thousands of people around the world. He has addressed the United Nations and spoken alongside Nelson Mandela. He believes he has a duty to keep talking.

> If I have learned nothing else in my life, I've learned that bitterness only consumes the vessel that contains it. And for me to permit bitterness to control or to infect my life in any way whatsoever would be to allow those who imprisoned me to take even more than the 22 years they've already taken. Now, that would make me an accomplice to their crime. ...
>
> Prison is a terrible, terrible place. It affects and infects every fibre of your being and once you've spent time there, you'll never be the same again. When there's a conviction shrouded in so much doubt as is the case with Guy Paul

Figure 11.11 *Rubin Carter (bottom right) talks with Steven Truscott (bottom left) and his children at a news conference in 2001, in which they called on the Canadian government to review Truscott's conviction for a 1959 murder.*

Morin, justice, compassion and human decency demand that he be allowed to remain at liberty until his appeal is finally decided. ...

You can't take back one day, one hour, one minute of the time you spend in jail. It's gone. Forever. But we can pull together and fight to end imprisonment as quickly as possible in cases where a prisoner is innocent. And we can work to eliminate conditions within the legal system that lead to miscarriages of justice.

Sources: http://www.magga.com/quotes/bitter.htm; Donna Laframboise, "Justice Not Blind But Blinded," *The Toronto Star*, February 8, 1993, p. A15; and http://www.aidwyc.org.

Questions

1. Do you believe that wrongful conviction is in itself a crime? Explain your answer.
2. What changes do you believe need to be made to the justice system to work toward preventing wrongful convictions?
3. Should the state compensate people who spend time in prison as a result of a wrongful conviction? How would you determine what is adequate compensation?

The cases of Marshall, Morin, and Milgaard fit the pattern of wrongful conviction perfectly. Marshall was an Aboriginal teenager already known to police. Milgaard was a drug-using, teenage "hippie," and police described Morin as "weird" because he played the clarinet and kept bees. In all three cases, once the suspect was identified, investigations focused on obtaining and manipulating evidence to prove their presumed guilt. Dianne Martin has written that "the ultimate challenge is to be morally ethical and intellectually honest during investigations, scrupulously fair during trials, and above all humble enough to admit error." Mistakes are inevitable in the justice system; the wrong lies in refusing to admit that mistakes happen.

To learn more about Steven Truscott and his case, visit www.emp.ca/dimensionsoflaw

Journalist Kirk Makin spent years studying the case of Guy Paul Morin. In his book *Redrum the Innocent: Wrongful Convictions*, he concludes with observations of how the criminal justice system failed:

> Those who insist the Morin case showed that the system ultimately works merely worsen the problem. ... What, for instance, if Morin had been an inarticulate immigrant unable to gain access to good legal help? ... What if his case had involved none of the sort of sensational human elements that attract media attention? The answer is simple. Morin would have become just another lost soul lying on a stained mattress in a dank cell, writing plaintive letters to politicians, reporters and lawyers who never responded. And if Canada had capital punishment, Guy Paul Morin would simply be dead.

WORKING FOR CHANGE *The Innocence Project: T-shirts, Bake Sales, and Bail*

At 64, Romeo Phillion is frail and lonely. Small wonder. He has been in prison for more than 31 years, convicted for the 1967 murder of an Ottawa fireman. Phillion has been eligible for parole for 20 years, but he insists he is innocent. If he does not admit guilt, he will not be paroled.

It is May 15, 2003. At a packed Toronto news conference, Phillion's claim of innocence is not being seen as evidence of incorrigibility. It is being championed by the Association in Defence of the Wrongly Convicted (AIDWYC) and a group of dedicated students from the Innocence Project of Osgoode Hall Law School. The Project has submitted a 450-page document supporting AIDWYC's rare formal bail appeal for Phillion. If Phillion is not released on bail, he could wait up to four years while the justice department considers his clemency appeal.

Professor Dianne Martin, co-director of the Innocence Project, calls the review process inhuman. "The hurdles are almost insurmountable," she says. "Documents are misplaced, censored, or simply disappear." Those words also describe what law students unearthed in five years of researching the justice system's treatment of Phillion.

Phillion contacted the Innocence Project after a prison guard gave him documents in 1998. They contained a 1968 police alibi report confirming that Phillion was 200 km away when the murder was committed. This was the keystone of the Project's efforts.

Figure 11.12 *Romeo Phillion kisses his cat Tiger, his pet in prison for two years, upon arriving at the home of his sister following his release on bail while the federal justice minister investigates his 1972 conviction.*

That same report had disappeared when Phillion was tried and convicted for the murder in 1972. The Crown never disclosed the existence of an alibi to Phillion's defence lawyer, Arthur Cogan. Two decades later, Cogan was stunned. "Anything favourable to [Phillion] that the police had in their possession should obviously have been disclosed," he told the *Globe and Mail* in November 2001. "The new evidence obviously casts real doubt as to whether he did it."

The Innocence Project students kept digging. Evidence that Crown witnesses had changed their testimony was covered up at the trial. Critical evidence—police notebooks and all the physical evidence, including the possible murder weapon—vanished before the trial. The case against Phillion was purely circumstantial. The Innocence Project has done everything but provide DNA evidence to prove Phillion's innocence. Tissue and hair were found under the victim's fingernails. They have vanished.

For the Innocence Project, Phillion's nightmare exposes a national disgrace. People alleging wrongful conviction must have access to a federally funded, independent tribunal. "This shouldn't be luck," Martin tells reporters. "Canadians in prison should not have to rely on volunteer law students selling T-shirts and holding bake sales to investigate their cases."

It is July 21, 2003. The Ontario Superior Court has just approved Romeo Phillion's bail application. Phillion is overjoyed. He will be free to live with his sister while the system processes his review application. James Lockyer, of AIDWYC, tells reporters it is more than a personal victory for Phillion. It could "affect the release of other people who were convicted of crimes they didn't commit in the future as well." Five years of work by the students of the Innocence Project have helped open one cell door. Soon others may follow.

Sources: Kirk Makin, "Man Jailed 29 Years Had Alibi, But Police Buried It," The Globe and Mail, *November 8, 2001, p. A1; "Phillion Case 'World Record' for Injustice: Lockyer," www.cbc.ca/storyview/CBC/2003/05/15/phillion_030515; and Darren Yourk, "Phillion Granted Bail," www.globeandmail.com, Monday, July 21, 2003.*

Questions

1. Do you agree that the federal government should fund a tribunal for prisoners claiming innocence? Why or why not?
2. Once a prisoner is eligible for parole, should it make a difference whether he or she claims innocence? Explain your answer.
3. Conduct research on the *Phillion* case to see (a) if and how it fits the classic pattern of wrongful conviction cases and (b) whether the case has been resolved.

Under s. 690 of the *Criminal Code*, people convicted of indictable offences, or their legal representatives, could apply to the federal minister of justice to have their cases reviewed for wrongful conviction. "Six-ninety," as it came to be known, was widely criticized because it did not clearly define who was eligible and when one could apply. Recently, s. 690 was repealed and replaced by Part XXI.1 of the *Criminal Code*, parts of which are found in the following feature.

Find out more about the Innocence Project in Canada and the United States at www.emp.ca/dimensionsoflaw

The Law Applications for Ministerial Review—Miscarriages of Justice

From Part XXI.1 of the *Criminal Code*:

696.1(1) An application for ministerial review on the grounds of miscarriage of justice may be made to the Minister of Justice by or on behalf of a person who has been convicted of an offence under an Act of Parliament or a regulation made under an Act

dangerous offender: a classification for a person convicted of an offence causing serious personal injury and who is likely to reoffend; may be sentenced to incarceration for an indefinite period of time (see s. 753.1 of the *Criminal Code*)

long-term offender: a court classification applied to a sexual offender who is likely to reoffend; may be sentenced to incarceration for an indefinite period of time

of Parliament or has been found to be a **dangerous offender** or a **long-term offender** under Part XXIV and whose rights of judicial review or appeal with respect to the conviction or finding have been exhausted. ...

696.3(3) On an application under this Part, the Minster of Justice may

(a) if the Minister is satisfied that there is a reasonable basis to conclude that a miscarriage of justice likely occurred,

(i) direct, by order in writing, a new trial before any court that the Minister thinks proper or, in the case of a person found to be a dangerous offender or a long-term offender under Part XXIV, a new hearing under that Part, or

(ii) refer the matter at any time to the court of appeal for hearing and determination by that court as if it were an appeal by the convicted person or the person found to be a dangerous offender or a long-term offender under Part XXIV, as the case may be; or

(b) dismiss the application.

(4) A decision of the Minister of Justice made under subsection (3) is final and is not subject to appeal. ...

696.5 The Minister of Justice shall within six months after the end of each financial year submit an annual report to Parliament in relation to applications under this Part.

Questions

1. Create an organizer that summarizes who can apply for ministerial review of a conviction, and under what circumstances.
2. After reading these excerpts from the *Criminal Code*, do you believe the provisions will help people who have been wrongfully convicted? Why or why not?
3. Some people may argue that s. 696.1 gives too much power to the minister of justice. Why would this argument be made? Do you agree or disagree with this viewpoint? Express your opinion in a paragraph.

Check Your Understanding

1. What did Commissioner Kaufman mean when he said that the Guy Paul Morin case "is not an aberration"?
2. What do you believe Kaufman meant by "systemic problems"? Give an example.
3. Describe the classic pattern of a wrongful conviction and its remedy.
4. What complaints led to the repeal of s. 690 of the *Criminal Code*?

CAREER PROFILE

Det. Rick Bunting, Toronto Police Forensic Identification Services

Detective Rick Bunting has been with the Toronto Police Forensic Identification Services for 17 years. A senior staff member, he now combines his work in forensics with personnel training responsibilities.

Q. What does a forensic identification specialist do?

A. We're storytellers of the crime. We gather the evidence that recreates what happened.

Q. What do you do in a typical week?

A. We do crime scene examination—one scene can take hours, and we handle 25 000 jobs a year. We do follow-up work, preparing reports and processing evidence that needs special treatment. And then there's court, where we testify to what we've found.

Q. Growing up, did you know you wanted to work in forensics?

A. Oh, no. I wanted to be a street cop. I was a regular officer for 16 years first. Then a guy in forensics wanted to try uniformed work. We arranged a lateral transfer—we switched jobs, essentially—and I discovered I love this work.

Q. What kind of education is needed?

A. I went into policing out of grade 12, but things have changed. Most recruits have college, some university. There's a point system on application: each level of education counts for a certain number of points. Other things count, too—height-to-weight ratio, physical standards, scores on psychological and aptitude tests.

Q. Can a person be hired directly into forensics?

A. No. Everybody here has had experience someplace else. Experience is essential to this work: you need to have worked in uniform, to have a feel for the street. Typically a person requests a transfer, works here awhile, and then if he or she is cut out for it, there's a nine-week course to take and an exam to pass.

Q. How do you know if you're cut out for it?

A. The work can weigh on some, knowing it's your evidence that puts people behind the pipes for life. And we have to observe autopsies, work with corpses, bloody crime scenes. Sometimes we have to cut a finger off to get a fingerprint. You need to be able to separate yourself, be able to forget that the body you're handling was once a person.

Q. What personal qualities are essential for this job?

A. You have to be methodical and thorough, and do things in the proper order. You can't rush into a crime scene, because your presence can destroy evidence. You need to be able to work independently and make judgments based on experience while keeping an open mind—you have to consider that the crime scene may tell a different story from the one you expected. But above all, you must to be willing to ask questions, to get help when it's needed.

And you have to be prepared to work without much recognition. When a crime is solved you hear all this praise in the media for, say, the homicide squad. You don't hear about the forensic people who did all that work, gathering the evidence that put the case together.

METHODS OF *Legal Inquiry*

Identifying Legal Issues

Identifying the issues in a case is an important legal skill. What exactly is a legal issue? It is a legal question that the parties in the case, who are usually represented by lawyers, ask the court to decide. An issue is often stated in the form of a question that applies to a particular set of circumstances. The court's judgment (called the decision or holding) answers the question or questions posed by the issue. The party whose questions are answered affirmatively by the court wins the case.

Using the *Latimer* case (see pages 325–327) as an example, consider what the accused, Robert Latimer, must prove in order to have the Supreme Court of Canada overturn his conviction. Since he admitted to killing his daughter, Latimer's only possible defence was the defence of necessity. The issue, therefore, was whether the facts of the case enabled Latimer to raise the defence of necessity successfully. This description, however, states the issue in its most general terms. It can also be broken down into more specific questions, or sub-issues. These would describe the elements of the defence of necessity and include the following points:

- Was there imminent peril or danger facing Latimer?
- Did the accused have a reasonable legal alternative to the course of action he followed?
- Was the harm inflicted on Tracey Latimer proportional to the harm avoided by Robert Latimer?

You know that Latimer was convicted. You also know, therefore, that the court answered "no" to all of the legal questions (issues) posed above.

Now, examine the issues raised in sentencing. Having convicted Latimer, the court had to determine an appropriate sentence. The *Criminal Code* mandates a minimum sentence for second-degree murder. However, the *Canadian Charter of Rights and Freedoms* came into force after the sentencing provisions of the Code. Rights guaranteed under the Charter take precedence over both federal and provincial legislation. The Charter guarantees against "cruel and unusual" punishment (s. 12). This provision raises a legal question, or issue: "Would imposing a mandatory minimum sentence on Robert Latimer violate his Charter guarantee against cruel and unusual punishment?"

As you saw with the first example, an issue can be taken to a deeper, or sub, level. At this level the legal question is: "Is the punishment prescribed in the *Criminal Code* so excessive or grossly disproportionate as to outrage society's standards of decency and, therefore, violate s. 12?" The issue is no longer a simple question about whether a sentence violates a Charter right; the issue is what, specifically, Latimer must prove to rely on this particular defence.

Being able to see the issues helps you understand what is relevant in a case. This ability then helps you focus on the part of the case that will become a precedent for subsequent cases. Because the Supreme Court rejected the Charter defence in *R v. Latimer*, it is now clearer in law what constitutes an excessive or grossly disproportionate sentence.

Applying the Skill

1. What is an issue in a case?
2. Choose a case from Unit 3: Criminal Law and state the issue. If appropriate, also state any related or sub-issues. Remember to state the issue as a legal question.
3. Courts have asked whether "excessive" or "grossly disproportionate" is a subjective test (that is, what Latimer believes) or an objective test (that is, what a reasonable person who is not involved in the case might believe). Given this further observation, list three levels of issues from the sentencing aspects of the *Latimer* case.

Reviewing Main Ideas

You Decide!

WHEN ARE CONDITIONAL SENTENCES APPROPRIATE?

R v. Proulx, [2000] 1 SCR 61

Judges must craft sentences that are "proportionate to the gravity of the offence and the degree of responsibility of the offender." Review the sentencing options described on pages 337–343, paying particular attention to the conditional sentence. This option was part of the 1996 reforms that were intended to reduce the use of incarceration. Now, consider the following facts.

Facts

The defendant, Jeromie Proulx, pleaded guilty to one count of dangerous driving causing death and one count of dangerous driving causing bodily harm.

After a night of partying, having consumed two beers, Proulx decided to drive some friends home. He was 18, had only seven weeks' experience as a licensed driver, and knew his car was unsound. Proulx drove erratically for 20 minutes, weaving through traffic, tailgating, and trying to pass without signalling. The roads were slippery, with steady oncoming traffic. As Proulx tried to pass another car, he drove into the oncoming lane, sideswiping two cars. The driver of the second car was seriously injured and one of Proulx's passengers was killed. Proulx himself was in a near-death coma, but recovered. He had no prior record. At the time of sentencing, he was employed and expecting a first child with his girlfriend.

Issue

All parties agree that a sentence of less than two years is appropriate for these offences. The issue is: should the sentence be served conditionally (in the community) or in jail?

Arguments in Favour of a Conditional Sentence

Section 742.1 of the *Criminal Code* sets out the criteria for a conditional sentence. Once a sentence of less than two years is determined as appropriate, the court must decide whether letting the offender serve the sentence in the community would threaten public safety. A conditional sentence must also conform to the fundamental purposes and principles of sentencing.

Proulx is young. He has no prior record and has had no convictions since the accident. He is extremely remorseful, and has suffered greatly by causing a friend's death. He himself was seriously injured. All these factors suggest that Proulx has been rehabilitated. There is no evidence that he presents a danger to the community. Sentencing him to jail would not further his rehabilitation, and it would separate him from his girlfriend and their new baby.

While dangerous behaviour must be denounced in order to deter others, these two objectives can be met by imposing conditions on Proulx while he serves his sentence in the community. He could be sentenced to house arrest, for example, and he could be required to perform community service by speaking to young people about the consequences of dangerous driving.

Arguments Against a Conditional Sentence

A conditional sentence would not be consistent with the fundamental purposes and principles of sentencing set out in s. 718 of the Code. Incarceration is necessary to denounce Mr. Proulx's conduct and to deter others from engaging in similar reckless behaviour. These are extremely serious offences. A person was killed.

Proulx knew he was driving an unsafe vehicle. Although the alcohol he consumed was probably not a factor, drinking and driving by young persons must not be condoned. A strong sentence sends a clear message to the community: dangerous driving will not be tolerated. Evidence suggests that severe sentences for driving offences do deter others. These offences are often committed by otherwise law-abiding citizens with families and good employment records. Arguably, such persons will be deterred by the threat of severe penalties.

A conditional sentence will be seen by the community as a "slap on the wrist," even if the judge imposes punitive conditions such as house arrest. It is important that sentencing judges be attentive to community attitudes. In this case, the objectives of denunciation and deterrence are paramount. Nothing less than jail time will suffice.

Make Your Decision

1. Create a chart in which you summarize the arguments for and against imposing a conditional sentence.
2. What do you believe would be an appropriate sentence in this case? You must give arguments as to why your sentence is fitting. Remember that your sentence needs to consider both the protection of society and the needs of the offender. You must achieve a balance.
3. Using either the Internet or a law library, research the Supreme Court's decision in this case. Re-examine your answer to question 2. Would you change your sentence in light of the Supreme Court's ruling? Why or why not?

Key Terms

Review the following terms to show that you understand the meaning of each and how it is applied in a legal context.

absolute discharge
aggravating circumstances
conditional discharge
dangerous offender
de facto
electronic monitoring
garnisheeing wages
incarceration
judicial discretion
long-term offender
mitigating circumstances
plea bargaining
pre-sentence report
recidivism
rehabilitation
restorative justice
statutorily prescribed minimum
victim impact statement

Understanding the Law

Review the following pieces of legislation mentioned in the text, and show that you understand the intent of each.

Criminal Code, ss. 255, 278, 486(1), 515(10)(b), 696.1, 718, 737, 738, 742.1
Canadian Charter of Rights and Freedoms, s. 12

Thinking and Inquiry

1. Each offence in the *Criminal Code* (other than those few with mandatory minimums) carries one of the following maximum penalties: six months, 18 months, two years, five years, 10 years, 14 years, or life. Try the following exercise to see if the maximum penalties for particular

offences conform to your own sense of their seriousness. First, determine what you believe the maximum penalty should be. Then examine the *Criminal Code* to find what the actual maximum penalty is.

- break and enter (a private dwelling)—s. 348
- robbery—s. 344
- sexual assault—s. 271
- perjury—s. 132
- public incitement of hatred—s. 319

2. You have been asked to review the Canadian Statement of Basic Principles of Justice for Victims of Crime. Part of your review should include recommendations for the inclusion of an additional principle. You must decide what the new principle should be and prepare a justification for your recommendation.
3. Go to www.emp.ca/dimensionsoflaw for a link to the Correctional Service Canada Web site. Check out the "Myths and Realities" section on Sentencing in Canada. Select those myths that you find most surprising and conduct a survey to find out how widely they are held to be true. Present your findings to the class.
4. Invite an Aboriginal speaker to your class to explain what a healing lodge is. Write a description of one of the ceremonies that may take place.

Communication

5. In small groups, create a dramatic scenario in which, as either a Crown attorney or a defence lawyer, you present your submissions for an appropriate sentence. Remember to highlight those factors that you consider to be mitigating or aggravating. Present your scenario to the class.
6. Debate the following statement: "*Resolved that: Parliament should disallow the use of mandatory minimum sentences.*"
7. Prepare a pamphlet concerning the rights of victims.

Application

8. Use resources such as the Internet, newspapers, magazines, and books to find information on sentencing in at least three other countries. Create a chart comparing these countries to Canada. In a one-page report, outline the similarities and differences between Canada's sentencing provisions and those of the other countries.
9. Using resources such as those suggested in question 8, compare how Canada and at least two other countries deal with appeals and cases of wrongful conviction. Summarize your findings in a PowerPoint presentation.
10. Visit the Web site of a group fighting for the wrongfully convicted. Conduct research on a case the group is supporting. In a one-page report on the case, include the following: who the accused is; what he or she was convicted of; what evidence was used to convict; and what problems point to a wrongful conviction.

Unit 4

Labour and Environmental Law

The units in this book have so far focused primarily on the development of the Canadian legal system and on individual rights, liberties, and responsibilities. This unit introduces the idea that collectivities—groups of individuals or a whole society—might require and be entitled to legal rights that protect the group and its members from harm. You will discover how individuals working in groups can use the law in ways that individuals acting alone could not. You will also see how economic forces and the law change the way individuals and groups interact, and how individual and group needs are balanced and adjusted.

Chapter 12 explores the way in which individuals and groups came to recognize, identify, and respond to environmental challenges and issues. The chapter identifies the problems that individuals acting alone faced in addressing problems that affected society as a whole. You will learn how groups were formed in order to identify and define problems, and in particular to press for the enactment of legislation to control environmental degradation and enhance sustainable development.

Chapter 13 focuses on the workplace, where most of us will spend one-third of our lives. You will learn about the relationship of employers and employees in a modern economy. You will also examine government efforts to set minimum standards for employees regarding wages, hours, working conditions, safety, and human rights in the workplace.

Chapter 14 introduces the idea of collective action by employees. You will learn how trade unionism attempts to balance power between labour and management, and trace how the law changed to give unions legal status. In exploring the idea of collective action and responsibility, you will also explore the ongoing tension between the goals of protecting the group and protecting the individual rights of group members.

Chapter 15 examines the way in which the changing workplace affects the lives and legal rights of workers. You will learn how globalization and free trade agreements have affected not only labour but also the environment and society generally, and investigate the extent to which the expansion of world trade may restrict the rights of governments, groups, and individuals. The chapter reflects the tension between group and individual rights that runs throughout this unit: How do we balance individual rights and freedoms with the maintenance of a stable and secure society?

Chapter 12 Protecting the Environment

CHAPTER *Focus*

In this chapter, you will

- evaluate the success of individuals and organizations that have lobbied for legislation to protect the environment
- explain how governments have responded to growing public concern about environmental issues
- explain avenues that individuals can use to take direct legal action to protect the environment
- analyze the effectiveness of the major environmental statutes in Ontario and Canada today
- evaluate emerging legal trends in environmental protection

This chapter examines the development and implementation of environmental law in the latter part of the 20th century. The cartoon below appeared in February 2002 after police raided a private environmental laboratory in Hamilton. The laboratory tested soil and water samples, including water samples for some municipalities in Ontario, and was suspected of falsifying test results. The Ontario government had previously shifted laboratory testing of water from Ministry of the Environment technicians to private facilities. Concerns about water testing by private laboratories were raised in the summer of 2000 when seven people died and at least two thousand became ill in the town of Walkerton after *E. coli* bacteria entered the water supply days before residents were informed of this danger.

Figure 12.1

At First Glance

1. What is the cartoonist's message concerning the reliability of environmental analysis in Ontario?
2. Explain how each of the images in the cartoon supports the cartoonist's overall message.
3. Which image is most effective, in your view?
4. Suggest some aspects of the environment that you think should have reliable monitoring.
5. How important is it to you that the government monitors your environmental surroundings? Explain your view.

The Environmental Movement

European settlers arriving in North America saw the continent and its surrounding waters as a warehouse of natural resources to be exploited with no regard for the impact of resource extraction on the environment. Over time, however, people began to raise concerns about the long-term future of natural resources and the health of the physical environment.

The first steps to preserve the environment were taken in the 1880s when individuals and groups began lobbying for the conservation and preservation of unspoiled wilderness areas. For example, the Sierra Club, now very active in environmental protection generally, started as a wilderness conservation lobby group in 1882. In 1885, the Canadian national parks system began when land was set aside for public use in what is now Banff National Park. Conservation and preservation were the main goals of environmental advocates for the next 80 years.

Learn more about the Sierra Club in Canada at www.emp.ca/dimensionsoflaw

By the middle of the 20th century, even though faced with evidence of damage to the environment, both government and business saw economic growth and improvements in standards of living as more important than environmental protection or preservation. They made decisions on the assumption that the solution to pollution was dilution—that is, environmentally destructive substances were to be dissipated by dumping them into large bodies of water or sending them up a chimney to be carried away by the wind. There was obvious damage in some areas, such as around Sudbury, where refinery emissions were killing the vegetation and acidifying lakes, and in water bodies such as Lake Erie, where phosphates from laundry detergents and other pollutants were affecting ecosystems. But there were few complaints outside the areas that were affected.

In fact, from the 1940s through the 1960s, the government of Ontario took steps to limit the rights of citizens to sue polluters who caused damage. For example, following one case heard in 1948, *McKie v. The KVP Co. Ltd.*, the Ontario government passed a law, *The KVP Act*, to limit the effects of

Figure 12.2 *Inco responded to concerns that emissions from its smelters were destroying lakes and vegetation in the Sudbury region by constructing a taller smokestack in 1970. The Sudbury "superstack" is 473 m high. It distributes pollutants over a much larger area than before.*

lawsuits by individuals to control pollution where such control might affect a company's productivity and profits. The view that economic development was more important than environmental protection was typical of governments in that period. Even now, while most governments pay more attention to public concerns about the environment, politicians' commitment often evaporates if environmental protection seems likely to slow economic growth.

Fyi The Cuyahoga River caught fire a number of times between 1936 and 1969. Photos from June 22, 1969, in particular, are famous for shocking the nation into demanding better pollution controls for waterways.

During the 1960s, the effects of environmental damage became obvious. Rachel Carson's book, *Silent Spring*, documented the damage that the spraying of the pesticide DDT had caused to birds and wildlife. Lake Erie had become so polluted that it was declared "dead." In June 1969, photographs of a burning oil slick on the Cuyahoga River close to downtown Cleveland in the United States shocked a complacent nation. Concerns were raised about urban sprawl, air and water pollution, the disposal of toxic wastes, and disposal of nuclear wastes. In Canada, federal and provincial governments were pressured to respond to these environmental concerns.

Figure 12.3 *By the 1960s, it became difficult to ignore the blatant destruction of the natural environment when instances like the Cuyahoga River's catching fire made the news. This photo shows the Cuyahoga on fire in 1952.*

Personal Viewpoint

Chief Dan George: An Aboriginal View of the Environment

Chief Dan George (Tes-wah-no) was born in 1899 on Burrard Reserve No. 3, on Vancouver's north shore, the son of a tribal chief. He was sent to a residential school at the age of five, where he was given the English surname of George. After school, he worked as a longshoreman, a construction worker, and a school bus driver. He became a film actor after he was 60 years old and used his fame to become a spokesperson for Aboriginal peoples. He wrote several books about his culture, comparing his views on the environment to those of the dominant North American culture. This excerpt is from his book, *My Heart Soars*.

> My father loved the earth and all its creatures. The earth was his second mother. The earth and everything it contained was a gift from See-se-am... and the way to thank this great spirit was to use his gifts with respect. ... And I shall never forget [my father's] disappointment when once he caught me gaffing for fish "just for the fun of it." "My Son," he said, "the Great Spirit gave you those fish to be your brothers, to feed you when you are hungry. You must respect them. You must not kill them just for the fun of it."...
>
> It is hard for me to understand a culture that not only hates and fights his brothers but even attacks nature and abuses her. I see my white brothers going about blotting out nature from his cities. I see him strip the hills bare, leaving ugly wounds on the face of mountains. I see him tearing things from the bosom of mother earth as though she were a monster, who refused to share her treasures with him. I see him throw poison in the waters, indifferent to the life he kills there; and he chokes the air with deadly fumes. ...
>
> My culture did not prize the hoarding of private possessions, in fact, to hoard was a shameful thing to do among my people. The Indian looked on all things in nature as belonging to him and he expected to share them with others and take only what he needed.

Figure 12.4 *Chief Dan George (1899–1981) at age 71 won an Oscar nomination for his role as a Cheyenne elder in the film* Little Big Man.

Source: Chief Dan George, *My Heart Soars*. Toronto: Hancock House Publishers, 1974.

Questions

1. What are Chief Dan George's key ideas concerning the environment?
2. Make a list of words or phrases from the excerpt that you feel capture the essence of the Aboriginal view of nature.
3. In a few sentences, describe your own views about nature. Identify at least two sources for your views, and describe what you learned from each source.
4. Do you agree with the view that the dominant Canadian culture "attacks nature"? Explain, providing evidence for your position.

Turning Points in the Law

"Green Wave" Triggers Global Legislative Action

As protests erupted around the world in the 1960s over contamination of waters and lands, many people began to develop a sense of responsibility for their natural surroundings. This evolution in social consciousness of environmental issues has been described as a "green wave"—an idea that seemed to develop a life and an impetus of its own.

One result was increased—and eventually overwhelming—pressure on governments to bring their economic and legislative resources to bear on the task of environmental protection. The green wave of the late 1960s produced a rare "critical mass" of public opinion. The result was the near-simultaneous passage of environmental protection legislation in legal jurisdictions all over the world (see Figure 12.5).

Our environment—the lands, water, air, and living things around us—is global in the simplest sense. Human beings from every nation have the potential to harm or to protect their common environment. It is perhaps this recognition of our individual, yet universal, responsibility that made it possible for governments around the world to make a united leap from public reaction to legal action.

Questions

1. Choose one of the actions listed in Figure 12.5 and conduct research to find out how it was intended to protect the environment. Present a short report on your findings.
2. Investigate one example of environmental pollution in the 1960s that resulted in public pressure for action in Ontario.

Environmental Protection Legislation Worldwide, 1967–1972

- 1967 • Sweden creates a National Environmental Protection Agency.
- 1967 • Japan passes its first general environmental protection statute.
- 1970 • Organisation for Economic Co-operation and Development (OECD) introduces its Environment Committee.
- 1970 • US federal government passes the *National Environmental Policy Act* of 1969 and creates the US Environmental Protection Agency.
- 1970 • US politician Gaylord Nelson founds Earth Day, the political act that is recognized by many as the "birth" of the environmental movement for citizens.
- 1971 • Government of France creates a Ministry of the Environment.
- 1971 • Ontario passes the *Environmental Protection Act*; similar legislation is proposed or would soon be passed by most other provinces in Canada as well.
- 1972 • United Nations holds a Conference on Human Environment in Stockholm, Sweden; later the same year, it creates the United Nations Environmental Programme (UNEP).

Figure 12.5

Concept of Sustainable Development

In the 1970s, with evidence of environmental damage and an appreciation of its causes, the idea of sustainable development was discussed. Sustainable development is an approach that seeks to preserve both a healthy economy and a healthy environment. This approach was re-examined by a UN committee, the World Commission on Environment and Development, in 1983. The committee's report, *Our Common Future*, defined sustainable development as "development that meets the needs of the present generation without compromising the ability of future generations to meet their own needs." Governments around the world, including federal and provincial governments in Canada, approved the concept. This approach requires:

- acceptance of a high value on environmental health as a key to continued economic performance
- recognition that the needs of the current generation must be balanced against the needs of future generations
- recognition that the needs of one group should not be met at the expense of another
- development of long-term economic and environmental policies instead of the short-term policies (planned for little more than a year at a time) used by most businesses and by government
- consideration of likely consequences of economic activity so that unwanted and negative environmental impacts can be prevented before they occur.

CHECK YOUR UNDERSTANDING

1. a) What changes occurred in the environmental movement in the mid-20th century?
   b) What factors do you think led to these changes?
2. What roles did non-governmental organizations and high-profile publications play in changing public attitudes toward the environment?
3. a) What is meant by sustainable development?
   b) How does this concept differ from previous ideas about the relationship between economic growth and environment? Give an example to illustrate the differences.
4. Suggest at least three changes that would have to take place in your home, school, and community for sustainable development to be adopted.
5. Explain why governments must assume some roles in protecting the natural environment.

Individual Legal Action to Protect the Environment

Individuals have some rights in taking legal action to protect the environment, but these rights are limited. Common-law rights allow individuals to take action against someone who interferes with their use or enjoyment of their own property. The individual's legal weapon is tort law. There are two torts that are often used in cases of environmental damage: nuisance and strict liability for the escape of a dangerous substance from another person's land. Two other, more general, torts can also be useful: **trespass**—that is, intentional and direct interference with another's land—and negligence. In cases involving land that borders on a water body, a landowner may sue a polluter who interferes with the water using the riparian rights doctrine (see discussion, next page).

trespass: the direct interference with land that is owned or occupied by another person

In all these types of lawsuits there are two principal common-law remedies: damages and injunctions. The first remedy, damages, requires the wrongdoer to pay for the harm actually done. To stop the objectionable behaviour, you may ask the court to grant an **injunction**, which is an order to prohibit someone from doing something.

injunction: a court order to prevent or stop someone from doing something; it may be a temporary order, effective until trial, when it may or may not be made permanent

Right to Sue for Nuisance

Private nuisance arises when there is unreasonable interference with the use and enjoyment of another person's land. The interference must be substantial. Common subjects of nuisance suits include noise, air and water pollution, vibrations, smells, soil contamination, and flooding.

private nuisance: an indirect interference with the use and enjoyment of land due to the actions or conduct of someone nearby

If the interference is caused by an activity of public importance and economic benefit to the community, and is difficult to prevent or avoid, the courts may tolerate behaviour that is a nuisance to the property owner. So, for example, a court may decide that the economic benefits and the public good attached to mass transit may outweigh the harm done to owners of a property next to a bus garage who are bothered by noise and diesel fumes. However, if the activities cause actual physical harm to the owner (rather than just inconvenience), damage the property, or reduce the owner's income, the court is much more likely to find the neighbour liable for nuisance, even if the activity gives rise to economic and public benefits.

If an activity interferes with a public right, such as the right to fish, one might assume that any member of the public who is affected by the harmful activity may bring an action in **public nuisance**. But there are problems with public nuisance lawsuits. The common law may deny any one person the right to sue, even if that person suffers damages, unless the plaintiff can show extraordinary damage above and beyond what his or her neighbours sustained. Usually, anyone wishing to sue for public nuisance must obtain the consent of the attorney general of the province to commence a lawsuit, or (more rarely) wait for the attorney general to start a lawsuit.

public nuisance: an interference with a public right, such as the right to fish or the right of navigation

These restrictions on what the law calls **standing** prevent public nuisance suits from being used by environmental groups to protect the public interest against harmful activities. However, in Ontario, since the *Environmental Bill of Rights, 1993* was adopted, the consent of the attorney general is not required to start a public nuisance lawsuit.

standing: a legal right to sue. A person who tries to bring suit where he or she has no standing will have the action dismissed

Right to Sue for Negligence

Negligence is conduct that falls below the standard of care that a reasonable person would consider acceptable in a given situation. If a person engaged in an activity should have foreseen the resulting damage, then that person would be liable. Negligence can be useful in environmental cases.

There are problems with using negligence law, especially in determining what a reasonable standard is. A defendant might well say that the production or processing techniques used in his or her plant are in accordance with industry standards. So even if industry standards are questionable, the defendant may successfully argue that he or she met the standard of care.

negligence: an act committed without intention to cause harm, but which a reasonable person would anticipate might cause harm

Riparian Rights

Owners or occupants of land bordering on a lake or stream all have **riparian rights** and obligations. This means that they have a right not to have the flow of the water or its quality interfered with by others who border on the body of water. For example, if one of the owners proposes to open a pulp mill or dump raw sewage into the water body, the other owners or occupants may sue for interference with riparian rights. A statutory body such as a municipality may have **legislative authority** to alter water flow or levels without the owners being able to sue. In the following case, you will see that an owner may be able to obtain an injunction simply by showing what might happen before there is any actual damage.

riparian rights: the right of an owner of land bordering on a lake, river, or stream to sue another person who interferes with the quantity or quality of the water

legislative authority: the power conferred on a person (usually a public body) to do something that would otherwise be prohibited by the common law

Case RIPARIAN RIGHTS

Gauthier v. Naneff (1970), 14 DLR (3d) 513 (Ont. HC)

Facts

Naneff proposed to hold a speedboat-racing regatta on Lake Ramsay in Sudbury. Lake Ramsay was a pristine lake. Gauthier and two others who owned land on the lake sought an injunction to prevent the race from being held on the ground that it would detrimentally affect water quality in the lake. The issue was whether the holding of the speedboat race would affect the plaintiffs' riparian rights, and in particular, affect the right not to have the lake water polluted.

The plaintiffs' evidence was that outboard motors would damage the purity of the water and that the harm would be irreparable. The court had to consider whether the defendant would unreasonably cause damage to water quality.

Decision

The court held that given present-day knowledge of and concern for pollution problems, riparian owners had the right to water quality that was not altered. The court refused to consider arguments by the defendant that the races would create economic benefits and raise funds for charity. These benefits, in the court's view, were not enough to justify pollution.

Questions

1. Summarize the arguments offered by the plaintiffs and the defendant in this case.
2. Why did the court decide in favour of the injunction?
3. Explain how the following circumstances might have affected the court's decision:
   a) the defendant offered to hold one race and not a series of races
   b) the defendant proposed a sailboat race
   c) the defendant offered to use part of the profits from the entry fees for the regatta to "beautify" parts of the lake.

Drawbacks to Using Common-Law Remedies

Individual lawsuits allow owners to be compensated for personal environmental damage or to stop activity that is harmful. The drawbacks are that lawsuits are expensive: plaintiffs have to pay for the lawyers and, if they lose, may have to pay the costs of the defence as well. Even if they are awarded damages, they may end up with a "paper judgment" if the defendant does not have the money to pay compensation. In the 1990s, the federal and provincial governments enacted some compensation schemes, set out in a variety of statutes, that allow owners to receive compensation without going to court.

Check Your Understanding

1. What limitations exist on individuals' rights to take legal action to protect the environment?
2. What is the difference between negligence and nuisance? Give several examples of each.
3. In your opinion, can individuals and groups effectively use nuisance and negligence law to protect the environment? Explain.

Government Actions

The Crown owns most of the undeveloped land in Canada. Governments also have at least partial control of most natural resource industries and many kinds of manufacturing. For these reasons, individual citizens and special-interest groups have pushed hard for government action to safeguard the environment.

Governments have responded in a piecemeal way to specific problems in the environment as they have been identified, trying to fix those problems with specific statutes. Confusion about jurisdiction between the federal government and provincial governments and the complexity of most environmental issues have led to a patchwork of legislation at both the provincial and federal levels. Legislation covers areas as diverse as land use planning and environmental assessments of the impact of proposed projects, preservation of wilderness and wildlife, preservation and management of natural resources, pollution control, and compensation for environmental damage. The federal statutes cover areas traditionally under federal jurisdiction, such as oceans and Aboriginal lands. For example, discharge of pollutants by an airport authority would likely be dealt with under a federal act. Figure 12.6 shows some of the federal and provincial statutes that focus on environmental problems.

Some Federal and Ontario Provincial Environmental Statutes

Federal Statutes

Canada National Parks Act, SC 2000, c. 32

Canadian Environmental Assessment Act, SC 1992, c. 37

Canadian Environmental Protection Act, 1999, SC 1999, c. 33

Clean Air Act, RSC 1985, c. C-32

Fisheries Act, RSC 1985, c. F-14

Migratory Birds Convention Act, 1994, SC 1994, c. 22

Navigable Waters Protection Act, RSC 1985, c. N-22

Nuclear Liability Act, RSC 1985, c. N-28

Nuclear Safety and Control Act, SC 1997, c. 9

Pesticide Residue Compensation Act, RSC 1985, c. P-10

Species at Risk Act, SC 2002, c. 29

Wild Animal and Plant Protection and Regulation of International and Interprovincial Trade Act, SC 1992, c. 52

Ontario Statutes

Brownfields Statute Law Amendment Act, SO 2001, c. 17

Drainage Act, RSO 1990, c. D.17

Endangered Species Act, RSO 1990, c. E.15

Environmental Assessment Act, RSO 1990, c. E.18

Environmental Bill of Rights, 1993, SO 1993, c. 28

Environmental Protection Act, RSO 1990, c. E.19

Fish and Wildlife Conservation Act, SO 1997, c. 41

Ontario Water Resources Act, RSO 1990, c. O.40

Pesticides Act, RSO 1990, c. P.11

Provincial Parks Act, RSO 1990, c. P.34

Wilderness Areas Act, RSO 1990, c. W.8

Figure 12.6

Some statutes were enacted long ago. Others, like the *Environmental Bill of Rights*, are much newer statutes. Some are narrow in focus, others broader. Some are aimed at assessing and planning for the future, others at regulating current activity, and others at prohibiting and punishing activity or encouraging it.

As well, there are general statutes that can be used to address environmental problems. For example, the federal *Income Tax Act*, which is applied primarily to collect taxes, may also be used to set a tax policy that encourages or discourages certain activities by taxing environmentally harmful activities and giving tax breaks for environmentally friendly ones.

Three major Ontario statutes are worthy of a closer look—the *Environmental Protection Act*, the *Environmental Assessment Act*, and the *Environmental Bill of Rights*. All have broad application, but they are very different in their approaches to environmental concerns.

Read provisions of Ontario's *Environmental Protection Act* at www.emp.ca/dimensionsoflaw

Environmental Protection Act

Ontario's *Environmental Protection Act* (EPA) was first introduced in 1971 and has been amended many times. It now consists of some 27 parts and nearly 200 sections. Its stated purpose is set out in s. 3: "...to provide for the protection and conservation of the natural environment." Yet, the Act has a narrow focus. Its chief purpose is to regulate the actual and potential sources of contaminants.

The provisions of the EPA fall into two broad categories. The first, containing its general provisions, creates a framework for preventing and controlling the discharge of pollutants into the environment. The second focuses on specific activities or pollutants where the risk from a spill or other polluting activity is high, for example, "Part VI: Ozone Depleting Substances" and "Part VII: Abandoned Motor Vehicles."

There are also provisions for reporting discharges and related offences, such as failure to report a polluting event to the Ministry of the Environment (MOE). The Act includes regulatory schemes, such as the licensing of businesses that handle potentially harmful substances like toxic waste, and the issuance of permits or approvals for environmentally hazardous activities. It provides for inspections, with powers given to inspectors to issue orders to prevent pollution or deal with discharges.

statutory authority: protection afforded by law; e.g., when a statute requires or authorizes a government agency to carry out an activity, the agency is deemed to be protected from civil liability related to that activity

The key section of the EPA is s. 14: "Despite any other provision of this Act or the regulations, no person shall discharge a contaminant or cause or permit the discharge of a contaminant into the natural environment that causes or is likely to cause an adverse effect." This section has been described as one of the strongest provisions in any Canadian pollution control legislation. There are two reasons for this claim. First, it covers private companies, individuals, and governments. There is no **statutory authority** for a government agency to pollute. Second, it overrides other provisions of the Act that permit pollutants to be discharged into the environment, and other provincial legislation as well as municipal bylaws that conflict with it. If s. 14 is breached, a company, its employees, officers, and directors may be convicted if they fail to take all reasonable steps to set up an adequate system of pollution control.

All prohibitions in the Act provide for large fines and imprisonment for negligent or deliberate discharge of contaminants. This provision suggests that there are defences for polluters: if the discharge occurred owing to forces beyond their control, or despite the taking of reasonable care to avoid an accident, there may be no punishment of the persons involved.

Case TOXIC WASTE BANNED AS DUST SUPPRESSANT FOR RURAL ROADS

Norampac Inc. and Brian Ward et al.
(unreported, February 21, 2002, Ont. CA)

Norampac, the largest containerboard manufacturer in Canada, produces a black, sticky, liquid waste byproduct from its corrugated cardboard manufacturing plant in Trenton, Ontario. The product is called Dombind, and contains toxic chemicals such as dioxin, furans, and phenols. These are known to affect human health as well as wildlife. Dombind was provided free of charge to Ontario municipalities, which used it as a dust suppressant on rural roads.

Conservationists started to work actively to stop this use of Dombind in 1993. In response, the company, then known as Domtar Packaging, signed a five-year letter of agreement with the Ministry of the Environment to install a new waste treatment plant and to reduce dioxin output to zero. It continued to supply the waste to municipalities. By 1998, little progress had been made on the waste treatment plant and the amount of dioxin used in Dombind had increased. In 1999, several environmental groups and individuals, represented by the Sierra Legal Defence Fund, joined the MOE in a legal battle to end the use of this material on Ontario's rural roads. Again, the company was ordered to purchase a new waste treatment facility for its Trenton plant and to stop using Dombind after October 31, 2002. (A previous environment minister had promised that Dombind use would stop by late 2000.)

The company appealed, but on February 21, 2002, the Ontario Court of Appeal upheld the ministry's decision. This was the fifth attempt by Norampac to overturn the ministry's directive. Any continued use of Dombind as a dust suppressant will lead to strict enforcement by the MOE.

Questions

1. What grounds did opponents use to work toward banning the use of Dombind?

2. What arguments could the company have used in its defence?
3. What role did environmental groups play in getting the material banned?
4. How effective was the action taken by the MOE, individuals, and groups in protecting the environment? Explain your view.

Problems with the EPA

The EPA focuses on remedies for environmental problems rather than on environmental sustainability. The Act is concerned with pollution, as if that were the only concern of environmental policy makers. It also grants broad powers to the Ministry of the Environment and gives that ministry broad discretion on how or whether to take action. The ordinary citizen cannot take individual action under the EPA, and must rely on the government to act. There is no government accountability for not acting, nor is there any real role for public participation or input.

Environmental Assessment Act

In Ontario, the main framework for conducting environmental assessments is the *Environmental Assessment Act* (EAA). The Ontario government passed the EAA in 1975, making it the first act of its kind in Canada.

Although the Act defines the environment very broadly, in reality the EAA covers only a short list of projects and activities (see Figure 12.7). Environmental assessments are usually required only for major projects such as dams, highways, and power plants. Between 1996 and 2000, the most significant and thorough assessment was of the Adams Mine landfill

Application of Ontario's *Environmental Assessment Act*

Act Applies To	Act Does Not Apply To
All public undertakings of the Ontario government with the exceptions noted opposite	A long list of undertakings exempted because of other statutes or regulations, for example, the Darlington nuclear power facility
Conservation authorities and major municipal undertakings	Most ordinary municipal works projects such as road repairs and sewer maintenance
In the private sector, waste disposal activities such as energy-from-waste operations, landfills, incinerators, waste management facilities, and private projects carried out on behalf of the Ontario government	The vast majority of private sector projects, activities, and developments
Certain private sector projects that are ordered into the assessment process on an individual basis, for example, a proposed power dam or pulp mill	Most private sector projects, unless there is considerable pressure from interest groups and/or individuals

Figure 12.7

project, a proposal to ship Toronto's waste north to an exhausted open-pit mine in Kirkland Lake.

Many projects outside the scope of the EAA have the potential for considerable environmental impacts, but because of the expense and complexity of assessment, the government does not require planners of these projects to go through the process. For instance, the Ministry of the Environment assesses and approves generalized requirements for some classes of activities such as municipal roads, sewage, and water works. Individual sites are not required to go through a separate, specific assessment. The generalized requirements may prove inadequate for a particular project, allowing environmentally questionable projects to slip through the assessment net.

The Assessment Process

There are several steps in the environmental assessment process. First, a large body of scientific data about the potential environmental impact of a proposed development or new activity is collected. Many physical characteristics—vegetation, animal and insect life, groundwater, drainage, and bird migration patterns, to name a few—of the proposed site are evaluated to determine its current condition. Then, all potential influences from the new activity are evaluated to determine how they might change the existing environment. These findings are considered, along with alternative plans that might reduce any environmental damage, and are weighed against the general economic benefits of the undertaking. The public is given an opportunity to examine the project documents, including scientific studies of environmental impact, and to comment on the proposal. The final decision is made by the MOE.

An environmental assessment is an expensive and time-consuming process, and requires considerable technical and scientific knowledge. Many project planners resent the cost and time required to complete assessments, and the result, in many cases, is an economy-versus-environment conflict, at least in the minds of those who believe in the project's value. As well, the process has been criticized as being too complicated and expensive to provide an effective opportunity for public comment. Those launching these projects often have the resources to promote the economic benefits (without, of course, publicizing the negative impacts). Groups that may be harmed, such as neighbourhoods, seldom have the organization and resources to discover the negative effects of a proposal or to communicate their findings. Those interest groups who have taken the opportunity to evaluate assessments have been criticized for trying to "stall" the process at considerable cost to its proponents.

The EAA does offer some degree of assistance by providing a structure for gathering information about environmental impacts and a forum for assessing and discussing those impacts, weighed against economic costs

Figure 12.8 *Individuals usually do not have the resources to intervene in environmental assessment, but organizations can sometimes manage the funding and have the expertise needed to get their views across. For example, the Coalition on the Niagara Escarpment (CONE) has contested the proposed expansion of this quarry.*

and benefits. Environmentalists have asked the government to provide funding to help individuals and groups that are granted standing to take part in the process as intervenors. There have been some government initiatives to provide funding for members of the public in a variety of types of hearings, including environmental assessments, but the arrangements continue to be made on a haphazard and temporary basis.

Environmental assessment, at least on paper, recognizes the concept of sustainable development. In an assessment, the decision maker is required to weigh the environmental costs and benefits of a proposed undertaking or activity, along with the economic costs and benefits. Does the project cause air or water pollution? How serious will the environmental degradation be? Are there alternative ways of carrying out the scheme that will do less damage? Is the damage level acceptable or not?

Environmental Bill of Rights

Ontario's *Environmental Bill of Rights* (EBR) was passed in 1993 after lobbying by environmental groups. It represented a radically new approach, describing environmental concerns in terms of human rights. The EBR is designed to empower members of the public in their efforts to take responsibility for the protection of the environment—for themselves and for future generations.

The EBR provides specific tools for public participation in environmental protection. Among these is the requirement that the government give notice of proposed governmental action that is subject to public consultation. This is done through the EBR registry, a public database available on the Internet. Members of the public can request a review of a policy, statute, regulation, or instrument that is in place, or request that one be developed if there is none. Any member of the public can ask for a review when an instrument (such as a licence or permit to conduct environmentally sensitive activity) has been granted, challenging both the government and the applicant. The legislation established an Environmental Commissioner to monitor statements of environmental values, to investigate environmental violations, and to report on ministry compliance with the legislature.

Problems with the EBR

Because it created important new tools for environmental protection, many commentators praised the passage of the EBR. It represented the high-water mark for environmental protection in this province. In practice, the EBR has resulted in very few actual investigations. The expansion of access to the courts was welcome, but lawsuits are expensive. Without dependable

The Law From the *Environmental Bill of Rights, 1993* [SO 1993, c. 28, as amended 1996, c. 27, s. 22; 1999, c. 5, s. 2; 2001, c. 9, Sched. G, s. 4; 2002, c. 17, Sched. F, table; and 2002, c. 24, Sched. B, ss. 25 and 34]:

Preamble

The people of Ontario recognize the inherent value of the natural environment.

The people of Ontario have a right to a healthful environment.

The people of Ontario have as a common goal the protection, conservation and restoration of the natural environment for the benefit of present and future generations.

While the government has the primary responsibility for achieving this goal, the people should have means to ensure that it is achieved in an effective, timely, open and fair manner. ...

Section 2(1) The purposes of this Act are,

(a) to protect, conserve and, where reasonable, restore the integrity of the environment by the means provided in this Act;

(b) to provide sustainability of the environment by the means provided in this Act; and

(c) to protect the right to a healthful environment by the means provided in this Act.

The subsection also includes these purposes:

- the reduction and elimination of pollutants that are an unreasonable threat to the environment
- the conservation and protection of sensitive areas, natural resources, and plant life, animal life, and ecological systems
- the wise management of natural resources.

Questions

1. Using the information above, explain how the EBR supports the concept of sustainable development.
2. How does the EBR empower citizens to take responsibility for protection of the environment?
3. Describe another example of the idea of a "bill of rights" being used to bring about positive change within society.

Information on the *Environmental Bill of Rights* can be found at www.emp.ca/dimensionsoflaw

financial assistance for those who start environmental lawsuits, these new rights are unlikely to be widely used.

More importantly, the scope of the EBR's application was severely curtailed in 1996 by the passage of the Ontario *Savings and Restructuring Act* (SRA), an **omnibus act** that made changes to several different Ontario statutes. The SRA, often referred to as Bill 26, changed the way in which

omnibus act: an act that contains statutes applying to many different areas of legislation

Explore the CELA Web site at www.emp.ca/dimensionsoflaw

environmental decisions are made in Ontario. It delegated what were previously provincial government decision-making roles—and thereby subject to the EBR—to municipalities and their conservation authorities, which are not subject to the legislation. This change effectively put a large number of environmental decisions beyond the reach of public intervention through the EBR.

WORKING FOR CHANGE *Lawyers Protect the Environment*

At the end of the 1960s, a group of law students, lawyers, and environmental activists formed the Canadian Environmental Law Association (CELA) as a means to promote changes in governmental policies and laws relating to the environment. CELA lawyers represent clients, individuals, and citizens' groups at hearings or in the courts. CELA has been both a training ground and a workplace for some of the best environmental lawyers, activists, educators, and scholars in Canada.

Requests for help come from such diverse groups as farmers living next to leaking landfills, First Nations protecting their natural resources, nature groups trying to preserve wetlands, and groups challenging government action or inaction. CELA represented citizens fighting proposals for disposing of Toronto's garbage. At the same time, it is seeking better landfill operating standards and laws to require aggressive waste reduction and recycling, as well as fair processes in environmental assessment laws.

CELA also works to protect public health. Its lawyers represented the mother of a young child sprayed with pesticides, and helped citizens' groups push for control of pesticide use by changing bylaws in their communities. It intervened in a Supreme Court of Canada case that found a municipal bylaw permitting pesticide use in Quebec to be lawful, and worked to obtain a better way for the federal government to register pesticides. In recent years, CELA has continued

Figure 12.9 *This is the logo of the Canadian Environmental Law Association. Explain the symbols that are incorporated into this logo.*

its longstanding watchdog role to ensure the protection of drinking water sources and systems, concentrating on the areas of water quality and toxic substances. It represented the local citizens' group in the Walkerton Inquiry (see page 374) into the *E. coli* contamination of the town's water supply. Working closely with doctors and others in the health-care field, CELA continues to seek stronger laws to control toxic substances implicated in such health disorders as cancer and developmental problems in children.

CELA has worked with many other organizations across Ontario and Canada on a wide variety of issues, including nuclear waste disposal, international trade, and land use planning. It is involved in large-scale issues (for example, intervening in cases involving an attempt to patent genetically modified animals) as well as location-specific matters, such as trying to save a small forest over which a local conservation group is challenging a developer.

While CELA can provide legal assistance, advocate for stronger laws and policy, and help the public to organize, its overall goal is to work with, and help empower, communities. The goal is to allow the public better access to justice and greater participation in decisions that affect environment and health.

Questions

1. What conditions prompted the establishment of CELA?
2. Give four examples of how CELA works to effect change in government policies.
3. a) Explain the reasons for CELA's overall goal.
   b) Why is this an important goal in a democratic society?

CHECK YOUR UNDERSTANDING

1. a) What is the purpose of the *Environmental Protection Act*?
   b) What are its strengths?
   c) What are its weaknesses?
   d) What kind of activity do you think might count as "permitting the discharge of a contaminant"? What distinguishes this activity from "discharging a contaminant"?
2. a) Identify some of the limitations of the *Environmental Assessment Act*.
   b) Describe the assessment procedure used in the EAA.
3. a) How is the EAA potentially a powerful tool for protecting the environment?
   b) Which aspects of the Act's implementation make it ineffective, in your opinion?
4. a) What public needs were addressed by the *Environmental Bill of Rights*?
   b) How has Bill 26 made the EBR less effective?

Environmental Protection in Retreat

In 1995, Ontarians elected a Progressive Conservative (PC) government that sought to reduce bureaucracy and public expense across a broad range of services. This policy resulted in a general government retreat from the previous "green wave" of governmental regulations. One step was the decision, in the name of economic restraint, to shift responsibility for enforcing compliance with environmental standards from the government to the polluters themselves. With the loss of hundreds of inspectors through budget cuts, the Ministry of the Environment's rate of enforcement of environmental regulations and investigation of complaints and incidents plunged dramatically, with as few as 10 percent of complaints being addressed. According to some analysts, despite enormous growth in environmental initiatives (and adjusting for inflation), the 1997–1998 MOE budget was barely above its budget for 1972–1973, its first full year of operation, and 68 percent lower than its peak in 1991–1992. Most of the cuts came from personnel, with the ministry being forced to lay off about 40 percent of its staff during the early years of the PC government.

Visit the site of the Ontario Ministry of the Environment at www.emp.ca/dimensionsoflaw

Fyi An example of the cuts made to the MOE since 1995 is the closure of a phytotoxicology laboratory in Brampton that tested the impacts of pollutants on plants. The laboratory was converted into a police tactical training centre.

Personal Viewpoint

One Perspective on Cuts to Government Regulation

In less than two years [1995–1997], both the dizzying pace and the huge volume of environmental de-regulation has been formidable. ... In responding to [critics of the cuts], the Minister of Environment and Energy and the Premier have said that the government is simply eliminating duplication and getting rid of useless regulations.

However, it is clear that a few positive proposals for change are overshadowed by obvious attempts to weaken environmental protection rules across the board. In defending the changes, the government is also clinging to the dubious argument that environmental regulations kill jobs. But, rigorous studies have proven that, on the contrary, environmental regulation promotes innovation and a company's competitive advantage. Environmental protection may in fact increase jobs, particularly in manufacturing, transportation, communications and utilities. ...

It is also clear that the many changes affecting environmental protection have occurred so quickly that the vast majority of the public is unaware of them. ...

The agenda of corporate globalization, de-regulation and privatization is undermining basic features of democracy and the role of government as a guardian of the public interest. The task for the environmental movement is to continue to reveal the environmental dimensions of this onslaught and ensure this information is part of the educational and advocacy efforts of the broader social justice community.

Source: Kathleen Cooper, Researcher with the Canadian Environmental Law Association, "Trashing Environmental Protection—Ontario's Four Part Strategy." In Luciana Ricciutelli, June Larkin, and Eimear O'Neill (eds.), *Confronting the Cuts: A Sourcebook for Women in Ontario*. Toronto: Inanna Publications and Education, 1998.

Questions

1. Identify words and phrases from this excerpt that signal the author's point of view.
2. Summarize the arguments that Cooper presents to support her view.
3. Do you agree with Cooper's assertion that the Ontario government's changes were "undermining basic features of democracy and the role of government as a guardian of the public interest"? Explain your opinion.

The Walkerton Tragedy

In 2001, the effects of the policy of government cutbacks were scrutinized in an official inquiry into the May 2000 *E. coli* outbreak in Walkerton, Ontario. The inquiry revealed the following chain of events that led to the outbreak.

- Early in April 2000, the chlorinator used to purify water in Well 7 at Walkerton began to break down. The Walkerton Public Utilities Commission (PUC), the local organization responsible for keeping water safe, ordered a new one since there was no backup available. Delivery was to take two months.

- Between April 7 and April 10, provincial environment officials received a fax from a private laboratory stating that four of eight routine tests of the Walkerton water supply indicated possible contamination. Three days later, they received additional evidence of contamination. When the officials contacted Stan Koebel, the manager of the Walkerton PUC, he assured them that there was no problem. Water samples taken on April 24 did not indicate contamination. Later, it was revealed that the samples were not taken from Well 7.
- On May 12, a severe storm caused floodwater, probably contaminated with *E. coli* bacteria from animal manure, to enter the town's water supply. Between May 15 and May 18, the PUC sent water to be tested at another laboratory, and three days later Koebel received a fax confirming *E. coli* contamination of Well 7.
- On May 19, the region's medical officer of health, Dr. Murray McQuigge, was informed that the local hospital had several cases of bloody diarrhea, a sign of *E. coli* infection, and questioned Koebel regarding the safety of the town's water supply. McQuigge was assured by Koebel that the water was safe, and other possible causes for the sickness were investigated. By May 20, 40 people were being treated for bloody diarrhea. An anonymous call to the Spills Action Centre of the Ministry of the Environment suggested that Koebel had received test results confirming contamination. This tip prompted calls from McQuigge and ministry officials to Koebel. He insisted the town's water supply was safe.
- On May 21, with more cases in the local hospital, McQuigge officially warned residents not to drink the water and took water samples for testing. Two days later, the laboratory confirmed *E. coli* bacteria pollution of the water supply. Koebel then admitted to McQuigge that he knew about the contamination as early as May 18, and cited the malfunctioning chlorinator. By this time, six people in hospital were near death or would soon die. Two thousand other residents would become ill.

For background information on Walkerton, visit www.emp.ca/dimensionsoflaw

The Walkerton incident led to a judicial inquiry, headed by Mr. Justice Dennis O'Connor, into the causes of the tragedy. Part of the investigation dealt with the question of what had gone wrong in Walkerton, part dealt with broader questions concerning the drinking water in Ontario, and part attempted to find solutions. Several factors were considered as possible causes:

1. *The system of rules and regulations.* The inquiry found that provincial regulations were not strict enough to prevent contamination of the water supply. During a critical time period, only Koebel was aware of the contamination.
2. *The absence of a national standard.* Water quality standards are currently the responsibility of provincial governments. Environmentalists

Figure 12.10 *A volunteer helps a Walkerton, Ontario resident load bottled drinking water into her car at an emergency water depot after townspeople were alerted about contamination of their water supply.*

have called on the federal government to establish binding regulations for water quality in all provinces. The federal and provincial governments have cooperated on subcommittees on drinking water and have developed suggested guidelines for water safety. These are not provincially binding, however, and only Alberta and Quebec have laws that enforce provincewide standards.

3. *Ineffective provincial monitoring of water quality.* Most provincial governments receive water test results directly from testing laboratories. The Ontario and Quebec governments depend on municipal water utilities to notify them of problems. No regulation specified that the municipality had to inform the government of *E. coli* contamination.

At the inquiry, lawyers for the Ontario government argued that Koebel was primarily to blame for the tragedy. Mr. Justice O'Connor rejected this argument because

> [i]t totally misconceives the role of the MOE [Ministry of the Environment] as overseer of communal water systems, a role that is intended to include ensuring that water operators and facilities perform satisfactorily. When there is a failure in the operation of a water facility, as there was in Walkerton, the question arises whether the MOE in its role as overseer should have prevented the failure or minimized the risk that would occur. ...
>
> I have concluded that the MOE failed in several respects to fulfill its oversight role in relation to Walkerton's water system. Some MOE programs or policies were deficient because they should have identified and addressed one or both of the two operational problems at Walkerton ... [inadequate chlorination and lack of continuous monitors], but did not do so.

Mr. Justice O'Connor made 28 recommendations that included an increased role for the MOE in coordinated efforts with local health officials, time-limited approvals of all waterworks, annual inspections of waterworks, and improved training and certification programs for MOE inspectors and waterworks operators. The premier and the MOE committed to implementing these recommendations.

Self-regulation versus Government Enforcement **Should governments rely more on voluntary compliance and self-regulation to protect the environment than on strict enforcement of regulations?**

The Ontario Progressive Conservative government after 1995 promoted the policy of voluntary compliance with environmental regulations and self-regulation for industries, farmers, and developers, saying that these parties were responsible citizens. It argued that voluntary and non-regulatory initiatives (VNRIs) could effectively protect the environment.

The following excerpts describe the positions of some individuals and groups on this issue.

Laws and regulations are among the most important instruments for transforming environment and development policies into action. ... It is essential to develop and implement enforceable and effective laws. ... It is equally critical to develop workable programs to enforce compliance with the laws, regulations, and standards that are adopted.

—1992 United Nations Conference on Environment and Development (the "Rio Conference")

Some Arguments for Voluntary Compliance and Self Regulatory Initiatives

- They provide incentives for industry to initiate environmental clean-up measures.
- They are more cost effective than regulations at achieving environmental protection, because they cost less to implement and enforce.
- They can be designed and implemented more quickly than Acts or regulations, and are thus more efficient for achieving environmental protection.
- They allow industries to design their own cost-effective environmental protection methods. Industries claim that they hold real potential for environmental benefits through emissions reductions.
- They provide greater flexibility in the process of how they are designed and implemented.
- They increase certainty for regulated industries.
- They can lead to a more cooperative climate among government, industry and other stakeholders.

—Environmental Commissioner of Ontario, "Discussion Paper for Round Table on Self Regulation, Voluntary Compliance and Environmental Protection," October 1996

Civil society is skeptical of governments backing away from their traditional role as environmental watchdog. Not trusting the business sector and generally unsympathetic to its concerns, many in the NGO [non-governmental organization] community are harsh critics of VNRIs. If VNRIs "do not work," civil society will demand a reversion to regulation.

—*Robert Kerr, Aaron Cosby, and Ron Yachnin,* Beyond Regulation: Exporters and Voluntary Environmental Measures. *Winnipeg: International Institute for Sustainable Development, 1998*

...voluntary programs lead to less accountability from industry due to serious problems of non-enforceability. It is not realistic to argue, as industry and government often do, that enforcement will come through "the court of public opinion." The public lacks the information, technical and legal advice, and funds necessary to even track company actions. Without a legal standard, there is nothing to enforce. Without mandatory reporting requirements, little relevant information will be accessible to the public. Nor is access to the media to publicize corporate actions necessarily available, particularly given the likelihood of corporate legal reprisals.

—*Michelle Swenarchuk and Paul Muldoon,* In Defence of Environmental Regulation. *Canadian Environmental Law Association, August 1996; www.cela.ca/law&dereg/Indef.htm*

Businesses need a new mind-set. How can companies argue shrilly that regulations harm competitiveness and then expect regulators and environmentalists to be flexible and trusting as those same companies request time to pursue innovative solutions?

—*Michael Porter and Claas van der Linde, "Green and Competitive: Ending the Stalemate." Denmark's International Study Program, International Business and Economics (no date); www.disp.dk*

Questions

1. Identify the two most effective arguments used by supporters of VNRIs. Explain your choices.
2. Identify the two most effective arguments used by supporters of government regulation and enforcement of environmental laws. Explain your choices.
3. Suggest one additional argument for either side of this issue.
4. What further information would you need to make a fully informed decision on this issue?
5. What is your opinion on this issue? Explain your view.

Proactive or Reactive?

Environmental researchers generally believe that reacting to environmental concerns—by trying to fix problems once they have occurred, or by punishing those who have caused environmental damage—is an inappropriate strategy for environmental protection. In many cases, environmental harm is irreversible: fining a polluter, for example, even where a cleanup is ordered, will not undo the harm caused by the release of the pollutant. Instead, the only effective way to protect the environment is to prevent damage in the first place. Preventing damage is complicated and requires long-term planning and coordination. It is nearly impossible to achieve a long-term, coordinated protection agenda by means of a complicated patchwork of legislation.

An alternative to regulating and punishing polluters is an approach that puts more emphasis on providing positive incentives to behave in ways that support sustainable development. Consider some of these ideas:

- Make people pay the real costs of environmentally damaging activities. For example, someone buying an SUV would have to pay an extra "gas-guzzling vehicle tax," a supplemental fee for licence plates, and an additional fee for each litre of fuel.
- Subsidize environmentally friendly practices. For example, give energy consumers who use solar or wind power a rebate on their electricity bills.
- Use more deposit and refund systems. Blue-box programs already encourage waste recycling. Build on these programs by paying people to recycle materials and reuse packaging (such as soft-drink containers).
- Instead of using expensive legal prosecutions, charge non-compliance fees, levied like a tax, to companies or enterprises that exceed pollution discharge levels.

It is likely that, as the concept of sustainable development is accepted and becomes better understood, more legislation will be passed to help address the economic–environmental balance. Ontario and a number of American states have already passed legislation such as the *Environmental Bill of Rights.*

Check Your Understanding

1. What changes in government policies, especially in Ontario, resulted in weaker protection for the environment?
2. a) Summarize the tragedy that occurred in Walkerton, Ontario, in May 2000.
   b) Where was the blame for the tragedy laid by the official inquiry?
   c) Suggest actions that should be taken to prevent a similar occurrence in the future.

3. a) What are the weaknesses and strengths of the regulatory model of environmental control?
   b) What are the weaknesses and strengths of the incentive model of environmental control?
   c) Which model would you recommend to the Ontario government for future environmental legislation? Explain your view.

METHODS OF *Legal Inquiry*

Interpreting Statutes

Imagine a conversation with a friend. As you speak, you attempt to convey information and meaning to the person with whom you are speaking. Sometimes you will be successful in getting your idea across, other times not. Statutes are a way in which the legislature attempts to "speak" to society (or to certain bodies or groups within society) on a particular issue, such as conservation or environmental protection. Sometimes the legislature speaks clearly and uses words unambiguously, and sometimes it does not. There are various reasons for this.

First, the ambiguity may simply reflect the difficulty that people or organizations have in speaking clearly to others. Second, statutes are the embodiment of several contributors—the draftsperson, the Cabinet committee members who review the draft act, the minister responsible for the act, the members of the governing party, and the members of the Opposition. When these different and sometimes contradictory voices are brought together in an act, the legislative intent may not always be clear.

Since there is no official source to which people may refer to resolve these statutory ambiguities, the courts have gradually taken on the responsibility of resolving them. This judicial function is known as "statutory interpretation," and the courts have developed a number of rules or principles to guide them when interpreting statutes.

The Referential Approach

The first approach that judges use is to refer to the provisions of the act itself. This is called the referential approach. This approach employs two rules of interpretation: the literal or plain-meaning rule, and the golden rule. The literal rule is a grammatical interpretation of the act that takes into account the words of the statute and nothing more. Under this rule, if the words are clear, then they will be adhered to, even if this approach leads to an absurdity.

The golden rule of interpretation is a modification of the literal rule. It states that the grammatical and ordinary words of the statute shall be adhered to, unless that approach would lead to an absurdity, in which case the words may be modified to avoid the absurdity, but no further.

The Purposive Approach

The purposive approach to statutory interpretation requires that a judge attempt to discover Parliament's intent by determining the purpose of the statute or the mischief that the statute was meant to correct, something that is often stated in the act itself. For example, s. 2(1)(a) of the Ontario *Environmental Bill of Rights, 1993* states that one purpose of the Act is "to protect, conserve and, where reasonable, restore the integrity of the environment." As with the referential approach, there are limits to using the purposive approach. The purpose of an act, like its grammar, may not be clear. For example, what is the difference (if any) between "protect" and "conserve," and what does "where reasonable" mean?

The Contextual Approach

The third approach is to interpret the ambiguous provision of a statute within the broader context of the statute. This is often described as the contextual approach. In following this approach, judges typically employ one or more of the following rules:

- When two or more specific words forming a class are followed by general words, the general words take their meaning from the specific words.
- Where a word or phrase is expressly mentioned, it implies the exclusion of others.
- Words of a statute must be given their contemporary meaning.

The Use of Presumptions

Finally, judges are assisted in interpreting statutes by relying on certain presumptions; for example, a statute does not operate retroactively, or a statute is deemed not to change the common law unless that intention is expressly stated in the statute. In the context of environmental protection, pollution that occurred before the Ontario *Environmental Protection Act* was passed is not regulated by the Act, unless the Act specifically addresses the issue. Thus, spills that occurred before November 29, 1985 (the date the Act was amended to regulate spills, such as those that occur when a train is derailed) are not regulated by the Act. However, the Ontario government can order the owner of contaminated land to clean up a site, even if the pollution occurred long before the owner purchased the land and even if it occurred before the *Environmental Protection Act* came into force. This is because the Act is clearly intended to apply to past pollution, regardless of who owns the land or when the pollution occurred.

Applying the Skill

1. What are the three principal approaches to statutory interpretation?
2. Explain why there is sometimes a dispute about a statute's meaning.
3. The golden rule of statutory interpretation is a sub-rule of the literal or plain-meaning rule. Explain how a judge might use these two rules to interpret a statute.
4. Why do judges today seldom use the literal rule of statutory interpretation?
5. Section 1(1) of the Ontario *Environmental Protection Act* states that "natural environment" means "the air, land and water, or any combination or part thereof, of the Province of Ontario." Soon after the Act came into force, in *Re Rockcliffe Park Realty Ltd. v. Ontario* (1975), 62 DLR (3d) 17 (Ont. CA), a company raised the question whether the Act applied only to public land or whether it also applied to private land. Using one or more of the approaches to statutory interpretation, how would you expect a court to interpret this definition in the Act?
6. Section 410 of the Quebec *Cities and Towns Act*, RSQ, c. C-19, empowers municipalities to pass bylaws for the "peace, order, good government, health and welfare ... of the municipality." Using the contextual approach, what arguments would you make to a court that this section should be interpreted in a way that authorizes a town in Quebec to pass a bylaw prohibiting pesticide use?

Reviewing Main Ideas

You Decide!

USING THE ENVIRONMENTAL BILL OF RIGHTS

Braeker et al. v. The Queen et al., court file no. 3332/98 (Owen Sound, Ont. Sup. Ct.)

This case involves an application for damages from a landowner whose use of the land resulted in polluted groundwater, and from the Ontario government for negligence in monitoring and enforcing protection measures.

Facts

In 1998, farmers Karl and Vicki Braeker of Grey County, Ontario, started legal proceedings against Max Karge, the owner of an adjacent property. They alleged that an illegal tire dump on the Karge property had contaminated the soil, groundwater, and surface water in the area, including the well on their own property.

Karge had sold this farm in 1990 to Thomas Sanders and held a second mortgage on it. Sanders did not pay the mortgage and laid waste to the property by cutting down the woodlot, selling off buildings, and ruining the house. In 1991, Sanders also allowed 15 000 used tires to be dumped on the farm. When Karge alerted the Ministry of the Environment to the illegal dumping activity, officials started an investigation. During the course of the investigation, another 20 000 tires were hauled to the property. After several letters to Sanders, the MOE agreed to allow the owner to bury the tires. They did not consult Karge or neighbouring landowners about this decision. Soon afterward, Sanders disappeared. MOE action to find him failed. To protect his interest in the property, Karge incorporated a numbered company and acquired title for the property from the first mortgage holder.

In 1995, the MOE ordered Karge to remove the tires. He appealed the order to the Environmental Appeal Board. The Board found that while Karge was responsible for the problem because he had made decisions about the property, he had also been victimized. The Board pointed out that the Ministry of the Environment was also to blame for the problem. They ruled that Karge should have to pay for removal of the tires, but only from net profits from the property after his mortgage had been recovered. The MOE was ordered to dig up and clean the tires and make them ready for removal.

Testing in 1997 revealed that the area of the tire dump was contaminated with chemicals in concentrations much higher than levels permitted by the Provincial Water Quality Objectives.

Removal of the tires finally began in 1998. The tires were recycled as part of an asphalt mix used on county roads. However, the MOE refused to clean up the groundwater, and the Braekers filed their claim under the *Proceedings Against the Crown Act*, the Ontario legislation that permits citizens to sue the government for torts and for breach of contract.

The Braekers and their lawyer, Rick Lindgren of the Canadian Environmental Law Association, sought damages for loss, injury, and harm caused by the government's regulatory negligence. Lindgren invoked Part VI of the *Environmental Bill of Rights* in the action.

The Law

The *Environmental Bill of Rights* in s. 84(1) stipulates that

> any person resident in Ontario may bring an action against the person in the court if that

> person or persons have contravened an act or regulation, and that contravention has caused or will imminently cause significant harm to a public resource of Ontario.

Section 84(2) requires that the plaintiff must already have applied for investigation into the contravention, an action the Braekers did not take. Lindgren argued that this requirement did not apply because s. 84(6) allows for an action to go ahead if delaying it would result in significant harm or serious risk of significant harm to a public resource.

Arguments of the Braekers and the Canadian Environmental Law Association (Appellants)

The Braekers maintained that the defendants unlawfully caused, permitted, or failed to stop the actual and imminent contamination of their property by contaminants released from the illegal tire dump. They sought a legal declaration to that effect, a permanent injunction preventing the use of the property for any non-rural use, and a declaration or injunction requiring an environmental restoration plan to restore the site to its prior condition. They also sought over a million dollars in damages. They maintained that the government failed to exercise its regulatory powers to protect the natural environment, and that it was negligent in its monitoring, inspection, and enforcement activities. They argued that their case was one in a growing list of instances in which the government was being sued to prompt it to exercise its statutory powers to protect the province's environment.

Arguments of the Ministry of the Environment and Mr. Karge (Respondents)

The MOE's statement of defence argued that the MOE and its staff had taken timely and prompt action to prevent environmental damage caused by the illegal dumping of tires. The burying of the tires had been a temporary measure until a permanent solution to the problem could be arranged. The respondents further claimed that the MOE "at all times acted diligently and within its statutory obligations" in responding to Sanders's illegal actions. Its letters to Sanders were within the standards set out by law. Because of their actions, the MOE did not owe any duty to the appellants.

Make Your Decision

As of August 2003, this matter was still before the courts and no judgment had been rendered.

1. Outline the important facts in this case.
2. Explain how the *Environmental Bill of Rights* was used by the appellants to prepare this legal action.
3. Summarize the arguments made by the appellants and respondents in this case.
4. Make a decision in this case, and provide reasons for your decision.

Key Terms

Review the following terms to show that you understand the meaning of each and how it is applied in a legal context.

injunction	public nuisance
legislative authority	riparian rights
negligence	standing
omnibus act	statutory authority
private nuisance	trespass

Understanding the Law

Review the following pieces of legislation mentioned in the text, and show that you understand the intent of each.

Environmental Assessment Act
Environmental Bill of Rights, 1993
Environmental Protection Act

Thinking and Inquiry

1. Make a list of at least five lifestyle changes your family could make to live in a more "sustainable" way.
2. Brainstorm a list of people and organizations that could play a role in protecting the environment. For each, assess their abilities to bring about substantial improvements in how we manage our impact on the environment.
3. a) In pairs, select one of the statutes in Figure 12.6 on page 365. Research and analyze it to determine the kind of approach it takes to the environment, for example, regulatory or prohibitive. Explain your findings to the class.
   b) What kinds of incentives does the statute use to achieve its goals?
   c) What improvements would you suggest in this statute to make it more effective?
4. Research a group that has organized to lobby for environmental change. Prepare a short report on the group, including the following:
   a) its origins and purpose
   b) the organization of the group
   c) actions that the group has taken or is taking to protect the environment.
5. Visit the Web site of Ontario's Ministry of the Environment and summarize three of its current initiatives in a short news release.
6. Poll a selection of students to find out their current concerns regarding the environment. Present these in a short report.

Communication

7. Suggest changes to environmental law in Ontario that you think would encourage sustainable development. Summarize your ideas in a one-page report.
8. Prepare arguments to debate the following proposition: "*Resolved that: There is no conflict between economic growth and environmental protection.*"
9. Prepare an "environmental bill of rights" for students in your school.
10. Prepare a script and videotape a one-minute public service message concerning the *Environmental Protection Act*, the *Environmental Assessment Act*, or the *Environmental Bill of Rights.*

Application

11. Prepare a request for a review of an environmentally sensitive practice in your community through the *Environmental Bill of Rights.* In your request, describe the practice and the reasons for your request.
12. Prepare a proposed bill that anticipates an environmental problem resulting from changing technologies. Determine the aspects of the bill that are regulatory and prohibitive.
13. Plan a Web site for a lawyer specifically concerned with environmental law. Include frequently asked questions, the areas in which the lawyer practises, and links to other significant sites.
14. Work in pairs to prepare a questionnaire to check public understanding of environmental law in Ontario, based on the learning you have acquired through this chapter. Interview an adult, and then give an oral report on your findings. What conclusions can you draw from this exercise about public understanding of environmental law?

The Government and the Workplace

All of us spend a high percentage of our lives "at work." This chapter examines the role that provincial and federal governments play in regulating employment standards in the workplace to satisfy the needs of both employees and employers. Employment legislation is concerned with issues such as wrongful dismissal, health and safety in the workplace, human rights in the workplace, workers' compensation, and minimum labour standards, such as wages and hours of work.

The cartoon in Figure 13.1 raises one contemporary issue in employee–employer relations that has not yet been resolved by government regulation.

Dilbert

Figure 13.1

CHAPTER *Focus*

In this chapter, you will

- explain how governments came to regulate employment standards
- explain the extent of the chief laws that the government uses to regulate employment standards, occupational health and safety, and human rights in the workplace
- understand how these laws are enforced

At First Glance

1. Who are the main characters in the cartoon? What is their relationship?
2. What issues in the workplace are raised by the cartoon?
3. In the situation shown in the cartoon, what do you think should be the rights of the employer? of the employee?
4. Do you think lawmakers should be concerned with the issues raised in the cartoon?
5. What do you think should be the major concerns of lawmakers when making laws for the workplace?

A Century of Change

In the last 100 years, federal and provincial governments have enacted a wide range of laws governing the workplace and regulating minimum wages, employment standards, occupational health and safety, human rights in the workplace, and workers' compensation.

The wages and living conditions described in the Personal Viewpoint feature on the next page were typical for many Canadian workers in the early 20th century. Many of those who were prospering believed that people were responsible for their own fortune or misfortune. The conditions for those who were poor were blamed on lack of "thrift," on laziness, or on "weakness of moral character." What social and economic factors led to changes that addressed the appalling conditions for workers, and what were the main changes that were made?

In the early and mid-19th century, governments were reluctant to make laws for the workplace when the "typical worker" was a self-reliant individual who worked on a farm but could easily survive in rural communities. By the 1870s, workers increasingly moved from farms to cities. Canada was moving rapidly from a pre-industrial society to a capitalist industrial society. Skilled workers such as blacksmiths were gradually being replaced by unskilled workers in factories.

Find out more about labour history in Canada at www.emp.ca/dimensionsoflaw

The first steps by governments toward change in working conditions came in the 1880s. The Ontario and Quebec governments introduced factory acts that prohibited child labour (boys under 12 years of age and girls under 14 years of age were prohibited from working in factories with more than five employees), but these laws were not very effective—in 1890 Ontario had only two factory inspectors to enforce its act. The *Report of the Royal Commission on Relations of Capital and Workers*, published in 1889, was the first official study by the federal government of workplace conditions.

The Beginning of Change

All provinces had passed laws for the protection of miners by the early 20th century, although this was still a very dangerous job. Quebec passed the first *Workmen's Compensation Act* in North America in 1909, but workers were not compensated if they were at fault for the injury. By the mid-1930s, seven other provinces had adopted workers' compensation. These steps were influenced by similar legislation that was enacted in Western European countries where industrialization was more advanced.

In the 1930s, during the Great Depression, all governments in Canada still took the position that the economic system, including labour standards in the workplace, was best left to work out its problems on its own, without interference. The influential British economist John Maynard Keynes had already suggested that governments and industry were the main players in the shaping of the economy, and that it might easily fall to

ersonal Viewpoint

A Worker in Early 20th-Century Canada

In 1913, J.S. Woodsworth, a minister and social worker at the time, described the life of a railroad worker:

> The man is a painter in the railroad shops of the Canadian Pacific Railway and is paid 36 cents an hour, eight hours a day and half a day on Saturdays for 44 hours each week. He has holidays off and nine days at Easter. In summer many railroad workers were laid off but he was lucky to keep his job. There is nothing for those who are laid off. His average income is $60 dollars a month. His only benefit from the company is the chance of a railroad pass, which he cannot use because he cannot afford the lost earnings. He sometimes can make a little extra money by mending broken dishes.
>
> He lives in a run-down six-room house beside the railroad tracks in a poor area of Winnipeg to save on money, with his wife and six children, none of whom are old enough to work. His youngest daughter is now in a provincial government home for the blind due to misdiagnosis at the hospital. She had been told to wear glasses but had gone blind. A specialist (with a fee of $10) had told him that the glasses had done nothing to solve her eyesight problems and that she would be permanently blind. He still hoped to save enough to pay the doctors' bills. His other children had no shoes and most of the their clothing had come from a church "mission."
>
> He listed his monthly expenses:
>
> - Rent: $23.00 a month
> - Heat: (coal) $11.00–$17.00, (wood) $7.00
> - Light: $.50–$1.97
> - Meat: $8.00–$10.00
> - Groceries: $20.00–$25.00 (for butter and eggs, vegetables, flour and condensed milk)
> - Miscellaneous: $.75 (to a fraternal society for burial costs), $.85 for union fees
>
> His wife is sometimes able to make $2.00 a week for dressmaking. He tries to take boarders in when it is possible, but says it does not pay.
>
> He wonders what he will do when he is too old to work. He hopes his children will be able to support him so he is not reduced to the position of the beggars he sees on the streets of the city.

Figure 13.2 *The lowest-paid workers in Canada's larger cities lived in cramped, unhealthy conditions.*

Source: Quoted in Ken Osborne, *R.B. Russell and the Labour Movement*. Toronto: Book Society of Canada, 1978.

Questions

1. Estimate the family's monthly expenses. How much, approximately, would the man have after he had paid these expenses?
2. Use the Internet or another source to find out what social programs exist today to help low-wage earners that were not available to the worker described by Woodsworth.

governments to provide the financial push to lift sagging economies (and workers) out of recession or depression conditions. They had a model for government intervention in the form of the "New Deal" initiative in the United States in the 1930s, where the government had already funneled money to start the recovery from the Depression in the form of public works projects for the unemployed, training for youth, and improving public utilities.

In Canada in 1935, the average workweek was still over 48 hours. Workweeks of 55 to 60 hours remained common. There were no laws setting minimum wages, maximum hours of work, severance pay, or paid vacations. Minimum-wage laws applied only to women in the workplace. The 1935 *Ontario Industrial Standards Act*, which set minimum wages and work standards in Ontario, was a response by employers to put a halt to "sweatshop" enterprises that were using workers desperate for employment and a wage, however low. Yet even the definition of wages and working hours in this Act was often subject to negotiation, and groups such as the local town council might act as mediators.

World War II brought an end to the Great Depression, and, led by trade union activity, workers pressed for better working conditions and higher wages. Average wages rose from 69.4 cents an hour to 91.3 cents between 1945 and 1948. Workers benefited from new labour standards and the right to organize unions and to strike (see Chapter 14: Organizing the Workforce). Yet most labour laws were narrow in scope, concerning mainly wages and a limited number of working conditions. Over the next 50 years employment standards slowly improved, with working hours being reduced, minimum wages raised, and safety standards enforced. More women entered the workforce, and issues such as gender equality and pregnancy leave were addressed. As you will see, employment standards today are vastly different from those described by Woodsworth.

Check Your Understanding

1. a) What areas of concern are addressed by employment law?
   b) Which area do you think is most important today?
2. Why were governments slow to make laws concerning the workplace?
3. Select three key "milestones" in the development of employment law from 1900 to 1945 and explain the importance of each.
4. What forces eventually led to legislation governing the workplace?

Employment Standards Legislation

Today, workplace conditions and employer–employee relations are covered by labour laws. Working conditions for federal government workers and private-sector industries that operate interprovincially or internationally, such as railways, telecommunications, ferries, tunnels, bridges and canals, banks, uranium mining and processing, and federal Crown corporations,

Figure 13.3

Main Employment Standards Concerns

- regular and overtime hours of work
- payment of minimum wage for the type of work performed
- extra pay (or extra time off) for overtime work
- time off for holidays and in lieu of working a holiday, or premium pay for working on a holiday
- meal breaks
- minimum time off work between shifts and per week
- a minimum annual vacation requirement and/or vacation pay
- equal pay for men and women for work of equal value
- non-discrimination with respect to benefits and benefit plan eligibility
- pregnancy, adoption, and/or parental leave (generally unpaid)
- continuity of employment, even if the business is transferred to a new owner, or its financial affairs are re-arranged
- minimum notice (in terms of time—weeks or months) of termination of employment (by either party—employer or employee), or payment of salary in lieu of working notice time
- severance pay on termination for employees in limited situations
- the right to refuse to work in unsafe conditions

are governed by the *Canada Labour Code*. All the provinces have labour code legislation that imposes minimum standards for the treatment of employees. These statutes regulate a variety of different issues (see Figure 13.3), and they have a wide scope of application. For example, the Ontario *Employment Standards Act* (ESA) applies to all contracts of employment where the work is performed in (or mainly in) Ontario.

Fyi The minimum wage in Ontario in 2003 was $6.85. In 1965, the minimum wage was the equivalent of $6.00 in 2003 dollars; in 1995, it was the equivalent of $7.89 in 2003 dollars.

The ESA and similar statutes seek to even out the negotiating power imbalance between employers and employees by establishing minimum standards for a number of contract issues. Historically, as you saw in J.S. Woodsworth's description, abuses in employment contract negotiations arose from unequal bargaining power between employers and employees. This situation still exists. For example, in a city or province with high unemployment, a person who must find work is at a tactical disadvantage compared to an employer who can select from a large pool of unemployed and willing workers.

The most important effect of the ESA and other employment standards legislation is to limit an employer's options when it comes to setting the terms of employment. For example, while an employer might theoretically be able to find an employee who is willing to work 16 hours a day, seven days a week for one hourly rate, the ESA establishes the concept of "overtime," and also limits the total number of hours per week that one person can be required to work on the job.

Employment standards prescribed by ESA and similar statutes are **inalienable**, that is, the parties cannot contract out of them. This stipulation is important, because if an employer were able, for example, to offer

inalienable: cannot be surrendered or transferred

unconscionable: unreasonable

an employee a wage premium (extra hourly pay) in exchange for that employee's promise never to take a vacation, the legislation would not work—in a tight employment market, employees would agree to **unconscionable** (unfair, in the opinion of the average observer) contracts just to get a job, and the unfair bargains made through such negotiations would quickly become labour market standards.

On the other hand, the minimum standards set by this type of legislation are exactly that—minimums. It is possible for the parties to negotiate, either individually or collectively (i.e., through labour unions), for higher standards, such as three weeks of annual vacation instead of two.

Learn more about the Ontario *Employment Standards Act* at www.emp.ca/dimensionsoflaw

Enforcing the Law

Most investigations into breaches of the ESA are in response to complaints from a worker or group of workers. Government inspectors then look into the complaint. In some cases, the government inspectors may investigate without a complaint being made.

Many of the issues relating to the enforcement of the employment standards set out in the labour codes are decided in courts of law. The following case illustrates how one situation was decided in the courts.

Case STRANDED IN DENVER

Horrill/Seller v. Garden Grove Produce Imports Ltd.
(1995), 97 di 145 (Can. LRB)

Facts

Greg Seller was hired by Garden Grove on December 27, 1994 as a long-haul truck driver. He left for his first trip—to Texas—on December 28, and delivered his load on December 31. He was then instructed to pick up two separate loads in two other Texas towns and to return with these to Calgary. The employer had promised delivery for January 5.

Seller left Donna, Texas on January 1, 1995 with his load of perishable fruit. He took a different route than that suggested by his employer. His route, though several miles west of the prescribed route, was on better roads, and the evidence was inconclusive as to whether there was a significant difference in travel time between the two routes. At any rate, Seller alleged that he was entitled to set his own route, subject to the employer's right to pay him for the mileage of the suggested route.

On January 3, 1995, Seller called his employer from Albuquerque, New Mexico, to advise that he was "running out of hours." While driving in the United States, Canadian truckers are subject to US legislation relating to maximum driving time without a rest day (or days). In this case, the legislation required a minimum of 48 hours' rest after 70 hours of driving time within any eight-day driving period of consecutive days' driving.

Seller, who had only five driving hours left, and his employer had a phone conversation, the facts of which were in dispute, Seller alleging he was offered no 24-hour break and Garden Grove alleging that Seller advised he could not deliver by January 7, already two days late. As a result of the conversation, Garden Grove arranged to fly a manager to Denver (allegedly the closest town to Albuquerque for which a flight could be arranged) and ordered Seller to drive to Denver (a nine-hour drive).

Seller drove to Denver and was met by the manager. What was said between the two was in dispute at trial, but the result was that Seller was left in Denver after being denied a ride back to Winnipeg and understood that he had either been dismissed or been forced to resign. He had no funds to travel back to Canada, and had to contact several agencies, including Traveller's Aid, the Salvation Army, and the Canadian Consulate Trade Office, for assistance getting home.

Upon his return, Seller filed a complaint under the *Canada Labour Code*, which regulates certain kinds of labour in the federal jurisdiction (including international trucking).

Issues

Seller alleged that he was dismissed as a result of exercising his right to refuse unsafe work (driving overtime without a rest period). The employer denied that it had dismissed Seller, but claimed that Seller had resigned. The employer also alleged that Seller failed to comply with the necessary procedure for a work refusal, which, under the Code, requires giving notice to a health and safety representative.

Decision

The court found, based on its review of the conflicting facts, that Seller was intentionally stranded in Denver, and that even though he may never have been told that he was fired, he was in fact dismissed.

The court also found that Seller's dismissal was indeed a reprisal for the exercise of his right to refuse unsafe work, and that it was reasonable on Seller's part to believe that the work was unsafe because of the legislated requirement for a rest period.

Finally, the court found that Seller's failure to follow the requirements of the legislation regarding work refusal did not mean his claim should be dismissed. No investigation could have been carried out at the time anyway, and the employer also failed to contact a representative, as it was required to do in light of Seller's refusal to work.

The court ordered Seller reinstated (if he wished to be) and compensated for lost wages and for the cost of returning to Winnipeg.

Questions

1. How did the application of the *Canada Labour Code* in this case affect (a) the employer and (b) the employee?
2. There was no evidence in this case about whether Seller was actually overtired at the time he pulled over. If there was evidence that he was feeling well rested despite being out of statutory driving hours, would he still have been legally able to refuse to keep driving? Explain your answer.
3. Do you think the decision in this case was fair? Explain your answer.

Problems Enforcing the Law

In some situations, enforcement of employment standards is difficult, especially when workers are not aware of the legislation. Conditions for contract workers, such as the pieceworkers described in the following Personal Viewpoint feature on homeworkers, are an example.

ersonal Viewpoint

Thirty-eight Cents a Shirt

With each step down the narrow, steep staircase of Rosanna Gonzalez's small detached house, the hum of sewing machines gets louder. A small room in the basement is crowded with three industrial machines, kitchen chairs, large spools of thread, an old fan, piles and piles of cut fabric and 42-year-old Rosanna and her 48-year-old co-worker Becky Perez, intently sewing away.

There's only a tiny window to deal with all the flying dust and thread particles. It looks like a run-down factory: concrete floors, fake-wood paneling and blinding fluorescent lights. Becky's eyes are locked on the bobbing needle of her machine. The third member of the group, Louisa Torres, is at home with her sick daughter, so Becky and Rosanna are on deadline to piece together 410 sweatshirts by Friday, and it's already Wednesday. To make it, they'll work well into the night. By Friday, they'll have easily put in 40 hours each. The women have kids to support, and Rosanna, whose husband does contract construction work, is sometimes the only source of income for her family.

Their "boss," a subcontractor who runs a small garment factory, doesn't care how many hours they work. They're homeworkers; he simply pays them by the piece. Each style comes with its own price, and by the end of one week when the shirts are made, delivered and inspected, Rosanna, Becky and Louisa will split about $400.

The three women met at their last job making shoes in a nearby factory. Becky, who emigrated from Chile 23 years ago, says there were things that she liked at the factory: set hours and decent (minimum-wage) pay. A year ago, when the business closed, setting up their own shop at home seemed the ideal solution. "The main advantage is that we work together so we help each other," says Becky, "and there is no boss around and sometimes in the factory we were treated like slaves."

After answering an ad in *The Toronto Sun*, Rosanna, Becky and Louisa filled a sewing order and have been employed by a menswear subcontractor ever since. Just three out of thousands of women who are eking out a living under substandard working conditions and earning well below the minimum wage.

Under the law, employers of homeworkers—in most cases, subcontractors who are getting work done for larger companies, which, in turn, will sell to retailers—must have a permit from the Ontario Ministry of Labour. Workers must be paid a minimum of $7.54 per hour (a premium of 10 percent above minimum wage, to account for the use of space and utilities in their home).

They must receive vacation pay. They must also be visited on a regular basis by a ministry inspector. They've never seen an inspector or a permit; their employer has never uttered a word about such things.

Amazingly, Becky didn't know what the minimum wage was until she recently met a representative from the Homeworkers' Association, a project of the 1000-member Union of Needletrades, Industrial and Textile Employees. The rep told her that she was being paid below Ontario standards. Homeworkers aren't unionized, for the simple reason that no one can find out how to unwind the tangle of retailers and subcontractors or even how many homeworkers there are. (In Toronto, the best estimate is that there are between 4000 and 8000.)

Rosanna, Becky and Louisa spend nine or 10 hours a day in front of their machines, for six, sometimes seven days a week. Rosanna leaves at four every afternoon so she can go to her other office-cleaning job. Sometimes, she says, when she comes home at eleven, Becky and Louisa are still at work. ...

Figure 13.4 *While factory workers receive an hourly wage, homeworkers in the garment industry are paid per item.*

Source: Adapted from Anne Bains, "Thirty-eight Cents a Shirt," *Toronto Life* (February 1998), pp. 41, 50.

Questions

1. What problems do Rosanna, Becky, and Louisa face in their job?
2. Suggest why they have accepted these working conditions.
3. a) What is the law concerning "homeworkers" in Ontario?
   b) Why is it difficult for the law to be applied?

Check Your Understanding

1. Outline the principal features of employment standards legislation.
2. Why is it necessary for employment standards in the ESA to be inalienable?
3. What enforcement problems exist with regard to this legislation?

Examine the Ontario *Occupational Health and Safety Act* at www.emp.ca/dimensionsoflaw

Safety in the Workplace

According to a study published by Human Resources Development Canada in 1999, an average of just under one million Canadian workers were injured on the job each year during the five-year study period (1993 through 1997). This translates into one injury for every 16 workers per year. The same study reported that there was an average of three fatal workplace injuries per working day in 1997. Young workers—those between the ages of 15 and 24—are at a greater risk than any other group, making up one-third of all workplace injury victims. In 1998, 116 young people died on the job in Canada.

The risks that accompany employment are as varied as jobs themselves. It would be impossible for the government to attempt to regulate all workplace risks, but the goal of protecting workers is an important one. Most provincial governments have adopted the position that managing risks in the workplace is the responsibility of both the employer and the employee, and that these workplace parties must work together to make work as safe as possible. Legislation to assist the parties has been enacted in each province.

Case LONDON YOUTH KILLED ON THE JOB

R v. Corporation of the City of London
(2000), 11 MPLR (3d) 273 (Ont. CJ)

Facts

Tim Hickman worked at the Silverwood hockey arena in London, Ontario. The arena was owned and operated by the city. Hickman's job included maintenance of the Olympia ice resurfacing machine. On March 23, 1996, he was working in the arena's ice room where equipment was kept. The Olympia was parked next to the ice room hot water tank, and Hickman was filling the vehicle's own tank with hot water.

He was called away briefly to another task, and when he returned to the ice room, he heard a hissing sound coming from the Olympia's gas cap. He opened the cap, and there was a sudden and fiery explosion. He was very severely burned. He was transferred to hospital, but died a few days later as a result of burn complications.

An investigation and a trial followed, and the experts were divided about the cause of the accident. An expert from the fire marshal's office suggested that the accident was caused when hot water from the machine's tank overflowed over the gas cap, causing the gas to expand and vapours to escape. The vapours, being heavier than air, dropped to the ground where they were ignited by the low-mounted pilot light of one or both of the room's two hot water tanks. Another pair of experts, hired by the City of London, were of the view that the leaking gas could have been ignited by either the pilot lights—regardless of their height—or by another source of current, such as the ceiling fan or even Hickman himself.

Decision

The justice of the peace at the trial agreed with the fire marshal expert's evidence, and found that the city had failed to comply with the *Occupational Health and Safety Act* (OHSA) by failing to provide for the safety of its workers. It had installed the water heaters at a height of 18 inches (46 cm) above the floor instead of 4.5 feet (1 m, 37 cm) as required by the *Gas Utilization Code*. All of the city's other arenas had their heaters installed at 4.5 feet, and the city, as the issuer of building permits, was in a position to know better. The justice of the peace also found that the city had unreasonably failed to install a mechanical ventilation system (which would have helped dissipate the gasoline vapours) for the facility. He fined the city $50 000 on each of eight counts of failure to protect under the OHSA, for a total fine of $400 000.

The city appealed on a number of issues, including the amount of the fines. The appeal court considered the standard of care required under the OHSA, and found that

> the [pilot light height] regulation raises a red flag about a hazardous situation and puts the employer on notice of the hazard. Failure to comply with the regulation may well lead to the conclusion that the employer failed to take reasonable precautions to protect the worker.

The existence of this regulatory "red flag" and the existence of large warning notices on the heaters themselves made it unreasonable for the city to approve the design of the ice room. The appeal court dismissed the appeal and declined to review the amount of the fines, finding that they were in the appropriate range.

Questions

1. Summarize the facts in this case.
2. What does the term "red flag" mean?
3. What were the reasons for
   a) the original decision?
   b) the decision on appeal?
4. Do you think that a city, as issuer of building permits, should be held to a higher standard of care than another builder? Explain your answer.

Enforcement

In Ontario, the *Occupational Health and Safety Act* and the regulations made under it have been put in place with the aim of preventing accidents and reducing risks for workers. The province has created an internal responsibility system (IRS) for managing risks within workplaces. All workplace parties have a role in making this system work.

The structure and sophistication of the IRS depends on the nature of the workplace. Small workplaces need only a health and safety representative—one person who works with both management and workers to identify and protect against risks particular to that workplace. Larger (or riskier) workplaces are required to create a Joint Health and Safety Committee (JHSC). These are made up of members from both the management and worker/union sides to assess risks, plan for risk management, and investigate workplace accidents and illnesses.

Fyi A worker is killed on the job almost every day in Ontario. Each year across Canada, almost 800 workers die on the job and about 800 000 are injured.

The government's role (implemented by the Ontario Ministry of Labour) is to supervise the work of the health and safety representative or the JHSC. Government officials intervene (by carrying out inspections and resolving disputes) when help is needed or when the system fails. The government also helps by researching and maintaining data on workplace injury rates, risks, and the effects of certain dangerous chemicals and substances that may be used in the workplace. The Ministry of Labour enforces the *Occupational Health and Safety Act* by imposing fines on parties who fail to protect the safety of workers.

Injured Workers' Compensation

Governments typically create a separate system with its own legislation to compensate people who have been hurt or become sick because of conditions at the work site (and also, in many cases, their dependents or survivors). These compensation systems are publicly supervised insurance schemes funded primarily by premiums and other payments from employers who require workers to take risks on their behalf.

Workers' compensation programs generally require different levels of employer premiums for different kinds of industries, based on the risks that are part of the job and the rate of injury in the industry. Individual employers can also reduce their premiums (or their payments relating to specific workers) by performing well—that is, by protecting workers and reducing injury rates. This strategy acts as an incentive for employers to take worker safety seriously.

When a worker is injured, a claim for compensation is submitted to a provincial workers' compensation board for investigation. In Ontario, this is the Workplace Safety and Insurance Board (WSIB). The use of a board promotes fairness in compensation throughout the province, and avoids the need for workers to negotiate compensation entitlements directly with their employers after an accident has occurred. Where disputes over workers' entitlements arise, compensation boards may provide mediation services. Where board decisions are challenged, the boards typically provide an appeal process. In most cases, workers' compensation legislation takes

WORKING FOR CHANGE *Paul Kells Promotes Safety*

In 1994, Paul Kells's son, Sean, was killed on his third day of work in a factory in Brampton, Ontario. The workplace violated many municipal, provincial, and federal health and safety regulations. The teenager, with no previous training, was pouring dangerous chemicals from one container into another. An electrical spark ignited the chemicals, and Sean later died of his burns.

Paul Kells, devastated by his loss, established the Safe Communities Foundation in 1996 with the goal to improve safety wherever people live, learn, work, or play. The program of the foundation, based on an idea from the World Heath Organization, is simple. Volunteers from the community, government, and business—including public service groups, school boards, police, and fire departments—work together with the province's safety associations and a plan from the Safe Communities Foundation. The Foundation provides a grant of up to $25 000 in the first year and up to $15 000 in the second year to participating cities and towns. This "coalition" identifies and analyzes the types of injuries that are causing the most serious problems (loss of work time, health problems) and develops a "business plan" to introduce programs to reduce injuries. The goal is to reduce injury costs by 20 to 30 percent in the first year.

It took enormous personal dedication to get this idea off the ground in its early days. Paul Kells went to the Ontario and Alberta ministries of labour, the five major banks, and various resource companies for support. The banks contributed $1.5 million in the first year of operation. Kells had to balance the running of his own communications management firm in Toronto with the needs of the Foundation, which often involved speaking in local communities to promote the growth of the movement. These opportunities also meant emotional strain for Kells as he relived the experience of his son's death.

Figure 13.5
Sean Kells

The first community to become part of the Safe Communities program was Brockville, Ontario, in April 1996. So far, in that community the program has been a success. In 1997, the police force lost only 20 hours to injury. In that same year, companies reduced their injury claims by 50 percent. By 2003, 32 communities across Canada had joined the movement, with 27 more under development. Paul Kells believes "Injury is a preventable disease—an epidemic disease but a preventable one."

Questions

1. Suggest why Paul Kells focused on safety in communities as well as in the workplace.
2. Do you agree with Paul Kells's statement that "Injury is a preventable disease"? Use evidence from the feature to support your answer.
3. Locate and visit the Web site for the Safe Communities Foundation. Write a paragraph in support of or against your community's becoming part of the Foundation.

away workers' rights to sue employers directly for compensation in case of an injury, so the program also provides employers with a measure of predictability when it comes to safety-related liability.

Workers' compensation legislation and programs also play an important role in helping injured workers return to the workplace by requiring employers to reinstate workers where possible. Workers are required to return to work as soon as they are able. The boards created under this legislation often play a role in funding safety research and agencies that provide medical care to injured workers, and also safety education and training.

Check Your Understanding

1. Why is it impossible for governments to attempt to regulate all workplace risks?
2. a) How does the internal responsibility system (IRS) work?
   b) What is the government's role in enforcing the *Occupational Health and Safety Act*?
3. From what you have learned so far, why do you think workers' compensation was one of the first areas in the workplace to be regulated by governments?

Fyi In Ontario, over 50% of all WSIB claims are a result of repetitive strain injuries (RSI). RSI is an umbrella term for a number of overuse injuries affecting the soft tissues (muscles, tendons, and nerves) of the neck, upper and lower back, chest, shoulders, arms, and hands, caused by a variety of factors including repetition, force, and awkward or static postures.

Human Rights Codes

Freedom from discrimination in employment is a key human right in Canada. It is guaranteed under the *Canadian Charter of Rights and Freedoms* and, in the provincial context, under the Ontario *Human Rights Code*. As you saw in Chapter 6, the Code prohibits discrimination on the following grounds:

> ...race, ancestry, place of origin, colour, ethnic origin, citizenship, creed, sex, sexual orientation, age, record of offences, marital status, same-sex partnership status, family status or disability.

Straightforward cases of discrimination—for example, where a person is turned down for a job because the employer refuses to hire Jews—are easy to identify. However, discrimination can be more subtle. An employer seeking to avoid hiring new immigrants may require applicants to pass a written English test, even though the job may require no written communication. In some cases, discrimination may even be unintentional: the wording of an advertisement for a job may, while seeming neutral, exclude a class of applicants. For example, a community centre looking to fill an administrative position may run an ad looking for someone to "join our hip, sporty, and fun-loving team." Qualified older or disabled job hunters might be deterred from applying by the perception that they would not fit in with the job culture. Interviewers might screen out applicants whom they perceive as a poor fit without actually being aware that they are discriminating on the basis of age or disability.

The Code addresses each of these forms of discrimination in employment. It also prohibits on-the-job harassment relating to any of the grounds of discrimination previously listed, and discrimination-based limits on membership in a vocational association.

The Code provides a system through which people who feel that they have been the victims of discrimination, either in the hiring process or on the job, can bring a complaint for consideration and adjudication by the Human Rights Commission, a tribunal capable of issuing binding orders on public and private sector employers.

Turning Points in the Law

A Decade of Change for Women

Despite the key roles played by women during World War II in the workplace and in the military, the two decades after that conflict were characterized by a sharp about-face in perceptions of the role of women. Returning soldiers took over the jobs that women had held, and a traditionalist turn in public sentiment meant most women returned to roles as homemakers after 1945.

But war had irrevocably changed the world of work and the aspirations of women. What is now described as the "women's liberation movement" was born in the late 1960s, as increasing numbers of women challenged outdated expectations and entered the labour force.

This influential movement created demands for social and legal changes to ensure the equality of women and men in the workplace. In 1967

Figure 13.6 *Women assemble the tail fuselage of a bomber, 1942.*

Legislation Affecting the Status of Women, 1977–1986

1977 • Parliament adopts the *Canadian Human Rights Act*, prohibiting sexual discrimination in employment and delivery of services under federal jurisdiction; women and men must receive equal pay for the same work.
• The *Canada Labour Code* amended to provide 17 weeks of maternity leave.

1978 • The *Canada Labour Code* amended to prohibit layoff or dismissal because of pregnancy.

1982 • The *Canadian Charter of Rights and Freedoms* entrenches equality rights based on sex in the constitution (s. 15(1)).

1983 • The *Canadian Human Rights Act* prohibits sexual harassment and discrimination based on pregnancy and marital or family status.

1986 • The *Employment Equity Act*, applying to Crown corporations, federal departments, and businesses under federal jurisdiction, is adopted. It aimed to eliminate historic and systemic discrimination against women, Aboriginal peoples, persons with disabilities, and members of visible minorities.

Figure 13.7 *Timeline of legislative changes affecting the status of women, 1977–1986.*

the federal government set up the Royal Commission on the Status of Women in Canada, and its final report contained 167 recommendations for change. Some consider this Commission to have been the single most important event to advance the status of women in Canada at that time. It led to the creation of Status of Women Canada, a federal department dedicated to the improvement of gender equality and the full participation of women in social, political, and working life. In the 1970s to 1980s, an ambitious array of legislative changes was made.

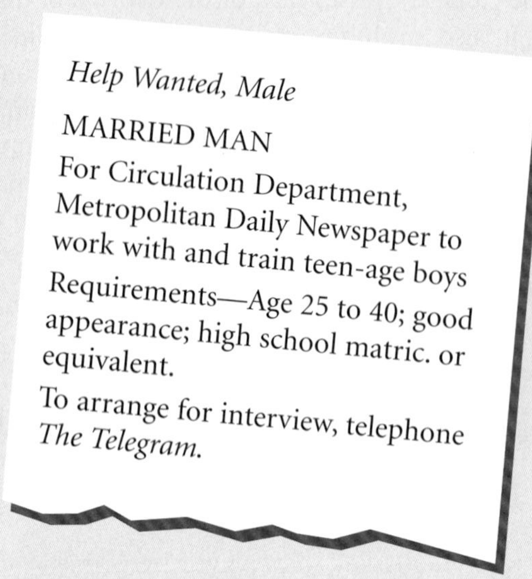

Help Wanted, Male

MARRIED MAN

For Circulation Department, Metropolitan Daily Newspaper to work with and train teen-age boys

Requirements—Age 25 to 40; good appearance; high school matric. or equivalent.

To arrange for interview, telephone *The Telegram.*

Figure 13.8 *This ad appeared in* The Toronto Telegram *on June 1, 1962. Advertisements such as this are now illegal in Canada.*

Because discrimination and systemic inequality still persist in Canada, the innovative legislation generated during this period remains vitally important to women today. The women's movement of the late 1960s and the decade that followed constituted a true turning point in the law: a time when a trend in public opinion was so universal and well focused that legal change, usually a slow and cautious process, was forced to take a sudden evolutionary leap if it was to keep pace.

Questions

1. Explain how each of the measures listed in Figure 13.7 affected the status of women in society and in the workplace.
2. Do you think these measures have significantly reduced the inequalities between men and women in the workplace? Explain your answer.

Gender Pay Equity

The issue of gender-based discrimination in employment compensation has received considerable media attention in recent years. The "gender gap" when it comes to earnings is typically expressed in the form of a percentage—a research firm may report that "women earn 78 cents to every dollar earned by men for similar work." While the gender pay gap has been steadily closing in the last three decades, women on average still earn less money than men do, even when they work in the same industry.

It is clearly illegal to pay women less money for doing exactly the same work as men. This kind of discrimination is a human rights issue and is easy to redress. The problem becomes more difficult, however, when traditional gender preferences are factored in. Although modern women are able to do exactly the same work as men with very few exceptions, workforce participation is still quite strongly segregated along gender lines. For example, administrative work, like secretarial work and filing, is much more often performed by women than by men. On the other hand, some aspects of manufacturing are very strongly male dominated.

In some workplaces, female-dominated and male-dominated jobs exist side by side. Both kinds of work contribute to the efficient operation of the business or industry, yet it is common for the male-dominated jobs to attract better pay. For example, a company may have a human resources

Figure 13.9 *Canadian annual average earnings by gender, 1992–2001 (in 2001 dollars). Suggest possible reasons why the gap in pay rates exists, and why it has been slow to change.*

Note: Data before 1996 are drawn from *Survey of Consumer Finances* (SCF) and data since 1996 are taken from the *Survey of Labour and Income Dynamics* (SLID). The surveys use different definitions; as a result, the number of people working full-year, full-time in the SLID is smaller than in the SCF.

Source: Statistics Canada, CANSIM, table 202-0102.

department (often female dominated) and also a technical support department (often male dominated). Both departments might be equally essential to the company's survival, yet the employees of the male-dominated department might earn significantly more money than those in the female-dominated department. The company may not have intended this difference. The employer may be completely free of gender discrimination in its hiring processes. Yet, the traditional compensation practices of the company and also the tendency of women and men to gravitate toward specific kinds of employment add up to what is called "systemic discrimination" in pay along gender lines. The problem is not with any specific discriminatory action, but rather with the system as a whole.

Addressing this kind of discrimination is very difficult. Ontario's answer is the *Pay Equity Act*, a complex and technical statute that requires certain employers to compare female- and male-dominated job classes in an attempt to bring company-wide compensation practices in line with the principle of pay equity or "equal pay for work of equal value."

The Law

From the Ontario *Pay Equity Act*:

Application

3(1) This Act applies to all employers in the private sector in Ontario who employ ten or more employees, all employers in the public sector, the employees of employers to whom this Act applies and to their bargaining agents, if any.

Purpose

4(1) The purpose of this Act is to redress systemic gender discrimination in compensation for work performed by employees in female job classes.

Identification of systemic gender discrimination

(2) Systemic gender discrimination in compensation shall be identified by undertaking comparisons between each female job class in an establishment and the male job classes in the establishment in terms of compensation and in terms of the value of the work performed.

Questions

1. Suggest why the *Pay Equity Act* does not apply to employers with fewer than 10 employees in the private sector. Identify some kinds of businesses that would be exempt from this Act.
2. How does the Act attempt to address the wage gap between men and women?

CHECK YOUR UNDERSTANDING

1. a) Explain what is meant by "systemic discrimination." Why is it difficult to eradicate?
   b) What is "systemic gender discrimination"? Why is this form of discrimination harder to redress?
2. According to what criteria might an organization compare "the value of work performed" by male and female job classes?
3. What difficulties exist in achieving pay equity?
4. As a group, discuss why the wage gap is persistent despite the *Pay Equity Act* and other legislation.

issue

Drug Testing in the Workplace **Should employers be allowed to conduct tests on workers to detect the presence of alcohol or drugs?**

In the United States, drug and alcohol-level testing of employees is common and, to many people, is acceptable. The most common form of drug testing involves analysis of urine samples, which employees must provide under surveillance. In Canada, the drug testing of employees is not acceptable, but some employers would like to have it adopted. How can our society ensure the safety of the workplace on the one hand and preserve the civil and human rights of workers on the other?

The following extracts explain the law and the positions of some individuals and groups on this issue.

Some research indicates that drug use leads to accidents in "high-risk" occupations such as construction work or among machine operators.

In several worksite studies, substance-abusing workers, compared with their nonabusing colleagues, are:

- Five times more likely to file a worker's compensation claim;
- 3.6 times more likely to be involved in on-the-job accidents; and
- Late for work three times as often.

—US Substance Abuse and Mental Health Services Administration (SAMHSA), Prevention Research: Injury/Disability/Workers' Compensation; www.drugfreeworkplace.gov/ResourceCenter/r115.pdf

Drug and alcohol testing ... is discriminatory and can only be used in limited circumstances. The primary reason should be to measure impairment. Even testing that measures impairment can be justified only if it is connected to the performance of the job. ... [B]y focusing on testing that actually measures impairment, especially in jobs that are safety sensitive, an appropriate balance can be struck between human rights and safety requirements... .

Section 5(1) of the Code prohibits discrimination in employment on grounds including "handicap" (...the more currently accepted term is "disability" ...). The Code adopts an expansive definition of the term "handicap" which encompasses physical, psychological and mental conditions.

—Ontario Human Rights Commission, "Policy on Drug and Alcohol Testing"

My company makes precision instruments that control hazardous materials... . If our equipment doesn't work right—people die. We can't tolerate workplace drug abuse—and we don't. But, we don't do drug-testing and we're not going to... .

We can attack workplace drug abuse with drug testing. It's quick, it's easy, and it's cheap. It just doesn't work. It gives us inaccurate and irrelevant information and undermines the trust of the good employees... . Or, we can take the time to learn about our employees, watch their job performance, and help them when it starts to slip. It's time-consuming, difficult, and expensive. But it works. Not just in preventing workplace drug abuse, but in creating a committed and productive workplace.

—Lewis Maltby, Vice-President, Drexelbrook Controls; www.ccsa.ca/wisearl3.htm

The advent of hair testing also has made pre-employment screening easier. Omega Labs ... for instance, can conduct as many as 5000 hair tests a week and averages a 24-hour turnaround. ... [T]he shaft of the hair is tested and for every 1.5 inches of hair, employers get a three-month drug history. Proponents of hair testing claim this type of test isn't easily compromised, like traditional urinalysis.

—Adena Whitman, "Pre-employment Drug Testing Pays Off," US Small Business Association, Online Women's Business Center; www.sba.gov/manage/drugtesting.html

The American Civil Liberties Union opposes indiscriminate urine testing because the process is both unfair and unnecessary. It is unfair to force workers who are not even suspected of using drugs, and whose job performance is satisfactory, to "prove" their innocence through a degrading and uncertain procedure that violates personal privacy. Such tests are unnecessary because they cannot detect impairment and, thus, in no way enhance an employer's ability to evaluate or predict job performance.

—American Civil Liberties Union, "Drug Testing in the Workplace," ACLU briefing paper; http://archive.aclu.org/library/pbp5.html

On August 28, 1991, a New York subway operator crashed his train near a station in lower Manhattan. Five people were killed and 215 others were injured. The operator admitted that he had been drinking prior to the crash. After the crash his blood alcohol content was .21, over twice the legal limit in New York.

—*US Substance Abuse and Mental Health Services Administration (SAMHSA), Employee Fact Sheet #1: "Why Have a Drug-free Workplace?"; http://workplace.samhsa.gov/WPWorkit/fs1.html*

...the push for workplace drug testing is much more driven by politics and power than by any serious belief that this is the appropriate way to deal with drug abuse. ... It is the stresses and conditions of society (which of course includes workplaces) that are the major cause of drug and alcohol abuse. ...

The fundamental problem ... is the damage that such a practice would do to our human rights and civil liberties. It would remove our privacy, destroy our dignity, and eliminate trust in our fellow workers and management. ...

—*Brian Kohler, National Representative, Health, Safety and Environment, Communications, Energy and Paperworkers of Canada*

Questions

1. What is your initial position on drug and alcohol testing by employers?
2. In your opinion, is drug and alcohol testing in the workplace a human rights issue? Why or why not?
3. Make a chart in your notebook comparing the arguments in favour of and against drug and alcohol testing.
4. Identify the best argument used by each side in the issue and explain your choice.
5. How should Canada deal with this issue in law? Explain the reasons for your position.

METHODS OF *Legal Inquiry*

Writing a Case Comment

One of the most important skills of a lawyer is the ability to examine issues critically. These skills might be directed toward a statute, a regulation, or a judicial decision. A critical analysis and evaluation of a court case is called a case comment. Case comments usually include an introduction, background information, the facts, the decision of the court, and analysis or discussion. *Scott v. Canada*, 1998 FCA 10327, is a good case for a comment.

Introduction Your introduction to the case should be informative. It should summarize the area of the law involved in the case (occupational safety) and note the issue that the case raises. In *Scott v. Canada*, the issue is whether a courier can deduct the cost of his food as a business expense. In general, the introduction should answer the question: Why is this case worth analyzing?

Background Information The background information lays the foundation for the analysis that is to follow, and provides a point of reference from which a reader can understand the implications of the case. The background should give the reader the context for your analysis and evaluation, which will be presented later in the comment.

Facts In the next section of your case comment, you summarize the "theory of the proceedings" and outline the facts of the case. The theory of the proceedings describes the cause of action or the alleged offence and the defence. Your statement of facts should be concise, accurate, and well organized. Chronological order is usually best. The theory of the proceedings and the facts will usually identify the issue raised by the case.

Decision of the Court In this section of your case comment, or at the conclusion of the Facts section, you state what happened in the case (the disposition of the case) and the reasons for the judgment. In *Scott v. Canada*, these appear under the heading Reasons for Judgment.

Analysis or Discussion The analysis or discussion is the most important part of the case comment and is also the most difficult to write. The following is a general guide to preparing an effective analysis and evaluation of a case.

Analysis

1. Identify the court's reasons for judgment. State both the majority and the dissenting (if any) opinions.
2. Describe the court's reasoning. Did it:
   a) follow, reinterpret, distinguish, or overrule an existing precedent?
   b) expand or narrow the interpretation of an act?
3. Did the court consider "extralegal" issues and factors such as: (a) policy? (b) social justice and equity? (c) moral values?

Evaluation

The evaluation or assessment of the significance of a case may include discussion of the following:

1. Your agreement (or disagreement) with the reasons of the court and the court's decision.
2. What you think the court's decision will mean for:
   a) the area of the law at issue in the case and whether the decision will affect other decisions that courts make in the future;
   b) society as a whole; and
   c) the promotion of justice.

Applying the Skill

1. What policy was the appeal court promoting in its decision in *Scott v. Canada*?
2. Write your own case comment on *Scott v. Canada*.

Reviewing Main Ideas

You Decide!

MARRIED TO A MURDERER

Saskatchewan (Human Rights Commission) v. Prince Albert Elks Club Inc. (2000), 193 DLR (4th) 549 (Sask. CA)

This case is an appeal by the Saskatchewan Human Rights Commission of the ruling, by a Board of Inquiry constituted under the *Saskatchewan Human Rights Code*, that the firing of a club manager because of her marriage to a convicted murderer did not constitute discrimination on the basis of marital status.

Facts

In June 1998, Heather Ennis, a 51-year-old woman, applied for and obtained the position of manager of the Elks Club in Prince Albert, Saskatchewan. She began work on July 15 and worked until she took three days off, beginning July 26.

On July 26, Ennis checked into the Saskatchewan penitentiary for a three-day conjugal visit with her husband of five years, David Ennis. In 1982, David Ennis had been convicted of the violent murder of his children and his children's grandparents, and was sentenced to 25 years without parole. He and Heather met through a common friend while David was incarcerated, and they were married in 1993.

When Ennis arrived at the penitentiary for her three-day visit, she was recognized by a member of the Elks Club working at the penitentiary. Inquiries on the part of the club revealed that Heather was the wife of David Ennis, a murderer. On July 29, the board of the club held a meeting that resulted in Heather's termination.

All the parties agreed that Ennis was qualified to do the job, and that during her short tenure as manager she did nothing that would provide grounds for termination for just cause. All the parties also agreed that the reason for Ennis's termination was her relationship with David Ennis.

The Law

The *Saskatchewan Human Rights Code* (the Code) has as its objects:

> s. 3(a) To promote recognition of the inherent human dignity and the equal inalienable rights of all members of the human family; and
>
> (b) To further public policy in Saskatchewan, that every person in Saskatchewan is free and equal in dignity and rights and to discourage and eliminate discrimination.

Discrimination in employment on the basis of marital status is prohibited under the Code. However, the definition of discrimination on the basis of marital status is limited by a regulation that reads as follows:

> Marital status means that state of being engaged [to be] married, married, single, separated, divorced, widowed or [living] in a common law relationship, but discrimination on the basis of a relationship with a particular person, is not discrimination based on marital status.

Case law in the area of discrimination on the basis of employment suggests that the essence of discrimination is the differential treatment of a person because of either:

- the fact of his or her status as a married or single person. For example, an employer cannot decide to hire only single people;

or

- the membership of a person's spouse in a particular class of people. For example, one case held that it was not acceptable for an employer to deny a person employment on the basis of a policy of not hiring spouses of existing employees (the person's wife was already working for the employer).

Consider the two arguments below.

Argument of the Saskatchewan Human Rights Commission (Appellant)

The Human Rights Commission argued that firing a competent and qualified employee on the basis of her marriage was unreasonable, and that this action fell within the definition of discrimination based on marital status—the firing had nothing to do with Ennis's qualifications or performance, and would not have been done had she not been married.

The Commission relied on a case in which the CBC's firing of an employee based on her marriage to a prominent local figure was overturned. In that case, the employer alleged that the employee's connection to the named individual affected the "perceived objectivity" of her reporting. The court held that this reason was not significant enough to excuse discrimination on the basis of marital status. (Note, however, that this case was decided under federal legislation that does not limit the definition of marital status discrimination in the way the Saskatchewan law does.)

Argument of the Elks Club (Respondent)

In coming to their decision to fire Heather Ennis, members of the club's board were motivated by two concerns: that her association with her husband posed a "security risk" for members in that confidential communications between members might be overheard by Heather and communicated to David, placing the members at risk. The second concern related to the fact that some members might be offended by the club's employment of a person who was married to a convicted murderer.

The club contended that it was not the fact that Ennis was married that mattered, rather the identity of the person she was married to, and they contended that the nature of the relationship—whether marital or otherwise—would have made no difference to their decision.

Make Your Decision

1. What were the facts in this case?
2. Explain how the *Saskatchewan Human Rights Code* limits the definition of discrimination with respect to marital status.
3. Summarize the key points made by both sides in the case.
4. Dismiss or allow the appeal. Provide reasons for your decision.

Key Terms

Review the following terms to show that you understand the meaning of each and how it is applied in a legal context.

inalienable
unconscionable

Understanding the Law

Review the following pieces of legislation mentioned in the text, and show that you understand the intent of each:

Canada Labour Code
Employment Equity Act
Ontario *Employment Standards Act*
Ontario *Industrial Standards Act*
Ontario *Occupational Health and Safety Act*
Ontario *Pay Equity Act*
Ontario *Workplace Safety and Insurance Act*

Thinking and Inquiry

1. With a partner or in a small group, interview someone who joined the workforce between 1950 and 1965 to gain his or her perspective on changes in working conditions over that person's lifetime. Present your findings in an oral report or video.
2. How would the present current employment standards legislation in Ontario improve the working conditions of men such as the one described in the Personal Viewpoint feature on page 387? Your answer may be in chart form.
3. The Ontario *Human Rights Code* prohibits discrimination on the basis of age, yet many workers are required to resign from their jobs at age 65. What arguments would you use to support the mandatory retirement rule? to argue against this ruling?
4. Read the employment advertisements in your local paper, and decide if any of these are in any way discriminatory based on the *Canada Human Rights Act* or the Ontario *Human Rights Code*. Justify your findings.

Communication

5. Investigate a recent case of youth injury in the workplace (see the Web site of the Safe Communities Foundation). Summarize the circumstances of the accident and suggest how it could have been avoided. Present your findings to the class.
6. Survey students who are employed to obtain their opinions on safety in the workplace. What recommendations do these students have to improve workplace safety?
7. Use the Statistics Canada Web site or another source to locate a table relating to labour conditions in Canada. Convert this information into graphic form to post in the classroom. Identify and comment on the trends shown in the graph.

Application

8. Research the changes to the Ontario *Employment Standards Act* made in 2001 regarding working hours and vacations. Whom do you think these changes benefited—employers or employees? Explain your answer.
9. Locate a cartoon that comments on a problem in the Canadian workplace today. Explain the cartoon using the analysis questions on page 385 as a guide. Do you agree with the cartoonist's view? Explain your answer.
10. Use resources such as the Internet, television, newspapers, and news magazines to find information on a recent issue that affects the workplace, either in your local area or in the province. Outline the issue and record at least two different viewpoints on it. Then state your own opinion on the issue, and explain how you think it should be resolved.

Organizing the Workforce

CHAPTER *Focus*

In this chapter, you will

- explain the history of labour relations in Canada
- investigate labour relations legislation in Ontario as it affects employer–union relationships
- understand how collective agreements are negotiated
- analyze contemporary challenges faced by unions

Labour unions in Canada have a rich history of organizing people in the workplace in order to protect their rights. This chapter studies the role that unions have played in fighting for and protecting the rights of workers. The relationship between unions and their members, and the relationship of both to the employer, will be studied through the examination of collective bargaining, labour sanctions, and the resolution of labour disputes. Because organizing the workplace depends on supporting labour legislation, this topic also will be examined.

Figure 14.1

At First Glance

1. Whom in the labour process does the character in the cartoon represent?
2. What does the cartoonist imply is the significance of a union contract in regulating employer–worker relationships?
3. Do you think that employers should have the right to dismiss employees whenever they wish? Explain your answer.

Emergence of Trade Unions

In the early 19th century, skilled craftspeople worked out of small shops, making consumer items such as boots and shoes or providing services such as blacksmithing. With industrialization and the introduction of the factory system in the mid-19th century, machines increasingly replaced skilled workers. The working conditions described in the previous chapter were typical in Canada. Under the common law that governed the relationship between masters (employers) and servants (workers), most workers had to accept an employer's conditions for work, or starve (see Figure 14.2 on the next page). There were always others more desperate for a wage who were prepared to take the job. This trend led skilled workers to try to protect their jobs, working conditions, and wages by forming **trade unions** that could bargain collectively with employers. Earlier trade associations of workers had provided members with such benefits as assisting the family if a worker were injured, but these groups had not acted as bargaining units with employers.

trade union: a group of workers who form an organization to bargain collectively with employers to improve working conditions, benefits, and wages

adversarial: a relationship in which the parties have clearly opposing interests and positions

strike: withdrawal of labour by workers during negotiations for a contract, a tactic designed to pressure employers to reach a new agreement

collective bargaining: a process in which individual workers in a union negotiate a contract between the union and the employer covering their wages, hours of work, and working conditions

Labour relations in Canada have tended to be **adversarial** in nature. From the beginning, employers resisted unionization of their workforce because it cut down on employers' freedom to manage their companies and treat employees as they saw fit. An individual employee usually does not have equal bargaining power with employers, who are much happier negotiating when they hold the stronger bargaining position. It is not surprising that employers opposed trade unions acting as bargaining agents.

The main tool that union workers could use to force employers to accede to their demands was to withdraw their labour, or go on **strike**. Employers argued in response that, under common law, **collective bargaining** restrained trade, that is, it limited the ability of the business to compete. They argued that individual workers and employers should be free to negotiate their own contracts in an open market, without interference by others. This argument meant that collective bargaining was a criminal offence—under the *Criminal Code*, it was an illegal conspiracy in restraint of trade. The result of this thinking was often legal prosecution and

Figure 14.2

Common Law Governing the Relationship Between Masters and Servants

- An employment contract was made between a master (employer) and a servant (worker) by which the servant agreed to serve the master in return for a wage.
- The servant agreed to submit to the direction of a master and carry out the master's orders in return for this wage.
- The servant did not share in the profits, own the tools used in the work, direct the work, or exercise independent judgment on how the work was to be done.
- The master could regulate the servant's behaviour and morality outside the workplace.
- If the servant harmed a third party in the course of the employment, the master was liable for the servant's acts.
- The servant could not sue the master if injured on the job, unless the injury was solely the fault of the master.
- The terms of an employment contract could include a specific purpose or period of time or an unspecified period (called a contract of indefinite duration).
- A servant ending an employment contract had to provide reasonable notice of intention to do so, so that he or she could be replaced. A servant who left without giving notice or who quit earlier than the agreed-upon time could be prosecuted by the master.

imprisonment for trade union members, dissolution of their workers' organizations, and loss of their jobs. Nevertheless, trade unions continued to grow in the 1860s in Canada. These small local unions, which were often affiliated with American unions, consisted mainly of skilled craft workers.

Learn more about Canada's labour history at www.emp.ca/dimensionsoflaw

Workers Struggle to Establish Unions

In the 1870s, the first efforts were made to establish a national organization of workers. A movement to limit work to nine hours a day (a 54-hour workweek) was formed in Hamilton, Ontario, and supported by unions in other cities. A strike in 1872 by typographic workers at the Toronto newspaper, *The Globe*, was successful in gaining a 54-hour workweek. The federal government then passed the *Trades Union Act*, which nullified conspiracy charges specified under the *Criminal Code* for union negotiators. However, to register as a trade union, members had to agree to be liable for any damage to the employer's property caused by union members during a strike. Few registered. There were still no laws to force employers to bargain collectively with unions. Union supporters could be fired, or employers could refuse to hire them.

Union membership fluctuated with the upswings and recessions in the economy. In times of recession, as in 1873 and 1893, membership declined because workers could not survive without work. The only legislation that was passed, following a Royal Commission inquiry in 1886 into appalling working conditions across the country, was the establishment of Labour Day, an official holiday for workers. The federal and provincial governments favoured employers and their actions, often calling out the militia and police forces to act against workers during strikes. Nevertheless, the number of strikes increased in the 1890s.

By 1907, strikes were a serious problem. The federal government passed the *Industrial Disputes Investigation Act*, which prohibited strikes in public utilities and mines until the dispute had been investigated by a party of three that consisted of one representative of the workers, one of the company, and a federal representative, who usually sided with the company. This meant in effect that workers could not strike. This Act was not declared unconstitutional until 1925.

Canadian Illustrated News

Vol. V.—No. 23. MONTREAL, SATURDAY, JUNE 8, 1872. SINGLE COPIES, TEN CENTS. $4 PER YEAR IN ADVANCE.

HAMILTON.—PROCESSION OF NINE-HOUR MOVEMENT MEN.—From a photograph.

Figure 14.3 *An artist's impression of the protest march held by workers in Hamilton, Ontario, on May 15, 1872, for a nine-hour workday*

The Winnipeg General Strike

The Winnipeg General Strike of 1919 is considered one of the most significant events in the labour movement in Canada, not because of its outcome but because of the demonstration of worker solidarity.

World War I had ended in 1918, and soldiers returning to Canada were unwilling to accept the low wages and long hours of work that prevailed before the war. In March 1919, there was a movement in Western Canada to form One Big Union (OBU). The organizers of this union wanted to unite all workers, skilled and unskilled, from all industries into one labour union. At the time, unions in Canada were organized by skill and trade. A main focus of this movement was the acceptance of the necessity for a general strike of all workers to obtain fair wages, the right to collective bargaining, and the right to safe workplaces. The OBU was widely opposed by employers, who accused the organization of being influenced by the Bolshevik or Communist Revolution of 1917 in Russia.

On May 15, 1919, in Winnipeg—at the time, Canada's third largest city—over 30 000 workers in both the private and public sectors walked off their jobs in support of fellow workers in the building and metal trades. The employers of these workers had refused to negotiate with their chosen representatives. In retaliation, the Winnipeg Trades and Labour Council called for a general strike. The situation rapidly deteriorated as tension grew on both sides of the dispute.

Figure 14.4 *Mounted police scatter protesters, Winnipeg, June 21, 1919.*

Fyi Police in Winnipeg were fired when they supported the strikers, and were replaced by untrained "special constables" who were paid more than the regular police. Some historians believe the violence during the strike was partially a result of the inability of the untrained "specials" to manage crowd control.

On June 17, the federal government ordered the arrest of 10 labour leaders who were part of the Central Strike Committee, which had organized to direct the strike and run some essential services in the city. Earlier in the month the mayor had banned all protest marches and demonstrations, but with the arrests, people took to the streets. On June 21, as police moved in to break up a parade of strikers, two people were killed and 30 were injured in a violent clash, a day now known as "Bloody Saturday." On June 25, six weeks after it began, the strike ended. The protesting workers failed to win any concessions on any of the principles for which they had fought. Seven of the arrested strike leaders were convicted and sentenced to jail terms ranging from six months to two years.

On many counts, the Winnipeg General Strike was a failure. One thing that was achieved, however, was recognition of a labour movement and the need for labour law reform. Voters realized that law reform was one of the best ways to bring about change. In 1920, four of the arrested strike leaders were elected to the Manitoba legislature. J.S. Woodsworth, a key leader of the strike, went on to be elected to Parliament, and in 1933 led the formation of the Co-operative Commonwealth Federation (CCF), which in 1961 became the New Democratic Party.

Trade Unions Recognized

After the lean years of the Great Depression of the 1930s, the need for factory workers and soldiers during World War II resulted in a labour shortage. Over 400 strikes occurred in 1943 in the face of wage controls and labour unrest.

In 1943, the first steps were taken to get management to recognize unions and undertake collective bargaining. Ontario passed the *Collective Bargaining Act*, which set up a means to allow employers and unions to

Personal Viewpoint

Organizing Ontario Miners in the 1930s

Ray Stevenson was a miner and union organizer in northern Ontario and Quebec for the Mine, Mill and Smelter Workers Union in the 1930s. Later, he joined the national executive board of the union. Here he describes working conditions in the mines and efforts in 1931 to organize the 8000 workers at the International Nickel Company in Sudbury.

> One of the jobs that I had was called "mucking in the drift." This was with shovels. You'd approach a 30- or 35-ton pile of broken rock with a little car on rails. You shovelled that rock into that little car, then you pushed the car as far as you had to, dumped it and brought it back. Two of you would manhandle 35 or 40 tons a day. You were in a constant state of near exhaustion, sweat, stripped-down. ...
>
> We kept working at trying to build the union. At an organizational level it meant seeking out those people in the workforce that you were with in each mine to get them to sign membership cards and agree to pay one dollar a month dues. ... But the main thing that had to be beaten was the fear—fear of reprisal by the company, fear of being fired, fear of not being able to provide for families. That was the essential thing. And from that point of view the people that we'd meet underground, or get out in a corner somewhere outside of the mine property to talk about the union, would be the most active and developed core. The idea was that if we got them organized there were a lot of other people who would follow them. We had to get into a position of challenging the absolute rights the company had. And in order to do that we had to bring these people together.
>
> The various companies were very well organized [in their attempts to quash union activity]. ...
>
> Many and many a fired worker changed his name and went to another place to get a job. But very efficient lists of "undesirables" were kept by all the companies and later there was some kind of centralized information that the companies shared with each other. ...
>
> There's no question that the blacklist thing operated and workers knew it. Companies didn't even go to too much trouble to hide it. They wanted workers to know they were being watched.

Source: Adapted from Gloria Montero, *We Stood Together: First-hand Accounts of Dramatic Events in Canada's Labour Past*. Toronto: James Lorimer & Company, 1979, pp. 72–73.

Questions

1. What difficulties did workers face when they signed up to join a union?
2. How did the positive aspects of joining a miners' union outweigh the risks?
3. Why did some workers, despite the working conditions they faced, refuse to join the union?
4. Research to find what laws exist today to protect workers in dangerous workplaces, such as mines.

Figure 14.5 *Miners in Kirkland Lake, Ontario, 1940s.*

bargain collectively. Disputes between the two groups were to be settled by the Ontario Labour Court, which was attached to the Supreme Court of Ontario. In 1944, the federal Cabinet passed Order-in-Council *PC 1003*, which has been described as the "Magna Carta" of the union movement because it finally abolished the common-law doctrines of conspiracy and restraint of trade regarding trade unions.

After the war ended, unions continued to strengthen their position. They worked for three main aims: wage increases for workers, industry-wide bargaining, and union security. Industry-wide bargaining aimed to have all workers within an industry work for similar wages under standard conditions, such as safety rules. Union security required that companies recognize unions where the majority of workers wanted a union. Unions wanted union dues to be automatically taken off paycheques, a system known as check-off. They also wanted compulsory union membership for all workers where the majority of workers wanted a union.

Turning Points in the Law

PC 1003: Trade Unions Recognized as Bargaining Agents

With an increasing number of strikes and rising labour discontent in the early 1940s, the federal government moved quickly to try to prevent further work stoppages across Canada. The federal Cabinet asked the governor general to sign into law the *Emergency Measure PC* (Privy Council) *1003*. *PC 1003* protected the right of workers to organize, and also required that all employers recognize unions chosen by the majority of workers in their place of employment. Until the passage of this emergency order, there were no laws in Canada that officially protected a union's right to engage in collective bargaining. In the United States, such legislation had already existed for almost 10 years with the passage of the *National Labor Relations Act (1935)*, otherwise known as the *Wagner Act*.

PC 1003 now formed part of the new *Wartime Labour Code*, which was drafted with the aim of preventing further labour unrest across Canada. The Code allowed for a process of conciliation should a contract agreement not be reached between the union and management.

With the enactment of *PC 1003*, unions began negotiating contracts across Canada. This law is seen as the turning point in labour law because it compelled employers to bargain with unions. The new labour law, which applied to all federal and provincial sectors, was seen as a major victory for unions and organized labour.

Questions

1. How was the status of trade unions affected by the passage of *PC 1003*? Explain your answer.
2. While *PC 1003* granted unions official status at the bargaining table, the law did not necessarily require that the employer bargain in good faith, that is, fully intend to make a collective agreement. Why did the lack of this requirement remain a concern for organized labour?
3. What do you think employer reaction was to *PC 1003*? Explain your answer.

The issue of union security came to a head in 1945 with a 100-day strike at the Ford Motor Company plant in Windsor, Ontario. The union wanted the check-off system in place and the compulsory union-membership system that had been accepted in Ford plants in the United States. For 16 months before the strike, union officials negotiated within the existing legal framework, without success. The strikers created a blockade of cars and trucks around the Ford plant and throughout the downtown streets of Windsor, virtually shutting down the city. There was widespread support for the strike, with sympathizers in Canada and the United States sending money to the workers. Attempts by governments to use force to end the strike merely increased support, and the possibility of a general strike loomed.

Figure 14.6 *Hundreds of cars and buses line the streets in front of the Ford Motor Company of Canada, as 20 000 workers blockade the company in sympathy with the eight-week-old strike by Ford employees, November 1945.*

On December 13, 1945, the union and the company agreed to accept **binding arbitration**. The federal government appointed Mr. Justice Ivan Rand of the Supreme Court of Canada to hear both sides of the dispute and render a decision. Rand interviewed all the parties concerned and then gave his ruling, now known as the **Rand formula**, on January 29, 1946:

> I doubt if any circumstance provokes more resentment in a plant than this sharing of the fruits of unionist work and courage by the non-union member. ... The company in this case admits that substantial benefits for the employees have been obtained by the union, some in negotiation and some over the opposition of the company. ... I consider it entirely equitable then that all employees should be required to shoulder their portion of the burden of expense for administering the law of their employment, the union contract; that they must take the burden along with the benefit.

Rand recommended compulsory dues check-off, regardless of whether a worker was a member of the union, arguing that all members benefited from the gains made by unions. In return, unions undertook not to strike while a collective agreement was in place. In the event of an illegal or **wildcat strike**, individual workers could be fined and the union could lose its check-off privileges.

Figure 14.7 (on the next page) lists some of the significant dates in the Canadian labour movement.

binding arbitration: a process in which a neutral third party, the arbitrator, hears from union and management representatives and makes a final decision that both sides must accept

Rand formula: the requirement that, in a bargaining unit in which the majority vote to join a union, all members must pay union dues whether or not they join the union

wildcat strike: an illegal strike that occurs while a collective agreement is still in force

Significant Dates in the Canadian Labour Movement	
1872	• *Trades Union Act* introduced, making it legal for workers to organize.
1886	• Trades and Labour Congress (TLC), a group of craft unions, founded.
1894	• Labour Day is made a national holiday.
1900	• Department of Labour established.
1907	• *Industrial Disputes Investigation Act* passed to aid in the prevention and settlement of strikes and lockouts in mines and industries connected with public utilities.
1919	• Winnipeg General Strike occurs.
1940	• Canadian Congress of Labour (CCL) founded.
1944	• *Privy Council Order 1003* (*PC 1003*) enacted by Cabinet.
1945	• Ford Motor strike results in the Rand formula.
1948	• *Industrial Relations and Disputes Investigations Act* establishes collective bargaining rights. Workers are protected against intimidation during union drives.
1955/ 1956	• TLC and CCL merge to form the Canadian Labour Congress (CLC).

Figure 14.7

Check Your Understanding

1. In the early stages of the labour movement, management made every effort to resist the formation of unions in their workplace. What was their motivation for this resistance?
2. What rights were workers fighting for in the early 1940s?
3. Why was it difficult for workers to organize into unions prior to *PC 1003*?
4. Do you agree with Mr. Justice Rand's decision and the explanation he offered in support of his ruling? Explain your answer.
5. Why is mandatory check-off of union dues essential for any union to exist?

Labour Relations Legislation

A trade union is a legal entity with rights and duties that are set out in the union's own constitution and bylaws, and in various statutes. The bargaining relationship between unions and their members, and between unions and employers, is regulated by labour relations legislation.

Learn more about the activities of the CAW at www.emp.ca/dimensionsoflaw

Most employers and about 90 percent of employees in Canada fall under the jurisdiction of provincial labour legislation. In Ontario, the principal statute is the *Labour Relations Act.* For industries or workplaces that are federally regulated, such as banking, transportation and communications, and First Nations' activities, the principal statute is the *Canada Labour Code.* In Ontario, the Ontario Labour Relations Board (OLRB) acts

WORKING FOR CHANGE *A Union Works for Social Change*

The Canadian Auto Workers (CAW) represents 250 000 workers in a wide range of industries, not just the automobile industry. From the beginning, the CAW has had a wider agenda than business unionism (unionism that is concerned only with traditional labour concerns, such as wage rates). The CAW has supported social unionism (unionism that is sensitive to broader concerns and the public interest) both locally and internationally.

The CAW's longstanding commitment to social unionism has resulted in a significant number of initiatives in the campaigns and issues that it has supported. The union has been involved with organizations that work for cancer prevention, blood banks, the eradication of child labour, preservation of universal health care, solutions for homelessness, and justice for the wrongfully convicted. The CAW annually supports women's shelters across Canada, and on International Women's Day, March 8, 2003, it donated $90 000 in support of 45 women's shelters across Canada.

CAW–Canada has made child care and support for working parents a key issue on the bargaining agenda. It has successfully negotiated paid time off for pregnancy and parental leaves in many workplaces. It has also recognized the need to create childcare spaces. In 1989, the CAW childcare centre opened in Windsor, Ontario, and in 1997 a second centre opened in Oshawa. "Child care is a right for all children of working parents," says CAW president Buzz Hargrove.

The CAW is committed to helping solve the problem of teenagers living on the streets and providing social housing and adequate women's shelters, as well as donating money to food banks across Canada. In September 2002, the CAW committed $50 000 to renovate a once-abandoned building in downtown Toronto and turn it into affordable housing as part of a solution to the crisis of homelessness.

Figure 14.8 *When asked what makes the CAW different from other unions, President Buzz Hargrove responded: "The CAW has a proud commitment to the overall social agenda. While some unions take on a cause, we see the need as much broader than that."*

The process of deciding which causes and issues the CAW should support is dealt with through its democratic structure. The CAW Council of Presidents, made up of presidents of union locals, submits proposals to the National Executive Board, which then decides. The CAW budget for social justice is substantial, at around $3 million per year.

Questions

1. In your own words, explain the difference between business unionism and social unionism.
2. What reasons can you give to explain the CAW's support for child care?
3. Do you believe all unions should have a broader "social agenda" similar to that of the CAW? Why or why not?
4. Locate and visit the CAW Web site and summarize some of the campaigns and issues with which it is presently involved.

certification: an order giving a union the right to negotiate for a collective agreement regulating wages and working conditions for employees

as an adjudicator in interpreting the various statutes covering labour relations, particularly the **certification** of trade unions. The OLRB is an independent tribunal.

Ontario's *Labour Relations Act*

Ontario has had an act governing labour relations for several decades. The main provisions of the most recent version, the *Labour Relations Act, 1995*, include regulations for a union to be certified as the bargaining agent for a group of workers, procedures for the negotiation of collective agreements, items that can be included in a collective agreement, guidelines for the operation of collective agreements, unfair practices by employers and employees, and regulations regarding work stoppages.

The Law

From the Ontario *Labour Relations Act, 1995*, SO 1995, c. 1, Schedule A:

2. The following are the purposes of the Act:
   1. To facilitate collective bargaining between employers and trade unions that are the freely-designated representatives of the employees.
   2. To recognize the importance of workplace parties adapting to change.
   3. To promote flexibility, productivity and employee involvement in the workplace.
   4. To encourage communication between employers and employees in the workplace.
   5. To recognize the importance of economic growth as the foundation for mutually beneficial relations amongst employers, employees and trade unions.
   6. To encourage co-operative participation of employers and trade unions in resolving workplace issues.
   7. To promote the expeditious resolution of workplace disputes.

Questions

1. What is meant in s. 2(1) by "freely-designated" representatives of the employees? How are these individuals selected?
2. How does "communication" (s. 2(4)) take place between employers and unions?
3. Name the purposes that stress general economic aims.
4. What kinds of "changes" (s. 2(2)) might legislators have been considering?

Certification of Unions

A trade union has to be certified by the Ontario Labour Relations Board before it can act as the bargaining unit for a group of employees. To become certified, the union must demonstrate to the OLRB that at least 40 percent of employees are members of the union. Fifty percent or more of the employees eligible to belong to the bargaining unit must support the union in a vote held by the Board. After certification, an employer cannot ignore the union by trying to settle contract matters directly with the employee.

To find out more about certification, read the *Labour Relations Act, 1995* at www.emp.ca/dimensionsoflaw

Case WORKER INTIMIDATION?

International Brotherhood of Painters and Allied Trades, Union Local 1891 v. Domus Industries Ltd., [1994] OLRB Rep. December 1630

Facts

The applicant union attempted to organize employees of the respondent by having an organizer visit the work site and attempt to persuade employees to join the union by signing union cards. If 55 percent were signed up, the union could apply to the Ontario Labour Relations Board to represent these workers in a bargaining unit. On discovering that some employees had signed up, the foreman dismissed those employees for the rest of the day, effectively laying them off. Many employees then called the union and attempted to withdraw or cancel their signed cards. Others signed a petition asking for their cards to be withdrawn. The foreman drew up the petition.

Issues

Did the actions of the foreman constitute unfair labour practices and violate provisions of the Ontario *Labour Relations Act, 1995*? If the company did violate the Act, did the violations make it unlikely that the Board would determine the true wishes of the workers regarding certification?

Decision

The Board found that the foreman's decision to lay the workers off after some of them had signed union cards in the certification drive, together with his participation in the petition to withdraw some of the signed cards, constituted an interference with the selection of the union. In the words of the Board's ruling:

> Having regard to all of the evidence before us, we are of the view that the employer committed numerous unfair labour practices contrary to the ... Act. These breaches of the Act were entirely the result of the conduct of [the foreman] ... who acts on behalf of the employer.

The Board also went on to find that the contraventions of the Act by the employer meant that the "true wishes of the employees are not likely to be ascertained." As a consequence, the Board ordered the immediate certification of the union as the bargaining agent for these employees.

Questions

1. Do you agree with the Board's ruling in this case? Explain.
2. Why might an employer not want a union in the workplace?
3. What other forms of intimidation do you think an employer might use to stop the certification of a union?

conciliation: an attempt to settle a contract dispute with the help of a government-appointed officer who meets with the parties during negotiations; this process is required prior to a union strike or a lock-out by an employer

mediation: a voluntary process that may follow conciliation, in which a third party attempts to help the parties reach an agreement before or during a strike or lock-out

bargain in good faith: negotiate with the honest intention of reaching a collective agreement

lock-out: an action in which an employer locks employees out of the workplace to pressure them to reach agreement on a new contract

scab: a derogatory term used to describe a worker hired as a temporary replacement during a strike or lock-out

Collective Bargaining

Once a union has been certified, it must negotiate a first contract with the employer on behalf of the bargaining unit. The contract covers wages, hours of work, and working conditions. It may also include pension and insurance benefits. This contract is in force for two years from the time it is negotiated. If the parties reach an impasse in which neither can convince the other of the merits of their respective cases, the contract negotiation process may become stalled. In most jurisdictions, and in Ontario under the *Labour Relations Act, 1995*, there are provisions to break the logjam and help the parties reach an agreement by using **conciliation** and **mediation**.

Section 17 of the *Labour Relations Act, 1995* says that the parties are required to **bargain in good faith** and make every effort to reach a collective agreement. If negotiations become stalled, either party can ask the Ministry of Labour to appoint a conciliator who is neutral but experienced in labour relations. The conciliator's role is to meet with the parties, identify issues on which they cannot agree, and help them find agreement. If the conciliator is unable to get the parties to agree, the minister of labour appoints one conciliator to represent the views of the unions involved and one to represent the views of the employer. Where agreement cannot be reached, the OLRB can act as arbitrator for the first collective agreement. If conciliation is unsuccessful and negotiations reach an impasse, the parties are free after 14 days to go on strike or resort to a lock-out.

Strikes and Lock-outs

Both the union and the employer can use economic sanctions as part of their bargaining strategy to pressure the other side to make a collective agreement. For the workers, the sanction is a strike. For the employer, the sanction is a **lock-out**. Strikes and lock-outs are prohibited during the life of an agreement.

In Ontario during a strike or lock-out, employers are free to hire replacement workers and attempt to carry on business. Unions call these workers **scabs**. The province of Quebec has outlawed the use of replacement workers since 1977, and so has the federal government in the *Canada*

Some Terms Used in Collective Agreements

Fringe benefits: Non-wage benefits such as paid vacations, pensions, health and welfare provisions, and life insurance, the cost of which is borne in whole or in part by the employer

Check-off: A clause in a collective agreement authorizing an employer to deduct union dues and ensuring that these funds are transmitted to the union

Bargaining unit: Group of workers designated by a labour relations board as appropriate for representation by a union for purposes of collective bargaining

Seniority: The term used to designate an employee's status relative to other employees to determine the order of layoffs, promotions, recalls, transfers, and vacations. Seniority can be based on length of service alone or other factors such as ability, needs of the employer, and union duties

Working conditions: Conditions pertaining to workers' job environment, such as hours of work, safety, paid holidays and vacations, rest periods, free clothing or uniforms, and possibilities of advancement

Shift: The stated daily working period for a group of employees

Premium pay: A wage rate higher than straight time, payable for overtime work, work on holidays, or scheduled days off, or for work under extraordinary conditions, such as dangerous, dirty, or unpleasant work

Cost-of-living allowance (COLA): Periodic pay increases based on changes in the Consumer Price Index (CPI) or inflation

Figure 14.9

Labour Code. The New Democratic Party government in Ontario also outlawed the practice for a few years in the early 1990s; the Progressive Conservatives restored it when they came to power in 1995.

The arguments in favour of preventing the use of replacement workers centre on the fact that the practice is a major irritant in the bargaining process. It creates more tension on picket lines as unions try to make it difficult for replacement workers to get in or out of a plant. Employers may feel that, if the plant can be kept running and they continue to earn profits, they can put further pressure on the union to settle, as the striking workers receive only strike pay from their union. Once a contract is reached, the unionized workers return to work and the replacement workers are let go.

The use of replacement workers may increase the bitterness and hostility of the union and its members toward the employer, making them less cooperative and post-settlement labour relations more difficult. Many employers avoid using replacement workers, even though they are legally permitted to use them, in the interest of maintaining cooperative and positive labour relations over the long term. Also, it is often difficult to find skilled replacement workers and both time-consuming and expensive to train them to a point at which they can operate efficiently.

issue

Public Service Strikes Should workers in essential services be allowed to strike?

The right to strike is a powerful tool for workers in their negotiations with employers. Without the threat of a strike, many employers would not feel pressed to negotiate a collective agreement at all, let alone one that confers benefits on employees. Certain workers are considered to be so essential to society that they are not allowed to engage in strikes as part of the negotiation process. Firefighters and police officers, for example, are prohibited from striking. But there are no clear criteria for determining who is "essential." Ambulance personnel may not strike, but doctors may—and have in Quebec, Newfoundland, and British Columbia. Are doctors less essential than ambulance paramedics, or do they simply have more political influence?

Where essential workers are barred from striking, governments by way of a compromise have often introduced binding arbitration as a means of solving the problem. An arbitrator hears the submissions of the union and the employer and decides the terms of the collective agreement. Otherwise, if an impasse is reached in negotiations, governments may use "back-to-work" legislation to order striking workers to return to their jobs.

The following extracts give the viewpoints of some individuals and groups on this issue.

> When we talk about how essential it is to have ambulance services, if there is someone in need, if there's a pregnant woman who needs to get to the hospital and calls an ambulance, it's essential that that woman be able to get an ambulance. Someone who has a heart attack and calls an ambulance—that's essential. It needs to be there for the people of Ontario.
>
> —*Tina Molinari, MPP, supporting the* Ambulance Services Collective Bargaining Act, 2001, *which designated ambulance services operated within municipalities as essential and removed the right of workers in the service to strike, June 12, 2001*

> Any time you legislate people back to work who aren't essential people by any stretch, then you're destroying collective bargaining. I'm not one who wants to do that.
>
> —*Morley Kells, Ontario Progressive Conservative backbencher, commenting on back-to-work legislation introduced in the Ontario legislature to end the Toronto strike by 24 000 striking workers in the waste-management service industry, July 9, 2002*

> Our government believes that collective bargaining is the best mechanism to resolve this situation. However, given the seriousness of the situation, the concerns raised, and the advice provided by the chief

medical officer of health ... we felt it was necessary to take the appropriate action in order to protect the health and safety of the residents and visitors of Toronto.

—Ontario Premier Ernie Eves on introducing back-to-work legislation to end the Toronto garbage strike in July 2002

We cannot treat people poorly—freeze their wages, increase workloads, refuse to bargain, and ... create the most stressful workplaces—and then claim they are essential. Either the work of public employees is unimportant, and thus cannot be labeled "essential"; or their work is vital, in which case they should be treated and remunerated on a scale that properly reflects their importance to a healthy and caring society—thereby eliminating the need to strike. Take your pick, but we cannot have it both ways. ... When the withdrawal of a service threatens life and limb, some restriction on strike activity is justified. But when it is merely inconvenient, or even temporarily costly, then superseding the right to strike represents a major blow to a fundamental democratic principle.

—Seth Klein, Director, BC Office of the Canadian Centre for Policy Alternatives, "Balancing Two Essentials—Public Services and the Right to Strike," http://www.policyalternatives.ca/bc/opinion43.html

Our position is the same as that of the United Nations: essential services protect life and limb. While education is vital and important, it's not an essential service.

—David Chudnovsky, President, BC Teachers' Federation, in a joint news release by the British Columbia Nurses' Union, British Columbia Teachers' Federation, and Canadian Union of Public Employees, BC Division, November 23, 2001

Last night [April 9] the OPSEU [Ontario Public Service Employees Union] turned down a government offer to re-open eight provincial schools for Deaf, Blind, Deafblind, and Learning Disabled Students. Hon. Minister [David] Tsubouchi, Chair of Management Board Secretariat states, "A week ago we asked OPSEU to declare these workers essential so that the provincial schools could reopen and families could get their children back into the classrooms. The union has rejected their (government) offer. As a result the schools will remain closed."

The Ontario Association of the Deaf is deeply concerned ... with the strike which is in its fifth week. This is jeopardizing students' lives. Students have stated they will not be able to attend college/university in the Fall because of the strike.

—Ontario Association of the Deaf, press release, April 10, 2002

Questions

1. Do you agree with legislation prohibiting workers employed in essential services from striking? Make a chart that summarizes arguments for and against such legislation.
2. If you could recommend a list of services to label "essential," which would you recommend?
3. If the right of workers to strike is removed, what other possibilities exist for them to show their frustration with the collective bargaining process?
4. If workers in essential services are not allowed to strike, what could motivate an employer to "bargain in good faith" and reach a fair collective agreement?

How frequently do strikes occur? There are more work stoppages in Canada than there are in many European countries, except for Italy. But 95 percent of all negotiated collective agreements are achieved without either side resorting to work stoppages.

It is illegal for workers to strike or for employers to lock out employees during the life of a collective agreement. But occasionally a workplace incident—for example, the firing of a popular union activist—triggers an angry reaction, resulting in a wildcat strike. Another form of industrial action, called **working to rule**, is less drastic than a general walkout. Here, workers adhere strictly to their duties as laid out in the collective agreement and refuse to perform informal functions that they might customarily do. For example, employees who normally work overtime may refuse this work because they have a legal right to do so under their agreement. In some cases, if workers refuse to engage in activities that are not specifically referred to in the collective agreement but that they have done customarily, this action may be held by the OLRB to be a wildcat strike and thus an unfair labour practice. In such a case, both workers and their union leaders may be fined. Because it is not always easy to tell when working to rule becomes an illegal strike, the OLRB proceeds on a case-by-case basis. Working to rule can also be used after a collective agreement has expired to pressure the employer to negotiate a new agreement.

working to rule: a form of work slowdown in which employees apply the collective agreement and workplace rules literally, with the intention of making the workplace less efficient

Case DEALING WITH AN UNFAIR LABOUR PRACTICE

St. Joseph's Health Centre and CUPE, Loc. 1144 (Re) (1982), 4 LAC (3d) 426 (Ont. Lab. Arb. Bd.)

Facts

The grievor was a long-serving employee with many years of seniority and an excellent work record. He was also the president of a local union that participated in a provincewide wildcat strike. He had a high profile locally and was a provincial leader in the union. He marched in the picket lines, led his members out on strike, and encouraged them to continue striking. His employer fired him. Other union leaders who had been discharged by their employers for participating in this provincewide strike had their dismissals reversed by arbitrators, who instead imposed suspensions on them. The question was whether the employee's conduct justified dismissal.

Decision

The arbitrator ruled that there should be some consistency in treatment of this grievor compared with others in similar situations. He ordered that the grievor be reinstated but with a suspension of 10 months, with the further provision that he would be discharged if he encouraged other unlawful strikes within the next year. This, the arbitrator felt, would be sufficient to mark the grievor's central role in provoking the rash of strikes.

Questions

1. Do you think the judgment in this case was fair and warranted?
2. As a sign of union solidarity, should the union reimburse the individual for loss of wages resulting from the suspension?

Workers establish picket lines during most strikes. One purpose of picketing is to inform the public of the issues involved in the strike and so gain public sympathy. Another may be to put pressure on the employer. Picketing can also hinder the employer's operations by delaying or preventing people and materials from entering the workplace. Court cases that may result from disturbances caused by picketing are dealt with under criminal law and trespass legislation. Courts try to strike a balance between the right of the union to get its message out and the right of the employer to run the business. In some cases, the courts will limit the number of pickets at particular sites, or set a limit on the time strikers can delay someone's entrance to a struck workplace.

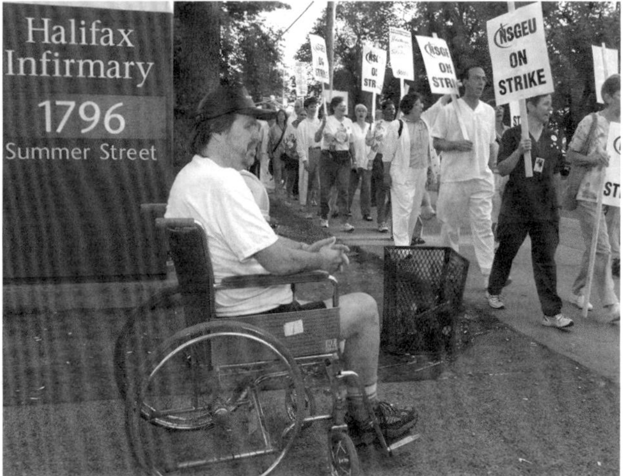

Figure 14.10 *A patient watches the picket line outside the Halifax Infirmary during a strike in June 2001.*

Settling Grievances During a Contract

Once a collective agreement is in place, the union and the employer need a mechanism to resolve disputes that arise under the contract agreement. These disputes are called grievances. Under Ontario's *Labour Relations Act,*

1995, and in other jurisdictions in Canada, the parties are required to submit contract disputes to binding arbitration. Members of the bargaining unit may file grievances—for example, a worker who believes he or she was improperly laid off can grieve the layoff. The union may also file a grievance, for example, where an individual ought to have grieved, but did not, and the union is concerned that failure to grieve might cause harm to the bargaining unit as a whole.

The grievance procedure usually allows for discussion of the alleged violation with the employer. If the problem is not resolved, then the parties agree that the grievance can be heard and decided by arbitration.

Check Your Understanding

1. What is meant by union certification? Explain the process of certification.
2. What is the difference between conciliation and mediation?
3. a) At what point in the negotiating process of collective bargaining might workers go on strike?
   b) What is the purpose of picketing?
4. Suppose that an employer and union cannot come to an agreement on the wage rates for workers, and a mediator is called in to assist in the bargaining process. What issues would the mediator take into consideration before making a decision?
5. The ability to strike is an important bargaining tool for unions. What are the advantages and disadvantages for workers if such a job action is used?
6. a) Do you agree with legislation that allows employers to hire replacement workers or "scabs" during a strike? Why or why not?
   b) Do you think the use of replacement workers or scabs is contrary to the purposes of the *Labour Relations Act, 1995* (page 420)? Explain your answer.
7. What is the function of the grievance mechanism in labour relations?

To identify the unions that have the most members in Canada, go to www.emp.ca/dimensionsoflaw

Challenges for Unions in the Workplace

By the beginning of the 21st century, the number of union members in Canada had declined by thousands. Governments in Alberta, British Columbia, and Ontario had weakened union recognition and labour legislation. The right of workers to organize was under attack. The move to privatize government services meant that many jobs that were formerly held by unionized workers were contracted out to non-union labour.

The main differences between a unionized and a non-unionized workplace in Ontario are shown in Figure 14.11. Figure 14.12 shows union membership in Canada over a 13-year period.

Figure 14.11 *Differences between unionized and non-unionized workplaces in Ontario.*

Unionized Workplace	Non-unionized Workplace
Wages, hours, and working conditions set by collective agreement	Each individual negotiates own wages, hours, and working conditions subject to minimums and floors set out in the *Employment Standards Act*
Workers may grieve dismissal or layoff and, if successful, may be reinstated	Workers may be dismissed and be paid an amount equivalent to pay for a reasonable notice period. No right to reinstatement
Layoff, promotion, benefits, vacation scheduling usually subject to seniority	Employers may lay off or promote whomever they wish, regardless of seniority
Workers may grieve and arbitrate contract violations, with cost of action paid by union	Workers can complain to the Employment Standards Branch of the Ministry of Labour about some employment contract violations, or sue, or quit. Any lawsuit is at employee's expense
Workers can use strikes and working to rule to pressure employer into making a favourable collective agreement for all members of the bargaining unit	Individual worker usually has to negotiate alone and has little leverage
Workers may have to be members of the union and must pay union dues in exchange for union's fair representation of all members of the bargaining unit	No union membership required; no dues paid

Figure 14.12 *Union membership in Canada, 1990–2002.*

Year	Union Membership (000s)	Non-agricultural Paid Workers (000s)*	Union Membership as % of Non-agricultural Paid Workers
1990	4031	11 598	34.8
1992	4089	11 414	35.8
1994	4078	11 310	36.1
1996	4033	11 764	34.3
1998	3938	12 031	32.7
2000	4058	12 707	31.9
2002	4174	13 414	31.1

* Non-agricultural paid workers shown for each year are annual averages of the preceding year; data shown for union membership are as of January of the years shown and as reported by labour organizations. Union membership as a percentage of non-agricultural paid workers is shown in parentheses.

Source: Human Resources Development Canada, "Union Membership in Canada—2002." *Workplace Gazette*, Vol. 5, No. 3, p. 39.

ersonal Viewpoint

Labour at the Crossroads

...Canada's unions ... are at a crossroads. Because no matter how you look at it, unions in Canada are on shaky ground, and have to make some tough choices about which direction they want to go.

On the upside, over the past six years, unions have organized on average some 50 000 to 60 000 new workers annually, and in 1999 the labour movement added some 146 000 new workers, one of its biggest increases ever.

Unions have also begun to organize in the hard-to-reach sectors of private service industries, and have concentrated more of their efforts on organizing women in low-wage manufacturing as well as home- and long-term care.

But on the downside ... the numbers of unionized workers are in decline, and in some cases, like construction or public administration, unions have lost hundreds of thousands of members. New job creation has also been primarily in non-unionized, low-wage and part-time sectors, and most provinces have made it harder for workers to join a union. ...

For the first time since the 1960s, the overall percentage of unionized workers in the workforce in Canada has fallen below 30 percent.

The cold reality is that the Canadian labour movement needs to add some 130 000 new workers every year, just to keep treading water. And if they want to grow even by 1 percent of the workforce, unions need to add roughly 325 000 annually. Given past results, the odds are against seeing numbers like these anytime soon.

The future doesn't look any brighter. The privatization of public services and the restructuring of the public sector means more unionized jobs will be lost. In the private sector, businesses now regularly conduct anti-union campaigns and hire legal teams to thwart organizing drives to keep unions out of their workplaces. ...

But if Canada's unions are to halt the decline and avoid the fate of labour movements elsewhere ... they will need to keep some key lessons in mind.

The first is that unions need to expand. Size matters. Because as countries like Sweden and Germany have shown ... : Wherever unionized workers make up the majority of the workforce, wages and working conditions are better, there are more social services, there is less poverty, and the standard of living is higher. ...

Canadian unions must commit new resources and money into organizing. ...

The second lesson is that the time to make changes is before a major crisis hits, not after. In both the U.S. and Britain, unions were slow to recognize their growing vulnerability, and only after it was too late and they had lost millions of members, did they begin to undertake major changes in how they recruited, bargained, and campaigned for better legal rights for workers.

The third lesson is that there are more direct and comprehensive ways of unionizing new workers. ...

Innovative ideas with the greatest possibility of success include: A national organizing commission as well as national organizing institute that can set and enforce national goals and objectives; provincial co-ordinating committees and organizing schools, which would allow the co-ordination of unions and the development of programs for the training of more organizers; and worker centres and the more extensive use of volunteer training programs that could actively reach out to youth and immigrants, and involve everyday workers in organizing. ...

Source: John Peters, "Labour at the Crossroads," *The Toronto Star*, August 30, 2002, p. A21.

Questions

1. Identify the statistical proof in Figure 14.12 that supports the article by Peters.
2. What reasons does Peters give for the decline in union membership? Can you think of any clear examples from your own community, or what you have read in the newspaper or heard on the news, that support his conclusions?
3. What does Peters think needs to take place for unions to halt their membership decline and increase membership? Do you agree with his opinions? Why or why not?
4. What evidence have you seen that unions are making an effort to inform the public and workers of the benefits of belonging to a union, as Peters suggests? What would you suggest is the best way for unions to convey such a message to the public?

Check Your Understanding

1. Despite the obvious disadvantages listed in Figure 14.11 for non-unionized workplaces, many workers remain content not to belong to a union. Why might this be so?
2. What reasons would you give for the decline of unions in the latter part of the 20th century?
3. Review Figure 14.12. What conclusions can you draw from this table?

Methods of *Legal Inquiry*

Conducting an Interview

As part of his investigation into the Windsor Ford strike, Mr. Justice Rand conducted a series of interviews with management, workers, and the union so that he could hear opinions from all sides in the dispute and render a fair decision. What kind of preparation did he have to make for these interviews?

To conduct a successful interview, you should

- learn as much as possible about the issues in advance
- prepare and write out questions, arranging them in a logical order, allowing for one question to lead into another
- go into the interview with an open mind
- listen attentively and be prepared to ask follow-up questions based on the responses from the person being interviewed
- take accurate notes throughout the interview
- review notes before ending the interview to make sure all points are covered
- thank the person interviewed for cooperating.

Applying the Skill

1. Working in a small group, make up at least six questions that Mr. Justice Rand might have asked a union organizer, a striker, a worker opposed to paying union dues, and the company president.
2. Select someone whom you know has been involved in a labour dispute, either on the side of the employee or that of the employer. Prepare your questions before interviewing your subject about his or her experience. You will want to find out the facts behind the dispute, the issues that were negotiated, the general mood of the parties involved in the negotiations, public perception of the dispute, and how the dispute was resolved. Upon completion of the interview, summarize your findings and provide your own opinion about what you learned.

CAREER PROFILE

Caroline V. ("Nini") Jones

Nini Jones practises law with the Toronto firm Paliare Roland. Nini put off law school in favour of a working stint in the "real world" of labour relations. Her experience as a labour organizer earned her both enhanced credibility with her future clients and valuable insights into her own personal and professional strengths and values.

Q. Have you always been interested in practising law?

A. Yes. I'd been planning to go to law school after I finished my undergraduate degree, but an opportunity came up to work for the Canadian Federation of Students, and I pursued that instead.

Q. How did that decision influence your career?

A. In hindsight, it was probably one of the smartest things I've ever done. Working for a number of years not only helped me decide what kind of work I wanted to do as a lawyer, but also why I wanted to go to law school in the first place.

Q. What is the Canadian Federation of Students? What kind of work did you do for them?

A. It's an organization that represents the interests of students: tuition fees, student debt, campus space, social issues, things like that. I was a field worker, travelling across the province to work with local student unions to promote the organization and benefits of membership. Another important thing about that job for me was that it was my first unionized job, and I got involved with the union (CUPE) early on, as the president of my local.

Q. And you later worked for a labour union?

A. For the Hotel and Restaurant Employees Union. It represents workers in a very wide range of hospitality workplaces, from hotels to fast food restaurants to casinos. I worked for them both as a rep and as an organizer.

Q. What is involved in helping a group of workers in becoming organized?

A. Essentially, workers need support to prepare for an eventual vote on the issue of whether they want to be in the union. One of the key jobs for an organizer is ensuring that we have identified potential leaders that represent all facets of the workforce. A workplace is like a school; there are groups of individuals who have common interests—

Q. Cliques?

A. Yes, if people still use that word. You need to tap into each of these cliques so that you can build a base of support that reflects the interests of the whole workplace.

Q. What is the most important thing students should know about the role of law in the employment context?

A. One thing? They should know everything. Law regulates every aspect of the employment relationship, and it's an employee's lifeline. Young workers, especially, can be very vulnerable. Access to employment law information is critical for them. Being part of a union offers the best protection. We should do much more than we're doing to educate young people about their rights, because when they get out of school, they're all going to work.

Reviewing Main Ideas

You Decide!

CHALLENGING THE RAND FORMULA

Lavigne v. Ontario Public Service Employees Union (OPSEU), [1991] 2 SCR 211

Facts

Francis "Merv" Lavigne had been a teacher at the Haileybury School, a college of applied arts and technology, since 1974. The official bargaining agent representing community college teachers was the Ontario Public Service Employees Union (OPSEU). For college employees in the Province of Ontario, the Council of Regents acted as the designated bargaining agent within a collective agreement that existed between OPSEU and the Council of Regents. Under the provision of the Rand formula, the employer was required to provide mandatory dues check-off for all employees and to forward all moneys collected to the union.

As an employee at the college, Lavigne was required under the Rand formula to pay union dues to OPSEU. He objected to the fact that some of the money collected by the union through union dues was not used for matters strictly relating to collective bargaining. Specifically, Lavigne objected to the union's financial contributions to the New Democratic Party's disarmament campaign, and a number of other political and social causes.

Lavigne filed an application in the Supreme Court of Ontario, arguing that his obligation to pay union dues that would in turn be used for purposes unrelated to collective bargaining violated his right to freedom of association and freedom of expression guaranteed by ss. 1 and 2 of the *Canadian Charter of Rights and Freedoms* and the ruling of the Rand formula.

The Supreme Court of Ontario agreed with Lavigne, indicating that the check-off provisions of the collective agreement were of no force or effect in so far as they compelled Lavigne to pay union dues that were then used for purposes not directly related to collective bargaining. The court further ruled that Lavigne's rights to freedom of association under s. 2(d) of the Charter had been violated.

The case then proceeded to the Ontario Court of Appeal, which reversed the decision. The court ruled that the use of union dues was deemed to be a private activity carried on by a private organization (OPSEU), and therefore was beyond the reach of the Charter. Lavigne appealed this decision to the Supreme Court of Canada.

The Supreme Court of Canada had to decide the following questions:

1. Did the *Canadian Charter of Rights and Freedoms* apply in this case?
2. If the answer to question 1 is yes, then were Lavigne's rights under ss. 2(b) and 2(d) of the Charter infringed?
3. If the answer to question 2, in any part, is yes, were such infringements reasonable and justified under s. 1 of the Charter?

The Law

From the *Canadian Charter of Rights and Freedoms*:

Guarantee of Rights and Freedoms

1. The *Canadian Charter of Rights and Freedoms* guarantees the rights and freedoms set out in it subject only to such reasonable limits prescribed by law as can be demonstrably justified in a free and democratic society.

Fundamental Freedoms

2. Everyone has the following fundamental freedoms: ...
   (b) freedom of thought, belief, opinion and expression, including freedom of the press and other media of communication; ...
   (d) freedom of association.

Arguments of Lavigne (Appellant)

Lavigne argued that he was willing to accept his obligation to remit union dues to OPSEU only under the condition that his dues be used only for collective bargaining purposes and not to support any cause unrelated to collective bargaining. Using his dues to support these causes violated his right to freedom of association under s. 2(d). He was being compelled to associate with an organization that he chose not to associate with.

Arguments of OPSEU (Respondent)

OPSEU argued that Lavigne's freedom of association was limited, but that this limitation was justified under s. 1 of the Charter. Unions need to participate in the broader political, economic, and social debates in society if they are to work for democracy in the workplace. Therefore, all members of a union should be required to pay union dues with no guarantee as to how their contributions will be used. All members should contribute to the union's financial base because all benefit. For the government to draw up guidelines to determine where union funds were to be spent would imply that unions were not capable of making sound decisions for the use of their funds.

Make Your Decision

1. Outline the important facts in this case.
2. Explain how the *Canadian Charter of Rights and Freedoms* and the Rand formula were important in this case.
3. Summarize the supporting arguments for both the appellant, Lavigne, and the respondent, OPSEU.
4. Make a decision in this case either in favour of Lavigne or dismissing his appeal. Provide support for your decision.

Key Terms

Review the following terms to show that you understand the meaning of each and how it is applied in a legal context.

adversarial	mediation
bargain in good faith	Rand formula
binding arbitration	scab
certification	strike
collective bargaining	trade union
conciliation	wildcat strike
lock-out	working to rule

Understanding the Law

Review the following pieces of legislation mentioned in the text, and show that you understand the intent of each.

Canada Labour Code
Collective Bargaining Act
Industrial Disputes Investigation Act
Ontario's *Labour Relations Act, 1995*
PC 1003
Trades Union Act

Thinking and Inquiry

1. Identify a labour dispute that is presently taking place either in your community, your province, or nationally.
   a) What are the key issues in the dispute?
   b) Summarize the positions taken by (i) the union, (ii) the employer, (iii) the media, and (iv) the government.
   c) If you were the arbitrator in this dispute, what recommendations would you make to settle it?
2. Review the progress in labour relations legislation from 1900 to 1950 (see Figure 14.7, page 418). What forces in society worked against union organizers?
3. a) Why were unions seen as a threat before 1950?
   b) Discuss whether unions are still seen as a threat in Canadian society. Present evidence to support your argument.
4. What is your view of the statement by Peters (page 430) that unions improve working conditions for all workers? Prepare to debate this view.
5. What costs could be associated with work stoppages for:
   a) the workers
   b) the union
   c) the company
   d) the community.

Communication

6. With a partner, interview two union members. Ask them to share their views on whether they believe the union serves an important purpose in their workplace and community. Summarize what you learned, and present it in a written report.
7. Select one significant event from the timeline shown in Figure 14.7 (page 418). Research the event further, decide why it is important, and assess its impact. Present a short oral report on the event.
8. Select and debate one of the following topics:
   - Unions have too much power in the workplace.
   - Workers should never be allowed to strike.
   - The negative effects of strikes always outweigh any positive outcomes.
   - Unions have benefited all workers in Canadian society.

Application

9. Research unions and labour relations laws in another developed country. Evaluate how well Ontario's labour relations legislation protects the right of workers to collective bargaining and their legal right to strike in comparison with the country you have chosen.
10. Select a union Web site to evaluate and review its contents under the following subheadings:
    a) Opinions Regarding Labour and Social Issues
    b) Views on How to Expand Membership

    Write a report summarizing your findings. What is your overall opinion on the Web site? Does it provide adequate and informative information for its members? Does the Web site effectively educate the public?
11. Write a letter to the provincial Ministry of Labour on a labour relations issue that you have studied. Your letter can be in support of or against a current piece of legislation or government policy.

Chapter 15 The Changing Workplace

CHAPTER Focus

In this chapter, you will

- investigate how the workplace has changed
- assess some effects of globalization on working conditions in developing countries
- analyze the effects of trade agreements such as NAFTA and the FTAA on workers' rights
- predict changes in collective bargaining and workplace regulations

The last two decades of the 20th century saw enormous changes in the workplace for Canadians. Long-term employees saw their jobs disappear as their local factories and offices closed to move south to the United States or to off-shore locations in developing countries. Robots replaced assembly-line workers in car factories. Firms and governments replaced full-time employees with contract or part-time workers. This chapter examines these and other trends in the workplace, and looks at the effects these changes have had, and are likely to continue to have, on the future of collective bargaining.

The cartoon in Figure 15.1 comments on one aspect of these trends.

Figure 15.1

At First Glance

1. What does the cartoonist mean by "new technology"?
2. What does he mean by the comment, "It's a distribution problem"?
3. Give examples of some specific jobs that have disappeared from the Canadian workplace as a result of technological innovations since 1985.
4. Give examples of jobs that have been created because of technological innovations since 1985.
5. Do you agree with the cartoonist's message? Why or why not?

Forces Shaping Canada's Workplace

The Canadian workplace has undergone tremendous change since the end of World War II. This change has been partly driven by technological developments in all fields, from industrial processes to transportation. Perhaps the most important technological changes have occurred in telecommunications, which have led to what is now called "the global village." We will consider these changes to understand the workplace today and how it may look in the future.

The Workforce Since 1945

Learn more about Canada's workforce in transition at www.emp.ca/dimensionsoflaw

At the end of World War II, Canada experienced a long period of economic expansion and growth. Workers tended to stay in a particular line of work, often remaining with the same employer for their entire career. Much of the workforce in mining, transportation, forestry, and larger manufacturing industries was unionized. Wages were relatively high, allowing families to have a single wage earner who supported a spouse and children at home. Domestic consumption increased as the high-wage economy allowed more and more people to buy consumer goods, such as electrical appliances and automobiles.

Many jobs carried benefit plans that covered medical costs and insurance, and provided pensions. As well, starting in the 1940s the federal government gradually added to its "social safety net," starting with the Family Allowance, a monthly payment to families with children. By the end of the 1960s, the government's social security program included a pension plan for retired workers, disability insurance, general welfare for those who could not earn an income, hospital insurance, and finally, universal health care (medicare). Educational opportunities increased with the expansion of universities and the establishment of a community college system in Ontario in the 1960s. Yet it was still possible for a semi-skilled worker to get a secure job with relatively high wages that would provide a decent standard of living for a family.

By the end of the 20th century, workers found themselves in quite a different situation. The gap between those earning higher incomes and those earning lower wages had widened. Job security in manufacturing and many service industries no longer existed, nor did lifetime employment. A career path based on promotion through seniority and loyalty to a company was no longer the norm. Workers changed jobs and careers regularly as employers introduced new technologies to increase productivity, downsized (by laying off workers or hiring fewer new employees), and otherwise tried to reduce labour costs. The proportion of workers employed in five-day, 40-hour-a-week jobs fell, and is still falling. Jobs for semi-skilled and unskilled workers were (and are) lower paying and are found mainly in service industries, such as the fast-food industry. For the first time, the number of contract and part-time workers in the labour force increased faster than the number of full-time workers.

For up-to-date statistics on labour trends in Canada, go to www.emp.ca/dimensionsoflaw

By 2000, 20 percent of all workers in Canada were part-time, compared with 15 percent in the late 1980s and 10 percent in the late 1970s. Employers used these part-time workers to keep labour costs to a minimum: they could hire skilled workers for a short time and not have to pay them benefits. This trend also led to a growth in self-employment, which accounted for over two-thirds of the jobs created in the 1990s. Self-employment accounted for almost 75 percent of net job growth in the 1990s, and by 2000 self-employed workers accounted for 16 percent of the workforce. Only 17 percent of these workers had benefits such as extended health and dental coverage or disability insurance, according to Statistics Canada. Richard Chaykowski of Queen's University sees this trend as a problem:

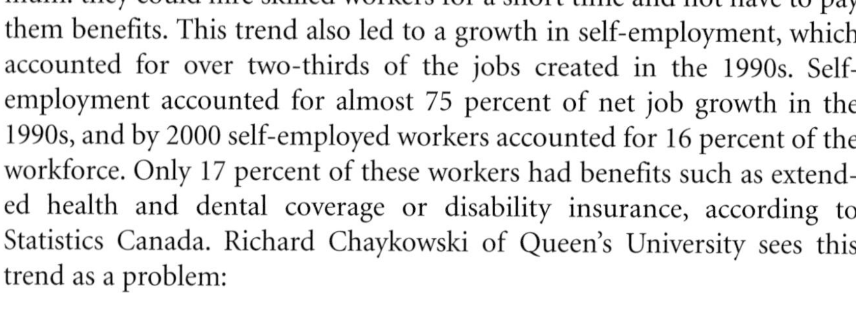

Figure 15.2

Full-time/Part-time Employment in Canada, Annual Averages, 1976–2002

Year	Full-time Employed % of Total Employed	Part-time Employed % of Total Employed	Voluntary Part-time % of Part-time Employed	Involuntary Part-time % of Part-time Employed
1976	87.4	12.6	89.4	10.6
1986	83.0	17.0	74.2	25.8
1996	80.1	18.9	65.1	34.9
2002	81.3	18.7	72.9	27.1

Source: Statistics Canada, Labour Statistics Division, Labour Force Survey.

> Our policies are designed in such a way that these people [the self-employed] fall through the cracks ... and you end up in some cases with two tiers of workers: those who are regular employees and have access to a much broader and more complete range of benefits, and those who don't.

Like all developed countries, Canada is now in a "post-industrial economy." The majority of workers are employed in the service sector rather than the goods-producing sector or the primary sector, which includes workers in mining, forestry, fishing, and agriculture (see Figure 15.3). In Ontario by 2000, 73 percent of the workforce was employed in service industries, with 18 percent in manufacturing and construction, and only 3 percent in agriculture, forestry, and mining.

The Impact of Technology

New technology has had a significant influence on the workplace since the early 1980s. The introduction of personal computers, advances in telecommunications, and the development of robotics have led to the replacement of many traditional jobs. Companies have shown greater productivity and efficiency as a result of introducing new technologies into the work environment. Those companies that did not invest in technology lagged behind, and in many cases closed down or were taken over by competitors. This trend will continue and even intensify. The introduction of advanced technology was not exclusive to the manufacturing sector. It also affected employees in the services sector, including clerical workers, bank tellers, and retail sales people.

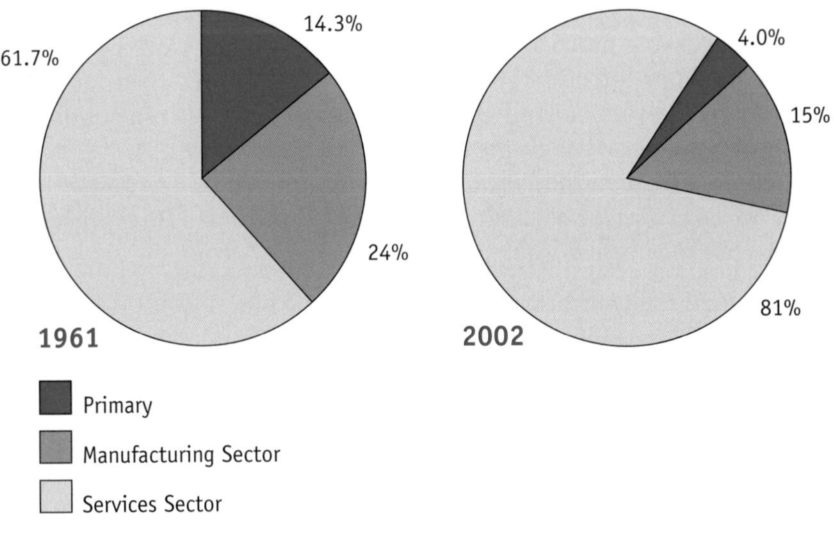

Figure 15.3 *Employment by sectors, Canada, 1961 and 2002.*

Source: Statistics Canada, Labour Statistics Division.

Figure 15.4 *Sparks fly as a robot welds parts on a Honda Odyssey at a plant in Alliston, Ontario. Robots have replaced many assembly-line workers in car plants. Companies hope that new manufacturing technology and smaller, more flexible factories will enable them to thrive in an increasingly competitive auto industry.*

New job opportunities have opened up in what is being called the "knowledge sector" of the economy. Many of these new jobs—for example, in Web design and computer programming—are geared toward workers who are educated in using new technologies. As yet, in Canada, these new job opportunities have not been created fast enough to help workers who have lost their former jobs.

Fyi According to a Statistics Canada survey of 25 000 employed Canadians between 1994 and 2000, the most common sources of stress in the workplace were too many hours or too many demands.

There is evidence from surveys that workers seem to be working longer and harder than before. Many workers who have full-time employment are working much longer hours in more stressful working environments. A labour force survey conducted in 1998 showed that one in five full-time employees worked overtime, averaging almost nine additional hours of work per week, or the equivalent of an extra day.

Jeremy Rifkin and Robert L. Heilbroner, authors of *The End of Work: The Decline of the Global Labor Force and the Dawn of the Post-Market Era*, summarize the impact of these changes:

> The hard reality that economists and politicians are reluctant to acknowledge is that manufacturing and much of the service sector are undergoing a transformation as profound as the one experienced by the agricultural sector at the beginning of the century, when machines boosted production, displacing millions of farmers. We are in the early stages of a long-term shift from "mass labour" to highly skilled "elite labour," accompanied by increasing automation in the production of goods and the delivery of services. Workerless factories and virtual companies loom on the horizon.

Effects of Changes on Unions

One impact of these changes is that unions in the manufacturing sector of the economy are struggling to maintain their memberships as the number of workers in that sector declines. Public service–sector unions, such as the Canadian Union of Public Employees, now have the largest memberships in the country. Other service workers, such as nurses and teachers, have organized unions based on their professional qualifications. The majority of service-sector workers, however, are not organized into unions. The challenge of organizing all auto mechanics or shop assistants, for example, is formidable.

Another challenge facing unions is organizing part-time workers. Collective bargaining has been used with some success to obtain a minimum number of work hours and some of the benefits, such as insurance, enjoyed by full-time workers. Contract workers are even harder to organize, as each has a separate contract with the employer.

Check Your Understanding

1. In what ways has the workplace in Canada undergone change since the end of World War II?
2. Examine Figure 15.2 (page 438) and compare statistics for 1976 and 2002. Write a short summary of the trends in employment shown in the table.
3. What is meant by a "post-industrial economy"? Provide some clear examples.
4. How has technology influenced the workplace since the early 1980s? Have any of these changes influenced your future career path? Explain.
5. What are some of the challenges facing unions as they try to maintain their membership numbers?

The Move to Freer Trade

The Great Depression of the 1930s caused a re-examination of world trade and financial policies. At the end of World War II, Canada was part of a system that kept the costs of foreign imports high to protect domestic production and raise tax revenues. This system was analyzed at the Bretton Woods Conference in New England in 1944, when representatives of 44 nations met to discuss how best to address the post-war global economy. What was evident was that there was no international financial structure in place to deal with a crisis such as the Depression.

Learn more about the Bretton Woods Conference at www.emp.ca/dimensionsoflaw

The response, led by the United States, the most powerful nation at the conference, was that the delegates agreed to set up three new economic institutions: the International Monetary Fund (IMF), the World Bank, and the General Agreement on Tariffs and Trade (GATT). The aim of the IMF was to facilitate the expansion and balanced growth of international trade. The World Bank was to transfer funds through loans from more prosperous countries to poorer countries to assist with the post-war rebuilding phase. GATT was to establish trade rules to govern foreign trade in the hope of reducing trade barriers among member countries.

multilateral: among many countries or parties

GATT was a **multilateral** trade treaty in which members undertook to grant "most favoured nation" status reciprocally to new trading partners. This meant that a new trading partner with Canada, for example, would get the same terms for trade as the "best" deal Canada had with another country. Canada was among the 23 countries that first signed GATT, and since then the country has remained committed to freer trade.

A business environment based on competition was created by the opening of Canada's borders to imports and by allowing Canadian-produced goods to be exported freely. The government, while knowing that some sectors would suffer and some jobs would be lost, still believed that the positive spin-offs would far outweigh any negative impact. The theory was that as barriers to international trade were removed all nations would benefit through increased access to international markets, exporting and importing goods freely. This general trend—liberalization of international trade by reducing trade barriers, such as taxes or duties on imports—continued over the balance of the 20th century and continues today. It is part of the trend known as **globalization**, which we will examine later in this chapter.

globalization: the trend toward an international free trade market in goods and services with minimal interference by national governments

bilateral: between two countries or parties

Free Trade in North America

The idea of reduced international trade restrictions was behind the negotiation of the **bilateral** Canada–US *Free Trade Agreement* in the late 1980s. In October 1987, the government of Canada, led by Prime Minister Brian Mulroney, reached an agreement with the United States on free trade between the two countries. Mulroney campaigned successfully on a free trade platform in the fall election of 1988. His return to office led to the signing into law of the *Free Trade Agreement* (FTA). The FTA officially came into effect on January 1, 1989.

At the time of its signing, the FTA established the world's largest free trade area. The objectives of the agreement are found in article 102:

a) [to] eliminate barriers to trade in goods and services between the territories of the Parties (the United States and Canada);
b) [to] facilitate conditions of fair competition within the free-trade area;
c) [to] liberalize significantly conditions for investment within this free-trade area;
d) [to] establish effective procedures for the joint administrators of this Agreement and the resolution of disputes; and
e) [to] lay the foundation for further bilateral and multilateral cooperation to expand and enhance the benefits of this Agreement.

Canada participated in the FTA to solidify its economic relationship with the United States through closer trade with the largest economy in the world. In a passionate speech debating the FTA in the House of Commons, Prime Minister Mulroney insisted that the FTA means "jobs, prosperity, regional growth, and a future for our children." The biggest concern of Canadians was the strong possibility of job losses once the FTA was implemented. The government promised to help with any dislocation caused as a result of the agreement, although it did not put into place any policies that addressed this problem.

For details of chapter 11 of NAFTA and the dispute resolution articles, visit www.emp.ca/dimensionsoflaw

The FTA opened the doors to the negotiation of the *North American Free Trade Agreement* (NAFTA) between Canada, the United States, and Mexico. This agreement came into full effect in January 1994, superseding the FTA. It went further than the FTA, as it required all internal barriers to an exporter doing business in Canada to be removed. The interpretation of chapter 11, article 102 of NAFTA sets out the basic obligations of each state's treatment of investors and its investments, including investors from the other two states that are party to the agreement. These investors are to be given the same treatment as domestic investors.

Interpretation of chapter 11 has led to some controversial decisions. For example, in April 1997 the Canadian government determined that a gasoline additive (MMT) posed a health risk and banned it from use in gasoline sold in Canada. The US company that produced the additive argued that under chapter 11 of NAFTA, the Canadian ban was a trade restriction. It successfully sued the Canadian government for its losses as the result of the ban.

NAFTA also permits a business operating in one country to move all or part of its business operations to one of the other two countries. For example, a Canadian company could move some or all of its operations to factories in Mexico along the US border, known as ***maquiladoras***, where labour is cheaper.

maquiladoras: factories set up in a free trade zone along the US border with Mexico, where foreign companies can move material across the border with minimal customs processing

Personal Viewpoint

Running on MMT

Three weeks ago, something happened in Canada. It could not have been very important because hardly anyone on this side of the Atlantic is even aware that it took place.

A total of four column inches in the British newspapers was devoted to the event. The handful of people who bothered to read them would have learnt that a company no one has heard of, which makes a product whose name no one can pronounce, received some money from the Canadian government and an assurance that it could continue making the product.

It is the butterfly's wing over North America that will cause a hurricane in Europe.

The company is called the Ethyl Corporation, and its product is a chemical called methylcyclopentadienyl manganese tricarbonyl, or—and let us thank God for acronyms—MMT.

MMT is a fuel additive [that] is mixed with petrol to prevent engine knocking. Many scientists believe it is also a dangerous neurotoxin. Manganese entering the body through the lungs causes nerve damage which can lead to psychosis, memory loss and early death.

Until last year, Canada was the only country on earth in which MMT was sold. It is legal to sell it in most of the US—but surveys suggest that suppliers will not stock it, not least because it appears to damage car engines, causing the release of other pollutants.

Canadian MPs questioned why their citizens should be exposed to this peculiarly unpleasant species of pollution. After a long and intelligent debate, the Parliament voted to ban it in April 1997. Had the vote taken place three years earlier, the Ethyl Corporation would have had to abide by the decision. A sovereign Parliament had decided to protect its citizens from a deadly poison, and that, you would imagine, would have been the end of the matter.

But, since 1994, corporations in Canada, the US and Mexico have enjoyed a new and astonishing power over elected authorities. The *North American Free Trade Agreement* (NAFTA) entitles companies to sue governments they believe to be raising unfair barriers to trade.

Ethyl sued the Canadian government for the "expropriation" of its "property" (namely, its anticipated profits) and the "damage" to its "good reputation" caused by the parliamentary debate. It took its suit to NAFTA, where a secret tribunal—whose records are not disclosed and whose decisions cannot be appealed—began to assess the case. Last month, the Canadian government, realising that its chances of success were approximately zero, settled with Ethyl.

It agreed to allow the corporation to resume sales of MMT in Canada. It agreed to pay Ethyl US$13 million [Cdn$20 million] in compensation. It agreed, too, to mislead its citizens. Upon settling, it announced that "MMT poses no health risk." ...

Yet MMT was banned in Canada irrespective of who produced it: the rules were precisely the same for foreign and domestic investors. This, as campaigners predicted, offered no protection at all to the sovereignty of the Canadian Parliament.

Source: George Monbiot, "Running on MMT: The Multilateral Agreement on Investments Will Force Governments to Poison Their Citizens," *The Guardian*, Thursday, August 13, 1998.

Questions

1. Summarize the facts in the case of Ethyl Corporation against the government of Canada.
2. Ethyl Corporation relied on chapter 11 of NAFTA to argue its case. Check the Web site for NAFTA through the link at www.emp.on.ca/dimensionsoflaw and summarize article 102 and what it means. How does chapter 11 limit the actions of governments?
3. United Parcel Service (UPS) is using chapter 11 of NAFTA to argue that Canada Post (a publicly run, federal Crown corporation) is enjoying unfair market control because it is funded and operated by the Canadian government.
   a) What is your opinion on this case?
   b) If UPS is successful, what might be the constitutional results? (See Chapter 4, p. 106.)
4. The hearings on the case regarding Ethyl Corporation are not available to the public, and the decisions of the tribunal are binding and cannot be appealed. What is your opinion of this process? Why do you think governments agreed to this arrangement?

Turning Points in the Law

Free Trade with the United States and Mexico

The negotiation of the *Free Trade Agreement* (FTA) with the United States and the subsequent *North American Free Trade Agreement* (NAFTA), which included Mexico, changed Canada's relationship with the United States. The United States had long been Canada's main trading partner, but by 2000 over 85 percent of Canada's exports went to the United States, and over 74 percent of imports came from there. The Canadian economy is now so closely bound to the US economy that some people are advocating that Canada abandon its currency and use the US dollar.

At the same time, US investment in Canada grew. US firms such as Home Depot, Wal-Mart, GAP, and Old Navy built stores in Canada, and in many cases replaced Canadian-owned stores. Branch plants of US firms such as Westinghouse closed their Canadian operations as the tariff advantages that had led them to invest in Canada were eliminated. In particular, American investment grew in the companies that supply raw materials to the United States, particularly oil, natural gas, and minerals.

NAFTA has also affected government policies. Because rules forbid subsidies or payments to help producers with export products, Canada's supply management system for dairy products has been challenged. US corporations that have invested in Canada can sue the Canadian government for any policies that cause them economic damage. In particular, there are fears that medicare in Canada will have to allow competition from US sources in sections that are privatized.

Some commentators feel that Canada's ability to make decisions in the best interests of its citizens has been compromised. The energy provisions in NAFTA, for example, specify that Canada cannot charge Canadian consumers less for energy than it charges US consumers. In the event of an energy shortage, Canada must continue to supply the United States with the same percentage of its resources, even if there is a shortage in Canada. Some fear that Canada will also have to divert fresh water to the United States in the future. To some Canadians, provisions such as these put the very existence of Canada as a separate, independent country in doubt.

Figure 15.5 *Prime Minister Brian Mulroney turns away from anti–free trade demonstrators after stopping to speak with them following a Progressive Conservative rally in Toronto in November 1988.*

Questions

1. Research newspaper articles written during the negotiation stages of the FTA and examine the mood of Canadians at the time. What were people who opposed the FTA saying? What were supporters saying?

2. Examine the opinions on both sides and identify predictions that you think were accurate.
3. Debate the following statement: "Free trade has a positive influence on the Canadian economy, resulting in better and higher-paying jobs."
4. What is your opinion of the prediction that Canada will lose its independence in the future and will be absorbed by the United States? Explain your views.

The Impact of Trade Agreements on Workers

NAFTA focuses primarily on trade rights and the right to do business in other countries that are party to the agreement. Labour is treated simply as a commodity, like raw materials or capital. Since NAFTA came into force, investment capital and employment opportunities have shifted from Canada to Mexico and to American states where labour is cheaper and employment standards are minimal—a pattern referred to as "social dumping." In the early 1990s, the American presidential candidate Ross Perot spoke of this trend when he opposed US involvement in hemispheric free trade, saying that the "giant sucking sound" Americans would hear would be jobs leaving the United States for Mexico. Events appear to have borne out Perot's prediction, at least to some extent. The *maquiladoras* on the Mexican side of the US border along the Rio Grande are run by American and multinational companies using cheap Mexican labour to assemble and finish goods that are then imported by the United States.

Fyi In 2002, the average work week for *maquiladora* workers was 60–75 hours; their pay averaged US$5.75 per day. The cost of living for workers was high—it took more than an hour of work to pay for 1 litre of milk.

NAFTA and Labour Issues

NAFTA includes a "side deal," the *North American Agreement on Labor Cooperation* (NAALC), to deal with labour issues. It came into force in 1994, and commits the parties to improving their labour conditions, complying with domestic labour legislation, and enforcing those laws in each country.

But does the NAALC protect labour? The agreement recognizes the right of each country to set its own labour legislation as part of its domestic law. The NAALC does not harmonize labour law or set minimum standards within the agreement area. It can review a country's enforcement of its own labour law. If there is a dispute about enforcement, an evaluation committee of experts investigates. If the matter is not resolved, then a member state may take the dispute forward for settlement before a panel of arbitrators. The panel may recommend remedies, including fines, together with suspension of some NAFTA trade rights. But it cannot compel a member state to adopt even minimal labour standards if it chooses not to.

The weakness of the NAALC has led the American Federation of Labor and Congress of Industrial Organizations (AFL–CIO) to the following conclusion:

The AFL–CIO's overall assessment of the NAALC is that for the first four years of its existence, it has failed to bring about substantial improvement in worker rights and standards in the three NAFTA countries. The NAALC, thus far, has been ineffective in promoting the concerns of workers beset by stagnant wages and job insecurity, which have been exacerbated [made worse] by economic integration in North America.

Learn more about the NAALC at www.emp.ca/dimensionsoflaw

The Law From the *North American Agreement on Labor Co-operation* between the government of the United States of America, the government of Canada, and the government of the United Mexican States:

Article 1: Objectives

The objectives of this Agreement are to:

1. improve working conditions and living standards in each Party's territory; ...
3. encourage cooperation to promote innovation and rising levels of productivity and quality;
4. encourage publication and exchange of information, data development and coordination, and joint studies to enhance mutually beneficial understanding of the laws and institutions governing labor in each Party's territory;
5. pursue cooperative labor-related activities on the basis of mutual benefit;
6. promote compliance with, and effective enforcement by each Party of, its labor law; ...

Article 2: Levels of Protection

Affirming full respect for each Party's constitution, and recognizing the right of each Party to establish its own domestic labor standards, and to adopt or modify accordingly its labor laws and regulations, each Party shall ensure that its labor laws and regulations provide for high labor standards, consistent with high quality and productivity workplaces, and shall continue to strive to improve those standards in that light.

Questions

1. How are the objectives of improving working conditions and living standards, as stated in objective 1 of the NAALC, related?
2. The objectives of the NAALC do not include any method for enforcement. Should such a method exist? Explain.
3. If you were asked to identify a set of high labour standards as outlined in article 2, what standards would you include? Identify at least five such standards in order of priority, and give a brief explanation as to why you have included each in your list.

Case VIOLATING NAALC PRINCIPLES

Echlin Case, US NAO (National Administration Office) Case No. 9703

Facts

In 1996, workers in an auto-parts factory then owned by the US-based Echlin company in Ciudad de los Reyes, Mexico State, were concerned about unhealthy and unsafe working conditions in the plant. As well as handling asbestos, workers were exposed to other toxic materials in poorly ventilated conditions. Wages were low, and workers endured sexual harassment and abuse from supervisors. The workers were represented by the CTM, a union associated with the ruling political party in Mexico, the Institutional Revolutionary Party (PRI). At the time, the PRI had governed Mexico continually since the 1920s. Its unions were perceived as ineffective and more attuned to the employers' interests than to the interests of its members.

When the workers tried to change their union representation from the CTM, company managers intimidated them, using such tactics as surveillance and heavier workloads for supporters.

Voting procedures for the new union were marked by irregularities, such as threats from management, and an open—not secret—ballot. The result was that the CTM won the election.

In December 1997, the petitioners, the Echlin Workers Alliance (made up of a group of US and Canadian unions, as well as human rights organizations and several non-governmental organizations), filed a complaint under the NAALC before a US panel. The petitioners alleged that the Mexican government was permitting violations of NAALC principles in respect of freedom of association, the right to organize into a trade union of one's choice, and the right to bargain collectively. There were also allegations of a failure to take basic steps to prevent occupational injuries and diseases, and against the Mexican government, for failing to maintain fair and impartial labour tribunals.

Issues

Were workers' rights to freedom of association and to collective bargaining interfered with by the employer or by the Mexican government? Did the Mexican government fail to enforce health and safety regulations in the plant?

Decision

The US panel held a public hearing on the case in March 1998 and published a report four months later. It confirmed that the workers faced threats of physical attack and dismissal, and that pro-PRI union thugs intimidated workers during union voting. Authorities turned a blind eye toward these abuses, and labour tribunals aided and approved the outcome of these flawed processes. As well, health and safety regulations were not enforced at the plant, largely due to what was described as a seriously flawed inspection system.

The outcome of these findings was that in May 2000, Mexico and the United States arrived at a ministerial agreement to hold several public seminars. The US and Mexican governments agreed jointly to discuss health and safety techniques. With respect to interference by PRI in the union organizing process, an action plan included overall goals for the Mexican government to pursue, without detailing how these were to be achieved. The plan stated:

> The Mexican Department of Labor and Social Welfare will continue promoting the registry of collective bargaining contracts in conformity with established labor legislation. At the same time, efforts will be made to promote that workers be provided information pertaining to collective bargaining agreements existing in their place of employment and to promote the use of eligible voter lists and secret ballot elections in disputes over the right to hold the collective bargaining contract.

Learn about other NAFTA labour disputes at www.emp.ca/dimensionsoflaw

A substantially similar case was filed at the same time in Canada (Canadian NAO Case No. 98-1).

Questions

1. As a result of the decision in this case, what—if anything—were (a) the Echlin company and (b) the Mexican government required to do?
2. Does the outcome in this case guarantee that workers in Echlin factories in Mexico now have the right to organize and the right to a safe workplace? Explain.
3. Although the NAALC can recommend changes to ensure workers' rights, its power to enforce these recommendations is limited. Should the NAALC continue to investigate, report on, and rule on such cases? Explain.
4. In July 1998, Echlin Inc. merged with Dana Corporation, creating one of the world's largest independent automotive equipment manufacturers. Conduct some research on Dana's record as it relates to workers' rights and the health and safety of workers in the workplace.

The European Union and Labour Issues

European Union (EU): the economic and political organization of 15 European nations into a common market (formerly the European Community)

The political and trade association of the **European Union (EU)** has created a set of common, enforceable labour standards that all member states must obey. Under its own powers, or through the complaint of a member state, the European Union can compel a member state to enact national labour legislation that meets the EU standard. If the member state fails to act, then a lawsuit may be brought before the European Court of Justice. Furthermore, individual citizens of member states may bring a complaint to the court if they can show a direct effect resulting from a member state's non-compliance with the EU standard.

The EU differs from NAFTA in that its powers are superior to those of the member states; thus, the EU can override the laws and the sovereignty of member states in some circumstances, for example, in the enforcement of labour standards. In general, EU members have been willing to create social and human rights standards that all must obey.

Free Trade Agreement of the Americas

Global Exchange is a US-based human rights organization that opposes globalization and the FTAA. Examine its arguments posted at www.emp.ca/dimensionsoflaw

The *Free Trade Agreement of the Americas* (FTAA) proposes to integrate the economies of the countries in the Western hemisphere, excluding Cuba. The FTAA was first discussed at the inaugural Summit of the Americas held in Miami, USA, in December 1994, with a second summit held in Santiago, Chile, in April 1998. Canada has played a significant role in the formation of the FTAA, and in Quebec City in April 2001, it played host to the third Summit of the Americas.

The FTAA's main focus is to create growth and development through enhanced economic integration of the countries involved. Other objectives of the FTAA include strengthening democracy, promoting human rights, and finding ways to address social and economic issues through hemispheric cooperation. The FTAA will, over a 10-year period, create a free trade area among its member countries. Members plan on having the FTAA take full effect by late 2005.

Figure 15.6
Anti-globalization protesters gathered in Quebec City to register their anger with what they see as the anti-democratic nature of summit discussions on the FTAA.

Like its predecessors—NAFTA and the FTA—the FTAA includes no guarantee that core labour standards will be protected. Without such protection, the rights associated with collective bargaining, such as the protection of wages and working conditions, are sure to come into question as businesses move capital from country to country. The FTAA will create an atmosphere of competition among corporations. Advocates of collective bargaining rights and workers' rights to freedom of association are concerned that these rights will be eroded or will not be implemented under these conditions.

For an assessment of NAFTA by the US trade representative, visit www.emp.ca/dimensionsoflaw

CHECK YOUR UNDERSTANDING

1. What was the significance of the Bretton Woods Conference of 1944?
2. How are the *Free Trade Agreement* and NAFTA both similar and different in nature and scope?
3. The *North American Agreement on Labor Cooperation* has had little or no influence in protecting workers' rights. Why is this so?
4. How is the European Union's treatment of labour disputes different from that of the NAALC? Are there more safeguards in place in the EU to protect workers' rights? Explain.
5. Workers in countries like Bolivia and Honduras earn low wages, and many are unemployed. Do you think these countries should join the FTAA? Why or why not?

For an assessment by the Economic Policy Institute on employment and workers in Mexico, the United States, and Canada, visit www.emp.ca/dimensionsoflaw

The Impact of Globalization

NAFTA and the FTAA are examples of an increasing trend toward globalization. This term has been used to describe the movement toward an international free market of goods, capital investment, and services moving across borders, with little or no hindrance from nation states. It is characterized by a global financial system linked by the top world banks, and an elaborate and sophisticated infrastructure of technological and communications systems.

Fyi The WTO meeting in Cancun, Mexico, in September 2003 ended when developing countries' representatives walked out in response to the refusal by the US, European, and Japanese representatives to end subsidies of $300 billion that they pay to their farmers. These subsidies distort world trade, and depress world prices for agricultural products so that developing countries cannot compete on world markets.

The World Trade Organization

The World Trade Organization (WTO), which in 1995 replaced GATT after almost eight years of negotiations, is the only international organization dealing with global rules of trade. This is why WTO meetings, as in Seattle in late November 1999 and Montreal in July 2003, have been the targets of protests by opponents of globalization. The WTO's main function is to make sure that trade flows as smoothly, predictably, and freely as possible. By April 2003, 146 nations had joined the WTO. The WTO goes further than GATT, because it deals with trade in services and intellectual property as well as goods. Participation in the WTO requires that member nations adhere to all the rules. Dispute resolutions are binding.

Learn more about the International Labour Organization at www.emp.ca/dimensionsoflaw

A significant topic of debate among WTO member nations is the issue of "core labour standards." Labour standards are not subject to WTO rules or disciplines. At the 1996 WTO conference held in Singapore, WTO members adopted a clear resolution that core labour standards, the essential standards to be applied to the way workers are treated, are not and will not form any part of the WTO. The members went further in saying that the International Labour Organization (ILO)—the organization made up of representatives from government, labour, and business, and affiliated with the United Nations—is the most competent body to deal with core labour standards rather than the WTO (most members of the WTO are also members of the ILO).

While the ILO tries to promote workers' rights, its power is limited. The organization can establish standards for labour, but its system of enforcement is weak. It can report violations of its standards; in 2000, it imposed sanctions on Myanmar (Burma) over the issue of forced labour. Labour legislation in Ontario has also been the subject of review by the ILO. School principals and vice-principals were denied the right to organize, bargain collectively, and strike under legislation passed in 1998. The ILO committee drew up interim conclusions in this case and requested the Ontario government to take the necessary measures to ensure that school principals and vice-principals could form and join the organization of their own choosing and could enjoy effective protection against anti-union discrimination and employer interference.

There are two opposing positions on the issue of whether making core labour standards a part of the WTO would benefit the global workplace and workers' rights. Industrial member countries of the WTO argue that the right to bargain collectively, freedom of association, freedom from workplace abuse (including forced labour and certain types of child labour), and the elimination of discrimination in the workplace should be entrenched with the WTO. These countries believe that the adoption of core labour standards by the WTO would provide incentives for member nations to improve workplace conditions.

On the other side of the argument, there are many developing and some developed member countries who believe strongly that core labour standards do not belong in the WTO. Making core labour standards a part of multilateral trade negotiations is another form of protectionism, clearly undermining the comparative advantage that lower-wage developing countries enjoy. These countries argue that if they have economic growth, conditions will improve and there will be better labour rights. They believe that sanctions against offending countries would only perpetuate poverty and delay any possible improvement in workplace standards.

The WTO leaders strongly believe that free trade among nations can lift workers in developing countries out of poverty and can address the mismatch that has been created in developed countries where many workers lack the skills demanded by a new knowledge-based economy. In his address on November 28, 1999 to the International Confederation of Free Trade Unions (ICFTU) in Seattle, WTO Director General Mike Moore said:

> I have never seen a contradiction between trade and labour because I don't believe one exists. Open economies, imperfect as they are, have delivered more jobs, opportunities and security to more people than alternatives. Countries that have embraced openness and freedom have increased the real incomes of their workers, which in turn has raised labour standards and reduced poverty.

Moore supports the position that the WTO results in freer-flowing and more stable trade, leading to stronger and more sustained economic growth. With this growth, he believes, will come job creation and the reduction of poverty.

Transnational Corporations and Globalization

Much anti-globalization feeling is directed against **transnational corporations (TNCs)**, sometimes known as multinationals. These are large corporations that usually have their head offices in one of the developed countries in Europe, North America, or Japan, and maintain several other branch-plant operations in other countries. They are truly global companies in terms of trade, their production processes, and their markets. By 1999, the 10 largest TNCs controlled assets representing three times the total income of the world's poorest 38 countries, which together had a population of over one billion people. Of the world's 100 largest economies, 50 are TNCs. The growth in assets of TNCs since the 1990s has occurred mostly as a result of mergers and takeovers, which have been aided by the trend toward globalization and the reduction of the powers of government to intervene in such mergers.

transnational corporation (TNC): a company that conducts its business in more than one country; also known as a multinational corporation

TNCs are free to invest in whatever country provides them with the most profitable location. Often they find that goods and services can be produced efficiently in places where labour is relatively cheap, and that different parts of the production process can be performed in a number of countries using multiple sources of labour. Often they use subcontractors to oversee production. Many of these companies choose not to have any involvement in the manufacturing process itself.

Fyi In 2000, sales of the world's largest TNC, General Motors, exceeded the gross domestic product of Poland.

The Impact of Globalization in Developing Countries

The production strategies of large multinationals have given rise to concerns about the working conditions of people, particularly women and children in developing countries, where wages are low, working conditions

Personal Viewpoint

Tackling Corporate Globalization Together

Collective bargaining has become one of the victims of mounting corporate dominance. International trade deals and the new communications technologies have given corporations the ability to transcend national borders. They can now set up shop anywhere in the world, preferably where the unions are weakest, or nonexistent, taxes the lowest, environmental laws the laxest. Even when [corporations] stay in Canada, the threat to relocate unless the union makes crippling concessions gives [employers] an overpowering advantage at contract renewal time. ...

In the public sector, governments subservient to corporate influence have obediently toughened their treatment of unions and either curtailed their right to strike or nullified it with strike-breaking legislation. Heeding their corporate masters, governments have also cut business taxes and the funding of public programs and institutions, providing an excuse for layoffs and wage freezes.

Unions, of course, must still try to resist this corporate or corporate-driven onslaught in contract negotiations. That's their long-established role. But if that is all they are doing, they risk becoming increasingly less capable of protecting their members.

Many union leaders ... now understand that all the problems they are grappling with internally—layoffs, contracting-out, privatization, contract concession demands, regressive labour law changes—have a single external origin. And that is the enormous growth of global corporate power, both economically and politically.

Corporations have always considered workers to be necessary evils, wages to be an erosion of profits, unions to be a hindrance to the exercise of managerial rights. Now that their power has been so enormously enhanced by free trade deals, capital mobility, servile politicians, and a corporate-controlled media, they can ride roughshod over organized labour—as they can over every other institution they oppose.

It is thus imperative that unions get involved in the broader battle against corporate globalization, because that is the source of all the troubles they are having with employers and governments. ...

What happens over the next few decades will probably determine which of two possible futures materializes: the further entrenchment and consolidation of corporate rule, or the achievement (or restoration) of true democracy. The contribution to be made by labour unions to the pro-democracy campaign could be crucial. If it is half-hearted, intermittent, and conditional, the momentous struggle against the corporate giants—already a daunting task—could fail. But if it is whole-hearted,

Figure 15.7 *What is the cartoonist implying about working conditions for the worker making clothes? the reasons for the purchaser's smile? Do you think the cartoonist would agree with Ed Finn? Explain.*

continuous, and unconditional, the labour-backed David could eventually topple the corporate Goliath.

Source: Ed Finn, "Tackling Corporate Globalization Together: Labour, 'Civil Society' Forging a Much-Needed Partnership," Canadian Centre for Policy Alternatives; www.policyalternatives.ca/publications/articles/article295.html.

Questions

1. a) What does Finn mean by "mounting corporate dominance"?
   b) How does he see this as threatening collective bargaining?
2. Identify statements in this article that show Finn's "anti-globalization" viewpoint.
3. Do you agree that unions should get involved in what Finn calls the "broader battle against corporate globalization"? Explain your answer.
4. What dilemmas do you think union leaders face as they look to define their new role in the labour movement?
5. Do traditional unions have a future in the new world of globalization, or are they doomed to extinction? Explain your answer.

often unsafe, and hours long. Increasingly, non-governmental organizations such as Free the Children and concerned consumers have been exposing the horrendous sweatshop working conditions in which name-brand products are made.

Child Labour

The abolition of child labour is one of the most pressing issues that face the world today. Estimates for 2000 indicated that more than 200 million child labourers existed worldwide, of which 180 million were suspected of being in what is considered the "worst forms" of child labour.

Globalization has in many cases increased the level of child labour, but it also has brought discussion of it to the forefront of the globalization debate. Child labour is acknowledged as a large-scale violation of children's rights, and as knowledge of its extent has increased there has been a growing worldwide movement against it.

In 1999, ILO member governments all agreed to **ratify** *Convention 182*, which would prohibit and eliminate what was considered to be the "worst forms" of slavery, child prostitution and pornography, the use of children to traffic drugs, and any work likely to harm the health, safety, or morals of children. What the ILO member countries accept is that child labour is a result of poverty. Any long-term solution or attempt to address the issue of exploitative child labour must rely on sustained economic growth. The global movement has intensified since the ratification of *Convention 182*. On June 12, 2002, the ILO marked the first World Day against Child Labour.

ratify: give formal consent to an agreement

To learn more about child labour and *Convention 182*, visit www.emp.ca/dimensionsoflaw

WORKING FOR CHANGE *Free the Children*

Children are among the least protected and most abused industrial workers in the world. According to a 1996 study in Pakistan, for example, 7000 children worked full time for 10- to 11-hour days in soccer ball factories in that country alone. Despite legislation of third-world governments, monitoring efforts by international organizations such as the ILO, and strategies such as the "FoulBall Campaign," child labour in the sports equipment sector is still rampant. And that is only one sector. Sports manufacturers have made changes, and some soccer balls now carry a stamp guaranteeing that no child labour was used in their production. However, as of June 2003, a group called Global March Against Child Labour reported that one out of every eight children in the world is still forced into hazardous labour.

One of the earliest organizations formed explicitly to combat abusive child labour is Free the Children (FTC). It was founded in 1995 by then 12-year-old Craig Kielburger of Thornhill, Ontario. Kielburger was moved by a story of the murder of Iqbal Masih, a Pakistani boy who had spoken out against child labour after being freed from six years of being shackled to a carpet-weaving loom 12 hours a day. Kielburger enlisted the support of some friends to start a children's movement. They called it Kids Can Free the Children. It had a twofold mission: to free children from abuse and exploitation, and to free young people from thinking they are powerless to change the world.

In one of his first public appearances, Kielburger spoke to 2000 union members at the Ontario Federation of Labour (OFL) convention and influenced the OFL to donate $150 000 to the FTC campaign. He then travelled to South Asia to see the extent of child labour at first hand. The media attention from that trip brought Free the Children into the spotlight at home and abroad. Kielburger's observations are documented in his acclaimed 1998 book, *Free the Children*, which has been translated into seven languages. Since that first trip, Kielburger has travelled to more than 40 countries to share his vision and message in defence of children's rights with over a million people.

Figure 15.8 *Craig Kielburger shakes hands with Governor General Romeo LeBlanc after receiving the Meritorious Service Medal at a 1998 ceremony in Ottawa. Kielburger received the medal for his campaign to raise public awareness of the exploitation of child labour in developing countries.*

In a 2002 statement responding to the nomination of Kids Can Free the Children for the Nobel Peace Prize, Kielburger said the organization then had a network of more than 100 000 members in 35 countries. FTC had raised funds to build more than 300 primary schools, providing education to over 20 000 children; shipped more than 100 000 school and health kits around the world; sent more than US$2.5 million worth of medical supplies to health clinics in developing countries; and led campaigns against sweatshops and child labour. It has also actively promoted the Rugmark emblem, which certifies that hand-woven rugs have been made without child labour.

Now preparing for a career in peace and conflict studies, Kielburger is much in demand as a speaker, and continues to finance Free the Children projects with money raised by speeches, awards, and royalties from his book. In a recent interview, when asked about the rewards of being an "active citizen," he replied: "After you have completed a massive fundraising or collected petitions with friends, you feel an indescribable sense of accomplishment. You are working on a cause greater than yourself, any one person. Most importantly, we learn that our voices count and that we can help bring about a change."

Source: "Craig Kielburger on Ending Child Labour and Being an Active Citizen," Global Tribe; *www.pbs.org/kcet/globaltribe/voices/voi_kielburger.html.*

Questions

1. Research some of the countries that Kielburger visited in South Asia to see what changes in labour laws have been enacted to protect children in the workplace.
2. Is child labour a problem in Canada? Examine your province's labour laws to determine how young workers' rights are protected.
3. Locate and visit the Free the Children Web site. What campaigns is FTC currently involved with? How can their effectiveness be assessed?
4. Free the Children encourages young people to take action at a local level. What can you do in your community to support Free the Children?
5. Factories in the developing world where children make goods for export are the most visible places for hazardous child labour. But UNICEF reports that most child workers are on the street, on farms, or hidden away in houses beyond the reach of labour inspectors. What strategies might help protect children in the informal sector?

Issue

Ethical Sourcing **Should the federal government enact legislation requiring apparel manufacturers to disclose the factory of origin of clothes sold in Canada?**

Consumer groups and humanitarian agencies have revealed that in some cases workers in developing countries making products that are sold under brand names are toiling in sweatshop conditions.

Under the Canadian *Textile Labelling Act, 1985*, clothing manufacturers wanting to sell in Canada are required to show the following information on clothing labels: the textile fibre content, the name of the country of origin, and the name or identification number of the dealer. There is no obligation to indicate exactly where the product was manufactured. Concerned consumers and suppliers of uniforms and sports gear are unable to confirm the conditions under which these products have been manufactured.

The Ethical Trading Action Group (ETAG), which includes the Canadian Labour Congress, the Union of Needletrades, the Industrial and

Textile Employees, and the Maquila Solidarity Network, among others, is proposing changes to the federal government's textile labelling regulations. In 2003, ETAG sent a letter to the minister of industry urging changes that would require companies intending to sell clothing in Canada to disclose the names and addresses of all their manufacturing locations in a publicly accessible database. Such a full-disclosure law would assure consumers that they were purchasing "Sweat Free" clothing, and encourage retailers to monitor the labour practices of their suppliers. It would also protect workers in countries where wages are higher.

To continue the pressure on the federal government, the Maquila Solidarity Network launched "Cut It Out" campaigns urging Canadians to cut the labels out of their clothes and send them to Industry Canada in Ottawa. In February 2003, they presented thousands of labels and petitions to the office of the minister. The following excerpts present opinions on this issue.

> This is a well-kept secret. Retailers don't want us to know the conditions that our clothes have been made under.
>
> *—Olivia Aynsley, "Cut It Out" organizer*

> Somehow we're led to believe it would be easy to simply track a source back to one of 150 000 factories. ... Twenty percent of them probably change names from year to year, or go out of business. Will we be able to actually construct a database to trace every single garment exactly to the factory where it's made?
>
> *—Bob Kirke, Executive Director, Canadian Apparel Federation, quoted by Martin Barry in "Anti-sweatshop Groups Have Apparel Makers Sweating,"* Canadian Apparel, *July/August 2002*

> Canadian companies are profiting from abusing the rights of people in many developing countries. It is time that we consumers hold retailers and manufacturers accountable for the conditions under which their clothes are produced.
>
> *—Bill Hynd, Oxfam "No Sweat" campaign coordinator*

> Retailers in Canada are getting more and more of their products made in countries with the worst human rights records, the worst labour practices, the worst respect for workers' rights.
>
> *—Bob Jeffcott, Maquila Solidarity Network*

> The administration of the thing is almost impossible. ... I think the issue here is to get the problem solved. None of us wants to be dealing with countries or factories where human beings are exploited.
>
> *—David Crisp, Senior Vice-President, Human Resources, Hudson's Bay Company, quoted by Sean O'Connor in "CA Lobby Targets Retail Industry,"* Canadian Retailer, *May 2002*

> Even if the proposal does become a government regulation, its life may be short-lived. Such regulations are liable to be knocked down in short order under international trade rules such as the *North American Free Trade Agreement*'s controversial chapter 11 provision, which allows companies to sue governments for practices seen as damaging to businesses. I believe that it is very likely that we would be challenged by our NAFTA partners.
>
> —*Bob Kirke, Executive Director, Canadian Apparel Federation, quoted by Sean O'Connor in "CA Lobby Targets Retail Industry,"* Canadian Retailer, *May 2002*

> We develop specifications ... and then we search out the best factories we can find globally. ... If I'm then to post a list for my competitors to just walk to that factory and take advantage of all of our research ... we'd be exposing our trade secrets to our competitors.
>
> —*Martin McCarthy, President, R.J. McCarthy Ltd., suppliers of school uniforms, quoted by Martin Barry in "Anti-sweatshop Groups Have Apparel Makers Sweating,"* Canadian Apparel, *July/August 2002*

Questions

1. Would you support changes to the *Textile Labelling Act, 1985* as proposed by ETAG? Why or why not?
2. Research garment companies to see what they are doing to ensure that their clothing is not being produced in sweatshops. Should Canada ban the sale of any clothing made in factories whose workers' rights are not protected?
3. The issue of monitoring international suppliers is relevant to many industries. Why are clothing manufacturers being specifically targeted?
4. Some companies argue that by setting up factories and creating jobs in poor countries, they have improved peoples' lives regardless of working conditions. Do you agree? Explain.

There have been numerous global social calls to action to try to stop worker exploitation in developing countries. Some argue that TNCs should be allowed to operate in developing countries, but should pay higher wages. TNCs argue that lower wages are paid to these workers because they are less skilled and less efficient than workers in developed countries. To pay such workers higher wages would eliminate the comparative advantage these workers enjoy. It would no longer be worthwhile for TNCs to employ them. Nevertheless, there is pressure on TNCs to pay workers in developing countries a "fair wage" equal to or better than existing wages in the country they are operating in.

Recent changes in trade legislation in both the United States and Europe support these possibilities. The United States passed trade legislation in 2003 allowing for the president to negotiate bilateral, regional, and global trade agreements, provided that there is a commitment by the US trading partner agreeing to honour internationally recognized labour rights. The partner's reward would be access to the US market. In January 2002, the European Union adopted a Generalized Scheme of Preferences that doubles the tariff cuts of developing countries if the EU determines that the country protects basic workers' rights.

What is very clear is that, while sweatshops with poor working conditions, unfair wages, and worker abuse were a significant part of the first wave of globalization and freer trade, there are signs of improvement. As companies' production methods are exposed, public and government pressure for change increases. The hope is that as the economies of developing countries become stronger, labour standards will also improve.

Check Your Understanding

1. a) How is the WTO different from GATT?
   b) Why do you think there are protests against the power of the WTO?
2. What role does the ILO play in protecting "core labour standards"? How effective do you think this role is? Explain.
3. There are two sides to the issue of whether core labour standards should form a part of the WTO. Explain both sides. Which position do you agree with? Why?
4. Give an example of a TNC. How have TNCs become a significant part of globalization?
5. What is the significance of *Convention 182*, passed by the ILO in 1999?

Methods of Legal Inquiry

Conducting a Debate

Debating is a skill that requires you to present and defend a clear argument on an issue. You have to learn to "think on your feet" in order to answer the person or persons presenting and defending an opposing position.

In a formal debate, the issue is worded in a particular form, for example:

> Resolved that: The right to unionize and engage in collective bargaining is essential to protect and enhance long-term human welfare in a globalized world environment.

Whether you are defending or refuting this resolution, you will have to make some preparations.

- Research the topic thoroughly.
- Understand both sides of the issue.
- Take detailed notes and document all your sources.
- Prepare step-by-step points to present your case and anticipate potential rebuttal.
- Elaborate in greater detail on the points that best support your position.
- If you are working as a team, outline your team strategy, deciding on the order of the speakers and which points each speaker will present.

According to traditional (parliamentary) rules of conduct, the speakers on each team have defined roles. Each team can present its own case and rebut the points made by the other team. Rebuttal is an art that requires quick and logical thinking. It is best directed at the other team's major points; avoid personal criticism.

This is the usual order of speakers:

- Speaker 1 (pro) defines resolution, presents key points of affirmative (government) team's case, and gives first half of argument
- Speaker 2 (con) accepts or rejects definition of resolution, presents key points of negative (opposition) team's case, and rebuts main points of first speaker
- Speaker 3 (pro) restates government team's position, rebuts points made by speaker 2, and presents final points of government's case
- Speaker 4 (con) restates opposition, rebuts points made by government speakers 1 and 3, and presents second half of opposition's case
- Speaker 5 (pro) reaffirms government case, rebuts remainder of opposition case, summarizes government's points, and rounds off argument
- Speaker 6 (con) reaffirms opposition case, rebuts remainder of government case, summarizes opposition points, and rounds off complete debate

At the end of the debate the listeners vote to accept or reject the resolution by a count of raised hands.

You can apply this skill to the You Decide! review exercise that follows.

Reviewing Main Ideas

You Decide!

UNIONS AND GLOBALIZATION

Choose teams of three and conduct a debate on the following resolution:

> Resolved that: The right to unionize and engage in collective bargaining is essential to protect and enhance long-term human welfare in a globalized world environment.

Unions and Collective Bargaining: Economic Effects in a Global Environment, a book by Toke Aidt and Zafiris Tzannatos (Washington, DC: World Bank, 2002), looks at the many aspects of this issue. Here are some arguments in support of unions found in the World Bank study:

- Higher wages come to those who are covered by collective agreements.
- Job tenure is longer in unionized firms compared with non-unionized firms.
- Fringe benefits are more common among unionized workers than among non-unionized ones.

These are some arguments against unions found in the World Bank study:

- Employment growth is slower in unionized firms than in non-unionized ones.
- Spending on research and development is lower in unionized firms compared with non-unionized ones.
- Unions have a potentially negative impact on productivity levels.

Here are two other opinions on the issue:

People join unions because it improves their standard of living and adds to their quality of life.

—*Ken Georgetti, President, Canadian Labour Congress, February 24, 2003*

Rigid labour contracts in most instances impede an employer's ability to adopt the right mix of capital, labour, and managerial discretion to changing market conditions.

—*Fazil Mihlar,* The Financial Post, *March 14, 2003*

Use these resources and others that you find, particularly on the Internet, to prepare your arguments. At the end of the debate, write a one-page report on what you learned about globalization and the future of collective bargaining.

Key Terms

Review the following terms to show that you understand the meaning of each and how it is applied in a legal context.

bilateral	multilateral
European Union (EU)	ratify
globalization	transnational corporation (TNC)
maquiladoras	

Understanding the Law

Review the following pieces of legislation (or organizations) mentioned in the text, and show that you understand the intent of each.

Free Trade Agreement
Free Trade Agreement of the Americas
General Agreement on Tariffs and Trade
North American Free Trade Agreement
World Trade Organization

Thinking and Inquiry

1. Use the Internet and your school or local library to research the protests at the Summit of the Americas held in Quebec City on April 20–22, 2001.
   a) What issues did the protesters raise?
   b) What was the Canadian government's response to the protesters' actions?
   c) How did corporate Canada react to the protests?
   d) Do you agree or disagree with the stand of the protesters on the FTAA? Explain your opinion.
2. Explain how the need for North American companies to remain competitive and maintain profits has affected North American workers.
3. Do you agree with the federal government's position that while freer trade may eliminate some jobs in Canada, newer and better jobs will be created? Explain and support your position with statistics on employment and income from the pre– and post–free trade eras.
4. Do you agree with WTO Director Mike Moore's statement that "countries that have embraced openness and freedom [in trade] have increased the real incomes of their workers, which in turn has raised labour standards and reduced poverty"? Respond in a two-page report.

Communication

5. Locate and visit the government of Canada's Web site. Search the archives and review the debates held in April 1997 in Parliament, when the Canadian government decided to ban the sale of MMT in Canada. What were some of the recurring comments made by MPs in support of banning MMT? Was there any support for MMT? If so, what did the supporter(s) say? Write a brief summary of the positions of MPs, and give your opinion of the arguments presented.

6. Compile a list that outlines the minimum labour standards for workers employed in a factory operating in a developing country that produces garments to be sold in Canada. Justify each standard, giving reasons why you think it is important.
7. Interview two people who were part of the labour force in the 1980s and 1990s, and find out how the introduction of the FTA and NAFTA affected their workplace. What are their opinions on these agreements? Share your findings with your class.
8. State your opinions on the following, and be prepared to defend your position.
   a) The WTO should include and enforce a set of core labour standards as part of its policy of global trade among its members.
   b) In order to protect workers' rights in Canada, the federal government should withdraw from NAFTA, the FTAA, and the WTO, effective immediately.
   c) Clothing sold by companies that have been accused of operating sweatshops should be banned from your school.

Application

9. Set up a petition and "Cut It Out" campaign within your school. Write a report on the response you receive from students, teachers, school administration, school council, school board, and the community. Contact your local Member of Parliament at the conclusion of the campaign and deliver the labels, your report, and a signed petition of support to him or her.
10. Using your understanding of NAFTA, identify specific industries in your immediate community that have experienced either an unfavourable or a favourable impact as a direct result of NAFTA. Summarize your findings.
11. Some people in business and government advocate a four-day workweek to solve the problem of job losses. Discuss this proposal with a partner, and draw up a list of pros and cons for this suggestion from the point of view of (a) employers and (b) unions.

Unit 5

International Law

What is international law? Unlike the law you have studied so far in this book, international law is a mass of agreements among nations that decide to be parties to these agreements. There is no international force to "police" nations that breach agreements they have signed, and international courts, as you will see, are limited in their jurisdictions. The United Nations most approximates a world law-making body, but it too is limited in its capabilities to make and enforce international law.

In this unit, you will explore the tensions between the idea of state sovereignty—that nations have the right to make and implement laws within their own boundaries without interference from other nations—and the idea of international rules that apply to all humanity and to common areas of the Earth, such as the oceans. As well, you will consider the effect of political developments on international law since the emergence of the United States as the single superpower after the collapse of its rival, the Soviet Union.

Chapter 16 starts by examining the traditional concept of state sovereignty and the reasons that international law developed in the 20th century to challenge this concept. The chapter looks at how and why treaties are negotiated and their role in international law, as well as the role of diplomacy in facilitating relationships among states.

In Chapter 17, a study of international organizations starts with considering the role of the United Nations as an international agency for facilitating the establishment of international norms. You will then judge the limitations of the United Nations and the International Court of Justice in enforcing these norms. The issue of human rights, a major concern of international law and international organizations, is explored. The chapter ends with an overview of regional organizations that are important to Canadians.

Chapter 18 considers how international law applies to various boundaries: land, the oceans, airspace, and outer space. Starting with the basic idea of state sovereignty over land, the chapter explores how new ideas, such as the "common heritage" of humankind, are changing international law. The chapter raises and probes difficult questions. For example, who owns the resources of the deep seabed and the moon? Should outer space be militarized?

In Chapter 19, you will consider the area of international law that governs military conflict between nations, as well as efforts to resolve conflict by peaceful means and to limit military actions and weapons. The issue of the unilateral use of military force without reference to the United Nations is raised, as well as the problems of dealing with terrorism.

Chapter 16 Principles of International Law

CHAPTER *Focus*

In this chapter, you will

- demonstrate an understanding of the concept of state sovereignty
- explain the evolution and development of international law
- evaluate the importance of treaties in national and international law
- examine the major conventions governing diplomatic relations

One of the main functions of international law is to govern the relations among sovereign states. States reach out to one another, negotiate, and make agreements; occasionally, they also harm one another, either deliberately or accidentally. International law smooths the process of state interactions by providing rules for conduct, mechanisms for the resolution of disputes, and substantive and procedural law to help guide decisions. But what is international law? This chapter examines some of the basic principles that have developed to manage relations among states and international organizations.

The cartoon in Figure 16.1 was published about one month before terrorist attacks on Washington and New York in 2001.

Figure 16.1

At First Glance

1. Give an example of a global treaty. What comment is the cartoonist making about the nature of global treaties?
2. Do you agree that the cooperation of the United States is necessary for global treaties to succeed?
3. Do you think the image of the nations of the world on the global treaties plane is an appropriate one? Why or why not?
4. Do you agree with the cartoonist's point of view? Why or why not?

International Law in Everyday Life

International law affects individuals and society in some very specific ways and touches on nearly all aspects of daily life. Consider, for example, an everyday activity such as a drive to the local Wal-Mart for a CD by a favourite British band. Many aspects of this simple excursion are affected by international rules.

- The ability of Wal-Mart, a US corporation, to invest securely in Canada is regulated by general international rules and the *North American Free Trade Agreement* (NAFTA).
- Many CDs sold in stores are manufactured in Asia or South America. Their sale in Canadian markets is regulated by international trade-law rules administered by the international World Trade Organization (WTO).
- The shipping of the CD (by air or sea) to Canada is heavily regulated by international agreements.
- The trademark of the multinational corporation that produced the CD is protected by international agreement, as is the copyright of the owner of the lyrics.
- The content, the format, and the conditions of the manufacture of the CD are all subject to international standards, for example, the Organisation for Economic Co-operation and Development (OECD) *Guidelines for Multinational Enterprises.*

The bottom line, in this scenario, is that in a globalized world even the most mundane activity is affected by international considerations.

state sovereignty: the lawful control by a state over its territory, right to govern in that territory, and authority to apply law there to the exclusion of other states

The Paradox of State Sovereignty

For centuries, the principle of **state sovereignty** has governed interactions among states. Originally, this concept meant that a state had the unfettered

Fyi In 1493, Pope Alexander VI settled the dispute between Spain and Portugal over land claims in the New World. Spain could claim land to the west of a line of longitude through the Atlantic Ocean, and Portugal could claim land to the east. The *Treaty of Tordesillas* in 1494 settled this Line of Demarcation. The eastern tip of Brazil was east of the line, which is why Portuguese and not Spanish is spoken in Brazil.

Fyi Starting in 1894, the Turkish Ottoman Empire began a campaign of genocide against the Christian Armenians. By 1918, about 1 800 000 had been killed and thousands had fled. No international body existed to intervene.

right to conduct itself in any manner it chose over its own territory. In addition, the concept meant that a state could exclude assertions of jurisdiction by other states in its territory or with respect to other rights that it enjoyed under international law. International law was seen as a guarantor of state sovereignty, but also as having the potential to limit sovereignty.

The idea of exclusive jurisdiction over the territory of a national state was developed and solidified from the 17th through 19th centuries. Vast tracts of "empty" or "unoccupied" land were partitioned and allocated to states. By the end of the 20th century, almost all land areas of the world were under the sovereignty of the states that constitute the international system. Yet, in this same period, states, by developing international law and entering willingly into treaties, limited their freedom of action and thus their sovereignty.

The World Becomes Smaller

Until the latter half of the 20th century, nations upheld the importance of state sovereignty. After World War II ended, this idea gave way to a broader view of the rights and responsibilities of states. Several factors contributed to this change.

Advances in technology, especially transportation technology and the communications revolution, affected the world community throughout the 20th century. Between the 1930s and 2000, world population more than tripled. With this growth, international travel and emigration increased. Many individuals now had multijurisdictional economic, legal, and personal ties that needed a legal framework within which to operate. More and more international commercial enterprises flourished. The activities of these new multinational corporations had to be regulated, and, in turn, the corporations demanded legally regulated investment and financial services and legal protection from arbitrary state action when they invested overseas.

Support for international law, especially as a tool for human rights protection, received a dramatic boost through the events of World War II. At least as far as the modern Western world was concerned, the Nazi atrocities uncovered in the last months of the war were Europe's first contemporary example of large-scale state-sanctioned genocide. The German government's murder and torture of Jewish and other prisoners during the war demanded a response that the fledgling international community was compelled, yet ill-equipped, to provide. Through an impressive effort, however, the international community organized itself to judge and punish "war criminals," creating the law that underlay the Nuremberg and Tokyo tribunals that put the leaders of German and Japanese policies on trial.

In the postwar period, the scope of international law expanded to include many activities that did not directly involve the state. It quickly became clear that a wide range of human activity needed to be regulated

Figure 16.2 *War crimes trial defendants charged with organizing genocide and gross violations against human rights listen at the Nuremberg trials in Nuremberg, Germany, on September 30, 1946. Defendants are seated in two rows before the line of helmeted military police.*

on an international basis. New technological developments, such as space vehicle overflight and remote sensing from satellites, meant that traditional ideas of exclusive territorial state sovereignty had to be reconsidered. The law governing outer space is an example of an international agreement spurred by technological developments. On October 4, 1957, the Soviet Union successfully launched *Sputnik I*, an unmanned space satellite that circled the Earth every 96 minutes. The international community responded by creating rules to govern this new activity.

Fyi *Sputnik I* incinerated on re-entering the Earth's atmosphere on January 4, 1958. *Sputnik II*, launched on November 3, 1957, carried a dog, Laika.

The Law From the *Treaty on Principles Governing the Activities of States in the Exploration and Use of Outer Space, Including the Moon and Other Celestial Bodies* (1967):

Article I

The exploration and use of outer space, including the moon and other celestial bodies, shall be carried out for the benefit and in the interests of all countries, irrespective of their degree of economic or scientific development, and shall be the province of all mankind.

Outer space, including the moon and other celestial bodies, shall be free for exploration and use by all States without discrimination of any kind, on a basis of equality and in accordance with international law, and there shall be free access to all areas of celestial bodies.

There shall be freedom of scientific investigation in outer space, including the moon and other celestial bodies, and States shall facilitate and encourage international co-operation in such investigation.

Article II

Outer space, including the moon and other celestial bodies, is not subject to national appropriation by claim of sovereignty, by means of use or occupation, or by any other means. ...

Article IV

States Parties [that have agreed] to the Treaty undertake not to place in orbit around the Earth any objects carrying nuclear weapons or any other kinds of weapons of mass destruction, install such weapons on celestial bodies, or station such weapons in outer space in any other manner.

The moon and other celestial bodies shall be used by all States Parties to the Treaty exclusively for peaceful purposes. The establishment of military bases, installations and fortifications, the testing of any type of weapons and the conduct of military manoeuvres on celestial bodies shall be forbidden. The use of military personnel for scientific research or for any other peaceful purposes shall not be prohibited. The use of any other equipment or facility necessary for peaceful exploration of the moon and other celestial bodies shall also not be prohibited.

Article V

States Parties [that have agreed] to the Treaty shall regard astronauts as envoys of mankind in outer space and shall render to them all possible assistance in the event of accident, distress, or emergency landing on the territory of another State Party or on the high seas. ...

Article VI

States Parties [that have agreed] to the Treaty shall bear international responsibility for national activities in outer space ... whether such activities are carried on by governmental agencies or by non-governmental entities. ... The activities of non-governmental entities in outer space ... shall require authorization and continuing supervision by the appropriate State Party to the Treaty. When activities are carried on in outer space ... by an international organization, responsibility for compliance with this Treaty shall be borne both by the international organization and by the States Parties to the Treaty participating in such organization.

Figure 16.3 *Astronauts Neil Armstrong and Buzz Aldrin plant the US flag on the lunar surface, July 20, 1969.*

Questions

1. Does article IV prohibit the passage of ballistic missiles (long-range rocket-powered missiles aimed at specific targets) through outer space? Explain your answer, referring to the article that addresses this issue.
2. Who is responsible under article VI for the acts or omissions of any private activities in space (e.g., by a telecommunications company)? Does the treaty imagine the possibility of activities by an international organization, for example, the European Space Agency?
3. In Figure 16.3, American astronauts are pictured raising the US flag on the moon in 1969. What are the political implications of this action, which took place only months after the United States ratified the outer space treaty?

The interdependent nature of the international community and the need to coordinate actions among states have given rise to a number of initiatives that limit action by individual states. States have willingly surrendered much of their freedom of action within their own territories in order to gain the political, economic, or scientific advantages of cooperation and standardization. The idea of absolute state sovereignty has given way to an international legal system under which many activities within the territory of a state are now regulated. The term "international law" now describes not only the relations among states, but also how states handle such matters as human rights within their borders.

Issues

Canada's Arctic and State Sovereignty

Should the Canadian government allocate more resources to solidify sovereignty claims to Arctic islands and establish claims over Arctic waters and ice?

Canada's Arctic occupies a strategic location politically and economically, and contains a vast storehouse of natural resources, including energy resources. It underlies important air communications routes between Japan and Europe and "great circle" airline routes from the United States to Europe. As well, it sits astride navigation routes from the eastern seaboard of the United States to Alaska. The population is sparse and communications links, especially those connecting the region to the south, are tenuous.

Canadian claims to sovereignty over the seas and ice-covered areas between the islands of the Far North have been challenged by the United States. The voyages of the *Manhattan*, an ice-strengthened US supertanker, through the Northwest Passage tested the possibility of oil transport from Alaska's North Slope to the US eastern seaboard in 1969 and 1970. The Canadian government reacted to the voyage of the *Polar Sea*, a US Coast Guard icebreaker, through Arctic waters in August 1985 by issuing a formal statement declaring the waters between the mainland and the Arctic islands internal Canadian waters. It announced plans to construct a Polar 8–class diesel-powered icebreaker, intended to demonstrate Canada's effective occupancy of the Far North, but in 1990 the project was cancelled.

The following excerpts show opinions on the issue of Canadian claims to sovereignty in the North.

> It is the first task of any national government worth its salt to assert, defend, and promote its territorial sovereignty. But apparently our federal government has neither the time nor the interest to do this in the Arctic.
>
> —*Canadian Arctic Resources Committee, "Sovereignty Over the Northwest Passage,"* Members Update, *Summer 1995*

> With the polar ice cap in the Canadian Arctic melting, a possible maritime route—the Northwest Passage—is opening up. In the next couple of decades, commercial ships may start plying the Arctic route instead of going through the Panama Canal—a shortcut of more than 4000 nautical miles.
>
> And so the question of Canadian sovereignty is, well, if not exactly heating up, then at least defrosting. The United States and other maritime powers do not accept Canada's claim to sovereignty over the waters of the Arctic archipelago. But an oil spill in such a fragile ecosystem would be a disaster. And so it matters whose environmental regulations hold sway at the top of the world.
>
> Christopher Sands, director of the Canada Project at the Center for Strategic and International Studies in Washington, worries aloud about the sort of power vacuum that could develop if the Arctic turned into a real shipping route without a universally accepted regulatory regime in place. ... His proposal: Despite US resistance, the international community should grant Canada special custodianship of the Arctic ecosystem, just as Australia has been granted a custodial role for the Great Barrier Reef, an ecosystem lying partly inside and partly outside Australian waters.
>
> —*Ruth Walker, "Arctic Thaw Opening Up Lucrative Shipping Route,"* The Christian Science Monitor, *June 7, 2000*

> Academics argue Canada's legal claim to the Arctic strait wouldn't hold up in the court of international public opinion. Military analysts claim the Canadian Forces lack the resources and personnel to effectively defend and patrol the area. ...
>
> "The Inuit should take the lead when it comes to protecting Canada's sovereignty in the North," said Franklyn Griffiths, a peace and conflict studies professor at the University of Toronto. ... He says since Canada uses the Inuit's historic claim to northern lands as proof

of Canadian sovereignty, it should allow northern peoples the right to control coastal waters.

> *—Matthew Van Dongen, "Stopping Canadian Sovereignty from Melting Away,"* Capital News Online, *http://temagami.carleton.ca/jmc/cnews/01022002/connections/c3.html*

Can Canada really claim that it has sovereignty over Arctic waters if there are sub-surface transits of the Northwest Passage undertaken without Canada's consent? Sovereignty implies authority and control, both of which are lacking if Canada is not in a position to determine whether such voyages are taking place. Failure to take steps to ensure that there is knowledge of what is happening both on and under the surface of the waters of the Arctic could lead to the loss by Canada of its claim to sovereignty over Arctic waters.

> *—Donald M. McRae, "Arctic Sovereignty: Loss by Dereliction?"* Northern Perspectives *(Vol. 22, No. 4), Winter 1994–95*

Learn about a trip taken by Canadian Rangers who patrol the Arctic at www.emp.ca/dimensionsoflaw

There's the whole area of the Arctic that we have to consider: how we continue to ensure that our interests are safeguarded in that area, because if you don't defend and you ignore certain parts of your land-mass, then you are in effect saying that it's not that important to you, and you are inviting others to establish a presence.

> *—David Collenette, Minister of National Defence, May 2, 1994; transcription of remarks at Canadian Defence Preparedness Association Defence 2000 seminar, Ottawa*

Over the last 35 years, Ottawa has failed to act on any of its promises to strengthen our grip on the Arctic—to build $500 million icebreakers, to buy 10 nuclear attack submarines to work under the polar ice, to establish five northern air force bases.

Two years ago, then foreign affairs minister Lloyd Axworthy unveiled the latest policy on Canada's North that would see Canada broaden its scientific and other activities in the Arctic to assert its interests.

"One of the most important ways of [asserting sovereignty over the Arctic] is not through the old traditional means of sending an icebreaker," he said. "I don't see this simply as ... standing there planting flags and glaring at each other across ice floes."

Nothing has happened to Axworthy's grand plan, either.

Maybe this time Canada will overcome its timidity and actually act on its dream of firmly establishing an independent claim to the Arctic. History, however, shows it will require real political will.

> *—Brendon Grunewald, "Northwest Passage a Shipping Lane?" Posted at* 70 South, *August 7, 2002; www.70south.com/news/1028712881/index_html*

Questions

1. Why does the prospect of global warming make the issue of sovereignty in Arctic waters more pressing?
2. How does the use of Arctic waters by US nuclear submarines affect Canada's claims to sovereignty?
3. Would you support measures by the Canadian government to assert sovereignty in Arctic waters? Why or why not?

Check Your Understanding

1. Explain the concept of state sovereignty.
2. Why is this concept important to the study of international law?
3. What factors in the 20th century led to support for a more limited notion of sovereignty? Explain each one.
4. Refer to Chapter 15 and explain how Canada has surrendered aspects of state sovereignty over its trade by membership in NAFTA and the WTO.

The Development of International Law

International law is a valid and often effective tool for shaping relations among states and, to some extent, between state governments and their peoples. However, it does not work in the same way as the domestic law that you have studied in earlier chapters of this book. To understand international law, you may need to set aside some assumptions about how "law" is supposed to work.

The narrow domain of early international law was restricted to the protection of diplomats, the establishment of state boundaries, and **treaty** law. Only very rarely was early international law seen as a tool for regulating the consequences of individual activity. The one striking example was the law respecting suppression of piracy on the high seas. Alberico Gentili, a 16th-century Italian, wrote: "Piracy is contrary to the law of nations and the league of human society. Therefore war should be made against pirates by all men." Pirates were deemed to be "enemies of humankind," and therefore subject to "universal jurisdiction," which meant that all states that captured them could put them on trial.

treaty: an agreement between or among nations, usually concluded in written form and governed by international law

How International Law Differs from Domestic Law

One of most important distinctions that sets international law apart from domestic law is that international law does not exist within a formal justice system. As you have seen, a country's domestic legal system is typically composed of a mechanism that creates binding rules, a judicial system for hearing civil lawsuits or prosecuting crimes, and an enforcement system. There is no international legislature passing laws like Parliament. In the international arena, while there are some judicial bodies of limited application, such as the International Court of Justice and the International Criminal Court, most of the mechanisms characteristic of a comprehensive judicial system simply do not exist, and enforcement measures are only sometimes available.

Personal Viewpoint

Hugo Grotius: Early Thoughts on International Law

In 1625, Hugo de Groot or Grotius, a Dutch lawyer, historian, poet, and theologian, published *De jure belli ac pacis Libri Tris* (*Three Books on the Law of War and Peace*). Grotius (1583–1645) was the first modern writer to write on the laws of states. He lived during a period of seemingly endless wars between nation states in Europe. In his book he describes his great desire to see peace and security in the world community:

> I saw prevailing throughout the Christian world a licence in making war of which even barbarous nations should be ashamed; men resorting to arms for trivial or for no reasons at all, and when arms were once taken up no reverence left for divine or human law, exactly as if a single edict [order having the force of law] had released a madness driving men to all kinds of crime.

To the scholar, there was a natural order, or natural law, found only by looking to past laws of other nations and civilizations. Four principles formed the foundation of the law of nations:

1. Neither state nor individual may attack another state or individual.
2. Neither state nor individual may take what belongs to another state or individual.
3. Neither state nor individual may disregard a treaty or contract of another state or individual.
4. Neither state nor individual may commit a crime.

Grotius wrote that if wars were fought for a moral purpose, then they were to be fought in the interests of a broader community. This premise imposed certain duties on the nations waging war:

Figure 16.4 *Hugo Grotius produced the first comprehensive study of international law.*

- Harm to people not taking part in the war was to be avoided.
- Care was to be taken of those conquered on the field of battle.
- Victory should not mean pillage and plunder; war is not a matter of revenge.

Questions

1. Give a contemporary example of each of the four principles that Grotius states form the foundation of the law of nations.
2. Do you think there can be a moral purpose for war? Explain your answer.
3. Do Grotius's duties on nations waging war exist today? Explain.

Nations are encouraged or persuaded to obey international law not because of the risk of legal sanctions, but because continued acceptance by the international community and participation in its activities serve the member nations' individual and community interests. For example, countries in which children are required or permitted to work under unacceptable conditions may find that countries opposed to child labour refuse to buy their products. The offending countries can often improve their export potential by working to comply with international labour standards—for example, by agreeing to abide by the International Labour Organization's Program on the Elimination of Child Labour.

Much of the time, international law depends on a state's voluntarily agreeing to be subject to particular rules. For example, much international law is treaty-based: a state must sign and ratify a treaty before it will be bound. States must choose to become members of organizations or alliances, or allow international institutions to exercise jurisdiction before their rules will apply. A good example of this is participation in the process of the International Criminal Court (ICC), established in 2002. The ICC, which is designed to deal with questions of individual criminal responsibility, was established by the United Nations' *Rome Statute of the International Criminal Court.* Members at an international conference, with 120 nations participating, agreed on this statute, which dealt with the issue of international criminal prosecutions. Unfortunately, a number of influential states, including the United States, China, and Russia, had not ratified the statute by the time it had come into force, making their participation in the ICC unlikely, at least for the moment. (You will learn more about the ICC in Chapter 19: Military Conflict and Conflict Resolution.)

To learn more about the Eichmann trial, visit www.emp.ca/dimensionsoflaw

Because of gaps in the international system, sometimes reliance must be placed on domestic enforcement. The case of Adolf Eichmann is an example of an individual state's undertaking the prosecution of a war criminal under circumstances that raised questions about state sovereignty and international law. This case underlines the dilemma of dealing with a problem within a system that has evident gaps and is designed to give precedence to sovereignty issues.

Case TRYING A MASS MURDERER

Attorney General of Israel v. Eichmann, 36 Intl. L Rep. 5 (Israel, Dist. Ct. Jerusalem 1961)

Facts

Adolf Eichmann, a high-profile member of the German SS and a war criminal, was tracked down in Argentina by Israeli nationals, seized, and abducted to Israel in May 1960. Argentina complained to the United Nations Security Council, which, while not condoning the crimes of which Eichmann was accused, declared that "acts such as [Eichmann's abduction], which affect the sovereignty of a Member State and therefore cause international friction, may, if repeated, endanger international peace and security." The UN Security Council ordered the government of Israel "to make appropriate reparation in accordance with the Charter of the United Nations and the rules of international law." Argentina did not, however, demand the return of Eichmann. On August 3, 1960, the Argentine and Israeli governments issued a joint statement in which they resolved "to regard as closed the incident which arose out of the action taken by citizens of Israel, which infringed the fundamental rights of the State of Argentina."

Eichmann was tried in Israel under Israel's *Nazi Collaborators (Punishment) Law*. He was convicted, and after the judgment was confirmed by the Supreme Court of Israel on appeal in 1962, he was executed.

Decision

In coming to its decision, the Israeli court considered the international-law aspects of the case. Eichmann's defence counsel argued that

> the Israel Law, by imposing punishment for acts done outside the boundaries of the State and before its establishment, against persons who were not Israel citizens, and by a person who acted in the course of duty on behalf of a foreign country ("Act of State"), conflicts with international law and exceeds the powers of the Israel Legislature...

and that

> the prosecution of the accused in Israel following his abduction from a foreign country conflicts with international law and exceeds the jurisdiction of the Court... .

The court found that national law would prevail over international law in an Israeli court. From the point of view of international law, the power of the state of Israel to pass the disputed law and Israel's "right to punish" were based on a dual foundation: the universal character of the crimes in question, and their specific character as intended to exterminate the Jewish people.

Questions

1. Summarize the facts in this case in relation to questions of state sovereignty and international law. Was the outcome satisfactory?
2. What arguments did the defence lawyers give? Do you agree with these arguments? Explain.
3. a) What do you understand the term "war criminal" to mean?
   b) Do you think the scope of Eichmann's crimes justified Israeli actions?

Regulating the International Impact of Domestic Law

In an interconnected world, activities in one state frequently have an impact on other states and their citizens. International law attempts to regulate situations in which activities in one state infringe on the sovereignty of another state, or cause damage to its territory, interests, or citizens.

Extraterritorial Legislation

To protect states' sovereignty, international law seeks to regulate extraterritorial legislation, that is, legislation passed by a state that affects citizens in other states. A prime example of the effects of extraterritorial domestic law is the impact on Canada of the 1996 US law the *Cuban Liberty and Democratic Solidarity Act*, better known as the Helms-Burton legislation.

nationalize: take over an industry, service, or land from private ownership on behalf of the state

After Fidel Castro came to power in Cuba in 1959, he **nationalized**, without compensation, property owned by Cuban and foreign (primarily US) companies and individuals. The former owners protested, and the US government challenged the action on their behalf, imposing crippling economic sanctions on Cuba. Still, there was no acceptable resolution of the situation.

The international law governing nationalization is complex. Many countries feel that their investments in other countries should not be subject to nationalization without compensation. Developing countries that have nationalized such investments often argue that nationalization, especially in cases where investors have benefited from an unjust and corrupt social, political, and economic system, is fair and necessary to achieve a just society. They point out that "investments" by nationals of richer countries are often made on very attractive terms secured by kickbacks to corrupt politicians, and that often, prior to nationalization, such "investments" are repaid many times over by excessive profits. They argue that "investors," by coming to a foreign country, submit to the local laws, including those with respect to nationalization.

Fyi The United States imposed sanctions against trade with Cuba in 1962. At the time, over 66% of the island's trade was with America. The sanctions were still in place in 2003.

In the 1990s, the United States passed laws with respect to the nationalized assets in Cuba to prevent their effective use. The Cuban government tried to sell or lease nationalized assets, such as mining operations, to corporations in countries that had relatively friendly relations with Cuba, such as Canada. However, the Helms-Burton legislation provided for civil suits in US courts against foreign nationals using, dealing, or "trafficking" in property in Cuba to which US nationals had claims. It also excluded certain foreign individuals from the United States by denying US visas to executives and majority shareholders (and their immediate families) of companies "trafficking" in such property.

Under this law, seven top executives and directors of Sherritt International Corp., a Canadian mining company, were in danger of exclusion from the United States and of being sued there for having carried out activities in Canada and Cuba that were perfectly legal under the laws of those two countries. Protest by Canada and other countries drew international attention to this legislation and stimulated lively debate about whether a state could impose penalties domestically on foreign nationals for activities that are legal in other states. (These provisions of the Helms-Burton legislation have since been suspended.)

Controlling Activities with Cross-Border Impacts

International law also seeks to regulate activities of a state that have an impact beyond its borders in a physical sense. The most famous case in this area of the law involves Canada. The *Trail Smelter* case of 1937 involved a metal-processing plant in Trail, British Columbia, that constantly released fumes that crossed the border and damaged apple orchards in the state of Washington. The United States brought a claim on behalf of the apple farmers against Canada (even though the government was in no way involved in running the plant, which was operated by a private corporation). An arbitrator who was asked to assist in resolving the dispute sided with the Americans, requiring Canada to pay damages and to take steps to prevent, or at least reduce, the fumes. The tribunal based its decision on the following principle:

> [U]nder the principles of international law, ... no State has the right to use or permit the use of its territory in such a manner as to cause injury by fumes in or to the territory of another or the properties or persons therein... .

Canada, in turn, has challenged activities of other states that have had an impact on its territory and interests. One example concerned the operation of the Soviet space program. In 1978, the Soviet nuclear-powered spy satellite *Cosmos 954* crashed in northern Canada. Canada sought compensation from the then Soviet Union for cleanup costs of radioactive materials scattered over 124 000 square kilometres. Although the Soviet Union balked at paying because it claimed that unnecessary costs were incurred by the involvement of American crew (which included intelligence agents eager to examine Soviet technology), eventually a settlement was reached and the Soviet Union paid the agreed amount.

Fyi According to the Atomic Energy Control Board of Canada, the cost of cleanup from the *Cosmos 954* crash was $14 million. The Soviet Union paid Canada $3 million.

CHECK YOUR UNDERSTANDING

1. How is international law different from domestic law? Give reasons for these differences.
2. Do you think the early principles of international law that applied to pirates should apply to contemporary international terrorists? Explain your answer.
3. What advantages do states gain by agreeing to be subject to international law?
4. Much polluted air from the United States affects air quality in Canada, and pollutants from Ontario affect the state of New York. Using the *Trail Smelter* ruling as a guide, should the state of New York be able to sue Ontario, or should Canada be able to sue the United States? Explain your reasoning.
5. Based on what you have learned, write your definition of international law. You will revisit this definition later in the chapter.

The Importance of Treaties

Treaties are one of the pillars of international relations. Rulers and officials representing peoples have entered into binding mutual commitments throughout history. Evidence has been found of a treaty dating to 1269 BCE. Signed by Hattusilis III, King of the Hittites, and Ramses II, the Egyptian Pharaoh, it pledged eternal friendship, lasting peace, territorial integrity, non-aggression, **extradition**, and mutual help.

extradition: the act of returning a person to a jurisdiction in which he or she is charged with a crime for trial in that jurisdiction

Treaties are in many ways similar to the contracts that regulate legal relations within individual nations. The international documents that are generally recognized as treaties may use the terms "treaty," "convention," "protocol," "agreement," "memorandum of understanding," "accord," "exchange of notes," or "arrangement." As long as these documents express agreement and are entered into by state governments, they will be generally subject to rules governing treaties.

Treaty-making often serves the same functions on the international level that legislation serves within countries. Relations between Canada and its closest neighbour, ally, and largest trading partner—the United States—are governed by hundreds of treaties on a wide range of topics (see Figure 16.5).

Canada is bound by many other treaties as well, by both bilateral (two-party) and multilateral (multiple-party) treaties covering nearly every conceivable area of human activity. For example, one of Canada's "hot" exports is ice wine. By 2003 an agreement was struck among wine trade groups from Canada, Austria, and Germany—all major producers of ice wine—to establish voluntary international standards for ice-wine production. Undoubtedly, an international agreement by various states will follow.

Selected Issues Covered by US–Canada Treaties

- Atomic energy
- Air traffic control
- Border security
- Boundary issues
- Protection of migratory birds
- Import of archaelogical/ethnological artifacts
- Educational exchanges
- Cooperative development of new technologies
- Environmental cleanups
- Extradition
- Refugees
- Great Lakes water quality
- Transboundary movement of hazardous waste
- Postal matters
- Suppression of smuggling

Figure 16.5

Basic Treaty-Law Principles

The law of treaties is complex. It is partly treaty-based, with the rest flowing from historical patterns of inter-state practice.

The 1969 *Vienna Convention on the Law of Treaties* and the 1986 *Convention on the Law of Treaties between States and International Organizations or between International Organizations* codify the main rules of treaty formation, application, and enforcement. These written rules were developed over the course of history through **customary law** and practice, and they are supported and interpreted by new applications and practices. To achieve its intended purposes, a treaty must be negotiated, signed, ratified, and implemented (enforced or put into effect) within each state that is a party to (has signed) the treaty.

customary law: a common pattern that has emerged over time to become binding in international law

Treaty Negotiations

The first stage is negotiation, which often occurs in a bilateral or multilateral context, such as an international forum or a diplomatic conference. The *Vienna Convention on the Law of Treaties* sets out the minimum standards of conduct for the negotiation process, and invalidates treaties "procured by the threat or use of force in violation of the principles of international law embodied in the Charter of the United Nations." These standards have been further elaborated by a UN resolution on the "principles and guidelines for international negotiations." Among other criteria, the resolution states that "[t]he purpose and object of all negotiations must be fully compatible with the principles and norms of international law, including the provisions of the Charter." To understand why this condition is important, consider the validity of "peace treaties" when one party state has militarily defeated another.

Signing, Ratification, and Reservations

At the end of negotiations, the negotiators produce a mutually agreed text. To give effect to the understandings that have been reached, the negotiators, on behalf of their respective countries, sign the treaty. Signing is a formal process that indicates the general (and sometimes temporary) agreement of the parties with the text of the treaty. To render a treaty fully binding, it must be ratified, or formally accepted. Ratification is done once the government has had a chance to review the work of its own ambassadors. Ratification of a treaty may be absolute, or may be accompanied by a (written) reservation. A reservation essentially modifies a party's obligation as described in the negotiated text. In some treaties, reservations may be prohibited; in other circumstances, other parties to the treaty might reject the reservation.

The ratification process varies from country to country. In Canada, ratification is done by the Cabinet, and does not go through the House of Commons and Senate. However, a practice has arisen to submit treaties of fundamental importance to Parliament for its opinion, prior to ratification by the government. For example, when faced with the decision whether to ratify the *Kyoto Protocol*, an environmental treaty with wide-ranging implications for Canadian industry (see Chapter 18: International Law and Common Heritage), the Canadian government chose to put the issue to a vote. The vote, which passed, was essentially a symbolic act; some commentators suggested that it was designed to deflect attention from more substantive debate about implementation.

In other countries, the ratification process is different. For example, in the United States, the president can ratify a treaty only with the "advice and consent of the Senate, ... provided two thirds of the Senators present concur" (article II(2) of the US constitution).

WORKING FOR CHANGE *International Campaign to Ban Landmines*

Anti-personnel landmines are designed to kill or injure people who step on or otherwise disturb them. These devices, buried in over 60 countries, have created a humanitarian problem of global proportions. Innocent victims attempting to use their land, travel, or even just play, can be killed or maimed by these horrific leftovers of war. Anti-personnel landmines are a costly burden on affected countries. They prevent development and drain the medical resources of the countries they infest.

Staff and volunteers of non-governmental organizations, working alongside people in landmine-contaminated areas, were the first to turn world attention to this terrible problem. Development projects in various sectors, including agriculture and water, were impossible where there were landmines. More gruesome were the lost lives and limbs, devastation that organizations such as the local affiliates of the International Committee of the Red Cross saw daily.

In October 1992, six of these organizations gathered in the New York office of Human Rights Watch to issue a "Joint Call to Ban Anti-Personnel Landmines," launching the International Campaign to Ban Landmines.

Figure 16.6 *Britain's Princess Diana tours a minefield dressed in a flak jacket and face shield in Huambo, central Angola, in January 1997. Diana visited Angola for the Red Cross to draw attention to the problems caused by landmines.*

Although the world celebrated when 122 states signed the *Ottawa Convention Banning Landmines* at a ceremony in Ottawa in December

1997, the real work to implement the convention was yet to begin. The Ottawa Convention provides a comprehensive framework for addressing the global landmine problem through formal acceptance of its terms.

Canada was an important founder of the Ottawa Convention and the first country to ratify it—on the same day it was opened for signature. As part of the ratification process, Canada has passed domestic legislation that makes it illegal for any Canadian to produce, use, transfer, or process anti-personnel mines.

Canada also takes its obligations under article 6 of the convention very seriously. This article says that "states in a position to do so" shall provide assistance for mine clearance, victim assistance, mine awareness, mine action planning and technology, and stockpile destruction. To this end, in December 1997, Prime Minister Jean Chrétien announced the establishment of the five-year, $100 million Canadian Landmine Fund to continue work on universalizing the ban and achieving its objectives. To coordinate this effort, and to signal the priority it places on these efforts, Canada appointed a special ambassador to serve as its international focal point on all matters pertaining to the implementation of the Ottawa Convention. Canada has also established a special unit in the Department of Foreign Affairs and International Trade dedicated to the landmine issue and the implementation of the convention.

Questions

1. Research to find out when and why anti-personnel landmines were used in the countries listed in Figure 16.7. Who produces anti-personnel mines?
2. What are the harmful effects of anti-personnel mines? Use evidence from the feature to support your answer.
3. Review the Web sites of organizations such as Handicap International, Human Rights Watch, Mines Advisory Group, and Physicians for Human Rights. Write a paragraph in support of ending the production, transfer, and use of anti-personnel mines.

Figure 16.7

Most Heavily Mined Countries, 1996

Country	Number of landmines per square mile	Estimated total number of landmines
Afghanistan	40	10 000 000
Angola	31	15 000 000
Bosnia and Herzegovina	152	3 000 000
Cambodia	143	10 000 000
Croatia	137	3 000 000
Egypt	60	23 000 000
Iran	25	16 000 000
Iraq	59	10 000 000
Rwanda	25	250 000

Note: One square mile = 2.59 kilometres. There is too little information about some countries, such as Vietnam, to include them in these estimates.

Source: United Nations Children's Fund; www.unicef.org/sowc96pk/hidekill.htm.

Read the latest reports on the progress of the *Ottawa Convention Banning Landmines* at www.emp.ca/dimensionsoflaw

Implementation

To implement a treaty means that a nation state takes steps to make the treaty's terms part of the domestic law of the land. How this is done depends on the content of the treaty. In Canada, boundary treaties can be implemented simply by having their effects recognized by the Crown. Other kinds of treaties may need to be supported by the enactment of new legislation, or the creation of new regulations under existing legislation.

In some countries, implementation flows automatically from ratification. For example, in the United States, once the Senate has ratified a treaty, it becomes "the Supreme Law of the Land" (article VI(2) of the US constitution). This is not the case in Canada, where most treaties must be implemented according to the normal legislative process, subject to the normal division of powers set out in ss. 91 and 92 of the Canadian constitution. In practical terms, this means that the federal government is incapable of implementing treaties that deal with matters under provincial jurisdiction.

The effect of this ruling has been that the federal government is now unwilling to enter into treaty obligations without the iron-clad assurance (usually obtained in advance) that it will not be left internationally liable by the failure of the provinces to pass implementing legislation. In most cases, provinces do give such assurances, making it possible for the federal government to participate in a treaty negotiation.

For more on the *Kyoto Protocol*, visit www.emp.ca/dimensionsoflaw

Problems can occur, however, if some provinces and not others support a treaty with provincial subject matter. This was the case in 2003 with the *Kyoto Protocol*, which Ontario and Alberta opposed because of concerns about the effects of emissions regulations on their industries. To help resolve this issue, Canada and other federal states have been working on a "federal state clause" for inclusion in treaties. The effect of the clause is that a treaty obligation applies only with respect to those provinces (or other sub-units within a federation) that have expressed a willingness to abide by the treaty.

Solving Treaty Disputes

A treaty relationship is an ongoing one. Most treaties have provisions for management of the relationship, including dispute resolution mechanisms.

Dispute resolution provisions can be as simple as a statement that disputes will be resolved by the International Court of Justice, or they can be much more specific. You will learn more about dispute resolution in Chapter 19: Military Conflict and Conflict Resolution.

Usually, a treaty dispute relates to problems with interpretation. International law has evolved a number of complex treaty-interpretation rules, some of which are codified in the *Vienna Convention on the Law of Treaties*. International law, in settling interpretation disputes, takes into account (1) the meaning that parties intended during the negotiation of the treaty and (2) actual practice in the application of the treaty. Actual practice is good evidence of what the treaty means to the parties who agreed to it.

Some treaties provide methods for amending processes. Some even establish elaborate institutional mechanisms for regular review and amendment. A good example of this is the regularly scheduled Conference of the Parties established under the *United Nations Framework Convention on Climate Change.* This is the conference that, in 1997, adopted the *Kyoto Protocol* (see Chapter 18).

Unfortunately, not all treaties, especially those concluded before 1945, have provisions for amendment or termination. This limitation can lead to problems if circumstances change and one of the parties seeks to avoid its obligations by claiming that strict application of the treaty is no longer appropriate. International law deals with such situations by permitting some parties to escape their historical obligations if a fundamental change of circumstance has occurred that was not foreseen when the treaty was made. This rule supports the current view that treaty relations should be seen as part of a continual adjustment in international relationships to keep pace with change.

CHECK YOUR UNDERSTANDING

1. In what ways are treaties a key part of international law? Consider how they are negotiated, ratified, and enforced.
2. What is a "federal state clause," and why does Canada need to include one in its treaties?
3. Why are dispute resolution mechanisms needed for treaties?
4. Use the *Ottawa Convention Banning Landmines* as an example to explain how an international issue may be addressed by a treaty.

Diplomatic Relations

International law is also expressed through state practice, which results in what is known as customary international law. Some of the oldest rules of international law deal with diplomatic protection. The protection of diplomatic representatives sent to foreign states was one of the first customs to be recognized as essential to the success of negotiations. The ancient rules applying to diplomats were codified in the 1961 *Vienna Convention on Diplomatic Relations*, and have been supplemented by other rules that take into account the growth of international organizations and missions (diplomatic bodies) interacting with these organizations.

States and international organizations interact with one another by communication and negotiation through an established network of diplomatic relations. Emissaries, ambassadors, and representatives travel the world on a regular basis, and embassies (the official residences and offices of these diplomatic representatives) are found in most major world cities. International relations have been made easier through advances in communications technologies such as telephone, e-mail, fax, and dedicated

Turning Points in the Law

The *Vienna Convention on Diplomatic Relations*, 1961

The expansion in the number of international organizations and areas covered by international law after 1945 meant that clear rules had to be established to deal with diplomatic relations among states. The ancient rules governing the treatment of envoys and diplomats were codified in the 1961 *Vienna Convention on Diplomatic Relations.* Since then, other rules have been added to take into account missions to international organizations.

The articles in the convention concern the immunity, inviolability, and protection afforded to the premises of the mission, to property relating to the mission's functioning, and to persons representing states diplomatically or those concerned with such representation.

Article 9, for example, allows for the receiving state to reject a representative sent by the sending state without explaining the reasons for that rejection. The sending state has to accept that decision.

Article 22 sets out the protections afforded to the mission buildings:

1. The premises of the mission shall be inviolable. The agents of the receiving State may not enter them, except with the consent of the head of the mission.
2. The receiving State is under a special duty to take all appropriate steps to protect the premises of the mission against any intrusion or damage and to prevent any disturbance of the peace of the mission or impairment of its dignity.
3. The premises of the mission, their furnishings and other property thereon and the means of transport of the mission shall be immune from search, requisition, attachment [seizure] or execution [seizure for debt].

Article 29 guarantees protection to diplomats:

The person of a diplomatic agent shall be inviolable. He shall not be liable to any form of arrest or detention. The receiving State shall treat him with due respect and shall take all appropriate steps to prevent any attack on his person, freedom or dignity.

Article 31 provides diplomatic immunity:

1. A diplomatic agent shall enjoy immunity from the criminal jurisdiction of the receiving State. He shall also enjoy immunity from its civil and administrative jurisdiction... .
2. A diplomatic agent is not obliged to give evidence as a witness.
3. No measures of execution may be taken in respect of a diplomatic agent... .
4. The immunity of a diplomatic agent from the jurisdiction of the receiving State does not exempt him from the jurisdiction of the sending State.

In return for these guarantees, diplomats and members of missions have a duty to respect the laws and regulations of the receiving state and not to interfere in its internal affairs.

Questions

1. Why might a receiving state reject a diplomat selected by the sending state?
2. Why is diplomatic immunity an important concept for international relations?
3. In the period of the Cold War hostilities between communist and non-communist states after World War II, there were instances of embassies being "bugged" and phone lines tapped. What recourse might a state have that was violated in this way?

"hotlines" such as the Kremlin–White House emergency line, or the video hotline between the US Department of Energy's Emergency Operations Center in Washington, DC, and the MinAtom Situation and Crisis Center in Russia. Despite these technologies, much diplomacy and negotiation are still carried on by professional diplomats on a face-to-face basis. The integrity and security of face-to-face communication has always required the support of legal rules for the protection of diplomats, their staff and families, embassies, consulates, and means of diplomatic communications.

The text of the *Vienna Convention on Diplomatic Relations* can be found at www.emp.ca/dimensionsoflaw

Diplomatic Immunity

The fundamental rule expressed in the Vienna Convention is that the "person of a diplomatic agent shall be inviolable." This means that diplomats are entitled to protection from physical harm and are not subject to arrest or detention (imprisonment or suspension of liberty) without recourse to the rules of international protocol set down by the Vienna Convention. Similarly, the premises of the mission or embassy shall be "inviolable" (note that, contrary to mistaken general belief, the territory of the embassy is not "foreign" territory of the sending state). In general, with respect to premises, this provision means that there can be no entry by agents or nationals of the host state without authorization from the sending state. The Vienna Convention extends this right of non-interference to such items as the files, documents, diplomatic bags (containers holding mail and other documents travelling to and from an embassy or consulate), diplomatic couriers, and means of communication. In the Iran hostages case that follows, the International Court of Justice noted:

> [T]here is no more fundamental prerequisite for the conduct of relations between States than the inviolability of diplomatic envoys and embassies. ... [T]he institution of diplomacy, with its concomitant [associated] privileges and immunities, has withstood the test of centuries and proved to be an instrument essential for effective co-operation in the international community.

Case US DIPLOMATIC HOSTAGES IN IRAN

US Diplomatic and Consular Staff in Tehran Case, [1979] ICJ Rep. 23 (Order);
US v. Iran, [1980] ICJ Rep. 3 (Merits)

Facts

On November 4, 1979, several hundred Iranian students and other demonstrators took possession of the US embassy in Tehran by force, in protest at the admission of the deposed Shah of Iran into the United States for medical treatment. The demonstrators were not opposed by the

Figure 16.8 *One of 60 American hostages—blindfolded and with his hands bound—is displayed to the crowd outside the US embassy in Tehran, November 1979.*

Iranian security forces. US consulates elsewhere in Iran were similarly occupied. The demonstrators, who had seized archives and documents, were still in occupation when this case was decided, holding 52 US nationals as hostages. The United States asked the International Court of Justice for a declaration calling for the release of the hostages, evacuation of the embassy and consulates, punishment of the persons responsible, and payment of **reparations.**

reparations: formal economic compensation, often from one sovereign state to another, for harm done in the course of armed conflict

Decision

The events that were the subject of the United States' claims fell into two phases. The first related to the armed attack on the United States' embassy by militants on November 4, 1979. No suggestion was made that the militants, when they executed their attack on the embassy, had any form of official status as recognized "agents" of the Iranian state. Their conduct in mounting the attack—overrunning the embassy and seizing its inmates as hostages—could not, therefore, be regarded as an act of the Iranian government. The militants' conduct might be viewed in this way only if it were established that they had acted on behalf of the state, having been directed by some Iranian government authority to carry out a specific operation. The court found no credible evidence of such a link.

However, this finding did not, in the court's view, absolve Iran of responsibility for the attacks. Under the Vienna Conventions of 1961 and 1963, and also under general international law, Iran was required to take appropriate steps to ensure the protection of the United States' embassy and consulates, their staffs, their archives, their means of communication, and the freedom of movement of their staffs. Iran failed to do this.

The second phase of the claim related to events that followed the occupation of the US embassy by the militants and the seizure of the consulates at Tabriz and Shiraz. Once the occupation had taken place, the Iranian government was required to take every appropriate step to bring it to a speedy end, to restore the consulates at Tabriz and Shiraz to US control, and in general to restore order and offer reparations for the damage. No such steps were taken.

For these reasons, the court decided by majority vote that the Islamic Republic of Iran violated obligations owed by it to the United States of America under international conventions in force between the two countries, as well as under long-established rules of general international law.

Fyi The Canadian embassy in Tehran sheltered six American embassy workers for 79 days during the hostage crisis, and supplied them with Canadian passports so that they could leave Iran. Ambassador Ken Taylor received a US Congressional Gold Medal in thanks for his actions.

Questions

1. Summarize the facts of this case.
2. What were the reasons for the decision of the International Court of Justice?
3. Do you think that this was a just decision? Explain your answer.
4. Is it necessary for all states to recognize and enforce rules of diplomatic relations? Explain.

While diplomatic protection is essential to the integrity of international relations, there have occasionally been problems related to abuses by diplomats of their special status. Such actions as smuggling drugs, selling duty-free liquor, avoiding legitimate debts, and drunk driving causing death threaten to tarnish the reputation of diplomacy. States concerned with public relations and the erosion of the principle of diplomatic immunity have often addressed these lapses by punishing misbehaving diplomats in the home country after refusing to allow a diplomat to be prosecuted in the receiving state (diplomats are generally considered immune to prosecution). In March 2002, a Russian diplomat was found guilty in Russia of involuntary manslaughter in the drunk-driving death of a woman in Ottawa and received a sentence of four years in a penal colony, although Russia was adamant that he should not be prosecuted in a Canadian court.

Diplomatic Asylum

The question of **diplomatic asylum** arises when a national from a given country seeks protection within the embassy of another country. When the United States invaded Panama in 1989, Panamanian leader Manuel Noriega sought refuge (or sanctuary) in the Vatican embassy in Panama City to avoid arrest by US troops. Ultimately, he gave up the protection of the embassy and surrendered to US authorities. One of the reasons (though not the only one) that he abandoned his safe haven was the fact that US soldiers played deafening rock music, 24 hours a day, over loudspeakers set

diplomatic asylum: protection sought in embassies of other countries by individuals fearing for their safety up around the Vatican embassy compound. It is obvious that this type of interference with embassy premises is questionable. In May 2002, two North Koreans managed to enter the Canadian diplomatic mission's compound in Beijing, China, seeking asylum and ultimately transfer to South Korea. This event strained the relations among the four governments involved.

Sometimes asylum is willingly given and respected. During the Hungarian revolution in 1956, Cardinal József Mindszenty sought asylum in the US embassy and lived there until 1971, when he was allowed to leave the country by the Hungarian communist authorities. Other times, countries refuse asylum. The institution of asylum is most highly developed in Latin America, where states have attempted to clarify the rules by agreeing to the *Convention on Diplomatic Asylum.*

Consular Relations

There is one embassy of a sending state in the receiving state. However, relations between states are managed by a number of officials other than those formally designated as diplomats and attached to the embassy. The most institutionalized of these officials are those charged with "consular" duties, the most important of which is protecting nationals of the sending state in the territory of the receiving state. Consulates and their staffs help obtain legal representation, act as "go-betweens" with local authorities, and generally protest if the rights of one of their citizens are in danger of being violated.

A current hot international issue with respect to consulates is access to prisoners, especially those charged with capital offences. Canada had to negotiate with Saudi Arabia about consular access to William Sampson, a Canadian who faced public beheading in Saudi Arabia after being charged, in 2001, with car bombings that killed a British man and injured several others. The International Court of Justice had to deal with similar issues in three applications against the United States (by Paraguay, Germany, and Mexico). In the case involving Mexico and the United States, Mexico alleged that

> [c]ompetent authorities of the United States ... have arrested, detained, tried, convicted, and sentenced to death no fewer than 54 Mexican nationals, who are currently under sentence of death in those states, following proceedings in which competent authorities failed to comply with their obligations under article 36(1)(b) of the *Vienna Convention* [*on Diplomatic Relations*].

The article mentioned requires that, upon detention of a foreign national, the government advise the "consular post" of the national's state of the detention. The arresting government must also help the detainee contact his or her consulate.

Personal Viewpoint

Saudi Justice, and Canadian Timidity

Canadian William Sampson was arrested in Saudi Arabia in December 2000, allegedly for his involvement in two car bombings related to illegal trade in liquor. One British man, Christopher Rodway, was killed in one of the bombings. Sampson confessed to the crime, but there was strong evidence that his confession was obtained through torture. He was sentenced to death. In mid-2002, it appeared that the Canadian government's attempts to secure Sampson's release would fail. In the spring of 2003, new hope for his release materialized through the efforts of Dan McTeague, MP for the riding of Pickering–Ajax–Uxbridge, who travelled to Britain to obtain a letter of forgiveness from Justin Rodway, the victim's son. This letter made a clemency appeal possible. (In Saudi law, a person may be forgiven if the persons harmed forgive the criminal.) On August 8, 2003, Sampson was released, along with five Britons who were also being held, after being granted a royal pardon by Saudi King Fahd. The focus of discussion then shifted to the extent of redress that Canada should pursue with respect to Sampson's allegations of torture.

Before this development, the Canadian government had been widely criticized for its ineffectiveness. The following editorial was written by a retired doctor, James Goodwin, who practised obstetrics in Iran, Saudi Arabia, the Sultanate of Oman, and Yemen.

> If an appeal court in the Kingdom of Saudi Arabia decides it, William Sampson, a Canadian citizen, will be beheaded in the capital city, Riyadh, at what a generation of expatriate Westerners indelicately called "Chop-Chop" Square.
>
> Let me tell you how they do this.
>
> The religious police bring the unfortunate prisoner in a little van at 1 p.m. on Friday, the Islamic holy day. ... The prisoner is then forced to kneel. ... The executioner stands at the ready with a very large sword. A little man, crouching to one side, jabs the prisoner in the middle of his back with a sharp stick, which causes his bowed head to jerk up. As soon as this happens, with one swift stroke, the head is off. ...
>
> [While working in Saudi Arabia] I witnessed or had first-hand knowledge of flagrant violations of human rights: harassment, intimidation, trumped-up criminal charges, summary incarceration, beatings, sexual assault and worse. ...

Figure 16.9 *James Sampson holds an old photograph of his son prior to William's release from a Saudi prison in August 2003.*

Most former expatriate workers from the West can relate similar stories. It's hardly a surprise that Canadians, visiting the kingdom on business, would see nothing of this.

During that time, regrettably, the diplomatic officials representing our Department of External Affairs (now Foreign Affairs) were hamstrung by operating policies [that] dictated caution to the point of impotence, in order to avoid ruffling Saudi feathers for fear of compromising Canadian business interests. Today, it seems that nothing has changed. When Crown Prince Abdullah cancelled his business trip to Canada in retaliation for our government's faint-hearted protest about Mr. Sampson's brutal treatment, the speed with which we retreated was shameful.

Why, in the name of humanity, can't we stop playing diplomatic games with these people and expose them for what they are? If Foreign Affairs Minister Bill Graham can protest the arrest and deportation to Syria of a Canadian citizen by the US government [Maher Arar, a Syrian-born Canadian on his way to Montreal from Tunisia via New York] with such passion and indignation, surely he and his officials can drum up enough outrage, energy, and backbone to demand that poor Mr. Sampson get a transparently fair trial, regardless of his guilt or innocence. That's the way we dispense justice in Canada and Mr. Graham must deliver this unequivocal message to the Saudi government without further delay.

Source: James Goodwin, "Saudi Justice, and Canadian Timidity," *Halifax Herald*, May 25, 2002.

Questions

1. Goodwin suggests that William Sampson deserves a trial consistent with "the way we dispense justice in Canada," even though his alleged crime took place in Saudi Arabia. Do you agree? Explain.
2. Why do you think people like Goodwin and a local MP felt the need to get involved with a diplomatic relations case? Would you get involved? Explain your response.
3. In your opinion, was the success of the clemency appeal a politically satisfactory resolution of this matter? Why or why not?
4. Visit www.emp.ca/dimensionsoflaw to learn more about the justice system in Saudi Arabia. What elements of this system would not be legal in Canada?

CHECK YOUR UNDERSTANDING

1. What is the role of embassies and consulates in facilitating international relations?
2. What are some of the problems that can arise from giving diplomats special privileges and protecting them from prosecution?
3. Do you think that it is essential to the smooth operation of international relations to allow for the practice of diplomatic asylum? Explain.

METHODS OF *Legal Inquiry*

Distinguishing between Opinion and Fact

The Personal Viewpoint feature, "Saudi Justice, and Canadian Timidity," was written as an editorial. Editorials express the opinions of writers on issues. It is important in evaluating such writings to identify opinions as distinct from facts. For example, it is a fact that William Sampson was arrested. Is it a fact that the Canadian government did not press his case because officials did not wish to upset business interests?

It is important—and not just in reading other writers' work—to distinguish instinctively between statements that are factual and those that are based on opinion. As a student presenting your views on issues, you need to make sure that your arguments are based on facts before you offer an opinion.

Applying the Skill

1. Read the Personal Viewpoint feature on pages 491–492. Identify key words that give clues to the writer's opinion. For example, the title of the piece uses the word "timidity." What does this word imply to you?
2. Re-read the feature and identify which facts indicate to you that the writer believes Sampson to be innocent of the charges against him.
3. Make a list of the facts that you would want to check in order to decide for yourself whether to support the writer's opinion or to oppose it.

Reviewing Main Ideas

You Decide!

THE NG EXTRADITION

United States v. Ng (1988), 93 AR 204 (QB)

The request for extradition of Charles Ng came before Justice Trussler of the Alberta Court of Queen's Bench in November 1987. It was not until almost a year later that the hearing itself took place. The evidence given by the US government consisted of 90 affidavits, 21 witnesses, and 39 exhibits. Counsel for Ng presented four witnesses.

Facts

Charles Ng, a British subject born in Hong Kong, was charged in California with several offences, including 12 counts of murder, kidnapping, and burglary. Prior to trial in California, Ng escaped from prison and fled to Calgary. On July 6, 1985, Ng was caught shoplifting in Calgary. During his apprehension, Ng resisted and shot a security guard in the finger. He was subsequently subdued and handcuffed. At the time of his apprehension, Ng was carrying a bag containing a mask, a knife, a rope, cyanide capsules, a gun, and ammunition.

The United States sought to extradite Ng. The extradition judge allowed the US application and committed Ng to custody. A *habeas corpus* application was heard and dismissed. If Ng was extradited to California, tried, and convicted, he faced the strong possibility of a death sentence.

In the United States, subject to some constitutional protections, the death penalty is permitted. In Canada, the death penalty—capital punishment—is not permitted.

The Law

Under article 6 of the extradition treaty between the United States and Canada, the minister of justice has the discretion to refuse extradition if the offence for which the accused is to be tried can result, on a finding of guilt, in the death penalty.

Issue

May the court refuse to issue a warrant for the extradition of Ng on the grounds that if he is convicted of the offences charged, the death penalty may be imposed? Consider the two arguments below.

Argument of the Minister of Justice

The power to seek assurances that the death penalty will not be imposed is discretionary, and is conferred on the minister of justice pursuant to s. 25 of the *Canada Extradition Act.* The minister of justice had decided not to seek these assurances. The minister stated that such assurances should be sought only under certain circumstances, which did not exist in Ng's case. The minister also stated that neither capital punishment nor the "death row phenomenon" (the subjection of a prisoner to inhuman or degrading treatment or punishment, particularly mental anguish) constitute cruel and unusual treatment. As a matter of public policy, the minister continued, Canada should not become a safe haven for those accused of murder in the United States.

Argument of Ng

Capital punishment for murder is prohibited in Canada. Section 12 of the *Canadian Charter of Rights and Freedoms* provides that no one is to be subjected to cruel and unusual punishment. The death penalty, the ultimate denial of human dignity, is *per se* a cruel and unusual punishment. The decision of the minister to surrender a fugitive who may be subject to execution without obtaining an assurance pursuant to article 6 is one that can be reviewed under s. 12 of the Charter. It follows that the minister must not surrender Ng without obtaining the undertaking described in article 6 of the treaty. To do so would render s. 25 of the *Canada Extradition Act* inconsistent with the Charter in its application to fugitives who would be subject to the death penalty.

Section 12 of the Charter prohibits cruel and unusual punishment. If capital punishment, that is, the death penalty, is not permitted under Canadian law, then would it not be cruel and unusual punishment to extradite a person who could be sentenced to death for violating the law of another nation?

Make Your Decision

1. What were the facts in this case?
2. Summarize the key points made by both sides in the case.
3. Would the surrender by Canada of an extradition fugitive to the United States, to stand trial for willful or deliberate murder for which the penalty upon conviction may be death, constitute a breach of the fugitive's rights guaranteed under the *Canadian Charter of Rights and Freedoms* and Canada's international law obligations?
4. Would the minister of justice, in deciding pursuant to article 6 of the extradition treaty between Canada and the United States to surrender the fugitive Charles Ng without seeking assurances from the United States that the death penalty would not be imposed on Charles Ng or, if imposed, that it would not be carried out, commit any of the errors of law and jurisdiction alleged in the statement of claim filed by Charles Ng?

Make your decision. Dismiss or allow the appeal, and provide reasons for your decision.

Key Terms

Review the following terms to show that you understand the meaning of each and how it is applied in a legal context.

customary law	reparations
diplomatic asylum	state sovereignty
extradition	treaty
nationalize	

Understanding the Law

Review the following treaties mentioned in the text, and show that you understand the intent of each.

Ottawa Convention Banning Landmines
Treaty on Principles Governing the Activities of States in the Exploration and Use of Outer Space, Including the Moon and Other Celestial Bodies (1967)
Vienna Convention on Diplomatic Relations (1961)
Vienna Convention on the Law of Treaties (1969)

Thinking and Inquiry

1. Write a one-page report to explain why the last 50 years of the 20th century resulted in a huge increase in treaties and international law.
2. Revisit your earlier definition of international law and amend it if your definition has changed.
3. How does international law differ from domestic law? Explain why these differences exist.
4. Is the principle of diplomatic immunity from court proceedings justified in the modern world? Should a diplomat's spouse be entitled to park the family car in a no-stopping zone while shopping, and ignore any parking tags received? Discuss from the standpoint of the requirements of international law and modern international relations.

Communication

5. Investigate a recent international law case (the Web site of the International Court of Justice will provide information). Summarize the facts of the case and explain how international law decided its outcome. Give a short oral presentation of your findings.
6. Research a treaty that is not mentioned in the text. Use an organizational chart to show
   - its official name
   - when it was created
   - the issue or issues that it addresses
   - the results it has achieved or will achieve.

   Give a short presentation to share your research with your group.
7. Identify a current international issue or dispute involving a treaty or treaties, and explain what effect it may have on Canada.
8. Use the government of Canada's Web site or other source to locate extradition treaties with any three countries. Convert this information into chart form to post in the classroom. Comment on any key points shown.

Application

9. If you were appointed to draft a constitution for Lower Freedonia, based on the knowledge you have gained in this chapter, what clauses dealing with treaties and international law would you recommend be adopted?
10. Find an editorial cartoon on a Web site or in a newspaper that comments on the need for changing an international law. State whether or not you agree with the cartoonist. Explain your answer.
11. Use resources such as the Internet, television, newspapers, and newsmagazines to find information on a recent issue involving treaty or extradition law. Outline the issue and record two different viewpoints on it. Then state your opinion on the issue, and explain how you think it should be resolved.

Chapter 17 International Organizations

CHAPTER *Focus*

In this chapter, you will

- examine some early international organizations, including the League of Nations
- outline the six main divisions of the United Nations, and analyze the UN's effectiveness in the 21st century
- evaluate the role of the International Court of Justice in resolving issues between nations
- analyze the role and jurisdiction of agencies responsible for defining, regulating, and enforcing international law
- demonstrate an understanding of how global issues such as human rights are covered in international law

International law requires a variety of organizations that work toward world peace, and international courts to apply the law. Certainly, the United Nations (UN) is the largest and most visible organization in the world arena, and you are probably familiar with the General Assembly and the Security Council. But the UN has many other divisions and agencies operating under its mandate. One of the most important is the International Court of Justice. This chapter also examines the role of non-governmental organizations in the international legal process. Although state sovereignty is a critical concept in international law (as you saw in Chapter 16), it has been refined to permit the protection of international human rights. The reality is that international law and human rights are inextricably linked in our ever-changing world.

The cartoon in Figure 17.1 illustrates a major area of concern, not only for the UN but for the world: the continuing crisis after the US-led invasion of Iraq in the spring of 2003.

Figure 17.1

At First Glance

1. What is the significance of the United Nations logo?
2. What is the cartoonist's message?
3. Why is Iraq an area of concern for the UN?
4. Research the current status of the UN in Iraq and describe the ongoing conflict in that country.

Early International Organizations

The rise of formal international organizations in the 19th century was the result of many factors, including changing technology, that made travel and communications faster and easier. With the telegraph and telephone, for example, news from Europe and other distant places could spread throughout North America within hours instead of months or even years. Some of these early organizations were not explicitly political. For instance, the International Red Cross was a non-governmental organization (NGO) founded by Swiss philanthropist Henry Dunant, who was moved to organize help in time of war by the sight of dead and injured on the battlefield in Italy in 1859 (see the Working for Change feature in Chapter 19: Military Conflict and Conflict Resolution, page 591). Other organizations, such as the League of Nations, were much more political.

Fyi NGOs that operate worldwide include humanitarian, medical, scientific, and sporting organizations. Examples include Amnesty International, Oxfam, Greenpeace, Doctors Without Borders, and the International Olympic Committee.

The League of Nations

The League of Nations was the first global permanent political organization that was formed to prevent war between nations by promoting international cooperation. It was founded in 1919 as part of the *Treaty of Versailles*, the peace treaty that officially ended World War I. Part I of this treaty included a provision for the creation of the League of Nations. When the United States entered the war in 1917, President Woodrow Wilson was horrified at the brutal slaughter that was taking place. He subsequently suggested that the only way to avoid a repetition was to create an international organization founded to maintain world peace and security, to reduce armaments, and to improve the quality of life for all people. Peace was to be preserved by **collective security**—states in the League would come to the defence of any other member that was attacked. At its largest, the League had 57 members, which in time included most of the combatants in World War I, with the glaring exception of the United States.

Fyi Total deaths in all nations that fought in World War I are estimated at 8.5 million, with 21 million wounded.

collective security: the concept that member states within an organization will provide military support and cooperation in the event of an attack on any other member state

The League of Nations was based in Geneva, Switzerland, a neutral country that had not fought in World War I. As well, Geneva was home to the International Red Cross, which was by now considered to be a neutral organization, and so the city was seen as a logical place for the League's

Learn more about the League of Nations at www.emp.ca/dimensionsoflaw

mandate: a government's or agency's scope of authority, as defined by law or democratic process

headquarters. Its organization included a council with permanent members, such as France and the United Kingdom, and non-permanent members, and an assembly in which each member state was represented. Assembly members would listen to disputes and reach a decision on what to do. But both these groups required unanimous votes for any action to be taken. Closely connected to the League of Nations, but autonomous entities, were the Permanent Court of International Justice, which later became the International Court of Justice (ICJ) and is discussed later in this chapter, and the International Labour Organization (ILO). The ILO's **mandate** was the promotion of social justice and internationally recognized human and labour rights, and this mandate continues today. In 1946, the ILO became associated with the United Nations. The League also established subsidiary bodies to promote cooperation in health, economic, and social matters among member states.

During the 1920s, the League dealt successfully with minor conflicts but, unfortunately, was unable to prevent the outbreak of World War II, largely because of structural weaknesses and the unwillingness of the international community to abandon notions of state sovereignty discussed in Chapter 16. As an international organization devoted to maintaining world peace, why did the League of Nations fail? Reasons include the following.

- The League of Nations had no armed forces at its disposal, and member states did not have to provide forces as a condition for joining (unlike the current UN).
- Although US President Wilson had been the main force behind the creation of the League, the United States never ratified the *Treaty of Versailles.* As the United States became economically the world's most powerful nation, its absence as a member state greatly undermined the League's prestige and influence.
- As the country that started World War I, Germany was not allowed at first to join the League. (It did become a member between 1926 and 1933.)
- Russia also was not allowed to join because Western European states feared its communist government, which promoted revolution by workers. As well, Russian revolutionaries had murdered the Tsar and royal family in 1918. (Russia did join in 1934, but was expelled when it invaded Finland in 1939.)
- Unanimous decisions were difficult to reach because of the self-interest of some member states.
- The League lacked the political will to persevere with sanctions.

Thus, without three of the world's leading powers as members, and with the other concerns noted above, the League had high ideals but little clout to enforce its decisions. On April 18, 1946, the League officially dissolved itself and transferred its mission and ideals to the United Nations.

Although the League was abandoned, most of its ideals and some of its structure were kept by the UN and outlined in its Charter.

CHECK YOUR UNDERSTANDING

1. Explain how improved transportation and communications technology affected the need for international law.
2. Outline the three main goals of the League of Nations.
3. Identify four reasons for the failure of the League of Nations.

The Modern Structure of the International Community

The international community operates through a wide-ranging system of organizations. These institutions reflect the community's diversity: some are global, some regional, and others non-governmental, but their relative stability helps channel international efforts in an organized way and allows all members of the international community to participate meaningfully. Each of these categories is discussed in the following pages, beginning with the United Nations and the International Court of Justice as global institutions.

The United Nations and Its Structure

The growth in the role of law in the international sphere following World War II was supported by the creation of an important institutional system: the United Nations. Even as World War II raged, the leaders of Britain, the United States, the former Soviet Union, and China met to discuss details of a post-war international organization dedicated to world peace. Toward the end of the war in 1945, representatives from 50 countries met in San Francisco to draft a text that became the *Charter of the United Nations*, signed on June 26, 1945. Poland, the 51st country, was not able to send a delegate to the San Francisco conference, but is considered an original member. The UN then came into existence on October 24, 1945, when the *UN Charter* was ratified by a majority of the original 51 member states. In the years following, nearly every other nation in the world has joined the UN. The only significant entities outside the system are Taiwan and the Vatican (the Holy See, an independent state in Italy), though they are recognized as states by some UN members and participate in some UN and international activities. Taiwan's membership is opposed by China, which claims Taiwan as part of its territory.

Fyi Switzerland and East Timor joined the UN as member states in 2002, bringing the total number of members to 191, of which more than two-thirds are developing countries.

In modern times, the foundational concepts of international law have been summarized in the *Charter of the United Nations*. The *UN Charter* outlines a number of basic international legal principles and the following purposes for this world organization:

- to maintain international peace and security
- to develop friendly relations among nations
- to solve international problems
- to promote respect for human rights and to be a centre for harmonizing the actions of nations.

norms: standards, customs, or accepted practices

The *UN Charter* also expresses the most fundamental **norm** of international law, which is found in article 2(4):

> All Members shall refrain in their international relations from the threat or use of force against the territorial integrity or political independence of any state, or in any other manner inconsistent with the Purposes of the United Nations.

Learn more about the United Nations at www.emp.ca/dimensionsoflaw

The United Nations is not a world government, and it does not make laws. However, it does provide a forum for the development of laws that generally find acceptance and for resolving international conflicts, and its members formulate policies on matters affecting us all. At the UN, all member states—large and small, rich and poor, with divergent political views and social systems—have a voice and a vote in this process.

The United Nations has six main organs. Five of them—the General Assembly, the Security Council, the Secretariat, the Economic and Social Council, and the Trusteeship Council—are based at UN headquarters in New York. The sixth, the International Court of Justice, is located at The Hague in the Netherlands. Figure 17.2 illustrates the broad range of activities that fall under the UN umbrella.

The General Assembly

Fyi Six official languages—Arabic, Chinese, English, French, Russian, and Spanish—are used at the UN.

The General Assembly of the United Nations is the central body in which each member state is represented and has one vote. By a one-nation, one-vote formula, the General Assembly, which has been described as the "town-hall meeting of the world," examines, debates, and promotes global consensus on issues of common concern. It is the closest thing to a world parliament. For many of its smaller and newer members, the General Assembly offers an indispensable arena for establishing contacts and forging common understandings.

The General Assembly can only adopt resolutions, except under certain specified circumstances. While none of its resolutions are legally binding, they do carry the weight of shared world governmental opinion. Still, the General Assembly is the most important norm-generating institution in the international legal system. Norms are prescribed either through the work of the General Assembly's subcommittees, in particular the Sixth (legal) Committee, or by the International Law Commission (ILC), established in 1947. The ILC operates as the world's "think tank" for the creation of new legal norms.

Figure 17.2 *The United Nations system*

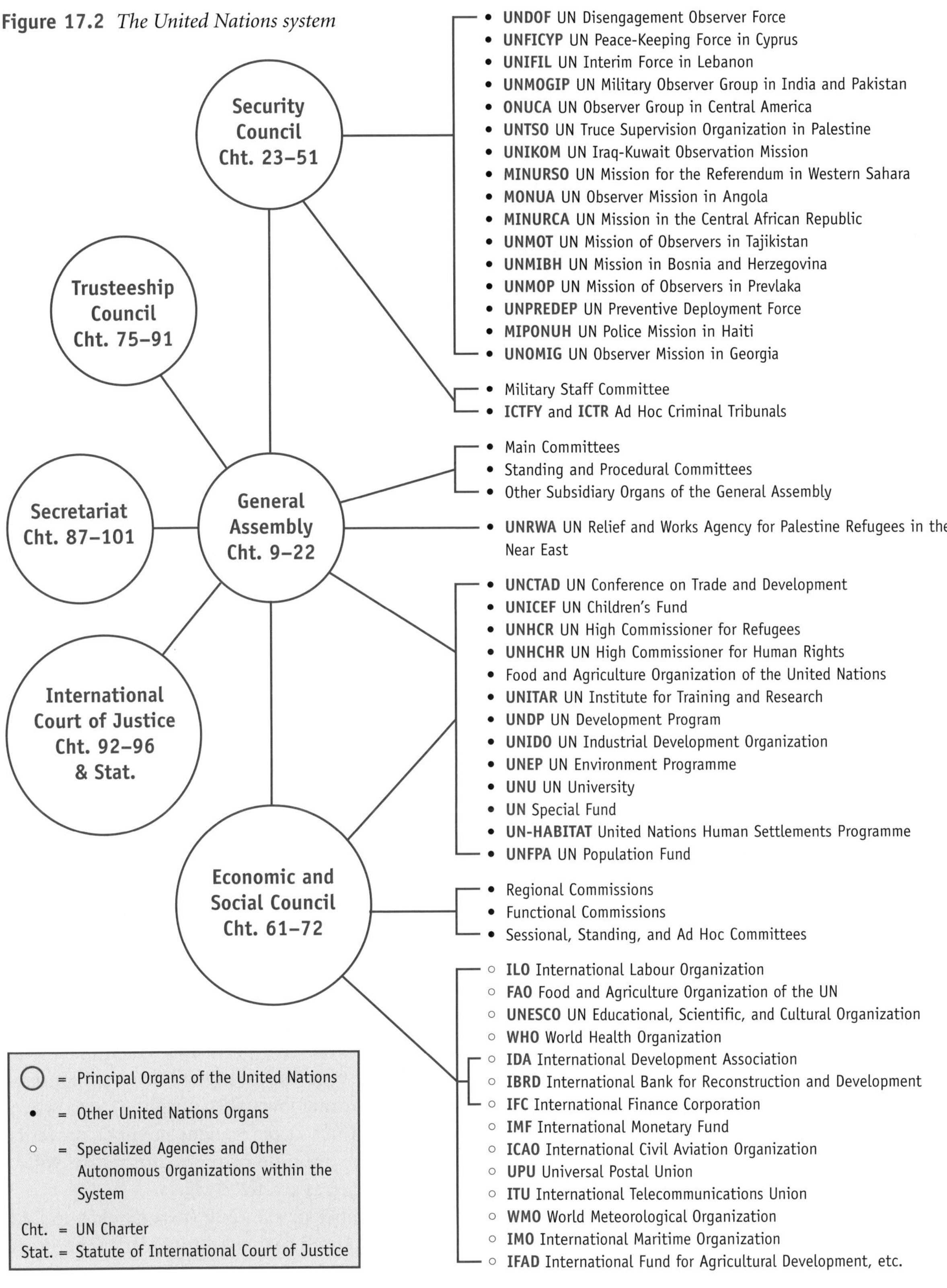

Figure 17.3 *Prime Minister Jean Chrétien speaks to the UN General Assembly in September 2002.*

Fyi On January 1, 2003, Angola, Chile, Germany, Pakistan, and Spain began their two-year membership term on the Security Council. Canada served a two-year term from 1999–2001.

The Security Council

As its primary responsibility, the Security Council maintains international peace and security, and is thus the most powerful organ of the UN. While other UN bodies simply offer recommendations to member states, the Security Council has the power to make decisions that are legally binding on all members under the *UN Charter*. Council decisions are supported by a system of **sanctions** for enforcing compliance.

sanctions: penalties or actions imposed as a means of influencing behaviour

The Security Council has 15 members. The victors of World War II became the five permanent members (China, France, Russia, the United Kingdom, and the United States), while 10 non-permanent members are elected every two years by the General Assembly. Member states sometimes lobby years in advance for a Security Council seat, both for its prestige and for the opportunity to express their national opinions on world issues.

Fyi In every decade since the founding of the UN, Canada has been elected to a two-year term on the Security Council.

Chapters VI and VII of the *UN Charter* describe the mandate and procedures of the Security Council. Chapter VI authorizes it to "investigate any dispute, or any situation which might lead to international friction or give rise to a dispute." Chapter VII empowers the Security Council to make decisions denouncing acts of aggression or other violations of the *UN Charter* and to take action and use force if necessary. Such action occurred in the 1990 resolution passed after Iraq invaded Kuwait, which led to the first Gulf War, in which US-led troops pushed Iraqi troops out of Kuwait.

Substantive matters, such as the use of force, require nine affirmative votes, which must include votes by the five permanent members. The Security Council's decision-making process is designed to reach consensus, and provides the five permanent members with a right of veto when consensus cannot be reached. A **veto** by a permanent member prevents adoption of a proposal, even if there are nine or more affirmative votes. Abstention from a vote is not regarded as a veto.

veto: a power to reject something, usually a law or a political measure

The Security Council has a number of standing (permanent) and ad hoc (temporary, issue-based) committees to assist in its work. The most important of the ad hoc committees are those that administer sanctions. One such committee is the Governing Council of the United Nations Compensation Commission, established by Security Council resolution 692 (1991), which arose out of the Iraqi invasion of Kuwait. The Security Council has also established two war crimes tribunals, which arose out of civil strife in the former Yugoslavia and Rwanda. (Chapter 19: Military Conflict and Conflict Resolution discusses these actions in greater detail.)

The Security Council supervises the ongoing peacekeeping operations of the UN, made up of troops and equipment supplied by member nations. Canada is highly regarded around the world for its continuing role in international peacekeeping (discussed further in Chapter 19). It also oversees UN disarmament programs, including the United Nations Monitoring, Verification and Inspection Commission (UNMOVIC). This commission was charged with monitoring and verifying Iraq's destruction of its weapons before and after the second Gulf War in 2003.

Fyi Since 1945, the veto has been used 250 times in the Security Council. Russia has used the veto the most times (120). The United States comes second, having used the veto 74 times.

The Secretariat

The Secretariat carries out the diverse day-to-day work of the UN and administers its programs and policies. It is the UN's civil service and is headed by the Secretary-General, who is appointed by the General Assembly on the recommendation of the Security Council for a five-year, renewable term. The functions of the Secretary-General have varied with the incumbent's personality, his own view of his role (to date, only men have held this office), and the scope of responsibility that is assigned to him by the General Assembly and Security Council.

Fyi Kofi Annan of Ghana, the seventh Secretary-General, was elected from UN staff in January 1997. The General Assembly awarded him a second term by acclamation from 2002 to December 31, 2006. In 2001, he and the United Nations shared the Nobel Peace Prize.

Figure 17.4 *UN Secretary-General Kofi Annan, right, accepts the Nobel Peace Prize in December 2001.*

Learn more about the Brundtland Report and the resulting international actions at www.emp.ca/dimensionsoflaw

The Secretariat's work includes administration of peacekeeping operations, mediation of international disputes, surveys of economic and social trends and problems, and preparation of studies on human rights and sustainable development. For example, the UN appointed the international commission that led to the Brundtland Report, titled *Our Common Future*, an investigation of the concept of sustainable development. This report led to the Earth Summit held in Rio de Janeiro in 1992, where world environmental problems were discussed.

The Secretariat has a staff of about 8900, drawn from some 170 countries. As international civil servants, staff members and the Secretary-General answer to the United Nations alone for their activities, and take an oath not to seek or receive instructions from any government or outside authority.

The Economic and Social Council

The Economic and Social Council (ECOSOC), under the overall authority of the General Assembly, coordinates the economic and social work of the United Nations and the UN system. It has become an increasingly important body as the centre of attention of the organization shifts to international economic, human rights, and social issues. The ECOSOC also consults with non-governmental organizations on issues such as the immunization of babies in Sudan against polio and the financing of refugee camps in Pakistan. The UN Children's Fund (UNICEF) and the International Labour Organization (ILO) are examples of organizations that report to the UN through ECOSOC.

Fyi Of the UN's 2002–2003 budget of $2.6 billion, 70% goes to the ECOSOC.

The ECOSOC has 54 members, elected by the General Assembly for three-year terms. Seats on the council are allotted based on geographical representation, with 14 allocated to African states, 11 to Asian states, 6 to Eastern European states, 10 to Latin American and Caribbean states, and 13 to Western European and other states. The ECOSOC's subsidiary bodies (see Figure 17.2, page 501) meet regularly and report back to the council.

The Trusteeship Council

When the UN was established in 1945, 750 million people—almost one-third of the world's population—lived in non–self-governing territories, dependent on colonial powers. The Trusteeship Council was established under chapter XIII of the *UN Charter* to administer colonial trust territories that had been under the mandate of the League of Nations. These territories included German East Africa (now Tanzania) and lands taken from enemy states at the end of World War I, such as island groups in the central Pacific, and Iraq, which was placed under British mandate with the collapse of the Ottoman Turkish empire.

The major goals of the Trusteeship Council were to promote the advancement of the territories' inhabitants and their progressive development toward independence and self-government. Since 1945, more than

80 former colonies have gained independence. Many administering authorities profited from the territories for which they were responsible. For example, Australia, New Zealand, and the United Kingdom all exploited the South Pacific island of Naura for its phosphate resources, while the United States conducted nuclear tests in the Bikini Atoll, part of the Marshall Islands (see Chapter 18: International Law and Common Heritage, page 542).

In late 1994, the Trusteeship Council suspended its operations because all these territories had attained independence and self-government, either as separate states or by joining neighbouring independent countries. Paulu, a group of islands in the North Pacific Ocean southeast of the Philippines, was the last to gain independence when it became the 185th member state of the UN in December 1994.

Is there a future for the Trusteeship Council? In Secretary-General Annan's 1997 reform plan, he recommended that this organ focus on the atmosphere, outer space, and the oceans. However, no action has yet occurred. Since it appears that the UN member states do not want to abolish the Trusteeship Council, some observers suggest that it be used to deal with collapsed and war-torn nations such as Afghanistan and Iraq. Would UN administrative structures be preferable to a US-led military mandate in the Middle East? The reconstruction of Iraq, a society of 23 million people, needs the direct help that only international organizations can provide, and the resurrection of the Trusteeship Council might be the vehicle to coordinate this massive international effort.

Fyi In September 2003, US President George W. Bush conceded that rebuilding and pacifying Iraq had proven more difficult and expensive than anticipated, and sought other countries' troops to assist with the process. He also requested $87 billion from the US Congress to finance the next year's operation.

Criticisms of the United Nations

Although the UN is the world's largest and most visible organization committed to world peace and security, it is not without its critics. Many people feel that the UN, and the Security Council in particular, are incapable of resolving conflicts because of the political manoeuvring that occurs. Many critics feel that action taken by the UN is often ad hoc and reactive, rather than planned and proactive. To be more effective, the UN must be able to respond to international problems before they escalate into full-scale crises. But this ability would require major reform and the political will of member states to commit much greater financial and human resources.

There is regular debate about the composition of the Security Council. Critics suggest that the permanent membership reflects the post–World War II period rather than the economic and political realities of the 21st century. Since two-thirds of member states represent developing countries, should this proportion be reflected in the Security Council? Should countries like Germany and Japan be considered for permanent membership, along with the dropping of France and the United Kingdom? These are some of the questions being raised today.

In addition, even if all members of the Security Council approve a resolution, a single veto by a permanent member can prevent its passage. Should the Security Council be paralyzed by use of the veto by one member?

This is a concern among developing states about the Security Council's power. Finally, if a legal question arises between the General Assembly and the Security Council, which body should resolve the issue? The *UN Charter* provides few answers, except to say in article 96 that these two bodies may request the International Court of Justice to give an advisory opinion on any legal question.

World Government? Should the world community establish a supranational (international) organization responsible for law making and enforcement?

The United Nations is not a supranational organization, nor is it a world government. It controls no citizens, taxes, or regular army. It is a voluntary association of sovereign independent states for the purpose of dialogue to keep peace in the world. Through its organizations, it attempts to foster peaceful relations among states and promote economic equality and human rights. Yet wars are still being fought, human rights are being violated, and economic parity seems ever more distant. Would the establishment of a supranational international body with law-making powers solve some of these problems? The following extracts offer some positions on this issue.

> As long as there are sovereign nations possessing great power, war is inevitable. There is no salvation for civilisation, or even the human race, other than the creation of a world government. (Quoted in *The Atlantic Monthly*, November 1945)
>
> . . .
>
> The United Nations is an extremely important and useful institution provided the peoples and governments of the world realize that it is merely a transitional system toward the final goal, which is the establishment of a supranational authority vested with sufficient legislative and executive powers to keep the peace. ("Open Letter to the General Assembly of the United Nations," October 1947)
>
> —*Albert Einstein*

> Perhaps national sovereignty wasn't such a great idea after all. ... But it has taken the events in our own wondrous and terrible century to clinch the case for world government.
>
> —*Strobe Talbott (Deputy Secretary of State under US President Bill Clinton), "The Birth of the Global Nation,"* Time, *July 20, 1992*

> The recommendations of the Commission [for Global Governance], if implemented, will bring all the people of the world into a global neighborhood managed by a world-wide bureaucracy, under the direct

authority of a minute handful of appointed individuals, and policed by thousands of individuals, paid by accredited NGOs, certified to support a belief system, which to many people—is unbelievable and unacceptable.

—Sovereignty International, "Report of the Commission of Global Governance: Our Global Neighborhood"; www.sovereignty.net/p/gov/gganalysis.htm

Because of globalization and the need to agree on basic common rules of civilized conduct in our global community, we would be remiss if we did not explore the possibilities of using the political technology of democracy to solve global problems.

—The World Citizen Foundation, www.worldcitizen.org

Could a global federalist government deliver an ideal world better than a world of nation states? It is very doubtful. A global government could only deliver world peace and harmony at the expense of the freedom of everyone to live their lives the way they want. ... If what passes for democracy in the European Union is any example of what this New World will be like, then, as someone ungrammatically remarked, "Include me out."

—Ralph Maddocks, "A World Government by Stealth," Le Québécois libre, *No. 55, February 5, 2000; www.quebecoislibre.org/000205-6.htm*

The UN leadership and heads of government must recognize that there is a big gap between the rhetoric stating the importance of civil society and the actual translation of that into practice. The UN, for a vast majority of civil society organizations, is a more acceptable manifestation of the global governance system, as compared to the WTO, the IMF or the World Bank. But this does not detract from the reality that the UN too is still stuck in a time warp. While embracing the language of democracy, it still has a long way to go before it can reflect this in its governance structures.

—Kumi Naidoo, CEO of Civicus: World Alliance for Citizen Participation, Amnesty International Bulletin 54, September 13, 2002

Questions

1. Assess the statements in each of the arguments presented above. What is your initial position on the issue of world government?
2. Is the idea of world government compatible with that of sovereignty of nations? Justify your position.
3. Should we have an international body invested with the authority to enact laws? Based on what you have learned about law making, present your arguments for or against this issue.

Check Your Understanding

1. What are the primary objectives of the United Nations? How does article 2(4) of the *UN Charter* tie into the UN's general objective(s)?
2. Why is the UN not considered a world government? Explain.
3. Outline the six main organs of the UN, and identify one distinguishing characteristic of each.
4. Explain the meaning of the following statement: "The Security Council is where the power lies." Do you agree? Why or why not?
5. What are the roles of the UN Secretariat and the Secretary-General?
6. Explain the meaning of the following statement: "Action taken by the UN is often ad hoc and reactive, rather than planned and proactive." Do you agree? Why or why not?
7. Should there be a one-country, one-vote policy in the UN? Explain your answer.

The International Court of Justice

The International Court of Justice (ICJ), or World Court, is the main judicial organ of the United Nations. The ICJ is composed of 15 judges, each elected to a nine-year term of office by the UN General Assembly and the Security Council, sitting independently of each other. The ICJ may not include more than one judge of any nationality. Elections are held every three years for one-third of the seats, and retiring judges may be re-elected. The members of the ICJ do not represent their governments but are independent lawmakers and judges, and the ICJ's composition is intended to reflect the principal legal systems of the world. The ICJ sits at the Peace Palace in The Hague in the Netherlands, hears cases brought before it by UN member states, and performs a dual role as it (1) settles the legal disputes submitted to it by states that have agreed to its jurisdiction and (2) gives advisory opinions on legal questions referred to it by international organs and agencies.

The ICJ was established under article 92 of the *UN Charter* and its own statute, based on the statutes of its predecessor—the Permanent Court of Justice, established by the League of Nations in 1922. The UN and the ICJ are also linked by article 94(2) of the *UN Charter*, which states:

> If any party to a case [decided by the ICJ] fails to perform the obligations incumbent upon it under a judgment rendered by the Court, the other party may have recourse to the Security Council, which may, if it deems necessary, make recommendations or decide upon measures to be taken to give effect to the judgment.

This provision means that the ICJ's jurisdiction is based on the consent of parties to the dispute, and its judgments are final and binding. If one state in a dispute fails to comply with a judgment, the other state may call on the UN Security Council to take measures to enforce that judgment.

Cases heard by the ICJ range from disputes regarding territorial sovereignty and land frontiers to establishing maritime boundaries. The ICJ has given advisory opinions on the status of human rights, the legality of the threat or use of nuclear weapons, and UN membership. Canada has put its position forward in cases requesting advisory opinions. A quorum of nine judges is needed to hear each case, but usually all 15 judges attend because the ICJ's caseload has not been large; countries have historically been reluctant to submit to its jurisdiction or ask its advice. Recently, the court has been attracting more cases, with 24 cases awaiting resolution in 2003.

Fyi In 56 years (1946–2002), the ICJ delivered 99 decisions—75 judgments and 24 advisory opinions.

Canada has been involved in the following three contentious cases before the ICJ.

- *Legality of Use of Force (Serbia and Montenegro v. Canada)* commenced in 1999 as a result of Canada's involvement in the NATO bombing of Serbia in the former Yugoslavia. Civil war had erupted when Josip Tito, the communist dictator who had governed Yugoslavia since the end of World War II, died in 1980. The former state fell apart as traditional ethnic nationalist sentiments were inflamed by leaders in Croatia and Serbia. Thousands of people died or were displaced in an orgy of "ethnic cleansing." In response to the march of Serbian militia into Kosovo, driving people from their homes, NATO bombed the Serbian capital of Belgrade and other targets.
- The *Fisheries Jurisdiction Case (Spain v. Canada)* (1995–1998) is summarized on pages 511–512.
- In the *Delimitation of the Maritime Boundary in the Gulf of Maine Area Case (Canada/United States of America, 1981–1984)*, the ICJ drew an international boundary off the east coast of the two countries (see Chapter 18: International Law and Common Heritage).

Typically, cases before the ICJ take years to resolve. An example is the *Oil Platforms Case (Iran v. US)*, commenced in 1992. This case arose after US military forces in the Persian Gulf attacked three oil-drilling platforms owned by the National Iranian Oil Company in 1987 and 1988. The conclusion of public hearings was not reached until March 2003, and a decision is not likely until 2004 or later.

To learn more about the International Court of Justice, visit www.emp.ca/dimensionsoflaw

Hearing Cases in the ICJ

The jurisdiction of the ICJ is limited to cases between states. In no circumstances can an individual, NGO, or corporation bring a matter before the ICJ or be "sued" in it. But this restriction does not mean that the ICJ cannot deal with a matter affecting an individual, NGO, or corporation. For example, when a number of NGOs (including the International Physicians for the Prevention of Nuclear War and the World Federation of Public Health Associations) started a campaign to abolish or limit nuclear weapons, they convinced the assembly of the World Health Organization and the UN General Assembly to put forward requests to the ICJ for an advisory opinion on aspects of the nuclear weapons question. Some portions of the matter were considered by the ICJ.

A matter can be considered by the ICJ only if the states concerned have accepted its jurisdiction. All UN member states are automatically members of the ICJ, but no state is subject to the ICJ's jurisdiction without that state's consent. Consent may be given in advance or after the dispute has arisen. Both parties must agree to be subject to the ICJ's jurisdiction.

In cases involving states that do not have judges of their nationality on the ICJ, ad hoc judges are appointed to sit only on that case. Canada does not have a current representative on the ICJ, but ad hoc judges have been appointed for cases in which Canada was a party. (Mark Lalonde, a former federal Cabinet minister, was chosen as an ad hoc judge by Canada in the case *Yugoslavia v. Canada.*) The ICJ can sit as a full court or in chambers. The chambers procedure allows the parties to select the judges who will sit on their case (as did Canada and the United States in the *Delimitation of the Maritime Boundary in the Gulf of Maine Area Case*).

A good case study to illustrate the ICJ's role is the dispute between Canada and Spain respecting fisheries jurisdiction beyond the 200-mile (370-km) limit. Historically, Canada had broadly accepted the ICJ's jurisdiction. However, commencing with the adoption of the *Arctic Waters Pollution Prevention Act* in the 1970s, Canada began to question whether it should continue to submit to the court's jurisdiction in matters involving environmental issues. On May 10, 1994, the Canadian government amended its *Coastal Fisheries Protection Act*, permitting the enforcement of Canadian fisheries regulations for the conservation of depleted fish stocks on the Grand Banks off Newfoundland, beyond 370 km, where Spanish and other non-Canadian fishing vessels regularly operated. The Canadian government, aware of the fact that its regulations and enforcement activities with respect to these fish stocks might be challenged in the ICJ, sought to preclude such a challenge by withdrawing the issue from the court's jurisdiction. Thus, before the legislation was introduced, Canada deposited a declaration on May 10, 1994 modifying its acceptance of the compulsory jurisdiction of the court so as to exclude "disputes arising out of or concerning conservation and management measures taken by Canada with respect to vessels fishing in the NAFO [Northeast Atlantic Fisheries Organization] Regulatory Area, as defined in the *Convention on Future Multilateral Co-operation in the Northwest Atlantic Fisheries*, 1978 [i.e., in an area beyond 370 km] and the enforcement of such measures."

Case A TRANSBOUNDARY RESOURCE CONFLICT

Fisheries Jurisdiction Case (Spain v. Canada) (December 4, 1998), International Court of Justice, General List No. 96

Facts

In 1994, the multilateral Northwest Atlantic Fisheries Organization (NAFO) set limits on the total allowable catch of Greenland halibut (or turbot), allocating national quotas for this resource. The European Union, pressured by Spain and Portugal, rejected the quotas as unfair. In March 1995, Canada, concerned with depleting turbot stocks, imposed a unilateral moratorium on turbot overfishing.

On March 9, 1995, Canadian government vessels intercepted and boarded the trawler *Estai*, a fishing vessel flying the Spanish flag and employing a Spanish crew, some 245 miles (454 km) from the Canadian coast, in Division L of the NAFO Regulatory Area (Grand Banks area). The vessel was seized and its master arrested on charges of violations of the (Canadian) *Coastal Fisheries Protection Act* and its implementing regulations. The *Estai* was brought into the Canadian port of St. John's, Newfoundland, where the master was charged with offences under the above legislation, and in particular with illegal fishing (violating the fish quota rules and using illegal fish nets in the process). Part of the ship's catch, including undersized fish, was confiscated. Crew members were released immediately; the master was released on March 12, 1995, following the posting of a bond.

Issues

On March 28, 1995, the Spanish government instituted proceedings against Canada related to the seizure of the *Estai* and the "lawless act against the sovereignty of a Member State of the European Com-

Figure 17.5 *Residents of St. John's watch as the Spanish trawler* Estai *arrives in port in March 1995.*

munity." It added, "Furthermore, the behaviour of the Canadian vessels has clearly endangered the lives of the crew and the safety of the Spanish vessel concerned." Spain accused Canada of violating a number of international laws, including the freedom to navigate and fish on the high seas.

Canada argued that the ICJ could not hear the case because the court lacked compulsory jurisdiction "over all disputes other than disputes arising out of or concerning conservation and management measures taken by Canada with respect to vessels fishing in the NAFO regulatory area and the enforcement of such measures."

Decision

The ICJ found that Canada's use of force to apply its legislation and regulation fell within the scope of what is commonly understood as "enforcement of conservation and management measures," and thus was legal under Canadian law (even though the regulation does not mention the use of force). Boarding, inspection, arrest, and minimum use of force for these purposes are all contained within the concept of enforcement of conservation and management measures.

Thus, the ICJ concluded that, in its view, Spain's complaint constituted a dispute "arising out of" and "concerning conservation and management measures taken by Canada with respect to vessels fishing in the NAFO Regulatory Area" and "the enforcement of such measures." This ruling meant that the dispute fell within the terms of the reservation contained in the Canadian declaration of May 10, 1994. For this reason the court, by 12 votes to 5, found that it had no jurisdiction to adjudicate upon Spain's complaint. (Since the ICJ did not include judges from Spain or Canada, each country appointed an ad hoc judge, bringing the total number of judges from 15 to 17.)

Questions

1. Summarize the facts that gave rise to this case.
2. What was Spain's argument?
3. Explain why the ICJ decided that it did not have jurisdiction to hear the case.
4. Explain the significance of this case.

Shortly after the seizure of the *Estai*, the dispute was negotiated. The Europeans agreed to conservation measures. On April 18, 1995, the proceedings against the *Estai* and its captain were discontinued by order of the Attorney General of Canada; on April 19, 1995, the bond was discharged and the bail was repaid with interest. Subsequently, the confiscated portion of the catch was returned. On May 1, 1995, the *Coastal Fisheries Protection Regulations* were amended to allow foreign fishing vessels to enter Canadian waters and offload fish only when a licence has been issued, or a treaty authorizes such activities. Finally, the negotiated *Proposal for Improving*

Fisheries Control and Enforcement, contained in the agreement of April 20, 1995, between Canada and Europe, was adopted by NAFO at its annual meeting held in September 1995 and became the basis for measures that would be binding on all parties from November 29, 1995. The "turbot war" was over. However, Spain would not let the matter drop: it proceeded with the case that it had instituted shortly after the *Estai* and its crew were seized.

Fyi In December 1995, the UN adopted the *Agreement Relating to the Conservation and Management of Straddling Fish Stocks and Highly Migratory Fish Stocks*. The Agreement legitimates activities such as those that Canada took with respect to the *Estai*.

CHECK YOUR UNDERSTANDING

1. What is the International Court of Justice? What are its two main functions?
2. What is the role of an ad hoc judge in this court?
3. What types of cases are most often heard by the ICJ?
4. Suggest why, in over 50 years, the ICJ has decided so few cases.
5. How effective do you think the ICJ is in resolving international questions of law? Explain your answer.

International Human Rights

Human rights have long been a central issue on the international legal agenda. The idea that people have certain universal, inalienable rights, at least from a Western perspective, dates back to classical (Greek and Roman) philosophy. On the international stage, recognition of such rights began to be made in the context of the treatment of combatants and civilians in times of war and civil strife, and was expanded to include a wider scope of recognized rights. The spread of colonialism raised issues about the status of minorities. In Western societies, changes in thinking about the status of women led to debates about their political rights. Industrialization in the 19th century led to initiatives to regulate factory working conditions, as you saw in Chapter 13.

There has always been a certain tension between the concept of inalienable individual rights and state sovereignty. States have traditionally opposed the suggestion that the rights of nationals should be dictated by international norms and not by state policy. However, the idea that human rights are "natural" (or moral, or neutral) has gained acceptance on an intellectual level across much of the international community.

Events between the world wars and during World War II led to the ready acceptance, by most people, of certain general expressions of what were beginning to be called "human rights." This eventually led to the adoption, both by the UN and by other international institutions, of norms that are now central to international law.

The earliest expression of these norms came in the form of the UN's *Universal Declaration of Human Rights* (UDHR), adopted in 1948. The proclamation of the UDHR was among the first acts of the newly formed UN, and the Declaration's widespread acceptance lent authority to the UN's role as a proponent of international law generally.

Turning Points in the Law

The *Universal Declaration of Human Rights*

In 1945, the United Nations became the world's first international governmental organization to gain the membership of nearly 90 percent of the states in the international community. The UN is a confederation of states—an emerging "town-hall meeting for all states" with its own legal personality, or sovereignty. Until 1945, only individual states were participants in the international system.

In 1945, the United Nations introduced the *Universal Declaration of Human Rights*, which contained the first-ever codified list of individual rights. On December 10, 1948, the UN General Assembly proclaimed the UDHR by resolution. Forty states voted for the resolution, the preamble of which reads in part:

> [R]ecognition of the inherent dignity and of the equal and inalienable rights of all members of the human family is the foundation of freedom, justice and peace in the world. ...
>
> [D]isregard and contempt for human rights have resulted in barbarous acts which have outraged the conscience of mankind, and the advent of a world in which human beings shall enjoy freedom of speech and belief and freedom from fear and want has been proclaimed as the highest aspiration of the common people. ...
>
> [I]t is essential, if man is not to be compelled to have recourse, as a last resort, to rebellion against tyranny and oppression, that human rights should be protected by the rule of law. ...
>
> [T]he peoples of the United Nations have in the Charter reaffirmed their faith in fundamental human rights, in the dignity and worth of the human person, and in the equal rights of men and women and have determined to promote social progress and better standards of life in larger freedom. ...

The adoption of the UDHR set the tone for the UN's priorities. Protection of human rights has been and continues to be a fundamental objective of the UN. Over the last 55 years, the UN has worked both to define the substantive content of these rights, and to devise effective procedures by which these rights can be enforced meaningfully and implemented into domestic legal systems.

Questions

1. Why was the *Universal Declaration of Human Rights* a turning point in the law?
2. Explain how each of these "global" rights has influenced the protection of individuals and peoples since 1945.
3. Read the complete UDHR in the Appendix. How has the UDHR been reflected in the drafting of the *Canadian Charter of Rights and Freedoms*?

The proclamation of the UDHR was actually the first stage of a three-part plan: the UN also intended to prepare a human rights treaty that could be ratified by its members (in contrast to the Declaration, which was a resolution passed by means of a vote), and to create a mechanism for enforcing human rights.

Work on the planned human rights treaty proved controversial. It ultimately led to the splitting of the proposed rights into two sets: civil and political rights, which were expressed in the *International Covenant on Civil and Political Rights*, and economic, social, and cultural rights, which formed the basis of the *International Covenant on Economic, Social and Cultural Rights.* These two covenants have since been ratified by a great majority of nations. Together with the UDHR, they form what is described as the *International Bill of Rights.* The following case illustrates how individuals can complain about human rights violations.

Case THE MI'KMAQ—SELF-DETERMINATION AND COLLECTIVE RIGHTS

UNHRC Communication No. 205/1986 (1990 and 1992)

Facts

In 1986, Donald Marshall, then Grand Chief of the Mi'kmaq tribal society, filed a letter with the UN Human Rights Committee (UNHRC) alleging that Canada was in violation of articles 1 and 25 of the *International Convenant on Civil and Political Rights* (ICCPR). According to Marshall, the Canadian government's refusal to grant standing to the Mi'kmaq representatives in the constitutional conferences of 1984, 1985, and 1987 violated the collective rights of the Mi'kmaq people to self-determination as prescribed under the ICCPR. In approaching the UNHRC, Marshall and his supporters sought a finding that the refusal to grant them status at these conferences was a violation of international human rights law.

The Mi'kmaq right to self-determination flowed, according to its proponents, from treaty rights that had been entrenched in Canada's constitution. The Mi'kmaq position was that the treaties forming the subject of these rights limited Canadian sovereignty over the Mi'kmaq people and their lands, and gave the Mi'kmaq the right to negotiate the way in which they would be governed.

In response, the Canadian government argued as follows.

- Any claim to self-determination by the Mi'kmaq could not be asserted in a way that would threaten Canadian unity.
- The Mi'kmaq society did not constitute a "people" within the meaning of the ICCPR.
- The right to self-determination, as a collective (and not an individual) right, was outside the jurisdiction of the UNHRC.
- The treaties upon which the Mi'kmaq were relying did not establish the tribal society as a separate national entity (with a claim to self-determination).

Decision

Marshall and his supporters were unsuccessful. After an analysis of the ICCPR and its Optional Protocol, the UNHRC determined that the

Optional Protocol "provides a procedure under which *individuals* can claim that their *individual rights* as set out in Part III [of the ICCPR] ... have been violated," but that "individuals cannot claim under the Optional Protocol to be victims of a violation of the right of self-determination, which is a [collective] right conferred upon peoples, as such." (Emphasis added.) The UNHRC also found that article 25(a) of the ICCPR (which guarantees certain individual rights of participation in public affairs) "cannot be understood as meaning that any directly affected group, large or small, has the unconditional right to choose the modalities [i.e., participation in constitutional conferences] of participation in public affairs."

Questions

1. Summarize the facts in this case.
2. Why did the Mi'kmaq representatives want to participate in Canada's constitutional conferences in the 1980s?
3. What were the reasons for the decision of the UN Human Rights Committee?
4. Was this a just decision? Explain your answer.

Selected UN Multilateral Human Rights Treaties

Components of the *International Bill of Human Rights*:

- *Universal Declaration of Human Rights*
- *International Covenant on Economic, Social and Cultural Rights*
- *International Covenant on Civil and Political Rights*

Other Key Instruments:

- *Declaration on the Granting of Independence to Colonial Countries and Peoples*
- *United Nations Declaration on the Elimination of All Forms of Racial Discrimination*
- *Discrimination (Employment and Occupation) Convention*
- *Convention against Discrimination in Education*
- *Declaration on the Rights of Persons Belonging to National or Ethnic, Religious and Linguistic Minorities*
- *Declaration on the Elimination of All Forms of Discrimination against Women*
- *Convention on the Rights of the Child*
- *Convention for the Suppression of the Traffic in Persons and of the Exploitation of the Prostitution of Others*
- *Convention against Torture and Other Cruel, Inhuman or Degrading Treatment or Punishment*
- *Declaration on the Protection of all Persons from Enforced Disappearance*
- *Declaration on Social Progress and Development*
- *Declaration on the Rights of Disabled Persons*
- *Universal Declaration on the Human Genome and Human Rights*
- *Convention Relating to the Status of Refugees*
- *Convention on the Prevention and Punishment of the Crime of Genocide*

Figure 17.6

Canada is a signatory to treaties forming the *International Bill of Rights*, and to many other UN human rights instruments. As a member of the UN and a signatory to these conventions, Canada's performance with respect to human rights is regularly reviewed by international bodies including the UN Committee on the Rights of the Child, the UN Committee on Economic, Social and Cultural Rights, the International Labour Organization, and the UN Committee on the Elimination of Racial Discrimination, among others.

WORKING FOR CHANGE *Amnesty International*

Amnesty International (AI) is a worldwide movement of people who campaign for internationally recognized human rights. Founded in 1961 by British lawyer Peter Benenson, its headquarters are in London, England. Benenson, horrified at the story of two Portuguese students sentenced to seven years' imprisonment for raising a toast to freedom, wrote to a British newspaper calling for an international campaign to bombard authorities around the world with protests for the "forgotten prisoners." Within months, this effort developed into the permanent international movement known as AI.

Today, AI is an international network of more than 1.5 million members in over 150 countries and territories in every region of the world. It is an NGO, independent of any government, political ideology, religion, or economic interest, and is concerned solely with a world in which all citizens enjoy all the rights enshrined in the *Universal Declaration of Human Rights* and the impartial protection of these rights. To ensure its independence, AI does not accept funds from governments or political parties but rather depends on members' donations and fundraising activities.

The main focus of AI's campaigning is

- to free all prisoners of conscience (persons imprisoned solely for the peaceful expression of their beliefs)

Figure 17.7 *A candlelight vigil is held during an Amnesty International march in Belleville, Ontario, observing International Human Rights Day, December 10, 2002.*

- to ensure a prompt and fair trial for all political prisoners
- to abolish the death penalty, torture, and other cruel, inhuman, or degrading treatment or punishment
- to end executions and "disappearances" that are not legally authorized
- to fight impunity (exemption from punishment) by working to ensure that perpetrators of such abuses are brought to justice in accordance with international standards.

AI research teams focusing on particular countries investigate reports of human rights abuses and send researchers on fact-finding missions to assess situations at first hand by interviewing prisoners, relatives, lawyers, witnesses to human rights violations, and human rights activists. AI's 2003 report documented human rights abuses in 151 countries and territories during 2002.

Even Canada, which has a good AI record, is not immune from scrutiny. For example, on September 4, 2003, AI released a report, "Canada: Why There Must Be a Public Inquiry into the Police Killing of Dudley George," renewing its call for a full, impartial public inquiry. Dudley George, aged 38, was killed by an OPP officer during an Aboriginal land protest at Ipperwash Provincial Park on September 6, 1995. The officer was subsequently convicted of criminal negligence causing death. But in the intervening eight years, the federal and Ontario governments have resisted continuous calls for a public inquiry into this incident. Evidence has emerged that the former Ontario premier and his ministers may have pressured the police to use lethal force, if necessary, during the Ipperwash protests. As AI concluded in its report, "To fail to [order a public inquiry] is to compound the injustice and also to flout (disrespect) the clear requirements of Canada's obligations under international law." The combined effect of AI publicity and the George family's use of domestic law may create conditions where the government will respond to calls for a public inquiry.

Questions

1. Why is Amnesty International effective as an agent of change?
2. Would AI be as effective if it were funded by world governments? Why or why not?
3. Review AI's Web site to research the September 2003 report on Dudley George and the need for a public inquiry. Prepare an oral report on the circumstances that led to the shooting, the reasons for the Ontario government's refusal to hold an inquiry, the possible violations of international law involved, and any other pertinent information that provides background on this case.

Learn more about Dudley George and the Ipperwash land protests at www.emp.ca/dimensionsoflaw

Recent examples in which internal Canadian laws have been found to be incompatible with international human rights obligations include the *Waldman* case and the ILO decision respecting Ontario legislation ending a teachers' strike.

- In *Waldman v. Canada*, the UN Human Rights Committee ruled that Canada was in violation of the *International Covenant on Civil and Political Rights* because of Ontario's funding of Roman Catholic schools and not those of other faiths. The Committee ruled against Canada even though the practice of funding only public and Catholic schools is provided for by the Canadian constitution. In response to the ruling, the Ontario government partially complied by creating a system of tax credits designed to pay some of the cost of sending children to other religious schools. (See the Issue, "Funding of Religious Schools," Chapter 4, page 110.)

- In the case of the teachers' strike, the International Labour Organization found that Ontario's back-to-work legislation, implemented to end strikes and lockouts in seven Catholic school boards and one public school board in September 1998, violated the *Freedom of Association and Protection of the Right to Organize Convention.*

Despite widespread ratification of the major UN human rights treaties, the legal, moral, and philosophical content of human rights remains a highly controversial topic. The international community enjoys tremendous cultural and religious diversity. Most religions are built upon their own codes of right and wrong, and many religious beliefs relate to human rights, or the expression of the role and status of individuals in society. These expressions and beliefs are not always perfectly consistent with the UN scheme of human rights—one that is strongly based in Western philosophy. For this reason, some state governments resist the application of certain human rights to the extent that they conflict with pre-existing religious and cultural norms. For example, freedom of religion is a commonly expressed human right, but it conflicts with the Islamic notion that it is not possible to change one's religion.

Taken to the extreme, rejections of "Western" human rights have occasionally been used to justify nation's mistreatment of their citizens under the umbrella of state sovereignty; but most objections to the content of human rights flow from legitimate philosophical differences.

It is important to recognize that the UN is not the only source of human rights norms. Many individual states have created their own expressions of human rights (consider, for example, the *Canadian Charter of Rights and Freedoms*, and Canada's provincial human rights codes). Human rights have also been codified on a regional basis. For example, in 1980, the Islamic Council of Europe sponsored the preparation of the *Universal Islamic Declaration of Human Rights*, based on the Qur'an and other sources of Islamic law. This document was addressed not only to the Muslim community but to the international community at large.

The Council of Europe addressed human rights in the form of the 1950 *European Convention for the Protection of Human Rights and Fundamental Freedoms.* The Organization of American States' *American Declaration on the Rights and Duties of Man* predated the UDHR by six months.

In some cases, regional organizations have sought to create expressions of human rights that reflect their own cultural norms. Documents such as the 1982 *African Charter of Human and Peoples' Rights* reveal subtle but significant differences in emphasis—the African Charter gives strong voice not only to individual rights but to community and family obligations. This perspective, which acknowledges the interconnectedness of individuals, stands in some degree of contrast to what many cultures (for example, communist states) believe to be the extreme individualism of Western conceptions of human rights.

Personal Viewpoint

Do Western Human Rights Speak for All?

The following extract represents a point of view that differs from traditional Western attitudes toward human rights.

> Asian religious traditions and cultures have their own spiritual and moral philosophies which ... can, and should, serve as the primary basis for human rights in Asian countries.
>
> It can be argued that the very concept of human rights is a recent Western idea not based in the Judeo-Christian-Islamic world view, but in post-enlightenment, secular culture. This concept, moreover, is based on an individualistic view of society, which is diametrically opposed to the Christian idea of the church as a "universal communion of saints" (*ecclesia*), as well as the Islamic concept of an *ummah* (community) enjoining the good, dissuading from evil, and having true faith in God. In contrast, the modern secular Western concept of human rights is a morally neutral concept based not on spiritual or religious principles, but on purely materialistic and social considerations. ...
>
> Asian religious traditions ... have their own profound moral principles that could serve as a framework for the realization of human rights in their own societies. It is high time that the West learn from the East the meaning of moral freedom and the true significance of non-material values rather than dictate to the peoples of Asia its own confused and highly selective principles of human rights. ...
>
> It is arrogant and hypocritical of any country, on the basis of its material wealth and military might, to dictate to selective countries how to live and how to develop and preserve their values and fundamental rights.
>
> On the other hand, it is the opportunistic cynicism of Asian and African dictators to ignore pleas to show greater respect for the most fundamental rights of their citizens on the ground of Western cultural neocolonialism. ...
>
> In today's religiously and culturally pluralistic world, nations must work together for the preservation of moral and spiritual values and the safeguarding of the fundamental rights of liberty, equality before God, and international law and human dignity.

Source: Mahmoud Ayoub, *Asian Spirituality and Human Rights*. Bangkok, Thailand: Asian Regional Resource Center for Human Rights Education, 2002.

Questions

1. Give examples of what the writer might mean by "extreme individualism" from cases you have studied in earlier chapters of this book.
2. Do you agree that the "Western concept of human rights is a morally neutral concept based on purely materialistic and social considerations"? Justify your answer.
3. Visit www.emp.ca/dimensionsoflaw for links to the *African Charter of Human and Peoples' Rights* and the *Universal Islamic Declaration of Human Rights*. For each of these documents, list three provisions that differ from those of the *Canadian Charter of Rights and Freedoms*, and three provisions that are similar.

CHECK YOUR UNDERSTANDING

1. Why has there been tension between the concept of universal inalienable rights and state sovereignty?
2. Identify the three components of the *International Bill of Rights*.
3. Why is the philosophical content of human rights a highly controversial topic?
4. Why have individual states created their own human rights legislation? Was this necessary? Why or why not?

Regional and Specialized Organizations

While the UN is the main focus of the international community, there are hundreds of organizations that influence international law. Some are made up of groups of states from a region and act as a means of defining and promoting the regional interests of those states. Others are created to advance a special interest, such as stewardship of the Arctic, the concerns of francophone countries, or economic cooperation and development among a group of countries. Below is a very brief overview of some regional and specialized international organizations that are of interest to Canada.

Regional International Organizations

Asia–Pacific Economic Cooperation

The Asia–Pacific Economic Cooperation (APEC) was established in response to the growing interdependence among Asian and Pacific economies, and the need to foster economic dynamism and a sense of community within the region. It was also seen as a way to establish a counterbalance to the emerging trading blocs of Europe and North America. APEC was not established in the conventional manner, that is, by treaty, but arose gradually from informal meetings, the first of which was held in Australia in 1989. At that time, representatives from 12 Asia–Pacific economies (including Canada) sought to discuss ways to increase cooperation and to establish a regular forum for consultation. An international organization was created with a permanent secretariat in Singapore and 21 "member economies." Although the main focus of the organization is economic and trade-related, APEC has now made environmental and women's issues part of its mandate.

Fyi In response to demands from Indonesia that its president, Suharto, not be exposed to protests over his abuse of human rights when he attended the APEC summit in Vancouver in November 1997, the RCMP used pepper spray on protesters. This action prompted an inquiry into the role of police and the Prime Minister's Office in the incident.

North American Free Trade Agreement

As you learned in Chapter 15, NAFTA is a trilateral agreement among Canada, Mexico, and the United States that came into full effect in January 1994. The agreement created "institutions" such as the *North American Agreement on Labour Cooperation*, 1993, and the *North American Agreement on Environmental Cooperation*, 1993. NAFTA also establishes processes for administering the complex economic relationship among the three countries.

Learn more about APEC and the OAS at www.emp.ca/dimensionsoflaw

Organization of American States

In 1990, Canada became a member of the Organization of American States (OAS), founded in 1948, which involves 35 countries of North, Central, and South America, as well as the Caribbean; its headquarters are in Washington, DC. For many years, Canada refused to join the OAS because of the possibility of having to oppose the United States on such issues as the exclusion of Cuba, or risk becoming a US puppet. Canada changed its position when major economic reforms created new opportunities for it throughout the region, and because emerging issues (such as drug control) meant that Canada could no longer afford to be excluded from this international forum.

The OAS is a full-fledged international entity with structures that resemble those of the UN; however, it also shares some elements of a collective security organization, such as NATO (although Canada does not participate in some of the OAS's security roles). The countries of the Western hemisphere use the OAS to promote their political and legal agenda internationally. Currently, the OAS focuses on consolidating the transition to democratic government in many countries of Latin America; advancing human rights; promoting peace and security; expanding trade; and tackling complex problems caused by poverty, drugs, and corruption.

Specialized International Organizations

Learn more about the Arctic Council at www.emp.ca/dimensionsoflaw

Arctic Council

The Arctic Council was inaugurated in Ottawa on September 19, 1996. Its eight members are Canada, Denmark, Finland, Iceland, Norway, Russia, Sweden, and the United States. (Greenland is a member as a province of Denmark.) All member countries have or administer territories that border the Arctic Ocean. The Arctic Council is a consensual organization, founded on the principles of cooperation, coordination, and interaction in matters of the Arctic, with the aim of addressing such issues as sustainable development and environmental protection. The Council also involves indigenous peoples' groups, such as the Inuit Circumpolar Conference, as permanent parties. Non-Arctic states and NGOs may become involved with the Arctic Council as observers.

Fyi Canada's Arctic encompasses about 40% of its total landmass and has about 85 000 residents. By comparison, Toronto's population is nearly 2.5 million.

La Francophonie

L'Agence intergouvernementale de la Francophonie (La Francophonie) is an international organization created by the Niamey (Niger) Convention of March 20, 1970, at the initiative of Senegal, Tunisia, and Niger. The

Figure 17.8 *Prime Minister Jean Chrétien speaks at a news conference during the Francophonie summit in Beirut, Lebanon, in 2002.*

organization now includes 50 "states and governments" including "Canada–Nouveau Brunswick" and "Canada–Quebec." Originally, La Francophonie was a cultural and educational organization, fulfilling the needs of primarily French-speaking nations. Since 1986, it has become more of a forum for political dialogue and exchange. In 1998, Boutros Boutros-Ghali, a former Secretary-General of the UN, became Secretary-General of La Francophonie, and the organization took on a much broader mandate.

Fyi At the 2002 G8 Summit in Kananaskis, Alberta, it was announced that Russia would host the 2006 G8 summit, thus completing its process of becoming a full member.

G7/G8

In 1975, the leaders of the world's six largest industrial countries (Britain, France, Germany, Italy, Japan, and the United States) met in France to deal with major economic and political issues. At that time, wildly increasing oil prices had destabilized the global monetary system. Canada joined in 1976 to make it the G7 ("group of seven"). Russia began meeting with the G7 in 1994, resulting in the birth of the G8 in 1998.

The G8 summits have consistently dealt with economic management, international trade, and relations with developing countries, especially Africa and the AIDS crisis there in recent years. Other topics of concern include the environment, crime and drugs, terrorism, and human rights. Since the 1998 summit in Birmingham, England, these annual meetings have become an opportunity for anti-globalization demonstrations. The 2001 Genoa summit resulted in the death of a protester.

Learn more about the G7/G8 at www.emp.ca/dimensionsoflaw

Personal Viewpoint

Stephen Lewis: "A Shocking Rejection of Africa"

In his long career, Stephen Lewis has been the leader of the Ontario New Democratic Party in the 1960s and 1970s, Canada's ambassador to the UN from 1984 to 1988, and a former deputy executive director of UNICEF. In June 2001, he was appointed UN Secretary-General's Special Envoy for HIV/AIDS in Africa. He was the keynote speaker at the G6B ("group of 6 billion") People's Summit. The G6B reflects the entire global citizenry and was organized by the International Society for Peace and Human Rights. The following is an excerpt of the speech delivered by Lewis, in his personal capacity, at the G6B People's Summit on June 21, 2002.

> It's simply self-evident truth, that in country after country, where the [AIDS] pandemic is grievously rooted, the development process has been dealt a mortal blow. The G8 Summit next week [at Kananaskis, Alberta] is, in a way, the last best chance for Africa. The G8 leaders ... must make a herculean effort to break free and provide a binding commitment to the continent. ... Sadly, inexplicably, the G8 is guilty of a profound moral default. They simply will not meet the commitments to which they have previously pledged... .
>
> Last year, at the AIDS summit in Abuja, Nigeria, the Secretary-General of the United Nations formally proposed the Global Fund, and asked for $7 to $10 billion dollars per year from all sources, but particularly from governments. After a great deal of cajoling and persuasion, the rich nations have contributed, thus far, $2.1 billion, but over three years. ... [I]t ... amounts to about 7 percent of the need... . It's a shocking piece of international financial delinquency, and it's a shocking rejection of Africa. ...

Figure 17.9 *Stephen Lewis speaks at a press conference at the United Nations after being named Special Envoy of the Secretary-General for HIV/AIDS in Africa, June 2001.*

> If the G8 Summit takes NEPAD [New Partnership for African Development] seriously, if it wishes to make development more than an "impossible dream," if it adds to international trade and investment a pledge to rescue the human condition in Africa, if it wants to redeem the Summit process, so tainted by previous posturing and irrelevance, then it will provide a guarantee, year by year, of the moneys that Kofi Annan has requested for the Global Fund. In one fell swoop, the entire Summit would then be credible. ...
>
> Somehow, this [2002] G8 Summit has to be a turning-point. Africa is coming to us, pledging reform, asking for help. If we raise it to the

intellectual and academic level, it really does become a question of globalization. ... In times of war, everything is a national emergency. In times of war, every apparatus of the state is conscripted into battle. In times of war, resources are somehow found that are thought not to exist—just think of the so-called war on terrorism, with scores of billions of dollars hurled into the fray overnight to avenge the horrendous deaths of three thousand people. So explain to me why we have to grovel to extract a few billion dollars to prevent the deaths of over two million people each year, year after year after year?

Why is the war against terrorism sacrosanct [most sacred], and the war against AIDS equivocal [questionable]? In the answer to that question lies the challenge for NEPAD and the true test for the G8.

Source: Stephen Lewis, Keynote Address to the G6B People's Summit, Calgary, Alberta, June 21, 2002; www.g6bpeoplessummit.org.

Questions

1. On what grounds does Lewis accuse the G8 of "moral default"? Do you agree with him? Why or why not?
2. Research and prepare a short report on the Global Fund proposed by UN Secretary-General Kofi Annan.
3. Explain the meaning of Lewis's statement: "In times of war, resources are somehow found that are thought not to exist ... [in order] to avenge the horrendous deaths of three thousand people."
4. Do you agree with Stephen Lewis's comments? Why or why not?

North Atlantic Treaty Organisation

To learn more about NATO, visit www.emp.ca/dimensionsoflaw

The North Atlantic Treaty Organisation (NATO) is an alliance of 19 countries from North America and Europe committed to fulfilling the goals of the *North Atlantic Treaty* signed in April 1949; its headquarters are in Brussels, Belgium. NATO's fundamental role is to safeguard the security and freedom of its member states by political and military means, but in recent years it has also played an increasingly key role in peacekeeping and the fight against terrorism.

In 1998, NATO countries and the international community became gravely concerned about the escalating conflict between Serbian military and ethnic Albanian forces in Kosovo, the humanitarian consequences of the conflict, and the risk of its spreading to other countries in the region. The UN Security Council was unable to achieve the support of its permanent members to intervene and, as a result, NATO—by a collective decision of the organization—intervened militarily by bombing Belgrade and other Serbian targets. Subsequently, forces of NATO and the Organization for Security and Co-operation in Europe were involved in actions to restore peace in Kosovo.

On September 12, 2001, NATO declared the terrorist attacks against the United States to be an attack against all 19 NATO countries within the terms of article 5 of the *North Atlantic Treaty*. This landmark decision was followed by practical measures aimed at assisting the United States in its campaign against terrorism.

Organisation for Economic Co-operation and Development

Learn more about the OECD at www.emp.ca/dimensionsoflaw

The Organisation for Economic Co-operation and Development (OECD) was established in 1961 by a core group of European and North American countries (including Canada) as a forum for discussing, developing, and perfecting economic and social policy. The OECD has 30 member countries, an active relationship with 70 other countries, and a permanent secretariat in Paris headed by a secretary-general. The main decision-making body is its council, which comprises one representative for each member country (as well as a representative of the European Commission). Members have used the OECD as a means of coordinating domestic and international policies designed to form a web of consistent business practices in an increasingly globalized world.

Organization for Security and Co-operation in Europe

Learn more about the OSCE at www.emp.ca/dimensionsoflaw

The Organization for Security and Co-operation in Europe (OSCE) was created in the early 1970s to lessen Cold War tensions in Europe and was designed to serve as a multilateral forum for dialogue and negotiation between East and West. It is now the largest regional security organization, with 55 participating states from Europe, Central Asia, and North America (including Canada). Headquartered in Vienna, Austria, the OSCE's primary role is to serve as an instrument for early warning, conflict prevention, crisis management, and post-conflict rehabilitation. The OSCE is actively involved in missions in southeastern Europe, including the former Yugoslavia.

Other Organizations

Learn more about NORAD at www.emp.ca/dimensionsoflaw

In environmental matters, Canada relies heavily on the work carried out by the International Joint Commission (IJC), created by the *Boundary Waters Treaty* of 1909. The IJC is but one example of the many international organizations that regulate, on an institutional basis, the complex Canada–US relationship. Others include the Seaway Authority, the Boundary Commission, fisheries commissions, and the various international bridge authorities. In addition, Canada and the United States have been partners in the North American Aerospace Defense Command (NORAD) since 1958 to administer continental defence.

International Regulation of Corporate and Individual Behaviour

International law and regulation tend to be directed at states and state actions rather than at individuals and corporations. How do states and international institutions regulate and, if necessary, punish corporations who break international law or international norms of good behaviour?

This question is especially challenging as the political and economic clout of these transnational corporations grows and, in some ways, exceeds that of the countries within which they operate. The OECD is one organization that has adopted guidelines for multinational enterprises. For example, the guidelines state that transnational corporations should work to eliminate child labour. These guidelines, however, are only that: guides, not binding rules. Other regulations that have been created by UN organizations to deal with individual issues related to transnational corporations include

- the Food and Agriculture Organization's *Code of Conduct for Responsible Fisheries*
- the World Health Organization's *International Code of Marketing of Breast-milk Substitutes*
- the United Nations Environment Program's *Code of Ethics on the International Trade in Chemicals.*

Codes of conduct are important, particularly for companies that sell directly to consumers and are therefore influenced by consumer criticism and, in some cases, consumer boycotts. In August 2003, a UN committee unanimously approved the first major draft of human rights standards for transnational corporations. The document outlines standards concerning labour rights, bribery, conduct of business in conflict zones, and environmental pollution. The draft will be sent to the UN Commission on Human Rights for formal adoption.

Learn more about Interpol at www.emp.ca/dimensionsoflaw

Transnational crime committed by individuals and by organized criminals is also a challenge for both state and international organizations. International law requires states to ensure that they enact and enforce laws that deal with such matters as terrorism, drug trafficking, arms trafficking, traffic in persons, obscene publications, and theft of cultural property, to name just a few of the topics addressed. International support and coordination for crime control are provided by Interpol, the world's police organization. Countries gain access to Interpol's services by applying for membership in Interpol and then by acceptance through a vote of its General Assembly. In 2003, 181 countries were members of Interpol.

Fyi In 1996, Justice Louise Arbour was appointed Chief Prosecutor of War Crimes before the International Criminal Tribunal for Rwanda and the former Yugoslavia in The Hague. In June 1999, Justice Arbour was appointed to the Supreme Court of Canada.

Criminal Prosecution of Individuals by International Courts

Recently, individuals who have been accused of directing or participating in gross violations of human rights have been prosecuted and tried by special criminal tribunals. In response to violations in the former Yugoslavia and Rwanda, the UN Security Council established two special international tribunals to try individuals accused of human rights crimes in those situations. These International Criminal Tribunals have tried a number of individuals, the most prominent being Slobodan Milosevic, the former president of Yugoslavia, for crimes committed in the name of "ethnic cleansing."

In Rome in July 1988, 120 member states of the UN adopted a treaty to establish a permanent international criminal court. This treaty came into effect on July 1, 2002, after 60 states ratified the *Rome Statute of the International Criminal Court* (ICC), an international court to deal with individual criminal responsibility, such as that being addressed by the special tribunals, but on a much broader scale. The ICC has become controversial because a number of high-profile states, including the United States, China, and Russia, had not ratified the *Rome Statute* by the time it had come into force, making their participation in the ICC unlikely, at least for the foreseeable future. (See Chapter 19: Military Conflict and Conflict Resolution for more information on these tribunals and the ICC.)

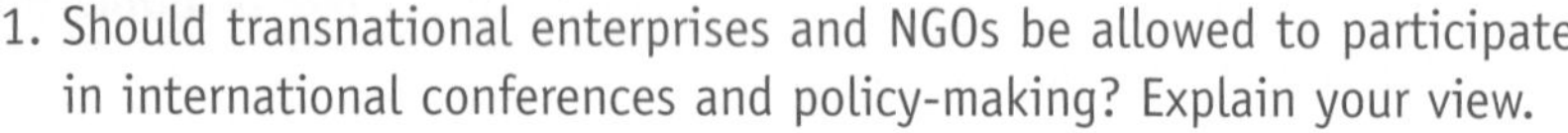

Learn more about NGOs at www.emp.ca/dimensionsoflaw

1. Should transnational enterprises and NGOs be allowed to participate in international conferences and policy-making? Explain your view.
2. Why do groups of nations seek to form regional arrangements such as the OAS and APEC?
3. Why, considering most nations' participation in the UN, do non-UN conferences, such as those held by APEC, continue to flourish?
4. Why do the annual G7/G8 summits attract demonstrators and protests?
5. How would you propose to regulate transnational corporations that fail to comply with international codes of conduct or guidelines of ethical behaviour?

METHODS OF *Legal Inquiry*

Preparing Graphic Presentations

It is often more effective in reports and presentations to translate statistics into graphic form than to reproduce a table of figures. For example, Figure 17.10 shows estimated figures for HIV/AIDS in the world for December 2002.

Figure 17.10

Global Cases of HIV/AIDS, December 2002 (thousands of people; est.)

Region	Epidemic started	Adults and children infected with HIV/AIDS	Adult prevalence rate*	% of HIV-positive adults who are women
Sub-Saharan Africa	Late '70s–Early '80s	29 400	8.8%	58%
North Africa and Middle East	Late '80s	550	0.3%	55%
South and Southeast Asia	Late '80s	6 000	0.6%	36%
East Asia and Pacific	Late '80s	1 200	0.1%	24%
Latin America	Late '70s–Early '80s	1 500	0.6%	30%
Caribbean	Late '70s–Early '80s	440	2.4%	50%
Eastern Europe and Central Asia	Early '90s	1 200	0.6%	27%
Western Europe	Late '70s–Early '80s	570	0.3%	25%
North America	Late '70s–Early '80s	980	0.6%	20%
Australia and New Zealand	Late '70s–Early '80s	15	0.1%	7%
Total		**42 000**	**1.2%**	**50%**

* The proportion of adults (15 to 49 years of age) living with HIV/AIDS in 2001, using 2001 population numbers.

Source: AVERTing HIV & AIDS, www.avert.org/worldstats.htm.

If you wanted to show the preponderance of people infected with HIV/AIDS in Sub-Saharan Africa, you would choose a pie graph to present these data (Figure 17.11). If you wanted to show the percentage of infected persons in each region who were women, you would use a bar graph (Figure 17.12, on the next page).

Figure 17.11 *People infected with HIV/AIDS, December 2002.*

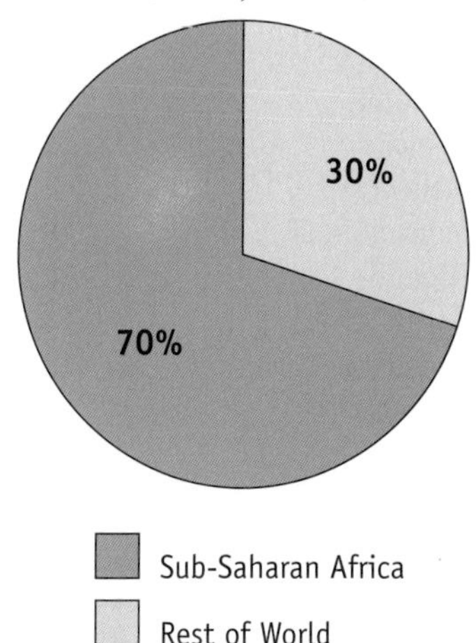

Applying the Skill

Use information from Figure 17.13 on the next page to show in graph form:

1. The number of orphans due to HIV/AIDS in each country as a proportion of total orphans in the country.
2. The total number of orphans in Africa as a proportion of the total number of children aged 0–14 years.
3. A comparison of data for Zambia and Burkina Faso.

Figure 17.12 *Percentage of HIV/AIDS-infected persons who are adult women, December 2002.*

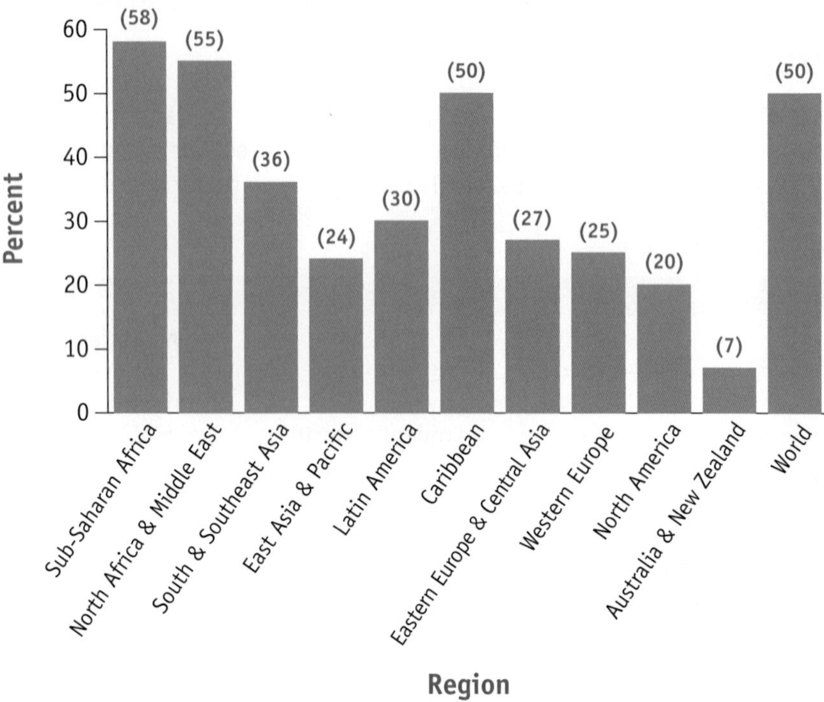

Figure 17.13

HIV/AIDS Orphans in Africa, 2001

Country	Number of children aged 0–14 (100s)	Total number of orphans (100s)	Total number of orphans due to AIDS	Orphans due to AIDS as a % of total orphans
Burkina Faso	5 769	769	268 000	35%
Côte d'Ivoire	6 806	905	420 000	46%
DR Congo	25 698	2 733	927 000	34%
Ethiopia	29 141	3 839	989 000	26%
Kenya	13 428	1 659	892 000	54%
Malawi	5 350	937	468 000	50%
Mozambique	8 196	1 274	418 000	33%
Nigeria	52 459	5 421	995 000	18%
South Africa	14 773	1 528	662 000	43%
Tanzania	16 094	1 928	815 000	42%
Uganda	11 852	1 731	884 000	51%
Zambia	4 961	874	572 000	65%
Zimbabwe	5 779	1 018	782 000	77%
African Total	**288 418**	**34 294**	**11 035 000**	**32%**

Source: AVERTing HIV & AIDS, www.avert.org/aidsorphans2.htm.

Reviewing Main Ideas

You Decide!

TRYING A HUMAN RIGHTS VIOLATOR

Britain's House of Lords v. Pinochet

Facts

Augusto Pinochet (1915–) was the military dictator of Chile from 1973 to 1990. In a campaign to destroy leftist political forces in Chile, Pinochet's government arrested thousands of people. Many were tortured, executed, or made to disappear, and others were imprisoned, allegedly on Pinochet's orders. Among these victims were 79 Spanish nationals. After surviving an assassination attempt in 1986, Pinochet dealt even more harshly with dissidents. In 1988, Chileans rejected a referendum that would have allowed Pinochet a second eight-year term beginning in 1989. In 1990, he stepped down from the presidency.

Pinochet retired from the army in 1998 and assumed a lifetime seat in the Chilean senate. As a senator, Pinochet was immune from prosecution for crimes carried out during his dictatorship. When he assumed his senate seat, thousands of Chileans protested.

Although the Chilean constitution shielded Pinochet from prosecution in Chile, it did not protect him from judicial proceedings overseas. While Pinochet was seeking medical treatment in the United Kingdom in 1998, a Spanish judge requested his extradition to Spain to face charges of murder, terrorism, torture, genocide, and other human rights violations committed during his regime. In an almost unprecedented move, British Prime Minister Tony Blair agreed to detain the dictator. The United Kingdom had signed the 1984 *UN Convention against Torture*, and Pinochet had violated that Convention by his acts. He was arrested under the UK *Extradition Act* and a case was commenced against him, which was ultimately appealed to the House of Lords. The Chilean government demanded Pinochet's release, arguing that, as a senator, he had diplomatic immunity.

Issues and Arguments

An initial decision of the House of Lords in November 1998 held that the "act of state" doctrine, which gave immunity to heads of state for acts required to govern, cannot make acts of torture and murder official government functions. This position was stated in the International Military Tribunal of Nuremburg (the Nuremburg Trials), which prosecuted Nazi war criminals at the end of World War II:

> Crimes against international law are committed by men, not by abstract entities, and only by punishing individuals who commit such crimes can the provisions of international law be enforced. ... It was submitted that ... where the act in question is an act of State, those who carry it out are not personally responsible, but are protected by the doctrine of the sovereignty of the State. In the opinion of the Tribunal, [this contention] must be rejected. ... The principle of international law, which under certain circumstances, protects the representative of a state, cannot be applied to acts which are condemned as criminal by international law. The authors of these acts cannot shelter themselves behind their official position in order to be freed from punishment in appropriate proceedings. (Judgment, pp. 41–42)

Pinochet's position as government leader therefore did not protect him against liability for acts of torture and murder, and this liability paved the way for his extradition. However, the decision was tainted by a successful allegation of bias (because of involvement on the part of the wife of one of the lords in Amnesty International, which was an intervenor in the case), and a new hearing was required.

The second decision in the House of Lords featured lengthy and complicated multiple reasons (separate reasons by individual lords). The majority position, put forward by Lord Browne-Wilkinson, was the same as in the first decision: that the "act of state" defence is not available to justify immunity when the crimes alleged are torture and murder.

While the decision provided for extradition in this situation, the majority placed limits on the general right to extradite by finding that the United Kingdom could extradite only for crimes committed after 1988, the year in which torture became a crime in that country (by the implementation of the *UN Convention against Torture* through UK domestic legislation).

Concurring in part, Lord Millett expressed the broader view that international law allows for extradition for crimes committed earlier than 1988, because a prohibition against torture is a longstanding norm of customary international law.

Decision

On March 24, 1999, Pinochet was found not to be immune to prosecution for his alleged crimes, and in October of the same year, a British magistrate ordered that the extradition could proceed. However, because of Pinochet's poor health, his prosecution was not pursued in either Britain or Spain. Pinochet returned to Chile, where half-hearted attempts to prosecute him also were not pursued.

Questions

1. Summarize the main facts of this case.
2. a) What is the "act of state" defence?
   b) What grounds did the House of Lords use for rejecting the act of state defence for Pinochet?
   c) Can and should international law outweigh the law of a nation?
3. Does the world community have the right to prosecute violations of international norms if a state cannot or will not prosecute?
4. Pinochet was not extradited to Spain for trial. Research to find out what happened after the House of Lords' finding, and give your opinion on these events.

Key Terms

Review the following terms to show that you understand the meaning of each and how it is applied in a legal context.

collective security
mandate
norms
sanctions
veto

Understanding the Law

Review the following pieces of legislation mentioned in the text, and show that you understand the intent of each.

Charter of the United Nations
International Covenant on Civil and Political Rights
International Covenant on Economic, Social and Cultural Rights
Rome Statute of the International Criminal Court
Universal Declaration of Human Rights

Thinking and Inquiry

1. Do you think the United Nations has become the "world government" that many people thought it would be? With a partner of an opposing viewpoint, discuss this issue.
2. In your opinion, do most states voluntarily observe international law? Consider aspects such as human rights as well as interaction with other states. Explain your answer.
3. List some of the legal and political shortcomings of the International Court of Justice.
4. To what extent do economic concerns and economic power influence the content and creation of international law? Give examples to justify your position.

Communication

5. The United Nations has established many special agencies, committees, commissions, and other organizations to deal with human rights. Research and prepare an oral report on the UN involvement in one of the following areas:
   - genocide
   - racial discrimination
   - right to food
   - torture
   - refugees
6. Research one of the following international organizations and report to the class on its composition, mandate, and the ways in which Canada interacts with this organization.
   - the European Union
   - the Council of Europe
   - the Economic Commission of Europe
   - the Group of 77 (G-77) representing the interests of developing countries
   - the African Union
   - the League of Arab States
   - the Association of Southeast Asian Nations
   - the Commonwealth of Independent States, composed of former Soviet republics
7. Locate a newspaper article examining an existing or a potential international law concern or violation. Research the item, and determine how international law applies. Prepare a short report, explaining your findings.

Application

8. Use the Internet to research a non-governmental organization with an international presence. Report to your group on any international impacts that this NGO has had on international law.
9. In groups, brainstorm what you personally can do to support international human rights violations and concerns. Present your findings in an oral report or a video.
10. Find an editorial cartoon that comments on an international organization or human rights issue that has become a major news story. Explain the cartoon, and outline the cartoonist's perspective. Do you agree with the artist's viewpoint? Why or why not?
11. How far has the international community progressed in developing a meaningful, just set of legal principles to establish personal liability for war crimes? Explain your answer.

Chapter 18 International Law and Common Heritage

CHAPTER *Focus*

In this chapter, you will

- identify global jurisdictional issues that may be governed by international law
- evaluate the effectiveness of treaties in protecting the environment
- examine the notion of common heritage and assess its applicability in international law
- describe the complexity of making, interpreting, and enforcing international law on a global scale

If you look at a globe, you will see the Earth's landmasses divided into a patchwork of nation states. State sovereignty is the primary principle used in international law to allocate jurisdiction over land. The oceans cover more than 70 percent of the Earth's surface and, apart from coastal waters, have historically not been subject to state sovereignty. As you will see, this principle is being challenged by extended claims to jurisdiction for various purposes. Antarctica, airspace, and outer space are also subject to doctrines that try to balance the interests of nation states and the world community. A third and still-evolving theme in international law goes further to state that some resources and zones are the common heritage of humankind and, as such, must be protected and developed for the benefit of all. The spectrum of international law, then, is broad: on one end lie the exclusionary demands of sovereignty; at the other, global needs for sharing and cooperation.

The cartoon in Figure 18.1 asks you to consider the relationship between world governments and the fate of the Earth.

Figure 18.1

At First Glance

1. What environmental protocol is the cartoonist satirizing?
2. What does the image say to you about the relationship between world governments and their commitment to (a) the protocol and (b) the globe?
3. Why do you think the cartoonist makes the arm of "World Governments" so much larger than the Earth?
4. Do you agree with the cartoonist's view? Explain your answer.

Modern Territorial Issues

As you learned in Chapters 16 and 17, the events of World War II catapulted the need for international law into public and political consciousness. As well, technology changed how people perceived the world. Developments in commercial and military aviation prompted the creation of a wave of new international rules, regulations, and organizations. Space exploration put humans into outer space, transforming it into a new frontier and a potential threat to human survival; the international community responded quickly with new laws and treaties. On and in the oceans, technological developments launched a new era of resource exploration and exploitation. The doctrine that the **high seas** should be open to all, which emerged in the 17th century, was no longer enough. Dramatically new international conditions demanded new laws.

For a history of the 8891-km Canada–US border, visit www.emp.ca/dimensionsoflaw

high seas: the portion of the oceans that is open to all and under no state's sovereignty

Boundaries and Canada

Boundaries between states are more than lines on a map. To understand how complex territorial issues can be, it is helpful to consider the Canada–US border. Although it may seem neat and simple, it took at least 17 international agreements, and many international commissions and arbitrations, to establish that border. Sometimes disputes almost led to war between Canada and the United States. Since 1925, the permanent International Boundary Commission has operated to maintain the boundary.

Interpretations of land boundaries affect the establishment of maritime (water) boundaries, which can be very complex and contentious. For example, in 1903 an international tribunal arbitrated the Alaska Panhandle dispute between Canada and the United States. The United States was allocated what the Canadian government declared to be too large a share of the West coast. The boundary, known as the A-B Line, is still in dispute. The Canadian position is that the A-B Line represents the boundary of both the United States' territorial and maritime possessions in the region. The

Fyi In this chapter, all references to miles in the context of the oceans and the law of the sea indicate nautical miles. One nautical mile is equivalent to 1.15 statute miles, or 1.85 km.

United States claims the boundary is territorial only and that it is entitled to **territorial sea** rights as measured from the A-B Line.

territorial sea: a belt of coastal waters and their resources under the sovereign control of the coastal state; set at 3 miles (5.55 km) and later extended to 12 miles (22.2 km)

On the Atlantic coast, Canada and the United States asked the International Court of Justice to set the maritime boundary through the Gulf of Maine in 1984. Ownership of the Machias Seal Island was left open. Until the matter is resolved, ownership of adjacent sea resources will also be contested. As you know, Canada's claim of Arctic sovereignty might be challenged in the future (see the Issue in Chapter 16, page 471).

Boundaries and Antarctica

Antarctica represents a unique situation in terms of sovereignty. Historically, it has been uninhabited by humans. Only limited territorial claims were made on Antarctica by the middle of the 20th century. After World War II, exploration increased, along with a Cold War–driven competition to make territorial claims.

Figure 18.2 *US Customs agents search vehicles entering the United States from Windsor, Ontario, on September 12, 2001. Cross-border traffic was backed up for 10 hours after security was tightened in the wake of the previous day's terrorist attacks on New York and Washington, DC.*

At the height of the Cold War, global negotiations attempted to "internationalize" Antarctica. These resulted in the *Antarctic Treaty*, which was signed in Washington, DC in 1959. (Canada did not become a party until 1988.) Essentially, this treaty suspended claims by the parties (originally Argentina, Australia, Belgium, Chile, France, Japan, New Zealand, Norway, the former Soviet Union, South Africa, the United Kingdom, and the United States) for the duration of the treaty. However, article IV made it clear that a state's signature did not amount to the abandonment of past or future claims on Antarctic territory. The treaty created something new—an international regime that would reserve (at least temporarily) an entire continent for the benefit of all the world's people.

The system worked for a quarter of a century, emphasizing scientific openness and environmental protection of the fragile land and marine ecosystem. In the late 1980s, Antarctica's great potential for resource extraction became apparent. Negotiations began in earnest for another treaty. The *Convention on the Regulation of Antarctic Mineral Resource Activities* (1988) outlined how mineral resources were to be extracted. It created an international furor. Shamed into retreat, the parties negotiated the *Protocol on Environmental Protection to the Antarctic Treaty* (1991).

This protocol established a commitment to the "comprehensive protection of the Antarctic environment" and designated Antarctica as "a natural reserve, devoted to peace and science." Perhaps more importantly, the protocol prohibits "any activity relating to mineral resources, other than scientific research" and states that the prohibition shall continue for at least 50 years.

To examine the *Antarctic Treaty*, visit www.emp.ca/dimensionsoflaw

CHECK YOUR UNDERSTANDING

1. Why did technological advances, such as those that made air travel possible, create the need for new international laws?
2. Why do boundaries exist between states?
3. How have Canada and the United States settled their land border issues in the past, and how is their boundary maintained today?
4. Describe two territorial disputes between Canada and the United States that are mentioned in the text and explain if, and how, they have been resolved.
5. a) How does state sovereignty in Antarctica differ from state sovereignty on other continents?
   b) What is the current legal status of Antarctica?
   c) What legal instrument creates and preserves the legal status of Antarctica?

The Oceans

The concept of territorial sovereignty co-exists with the idea of **non-appropriation**, a very different notion that is the foundation of the doctrine of the high seas. The law of the sea is one of the oldest and most complex areas of international law. The Romans believed the high seas were common to all men and should be open to all. In 1609, Grotius (see the Personal Viewpoint in Chapter 16, page 475) re-established this idea in his book *Mare Liberum* (*Free Seas*). The doctrine of non-appropriation of the oceans was quickly adopted, and Grotius is now known as the father of the modern law of the sea.

non-appropriation: the doctrine that no state may subject any part (of the high seas) to its sovereignty

The doctrine of non-appropriation reflects the technology of the 17th century, which did not permit occupation or control over ocean areas except for a narrow coastal belt. As well, the freedom of the high seas reflected the military, fishing, and commercial interests of the dominant powers of the time. In practical terms, all nations had the freedoms of navigation (and, later, overflight), fishing, and scientific research on the high seas.

Fyi Because Canada has the longest coastline of any nation in the world, the law of the sea has been extremely important to its governments.

The history of international law in the oceans has been characterized by a struggle between rights asserted by coastal states and the rights of the international community. This struggle has had two major consequences. The first has been the creation of various maritime zones that mix coastal state and world community rights. The second has been the increasing appropriation of marine resources by politically and economically dominant

partition: to create separate areas or divisions under the control of different governments

cannon-shot rule: used to define a state's territorial seas—the band of ocean extending from a state's shore over which it may claim sovereignty (the three-mile rule)

internal waters: bays, rivers, harbours, and lakes over which a state has (or claims) complete sovereignty

innocent passage: a doctrine that allows international navigation of territorial seas on the condition that no fishing or illegal activities occur

coastal states. In the last few decades, there has been a level of **partitioning** on the seas and oceans unknown in history.

Maritime Zones

In the early 18th century, a provision known as the **cannon-shot rule** became widely accepted in Europe. This rule allowed states to safeguard their security and resource interests by asserting sovereignty over a maritime zone surrounding their territory and **internal waters**. The limit of this zone, the territorial sea, was set at three miles (5.5 km)—the range of a land-based cannon at the time. The doctrine of the territorial sea was the classic balancing of legitimate coastal state and world community interests.

A second accommodation was needed to protect the community interest in navigation, especially in narrow waters and straits. The doctrine of **innocent passage** was later developed to allow ships to pass through another nation's territorial sea. Ships exercising the right of innocent passage could not fish or threaten the security of the coastal state. In exchange, the coastal state could exercise only very limited control over the passing ships. In some circumstances, interventions under international law were needed.

As you learned in Chapter 16, under international law, states are allowed to take actions to repress and prosecute piracy. Similarly, states can pursue ships that commit offences in their territorial sea, even if those ships escape into the high seas. This is known as the doctrine of hot pursuit, and it later applied to contiguous (adjacent) and economic zones extending beyond the traditional three-mile limit. One famous case involved the *I'm Alone*, a ship that was pursued and sunk by US ships in 1929.

Figure 18.3 *On July 1, 2003, the shipping lanes in the Bay of Fundy (used mainly by Irving oil tankers) were shifted to protect the endangered North Atlantic right whale—an environmental first. Although Canada considers the Bay to be internal waters, the United States has disputed this claim.*

Case THE SINKING OF THE *I'M ALONE*

Canada v. United States, 2 Hackworth, International Law 703–708 (1941), Dept. of State Arb. Ser. No. 2

Facts

On March 20, 1929, the US Coast Guard cutter *Wolcott* sighted the *I'm Alone*, a British schooner of Canadian registry, about 10.5 miles (19.4 km) off the coast of the United States and within an hour's sailing distance of shore. The Coast Guard suspected the *I'm Alone* of transporting alcohol for sale in the United States in contravention of the *Volstead Act* (*National Prohibition Enforcement Act*), 1919. The *Wolcott* ordered the ship to stop, but the *I'm Alone* put to sea. The *Wolcott*'s gun jammed, and the US Coast Guard cutter *Dexter* took up the pursuit. On March 22, about 200 miles (370 km) offshore, the *I'm Alone* refused to stop. The *Dexter* fired, sinking the *I'm Alone*. One person on board drowned. The dispute was submitted to two commissioners, one appointed by Canada, the other by the United States.

The Canadian legation (legal group) cited the doctrine of hot pursuit: "it is agreed that international law recognizes that pursuit begun within territorial waters may be continued on the high seas, if immediate and continuous." However, this doctrine did not apply because "the pursuit did not begin within the territorial three-mile limit." Furthermore, "the cutter [that] sank the schooner had not participated in the original pursuit, but had come up from an entirely different direction two days later."

The US Department of State replied that the doctrine of hot pursuit applied when the chase began within the one-hour sailing limit:

> In the estimation of this Government, the correct principle underlying the doctrine of hot pursuit is that if the arrest would have been valid when the vessel was first hailed, but was made impossible through the illegal action of the pursued vessel in failing to stop when ordered to do so, then hot pursuit is justified and the locus [point] of the arrest and distance of the pursuit are immaterial provided:
>
> (1) that it is without [not in] the territorial waters of any other state;
> (2) that the pursuit has been hot and continuous.
>
> With regard to the duration of pursuit I may state that it is the view of this Government that this is unimportant, provided the other elements of hot pursuit are always present.

Decision

In a joint interim report dated June 30, 1933, the commissioners were "not in agreement." Neither had they reached "final disagreement" as to whether the convention of 1924 (an agreement between the United States and Britain to prevent the smuggling of intoxicating liquors into the United

To learn more about the *I'm Alone* case, visit www.emp.ca/dimensionsoflaw

States) gave the United States the right of hot pursuit when the offending vessel was within an hour's sailing distance of the shore at the start of the pursuit and beyond that distance when it ended. The commissioners further stated that assuming the United States government did have the right of hot pursuit in the circumstances, the "admittedly intentional sinking of the suspected vessel was not justified by anything in the Convention." The joint final report of January 5, 1935 stated: "The Commissioners now add that it [the intentional sinking of the *I'm Alone*] could not be justified by any principle of international law."

Questions

1. Summarize the facts in this case.
2. In this circumstance, did the United States have the right of hot pursuit of the alleged offending vessel, the *I'm Alone*?
3. Why are the phrases "intentional sinking" and "suspected vessel" legally significant?
4. Should the United States have been forced to pay compensation for the loss of the ship and its cargo? Using information from the case, write a paragraph defending your position.

After World War II, the issue of maritime zones and marine resources became much more complex and contested. In 1945, US President Harry Truman unilaterally extended his country's jurisdiction over all natural resources—including oil, gas, minerals, and so on—on the US **continental shelf**. It was the first major challenge to the freedom-of-the-seas doctrine, and other countries soon made similar claims.

continental shelf: the gently sloping crust of the Earth that extends from a coastal state into the ocean and is submerged by no more than 200 m of water

Coastal states were soon facing new problems, from the pollution of passing ships (particularly oil spills) to electronic technology that allowed eavesdropping on shoreline installations. Fishing stocks just beyond the three-mile limit were being depleted and destroyed by technologically advanced distant-water fishing fleets. These fleets are made up of massive "factory ships," which are equipped to process and store fish and remain at sea for months.

To learn more about the devastation caused by distant-water fishing fleets, visit www.emp.ca/dimensionsoflaw

The governments of many coastal states faulted the international community for failing to develop effective fishery management institutions and pollution control. The freedom of the seas had become a lawless free-for-all that would devastate the oceans. Well-financed distant-water fishing fleets, however, needed access to fish, a vital protein source for their populations. They zealously asserted that the right to fish was a fundamental freedom of the high seas.

Many coastal states found that the traditional three-mile zone did not allow them to protect critical interests such as customs, immigration, and sanitary laws. States, including Canada, began to establish "special-purpose" zones of jurisdiction to enforce these laws. Generally, the international community accepted the zones, as long as they were a response to genuine community interests, such as the prevention of ship-borne disease.

Some maritime states detected a trend: their commercial and military fleets were facing increased limitations on the freedom of innocent passage. They disputed the right of powerful coastal states to impose new limits unilaterally. Claims that the new zones and regulations were needed to control pollution and preserve resources were criticized as a disguise for purely political attempts to seize control of the oceans and seabed.

By the late 1960s, the harvesting of ocean and seabed resources—including fish, oil and gas, diamonds, metals, and minerals—was reaching unheard of levels. Military rivalry between the superpowers was affecting the oceans and **deep seabed** through nuclear testing, nuclear submarines, and plans for nuclear installations. In 1967, the *Torrey Canyon*, one of the first oil supertankers, struck a reef off the coast of England. The disaster exposed the world to the environmental horrors of oil slicks and the difficulties of dealing with them under international law. More than 120 000 tonnes of oil started leaking, killing marine life along the south coast of Britain and the shores of Normandy in France.

In late 1967, Maltese ambassador Arvid Pardo addressed the United Nations. He described the situation on the oceans and in the deep seabed as a crisis for humankind.

Fyi A 1998 World Wildlife Fund study estimated that government subsidies for distant-water fishing fleets have inflated the size of the fleets to 2.5 times what the fishing stocks of oceans can sustain.

deep seabed: the seabed and ocean floor and their subsoil beyond the limits of national jurisdiction

Turning Points in the Law

The Common Heritage of Humankind

When Arvid Pardo addressed the UN General Assembly on November 1, 1967, he spoke as the Ambassador of Malta, a 316-square-kilometre Mediterranean archipelago that is tiny by Canadian standards. The impact of Pardo's speech, however, was enormous. He asserted that the deep seabed and ocean floor must be seen as the "common heritage of mankind." He expounded the following principles.

- The seabed and the ocean floor underlying the seas beyond the limits of national jurisdiction are not subject to national appropriation in any manner whatsoever.
- The seabed and the ocean floor beyond the limits of national jurisdiction shall be reserved exclusively for peaceful purposes.
- Scientific research with regard to the deep seas and ocean floor, when not directly connected with defence, shall be freely permissible and its result available to all.
- The resources of the seabed and ocean floor beyond the limit of national jurisdiction shall be exploited primarily in the interest of humankind with particular regard to the needs of poor countries.
- The exploration and exploitation of the seabed and ocean floor beyond the limits of national jurisdiction shall be conducted in a manner consistent with the principles and purposes of the *UN Charter* and in a manner not causing obstruction of the high seas or serious impairment of the marine environment.

Pardo appealed "to moral concepts, to reason, and to well-understood national interests." Using the language of diplomacy, he launched a process that lasted 15 years and changed the course of international law. On December 17, 1970, the UN General Assembly voted overwhelmingly in favour of Resolution 2749 (XXV). It declared that "the seabed and ocean floor (hereinafter referred to as 'the Area'), as well as the resources of the Area, are the common heritage of mankind."

Many sessions later, on December 10, 1982, the *United Nations Convention on the Law of the Sea* (UNCLOS) was completed. It is the most ambitious effort to codify international law that the UN has ever undertaken, and has been called "the constitution of the seas." Pardo's concerns helped shape the massive document, including the following articles:

> **Article 135**
> Neither this Part (XI) nor any rights granted or exercised pursuant thereto shall affect the legal status of the waters superjacent [lying immediately above] to the Area (the seabed and ocean floor and subsoil thereof beyond the limits of national jurisdiction) or that of the air space above the waters.

> **Article 136**
> The Area and its resources (all solid, liquid or gaseous mineral resources *in situ* [in their original place] the area at or beneath the seabed, including polymetallic or manganese nodules) are the common heritage of mankind.

Questions

1. In your own words, explain Pardo's concept of the "common heritage" of humankind.
2. Do you agree with the principle of common heritage, or do you find it too idealistic? Use evidence from the article to support your answer.
3. Do you believe that the equitable sharing of the benefits derivable from the exploitation of deep-seabed resources should and could become an international reality? Explain your response.
4. What environmental areas of the planet do you think should be defined as the common heritage of humankind?

Figure 18.4 *A gigantic water column reaching to a height of over 1500 metres rises in a mushroom cloud following the first underwater explosion of an atomic bomb near the island of Bikini in July 1946. Underwater nuclear testing, which disrupts the ecology of the deep seabed, continued through the 1980s.*

United Nations Convention on the Law of the Sea (1982)

Perhaps the first task facing negotiators of the *United Nations Convention on the Law of the Sea* was to establish consistent offshore jurisdictional areas (see Figure 18.5). States were claiming anything from the traditional three-mile limit to a major group that had imposed a 200-mile limit. Eventually, a 12-mile (22.2-km) limit was universally accepted as the limit of the territorial sea. UNCLOS also permits the establishment of an additional 12-mile contiguous zone (adjacent to the territorial-sea limit), which gives coastal states wider powers to police and enforce laws.

UNCLOS also clarifies the notion of innocent passage. For international straits narrower than 24 miles (44.4 km), such as the Strait of Gibraltar, the regime of **transit passage** is established. This allows uninterrupted navigation and overflight in and above international straits and stipulates that the coastal state cannot use the guise of environmental or other concerns to interfere with a ship's or aircraft's right of passage.

UNCLOS has also created the **exclusive economic zone (EEZ)**, which extends up to 200 miles (370 km) from the shores (from straight **baselines**) of coastal states. It has also been argued that the economic-zone concept marks a victory for the effective management of the marine environment and its resources. Entrusting the management of "community interests" to individual states is preferable to the free-for-all that had

transit passage: a regime that allows for uninterrupted navigation and overflight in and above international straits narrower than 24 miles

exclusive economic zone (EEZ): a 200-mile (370-km) coastal marine zone in which a coastal state has exclusive control of resource exploitation and environmental management

baseline: a line that is drawn to simplify the mapping of marine zones, small bays, and coastal indentations

Figure 18.5 *Contemporary diagram of offshore jurisdictional areas.*

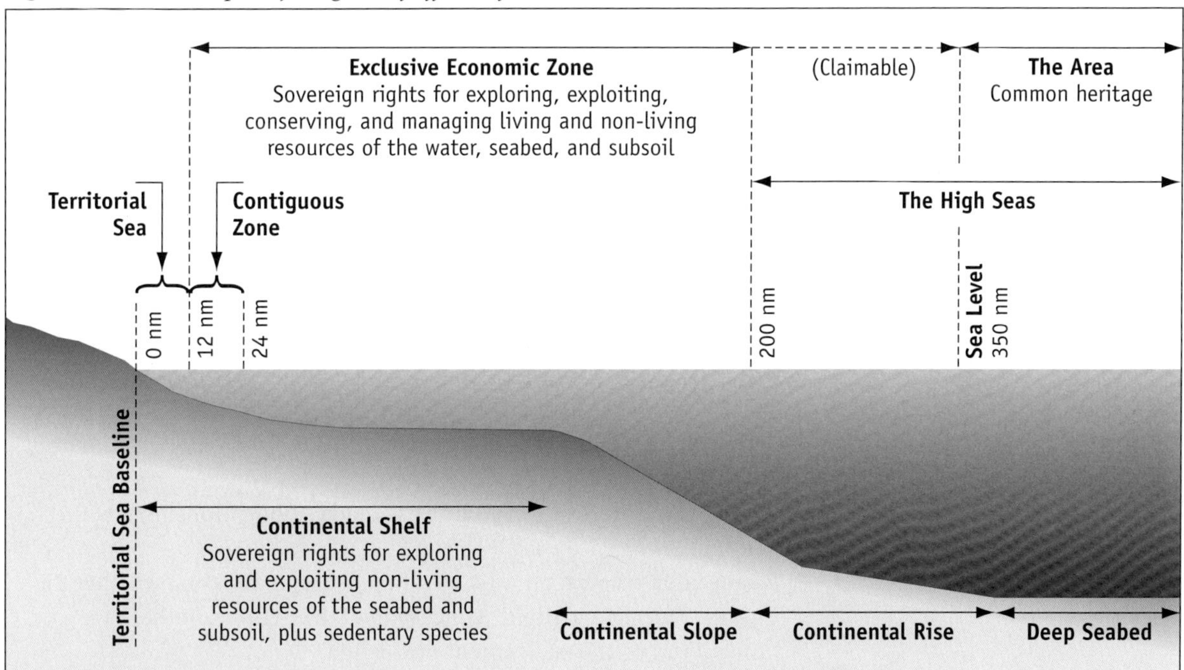

Note: all measures are in nautical miles (nm); 1 nautical mile = 1.15 statute miles or 1.85 km.

emerged. Some developing countries have acclaimed the economic zone as recognition of their sovereignty over their own resources. Canada sees it as a vindication of its struggles to have the rights of coastal states recognized and a zonal approach adopted for effective management of resources and the environment.

The Law

Canada has asserted an exclusive fishing zone of 200 miles since 1977 and a pollution control zone over the same area. It did not formally create an exclusive economic zone, however, until the adoption of the *Oceans Act* in 1996.

From the *Oceans Act* (1996):

14. Canada has
    (a) sovereign rights in the exclusive economic zone of Canada for the purpose of exploring and exploiting, conserving and managing the natural resources, whether living or non-living, of the waters superjacent to [above] the seabed and of the seabed and its subsoil, and with regard to other activities for the economic exploitation and exploration of the exclusive economic zone of Canada, such as the production of energy from the water, currents and winds;
    (b) jurisdiction in the exclusive economic zone of Canada with regard to
        (i) the establishment and use of artificial islands, installations and structures,
        (ii) marine scientific research, and
        (iii) the protection and preservation of the marine environment; and
    (c) other rights and duties in the exclusive economic zone of Canada provided for under international law.

Questions

1. Create a chart that lists the activities and marine areas and resources that s. 14 claims exclusively for Canada.
2. The *Oceans Act* is a statute of the Parliament of Canada. Can a state, by its own legislation, assign itself jurisdiction over a part of the ocean? Why or why not?
3. In what ways does s. 14 recognize Canada's obligations under international law?
4. Basing your opinion on s. 14, write a paragraph assessing whether the *Oceans Act* is guided by concern for the "common heritage" of humankind or the enrichment of Canada.

For critics like Arvid Pardo, the creation of the exclusive economic zone effectively legalized partitioning of the oceans, the very thing he stood against. Critics say partitioning denies to the world community the benefits of a maritime area that was once considered community property, or at least was not susceptible to appropriation. The zone may further enrich powerful developed coastal states by extending their sovereignty into the oceans. As well, it is probable that only developed states will have the capital needed to explore and exploit deep-seabed resources. In this way, they may exploit the economic weakness of developing coastal states.

The economic-zone concept may also prove to be ineffectual in protecting the resources themselves. Developing coastal states may favour short-term, predatory exploitation of resources to raise much-needed cash. They may be unable to afford to manage their marine areas.

What cannot be disputed is that the adoption of the economic zone has shrunk the area designated as the high seas. UNCLOS defines the high seas as those portions of the ocean "that are not included in the exclusive economic zone, in the territorial sea or in the internal waters of a State, or in the archipelagic waters of an **archipelagic State**."

archipelagic state: a state consisting of a group of islands and the waters separating them; examples are Malta and Indonesia

The Continental Shelf

Canada's continental shelf and **continental margin** are huge, equalling roughly 40 percent of the country's landmass. In some places, the continental margin extends 600 miles (1000 km) from shore. Canada has assertively advocated coastal state control of the whole of the continental shelf, even if it goes well beyond the 200-mile exclusive economic zone. During the Law of the Sea Conference, Canada and other wide-margin states (the United States, Australia, and the former Soviet Union) argued that they had "vested rights" in their continental shelves, which formed the "submerged portions of the continental landmass." One Canadian politician described the continental margin as "the portion of Canada that no one sees."

continental margin: the seabed and subsoil of the continental shelf, continental slope, and continental rise; does not include the deep seabed or its subsoil

These arguments were seen as self-serving. It was pointed out that most wide-margin states are developed and control a disproportionate share of the world's resources. Critics said that granting them control over resources beyond the 200-mile limit without some recognition of world community interest would be unconscionable. A compromise was struck. The "margineer" state could retain claims as long as geological criteria confirmed that the area was part of its continental shelf. Stringent controls were also put in place to limit the claims that the world community could make to payments and contributions with respect to exploitation of the shelf beyond the 200-mile limit.

Canada has signed UNCLOS, but had not yet ratified it by 2003. The UNCLOS provision requiring contributions to a world community fund from oil production beyond the 200-mile limit has remained a stumbling block. The production platform of Hibernia, one of the major offshore oil fields, is located 315 km east-southeast of the island of Newfoundland, and related resource fields straddle the 200-mile line. The Terra Nova oil field, where production started in 2002, is even farther from shore.

Internal Waters

Coastal states have argued that certain bodies of water are so closely associated with the land that they should be sovereign "internal waters." The argument makes sense when dealing with areas landward of baselines. However, some coastal states have pushed the concept to the limit. Canada, for example, has claimed sovereignty over vast areas of water such as Hudson Bay and the waters of the Arctic Archipelago (see the Issue in Chapter 16, page 471).

The Canadian argument for extending the range of internal waters is shared by other coastal states, and is often supported by referring to practical issues and history. Canada has claimed these large saltwater bodies as historic bays and, thus, internal waters:

- Bay of Fundy
- Gulf of St. Lawrence
- Hudson Bay
- straits of Juan de Fuca, Georgia, and Haro
- Dixon Entrance, Hecate Strait, and Queen Charlotte Sound.

Whether justified or not, the act of claiming portions of the oceans as internal waters blocks the rights of other states to navigation and resources. It contributes to the partitioning of the oceans and has been opposed by states with resource and navigational interests, and by states supporting world community concerns. In many cases, objections also serve narrow national interests, such as distant-water fishing, transportation of dangerous cargoes, and protection of maritime military power.

The Fisheries

Even with economic-zone rights, the Canadian government wants greater control of neighbouring waters for both the exploitation and protection of resources. It reserves the right to create fishing zones beyond the 200-mile limit in order to implement conservation and management measures. It exercised this right in 1994 by amending the *Coastal Fisheries Protection Act*. In March 1995, Canadian fishery officials and RCMP officers boarded and seized the Spanish fishing vessel *Estai* for fishing contrary to Canadian law (see Chapter 17, page 511). The vessel was well outside the 200-mile zone, and the arrest of the *Estai* crew flared into an international incident.

The standoff was defused by the *Agreement Relating to the Conservation and Management of Straddling Fish Stocks and Highly Migratory Fish Stocks* of 1995, in which Canada played a key role. Because the 200-mile economic

Figure 18.6 *Fish harvesters and plant workers from all over western Newfoundland protest the ongoing closure of the cod industry at the Department of Fisheries and Oceans office in Corner Brook, Newfoundland, May 2003.*

zone does not allow coastal states to protect these two types of fisheries, the agreement lets coastal states set greater limits, as mandated by international fisheries organizations.

To learn how the North Atlantic Salmon Conservation Organization (NASCO) is trying to preserve wild Atlantic salmon stocks, visit www.emp.ca/dimensionsoflaw

"Straddling fish stocks" are composed of anadromous species (those that swim from the sea into freshwater rivers to spawn), such as salmon. Most of the costs associated with salmon resources—such as fish ladders and pollution control measures—relate to river management. As salmon return to the state that controls the waters, they can be caught and harvested in the economic zone of another state or on the high seas. The *UN Convention on the Law of the Sea* sets out a special regime for anadromous stocks. Currently, the matter for Canada is regulated by bilateral arrangement with potential harvesters of Canadian migratory stocks, including

- the *Canada/Spain Mutual Fisheries Relation Agreement* (1976), article III
- the *Canada–Japan Fisheries Agreement* (1978), article V(i)
- the *Canada–US Salmon Agreement* (1999)
- the *Yukon River Salmon Agreement* (2002).

Highly migratory fish stocks include such species as tuna, shark, and sailfish. Numerous treaties and international commissions are in place to deal with their management, including the International Commission for the Conservation of Atlantic Tunas (ICCAT), to which Canada belongs, and the Inter-American Tropical Tuna Commission (IATTC).

Fisheries worldwide are in crisis. Too many fishers are chasing too few fish. Great fish, such as tuna and shark, are facing extinction. The Food and

Agriculture Organization (FAO) of the United Nations has created a number of initiatives to try to reverse the global crisis, including

- the *FAO Agreement to Promote Compliance with International Conservation and Management Measures by Fishing Vessels on the High Seas* (1993)
- the *Code of Conduct for Responsible Fisheries* (1995)
- the *2001 International Plan of Action to Prevent, Deter and Eliminate Illegal, Unreported and Unregulated Fishing.*

A lack of effective enforcement institutions suggests that these initiatives are unlikely to succeed.

Check Your Understanding

1. Using Canada as an example, describe how the concept of the territorial sea changed during the 20th century, and briefly explain why these changes took place.
2. a) Describe problems that some coastal states have experienced since World War II.
   b) What has been the response of the international community to these problems?
3. In your opinion, is there a conflict between Canadian law and UNCLOS, which Canada has signed? Explain your answer.
4. a) What is meant by the term "exclusive economic zone"?
   b) Why do some see the EEZ as a great victory for internationalism?
   c) Why do others see the EEZ as a tragedy?
5. a) Describe Canada's use of the concept of "internal waters."
   b) Do you think large bodies of water, such as Hudson Bay, should be under the exclusive control of the coastal state? Explain your answer.
6. a) How has the idea of the right of all to use the high seas affected the fisheries worldwide?
   b) What three international initiatives are in place to deal with the global crisis in the fisheries?
   c) How effective are they likely to be?

Airspace and Outer Space

Soon after the beginnings of manned flight, legal debates commenced about international controls on the use of airspace. Three potential regimes were proposed:

- freedom of the air (similar to freedom of the high seas)
- the subjection of airspace to the absolute sovereignty of the subjacent (immediately below) state
- sovereignty over airspace subject to a right of passage (similar to the right of innocent passage as understood by the law of the sea).

In 1911, the Institute of International Law adopted a resolution that was intended to serve as the basis of an international convention. It stated that international "aerial circulation is free, saving the right of subjacent states to take certain measures, to be determined, to ensure their own security and that of the persons and property of their inhabitants." World War I intervened. As civilian targets were bombed by early aircraft, it became clear that more international regulation of airspace was needed, and soon.

By 1919, an international convention recognized that "every Power has complete and exclusive sovereignty over the airspace above its territory." By 1944 the well-accepted principle was reiterated in the *Chicago Convention on Civil Aviation*, which is generally regarded as a statement of the customary law on the subject. A variation on the doctrine of innocent passage also emerged to foster the growth of civil aviation, but airspace still remains within the exclusive sovereignty of the subjacent state. Exclusive sovereignty extends to airspace above the territorial sea of coastal states, but now a rule of transit passage permits aircraft to fly over narrow international straits.

States have downed aircraft for violating their airspace. On May 1, 1960, at the height of the Cold War, the Soviet Union shot down an American U-2 spy plane flying deep in Soviet airspace above Moscow. The US pilot was tried, convicted, and imprisoned by the Soviets. The "U-2 incident" threatened to trigger a major confrontation between the nuclear powers. On September 1, 1983, the Soviet military shot down an aircraft in its airspace that it alleged was on a spying mission. This time, the aircraft was a Korean

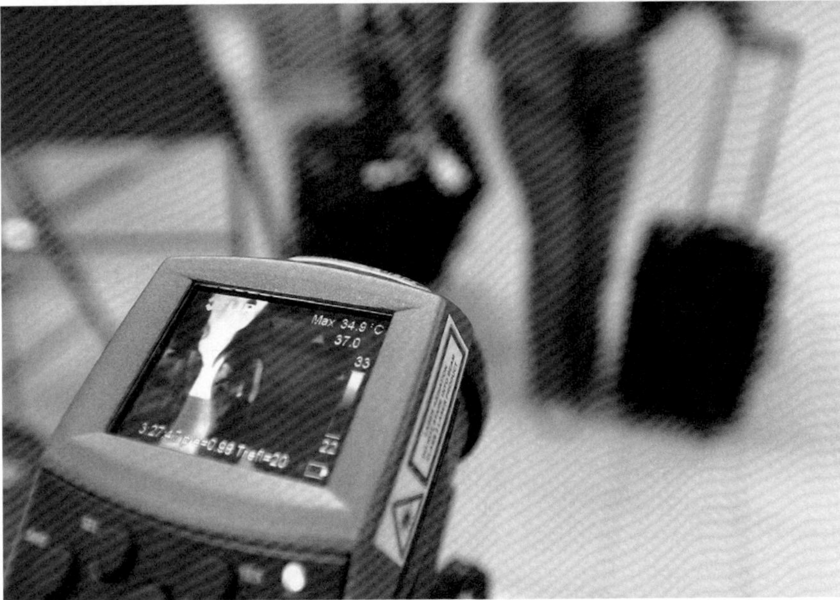

Figure 18.7 *A passenger is shown on the monitor of a thermal scanner at Pearson International Airport in Toronto, May 2003. Thermal scanners, used to detect people with a high fever, were installed at the airport in response to the SARS outbreak in 2003.*

Learn how the ICAO is responding to terrorism at www.emp.ca/dimensionsoflaw

Airlines jumbo jet on a civilian flight from Anchorage, Alaska, to Seoul, Republic of Korea. All 269 passengers were killed. Airline officials and the South Korean and American governments strenuously denied Soviet allegations. The international outcry forced a redefinition of international airspace law. States are prohibited from using weapons against civilian aircraft suspected of spying, and instead must demand that such aircraft land and comply with local regulations.

Unlawful acts also threaten civil aviation. In 1969 and 1970, a series of bloody terrorist hijackings created the impetus for the *Convention for the Suppression of Unlawful Acts Against the Safety of Civil Aviation* (Montreal Convention), 1971. This convention defines as offences any act of violence against a person on board a civilian aircraft and any acts or threats that endanger the safety of an aircraft in flight. It requires that states make these offences punishable and that they comply and cooperate with other states in prosecuting offences. The convention is administered by the Montreal-based International Civil Aviation Organization (ICAO). (You will examine the Montreal Convention more closely as you study the aerial incident at Lockerbie, Scotland, later in this chapter.)

The ICAO, which dates back to the *Chicago Convention on Aviation Rights*, administers the international civil air travel system. It is the only specialized United Nations agency located in Canada.

After the September 11, 2001 attacks on the United States, the ICAO developed an action plan to combat new forms of terrorism. At the core of the plan are regular mandatory evaluations of the levels of aviation security in place for all 187 member states.

Outer Space

To learn more about the hazards of space junk, visit www.emp.ca/dimensionsoflaw

As you saw in Chapter 16, international law with respect to outer space evolved so quickly that the process has been described as the creation of "instant" customary law, a contradiction in terms. The general principles set down in the 1963 *Declaration of Legal Principles Governing the Activities of States in the Exploration and Use of Outer Space* won broad acceptance and were confirmed and extended in other instruments, including the following:

- *Treaty on Principles Governing the Activities of States in the Exploration and Use of Outer Space, Including the Moon and Other Celestial Bodies* (1967) (see Chapter 16, page 469)
- *Agreement on the Rescue of Astronauts, the Return of Astronauts and the Return of Objects Launched into Outer Space* (1968)
- *Convention on International Liability for Damage Caused by Space Objects* (1972)
- *Convention on Registration of Objects Launched into Outer Space* (1976).

Fyi In 2003, an estimated 1814 tonnes of human-made debris was orbiting the Earth.

Although these treaties and conventions form the core of contemporary outer space law, they leave some areas in doubt. For example, does the principle of non-appropriation allow mining of the moon (or a planet) as long as no claim to sovereignty is made? Whom should such resources benefit? To resolve these issues, the *Agreement Governing the Activities of States on the Moon and Other Celestial Bodies* (1967) was drawn up. The "Moon Agreement," as it is known, was negotiated at the same time as UNCLOS, and the concept of the common heritage of humankind had an impact.

McGill University's Institute of Air and Space Law is devoted to research and education in these areas of international law. For more information, visit www.emp.ca/dimensionsoflaw

The United States and other developed countries argued for the high-seas model, with perhaps some royalty being payable to an international fund. The majority of states at the United Nations were then, and are now, developing nations. They demanded that their rights be recognized. As a result, the agreement explicitly states in article XI, "The moon and its natural resources are the common heritage of mankind, which finds its expression in the provisions of this Agreement." The same article states that "Neither the surface nor the subsurface of the moon, nor any part thereof or natural resources in place, shall become property of any State, international intergovernmental or non-governmental organization, national organization or non-governmental entity or of any natural person... ."

Only 10 states (Australia, Austria, Chile, Kazakhstan, Mexico, Morocco, the Netherlands, Pakistan, the Philippines, and Uruguay) ratified the Moon Agreement (1984). For now, it is essentially dead. Another five states (France, Guatemala, India, Peru, and Romania) have signed but not ratified the agreement. Few states in either group can be described as among the great space powers. In light of the 1994 "reforms" to UNCLOS, it is unlikely that the common heritage of humankind will dominate concerns when the Moon Agreement is revisited.

The law of outer space is in its infancy, and existing legal norms have yet to be tested. For the international community, other important issues include

- the use of nuclear power for satellites
- the militarization of outer space
- the proliferation of "space junk"
- jurisdictional issues with respect to the International Space Station (for example, who deals with a drunken brawl between astronauts from different states?).

Another controversial question lingers about the limits of outer space: Where does airspace under national jurisdiction end and outer space begin? The answer has serious implications. It affects the ability of landlocked states to launch space vehicles over the airspace of neighbouring states. Some parties suggest the limit should be set 100–110 km

Figure 18.8 *China's Shenzhou II unmanned experimental spacecraft is lowered onto a Long March II-F rocket in preparation for launch, January 10, 2001. With the entry of developing nations such as China and India, the "race for space" has only just begun.*

above sea level, with the proviso that states retain the right to fly space vehicles at lower altitudes over the territory of other states for the purpose of reaching orbit or returning to Earth.

CHECK YOUR UNDERSTANDING

1. a) In what ways is the regulation of airspace different from the doctrine of the high seas?
   b) What reasons explain these differences?
2. What organization administers the international civil air system?
3. a) When and how has the international community created rules and laws on outer space?
   b) Which treaties make up the core of current outer space law?
4. Under the "Moon Agreement," what resources of the moon are claimed to be the common heritage of humankind?
5. a) What are some of the issues that are being discussed with respect to outer space and law?
   b) Do you foresee any new issues and problems that may arise with regard to outer space in the next few decades? Explain your answer.

The Atmosphere and Other Global Resources

The atmosphere is the mixture of gases that lie between the Earth's surface and outer space. Earth's atmosphere is unique in that it creates the conditions and climate that support the enormous diversity of biological life. No other planet has yet been proven to support life. The survival of Earth's spectacular ecology depends on the preservation of the atmosphere. Although the nature of this ecosystem still requires much study, present scientific knowledge on the impact of human activities is enough to justify alarm.

The environmental movement has been advocating for the health of the atmosphere since the 19th century. Evidence of atmospheric change is widespread. Steep increases in the concentration of **greenhouse gases** threaten to advance global warming. Even a small increase in Earth's temperature disrupts the delicate ecological balance. In the Arctic, for instance, researchers predict that polar bears will become extinct as the polar ice cap melts. As a result of the use of chlorofluorocarbons (CFCs) in refrigerators and air conditioners, holes have developed in the ozone layer of the atmosphere above Antarctica and the Arctic. The ozone layer protects life from the damaging effects of ultraviolet radiation.

greenhouse gases: gases that cause the atmosphere to reflect heat back to the Earth, including water vapour, carbon dioxide, methane, nitrous oxide, and hydrofluorocarbons

Greenhouse gases result from many processes, some naturally occurring. Researchers are especially concerned with anthropogenic causes (those resulting from human activity), which can have a staggering impact. Key anthropogenic causes of greenhouse gases include the burning of fossil fuels for energy, deforestation, and changes in land use (for example, raising livestock instead of crops on farmland results in much greater emissions of methane).

WORKING FOR CHANGE *Greenpeace: Daring to Make a Difference*

In the fall of 1971, a handful of young activists hired a boat, invited some journalists along, and set out from Vancouver. They were on an outrageous mission: to "bear witness" to (and stop) the testing of a nuclear bomb. The activists sailed to a forbidden area off Amchitka Island, Alaska, as the underground blast was scheduled to take place. The US military ordered them to leave, but they stayed put. The tense standoff captured the hearts and minds of people around the world.

The little boat lost the battle—the United States finally did test the bomb—but Greenpeace was born. More than 30 years later, this independent non-governmental organization (NGO) is truly global, with a small fleet of its own. Greenpeace exists to expose environmental criminals and to challenge governments and corporations when they fail to safeguard the environment and protect the Earth's biodiversity.

In addition to its work against nuclear testing and contamination, Greenpeace organizes campaigns to

- protect the oceans and ancient forests
- phase out the use of fossil fuels
- promote the use of renewable energy
- eliminate toxic chemicals
- prevent the release of genetically modified organisms (GMOs)
- support safe and sustainable trade.

Greenpeace has also played a pivotal role in the adoption of

- a ban on toxic waste exports to less developed countries
- a moratorium on commercial whaling and the creation of a Southern Ocean Whale Sanctuary
- a UN convention providing for better management of world fisheries
- a 50-year moratorium on mineral exploitation in Antarctica
- bans on dumping radioactive and industrial waste and disused oil installations at sea.

Since 1971, Greenpeace's work and actions have contributed to many environmental achievements (see Figure 18.10, on the next page).

Figure 18.9 *A Greenpeace activist starts a hovercraft beside the NGO's vessel* Rainbow Warrior *in March 1982. In 1985, French secret agents sank the ship while it was docked in New Zealand; a photographer on board perished. Greenpeace had been protesting French nuclear tests in the South Pacific. In 1987, France was ordered to pay Greenpeace US$8 million in compensation.*

Results of Greenpeace Activities, 1972–2002

- 1972 • US stops testing nuclear bombs at Amchitka Island, Alaska.
- 1975 • France ends atmospheric nuclear tests in the South Pacific after Greenpeace protests.
- 1978 • The grey seal slaughter in the Orkney Islands, Scotland, is halted.
- 1989 • UN declares a moratorium on high seas large-scale driftnets after Greenpeace exposes indiscriminate fishing practices.
- 1993 • London Dumping Convention permanently bans the dumping of radioactive and industrial waste at sea.
- 1996 • UN adopts the *Comprehensive Nuclear Test Ban Treaty*.
- 1998 • Shell Oil agrees to bring its offshore installation, the Brent Spar, to land for recycling.
- 1999 • International Law of the Sea Tribunal orders Japan to stop its "experimental" fishing of southern bluefin tuna.
- 2000 • *Biosafety Protocol*, designed to protect the environment and human health by controlling the international trade of genetically modified organisms, is adopted in Montreal.
- 2001 • A UN treaty bans the use of highly toxic persistent organic pollutants (POPs) in pesticides and industrial processes.
- 2002 • The European Union, followed by Japan and Canada, ratifies the *Kyoto Protocol*.

Figure 18.10

Questions

1. Where does Greenpeace get its political power?
2. In a paragraph, describe the tactics that Greenpeace has used to further its objectives. State whether you think these tactics were justified or not, and explain your view.
3. a) What makes Greenpeace influential as an agent for change?
   b) Why might some people and groups find Greenpeace to be too influential?
4. Would Greenpeace be as effective if it were funded by governments? Create a short presentation, using computer software if possible, to support your position.

Greenhouse gas emissions affect the atmosphere as a whole. Activities in one part of the globe affect the atmosphere over other regions. For this reason, it can be argued that the atmosphere should be viewed in international law as a global resource.

In 1988, the World Meteorological Organization and the United Nations Environment Program established the Intergovernmental Panel on Climate Change (IPCC). The IPCC is charged with collecting data on climate change, researching the causes and impact of such change, and predicting the rate and consequences of future change based on current human activity.

The IPCC releases periodic reports of its findings. In 1992, one report led to the adoption of the *UN Framework Convention on Climate Change*. Parties to the framework, including Canada, have held conferences to plan programs to reduce emissions of gases suspected of contributing to climate change. The 1997 *Kyoto Protocol* emerged from these conferences and was negotiated with the participation of over 160 countries.

Fyi Inuit hunters have helped environmental researchers studying climate change by recording such changes in their areas as thinning ice and the appearance of birds (for example, robins) not previously seen in the region.

The *Kyoto Protocol* is a complex plan for reducing gas emissions that damage the atmosphere. The highest levels of these gases are released by developed nations. In simplest terms, the Protocol requires signatories to reduce their emissions to at least 1990 levels. The target date for achieving this result is 2012. Emissions can be reduced in many ways, including innovative methods that let countries cooperate to meet their obligations. One formula allows a state to get credits for activities in other countries. For example, a Canadian company helps a utility in a developing country to switch from a coal-burning power plant to wind generation. The reduction in emissions that results can be claimed as a credit to achieve Canada's Kyoto targets. Such credits can also be traded and sold.

To come into force, the *Kyoto Protocol* must be ratified by parties whose combined emissions account for at least 55 percent of the total world carbon dioxide emissions for 1990. Late in 2003, the total emissions of parties to the agreement accounted for only 43.9 percent, far short of the target. Canada, representing 3.3 percent of the target, ratified the agreement on December 17, 2002. The United States, accounting for a 36.1 percent share of the 1990 emissions figure, has signed but not ratified the *Kyoto Protocol.* If it does ratify, the *Kyoto Protocol* will come into force.

For Canada, as for many other counties, ratifying the *Kyoto Protocol* has been and will continue to be controversial. The treaty requires Canada to cut emissions by 240 megatonnes a year in the 2008–2012 compliance

Learn more about Canada's Kyoto commitments and the current state of the *Kyoto Protocol* internationally at www.emp.ca/dimensionsoflaw

Fyi Alberta and Ontario account for about 60% of Canada's greenhouse gas emissions. Quebec and British Columbia are next, but far behind.

Carbon Dioxide Emissions, 1990–2025 (million metric tonnes carbon equivalent)

	History		Projections						Average Annual % Change, 2001–2025
	1990	**2000**	**2001**	**2005**	**2010**	**2015**	**2020**	**2025**	
Industrialized Countries	2844	3191	3179	3296	3572	3817	4048	4 346	1.3
EE/FSU*	1337	842	856	977	1038	1120	1187	1 267	1.6
Developing Countries	1691	2385	2487	2635	3075	3575	4137	4 749	2.7
World	5872	6417	6522	6908	7685	8512	9372	10 361	1.9

* EE/FSU = Eastern Europe/Former Soviet Union.

Industrialized: United States, Canada, Mexico, United Kingdom, France, Germany, Italy, the Netherlands, other Western Europe, industrialized Asia, Japan, Australia/New Zealand.

Developing: China, India, South Korea, other Asia ,Turkey, other Middle East, Africa, Central and South America.

Source: Energy Information Administration, US Department of Energy; www.eia.doe.gov/oiaf/ieo/tbl_a10.html.

Figure 18.11

period. That figure is about 20 percent less than what levels might reach without the Protocol. While public support has been high, some provincial governments and business groups have been critical. They have questioned the science behind the concept of climate change that led to the *Kyoto Protocol*, and described the costs of reducing emissions as far too high.

Personal Viewpoint

Alberta Premier versus the *Kyoto Protocol*

On September 3, 2002, Alberta Premier Ralph Klein released an open letter to Prime Minister Jean Chrétien, strongly opposing ratification of the *Kyoto Protocol*. An excerpt from that letter follows.

> Dear Prime Minister:
>
> I am writing in response to your announcement in Johannesburg that your government intends to bring ratification of the *Kyoto Protocol* to a vote in the Commons. ... Specifically, Alberta's concerns are four-fold:
>
> - With Canada producing only two percent of the world's greenhouse gases, the commitment called for in the protocol ... will have little discernible impact on global warming, but will result in the unnecessary loss of thousands of Canadian jobs, and an overall slowdown in Canadian economic growth. Because countries such as the United States and Australia are not signatories to the protocol, Canada will be put at an untenable disadvantage in the global marketplace. ...
> - The *Kyoto Protocol* will not result in substantive reductions in greenhouse gases around the world, but will see simply a shift in where the gases are produced and in billions of dollars from nations such as Canada to other countries.
> - As the principal supplier of Canada's energy, Alberta will be especially hurt by federal ratification of Kyoto. ...
> - ...Canadians will feel the effects of Kyoto—at the pump, on their utility bills, at the workplace, and on their ability to find jobs. ...
>
> [I]n your Johannesburg statement, you said that there would be further consultation with Canadians before a vote on ratification is held in Parliament. ... Specifically, three items need to be evaluated thoroughly:
>
> - A clear, thorough, honest and public understanding of the costs of Kyoto... .
> - A detailed plan on how Kyoto will be implemented without unduly penalizing any region or sector of the country... .
> - Other options to address climate change in Canada... .
>
> Alberta believes that a made-in-Canada approach to climate change can be developed that would achieve the intent of the *Kyoto Protocol*, but on different timelines and in ways that would not hurt the national economy or individual Canadians' jobs. ... Other provinces and other Canadians have other ideas. If your government fails to give other options a fair hearing ... then it will do a disservice to the country and to the cause of addressing climate change.
>
> Alberta recognizes your government's constitutional right to negotiate and sign international treaties. At the same time, the Government of Canada does not have the constitutional authority to implement international treaties in areas of provincial jurisdiction. ...

Source: Government of Alberta news release; www.gov.ab.ca/acn/200209/13052.html.

Questions

1. Create a chart that lists (a) Premier Klein's objections to the *Kyoto Protocol*, (b) your agreement or disagreement with these objections, and (c) your reason(s).
2. Would a loss of "competitive advantage" because of the United States' and Australia's failure to sign the *Kyoto Protocol* have been an acceptable reason for Canada not to ratify it? Explain your answer.
3. Write two brief arguments, one supporting and one refuting a "made-in-Canada" approach to climate change as an alternative to the *Kyoto Protocol*.
4. Explain the last paragraph of Premier Klein's letter in your own words. What does he seem to be threatening?

In an effort to create support for the *Kyoto Protocol*, the federal government brought the issue of ratification before the House of Commons for debate. As you learned in Chapter 16, such debate is not required by Canadian international law. The motion passed easily in December 2002 in a 195–77 vote, and many commentators criticized it as an empty political move. Some critics worry that Canada ratified the agreement without enough research on its technical and economic implications. Now other critics are saying the *Kyoto Protocol* has been so diluted that it will be too little, too late.

Personal Viewpoint

Alberta Scientists for the *Kyoto Protocol*

On October 22, 2002, 58 prominent Alberta scientists sent a letter to Premier Ralph Klein rebutting his open letter to Prime Minister Chrétien berating ratification of the *Kyoto Protocol*. Excerpts from their rebuttal follow.

> Dear Premier Klein:
>
> ...We are writing to express our concerns about Alberta's position with respect to decreasing emissions of greenhouse gases. ... Contrary to the views often portrayed by the press and industry spokespersons, there is little disagreement in the scientific community on climate warming. ... Virtually all scientific models agree that we are faced with 1–2° Celsius of additional warming by mid-century, and considerably more by the year 2100... .
>
> There has been much publicity about the alleged economic losses that will be suffered by the oil and gas industries if *Kyoto* is ratified and implemented. But losses that will be suffered by other resource sectors if climate continues to warm must also be considered. Of particular concern is the fate of agriculture on the western prairies, which contain 60 percent of Canada's agricultural land. ... Recent analyses predict that by mid-century the arid and semi-arid areas of Alberta and Saskatchewan will increase by 50 percent... .
>
> Another example is forestry. In the 1980s and 1990s, the incidence of forest fire doubled in Canada compared to the 1960s and 1970s, burning an area equal to 80 percent of the province of Alberta during this 20-year period.

In the worst fire years of the 1990s, the CO_2 [carbon dioxide] emitted by forest fires almost equaled that from burning fossil fuels in Canada. The area burned was enough to turn our boreal forests from a "sink" for atmospheric CO_2 before 1980 to a "source" of carbon to the atmosphere in the 1990s. ...

Climate warming will increase the problem of fresh water for the prairies, and the water that remains will decline in quality. Already, wetlands are dry and many lakes have lost most of their water. Summer river flows are already flowing at 20–60 percent of historical values. ...

We believe that direct losses to Alberta's petroleum industry can be more than offset by new developments in science and technology. Incentives to consumers to buy fuel-efficient automobiles and energy-saving electrical and heating appliances, to move more freight by rail, and [to] increase the energy efficiency of homes and businesses are among the measures that can be implemented even with existing technology. Much could also be done to encourage renewable energy sources, or even to substitute switches from coal to natural gas, with its lower GHG [greenhouse gas] emissions. These are but a few of the many measures that can help to meet targets for greenhouse gases. They offer enormous opportunities for technical innovation... .

It is imperative that we get serious about reducing emissions of greenhouse gases now. ... We are optimistic that Alberta and Canada have the technical expertise to meet the Kyoto targets, if efforts are made to mobilize it.

Many members of our group have contributed directly to the scientific understanding of climate warming and its impacts. We would be delighted to discuss the evidence for climate warming, its effects on Alberta, and possible solutions to reducing greenhouse gases with you at your convenience.

Source: University of Alberta, *Express News*; http://www.expressnews.ualberta.ca/expressnews/articles/ideas.cfm?p_ID=3250&s=a.

Questions

1. Suggest why the scientists start their letter by stressing that global warming exists.
2. What effects of global warming are the scientists predicting for the agricultural sector in the prairies? For the forestry industry? For freshwater resources?
3. What proposals do the scientists make to reduce greenhouse gas emissions?
4. Compare the scientists' arguments with those of Premier Klein. Whose position do you support? Explain your answer.

Figure 18.12 *A forest fire rages near Chase, BC, in August 2003. Scientists have predicted that as global warming increases, forest fires will become more widespread and uncontrollable. Fires, in turn, will emit huge amounts of carbon dioxide into the atmosphere.*

Other Global Resources

Getting international agreement to protect the air, which is required for life, is a continuing legal challenge (some would say battle) involving thousands of lawyers and experts. What of other global—or transnational and common—resources that require collective management and allocation? How do we allocate an oil deposit that straddles borders, such as that between Iraq and Kuwait? How should scarce water resources be allocated among states that rely on one river, such as the Nile? How can international law deal with, let alone protect, such global resources as biodiversity, the electromagnetic spectrum (the full range of electromagnetic radiation, including radio waves), geostationary orbits (for example, satellites), medicinal plant species, technology, food, and water?

Visit www.emp.ca/dimensionsoflaw for United Nations Environmental Network maps, graphs, and charts on emissions around the world. See how Canada compares.

issue

Canada's Freshwater Resources **Should the Canadian government allow businesses to bulk export fresh water?**

Throughout its history, Canada has prospered by exploiting its rich resources. It continues to do so today. One exploitable resource has been the subject of decades of debate: fresh water. Quebec alone already exports over 250 million litres of bottled water each year. Should entrepreneurs be allowed to export water in bulk for profit? Consider the following opinions on this issue.

Each day in British Columbia 294 billion gallons [1.337 trillion litres] of fresh water flow into the Pacific Ocean... . This amounts to a renewable supply of fresh water equal to 195 times the requirement of every person in Canada... . [T]he current moratorium on bulk water exports is unacceptable. ... British Columbia should share a proportion of its surplus water for economic as well as humanitarian reasons. ... Shipping bulk water by marine tanker has passed all environmental tests required by the federal and provincial governments. Water export by marine tanker offers a new environmentally sound industry to British Columbia, utilizing a commodity which is available in vast supply and continually replaces itself.

—Fred Paley, CEO of Global H2O Resources, in a 1992 speech to the Canadian Water Resources Association

The truth is that Canada, which occupies 7 percent of the world's land mass, has 9 percent of its renewable water. So, we have just about our fair share. ... That is why the Government of Canada emphatically opposes large-scale exports of our water. We have another reason for our opposition; the interbasin [between watersheds] diversions necessary for such exports would inflict enormous harm on both the environment

Learn more about selling Canada's water at www.emp.ca/dimensionsoflaw

and society, especially in the North, where the ecology is delicate and where the effects on Native cultures would be devastating.

—*Federal Water Policy, Environment Canada, 1987*

The key to [one proposed] project is the diversion of water by the damming of three rivers—the Peace, Kootenay, and Columbia Rivers in southwestern British Columbia and Montana—to create a huge lake to be called the Rocky Mountain Reservoir in the Rocky Mountain Trench… . In British Columbia alone, 19 lakes or reservoirs and 38 000 megawatts of hydroelectric power would be created. Just in Mexico, the 20 million acre feet [24.7 cubic metres] [of water transfers created by the project] would allow that country to develop eight times more new irrigated land than the Aswan [High] Dam provides for Egypt [about 2.25 million acres, or 910 000 hectares].

—*Francis L. Dale, in a 1992 speech to the Canadian Water Resources Association*

Under the trade regimes now in place, once Canada starts large scale transfers of water, we will simply lose control over it. The interplay of both the NAFTA and GATT ... makes it difficult for Canada to ban water exports outright. ... Canada could rely on an exception in the trade regime and ban water exports by basing its actions on well supported evidence that such measures were needed to protect human and environmental health and conserve the resource. A national conservation strategy would not only serve the purpose of protecting our future water supply but provide a foundation for Canada to assert its sovereignty over its own resources and withstand any trade challenges which come our way.

The ability to control the destiny of one's water resources will be of profound importance this century.

—*Paul Muldoon, "The Case Against Water Exports," Canadian Environmental Law Association, March 2000*

Questions

1. Under what international agreements does Canada have an obligation to sell water?
2. Summarize the main arguments for and against bulk water exports.
3. Should fresh water be treated in a different way from other resources? Why or why not?
4. Does Canada have a responsibility to conserve and protect its freshwater resources? Support your answer with references to this feature and other materials in the chapter.

The common theme running through these examples of global resources, and indeed throughout this chapter, is the need to reconcile state and community interests in the world surface and its resources. A proper solution may ensure that scarce and fragile resources are not mismanaged and that equitable principles are used to divide benefits between particular states and the wider community.

To learn more about water scarcity worldwide, visit www.emp.ca/dimensionsoflaw

As you have learned, Canada is 7 percent of the Earth's landmass and holds 9 percent of its fresh water. Yet less than 0.5 percent of the world's population lives in Canada. Fresh water is a sensitive issue for Canada, even beyond export and sovereignty considerations. At least 20 nations today are classified as water-scarce. By 2025, between 10 and 15 nations will be added to that list. According to UN projections, between 1990 and 2025 the number of people living in countries in which renewable water is a scarce resource will rise from 131 million to somewhere between 817 million and 1.079 billion. How should Canada respond?

Is fresh water a common heritage of humankind? It cannot be disputed that Arvid Pardo's common-heritage concept has had an impact on the development of international law. But, as evidenced by the reaction to the *Kyoto Protocol*, it has been only selectively embraced by individual states.

CHECK YOUR UNDERSTANDING

1. What category of resource is the atmosphere accorded in international law?
2. a) What is the Intergovernmental Panel on Climate Change (IPCC)?
   b) How did the work of the IPCC lead to the *Kyoto Protocol*?
3. Suggest why, under the *Kyoto Protocol*, developing countries will be allowed to increase their emissions while developed countries must decrease theirs.
4. a) What is the goal, and target date, of the *Kyoto Protocol*?
   b) What major obstacles does it face in achieving those goals?
5. List a few global resources, and describe how have they been managed in the past.
6. Use what you have learned in this chapter to explain why it is difficult to get international action on environmental problems such as overfishing and pollution of the air and oceans.

METHODS OF *Legal Inquiry*

Bibliographic Documentation

In Chapter 2, you learned to read and create full case citations using the *Canadian Guide to Uniform Legal Citation* (now the *McGill Guide*). It is equally important to follow only one recognized style in writing essays or reports. There are several styles for text citation—including those of the American Psychological Association (APA), the Modern Language Association (MLA), and the *Chicago Manual of Style*. Which is used depends on the discipline. For example, history most often uses *Chicago* style, while psychology uses APA. For law, the *McGill Guide* is the standard. Many schools have their own departmental or cross-departmental style guide. Check with your teacher to see which style of documentation your school uses.

Footnotes

Not all styles include footnotes. Carleton University's Department of Law uses a legal style sheet that treats footnotes in the following way:

Each footnote should be listed in the text by a superscript Arabic figure (that is, placed on the same level as apostrophes) at the end of the passage to which it refers. Footnotes should be numbered consecutively throughout the paper. The footnotes themselves should be placed at the bottom of each page and identified in order by number. Endnotes should be placed at the end of the paper (before the bibliography) and also identified by number.

In order to avoid charges of plagiarism, use footnotes or endnotes whenever

- quoting directly from another's work
- paraphrasing
- discussing opinions and theories of others
- presenting information that is not a matter of general knowledge
- explaining and amplifying statements made in your text.

The Complete Citation

The first time a work is cited in a footnote or endnote, complete bibliographical information should be given.

Statutes and Regulations

Legal writing often refers to legislation. Such citations must include short title, abbreviation for the volume, chapter number, and section number. For example: *Criminal Code* (RSC 1985, c. C-46).

Books

A full citation includes the author's name, book title (underlined or italicized), volume number (if any), place of publication, publisher, date, and pinpoint. (A pinpoint is a reference to a specific page or paragraph number.)

One author:
[1] P. Sworden, *An Introduction to Canadian Law* (Toronto: Emond Montgomery Publications, 2002) at 103.

Joint authors:
[2] J.L. Brierly & H. Waldock, *Law of Nations: An Introduction to the International Law of Peace* (London: Oxford University Press, 1997).

More than three authors (cite only the first author, followed by et al., which is Latin for "and others"):
[3] G. Alexandrowicz *et al.*, *Dimensions of Law: Canadian and International Law in the 21st Century* (Toronto: Emond Montgomery Publications, 2003).

Editor of a collection as author:
[4] H.M. Kindred, ed., *International Law, Chiefly as Interpreted and Applied in Canada*, 6th ed. (Toronto: Emond Montgomery Publications, 2000).

Journal Articles

A full citation includes author's name, title of article (in quotation marks), year of publication, volume number, name of journal, page, and pinpoint.

One author:
[5] N. Goyette, "Tax Treaty Abuse: A Second Look" (2003) 51 *Canadian Tax Journal* 764 at 768.

Internet Sources

When citing Internet sources, you must cite not only the Web site, but include the following information: traditional citation, online, host organization, uniform resource locator (URL), and last modified or date accessed. For example:

[6] K. Ramsland, "The Crime Scene," online: Court TV's Crime Library http://www.crimelibrary.com/criminal_mind/forensics/crimescene/1.html (date accessed: 19 June 2003).

The Shortened Citation

When a complete citation has been used in an earlier footnote or endnote, the shortened form is used. It includes only the author's surname, a reference to the earlier footnote or endnote, and the page references. For example:

[7] Sworden, *supra* note 1 at 8. (Note: *supra* is Latin for "above.")

If the work being cited is the same as that immediately above it, *ibid.* (an abbreviation of the Latin, *ibidem*, "in the same place") may be used. For example:

[7] Sworden, *supra* note 1 at 8.
[8] *Ibid.* at 10.

Bibliography

After footnotes and endnotes at the end of the paper, a bibliography should list all books, pamphlets, articles, newspapers, documents, legislation, and so on that have been used in preparing the essay or report. Any interviews conducted should also be included. All but the first line of each reference should be indented. Authors are cited alphabetically, placing the last name first. Cases and legislation may be listed separately from other sources. For example:

Sworden, P., *An Introduction to Canadian Law* (Toronto: Emond Montgomery Publications, 2002).

Brierly, J.L. & H. Waldock, *Law of Nations: An Introduction to the International Law of Peace* (London: Oxford University Press, 1997).

Source: Adapted from "Legal Style Sheet," Department of Law, Carleton University; www.carleton.ca/law/style.htm.

Applying the Skill

Select a legal topic, locate the following sources, and give the proper citation for each:

1. a book with one author
2. a book with two authors
3. a journal article
4. a statute
5. an Internet site.

Reviewing Main Ideas

You Decide!

HOLDING A STATE ACCOUNTABLE FOR AIRSPACE TERRORISM

Case Concerning Questions of Interpretation and Application of the Montreal Convention arising out of the Aerial Incident at Lockerbie: *Libya v. UK*, [1992] ICJ Rep. 3

Facts

In 1988, Pan Am flight 103, flying from Frankfurt to New York, exploded over Lockerbie, Scotland. The crew and all 259 passengers were killed, as were 11 persons on the ground. The dead were nationals of 21 states; almost two-thirds were American and a quarter were British. On November 14, 1991, arrest warrants were issued in Scotland for two Libyans accused of conspiracy, murder, and an offence under the *Aviation Security Act*, 1982, in connection with the explosion. It was believed they were officers of the Libyan Intelligence Service. A similar warrant was issued in the United States. France issued warrants against Libyan officials accused of involvement in a 1989 explosion of UTA flight 772, which killed 192 people.

In a joint declaration in November 1991, the United Kingdom, the United States, and France called upon Libya, *inter alia* (among other things), (1) to hand over the two Libyans for trial in Scotland or the United States and to satisfy the requirements of French justice and (2) to renounce international terrorism. Libya did not comply. Instead, acting in accordance with the *Convention for the Suppression of Unlawful Acts Against the Safety of Civil Aviation* (the Montreal Convention), to which it and the other three states were parties, Libya took the steps required of it to establish its own jurisdiction in the cases. It ensured the presence of the accused in Libya and initiated an inquiry into the facts. Libya submitted the cases to competent authorities for prosecution and sought the assistance of the United Kingdom in the proceedings. The United Kingdom refused, insisting on extradition even though the two countries had no extradition treaty. Libyan law did not permit extradition of its nationals. In early 1992, the United Kingdom, the United States, and France took the case to the UN Security Council, which passed resolutions urging Libya to "provide a full and effective response" to their requests.

On March 3, 1993, Libya instituted proceedings against the United States and the United Kingdom before the International Court of Justice under article 14 of the Montreal Convention. Libya asked the Court to declare (1) that it had complied with its obligations under the Montreal Convention and (2) that the United Kingdom had breached the Convention by seeking to force Libya to return the alleged offenders and by not providing for the Libyan proceedings.

After the oral hearing of this application, the Security Council, at the request of the United States, the United Kingdom, and France, adopted resolution 748 under chapter VII of the *UN Charter*. It required Libya to hand over the alleged offenders and then imposed sanctions against it for not doing so. The Council acted on the basis that Libya had been engaged in international terrorism, which was a "threat to the peace" under article 39 of the *UN Charter*.

The Law

From the *Convention for the Suppression of Unlawful Acts Against the Safety of Civil Aviation*, 1971:

Article 14

1. Any dispute between two or more Contracting States concerning the interpretation or application of this Convention that cannot be settled through negotiation, shall, at the request of one of them, be submitted to arbitration. If within six months from the date of the request for arbitration the Parties are unable to agree on the organization of the arbitration, any one of those Parties may refer the dispute to the International Court of Justice by request in conformity with the Statute of the Court.
2. Each State may at the time of signature or ratification of this Convention or accession [later agreement] thereto, declare that it does not consider itself bound by the preceding paragraph. The other Contracting States shall not be bound by the preceding paragraph with respect to any Contracting State having made such a reservation.
3. Any Contracting State having made a reservation in accordance with the preceding paragraph may at any time withdraw this reservation by notification to the Depositary Governments [states where treaty documents are held and where notifications are received].

From UN Security Council Resolution 731 (January 21, 1992):

The Security Council, ...

Determined to eliminate international terrorism,

1. Condemns the destruction of Pan Am flight 103 ... and the resultant loss of hundreds of lives;
2. Strongly deplores the fact that the Libyan Government has not yet responded effectively to ... requests to cooperate fully in establishing responsibility for the terrorist acts ... ;
3. Urges the Libyan Government immediately to provide a full and effective response to those requests so as to contribute to the elimination of international terrorism; ...

From UN Security Council Resolution 748 (March 31, 1992):

The Security Council, ...

1. Decides that the Libyan Government must now comply without any further delay with paragraph 3 of resolution 731 (1992) regarding the requests addressed to the Libyan authorities by France, the United Kingdom of Great Britain and Northern Ireland, and the United States of America,
2. Decides also that the Libyan Government must commit itself definitely to cease all forms of terrorist action and all assistance to terrorist groups and that it must promptly, by concrete actions, demonstrate its renunciation of terrorism.

Issue

Did the United Kingdom breach its obligations under the Montreal Convention in trying to force Libya to extradite the alleged terrorists after Libya had tried them under its own jurisdiction?

Make Your Decision

1. What were the facts in this case?
2. Explain whether or not Libya or the United Kingdom infringed the Montreal Convention.
3. How do Security Council Resolutions 731 and 748 affect the issue?
4. Make a decision in this case, providing your reasons.
5. Using Internet, library, or other resources (including www.emp.ca/dimensionsoflaw), research the developments in the case of the Lockerbie incident. Prepare a report, including your assessment of whether justice has been done.

Key Terms

Review the following terms to show that you understand the meaning of each and how it is applied in a legal context.

archipelagic state	high seas
baseline	innocent passage
cannon-shot rule	internal waters
continental margin	non-appropriation
continental shelf	partition
deep seabed	territorial sea
exclusive economic zone	transit passage
greenhouse gases	

Understanding the Law

Review the following pieces of legislation mentioned in the text, and show that you understand the intent of each.

Agreement Governing the Activities of States on the Moon and Other Celestial Bodies (1967)
Agreement Relating to the Conservation and Management of Straddling Fish Stocks and Highly Migratory Fish Stocks (1995)
Chicago Convention on Civil Aviation
Code of Conduct for Responsible Fisheries (1995)
Comprehensive Nuclear Test Ban Treaty (1996)
Convention for the Suppression of Unlawful Acts Against the Safety of Civil Aviation (Montreal Convention) (1971)
Convention on the Regulation of Antarctic Mineral Resource Activities (1988)
Kyoto Protocol
UN Framework Convention on Climate Change

Thinking and Inquiry

1. With a partner or in a small group, examine a recent international treaty that has been established to protect the environment. Consider pollution control a top priority, especially if it affects your area. Describe the treaty's aims and effectiveness. Present your findings in an oral report or video.
2. Select a newspaper article that deals with an environmental issue or disaster. How has national or international law dealt with the issue or problem?
3. The *United Nations Convention on the Law of the Sea* and recent UN conferences on the law of the sea have challenged the long-established order—including Canada—with respect to maritime jurisdiction. They have effected fundamental changes that reflect new legal and political realities in the world community. Create arguments that both refute and support these statements. Discuss with specific reference to Canada's role.
4. Should all the world's industrialized states support and ratify the *Kyoto Protocol*? Is this agreement the only means available to the international community to protect the atmosphere? Support your argument, referring to facts and legislation found in this chapter.

Communication

5. Investigate an international case that involves a boundary dispute between two states. Summarize the facts of the dispute and comment on (a) whether or not both sides have accepted the court's decision, and (b) the ways in which the states have tried to avoid the binding nature of the decision. Give a short oral presentation of your findings.
6. Survey students in your classes on the most pressing environmental issue that must be addressed by the international community in the next five years. What recommendations do these students have to improve the health of the environment and to avert environmental collapse?
7. Use the Internet, library, or any other source to find out what citizens and NGOs around the world are doing to improve local ecologies and environmental conditions. Convert your findings into graphic form to post in the classroom.

Application

8. Research the various international rights that states enjoy with respect to the territorial sea, the high seas, and exclusive economic zones. Explain your answer.
9. Using resources such as the Internet, television, and print media, research the status of the *Kyoto Protocol*. What states have and have not ratified it? Check the positions of various provinces, such as Alberta and Ontario, to see if they support or oppose the Protocol. Find out what kind of pressure is being applied to hold-out states such as the United States and Australia. Prepare a report using computer software to include slides, charts, quotes from individuals, and points of international law.
10. Find two editorial cartoons that comment on one environmental or territorial issue that has become a top news story. Explain the cartoons and describe their messages. Which one do you agree with most? Explain.
11. In opposing the *Kyoto Protocol*, Premier Ralph Klein wrote that "the Government of Canada does not have the constitutional authority to implement international treaties in areas of provincial jurisdiction." Disputes over control of resources can also erupt between provinces. Using the Internet and the library, research recent disputes (for example, between Newfoundland and Labrador and Nova Scotia over Atlantic oil beds) and list the two or three most important, giving reasons for your selections.

Military Conflict and Conflict Resolution

CHAPTER *Focus*

In this chapter, you will

- explain how and why the use of force is limited in international law
- compare methods of resolving conflicts by peaceful means
- evaluate the difficulties and effectiveness of international intervention in conflicts between nations
- evaluate Canada's role in peacekeeping

There is a tendency to judge international law based on its effectiveness in controlling conflict. As a result, critics point to every breach of the peace as evidence of the ineffectiveness of international actions and institutions. However, international law has had many important successes, which unfortunately generate fewer headlines than the failures do. International peacekeeping initiatives have avoided conflicts, ended wars, and aided reconstruction.

Changes in patterns of conflict over the last half century suggest that the agenda of war elimination has made some slow but steady progress, as illustrated in Figure 19.1.

Figure 19.1

At First Glance

1. What is the cartoon's message?
2. What symbols has the cartoonist used to convey this message?
3. Do you agree with the point that the cartoon is making about the role of the UN in keeping peace?
4. Work with a partner to generate a list of issues and problems that are related to international law and peace and security.

Peaceful Resolution of Disputes

One of the fundamental purposes of international law is to create rules and mechanisms that will lead to the peaceful resolution of disputes. This legal obligation is expressed in a number of ways, such as article 2(3) of the *UN Charter*, which states: "All Members shall settle their international disputes by peaceful means in such a manner that international peace and security, and justice, are not endangered." This principle has been elaborated in a variety of instruments, including the *Declaration on Principles of International Law Concerning Friendly Relations and Co-operation among States in Accordance with the Charter of the United Nations* (1970), which reads:

> States shall accordingly seek early and just settlement of their international disputes by negotiation, inquiry, mediation, conciliation, arbitration, judicial settlement, resort to regional agencies or arrangements or other peaceful means of their choice. In seeking such a settlement the parties shall agree upon such peaceful means as may be appropriate to the circumstances and nature of the dispute.

The use of diplomacy, discussed in Chapter 16, has been the traditional first step in international dispute resolution. Through diplomacy, parties can outline the legal and factual basis of their positions and take advantage of opportunities for response, clarification, and so on. Where strained relations make diplomacy impossible, a third party or an international organization such as the United Nations may offer a forum for negotiation. This is known as "good offices." In some instances, the third party may offer creative solutions to bridge the gap between the parties.

The Law From the *UN Charter*, chapter VI: Pacific [peaceful] Settlement of Disputes

Article 33

1. The parties to any dispute, the continuance of which is likely to endanger the maintenance of international peace and security, shall, first of all, seek a solution by negotiation, enquiry, mediation, conciliation,

arbitration, judicial settlement, resort to regional agencies or arrangements, or other peaceful means of their own choice.

2. The Security Council shall, when it deems necessary, call upon the parties to settle their dispute by such means.

Article 34

The Security Council may investigate any dispute, or any situation which might lead to international friction or give rise to a dispute... .

Article 36

1. The Security Council may, at any stage of a dispute of the nature referred to in Article 33 or of a situation of like nature, recommend appropriate procedures or methods of adjustment.
2. The Security Council should take into consideration any procedures for the settlement of the dispute which have already been adopted by the parties.
3. In making recommendations under this Article the Security Council should also take into consideration that legal disputes should as a general rule be referred by the parties to the International Court of Justice in accordance with the provisions of the Statute of the Court.

Article 37

1. Should the parties to a dispute of the nature referred to in Article 33 fail to settle it by the means indicated in that Article, they shall refer it to the Security Council.
2. If the Security Council deems that the continuance of the dispute is in fact likely to endanger the maintenance of international peace and security, it shall decide whether to take action under Article 36 or to recommend such terms of settlement as it may consider appropriate.

Article 38

Without prejudice to the provisions of Articles 33 to 37, the Security Council may, if all the parties to any dispute so request, make recommendations to the parties with a view to a pacific settlement of the dispute.

Questions

1. a) How are parties to a dispute expected to resolve their differences? What methods are they encouraged to use?
   b) What role does the Security Council play in this process?
2. a) Under which article can the Security Council recommend procedures or methods of adjustment? What is your opinion of this process?
   b) Identify some factors that might hinder this process from stopping conflicts.

3. a) Summarize the role of the Security Council in the peaceful settlement of disputes, according to law.
   b) How has the power of veto held by the five permanent members of the Security Council (see Chapter 17, page 502) limited the effectiveness of the Security Council in resolving disputes?

An International Framework for Conflict Resolution

During the 19th century, a practice evolved of creating temporary arbitration tribunals to deal with a wide range of international disputes. By the end of the century, this was recognized as a normal way of settling disputes, and a system was established. *The Hague Convention for the Pacific Settlement of International Disputes* (July 1899 and October 1907) set a wide range of rules and established a permanent panel of arbitrators. The system was called the Permanent Court of Arbitration. So far, almost 100 nations have signed the two conventions. For Canada, the arbitration process has played an important role, especially with respect to boundary definition. Famous arbitrations that have involved Canada include the 1903 *Alaskan Boundary Arbitration* (see Chapter 18, page 535) and the 1937 *Trail Smelter* case (see Chapter 16, page 479).

International Courts

International courts also have an important role to play in the process of peaceful dispute resolution. As you saw in Chapter 17, in 1999, Canada was involved in a case brought before the International Court of Justice (ICJ) by the former Yugoslavia, questioning the use of force in the NATO bombing during the civil war that followed the break-up of that country.

Individuals have also been prosecuted in international arenas. The International Criminal Court (ICC) was established in July 2002 specifically to try persons charged with **genocide** and crimes against humanity. In addition, article 8 of the ICC's constituting statute, the *Rome Statute of the International Criminal Court*, provides a definition of "war crimes." Acts that count as war crimes include: intentionally launching an attack that will cause loss of life or injury to civilians, or damage to civilian or cultural objects; widespread, long-term, and severe damage to the natural environment; the use of prohibited weapons, including poisonous or other gases; and methods of warfare that cause unnecessary suffering or are inherently indiscriminate in claiming victims. Note that "war crimes" may be committed not only in international conflicts but also in armed conflicts "not of an international character," that is, civil wars.

Prior to the establishment of the ICC, former UN High Commissioner of Human Rights Jose Ayala Lasso had said, "A person stands a better

genocide: the deliberate and systematic killing of a whole ethnic or racial group

Fyi In the 1990–91 Gulf War, Iraqi troops set fire to 650 Kuwaiti oil wells, and six to eight million barrels of oil were spilled into the Persian Gulf.

chance of being tried and judged for killing one human being than for killing 100 000." International criminal courts were first established over 50 years earlier, at the end of World War II, to deal with crimes committed in Europe and the Far East, but there was little progress in setting up a permanent one until the 1990s. In 1993, civil war broke out in the former Yugoslavia, and the policy of "**ethnic cleansing**"—driving people from their homes, murdering them, and taking over their lands and properties—was implemented by invading forces (you will learn more about this event later in this chapter).

ethnic cleansing: the forced removal of other ethnic groups from an area in order to leave only one group

This was not the first instance of genocide since the end of World War II. It is estimated that two million people died in Cambodia under the brutal regime of the Khmer Rouge. In Africa, thousands died at the hands of dictators such as Idi Amin of Uganda. There was no mechanism in international law to try such criminal acts. The events in Yugoslavia and, in 1994, in Rwanda—where the ruling Hutus slaughtered hundreds of thousands of Tutsis and moderate Hutus in the face of inaction by the United Nations—spurred the international community to set up tribunals to deal with those situations. This also spurred the world to set up a permanent international court to try such acts. The idea of an international criminal court was enthusiastically received. By 2003, over 90 states had ratified the *Rome Statute*. The United States was not among them.

Learn more about the International Criminal Court at www.emp.ca/dimensionsoflaw

Personal Viewpoint

Romeo Dallaire: "Nothing Will Ever Wash the UN's Hands Clean of Rwandan Blood"

Lieutenant-General Romeo Dallaire joined the Canadian Army in 1964 and was commander of the UN Assistance Mission for Rwanda (UNAMIR) during one of the darkest hours for UN peacekeeping. In 1993, Dallaire headed off on what he thought would be a straightforward peacekeeping mission, but 13 months later he flew home from Africa, disillusioned and suicidal, having witnessed the worst genocide of the late 20th century.

In April 1994, Hutu extremists massacred over 800 000 Tutsis and moderate Hutus. Dallaire did everything he could, pleading for more peacekeepers to add to his forces. If the UN had answered his request, the massacre might have been much less extensive. General Dallaire was medically released from Canada's armed forces in April 2000 because of post-traumatic stress disorder. Following is an excerpt from a BBC interview with Dallaire in September 2000.

> Everything that possibly could have [gone wrong did go wrong]. ... I have [taken] the position from the start that the United Nations is nothing but the front man in this failure. The true culprits are the sovereign states that influence the Security Council, that influence other nations into participating or not. And I would say that there are a number of countries who absolutely did not want to get embroiled in any possible complex mission, and brought their

> weight to prevent others who were ready to go, as, for example, a number of African nations.
>
> And so here I am, commencing a third week of war. The mass slaughter is ongoing. What is the trip wire? 50 000? 100 000? 200 000? What have you got to put on the table to get the Western world to realize that maybe this is not acceptable within the human race?

The following excerpts come from Dallaire's book, *Shake Hands with the Devil*, an account of his time in Rwanda.

> Ultimately, led by the United States, France, and the United Kingdom, this world body [the UN] aided and abetted genocide in Rwanda. No amount of its cash and aid will ever wash its hands clean of Rwandan blood.
>
> The Security Council and the office of the secretary-general were obviously at a loss as to what to do. ... I continued to receive demands to supply them with more information before they would take any concrete action. What more could I possibly tell them that I hadn't already described in horrific detail? The odour of death in the hot sun; the flies, maggots, rats and dogs that swarmed to feast on the dead. At times it seemed the smell had entered the pores of my skin. ... We had sent a deluge of paper and received nothing in return; no supplies, no reinforcements, no decisions. ...
>
> My story is not a strictly military account nor a clinical, academic study of the breakdown of Rwanda. It is not a simplistic indictment of the many failures of the UN as a force for peace in the world. It is not a story of heroes and villains, although such a work could easily be written. This book is a *cri de coeur* for the slaughtered thousands, a tribute to the souls hacked apart by machetes because of their supposed difference from those who sought to hang on to power. ... This book is the account of a few humans who were entrusted with the role of helping others taste the fruits of peace. Instead, we watched as the devil took control of paradise on Earth and fed on the blood of the people we were supposed to protect.

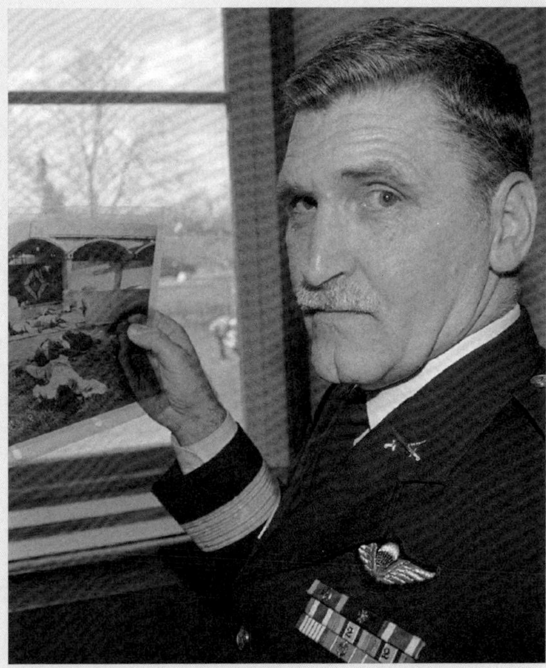

Figure 19.2 *General Romeo Dallaire holds a photo showing the shocking conditions under which Canadian troops in Rwanda had to work.*

Sources: "Eyewitness: UN in Rwanda 1994," http://news.bbc.co.uk/1/world/africa/911232.stm; Stephanie Nolen, "Dallaire Book Slams US, UN, on Rwanda," *The Globe and Mail*, August 21, 2003, A1; and Romeo Dallaire, *Shake Hands with the Devil: The Failure of Humanity in Rwanda*. Toronto: Random House Canada, 2003.

Questions

1. Research the circumstances that led to the establishment of UNAMIR at www.emp.ca/dimensionsoflaw. Write a short paragraph to summarize your findings.
2. What did Dallaire mean when he said, "I have taken the position ... that the United Nations is nothing but the front man for this failure"?
3. Should somebody of Dallaire's status and background be publicly critical of the UN and the Security Council? Explain your answer.
4. Explain the significance of the title of Dallaire's book, *Shake Hands with the Devil*.

Learn about the ICTR and ICTY at www.emp.ca/dimensionsoflaw

In response to the gross violations of human rights in the former Yugoslavia and Rwanda, the UN Security Council set up two special international tribunals to try individuals accused of crimes in those situations. The International Criminal Tribunal for Rwanda (ICTR) and the International Criminal Tribunal for the Former Yugoslavia (ICTY) have tried a number of individuals, the most prominent being Slobodan Milosevic, the former president of Yugoslavia.

Slobodan Milosevic and the International Criminal Tribunal **Will the ICTY deliver real or "victors' justice" in the Milosevic trial?**

Slobodan Milosevic was charged with crimes against humanity in the course of civil war in the former Yugoslavia. As president of Yugoslavia, he led the unsuccessful military opposition to independence movements in Slovenia and Croatia in the early 1990s. His regime carried on a brutal resistance during the long struggle by Bosnia and Herzegovina for independence in the mid-1990s. Finally, after a US-led NATO bombing campaign in 1999 that followed the invasion of Kosovo by Serbian troops, he was ousted as president of Serbia, the remaining part of Yugoslavia.

In April 2001, Milosevic was arrested for war crimes; in February 2002, he was brought before the International Criminal Tribunal for the Former Yugoslavia, a specially constituted war crimes tribunal based in The Hague, Netherlands. While there is general acceptance that Milosevic deserved to be prosecuted and punished for his crimes, some observers have criticized the close ties between the North Atlantic Treaty Organisation (NATO)—the military alliance that led the efforts to bring down Milosevic—and the ICTY, alleging that the Tribunal's process amounts to "victors' justice." The following excerpts express opinions on this issue.

> While the tribunal is not perfect (no court is), the ICTY functions according to the highest standards of international justice. This means that Mr. Milosevic will receive all the guarantees necessary for a fair trial. Its proceedings have to date resulted in the acquittal of a number of defendants, including Serbs, on various charges. If the Tribunal falls short in protecting any of Milosevic's rights to mount a vigorous defense, it should be criticized and change its practice.
>
> The ICTY is an international court. The pre-trial judges hearing the initial proceedings are from the United Kingdom, Jamaica, and Morocco. As of April 2001, the Tribunal employed a staff of 1103 from 74 different countries. While certainly there are citizens from NATO countries serving at all levels of the Tribunal, if there is a specific

conflict of interest, that individual should excuse him- or herself from the proceedings.

—*"The Milosevic Case: Questions and Answers," from the* World Report 2001 *of Human Rights Watch, a US-based non-governmental organization*

[S]upporters of the Hague tribunal argue, even if the former Yugoslav president was effectively kidnapped on behalf of those western states which like to describe themselves as the international community, that was a necessary price to pay for justice to be done. What they seem unable to grasp is that justice will never be seen to have been done, because the tribunal for the former Yugoslavia cannot seriously be regarded as a genuinely independent court. ... This is a court which itself lays the charges it judges, accepts hearsay evidence and is heavily staffed by political appointees of the very states which led the onslaught against Milosevic's Yugoslavia—attacks which were not supported by the UN, are widely regarded as having been illegal and are themselves the subject of war crimes allegations.

—*Seumas Milne, "Hague Is Not the Place to Try Milosevic,"* The Guardian, *August 2, 2001*

The taunt of "victors' justice" is facile [superficial]. Victory in war can provide the opportunity to do justice—as it did to the authors of the Holocaust and may yet to the perpetrators of ethnic cleansing. ... The acid test of the Milosevic trial is not whether it will "be victors' justice" but whether it will be "justice." That test was passed by the judgment at Nuremberg because it produced an indelible historical record to confound future Holocaust deniers.

—*Geoffrey Robertson, "This Needn't Be Victor's Justice,"* The Guardian, *February 12, 2002*

That justice is being served on Milosevic is good. What cannot be pretended is that this form of international justice is anything approaching perfect. First, it is more Western than international. To watching eyes in the world beyond the borders of Europe, there is too much about the proceedings at The Hague that smacks of victors' justice. The trial is being financed by the NATO nations, some of whom appeased Milosevic's ambitions to create a Greater Serbia, and then belatedly moved to eject him when he unleashed his killing squads on Kosovo. ... [W]e wonder how having a judge and prosecutor from one of the most actively combatant countries [the UK] in the war for Kosovo must look to non-Western eyes. Does it convince every African, Arab or Asian onlooker that the business at The Hague is entirely fair? Or

For background information on Milosevic, his war crimes trial, and the ICC, visit www.emp.ca/dimensionsoflaw

will it arouse understandable suspicions that this is a demonstration of Western powers using justice only when it suits them?

—*"Justice Is on Trial,"* The Observer, *February 17, 2002*

Questions

1. What is "victors' justice"?
2. In one or two sentences, summarize the arguments made in each of the readings. Note whether or not the points made are supported by logic and evidence.
3. Why have some commentators questioned the neutrality of the ICTY?
4. What is your opinion on this issue? Give reasons to support your answer.

Dispute resolution mechanisms serve a useful purpose by substituting the rule of law for the use of force. Unfortunately, the doctrine of state sovereignty usually allows states not to participate in dispute resolution processes if they so choose. International peace and stability will not be fully achieved until members of the international community are required to submit to the jurisdiction of all institutions designed to ensure the peaceful resolution of disputes.

WORKING FOR CHANGE *Louise Arbour*

In May 1999, the international spotlight was turned on Canadian Louise Arbour. From The Hague, site of the International Criminal Tribunal for the Former Yugoslavia, Arbour announced that international warrants had been issued for the arrest of Yugoslav President Slobodan Milosevic for crimes against humanity, including murder. As prosecutor, it was Arbour's decision to start the process to bring Milosevic to justice. She told prominent TV news anchor Peter Jennings: "I wouldn't want anybody to believe that an indictment against Mr. Milosevic is an end game. As far as I'm concerned, this indictment is the first chapter. The next chapter is arrest and trial." Milosevic was arrested in 2001 and tried in 2002–2003.

The charges against Milosevic were issued against a background of controversy. Globally, there was great frustration with the prosecution of war criminals. In places like Rwanda—where hundreds of thousands of people had been slaughtered by rival ethnic clans—and Yugoslavia, well-publicized atrocities suggested that the international community was powerless to bring war criminals to justice. Arbour set about changing that impression, calling the tribunal "the most important chapter in the history of criminal and international humanitarian law." On her appointment to the Tribunal in 1996, she stated, "there is no single issue more important ... than the actual arrest of indicted war criminals. That will be my very top priority."

Arbour was no stranger to controversy when she took the position on the Tribunal. She was professor of law and associate dean of Osgoode Hall Law school of York University when she was appointed to the Ontario Supreme Court in 1987. In 1990, Arbour moved to the Ontario Court of Appeal, where a number of her decisions

Figure 19.3 *Louise Arbour announces the indictment of Yugoslav President Slobodan Milosevic for atrocities in Kosovo at the International Criminal Tribunal for the Former Yugolavia, May 1999.*

attracted public attention, including her decision to give prisoners the right to vote, her ruling as unconstitutional a law that prevented the defence from bringing up the sexual past of a rape victim, and her support for the acquittal of a Hungarian living in Ontario accused of war crimes. In 1995, Arbour wrote a highly critical report of Canada's prison system and its handling of violent incidents at the Kingston Penitentiary for Women. She has also written widely on the *Canadian Charter of Rights and Freedoms.*

Soon after issuing the indictments against Milosevic in 1999, Arbour was appointed to Canada's Supreme Court.

Questions

1. A spirit of independence has characterized Louise Arbour's legal career. In what ways is this an important characteristic for prosecutors in an international criminal tribunal?
2. Is a spirit of independence an important characteristic for a Canadian Supreme Court justice? Explain your ideas.
3. Conduct research to find out the results of the charges against Slobodan Milosevic. Was he found guilty? What were some of the issues in the trial?
4. Conduct research on Arbour's career with the Supreme Court. Identify some of her decisions that have been important and interesting. What impact has she had on the law in Canada?

"Just War" and the Legitimate Use of Force under Modern Law

The old idea that wars can be classified as legally (and morally) legitimate or illegitimate is ancient. However, the modern idea that war is not a just or legitimate way to conduct international relations was expressed in such treaties as *The Hague Convention for the Pacific Settlement of International Disputes* (Hague I, 1899); the *Covenant of the League of Nations* (1919); and the *General Treaty for the Renunciation of War as an Instrument of National Policy* (Kellogg-Briand Pact, 1928).

Wide acceptance of the principle that waging war on another state is an unacceptable act resulted in the enshrinement of the principle in the *UN Charter.* The only justification for the use of force was restricted to the right of a nation to protect its own people or territory. Of course, the extent of a nation's territory and the actions that may be necessary for self-defence are often matters of disagreement at the international level. The issue of self-defence and "pre-emptive self-defence" figured prominently in the discussion of the legitimacy of the use of force in Afghanistan and in the Iraq wars.

With the advent of the United Nations—an institution created for the protection of world peace—a second justification for the use of force has emerged: members of the international community will accept as legitimate military actions that have received authorization by the UN Security Council. A classic example is Security Council Resolution 83 (1950), which authorized the use of force in Korea in 1950. At the end of World War II in 1945, the Korean peninsula was divided, with troops from the former Soviet Union occupying the northern part and US troops occupying the southern part. The north adopted a communist, totalitarian regime, while the south embraced capitalism and democracy. Tensions between these two increasingly hostile governments led to the Korean War (1950–1953).

The Security Council resolution that authorized the use of force reads as follows:

> The Security Council,
>
> HAVING DETERMINED that the armed attack upon the Republic of Korea by forces from North Korea constitutes a breach of the peace,
> HAVING CALLED FOR an immediate cessation of hostilities, and
> HAVING CALLED UPON the authorities in North Korea to withdraw forthwith their armed forces to the 38th parallel, and
> HAVING NOTED from the report of the United Nations Commission on Korea that the authorities in North Korea have neither ceased hostilities nor withdrawn their armed forces to the 38th parallel and that urgent military measures are required to restore international peace and security, and
> HAVING NOTED the appeal from the Republic of Korea to the United Nations for immediate and effective steps to secure peace and security,
> RECOMMENDS that the Members of the United Nations furnish such assistance to the Republic of Korea as may be necessary to repel the armed attack and to restore international peace and security in the area.

Fyi A ceasefire agreement in 1953 ended the Korean conflict, but the two countries have technically been in a state of war for over 50 years. The United States has continued to support South Korea and it has prospered, becoming an important trading nation, in contrast to the poverty and isolation that exist in North Korea.

As the law stands now, the rule for a determination of whether use of force is permissible is deceptively simple: use of force is permissible only if it is either (1) used in self-defence or (2) authorized by Security Council resolution.

Claiming Self-Defence

Applying the rule described above is far more complicated than stating it. The concept of self-defence is very difficult to define from both a practical and a legal standpoint. It also demands frequent revision in response to changes both in what is considered to be a threat to sovereignty and in warfare technology.

The international community has tried to develop the principle of self-defence through legal instruments, including

- the *Declaration on Principles of International Law Concerning Friendly Relations and Co-operation among States in Accordance with the Charter of the United Nations* (1970)
- the *Declaration on the Enhancement of the Effectiveness of the Principle of Refraining from the Threat or Use of Force in International Relations* (1987)
- the *Definition of Aggression* (General Assembly Resolution, 1974).

Clarifications of the scope of self-defence have also resulted from court decisions, especially decisions from the International Court of Justice. In the case *Military and Paramilitary Activities in and against Nicaragua (Nicaragua v. United States of America)* (1984–1991), Nicaragua accused the United States of taking military actions against that country, including mining harbours and funding rebel paramilitary organizations. The United States claimed that these actions were taken in collective self-defence against Nicaragua's socialist government. The United States contended that Nicaragua was supporting armed groups in neighbouring El Salvador as well as Honduras and Costa Rica. The ICJ found that Nicaragua's supplying weapons to rebels or making limited incursions into neighbouring countries did not justify an armed response under the guise of "collective self-defence."

Learn more about *Nicaragua v. United States of America* at www.emp.ca/dimensionsoflaw

In the *Legality of the Threat or Use of Nuclear Weapons (1994–1996) Advisory Opinion*, a divided ICJ offered the following comment on the use of nuclear weapons in the context of self-defence:

> However, in view of the current state of international law, and of the elements of fact at its disposal, the Court cannot conclude definitively whether the threat or use of nuclear weapons would be lawful or unlawful in an extreme circumstance of self-defence, in which the very survival of a State would be at stake.

International practice helps define the acceptable limits of self-defence. When Israel attacked an Iraqi nuclear reactor under construction in 1981, invoking the principle of self-defence, this claim was rejected by the Security Council, which "strongly condemn[ed] the military attack by Israel in clear violation of the Charter of the United Nations and the norms of international conduct." However, a similar pre-emptive action by Israel prior to the 1967 war with its Arab neighbours met with general acceptance by the international community. In that case, Egypt's potential threat to Israel was considered to be imminent, and the timing of Israel's actions given the impending risk made pre-emptive action more acceptable in international eyes.

The claim of pre-emptive self-defence was one of the justifications that the "coalition of the willing" (including the United States and Britain) presented prior to the attack on Iraq in the spring of 2003. At the time, even the United States conceded that the Iraqi threat was "one to five years" in the future. In that case, the attack proceeded without Security Council

Figure 19.4 *Prime Minister Jean Chrétien receives a standing ovation in the House of Commons after defending his government's refusal to send troops to Iraq, April 2003.*

authorization. The fact that the US-led action was not authorized by the Security Council and that it did not fall clearly within the self-defence exception were key reasons for Canada's decision not to participate in the attack on Iraq.

Are There Exceptions to the Rule?

Alongside the debate over the scope of self-defence, another question has emerged. Certain recent military actions have met neither the condition of self-defence nor that of Security Council authorization for legitimacy, yet have enjoyed significant support from some members of the international community. These conflicts have included

- the United States' interventions in Grenada in 1983 and Panama in 1989
- the intervention by NATO in Kosovo in 1999
- the US–UK invasion of Iraq in the spring of 2003.

In some of these cases, the international community has acknowledged the role of the invading state in defusing or improving an unacceptable situation. This moral acceptance of technically "illegal" wars has led many people to ask whether there is—or ought to be—an exception to the "self-defence or authorization" rule.

Deciding on conditions that would allow such exceptions presents a daunting challenge. Reasons proposed for interventions have been diverse: some were dubbed "pro-democratic," others were carried out on humanitarian grounds, and the 2003 invasion of Iraq was subsequently promoted as a means of "regime change" to remove an oppressive dictator. It would be very difficult to obtain international consensus on which of these motives might form legitimate grounds for interference in the affairs of a state. If the international community does decide to make exceptions, these may apply only in situations where the proposed intervention is to be undertaken by a widely representative, legitimate, international body. This was the case at the time of the NATO intervention in Kosovo in 1999.

The Kosovo intervention arose in response to widespread ethnic cleansing of Albanians in the Serbian province of Kosovo. Serbian forces under Slobodan Milosevic had killed thousands and caused an estimated 800 000 refugees to flee Kosovo. The US-led NATO bombing campaign ended when Serbian troops withdrew from the region. An assessment of the Kosovo intervention was made by the Independent International Commission on Kosovo, a non-governmental group of distinguished international observers, including critic and writer Michael Ignatieff. The Commission concluded:

Read the report of the Independent International Commission on Kosovo at www.emp.ca/dimensionsoflaw

> [T]he NATO intervention in Kosovo was illegal [because it did not receive prior approval from the UN Security Council] but legitimate; it was legitimate because [given human rights violations and the failure of diplomatic avenues] Kosovo was liberated as a consequence of the intervention; the oppression of Kosovar Albanians was ended, and all those who had been expelled by Serbian forces during the war ... were able to return to their homes.

Such approaches to intervention undermine the central authority of the Security Council. Canada became interested in the question of intervention, particularly after Canadian peacekeepers in Rwanda were unable to stop the genocide in 1994. In 2000, the government sponsored the International Commission on Intervention and State Sovereignty (ICISS), an independent body composed of distinguished international policy makers and jurists whose purpose was to report to the UN. The Commission's report, entitled *The Responsibility to Protect*, concluded that "sovereign states have a responsibility to protect their own citizens from avoidable catastrophe, but when they are unwilling or unable to do so, that responsibility must be borne by the broader community of states."

Learn more about the ICISS at www.emp.ca/dimensionsoflaw

The United States: Going It Alone **Should the United States follow a policy of unilateralism in international affairs?**

With the collapse of the communist regime in the former Soviet Union in 1991, the United States became the world's only superpower. Within years, people were beginning to suspect that US commitment to the international community was fading. The White House had not signed important treaties, such as the *Kyoto Protocol* to reduce greenhouse gas emissions or the *Ottawa Convention Banning Landmines*, and owed US $2.3 billion to the United Nations, over 60 percent of that organization's outstanding debt. These suspicions

Figure 19.5 *This cartoon, published in July 2001, suggests that the United States under the Bush administration was not enthusiastic about supporting international efforts to solve problems. Which images help create this idea?*

were reinforced when the United States took military action against both Afghanistan (2001) and Iraq (2003) without the approval of the UN Security Council. Here are some views on the Americans' unilateralist or "go-it-alone" foreign policies.

[T]he end of the cold war had breathed new life into traditional American isolationism. With no great security threat from abroad, American conservatives were even less likely to accept the constraints of international institutions and obligations. With no need for allies, why accept the constraints necessary to lure and mollify them?

The extraordinary range of American military power also undermined postwar commitment to multilateralism. With America towering over others militarily, could we not do what we wanted? Was there a need to accept the constraints of alliances and membership? Why not act as we saw fit to protect American interests... ?

Because the United States currently enjoys a surplus of power, it is now possible for Washington to have a very ambitious foreign policy and still remain unilateral in its approach toward the outside world. The United States is perhaps now the only country in the world that can, to a very significant measure, get its way internationally if it is absolutely determined to bend others to its will.

—*Charles William Maynes, "America's Fading Commitment to the World," from* Global Focus: US Foreign Policy at the Turn of the Millennium*; Foreign Policy in Focus, 1998*

Since September 11, 2001 [the date of the terrorist attacks on New York and Washington, DC], there have been calls from various quarters to embrace nation building as a tool for combating terrorism. The logic behind the idea is that "good" states do not do "bad" things, so that Washington should build more "good" states. ...

In reality, combating terrorism is tied to the realist perspective, which says that it increasingly makes sense for states to use or condone violence, including terrorism, when they fall prey to the idea that violence will succeed. A realist approach to combating terrorism, therefore, does not hinge on nation building or making the world safe for democracy. It hinges on a policy of victory and credible deterrence.

—Gary T. Dempsey, "Old Folly in a New Disguise: Nation Building to Combat Terrorism," The Cato Institute, March 21, 2002

Growing unilateralism in the conduct of US foreign policy has never been as sharply in evidence as in the ultimatum by President George Bush to Iraqi leader Saddam Hussein to leave his country or face imminent military attack.

A nation that has always prided itself as the custodian of democratic values is now displaying many of the less appealing characteristics of a 19th century imperial power. America's pre-eminence in today's uni-polar world has emboldened it to demonstrate its hyper-power status in conflict after conflict. ...

Given current political realities, a unilateralist foreign policy approach may not prove too costly for the US in the short run. But in the long term, the arrogance of power, which has already begun to undermine the effectiveness of multilateral institutions, will erode US credibility. This in turn will stoke anti-American sentiment, already widespread in several parts of the world, and encourage the very forces of extremism which the Bush administration valiantly seeks to counter.

—From an editorial in The Times of India, *March 20, 2003*

The Bush administration has made its decision to invade Iraq, an action that will inevitably result in the deaths of untold numbers of people, create a more unstable world, and decrease the safety of Americans everywhere. It has done so despite overwhelming, worldwide opposition and the lack of a UN mandate for his planned attack. ...

The negative consequences of this action will be enormous and long-lasting. We are deeply concerned that the use of US military force will do permanent damage to the rule of law and international cooperation. ... It confirms the fears of hundreds of millions around the world that the Bush government has transformed the US into a rogue military superpower—outside the rule of law—that uses violence to attain its political goals.

Bush's radical, unilateralist foreign policy is as unsustainable as it is dangerous.

—Position statement of Peace Action of Central New York, a local chapter of Peace Action, the United States' largest peace and disarmament organization, March 20, 2003

Questions

1. Identify the main idea in each of the excerpts.
2. Based on the views given here, how would you define "policy of unilateralism"? What other views might support this policy?
3. Suggest some reasons why the United States might prefer a unilateralist foreign policy over a commitment to the international community.
4. For what reasons might a US policy of unilateralism in foreign affairs concern people and nations around the world?

Check Your Understanding

1. What main options or mechanisms are available at the international level for peaceful dispute resolution?
2. Define "legitimate use of force." In modern times, what criteria must a nation meet before its military actions will be accepted within the boundaries of international law?
3. Does the international community accept the notion of pre-emptive self-defence? Explain your answer.
4. Under what circumstances have military actions received the informal support of the international community despite a failure to meet existing criteria for legal legitimacy?

Methods and Strategies for Conflict Prevention and Resolution

The international community, through the United Nations and other institutions, employs a variety of strategies to prevent armed conflict. These include

- consensus-building measures, such as the UN's *Declaration and Programme of Action on a Culture of Peace* (1999)
- institutional defence arrangements, such as NATO
- arms control initiatives, for example, the *Treaty on the Non-Proliferation of Nuclear Weapons* (1968)
- commercial and trade measures, such as multilateral arms embargoes, which stop the shipment of arms to warring countries
- restrictions on particular tools of warfare, such as the *Protocol for the Prohibition of the Use in War of Asphyxiating, Poisonous or Other Gases, and of Bacteriological Methods of Warfare* (1925) and the Chemical Weapons Convention (1993)

- imposition of personal criminal responsibilities for the waging of war in violation of international treaties and the crime of "aggression" as defined under customary law and the *Rome Statute*.

Learn more about the *Declaration and Programme of Action on a Culture of Peace* at www.emp.ca/dimensionsoflaw

This section of the chapter focuses on practical measures that have been used to prevent conflict, such as arms control.

After World War II, the international focus for conflict prevention between the two superpowers—the former Soviet Union and the United States—and their allies was to control available weapons, particularly atomic weapons. The process of disarmament became part of the UN system by the establishment of the Conference on Disarmament (CD) in 1979. The CD is currently composed of 66 members, including Canada. Its activities are supported by various UN organizations and are aimed at ensuring that the supply of weapons is controlled, particularly the most destructive weapons.

Weapons of Mass Destruction

The most active current focus of international arms control is on **weapons of mass destruction** and their delivery systems (long-range missiles and nuclear, chemical, and biological weapons). The question of nuclear weapons and their limitation has been on the international agenda since the formation of the UN and the dropping of atomic bombs by the United States on Hiroshima and Nagasaki in 1945 to bring about Japan's surrender and an end to World War II. In 2003, the United States and Britain justified their invasion of Iraq with the accusation that dictator Saddam Hussein was building weapons of mass destruction.

weapons of mass destruction: military weapons that have the potential to kill large numbers of people and that cannot distinguish between soldiers and civilians

Arms Control Initiatives

Various arms control initiatives were proposed in the years following World War II, but little was achieved until the 1968 adoption of the *Treaty on the Non-Proliferation of Nuclear Weapons* (NPT), a landmark instrument designed to prevent the spread of nuclear weapons and weapons technology. The five nuclear-weapon states as identified by the NPT were China, France, the Soviet Union (now Russia), the United Kingdom, and the United States. These countries were allowed to keep their nuclear weapons, but with a commitment to proceed toward nuclear disarmament. The 183 non–nuclear-weapon states that are party to the NPT have pledged not to develop or otherwise acquire nuclear weapons. However, India and Pakistan now have them, and Iran, Libya, North Korea, and Israel are believed to have acquired nuclear capability or to possess undeclared nuclear weapons.

In practical terms, not much progress has been made to eliminate holdings of nuclear weapons. One initiative, however—the *Strategic Offensive Reductions Treaty* (2002)—requires the United States and Russia to slash nuclear arsenals by roughly two-thirds by 2012.

Nuclear-Free Zones

Another anti-proliferation initiative has been the establishment, by treaty, of nuclear-weapons-free zones. Such zones have been created in Latin America, the Caribbean, the South Pacific, Southeast Asia, Africa, and Antarctica. The *Antarctic Treaty* is the most comprehensive, prohibiting "any measures of a military nature, such as the establishment of military bases and fortifications, the carrying out of military maneuvers, as well as the testing of any type of weapons." There are also treaties prohibiting the creation of military installations on the seabed and on the moon (see Chapter 18).

New initiatives include the creation of nuclear-free zones in Central Asia and in the Middle East, though progress on the latter will likely be limited until a realistic prospect for peace exists in the region. Mongolia set an interesting precedent in notifying the UN of its intention to be a one-country nuclear-free zone.

Transfer Limitations

Prohibiting the transfer of nuclear technologies from country to country is another arms control strategy. Under the 1996 *Wassenaar Arrangement*, each member country has the responsibility to ensure that its exports do not contribute to arms proliferation. Canada has tightened its transfer policies following criticisms that its technological exports to India helped that country acquire nuclear weapons. Now, Canada's Export and Import Controls Bureau (EICB) within the Department of Foreign Affairs authorizes, regulates, and monitors the import and export of restricted goods. Canada's Nuclear Non-Proliferation List, which sets out controlled nuclear material, includes a vast array of equipment, beginning with complete nuclear reactors.

Test Bans

The NPT may soon be supplemented by the *Comprehensive Nuclear Test Ban Treaty* (CTBT, 1996), which, if it comes into force (upon ratification by 44 nuclear-capable states), will ban all nuclear explosions for military or civilian purposes. This ban limits proliferation by making it difficult to design and test new generations of nuclear weapons. So far, the CTBT has not been signed by North Korea, Pakistan, and India, and has not been ratified by China, Israel, the United States, and Vietnam, among others.

Security Guarantees

A common motive for acquiring nuclear weapons is concern about potential attacks by another nuclear-armed state. One non-proliferation strategy involves the provision of guarantees of security. There are two types of guarantees. "Negative" security assurances require parties "not to use or threaten to use nuclear weapons against the Contracting Parties of the Treaty." "Positive" guarantees include those made by NPT-listed nuclear weapons states, to the effect

> that they will provide or support immediate assistance, in accordance with the Charter, to any non–nuclear-weapon State Party to the *Treaty on the Non-Proliferation of Nuclear Weapons* that is a victim of an act of, or an object of a threat of, aggression in which nuclear weapons are used.

In 2003, one of the testing points for the non-proliferation approach was North Korea. This country has been pursuing a program of weapons acquisition (and has declared that it possesses some nuclear weapons) since the United States refused its proposal for a formal non-aggression pact. Tensions have been high as the international community considers its options in dealing with what some describe as a renegade nuclear state.

Weapons in Terrorists' Hands

Currently, there is concern about the proliferation of nuclear weapons among non-governmental groups such as terrorists, criminal gangs, and rebel movements. The greatest concern is the vulnerability of Russia's nuclear installations and arms dumps. There is fear also that cash-starved governments and military organizations may resort to sales of old Soviet weapons technologies to non-state organizations that will use the weapons for terrorism. With the disintegration of the Soviet Union in 1991, the United States and Russia established the Cooperative Threat Reduction program in an attempt to secure and destroy Russia's nuclear weapons. The 1980 *Convention on the Physical Protection of Nuclear Material* is aimed at preventing the theft of nuclear material.

Learn more about the Cooperative Threat Reduction program at www.emp.ca/dimensionsoflaw

Missile Defence Systems

Missile testing by North Korea, India, and Pakistan has revived the interest of some countries, particularly the United States, in anti-ballistic missile (ABM) defence systems—long-range networks that are designed to detect and destroy missiles fired from hundreds or even thousands of kilometres away. The problem of ABMs is a complex one, as it has implications for international relationships among countries that must cooperate with one another. Current US plans envisage land-based interceptor rockets that could knock out ballistic-missile warheads before they can hit North America. Canada is seen as playing an important role in this defence system because of its proximity to the United States.

The United States is also developing plans for a defence system using weapons based in space, dubbed "Star Wars." High-tech weapons mounted on satellites would be able to shoot down attacking missiles anywhere in the world. The Moon Agreement (1967) prohibits nuclear weapons in space, but there are many questions of interpretation over the use of other types of weapons. Many people are suspicious of this technology, arguing that it could be used for offensive purposes. At the very least, they suggest, the control of such far-reaching weapons technology by one country dramatically alters international power relationships and the concept of national sovereignty.

Fyi Chlorine and mustard gases were first used in 1915 during World War I. Chlorine gas inhalation resulted in violent choking and death. Mustard gas produced horrible internal and external burns. Soldiers who survived gas attacks were often left with disfiguring scars and damaged lungs.

Chemical and Biological Weapons

Chemical weapons have always been considered particularly abhorrent, even before their first organized use by the Germans in World War I. After the war, an initiative was undertaken to ban chemical weapons. This resulted in the adoption of the *Protocol for the Prohibition of the Use in War of Asphyxiating, Poisonous or Other Gases, and of Bacteriological Methods of Warfare* (1925), commonly referred to as the *Geneva Protocol.*

Turning Points in the Law

The *Geneva Protocol*, 1925

On April 22, 1915, during World War I, German forces at Ypres made the first large-scale wartime use of chemical weapons through the deployment of "asphyxiating bombs" against Allied—largely French and Canadian—troops. The following report appeared in the *New York Tribune* on April 27, 1915, before the nature of the "noxious gas"—chlorine—was determined:

> The attack of last Thursday evening was preceded by the rising of a cloud of vapor, greenish gray and iridescent. That vapor settled to the ground like a swamp mist and drifted toward the French trenches on a brisk wind. Its effect on the French was a violent nausea and faintness, followed by an utter collapse. It is believed that the Germans, who charged in behind the vapor, met no resistance at all, the French at their front being virtually paralyzed.

Before the Ypres attack, the potential for use in warfare of chemical and biological weapons had already been raised on a theoretical level, and had been the subject of a prohibition in The Hague Conference (1907).

The threat of chemical and biological warfare has always inspired a unique level of fear and revulsion on the part of soldiers and civilians alike. Support for a prohibition on the use of such weapons has been almost universal in the international community. In 1925, this consensus led to the passage of the *Geneva Protocol.* The Protocol, with 133 parties, stood as the primary legal authority on chemical and biological weapons until 1993. It provided, in part, as follows:

> Whereas the use in war of asphyxiating, poisonous or other gases, and of all analogous liquids, materials or devices, has been justly condemned by the general opinion of the civilized world; and ...
>
> To the end that this prohibition shall be universally accepted as a part of International Law, binding alike the conscience and the practice of nations;

Declare:

That the High Contracting Parties, so far as they are not already Parties to Treaties prohibiting such use, accept this prohibition, agree to extend this prohibition to the use of bacteriological methods of warfare and agree to be bound as between themselves according to the terms of this declaration.

Questions

1. Why are chemical and biological warfare considered to be particularly abhorrent?
2. Describe the international strategy that was used to try to control chemical weapons.
3. Identify some of the reasons why this strategy has not stopped all use of chemical weapons.

Figure 19.6 *German prisoners are shown with gas masks in April 1915. Canadian troops were ill prepared for German gas attacks on the Allied lines around Ypres.*

The *Geneva Protocol* banned only the use and not the possession of chemical agents. It was superseded in 1993 by the *Convention on the Prohibition of Development, Production, Stockpiling, and Use of Chemical Weapons and on Their Destruction* (the Chemical Weapons Convention, or CWC). An impetus for this new treaty was the use of chemical weapons by Iraq against both Iran and its own Kurdish citizens in Halabja.

The CWC established an elaborate verification system and provided for the creation of the Organisation for the Prohibition of Chemical Weapons (OPCW). The treaty's stringent verification requirements helped to overcome a major hurdle to the acceptability of disarmament treaties—the fear of cheating by potential adversaries. The CWC requires that each state establish a national authority to serve as the country's focal point for effective liaison with the OPCW and with other countries. The Canadian National Authority is part of the Department of Foreign Affairs and International Trade.

To learn more about the Organisation for the Prohibition of Chemical Weapons, visit www.emp.ca/dimensionsoflaw

CHECK YOUR UNDERSTANDING

1. List at least three different conflict prevention strategies employed by the international community. Conduct research and list examples of the application of these strategies in recent conflicts.
2. Why has the international legal community focused its preventive efforts on nuclear and chemical weapons control initiatives?
3. List two current arms control issues that present a challenge to the international community.

For in-depth background on Afghanistan, visit www.emp.ca/dimensionsoflaw

War and Peace

In spite of a host of efforts to prevent war, it happens with uncomfortable regularity. An estimated 110 million people died in both large and small wars during the 20th century, and the first years of the 21st century saw international wars in Afghanistan and Iraq and civil wars in a number of African countries, including Liberia and Sudan. At times, peace is an elusive goal, and war a brutal reality.

Wartime Law

When preventive strategies fail and war breaks out, the international community's focus shifts. The notion that the normal course of the law does not apply in wartime is ancient and is reflected in the Latin maxim, *inter arma enim silent leges* (even law falls silent during hostilities). In modern times, of course, law is not silent during the course of a conflict. Law during conflict is now characterized by unique principles rooted in tradition, and expressed in comprehensive norms setting out what is permissible and what is not in times of war.

By the Middle Ages, the code of chivalry and Church-sanctioned limitations, such as the Truce of God (no fighting on Sundays), served to control some aspects of warfare to protect combatants and non-combatants. Modern law, however, has its roots in the second half of the 19th century, in documents such as the 1863 *Lieber Code*, drafted by Professor Francis Lieber and issued as General Orders No. 100 of the Union Army during the US Civil War. This and other early attempts culminated with international peace conferences at The Hague in 1899 and 1907. These conferences adopted a series of conventions dealing with the conduct of war and the treatment of combatants. The rules were continually updated to take into account technological development, such as aerial warfare, and the experience of major conflicts, such as the two World Wars.

The Geneva Conventions

Our current law originated in the updating conference held in Geneva in 1949. This conference adopted a series of conventions that now have virtually universal acceptance (190 parties):

- *Geneva Convention for the Amelioration of the Condition of the Wounded and Sick in Armed Forces in the Field* ("Convention I")
- *Geneva Convention for the Amelioration of the Condition of the Wounded, Sick and Shipwrecked Members of Armed Forces at Sea* ("Convention II")
- *Geneva Convention Relative to the Treatment of Prisoners of War* ("Convention III")
- *Geneva Convention Relative to the Treatment of Civilian Persons in Time of War* ("Convention IV").

These conventions were later supplemented by protocols. The intention of the Geneva Conventions was to limit the impact of wars on combatants and minimize the damage for civilians. Countries engaging in either civil or international war are required to control their activities and to make efforts to ensure that civilian populations are not attacked. In a sense, the Geneva Conventions were attempts to put limits on behaviour in warfare.

WORKING FOR CHANGE *The Red Cross—"Even War Has Limits"*

The Red Cross, founded in 1863, was dedicated from the outset to aiding combatants on both sides of wars. The movement arose from suggestions of Henry Dunant, who described in his book, *A Memory of Solferino*, the horrors faced by those wounded in battle. He suggested that societies made up of volunteers care for the wounded. An International Committee for Relief to the Wounded was founded, with Dunant sitting on the committee. This became the International Committee of the Red Cross (ICRC) when volunteers were distinguished from combatants by wearing a white armband with a red cross on it. This emblem was a reversal of the Swiss flag (a white cross on a red background), and so is also known as the Geneva Cross. In time it became the internationally acknowledged emblem of the ICRC, and a sign of impartial humanitarian aid in times of war and natural catastrophe. Because of the perceived (although unintended) religious significance of the cross, national societies choose to be either an International Red Cross or a Red Crescent Movement affiliate; there is no difference in their service.

Figure 19.7 *A Red Cross worker escorts a young Kosovar refugee, carrying his Canadian flag, as he prepares to board an aircraft to return home.*

The link between the ICRC and the international legal system was established in 1864 when the ICRC sponsored the conference that adopted the *Geneva Convention for the Amelioration of the Condition of the Wounded in Armies in the Field.* Headquarters for the organization are still in Geneva, Switzerland. The ICRC has since become a significant influence on the advancement of international humanitarian law, has been accepted by all combatants, and has done its work in the field in every major conflict. The seven principles that shape its service are humanity, impartiality, neutrality, independence, voluntary service, unity, and universality.

National societies conduct work in their home countries. They are on hand to provide aid in national and international emergencies, such as floods, earthquakes, and fires. The ICRC works in these emergencies to repair infrastructure such as wells, provides food and household supplies for refugees, supplies medical equipment such as prostheses, and works to reunite families. The Canadian Red Cross is a vital branch of the Red Cross family, providing important services in accordance with the seven principles.

Questions

1. Why is it important that the ICRC be neutral, independent, and impartial?
2. In what sense is the ICRC an international organization?
3. In your opinion, what is the meaning of the Red Cross slogan, "Even War Has Limits"?
4. The UN has many organizations that supply services such as those of the ICRC. Why is an organization like the ICRC needed?

For more information on the International Red Cross, visit www.emp.ca/dimensionsoflaw

War's Aftermath

The aftermath of hostilities is closely regulated by international law. The Geneva Conventions (and also customary law) prescribe, to some extent, the duties that arise through an occupying power's control of foreign territory. Generally, these have to do with public order and safety, and the protection and care of the civilian population. In addition, the occupying power has the obligation to refrain from and prevent:

> (a) violence to life and person, in particular murder of all kinds, mutilation, cruel treatment and torture; (b) taking of hostages; (c) outrages upon personal dignity, in particular humiliating and degrading treatment; [and] (d) the passing of sentences and the carrying out of executions without previous judgment pronounced by a regularly constituted court, affording all the judicial guarantees which are recognized as indispensable by civilized peoples.

Unfortunately, the Geneva Conventions do not prevent all instances of violence against a defeated people. In Africa, where legitimate governments often fall to rebel forces, there have been many reports of atrocities committed on rival populations. In such places as Sierra Leone, the hands and feet of civilians were systematically hacked off by rival forces as a method of instilling terror. The United States has not escaped criticism for its poor handling of over 600 prisoners during the wars in Afghanistan and Iraq. Alleged members of al-Qaeda, the terrorist organization that carried out the September 11, 2001, attacks on New York City and Washington, DC, were imprisoned at the US military base at Guantanamo Bay, Cuba. Under security measures adopted by the United States following the attacks, the military was not required to provide the legal rights that are routinely afforded to domestic prisoners and prisoners of war under the Geneva Conventions. In its own defence, the US administration argued that al-Qaeda members were terrorists and not prisoners of war (see You Decide! on page 599).

Peacekeeping

Learn more about Canada's role in peacekeeping at www.emp.ca/dimensionsoflaw

In some cases, hostilities may be ended through intervention by an international authority such as the UN or other international peacekeeping or peace-maintenance forces.

The concept of peacekeeping emerged after the 1956 war in the Middle East to deal with the conflict between Egypt and Israel. Lester B. Pearson, then Secretary of State for External Affairs and later Prime Minister of Canada, proposed the deployment of an international peace force under the UN flag. The idea proved to be a success in managing the aftermath of that conflict, and Pearson received the Nobel Peace Prize for his idea. Since that time, there have been numerous UN peacekeeping missions, most with the involvement of Canadian troops. Canada has embraced this role enthusiastically, and peacekeeping figures prominently in governmental defence and foreign policy objectives. Practical aspects of peacekeeping are dealt with at the Pearson Peacekeeping Centre, an independent, internationally recognized training centre, established by Canada in 1994.

Peacekeeping law has faced a number of changes, especially in the scope of peacekeeping activities. These have evolved from observation to more active roles characterized by "peace making" and "nation building," as well as the use of force in such places as Somalia and Afghanistan. Some of the new roles assigned to peacekeeping forces and their civilian partners (police, administrators of justice, and so on) have been dubbed "peace building" or "peace maintenance." These activities raise complex legal issues, for example, the imposition of policies that may not coincide with local wishes.

ersonal Viewpoint

Canada Should Push for a Rapid Deployment Force in the Congo

Peter Langille is senior research associate at the Centre for Global Studies, University of Victoria. He is the author of *Bridging the Commitment-Capacity Gap: Existing Arrangements and Options for Enhancing UN Rapid Deployment*. In this 2003 article, he makes a case for Canada's increased participation in peacekeeping efforts, particularly through the use of a UN military force that can respond rapidly to conflicts before there is extensive loss of life.

Few places on Earth need help more than the Democratic Republic of Congo. Civilians, including thousands of panicked refugees, are at the mercy of armed, drugged militias, which appear intent on slaughter. ... UN commanders in the present mission have cabled New York daily, pleading for reinforcements. ...

Already this messy five-year war has led to the deaths of at least three million people. ...

UN Secretary-General Kofi Annan has asked UN member states to provide troops and deploy an emergency international force through a "coalition of the willing." France will, if supported, lead the coalition, and Canada has said it could contribute two military transport planes or perhaps 200 soldiers. ...

This isn't good enough. Canada could and should be doing more. Despite cutbacks, Canada retains a regular force of 19 500 soldiers ... augmented by 15 500 reserves, which provides a total force of 35 000 troops. ... Our total deployment abroad is 1500 troops. ... [I]t appears that 4500 soldiers are already committed [elsewhere]. ... Why can't two battalions of mechanized (wheeled) infantry (approximately 1200 troops) be sent to the Congo?

Our government might also consider a mechanism designed specifically for such an emergency. Canada is one of 15 countries participating in the multinational Standby High Readiness Brigade (SHIRBRIG) for UN peace operations, which has been operational since 1999. ...

The objective underlying the brigade's eight years of cooperative planning was to provide the UN with a jump-start, rapid deployment force of as many as 5000 troops within 30 days' notice (each participating state reserves the right to decide whether to deploy national personnel on a case-by-case basis).

SHIRBRIG, unlike most national contributors, is a complete, self-sufficient brigade with its own headquarters, logistics and communications. The participating militaries are familiar with one another and work to common doctrine and standards. ...

According to polls, Canadians support further participation in UN peace operations. Having once been a world leader and major contributor to peacekeeping, Canada now ranks 31st in contributions to UN operations. But given Congo's crisis, it's unlikely that the Canadian people would be satisfied with sending military observers or even 200 troops.

The Canadian Forces can help in the Democratic Republic of Congo. We have options and resources.

Source: Peter Langille, "Canada Should Push for a Rapid Deployment Force in the Congo," *The Human Security Bulletin*, Canadian Consortium on Human Security, www.humansecuritybulletin.info/editorial_1.htm.

Questions

1. a) What is a "rapid deployment force"?
   b) Why is rapid deployment capability important in resolving conflicts such as the one in Congo that was ongoing in the spring of 2003? (To learn more about this conflict, visit www.emp.ca/dimensionsoflaw.)
2. Identify some other possible ways for the international community to deal with conflicts similar to the one in Congo. Explain your ideas.
3. Should Canada dedicate significant economic and human resources to intervening in civil wars such as the one in Congo? Why or why not?

Learn more about terrorism and war in the 21st century at www.emp.ca/dimensionsoflaw

Terrorism

So far, this chapter has focused on state-to-state aggression and civil war. However, since the last quarter of the 20th century, a different use of force has come to the fore, most notably in the events of September 11, 2001. The international community has responded to terrorist threats through a variety of measures, including the unilateral use of force (in Afghanistan and Iraq). The community has also put into place a legal response composed of domestic legislation (such as Canada's *Anti-terrorism Act*), international organization resolutions, and a series of treaties to deal with the problem.

International Agreements to Combat Terrorism

Treaties Dealing with Terrorism Generally

- *Inter American Convention to Prevent and Punish the Acts of Terrorism Taking the Form of Crimes Against Persons and Related Extortion That Are of International Significance* (1971)
- *European Convention on the Suppression of Terrorism* (1977)
- *South Asian Association for Regional Cooperation Regional Convention on Suppression of Terrorism* (1987)
- UN *International Convention for the Suppression of Terrorist Bombings* (1997)
- *Arab Convention on the Suppression of Terrorism* (1998)
- *International Convention for the Suppression of the Financing of Terrorism* (1999)
- *Convention of the Organization of the Islamic Conference on Combating International Terrorism* (1999)
- *Organization for African Unity Convention on the Prevention and Combating of Terrorism* (1999)
- *Treaty on Cooperation among the States Members of the Commonwealth of Independent States in Combating Terrorism* (1999)

Treaties Dealing with Terrorism on Aircraft

- *Convention on Offences and Certain Other Acts Committed on Board Aircraft* (Tokyo Convention) (1963)
- *Convention for the Suppression of Unlawful Seizure of Aircraft* (Hague Convention) (1970)
- *Convention for the Suppression of Unlawful Acts Against the Safety of Civil Aviation* (Montreal Convention) (1971) and *Protocol for the Suppression of Unlawful Acts of Violence at Airports Serving International Civil Aviation* (1988)

Treaties Dealing with Terrorism at Sea

- *Convention for the Suppression of Unlawful Acts Against the Safety of Maritime Navigation* (Rome Convention) (1988)
- *Protocol for the Suppression of Unlawful Acts Against the Safety of Fixed Platforms located on the Continental Shelf* (1988)

Other Related Treaties

- *International Convention Against the Taking of Hostages* (1979)
- *Convention on the Marking of Plastic Explosives for the Purpose of Detection* (Montreal Convention) (1991)

Figure 19.8 *The struggle against terrorism has been going on for years. In what ways have international efforts sought to catch up to changing conditions and events?*

Perhaps the most definitive statement of states' obligations with respect to terrorism is Security Council Resolution 1373 (2001), adopted days after the September 11 attacks. It concentrates on the prevention and suppression of the financing of terrorist acts and requires states to refrain from providing any form of support, active or passive, to terrorist entities. It also declares that "acts, methods, and practices of terrorism are contrary to the purposes and principles of the United Nations... ." Whether these measures will aid in stopping terrorism remains to be seen.

Check Your Understanding

1. Why is there reasonably strong consensus in the international community about the need for humane treatment of combatants?
2. In your opinion, what are some significant hurdles encountered in making and enforcing wartime law?
3. List four duties of an occupying power under international law.
4. How was Canada instrumental in developing the concept of international peacekeeping?
5. To what extent are governments responsible for the terrorist actions of their nationals? How does international law enforce this responsibility?

CAREER PROFILE

Maj. Christopher Young, Lord Strathcona's Horse (Royal Canadians) Armoured Unit

Christopher Young completed two tours of peacekeeping duty (1993–1994 and 1997–1998) in the former Yugoslavia.

Q. How do you become a peacekeeper in the Canadian Forces?

A. First, I'm not a peacekeeper—I'm a soldier. Like all Canadian Forces personnel, I'm trained to fight. Peacekeeping is just one facet of my work. Canadian Forces personnel make a highly respected contribution to peacekeeping missions largely because the international community recognizes their high-quality combat training and experience.

Q. During your deployments in the former Yugoslavia, what kinds of things would you do in a normal work week?

A. We'd review reports coming in from various Canadian battalion troops. Then we'd look at requests for information coming in from Ottawa National Defence headquarters, and respond to urgent logistical issues. Then, typically two days a week, we would be on the road, travelling from Zagreb to Daruver, visiting with the Canadian Contingent Support Group [later the Canadian Logistics Battalion]. We'd have to travel through what were essentially front lines—belligerent lines—into the Serbian-controlled zone. It could be a pretty interesting trip.

Q. Which aspects of your work did you find the most rewarding? The least?

A. I felt we were really getting something done when we could make a practical difference to the troops. For example, at one point, we coordinated a procurement for wet-weather boots to replace the usual Mark 5 leather boot that was just not cutting it in the cold and wet environment. It meant developing specifications, then dealing with a couple of potential contractors, then getting the men to try out the boots in the theatre before we could get the contract awarded. It seems like a simple thing, but it made a big difference.

I guess one of the most frustrating things, at least from our perspective, was the perception that there was a lack of decisive action from a combat standpoint. We were watching things happen—ethnic cleansing, forced migrations—while the UN was trying to respond through negotiation. But the parties would sign an agreement one day and then violate it the next. There was clearly no good faith there.

Q. What was the most unexpected aspect of your work in the former Yugoslavia?

A. You can never really be prepared for the impact a war zone has on you. You go into it complaining about home things, like high taxes or bureaucracy. But after spending time in a country where you can get shot on the spot just for saying the wrong thing to the wrong neighbour, where the people have nothing, I couldn't stop thinking how good we have it here.

Q. If you could suggest one change in international law or policy that would make the peacekeeping function easier, what would it be?

A. One issue that was politically awkward was the UN's policy of intervening only with the permission of the receiving state. In the former Yugoslavia, the invitation came from the Croatian faction. In a civil war, it's difficult to maintain the appearance of neutrality when you come in with the political support of one of three warring factions. I think our job would be easier if the UN did not need to wait to be invited, but was more proactive about its involvement in these situations where we can clearly be of help.

Q. What would you say to Canadian teenagers interested in a career in the Canadian Forces?

A. I'd recommend it simply because of the enormous diversity in work and life experiences. The work of a soldier is so much more than combat. I found myself doing things from negotiating with two factions over weapons holdings, to writing a short book on stress injuries, and so much more. It's rewarding work, and it's never, ever dull.

Questions

1. According to Maj. Young, why are soldiers effective peacekeepers?
2. What are some peacekeeping activities that Young identified in the interview? Why might these be important activities for keeping the peace in a place like the former Yugoslavia?
3. After reading this interview, what might you identify as important issues facing peacekeepers on missions? Explain your answer.

METHODS OF *Legal Inquiry*

Writing a Research Essay

A research essay differs from other types of essays that you may write to express an opinion or explore an idea. A research essay provides the evidence that supports your view or understanding of a topic. Evidence may take two forms: facts and the opinions of learned people on the topic. Your own opinions are not evidence and should not form part of a research essay.

Step 1

The first step in a research essay is to decide what it is that you want to prove. Your idea is stated as a thesis—a clear, concise statement of your understanding of the topic. (See Methods of Legal Inquiry, Chapter 4, page 123, for help in developing a thesis statement.) Your thesis can be based on readings and research that you have already done, on classroom discussions, or from examining the theses of others on similar topics.

Step 2

Next, gather evidence that helps to prove that your thesis statement is correct. Several Methods of Legal Inquiry features in this book will be helpful here, including:

- Internet Research (Chapter 1, page 29)
- Analyzing and Interpreting Data (Chapter 5, page 154)
- Determining Factual Relevance (Chapter 6, page 185)
- Reading Statistics Critically (Chapter 8, page 254)
- Detecting Bias in the Media (Chapter 9, page 286)

- Conducting an Interview (Chapter 14, page 431)
- Distinguishing between Opinion and Fact (Chapter 16, page 493)

At this stage you are actively searching for relevant sources of information, making judgments about the worth of evidence, summarizing useful information, and recording sources carefully and completely. It is important to have the time to explore a wide variety of sources and be able to reflect on the information that you uncover. Effective time management and organizational skills are critical! Spread your research activities over a number of sessions and review your progress frequently, including checking the validity of your thesis. Be aware that your research may show that your thesis is incorrect or imprecise; you may have to modify it to bring it into line with your evidence, or you may decide that even more research is necessary.

Step 3

Organize your evidence and prepare to begin writing. You should look for themes or subtopics that logically work together to create a strong argument in support of your thesis.

Step 4

Produce the rough draft of your essay. Your introduction should identify the importance of the topic, reflect on the range of possible opinions, and state your thesis. Organize the body of the essay by themes or subtopics: within each subtopic, give the relevant evidence and discuss its importance to proving the thesis. The conclusion restates the thesis, summarizes your arguments, and, perhaps, offers ideas for further research on the topic.

When your rough draft is complete, it is a good idea to go over it carefully, checking that all sources are cited. You must identify the sources for all the evidence that you included in your essay, whether quoted directly or paraphrased. Failure to cite your sources leaves you open to charges of plagiarism—claiming the work of others as your own. Your teacher may require a particular style for citing references, or may accept any one of the common styles. The Modern Language Association (MLA) and the American Psychological Association (APA) are two well-known styles. (For additional help, see the Methods of Legal Inquiry feature on bibliographic documentation in Chapter 18, page 562.)

Many people find it helpful to put the draft essay aside for a day or so and come back to it with fresh eyes. It is amazing how many grammar, spelling, and structural problems jump out at you when you read the essay after a short break.

Step 5

When you are satisfied with your draft, produce the final paper, taking care to check for typographical and other errors, such as pages out of order or the teacher's name misspelled on the title page. Take the view that this paper represents you to the teacher and to your classmates. Make sure the impression you create is the one you want!

Reviewing Main Ideas

You Decide!

US TREATMENT OF SUSPECTED TERRORISTS

Facts

The September 11, 2001, terrorist attacks on the World Trade Center in New York and the Pentagon in Washington, DC, prompted the United States to take a more aggressive approach to national security. Evidence suggested that the terrorists who targeted the United States belonged to al-Qaeda and had received support and protection from the Taliban government of Afghanistan.

In October 2001, the United States led a coalition of nations—including Canada—in a military campaign against Afghanistan and quickly defeated the Taliban forces. Captured al-Qaeda members and Taliban officials suspected of supporting terrorism were rounded up and detained. Elsewhere in the world, people believed to be al-Qaeda or Taliban members were also arrested. In early 2002, the prisoners were shipped to the US military base at Guantanamo Bay, Cuba.

Over 600 prisoners from 43 different countries were transferred to Guantanamo Bay. While being moved, they were handcuffed, blindfolded, made to wear earmuffs, and clamped in leg irons. At the base they were housed in 1.8 m by 2.4 m cages made out of chain-link fencing, with corrugated metal roofs. They were interrogated by military officials.

The prisoners were not charged with crimes, nor were they represented by legal counsel. A military commission determined their guilt or innocence. Details of the evidence against each prisoner were not published, nor was the verdict of the tribunal. There was no right to appeal the verdict of the commission. An execution chamber was built on the base soon after the prisoners arrived. US officials announced that the prisoners were to be held at Guantanamo Bay "until the end of the war against terrorism."

Arguments Offered by the US Administration

The US government claimed that the Taliban and al-Qaeda prisoners were "unlawful enemy combatants"; therefore, the Third Geneva Convention did not apply because they were not prisoners of war. They were also not protected by US human rights guarantees for criminals, because they were not US citizens and they were not in the United States. (The Guantanamo Bay base is on Cuban soil under a lease that has existed for over 90 years.) The stringent use of force and restraint was necessary because of the prisoners' threat to the United States. As one member of the Joint Chiefs of Staff pointed out: "They are bad guys. They are the worst of the worst and if let out on the street, they will go back to the proclivity of trying to kill Americans and others." According to US officials, the prisoners were sheltered from the weather, given culturally appropriate food, had access to medical treatment, and were given copies of the Qur'an.

US officials argued that a high degree of secrecy was necessary in order to combat the threat of terrorism. Information gained through interrogation led to further arrests. Allowing outside observers or participants in the prosecution process might have undermined American efforts to strengthen their own security.

Arguments Offered by Critics

Numerous organizations and governments condemned the United States' treatment of the prisoners. Conditions in the prison were not up to a level expected for prisoners of war, and even US prison officials agreed that the conditions did not meet standards for prisoners in the US justice system. The NGO Human Rights Watch argued: "As a party to the Geneva Conventions, the United States is required to treat every detained combatant humanely, including unlawful combatants. The United States may not pick and choose among them to decide who is entitled to decent treatment."

Amnesty International wrote: "The USA has variously used hooding, blindfolding, handcuffing, and shackling of detainees in Afghanistan, Guantanamo Bay (Cuba), and Iraq. ... The administration has sought to insulate its actions ... from the eyes of the international community. The USA is undermining the rule of law, and setting a dangerous example in so doing."

Critics decried the legal limbo in which the prisoners existed, a situation for which there was no provision under international law. According to international and human rights law, legal status as a prisoner of war or criminal should be determined by a competent, independent tribunal, not by the US captors. This lack of status meant that the prisoners could be held indefinitely without being charged or brought to trial.

Critics were outraged by the lack of prisoners' rights to a fair trial and representation by counsel. Under article 10 of the *Universal Declaration of Human Rights* and subsequent conventions, every person has the right to a fair and public trial. At Guantanamo Bay, the fate of the prisoners was determined in secret by military commissions with the power to convict based on hearsay, with no opportunity for appeal.

Make Your Decision

1. Summarize the arguments that the United States used to justify its treatment of the prisoners.
2. Summarize the arguments that critics used to pressure the United States into changing its treatment of the prisoners.
3. Identify some important issues of international law raised by this situation.
4. In your opinion, was the United States justified in its treatment of al-Qaeda and Taliban prisoners? Explain your viewpoint.
5. Conduct research to find out what has happened to the prisoners at Guantanamo Bay and what principles of international law were developed by the experience.

Key Terms

Review the following terms to show that you understand the meaning of each and how it is applied in a legal context.

ethnic cleansing
genocide
weapons of mass destruction

Understanding the Law

Review the following entities mentioned in the text, and show that you understand the intent of each.

Conference on Disarmament
Geneva Conventions
International Court of Justice
International Criminal Tribunal for the Former Yugoslavia
United Nations Charter, chapter VI

Thinking and Inquiry

1. Summarize the methods for maintaining peace and discouraging wars that have been developed by the international legal community.
2. In your opinion, why have international efforts failed to prevent all international and civil wars?
3. Construct a table showing the advantages and disadvantages of the use of arms limitation strategies in preventing or minimizing conflicts.
4. There have been efforts to control conventional weapons as well as weapons of mass destruction. Conduct research and write a one-page summary of international efforts toward control of one of these topics:
   - light weapons, such as machine guns
   - use of child soldiers
5. The questions that people ask about a topic reflect their understanding of the subject. Using the information in this chapter, make up three questions on each of these topics:
   a) justification for the use of force
   b) arms limitations
   c) Geneva Conventions
   Explain how the questions that you ask show your understanding of the topic.

Communication

6. Imagine that you want to take action to encourage peace and stop armed conflicts around the world. Identify three organizations that you could contact for information and ideas. Summarize the strategies that each of the organizations might suggest.
7. Create a photographic essay of a current conflict somewhere in the world. Use Internet, newspaper, and magazine sources to gather photographs to show the impacts of the conflict on people.
8. Conduct research on a broad international issue related to peace and security, such as terrorism, control of nuclear weapons, or weapons in space. Describe international efforts to control or minimize the damage or aggression, and the role of international law in the issue.
9. Suppose you were asked to debate the following question: "*Resolved that: The United Nations should take military action in every case to stop both international and civil war, in order to prevent human suffering.*" Outline the arguments that might be made by both sides of this debate. Which side do you find more compelling?

Application

10. Identify one action that you could take in your local area to support international legal efforts to ensure peace and security.
11. Evaluate the effectiveness of international intervention in conflicts between nations by creating a table listing conflicts that have been avoided or prevented, those that have been stopped, and those that are still ongoing in spite of international efforts. Use encyclopedias or other summary sources to get brief overviews of conflicts. Based on your table, decide whether or not international intervention has been effective.
12. Prepare a case study of a current civil or international war. Describe the sources of the conflict, the groups that are contributing to the problem, and attempts made to improve the situation. Try to find statements illustrating the views of both sides of the conflict. Speculate on the outcome, outlining your view of the likely situation over the next five years.
13. One reason given by the United States for not supporting the International Criminal Court is that the United States refuses to expose its soldiers to the possibility of criminal prosecution by an international body. Should soldiers who act as peacekeepers or who are part of a multilateral body, such as those in Iraq and Afghanistan, be immune from prosecution by the ICC for criminal acts that they may commit? Why or why not?

Appendix

Canadian Charter of Rights and Freedoms
Universal Declaration of Human Rights
Legal Citation Reference
Table of Cases

The Appendix includes two essential human rights documents, the *Canadian Charter of Rights and Freedoms* and the *Universal Declaration of Human Rights*, and two useful resources for the study of *Dimensions of Law* and of the law generally.

The full text of the *Canadian Charter of Rights and Freedoms*, Part I of the *Constitution Act, 1982*, is set out first, complete with marginal notes.

The *Universal Declaration of Human Rights*, as adopted and proclaimed by the United Nations' General Resolution 217 A (III) of December 10, 1948, is set out next.

The Legal Citation Resource includes abbreviations of courts, case reporting series, and jurisdictions, as well as selected neutral citation tribunal identifiers for federal and provincial courts and the meaning of terms and abbreviations commonly encountered in case citations.

The Table of Cases lists all cases cited in the text of *Dimensions of Law* for which complete citations are provided.

Canadian Charter of Rights and Freedoms

Part I of the *Constitution Act, 1982*

Whereas Canada is founded upon principles that recognize the supremacy of God and the rule of law:

Guarantee of Rights and Freedoms

Rights and freedoms in Canada

1. The *Canadian Charter of Rights and Freedoms* guarantees the rights and freedoms set out in it subject only to such reasonable limits prescribed by law as can be demonstrably justified in a free and democratic society.

Fundamental Freedoms

Fundamental freedoms

2. Everyone has the following fundamental freedoms:

(a) freedom of conscience and religion;
(b) freedom of thought, belief, opinion and expression, including freedom of the press and other media of communication;
(c) freedom of peaceful assembly; and
(d) freedom of association.

Democratic Rights

Democratic rights of citizens

3. Every citizen of Canada has the right to vote in an election of members of the House of Commons or of a legislative assembly and to be qualified for membership therein.

Maximum duration of legislative bodies

4. (1) No House of Commons and no legislative assembly shall continue for longer than five years from the date fixed for the return of the writs at a general election of its members.

Continuation in special circumstances

(2) In time of real or apprehended war, invasion or insurrection, a House of Commons may be continued by Parliament and a legislative assembly may be continued by the legislature beyond five years if such continuation is not opposed by the votes of more than one-third of the members of the House of Commons or the legislative assembly, as the case may be.

Annual sitting of legislative bodies

5. There shall be a sitting of Parliament and of each legislature at least once every twelve months.

Mobility Rights

Mobility of citizens

6. (1) Every citizen of Canada has the right to enter, remain in and leave Canada.

Rights to move and gain livelihood

(2) Every citizen of Canada and every person who has the status of a permanent resident of Canada has the right

(a) to move to and take up residence in any province; and
(b) to pursue the gaining of a livelihood in any province.

Limitation

(3) The rights specified in subsection (2) are subject to

(a) any laws or practices of general application in force in a province other than those that discriminate among persons primarily on the basis of province of present or previous residence; and
(b) any laws providing for reasonable residency requirements as a qualification for the receipt of publicly provided social services.

Affirmative action programs

(4) Subsections (2) and (3) do not preclude any law, program or activity that has as its object the amelioration in a province of conditions of individuals in that province who are socially or economically disadvantaged if the rate of employment in that province is below the rate of employment in Canada.

Legal Rights

Life, liberty and security of person

7. Everyone has the right to life, liberty and security of the person and the right not to be deprived thereof except in accordance with the principles of fundamental justice.

Search or seizure

8. Everyone has the right to be secure against unreasonable search or seizure.

Detention or imprisonment

9. Everyone has the right not to be arbitrarily detained or imprisoned.

Arrest or detention

10. Everyone has the right on arrest or detention

(a) to be informed promptly of the reasons therefor;

(b) to retain and instruct counsel without delay and to be informed of that right; and

(c) to have the validity of the detention determined by way of *habeas corpus* and to be released if the detention is not lawful.

Proceedings in criminal and penal matters

11. Any person charged with an offence has the right

(a) to be informed without unreasonable delay of the specific offence;

(b) to be tried within a reasonable time;

(c) not to be compelled to be a witness in proceedings against that person in respect of the offence;

(d) to be presumed innocent until proven guilty according to law in a fair and public hearing by an independent and impartial tribunal;

(e) not to be denied reasonable bail without just cause;

(f) except in the case of an offence under military law tried before a military tribunal, to the benefit of trial by jury where the maximum punishment for the offence is imprisonment for five years or a more severe punishment;

(g) not to be found guilty on account of any act or omission unless, at the time of the act or omission, it constituted an offence under Canadian or international law or was criminal according to the general principles of law recognized by the community of nations;

(h) if finally acquitted of the offence, not to be tried for it again and, if finally found guilty and punished for the offence, not to be tried or punished for it again; and

(i) if found guilty of the offence and if the punishment for the offence has been varied between the time of commission and the time of sentencing, to the benefit of the lesser punishment.

Treatment or punishment

12. Everyone has the right not to be subjected to any cruel and unusual treatment or punishment.

Self-crimination

13. A witness who testifies in any proceedings has the right not to have any incriminating evidence so given used to incriminate that witness in any other proceedings, except in a prosecution for perjury or for the giving of contradictory evidence.

Interpreter

14. A party or witness in any proceedings who does not understand or speak the language in which the proceedings are conducted or who is deaf has the right to the assistance of an interpreter.

Equality Rights

Equality before and under law and equal protection and benefit of law

15. (1) Every individual is equal before and under the law and has the right to the equal protection and equal benefit of the law without discrimination and, in particular, without discrimination based on race, national or ethnic origin, colour, religion, sex, age or mental or physical disability.

Affirmative action programs

(2) Subsection (1) does not preclude any law, program or activity that has as its object the amelioration of conditions of disadvantaged individuals or groups including those that are disadvantaged because of race, national or ethnic origin, colour, religion, sex, age or mental or physical disability.

Official Languages of Canada

Official languages of Canada

16. (1) English and French are the official languages of Canada and have equality of status and equal rights and privileges as to their use in all institutions of the Parliament and government of Canada.

Official languages of New Brunswick

(2) English and French are the official languages of New Brunswick and have equality of status and equal rights and privileges as to their use in all institutions of the legislature and government of New Brunswick.

Advancement of status and use

(3) Nothing in the Charter limits the authority of Parliament or a legislature to advance the equality of status or use of English and French.

English and French linguistic communities in New Brunswick

16.1. (1) The English linguistic community and the French linguistic community in New Brunswick have equality of status and equal rights and privileges, including the right to distinct educational institutions and such distinct cultural institutions as are necessary for the preservation and promotion of those communities.

Role of the legislature and government of New Brunswick

(2) The role of the legislature and government of New Brunswick to preserve and promote the status, rights and privileges referred to in subsection (1) is affirmed.

Proceedings of Parliament

17. (1) Everyone has the right to use English or French in any debates and other proceedings of Parliament.

Proceedings of New Brunswick legislature

(2) Everyone has the right to use English or French in any debates and other proceedings of the legislature of New Brunswick.

Parliamentary statutes and records

18. (1) The statutes, records and journals of Parliament shall be printed and published in English and French and both language versions are equally authoritative.

New Brunswick statutes and records

(2) The statutes, records and journals of the legislature of New Brunswick shall be printed and published in English and French and both language versions are equally authoritative.

Proceedings in courts established by Parliament

19. (1) Either English or French may be used by any person in, or in any pleading in or process issuing from, any court established by Parliament.

Proceedings in New Brunswick courts

(2) Either English or French may be used by any person in, or in any pleading in or process issuing from, any court of New Brunswick.

Communications by public with federal institutions

20. (1) Any member of the public in Canada has the right to communicate with, and to receive available services from, any head or central office of an institution of the Parliament or government of Canada in English or French, and has the same right with respect to any other office of any such institution where

(a) there is a significant demand for communications with and services from that office in such language; or

(b) due to the nature of the office, it is reasonable that communications with and services from that office be available in both English and French.

Communications by public with New Brunswick institutions

(2) Any member of the public in New Brunswick has the right to communicate with, and to receive available services from, any office of an institution of the legislature or government of New Brunswick in English or French.

Continuation of existing constitutional provisions

21. Nothing in sections 16 to 20 abrogates or derogates from any right, privilege or obligation with respect to the English and French languages, or either of them, that exists or is continued by virtue of any other provision of the Constitution of Canada.

Rights and privileges preserved

22. Nothing in section 16 to 20 abrogates or derogates from any legal or customary right or privilege acquired or enjoyed either before or after the coming into force of this Charter with respect to any language that is not English or French.

Minority Language Educational Rights

Language of instruction

23. (1) Citizens of Canada

(a) whose first language learned and still understood is that of the English or French linguistic minority population of the province in which they reside, or

(b) who have received their primary school instruction in Canada in English or French and reside in a province where the language in which they received that instruction is the language of the English or French linguistic minority population of the province,

have the right to have their children receive primary and secondary school instruction in that language in that province.

Continuity of language instruction

(2) Citizens of Canada of whom any child has received or is receiving primary or secondary school instruction in English or French in Canada, have the right to have all their children receive primary and secondary school instruction in the same language.

Application where numbers warrant

(3) The right of citizens of Canada under subsections (1) and (2) to have their children receive primary and secondary school instruction in the language of the English or French linguistic minority population of a province

(a) applies wherever in the province the number of children of citizens who have such a right is sufficient to warrant the provision to them out of public funds of minority language instruction; and

(b) includes, where the number of those children so warrants, the right to have them receive that instruction in minority language educational facilities provided out of public funds.

Enforcement

Enforcement of guaranteed rights and freedoms

24. (1) Anyone whose rights or freedoms, as guaranteed by this Charter, have been infringed or denied may apply to a court of competent jurisdiction to obtain such remedy as the court considers appropriate and just in the circumstances.

Exclusion of evidence bringing administration of justice into disrepute

(2) Where, in proceedings under subsection (1), a court concludes that evidence was obtained in a manner that infringed or denied any rights or freedoms guaranteed by this Charter, the evidence shall be excluded if it is established that, having regard to all the circumstances, the admission of it in the proceedings would bring the administration of justice into disrepute.

General

Aboriginal rights and freedoms not affected by Charter

25. The guarantee in this Charter of certain rights and freedoms shall not be construed so as to abrogate or derogate from any aboriginal, treaty or other rights or freedoms that pertain to the aboriginal peoples of Canada including

(a) any rights or freedoms that have been recognized by the Royal Proclamation of October 7, 1763; and

(b) any rights or freedoms that may be acquired by the aboriginal peoples of Canada by way of land claims settlement.

Other rights and freedoms not affected by Charter

26. The guarantee in this Charter of certain rights and freedoms shall not be construed as denying the existence of any other rights or freedoms that exist in Canada.

Multicultural heritage

27. This Charter shall be interpreted in a manner consistent with the preservation and enhancement of the multicultural heritage of Canadians.

Rights guaranteed equally to both sexes

28. Notwithstanding anything in this Charter, the rights and freedoms referred to in it are guaranteed equally to male and female persons.

Rights respecting certain schools preserved

29. Nothing in this Charter abrogates or derogates from any rights or privileges guaranteed by or under the Constitution of Canada in respect of denominational, separate or dissentient schools.

Application to territories and territorial authorities

30. A reference in this Charter to a province or to the legislative assembly or legislature of a province shall be deemed to include a reference to the Yukon Territory and the Northwest Territories, or to the appropriate legislative authority thereof, as the case may be.

Legislative powers not extended

31. Nothing in this Charter extends the legislative powers of any body or authority.

Application of Charter

Application of Charter

32. (1) This Charter applies

(a) to the Parliament and government of Canada in respect of all matters within the authority of Parliament including all matters relating to the Yukon Territory and Northwest Territories; and

(b) to the legislature and government of each province in respect of all matters within the authority of the legislature of each province.

Exception

(2) Notwithstanding subsection (1), section 15 shall not have effect until three years after this section comes into force.

Exception where express declaration

33. (1) Parliament or the legislature of a province may expressly declare in an Act of Parliament or of the legislature, as the case may be, that the Act or a provision thereof shall operate notwithstanding a provision included in section 2 or sections 7 to 15 of this Charter.

Operation of exception

(2) An Act or a provision of an Act in respect of which a declaration made under this section is in effect shall have such operation as it would have but for the provision of this Charter referred to in the declaration.

Five year limitation

(3) A declaration made under subsection (1) shall cease to have effect five years after it comes into force or on such earlier date as may be specified in the declaration.

Re-enactment

(4) Parliament or a legislature of a province may re-enact a declaration made under subsection (1).

Five year limitation

(5) Subsection (3) applies in respect of a re-enactment made under subsection (4).

Citation

Citation

34. This Part may be cited as the *Canadian Charter of Rights and Freedoms.*

Universal Declaration of Human Rights

Adopted and proclaimed by General Assembly Resolution 217 A (III) of December 10, 1948

Preamble

Whereas recognition of the inherent dignity and of the equal and inalienable rights of all members of the human family is the foundation of freedom, justice and peace in the world,

Whereas disregard and contempt for human rights have resulted in barbarous acts which have outraged the conscience of mankind, and the advent of a world in which human beings shall enjoy freedom of speech and belief and freedom from fear and want has been proclaimed as the highest aspiration of the common people,

Whereas it is essential, if man is not to be compelled to have recourse, as a last resort, to rebellion against tyranny and oppression, that human rights should be protected by the rule of law,

Whereas it is essential to promote the development of friendly relations between nations,

Whereas the peoples of the United Nations have in the Charter reaffirmed their faith in fundamental human rights, in the dignity and worth of the human person and in the equal rights of men and women and have determined to promote social progress and better standards of life in larger freedom,

Whereas Member States have pledged themselves to achieve, in co-operation with the United Nations, the promotion of universal respect for and observance of human rights and fundamental freedoms,

Whereas a common understanding of these rights and freedoms is of the greatest importance for the full realization of this pledge,

Now, therefore,

The General Assembly

Proclaims this Universal Declaration of Human Rights as a common standard of achievement for all peoples and all nations, to the end that every individual and every organ of society, keeping this Declaration constantly in mind, shall strive by teaching and education to promote respect for these rights and freedoms and by progressive measures, national and international, to secure their universal and effective recognition and observance, both among the peoples of Member States themselves and among the peoples of territories under their jurisdiction.

Article 1

All human beings are born free and equal in dignity and rights. They are endowed with reason and conscience and should act towards one another in a spirit of brotherhood.

Article 2

Everyone is entitled to all the rights and freedoms set forth in this Declaration, without distinction of any kind, such as race, colour, sex, language, religion, political or other opinion, national or social origin, property, birth or other status.

Furthermore, no distinction shall be made on the basis of the political, jurisdictional or international status of the country or territory to which a person belongs, whether it be independent, trust, non-self-governing or under any other limitation of sovereignty.

Article 3

Everyone has the right to life, liberty and security of person.

Article 4

No one shall be held in slavery or servitude; slavery and the slave trade shall be prohibited in all their forms.

Article 5

No one shall be subjected to torture or to cruel, inhuman or degrading treatment or punishment.

Article 6

Everyone has the right to recognition everywhere as a person before the law.

Article 7

All are equal before the law and are entitled without any discrimination to equal protection of the law. All are entitled to equal protection against any discrimination in violation of this Declaration and against any incitement to such discrimination.

Article 8

Everyone has the right to an effective remedy by the competent national tribunals for acts violating the fundamental rights granted him by the constitution or by law.

Article 9

No one shall be subjected to arbitrary arrest, detention or exile.

Article 10

Everyone is entitled in full equality to a fair and public hearing by an independent and impartial tribunal, in the determination of his rights and obligations and of any criminal charge against him.

Article 11

1. Everyone charged with a penal offence has the right to be presumed innocent until proved guilty according to law in a public trial at which he has had all the guarantees necessary for his defence.
2. No one shall be held guilty of any penal offence on account of any act or omission which did not constitute a penal offence, under national or international law, at the time when it was committed. Nor shall a heavier penalty be imposed than the one that was applicable at the time the penal offence was committed.

Article 12

No one shall be subjected to arbitrary interference with his privacy, family, home or correspondence, nor to attacks upon his honour and reputation. Everyone has the right to the protection of the law against such interference or attacks.

Article 13

1. Everyone has the right to freedom of movement and residence within the borders of each State.
2. Everyone has the right to leave any country, including his own, and to return to his country.

Article 14

1. Everyone has the right to seek and to enjoy in other countries asylum from persecution.
2. This right may not be invoked in the case of prosecutions genuinely arising from non-political crimes or from acts contrary to the purposes and principles of the United Nations.

Article 15

1. Everyone has the right to a nationality.
2. No one shall be arbitrarily deprived of his nationality nor denied the right to change his nationality.

Article 16

1. Men and women of full age, without any limitation due to race, nationality or religion, have the right to marry and to found a family. They are entitled to equal rights as to marriage, during marriage and at its dissolution.
2. Marriage shall be entered into only with the free and full consent of the intending spouses.
3. The family is the natural and fundamental group unit of society and is entitled to protection by society and the State.

Article 17

1. Everyone has the right to own property alone as well as in association with others.
2. No one shall be arbitrarily deprived of his property.

Article 18

Everyone has the right to freedom of thought, conscience and religion; this right includes freedom to change his religion or belief, and freedom, either alone or in community with others and in public or private, to manifest his religion or belief in teaching, practice, worship and observance.

Article 19

Everyone has the right to freedom of opinion and expression; this right includes freedom to hold opinions without interference and to seek, receive and impart information and ideas through any media and regardless of frontiers.

Article 20

1. Everyone has the right to freedom of peaceful assembly and association.
2. No one may be compelled to belong to an association.

Article 21

1. Everyone has the right to take part in the government of his country, directly or through freely chosen representatives.
2. Everyone has the right of equal access to public service in his country.
3. The will of the people shall be the basis of the authority of government; this will shall be expressed in periodic and genuine elections which shall be by universal and equal suffrage and shall be held by secret vote or by equivalent free voting procedures.

Article 22

Everyone, as a member of society, has the right to social security and is entitled to realization, through national effort and international co-operation and in accordance with the organization and resources of each State, of the economic, social and cultural rights indispensable for his dignity and the free development of his personality.

Article 23

1. Everyone has the right to work, to free choice of employment, to just and favourable conditions of work and to protection against unemployment.
2. Everyone, without any discrimination, has the right to equal pay for equal work.
3. Everyone who works has the right to just and favourable remuneration ensuring for himself and his family an existence worthy of human dignity, and supplemented, if necessary, by other means of social protection.
4. Everyone has the right to form and to join trade unions for the protection of his interests.

Article 24

Everyone has the right to rest and leisure, including reasonable limitation of working hours and periodic holidays with pay.

Article 25

1. Everyone has the right to a standard of living adequate for the health and well-being of himself and of his family, including food, clothing, housing and medical care and necessary social services, and the right to security in the event of unemployment, sickness, disability, widowhood, old age or other lack of livelihood in circumstances beyond his control.
2. Motherhood and childhood are entitled to special care and assistance. All children, whether born in or out of wedlock, shall enjoy the same social protection.

Article 26

1. Everyone has the right to education. Education shall be free, at least in the elementary and fundamental stages. Elementary education shall be compulsory. Technical and professional education shall be made generally available and higher education shall be equally accessible to all on the basis of merit.
2. Education shall be directed to the full development of the human personality and to the strengthening of respect for human rights and fundamental freedoms. It shall promote understanding, tolerance and friendship among all nations, racial or religious groups, and shall further the activities of the United Nations for the maintenance of peace.
3. Parents have a prior right to choose the kind of education that shall be given to their children.

Article 27

1. Everyone has the right freely to participate in the cultural life of the community, to enjoy the arts and to share in scientific advancement and its benefits.
2. Everyone has the right to the protection of the moral and material interests resulting from any scientific, literary or artistic production of which he is the author.

Article 28

Everyone is entitled to a social and international order in which the rights and freedoms set forth in this Declaration can be fully realized.

Article 29

1. Everyone has duties to the community in which alone the free and full development of his personality is possible.
2. In the exercise of his rights and freedoms, everyone shall be subject only to such limitations as are determined by law solely for the purpose of securing due recognition and respect for the rights and freedoms of others and of meeting the just requirements of morality, public order and the general welfare in a democratic society.
3. These rights and freedoms may in no case be exercised contrary to the purposes and principles of the United Nations.

Article 30

Nothing in this Declaration may be interpreted as implying for any State, group or person any right to engage in any activity or to perform any act aimed at the destruction of any of the rights and freedoms set forth herein.

Legal Citation Reference

Courts

CA	Court of Appeal
CJ	Court of Justice
Dist. Ct.	District Court
Div. Ct.	Divisional Court
EAB	Environmental Appeal Board
FCA	Federal Court of Appeal
FCTD	Federal Court Trial Division
Gen. Div.	General Division
HC	High Court
HL	House of Lords
JCPC	Judicial Committee of the Privy Council (UK)
KB	Court of King's Bench
Lab. Arb. Bd.	Labour Arbitration Board
LRB	Labour Relations Board
OLRB	Ontario Labour Relations Board
PC	Privy Council (UK)
Prov. Div.	Provincial Division
QB	Court of Queen's Bench
SC	Supreme Court
SCC	Supreme Court of Canada
Sup. Ct.	Superior Court
TCC	Tax Court of Canada
TD	Trial Division
Terr. Ct.	Territorial Court

Case Reporting Series

AC	*Appeal Cases* (UK)
All ER	*All England Law Reports* (UK)
Alta. LR	*Alberta Law Reports*
APR	*Atlantic Provinces Reports*
AR	*Alberta Reports*
BCLR	*British Columbia Law Reports*
CCC	*Canadian Criminal Cases*
CELR	*Canadian Environmental Law Reports*
CPR	*Canadian Patent Reporter*
CR	*Criminal Reports*
CTC	*Canada Tax Cases*
di	*Décisions information* (Quebec)
DLR	*Dominion Law Reports*
ETR	*Estates and Trusts Reports*
FC	*Federal Court Reports*
ICJ Rep.	*International Court of Justice Reports*
Intl. L Rep.	*International Law Reports*
Man. R	*Manitoba Reports*
MPLR	*Municipal and Planning Law Reports*
MVR	*Motor Vehicle Reports*
NBR	*New Brunswick Reports*
Nfld. & PEIR	*Newfoundland and Prince Edward Island Reports*
NR	*National Reports*
NSR	*Nova Scotia Reports*
NWTR	*Northwest Territories Reports*
OLR	*Ontario Law Reports*
OR	*Ontario Reports*
RCJ	*Recueils de jurisprudence du Québec*
RFL	*Reports of Family Law*
S Ct.	*Supreme Court Reporter* (US)
Sask. R	*Saskatchewan Reports*
SCR	*Supreme Court Reports* (Canada)
US	*United States Reports* (US)
WCB	*Workers' Compensation Board Reports* (Ontario)
WLR	*Weekly Law Reports* (UK)
WWR	*Western Weekly Reports*

Jurisdictions

Alta.	Alberta
BC	British Columbia
Can.	Canada
Man.	Manitoba
NB	New Brunswick
NL	Newfoundland and Labrador
NS	Nova Scotia
NU	Nunavut
NWT	Northwest Territories
Ont.	Ontario
PEI	Prince Edward Island
Que.	Quebec
Sask.	Saskatchewan
Yuk.	Yukon

Selected Neutral Citation Tribunal Identifiers

Federal Courts (in order of level)

SCC	Supreme Court of Canada
FCA	Federal Court of Appeal
FCT	Federal Court Trial Division
TCC	Tax Court of Canada
CACT	Competition Tribunal of Canada

Alberta Courts (in order of level)

ABCA	Alberta Court of Appeal
ABQB	Alberta Court of Queen's Bench
ABPC	Alberta Provincial Court

British Columbia Courts (in order of level)

BCCA	British Columbia Court of Appeal
BCSC	Supreme Court of British Columbia
BCPC	Provincial Court of British Columbia

Ontario Courts (in order of level)

ONCA	Court of Appeal for Ontario
ONSC	Ontario Superior Court of Justice
ONSCDC	Ontario Superior Court of Justice—Divisional Court
ONLRB	Ontario Labour Relations Board

Quebec Courts (in order of level)

QCCA	Quebec Court of Appeal
QCCS	Quebec Superior Court
QCCQ	Court of Quebec
QCTDP	Quebec Human Rights Tribunal

Miscellaneous

aff'd./aff'g.	affirmed/affirming; used in citations that include case history
c.o.b.	carrying on business
et al.	*et alii* (Latin, "and others"); used if a case involves multiple parties
rev'd./rev'g.	reversed/reversing; used in citations that include case history
sub nom.	*sub nomine* (Latin, "under the name"); used if a case is reported under different styles of cause
var'd./var'g.	varied/varying; used in citations that include case history
unreported	not published in a case reporting series

Table of Cases

Glossary

A

Aboriginal rights: rights that some Aboriginal peoples of Canada hold as a result of their ancestors' longstanding use of the land. Aboriginal rights vary from group to group depending on the customs, practices, and traditions that have formed part of these distinct cultures

absolute discharge: a sentence that frees the offender with no conditions and no criminal record

absolute liability: culpability based on the commission of an *actus reus* without regard to the *mens rea*

acquitted: found not guilty of offence

***actus reus*:** the wrongful act or omission in a criminal offence

ad hoc organization: an organization created for a specific purpose

administrative law: the category of public law that governs relations between people on the one hand and government agencies, boards, and departments on the other

adversarial: a relationship in which the parties have clearly opposing interests and positions

affirmative action: a policy designed to increase the representation of groups that have suffered discrimination

affirmative defence: a defence that justifies an accused's criminal conduct

aggravating circumstances: factors that increase criminal responsibility, for example, the use of violence

ambit of the offence: scope of a legal prohibition

amending formula: a method for making changes to a constitution; in Canada's case, a method that would no longer involve the British parliament

anglophone: in a bilingual country, a person whose principal language is English

apartheid: a former policy of the South African government that involved discrimination and segregation directed against non-whites

appearance notice: a document designed to ensure an accused's attendance in court; issued by a police officer where no arrest is made

archipelagic state: a state consisting of a group of islands and the waters separating them; examples are Malta and Indonesia

B

balance of probabilities: the basis of greater likelihood; the degree of proof in civil law, in comparison with proof beyond a reasonable doubt in criminal law

bargain in good faith: negotiate with the honest intention of reaching a collective agreement

baseline: a line that is drawn to simplify the mapping of marine zones, small bays, and coastal indentations

bilateral: between two countries or parties

binding arbitration: a process in which a neutral third party, the arbitrator, hears from union and management representatives and makes a final decision that both sides must accept

bona fide: (Latin) "in good faith"; legitimate, genuine

C

cannon-shot rule: used to define a state's territorial seas—the band of ocean extending from a state's shore over which it may claim sovereignty (the three-mile rule)

case law/common law: a type of law developed in England that is based on following previous judicial decisions and is common to all the people of a country

case officer: officer in charge of an investigation

case to meet: a case for the Crown that is sufficiently strong to support a conviction

certification: an order giving a union the right to negotiate for a collective agreement regulating wages and working conditions for employees

challenge for cause: procedure for challenging a potential juror for a reason listed in s. 638 of the *Criminal Code*

civil disobedience: a peaceful form of protest by which a person refuses to obey a particular law as a matter of conscience

code: a systematic collection of laws, written down and organized into topics

collective bargaining: a process in which individual workers in a union negotiate a contract between the union and the employer covering their wages, hours of work, and working conditions

collective rights: rights acquired as a result of membership in a group; all members of the group share the same rights

collective security: the concept that member states within an organization will provide military support and cooperation in the event of an attack on any other member state

comprehensive land claims: claims based on the recognition that there are continuing Aboriginal rights to lands and natural resources; these claims occur where Aboriginal title has not been previously dealt with by treaty or other means

conciliation: an attempt to settle a contract dispute with the help of a government-appointed officer who meets with the parties during negotiations; this process is required prior to a union strike or a lock-out by an employer

conditional discharge: a sentence that frees the offender with no criminal record but with court-ordered conditions that must be followed

Confederation debates: debates held in the legislative assembly of the Province of Canada to discuss the terms of Confederation drafted at conferences held by the Fathers of Confederation in Charlottetown and Quebec

constitutional law: in Canada, the body of written and unwritten laws that set out how the country will be governed. This type of law sets out the distribution of powers between the federal government and the provinces and embodies certain important legal principles

continental margin: the seabed and subsoil of the continental shelf, continental slope, and continental rise; does not include the deep seabed or its subsoil

continental shelf: the gently sloping crust of the Earth that extends from a coastal state into the ocean and is submerged by no more than 200 m of water

continuity of evidence: continuous chain of possession designed to ensure the safekeeping of evidence

contract law: the area of private law that governs agreements between people or companies to purchase or provide goods or services

convention: a way of doing something that has been accepted for so long that it amounts to an unwritten rule

criminal law: the category of public law that prohibits and punishes behaviour that injures people, property, and society as a whole

cross-examination: oral examination of a witness by a lawyer who did not summons the witness to testify, designed to challenge the witness's evidence

Crown (attorney): lawyer employed by the state to prosecute a criminal offence

culpability: guilt; blameworthiness

cultural genocide: deliberate and systematic destruction of the culture, traditions, language, and customs of a specific cultural group

custom: a long-established way of doing something that, over time, has acquired the force of law

customary law: a common pattern that has emerged over time to become binding in international law

D

dangerous offender: a classification for a person convicted of an offence causing serious personal injury and who is likely to reoffend; may be sentenced to incarceration for an indefinite period of time (see s. 753.1 of the *Criminal Code*)

***de facto*:** (Latin) exists in actuality, whether legally accepted or not

deep seabed: the seabed and ocean floor and their subsoil beyond the limits of national jurisdiction

defendant: in civil law, the party being sued; in criminal law, the person charged with an offence

deoxyribonucleic acid (DNA): biological compound that forms cell chromosomes, from which genetic information can be obtained

dialectic: the process of clarifying an idea through discussion

diplomatic asylum: protection sought in embassies of other countries by individuals fearing for their safety

directed verdict: a verdict acquitting the accused after the Crown closes its case where there is insufficient evidence to support a conviction

discretion: freedom to decide a matter in accordance with the principles of fairness

discrimination: treating a person differently or adversely for no valid reason

domestic law: a law that governs activities within a particular country

duress: illegal threats; coercion through threats

E

electronic monitoring: a device or system that ensures an offender follows a court order; usually used to regulate home confinement (also known as house arrest)

empanelling a jury: process of jury selection for individual trials, governed by the *Criminal Code*

entrenched in the constitution: forming part of the constitution, and amended only through the formal constitutional process

entrenchment: protecting a portion of a constitution by ensuring that it can be changed only through constitutional amendment

estate law: the area of private law that regulates wills and probates, and determines what happens to a person's property after death

ethnic cleansing: the forced removal of other ethnic groups from an area in order to leave only one group

European Union (EU): the economic and political organization of 15 European nations into a common market (formerly the European Community)

examination in chief: oral examination of a witness by the lawyer who summonsed the witness to testify

exclusive economic zone (EEZ): a 200-mile (370-km) coastal marine zone in which a coastal state has exclusive control of resource exploitation and environmental management

exculpating factor: a factor that clears a defendant of blame

extradition: the act of returning a person to a jurisdiction in which he or she is charged with a crime for trial in that jurisdiction

F

family law: the area of private law that governs relations among members of a family

federalism: Canada's form of political organization in which the federal government governs the country as a whole, while the provinces and territories have specific, limited powers

feminist jurisprudence: the theory that law is an instrument of oppression by men against women

francophone: in a bilingual country, a person whose principal language is French

G

garnisheeing wages: taking money directly from a defendant's wages under court order

general intent offence: an offence in which the accused's intent is limited to the prohibited act itself, with no other criminal purpose

genocide: the deliberate and systematic killing of a whole ethnic or racial group

globalization: the trend toward an international free trade market in goods and services with minimal interference by national governments

greenhouse gases: gases that cause the atmosphere to reflect heat back to the Earth, including water vapour, carbon dioxide, methane, nitrous oxide, and hydrofluorocarbons

gunshot residue (GSR): trace substances left on surfaces, including the hand of the shooter, after the discharge of a firearm

H

hearsay: evidence consisting of matters that a witness was told

high seas: the portion of the oceans that is open to all and under no state's sovereignty

human rights: the rights of an individual that are considered basic to life in any human society, including the right to religious freedom and equality of opportunity; when such rights require protection, intervention by the state is necessary

hybrid offence: term used to describe an offence under the *Criminal Code*, prosecuted as either an indictable or a summary conviction offence at the discretion of the Crown

I

inalienable: cannot be surrendered or transferred

incarceration: imprisonment

indictable: term used to describe a serious offence under the *Criminal Code*, prosecuted in a manner more complex and carrying penalties more severe than a summary conviction offence

inferior jurisdiction: jurisdiction exercised by court with provincially appointed judges

information: sworn statement setting out reasonable and probable grounds to believe that an offence has been committed; used as a basis for obtaining a warrant

injunction: a court order to prevent or stop someone from doing something; it may be a temporary order, effective until trial, when it may or may not be made permanent

innocent passage: a doctrine that allows international navigation of territorial seas on the condition that no fishing or illegal activities occur

internal waters: bays, rivers, harbours, and lakes over which a state has (or claims) complete sovereignty

international law: a law that has jurisdiction in more than one country

internment: confinement, such as in wartime, when a country forces people considered enemies to live in a special area or camp

interpretive presumption: inference that must accompany the interpretation of a law

intervenor: an individual, agency, or group of people not directly involved in a case but who, as a third party, has a special interest in its outcome; sometimes called "friend of the court"

***intra vires*:** (Latin) within the power of

J

judicial activism: the perception that judges, rather than Parliament, are making laws and imposing their personal values in their judgments

judicial discretion: freedom of judges to determine a sentence

judicial independence: the principle that judges function independently of the government

judicial interim release: release of an accused pending trial or appeal

jurisprudence: philosophical interpretations of the meaning and nature of law

jury array: pool of potential jurors assembled under provincial legislation; also called jury panel or jury roll

justice: in Plato's theory of natural law, the state or condition that exists when all the powers of an individual or society are working together in harmony for the good of the whole

L

land claims: formal demands made by Aboriginal peoples for ownership and control of lands on which they live or have traditionally lived

legal realism: the school of legal philosophy that examines law in a realistic rather than a theoretical fashion; the belief that law is determined by what actually happens in the courts as judges interpret and apply law

legislative authority: the power conferred on a person (usually a public body) to do something that would otherwise be prohibited by the common law

lobby group: a number of people trying to influence legislators on behalf of a particular cause or interest

lock-out: an action in which an employer locks employees out of the workplace to pressure them to reach agreement on a new contract

long-term offender: a court classification applied to a sexual offender who is likely to reoffend; may be sentenced to incarceration for an indefinite period of time

M

mandate: a government's or agency's scope of authority, as defined by law or democratic process

***maquiladoras*:** factories set up in a free trade zone along the US border with Mexico, where foreign companies can move material across the border with minimal customs processing

Marxism: an economic and political theory that states that law is an instrument of oppression and control that the ruling classes use against the working classes

mediation: a voluntary process that may follow conciliation, in which a third party attempts to help the parties reach an agreement before or during a strike or lock-out

***mens rea*:** the blameworthy mental element in a criminal offence

Métis: French-speaking descendants of fur traders or voyageurs and Aboriginal peoples

mitigating circumstances: factors that reduce criminal responsibility, for example, a first offence

multilateral: among many countries or parties

N

national organization: an organization that represents a particular group of people on a permanent basis and has more than one purpose or goal

nationalize: take over an industry, service, or land from private ownership on behalf of the state

natural law: the theory that human laws are derived from eternal and unchangeable principles that regulate the natural world, and that people can become aware of these laws through the use of reason

NCR acquittee: a person found not criminally responsible at trial

negativing defence: a defence that raises a reasonable doubt about whether the accused committed the offence charged

negligence: an act committed without intention to cause harm, but which a reasonable person would anticipate might cause harm

non-appropriation: the doctrine that no state may subject any part (of the high seas) to its sovereignty

norms: standards, customs, or accepted practices

notwithstanding clause: a clause in the Charter that may be invoked by Parliament or provincial legislatures to override basic Charter provisions

O

ombudsman: an official appointed to receive and investigate citizens' grievances against the government

omnibus act: an act that contains statutes applying to many different areas of legislation

P

parliamentary supremacy: the principle that Parliament has the supreme power of making Canadian laws

partition: to create separate areas or divisions under the control of different governments

patriate: bring decision-making powers regarding the constitution under Canadian control

peremptory challenge: the procedure by which the defence or Crown can reject a potential juror without giving reasons, as authorized by the *Criminal Code*

pith and substance: the main purpose of a law, as opposed to its incidental effects

plaintiff: in civil law, the party suing

plea bargaining: a process in which the accused (defence) negotiates with the Crown, usually agreeing to plead guilty in exchange for a lesser charge and a recommendation for a lighter sentence

positive law: the theory that law is a body of rules formulated by the state, and that citizens are obliged to obey the law for the good of the state as a whole

power of disallowance: a power granted to the federal government by s. 90 of the *Constitution Act, 1867* that gave it the right to disallow provincial legislation (declare it void) within one year of its passage; a type of veto power that has not been used since World War II and that is generally considered to be no longer valid

pre-sentence report: a report that describes the offender and the offence and that may also recommend a sentence; usually prepared by a probation officer

pre-trial conference: conference attended by judge, Crown, and the accused or accused's lawyer to promote a fair and expeditious trial

precedent: a legal decision that is taken as a guide for subsequent cases

prejudice: an opinion or judgment, especially an unfavourable one, based on irrelevant considerations or inadequate knowledge

preliminary inquiry: a hearing held to determine whether sufficient evidence exists to commit an accused for trial in a court of superior jurisdiction

primary sources of law: those parts of a legal system that have the longest historical development and represent the system's cumulative values, beliefs, and principles

private law: the body of law that regulates disputes between individuals, businesses, or organizations; sometimes called civil law

private nuisance: an indirect interference with the use and enjoyment of land due to the actions or conduct of someone nearby

procedural law: a law that outlines the methods or procedures that must be followed in enforcing substantive laws

promise to appear: a document designed to ensure an accused's attendance in court; issued by the officer in charge of a police station after an arrest

property law: the area of private law that applies primarily to the buying, selling, and renting of land and buildings and the use to which lands may be put

public law: the area of law that regulates activities between a state and its citizens

public nuisance: an interference with a public right, such as the right to fish or the right of navigation

R

racial profiling: a practice relying on racial stereotypes rather than reasonable suspicion to single out persons for greater scrutiny in law enforcement

Rand formula: the requirement that, in a bargaining unit in which the majority vote to join a union, all members must pay union dues whether or not they join the union

ratify: give formal consent to an agreement

read down: to rule that, while a piece of legislation may generally be consistent with the Charter, it is inconsistent in the particular case at hand

reasonable limits: restrictions on rights and freedoms that are imposed if the merits of the limits are determined to advance society's interests

recidivism: returning to crime

recognizance: a document designed to ensure an accused's attendance in court; issued by the officer in charge of a police station after an arrest in which the accused promises to pay a sum of money if he or she fails to appear

rehabilitation: a sentencing goal that seeks to restore a person to moral, physical, social, and mental health through training and treatment

reparations: formal economic compensation, often from one sovereign state to another, for harm done in the course of armed conflict

requisite intention: the *mens rea* that the Crown is required to establish in order to convict an accused of an offence

restorative justice: a philosophy of criminal law that views offences as conflicts among offenders, victims, and their communities that should be resolved through the broad and active participation of all involved

riparian rights: the right of an owner of land bordering on a lake, river, or stream to sue another person who interferes with the quantity or quality of the water

Royal Commission: a board of inquiry appointed by the government to investigate and report on a particular issue

rule of law: the fundamental principle that society is governed by laws applying equally to all persons and that neither any person nor the government is above the law

S

sanctions: penalties or actions imposed as a means of influencing behaviour

scab: a derogatory term used to describe a worker hired as a temporary replacement during a strike or lock-out

search incidental to arrest: search following an arrest that must be conducted to achieve a valid purpose connected to the arrest

secondary sources of law: current laws that enshrine a society's values in written rules and regulations that have been formulated by legislators and judges

separatism: the desire to establish a politically independent Quebec and to withdraw from Confederation

sovereignty-association: the concept put forth by the Parti Québécois government of René Lévesque, whereby Quebec would become a sovereign jurisdiction in all areas of law making, but would maintain economic association with the rest of Canada

specific intent offence: an offence in which the accused's intent goes beyond the prohibited act itself to include another, criminal purpose

specific land claims: claims that deal with specific grievances that Aboriginal peoples may have regarding the fulfillment of treaties and administration of lands and assets under the *Indian Act*

standing: a legal right to sue. A person who tries to bring suit where he or she has no standing will have the action dismissed

***stare decisis*:** (Latin) to stand by the decision

state sovereignty: the lawful control by a state over its territory, right to govern in that territory, and authority to apply law there to the exclusion of other states

statute law: laws passed by legislatures

statutorily prescribed minimum: the minimum penalty set by a statute

statutory authority: protection afforded by law; e.g., when a statute requires or authorizes a government agency to carry out an activity, the agency is deemed to be protected from civil liability related to that activity

stereotyping: judging one person of a group and applying that judgment to all group members

strict liability: culpability based on the commission of an *actus reus* and inability to prove the defence of due diligence

strike: withdrawal of labour by workers during negotiations for a contract, a tactic designed to pressure employers to reach a new agreement

strike down: to rule that a piece of legislation is inconsistent with the Charter and is no longer valid

substantive law: a law that identifies the rights and duties of a person or level of government

summary conviction: term used to describe an offence under the *Criminal Code*, prosecuted in a manner less complex and carrying penalties less severe than an indictable offence

summons: a document designed to ensure an accused's attendance in court; issued by a justice or judge after an arrest is made

superior jurisdiction: jurisdiction exercised by court with federally appointed judges

T

territorial sea: a belt of coastal waters and their resources under the sovereign control of the coastal state; set at 3 miles (5.55 km) and later extended to 12 miles (22.2 km)

tort law: the area of private law covering civil wrongs and damages that one person or company causes to another, when the wrongs or damages arise independently of a contractual relationship

trade union: a group of workers who form an organization to bargain collectively with employers to improve working conditions, benefits, and wages

transit passage: a regime that allows for uninterrupted navigation and overflight in and above international straits narrower than 24 miles

transnational corporation (TNC): a company that conducts its business in more than one country; also known as a multinational corporation

treaty: (1) a formal agreement between two autonomous entities to conduct themselves in certain ways or to do certain things; (2) an agreement between or among nations, usually concluded in written form and governed by international law

trespass: the direct interference with land that is owned or occupied by another person

trier of fact: the determiner, whether judge or jury, of the facts on the basis of admissible evidence

U

***ultra vires*:** (Latin) beyond the power of

unconscionable: unreasonable

undue hardship: the result of a change that would affect the economic viability of an employer or produce a substantial health or safety risk that outweighs the benefit of accommodating someone

utilitarianism: the theory that the law should achieve the greatest good for the greatest number of people

V

veto: a power to reject something, usually a law or a political measure

victim impact statement: verbal or written statement given by a victim or victim's family to describe the personal consequences of the crime

vitiated by fraud: made invalid as a result of fraud on the part of the accused

***voir dire*:** trial within a trial to determine whether evidence is admissible

W

warrant: grant of judicial authority to arrest or search

weapons of mass destruction: military weapons that have the potential to kill large numbers of people and that cannot distinguish between soldiers and civilians

wildcat strike: an illegal strike that occurs while a collective agreement is still in force

working to rule: a form of work slowdown in which employees apply the collective agreement and workplace rules literally, with the intention of making the workplace less efficient

writ of *habeas corpus*: common-law remedy to test the legality of detention or imprisonment

Index

D

G

H

I

J

K

L

M

N

O

P

T

U

Credits

Images

Page 3: Robert Cooper/CP Photo Archive; Page 4: Graeme Mackay; Page 8: © Chris Collins/CORBIS/MAGMA; Page 10: © Bettman/CORBIS/MAGMA; Page 15: National Archives of Canada, PA-139073; Page 18: Chuck Stoody/CP Photo Archive; Page 19: Boris Spremo/CP Photo Archive; Page 27: Chuck Stoody/CP Photo Archive; Page 32: © 2003 The New Yorker Collection from cartoonbank.com. All Rights Reserved; Page 35: Toronto Public Library; Page 38: Courtesy of Sandeep Dave; Page 39: Courtesy of the Canadian Museum of Civilization; Page 41: Shaun Best/CP Photo Archive; Page 44: Robert Cooper/CP Photo Archive; Page 46: National Archives of Canada, PA-107943. Reprinted with permission by the Montreal Gazette; Page 51: Jacques Boissinot/CP Photo Archive; Page 57: Darko Zeljkovic/CP Photo Archive; Page 68: By permission of John L. Hart FLP, and Creators Syndicate, Inc.; Page 71: © Francis G. Mayer/CORBIS/MAGMA; © Bettman/CORBIS/MAGMA; Page 74: © Bettman/CORBIS/MAGMA; Page 78: © Bettman/CORBIS/MAGMA; Page 79: © Bettman/CORBIS/MAGMA; Page 80: © Bettman/CORBIS/MAGMA; Page 84: Tom Hanson/CP Photo Archive; Page 87: Damian Dovarganes/CP Photo Archive; Page 93: Ron Bull/CP Photo Archive; Page 101: Mark Gallant/CP Photo Archive; Page 102: Reprinted by permission of Bob Kreiger; Page 107 left: Peter Bregg/CP Photo Archive, right: Mark Gallant/CP Photo Archive; Page 109: Malcolm Mayes/artizans.com; Page 112: Peter Power/CP Photo Archive; Page 116: © NCC/CCN; Page 122: Wayne Glowacki/CP Photo Archive; Page 128: Reprinted with permission from The Globe and Mail; Page 130: CP Photo Archive; Page 132: Drew Gregg/CP Photo Archive; Page 137: Frank Gunn/CP Photo Archive; Page 147: Jonathan Hayward/CP Photo Archive; Page 152: Frank Gunn/CP Photo Archive: Page 158: Alan King/artizans.com; Page 163: Vancouver Public Library #1397; Page 169: Archives of Ontario, 10009039; Page 175: Andrew Stawicki/CP Photo Archive; Page 182: Tom Hanson/CP Photo Archive; Page 184: Courtesy of the Hon. Madam Justice Maryka Omatsu; Page 186: Wayne Roper/CP Photo Archive; Page 192: Wojtek Kozak/Artizans.com; Page 195: Bill Grimshaw/CP Photo Archive; Page 199: CP Photo File; Page 200: Ryan Remiorz/CP Photo Archive; Page 201: Jacques Boissinot/CP Photo Archive; Page 206: P75-103-S7-300 MSCC – St. Phillip's School, Girls 1. Reprinted with the permission of the General Synod Archives, Anglican Church Archives; Page 210: Nick Procaylo/CP Photo Archive; Page 214: Andrew Vaughan/CP Photo Archive; Page 229: Deborah Baic/CP Photo Archive; Page 230: © Tribune Media Services, Inc. All Rights Reserved. Reprinted with permission; Page 233: Chuck Mitchell/CP Photo Archive; Page 237: Library of the Religious Society of Friends; Page 238: Ron Bull/CP Photo Archive; Page 243: John Mahler/CP Photo Archive; Page 260: © The New Yorker Collection 2002, Alex Gregory from cartoonbank.com. All Rights Reserved; Page 262: Deborah Baic/CP Photo Archive; Page 265: Itsuo Inouye/CP Photo Archive; Page 268: Sean Dempsey/CP Photo Archive; Page 290: © The New Yorker Collection 1997. Michael Maslin from cartoonbank.com. All Rights Reserved; Page 293: Bruce Stotesbury/CP Photo Archive; Page 303: David Moll/CP Photo Archive; Page 308: Scott Gardner/CP Photo Archive; Page 313: Tom Hanson/CP Photo Archive; Page 320: © The New Yorker Collection 2000. Robert Mankoff from cartoonbank.com. All Rights Reserved; Page 325 top: Tom Hanson/CP Photo Archive, bottom: Brent Linton/CP Photo Archive; Page 333: Dave McCord/CP Photo Archive; Page 339: Chuck Stoody/CP Photo Archive; Page 341: Doug Crawford/CP Photo Archive; Page 345: Aaron Harris/CP Photo Archive; Page 346: J.P. Moczulski/CP Photo Archive; Page 349: Courtesy Rick Bunting; Page 355: Andrew Vaughan/CP Photo Archive; Page 356: Graeme MacKay; Page 358 top: Dennis Bueckert/CP Photo Archive, bottom: Special Collections, Cleveland State University; Page 359: © Bettmann/CORBIS/MAGMA; Page 370: Courtesy of the Niagara Escarpment Commission; Page 372: Courtesy of CELA; Page 376: © Reuters NewMedia Inc./CORBIS/MAGMA; Page 385: DILBERT reprinted by permission of United Feature Syndicate, Inc.; Page 387: Provincial Archives of Manitoba, #N2438; Page 393: Dick Hemingway; Page 397: Courtesy Paul Kells; Page 399: © CORBIS/MAGMA; Page 410: Reprinted by permission of Gary Huck; Page 413: National Archives of Canada, C-058640; Page 414: Provincial Archives of Manitoba, N#2757; Page 415: Canada Science and Technology Museum CN000692; Page 417: © Bettmann/CORBIS/MAGMA; Page 419: Jason Kryk/CP Photo Archive; Page 427: Andrew Vaughan/CP Photo Archive; Page 432: Courtesy Caroline V. ("Nini") Jones; Page 436: Courtesy of Malcolm Evans; Page 440: Fred Lum/CP Photo Archive; Page 445: Toronto Sun/CP Photo Archive; Page 450: Ryan Remiorz/CP Photo Archive; Page 454: Kirk Anderson/Artizans.com; Page 456: Fred Chartrand/CP Photo Archive; Page 465: AP Photo/CP Photo Archive; Page 466: Bruce MacKinnon/Artizans.com; Page 469: AP Photo/CP Photo Archive; Page 470: AP Photo/CP Photo/NASA; © CORBIS/MAGMA; Page 482: John Stilwell/CP Photo Archive; Page 488: AP Photo/CP Photo Archive; Page 491: John Lehman/CP Photo Archive; Page 496: Malcolm Mayes/Artizans.com; Page 502: Kevin Frayer/CP Photo Archive; Page 503: Heiko Junge/CP Photo Archive; Page 510: Fred Chartrand/CP Photo Archive; Page 517: Belleville Intelligencer (Darko Zeljkovic)/CP Photo Archive; Page 523: Fred Chartrand/CP Photo Archive; Page 524: Stephen Chernin/CP Photo Archive; Page 534: Malcolm Mayes/Artizans.com; Page 536: Paul Sancya/CP Photo Archive; Page 538: Tim Krochak/CP Photo Archive; Page 542: © Bettmann/CORBIS/MAGMA; Page 547: Gary Kean/CP Photo Archive; Page 549: Aaron Harris/CP Photo Archive; Page 551: Xinhua/CP Photo Archive; Page 553: CP Photo Archive; Page 558: Murray Mitchell/CP Photo Archive; Page 568: Bado/Artizans.com; Page 573: Tom Hanson/CP Photo Archive; Page 577: AP Photo/CP Photo; Page 580: Jonathan Hayward/CP Photo Archive; Page 582: Courtesy of the Toronto Star Syndicate. Reprinted by permission of Patrick Corrigan; Page 589: CP Photo Archive; Page 591: Andrew Vaughan/CP Photo Archive; Page 596: Courtesy Major Christopher Young.

Text

Page 6: Wayne W. McVey, Jr. and Warren E. Kalbach, *Canadian Population.* Toronto: Nelson, 1995, p. 149; Page 24: Adapted from Haroon Siddiqui, *The Toronto Star,* June 25 and 29, 2000; and from the CCLA's Web site at http://ccla.org/peop/bovory.shtml; Page 28: Adapted from Ted Tjaden, *Legal Research and Writing.* Toronto: Irwin Law, 2001, pp. 94–95; Page 38: Reprinted by permission of Sandeep Dave; Page 40: From the Iroquois Constitution, "Laws of Adoption." Available at the University of Oklahoma Law Center, www.law.ou.edu/hist/iroquois.html; Page 51: From *In the Rapids: Navigating the Future of First Nations* by Ovide Mercredi and Mary Ellen Turpel. Copyright ©1993 by Ovide Mercredi and Mary Ellen Turpel. Reprinted by permission of Penguin Books Canada Limited; Page 70: "The Apology" from *The Great Dialogues of Plato* by Plato, translated by W.H. Rouse, copyright © 1956, renewed © 1984 by J.C.G. Rouse. Used by permission of Dutton Signet, a division of Penguin Group (USA) Inc.; Page 75: Reprinted by permission of *The Vancouver Sun*; Page 83: Reprinted by permission of the Hon. Bertha Wilson; Reprinted by permission of *The National Post*; Page 85: Reprinted by permission of *The Toronto Star* Syndicate and *The National Post*; Page 110: Reproduced with the permission of the Minister of Public Works and Government Services Canada, 2003; Page 111: Reprinted by permission of the Ontario Secondary School Teachers' Federation; Page 113: Reprinted by permission of The City of Toronto; Page 123: With permission from the *London Free Press*; Page 144: Patrick Nugent: "Wrong Use of the Notwithstanding Clause," Opinion Guest Column, *University of Alberta Folio* (Vol. 37, No. 15). March 31, 2000; www.ualberta.ca/~publicas/folio/37/15/opinion.html. Reprinted by permission; Page 147: Adapted by permission of *The Toronto Star* Syndicate; Page 148: Reprinted by permission of *The National Post*; Page 154: Patrick J. Monahan, *Constitutional Law,* 2nd ed. Toronto: Irwin Law, 2002, p. 393; Page 166: Reprinted by permission of Dr. Barnet Berris; Page 176: Excerpt from Centre for Equality Rights in Accommodation, "Challenging Homelessness and Poverty as Human Rights Violations: An Update on CERA's Test Case Litigation," Winter 2002, www.equalityrights.org/cera/docs/tcupdate.rtf. Reprinted with permission; Page 239: Adapted from "The Female Refugees Act," *Opening the Doors*: The Newsletter of the Council of Elizabeth Fry Societies of Ontario, Spring 2001 and Michelle Landsberg, "Plight of 'Incorrigible' Women Demands Justice," *The Toronto Star,* Sunday, May 6, 2001. Reprinted with permission; Page 240: From *Justice and the Poor: A National Council of Welfare Publication.* Spring 2000. Reproduced with the permission of the Minister of Public Works and Government Services Canada, 2003; Page 255: "Youths and Adults Charged by Type of Offence, Canada 2001," adapted from the Statistics Canada Web site, www.statcan.ca/english/Pgdb/legal17a.htm; Page 264: Reprinted by permission of International Creative Management Inc. Copyright © 2002 by Michael Specter. First appeared in *The New Yorker*; Page 313: *The Globe and Mail,* October 17, 2001, p. 6; Page 359: Chief Dan George, *My Heart Soars.* Toronto: Hancock House Publishers, 1974. Reprinted by permission of Hancock House Publishers; Page 374: Kathleen Cooper, Researcher with the Canadian Environmental Law Association, "Trashing Environmental Protection—Ontario's Four Part Strategy." In Luciana Ricciutelli, June Larkin, and Eimear O'Neill (eds.), *Confronting the Cuts: A Sourcebook for Women in Ontario.* Toronto: Inanna Publications and Education, 1998; Page 387: Quoted in Ken Osborne, *R.B. Russell and the Labour Movement.* Toronto: Book Society of Canada, 1978; Page 393: Reprinted by permission of Anne Bains; Page 401: "Canadian Annual Average Earnings by Gender, 1992–2001," adapted from the Statistics Canada Web site, www.statcan.ca/english/Pgdb/labor01a.htm; Page 415: Reprinted by permission of James Lorimer & Company; Page 429: Reproduced with the permission of the Minister of Public Works and Government Services Canada, 2003; Page 430: Reprinted by permission of John Peters, The Centre for Social Justice; Page 438: "Full-time/Part-time Employment in Canada, Annual Averages, 1976–2002," adapted from the Statistics Canada Labour Force Survey; Page 444: George Monbiot, "Running on MMT: The Multilateral Agreement on Investments Will Force Governments to Poison Their Citizens," *The Guardian,* Thursday, August 13, 1998; Page 454: Ed Finn, "Tackling Corporate Globalization Together: Labour, 'Civil Society' Forging a Much-Needed Partnership," Canadian Centre for Policy Alternatives, www.policyalternatives.ca/publications/articles/article295.html; Page 456: "Craig Kielburger on Ending Child Labour and Being an Active Citizen," *Global Tribe,* www.pbs.org/kcet/globaltribe/voices/voi_kielburger.html; Page 472: This article first appeared in *The Christian Science Monitor* on June 7, 2000 and is reproduced with permission. Copyright © 2000 *The Christian Science Monitor* (www.csmonitor.com). All rights reserved; Page 483: United Nations Children's Fund; Page 491: James Goodwin, "Saudi Justice, and Canadian Timidity," *Halifax Herald,* May 25, 2002; Page 520: Reprinted by permission of Asian Regional Resource Center for Human Rights Education, Bangkok, Thailand; Page 525: Stephen Lewis, Keynote Address to the G6B People's Summit, Calgary, Alberta, June 21, 2002, www.g6bpeoplessummit.org; Pages 529, 530: AVERTing HIV & AIDS, www.avert.org/worldstats.htm; Page 555: Energy Information Administration, US Department of Energy; Page 556: Reprinted by permission of the Office of Premier Ralph Klein; Page 557: Reprinted by permission of *ExpressNews*; Page 573: "Eyewitness: UN in Rwanda 1994," http://news.bbc.co.uk/1/world/africa/911232.stm; Stephanie Nolen, "Dallaire Book Slams US, UN, on Rwanda," *The Globe and Mail,* August 21, 2003, A1; and Romeo Dallaire, *Shake Hands with the Devil: The Failure of Humanity in Rwanda.* Toronto: Random House Canada, 2003; Page 593: Reprinted by permission of Dr. H. Peter Langille. Article first appeared in *The Globe and Mail.*